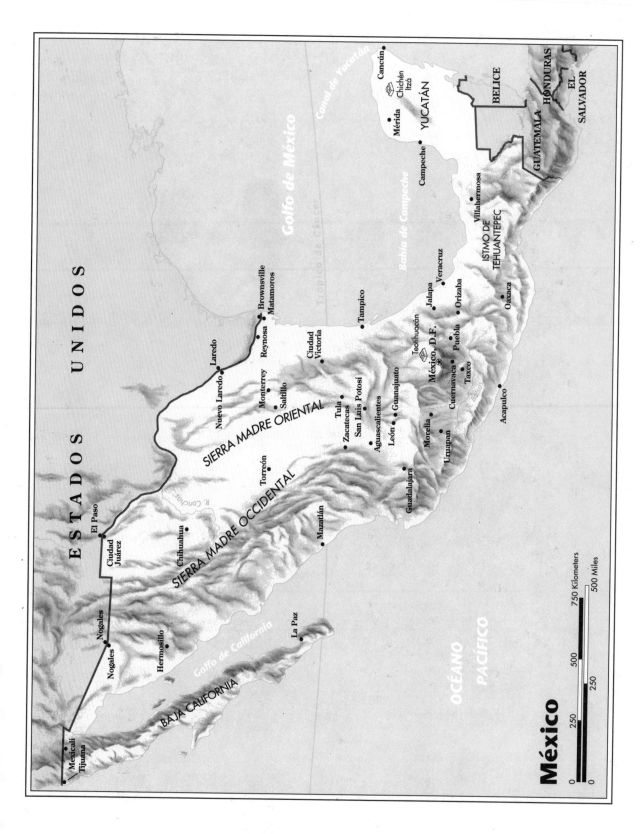

México

ESTADOS UNIDOS

BAJA CALIFORNIA

SIERRA MADRE OCCIDENTAL

SIERRA MADRE ORIENTAL

Golfo de México

Golfo de California

OCÉANO PACÍFICO

Bahía de Campeche

Canal de Yucatán

Trópico de Cáncer

R. Conchos

R. Bravo

ISTMO DE TEHUANTEPEC

YUCATÁN

BELICE

GUATEMALA

HONDURAS

EL SALVADOR

Tijuana
Mexicali
Nogales
Nogales
Hermosillo
La Paz
Ciudad Juárez
El Paso
Chihuahua
Nuevo Laredo
Laredo
Mazatlán
Torreón
Monterrey
Saltillo
Reynosa
Matamoros
Brownsville
Ciudad Victoria
Tampico
Zacatecas
Tula
San Luis Potosí
Aguascalientes
León
Guanajuato
Guadalajara
Morelia
Uruapan
Teotihuacán
México, D.F.
Cuernavaca
Taxco
Puebla
Jalapa
Veracruz
Orizaba
Oaxaca
Acapulco
Villahermosa
Campeche
Mérida
Chichén Itzá
Cancún

250
500
750 Kilometers
0
250
500 Miles
0

¿Cómo se dice...?

SIXTH EDITION

ANA C. JARVIS

CHANDLER-GILBERT COMMUNITY COLLEGE

RAQUEL LEBREDO

CALIFORNIA BAPTIST COLLEGE

FRANCISCO MENA-AYLLÓN

UNIVERSITY OF REDLANDS

HOUGHTON MIFFLIN COMPANY

BOSTON   NEW YORK

Director, Modern Language Programs: E. Kristina Baer
Senior Development Editor: Sharon Alexander
Project Editor: Helen Bronk
Senior Production/Design Coordinator: Jennifer Waddell
Manufacturing Coordinator: Sally Culler
Marketing Manager: Elaine Uzan Leary

Cover Design: Harold Burch, Harold Burch Design, New York City.

Printed in the U.S.A.

Library of Congress Catalog Card Number: 97-72493

Student Text ISBN: 0-395-85792-9

3456789-VH-01 00 99

Ana C. Jarvis, a native of Paraguay, was born in Asunción and attended school in Buenos Aires, Argentina. She received her Ph.D. in Spanish from the University of California, Riverside, in 1973. Presently an instructor of Spanish at Chandler-Gilbert Community College in Chandler, Arizona, Dr. Jarvis previously taught at Mesa Community College, the University of California, Riverside, San Bernardino Valley College, Brigham Young University, and Riverside City College. In addition to authoring numerous Spanish textbooks, she has published several short stories in Spanish and is presently at work on a novel. In 1988 she was chosen "Faculty Member of the Year" at Chandler-Gilbert Community College.

Raquel Lebredo was born in Camagüey, Cuba. She attended school in Havana and later enrolled at the University of Havana, where she received a Ph.D. in Education in 1950. She was subsequently employed as an elementary school principal, and taught literature and language at a preparatory school in Havana. After living in Spain for a period of time, she moved in 1968 to the United States. Dr. Lebredo was awarded a Ph.D. in Spanish from the University of California, Riverside, in 1973. Since then she has taught Spanish at Claremont Graduate School, Crafton Hills College, the University of Redlands, and California Baptist College, and has authored several Spanish textbooks. In 1985 she was chosen "Faculty Member of the Year" by the student body at California Baptist College, and in 1991 she received a YWCA "Women of Achievement" award.

Francisco Mena-Ayllón, a native of Madrid, Spain, received his Ph.D. in Spanish from the University of California, Riverside, in 1973. He has taught Spanish language and literature courses at the University of California, Riverside, Oberlin College, California State University, Chico, the University of Redlands, and Crafton Hills College. In addition to authoring numerous Spanish textbooks in the United States, he has published a book about Federico García Lorca and several volumes of his own poetry. His poetry has been published in Spain, Latin America, and the United States. His work has also been included in several anthologies of contemporary Spanish poets, and he is listed in *Quién es quién en las letras españolas, 1978* (Who's Who in Spanish Letters), as an important contributor to contemporary Spanish literature.

PREFACE

¿Cómo se dice...?, Sixth Edition, is a complete, flexible program designed to present the fundamentals of Spanish to two- and four-year college and university students. This edition continues to feature the balanced, eclectic approach to language instruction that has made ¿Cómo se dice...? one of the most widely used programs of its kind. To achieve its goal of helping students attain linguistic proficiency, ¿Cómo se dice...?, Sixth Edition, systematically involves them in activities requiring the communicative use of all four language skills: listening, speaking, reading, and writing. Because cultural awareness is as important to successful communication as linguistic competence, special care has been devoted in the Sixth Edition to providing up-to-date, practical insights into the cultural diversity of the Spanish-speaking world. Since it is essential to understand the underlying philosophy and organization of the program to use it to greatest advantage, the student's text and other components are described in detail below.

The Student's Text

The organization of this central component of the ¿Cómo se dice...?, Sixth Edition, program reflects its emphasis on the active use of Spanish for practical communication in context. The student's text is organized as follows:

■ An introductory *Lección preliminar* enables students to communicate in Spanish using basic, high-frequency language from the outset of the course.

■ Each of the eighteen regular lessons focuses on a high-frequency communicative situation and contains the features listed below.

Objectives: Each lesson begins with a list of grammatical and communicative objectives.

Dialogues and *¡Conversemos!*: New vocabulary and structures are first presented in the context of a conversation in idiomatic Spanish dealing with the high-frequency situation that is the lesson's central theme. An English translation of the dialogues is provided in Appendix D for students to verify meaning deduced from context. A cassette icon indicates that the dialogues are recorded on the Student Cassette. Comprehension questions on the dialogue (*¡Conversemos!*) follow the vocabulary section to provide immediate reinforcement of the vocabulary and communicative functions presented in the dialogue.

Vocabulario: All new words and expressions introduced in the dialogues are listed by parts of speech or under the headings *Cognados* and *Otras palabras y expresiones*. The *Vocabulario adicional* section offers thematic groupings of other words and phrases related to the lesson theme; many are presented through illustrations to help students assimilate them more readily. Entries in these lists are to be learned for active use.

¿Lo sabía Ud.?: These notes expand on cultural information and themes introduced in the dialogues in simple, easy-to-read Spanish.

Pronunciación: Lessons 1–9 present and practice the sounds of the Spanish language with special attention to features that pose difficulty for English speakers. A cassette icon indicates that the section is recorded on the Student Cassette.

Estructuras **and** ***Práctica:*** Each new grammatical structure featured in the dialogue is explained clearly and concisely in English so that the explanations may be used independently as an out-of-class reference. All explanations are followed by numerous examples of their practical use in natural Spanish. The *¡Atención!* head signals exceptions to the grammar rules presented or instances where knowledge of an English structure may interfere with learning the equivalent Spanish structure. After each explanation, the *Práctica* activities offer immediate reinforcement of new concepts through a variety of structured and communicative activities.

¡A ver cuánto aprendió!: This series of progressively less structured activities allows students to synthesize the lesson's new vocabulary and structures. *¡Repase el vocabulario!* uses a variety of proven activity formats to review new vocabulary presented in the lesson. *Entrevista* has students interview one another on topics related to the main lesson theme. *Situaciones* involves pairs or small groups of students in using new structures and vocabulary in brief conversational exchanges. *Para escribir* guides students to express themselves in writing in a variety of formats, such as notes, postcards, letters, dialogues, and compositions.

En la vida real: This section develops oral proficiency by using authentic documents and role-plays to involve students in more complex and extended communicative tasks, such as planning an event, asking for information, or solving a problem. Each lesson includes an activity that involves reading and using information gained from an authentic text, for example, a newspaper ad or a travel brochure. Most of the activities are designed for work in pairs or small groups, and all of them require spontaneous use of Spanish in practical, meaningful, communicative tasks intended to motivate learners and to underscore the usefulness of language study.

In addition, the following features appear at regular intervals throughout the student's text:

Así somos: All odd-numbered lessons end with a series of activities designed for use with the candid interview segments of the *Así somos* modules of the ¿Cómo se dice...? Video, which reinforce the lesson themes. The previewing, post-viewing, and expansion activities use a variety of formats, including true/false, sentence completion, questions, matching, and multiple choice. A supplementary vocabulary list facilitates students' comprehension of the video.

¡Vamos a leer!: All even-numbered lessons end with a reading section that reinforces the structures and vocabulary presented in the text. Five readings are new to the Sixth Edition. The first four readings are related to the lesson themes; the final five readings consist of authentic literary selections that provide an appealing introduction to reading literature in Spanish. To develop students' reading skills, *Antes de leer,* a series of pre-reading questions, precedes each selection. Personalized, open-ended questions *(Díganos)* follow each reading and provide opportunities for students to discuss their own opinions and experiences in relation to the reading topic or theme.

Self Tests: The Self Tests, which appear after Lessons 3, 6, 9, 12, 15, and 18, enable students to review the structures, vocabulary, and cultural information of the three preceding lessons. Organized by lesson and by grammatical structure, the Self Tests enable students to determine quickly what material they have mastered and which concepts to target for further review. An answer key is provided in Appendix E for immediate verification.

Panorama hispánico* and *Teleinforme: These sections, which appear after each even-numbered lesson, focus on the life-style, culture, geography, economy, and history of specific regions of the Spanish-speaking world. The full-color *Panorama hispánico* photo essays feature captions in simple Spanish that are accessible to students; each caption ends with a question that invites cross-cultural comparison. The *Teleinforme* sections, which reinforce the content of the photo essays, include a supplementary vocabulary list and previewing, post-viewing, and expansion activities designed to enhance students' comprehension of the authentic footage featured in the *Teleinforme* modules of the **¿Cómo se dice…?** Video.

Reference Materials: The following sections provide learners with useful reference tools throughout the course:

- *Maps:* Colorful, up-to-date maps of the Hispanic world appear on the inside front and back covers of the textbook for quick reference.

- *Appendixes:* Appendix A summarizes the sounds and key pronunciation features of the Spanish language, with abundant examples; this section is also recorded on the Student Cassette so students can hear and practice proper pronunciation of the Spanish sounds outside of the classroom. Conjugations of high-frequency regular, stem-changing, and irregular Spanish verbs constitute Appendix B. Appendix C is a glossary of all grammatical terms used in the text, with examples. Appendix D provides English translations of the lesson dialogues. Appendix E is the answer key to the Self Tests. Appendix F provides a list of the Spanish names of more than 100 professions and occupations to facilitate personalized classroom discussion.

- *Vocabularies:* Spanish-English and English-Spanish glossaries list all active, core vocabulary introduced in the *Vocabulario* lists that follow the dialogues and in the *Estructuras* sections. Active vocabulary is identified by the number of the lesson in which the word or phrase first appears. The Spanish-English vocabulary also lists passive vocabulary, which consists of those words glossed by an English equivalent in the text.

Supplementary Materials for the Student

Student Cassette: A free ninety-minute tape containing recordings of the dialogues, the pronunciation sections, and the introduction to Spanish sounds from Appendix A is packaged with each copy of the student's text. This cassette is designed to maximize learners' exposure to the sounds of natural spoken Spanish and improve their pronunciation.

Workbook/Laboratory Manual: Each lesson of the Workbook/Laboratory Manual is correlated to the corresponding lesson in the student's text and is divided into two sections. The *Workbook Activities* section offers an array of writing activities—sentence completion, sentence transformation, fill-in charts, dehydrated sentences, answering questions, crossword puzzles, and illustration-based exercises—that reinforce the structures and vocabulary presented in the textbook. Reading comprehension passages appear after each odd-numbered lesson to further skill development in that area. *Check Your Progress* sections provide a comprehensive review of key vocabulary and structures after every two lessons. The *Laboratory Activities* section includes pronunciation, structure, listening comprehension, and dictation exercises to be used in conjunction with the Cassette Program. An answer key for all written exercises with discrete answers in both the Workbook and the Laboratory sections is provided for self-correction.

Cassette Program: The complete Cassette Program to accompany the ¿Cómo se dice...? Workbook/Laboratory Manual, Sixth Edition, is available for student purchase. The textbook dialogues are included as listening and pronunciation exercises in each lesson; they are dramatized once at natural speed, then reread with pauses for repetition. They are followed by comprehension questions on the dialogues, an open-ended activity that elicits responses appropriate to given situations, structured grammar exercises, a listening comprehension activity, and a dictation. A comprehensive review section of questions follows Lessons 9 and 18. Answers to all exercises, except for those that require a written response, are provided on the cassettes.

Computer Study Modules: Available in Windows® and Macintosh® versions, this text-specific software offers additional, computer-aided practice of grammar structures and vocabulary from the textbook as well as supplemental reading comprehension activities. The program provides immediate feedback so users can monitor their progress in Spanish, and the package includes a User's Guide.

¿Cómo se dice...? **CD-ROM:** New to the Sixth Edition, this state-of-the-art multimedia program develops all four language skills and cultural awareness in a self-paced, user-friendly environment. This interactive learning tool includes eighteen modules correlated to the textbook lessons and features seventy-two full-motion video clips of exclusive interviews with native speakers from around the Spanish-speaking world. Each video clip has two activities. True/false or multiple-choice exercises check basic understanding of the interview. Click-and-drag activities require users to listen to a brief passage in Spanish and then manipulate words or images on screen in response to what they heard. In the interview activities, users listen to personal questions based on the interview topic and record their responses. The task-based writing activities provide a topic related to the interview; the composition may be printed and submitted to the instructor for evaluation. The program also contains supplemental cultural information, a list of key words for understanding each video clip, a transcript of each clip in

Spanish, sample answers for the interview activities, and useful tips for the writing activities. The CD-ROM runs on both Windows® and Macintosh® platforms.

Supplementary Materials for the Instructor

Instructor's Annotated Edition: The Introduction to the Instructor's Annotated Edition provides a detailed description of the entire **¿Cómo se dice...?** program with suggestions for its implementation. In the annotated version of the student's text that follows the introductory material, specific suggestions for implementing and supplementing the features of the lesson are supplied right on the appropriate textbook page.

¿Cómo se dice...? Video: Completely revised for the Sixth Edition, this captivating two-hour video provides a unique opportunity to develop listening skills and cultural awareness through multiple levels of viewing materials: unrehearsed interviews with native speakers from sixteen Spanish-speaking countries on a wide variety of topics, authentic footage, and images of everyday life. The video consists of eighteen modules that correlate to the *Así somos* and *Teleinforme* sections in the student's text. Filmed during the Semana Panamericana at the Universidad Autónoma de Guadalajara in Mexico, the nine *Así somos* modules reinforce the lesson themes, vocabulary, and language functions. They enable students to see, hear, and interact with Hispanics in authentic settings. In each module, students listen to a series of basic questions posed by María Isabel, the host, and the interviewees' responses. The segment concludes with María Isabel asking the viewers a question to which they provide a personalized response. The special *Entrevista* section, which appears at the end of Lessons 3, 7, 13, 15, and 17, features interviews with selected professionals. The nine *Teleinforme* modules present a broad cultural overview of the Hispanic world through authentic television footage from a number of Hispanic countries. Each *Teleinforme* includes two to four clips with a wide range of content: interviews, travelogues, festivals, and commercials. The content reinforces in a visually appealing and lively manner the material presented in the *Panoramas hispánicos*.

Instructor's Resource Manual: This new component contains the printed version of the Testing Program, the Cassette Program Tapescript, the Videoscript, and the answer key to the *Check Your Progress* sections of the Workbook. Completely revised, the Testing Program now features two versions (A and B) of all quizzes and exams. It includes quizzes for each of the eighteen regular lessons and the preliminary lesson of **¿Cómo se dice...?**, midterm examinations designed to be given after Lessons 4 and 13, final examinations to be given after Lessons 9 and 18, and an answer key for each quiz or exam. Each test evaluates students' mastery of target vocabulary and grammar as well as their listening comprehension and writing skills.

Instructor's Activities Manual: New to the Sixth Edition, this component provides a wide range of supplementary material that allows instructors the flexibility to tailor their classes to meet specific needs of their students. It contains communicative and listening comprehension activities, games, and vocabulary and grammar exercises that can be photocopied and distributed to students for additional practice.

Computerized Test Bank: This component enables instructors to customize the existing Testing Program by selecting specific items and by adding, deleting, or modifying items. The Computerized Test Bank is available in Windows® and Macintosh® versions.

***¿Cómo se dice...?* Overhead Transparencies:**   This new supplement contains fifty-five, full-color, text-specific or thematic visuals and a series of maps of the Spanish-speaking world. The overhead transparencies facilitate vocabulary presentation or provide visual cues for activities that reinforce the vocabulary and structures in the textbook.

Situation Cards Kit: This set of 120 cards with its own Instructor's Guide enables instructors to monitor students' development of oral proficiency.

Spanish History Booklet: This booklet contains supplementary information on the history, politics, and cultures of Spain and Hispanic America.

Instructor's Resource Kit: This conveniently boxed supplement package assists the instructor in presenting, reviewing, expanding, and reinforcing the materials in the textbook. The Instructor's Resource Kit for ¿Cómo se dice...?, Sixth Edition, contains the following materials:

- The Instructor's Resource Manual
- The Instructor's Activities Manual
- The ¿Cómo se dice...? Overhead Transparencies
- The Situation Cards Kit
- The Spanish History Booklet

We would like to hear your comments on and reactions to ¿**Cómo se dice...?**, Sixth Edition. Reports on your experiences using this program would be of great interest and value to us. Please write us care of Houghton Mifflin Company, College Division, Modern Languages, 222 Berkeley Street, Boston, MA 02116–3764.

Acknowledgments

We wish to express appreciation to the following colleagues for the many valuable suggestions they offered in their reviews of the Fifth Edition and of the revised manuscript of the Sixth Edition.

Jon Amastae, The University of Texas at El Paso
Graciela Buschardt, St. Louis Community College at Meramec
Octavio de la Suarée, William Paterson College
Ronna S. Feit, Nassau Community College
Carmen Forner, Community College of Southern Nevada at Las Vegas

Mark Forrester, Burlington County College
Peg Haas, Kent State University
Virginia Morris, Broward Community College
Eileen Nelson, Brookhaven College
Verónica Mejía Noguer, Chaffey College
Loknath Persaud, Pasadena City College
Wendy L. Rolph, University of Toronto
Ruth E. Smith, Northeast Louisiana University
Rosa L. Stewart, University of Victoria
Edda Temoche-Weldele, Grossmont College

We also extend our sincere appreciation to the Modern Languages Staff of Houghton Mifflin Company, College Division: E. Kristina Baer, Director of Modern Language Programs; Sharon Alexander, Senior Development Editor; Helen Bronk, Project Editor; Jennifer Waddell, Senior Production/Design Coordinator; Sally Culler, Manufacturing Coordinator; and Henry Rachlin, Designer.

Ana C. Jarvis
Raquel Lebredo
Francisco Mena-Ayllón

CONTENTS

LECCIÓN 6

UN VIAJE A PERÚ   132

LECCIÓN 7

HABLANDO DE LAS VACACIONES   164

LECCIÓN 13

SE ALQUILA UN APARTAMENTO   315

LECCIÓN 14

PLANEANDO UNA CENA   333

Saludos y despedidas

▄▄ EN LA UNIVERSIDAD

—Buenos días, profesora.
—Buenos días, señorita.
  ¿Cómo se llama usted?
—Me llamo María Teresa Rojas.

—Buenas tardes, doctor Vega.
—Buenas tardes, señora.
  ¿Cómo está usted?
—Muy bien, gracias. ¿Y usted?
—Bien, gracias.

—Buenas noches, señor Acosta.[1]
—Buenas noches, Ana María.
  ¿Qué tal?
—Bien, ¿y usted?
—No muy bien...
—¡Caramba! ¡Lo siento!

---

[1] In Spanish-speaking countries, young people frequently address their elders as **señor** or **señora**.

EN EL CLUB

—Hola, Juan Carlos.
—Hola, Silvia. ¿Cómo estás?
—Bien, ¿y tú?
—Bien, gracias.
—¿Qué hay de nuevo?
—Nada.
—Hasta luego.
—Adiós.

—Hasta mañana, Mirta.
—Hasta mañana, Daniel.
  Saludos a Roberto.

—Chau, Tito.
—Chau. Nos vemos el lunes.

VOCABULARIO (vocabulary)

■ TÍTULOS (titles)

doctor (Dr.)   doctor[1] *(masculine)*
doctora (Dra.)   doctor *(feminine)*
profesor   professor, teacher,
  instructor *(masculine)*
profesora   professor, teacher,
  instructor *(feminine)*

señor (Sr.)   Mr., sir, gentleman
señora (Sra.)   Mrs., madam, lady
señorita (Srta.)   Miss, young lady

■ SALUDOS Y DESPEDIDAS (greetings and farewells)

adiós   good-bye
buenas noches   good evening,
  good night
buenas tardes   good afternoon

buenos días   good morning
chau[2]   bye
hasta luego   see you later
hasta mañana   see you tomorrow

hola   hello, hi
Nos vemos.   See you.
Saludos a...   Say hello to . . .

■ OTRAS PALABRAS Y EXPRESIONES (other words and expressions)

¡caramba!   gee!
el lunes[3]   Monday
en la universidad   at the university
en el club   at the club

gracias   thanks, thank you
lo siento   I'm sorry
muy   very
¿qué?   what?

tú   you *(informal)*
usted (Ud.)   you *(formal)*
y   and

■ PREGUNTAS Y RESPUESTAS ÚTILES (useful questions and answers)

¿Cómo se llama usted?   What is your name?
Me llamo...   My name is . . .
¿Cómo está usted?   How are you? *(formal)*
¿Cómo estás?   How are you? *(informal)*
¿Qué tal?   How's it going? *(informal)*
¿Qué hay de nuevo?   What's new?

bien   fine
muy bien   very well
no   no, not
no muy bien   not very well
nada   nothing

---

[1] In most Spanish-speaking countries, lawyers and members of many other professions who hold the
  equivalent of a Ph.D. are addressed as **doctor** or **doctora**.
[2] from the Italian "*ciao*"
[3] The definite article **el** *(the)* is used in Spanish as the equivalent of *on* with the days of the week.

Useful expressions for the class *(Expresiones útiles para la clase)*

You will hear your teacher use the following directions and general terms in class. Take time to familiarize yourself with them.

■ When the teacher is speaking to the whole class:

Abran sus libros, por favor.	*Open your books, please.*
Cierren sus libros, por favor.	*Close your books, please.*
Escriban, por favor.	*Write, please.*
Escuchen, por favor.	*Listen, please.*
Estudien la Lección...	*Study Lesson . . .*
Hagan el ejercicio número...	*Do exercise number . . .*
Levanten la mano.	*Raise your hands.*
Repasen el vocabulario.	*Review the vocabulary.*
Repitan, por favor.	*Repeat, please.*
Siéntense, por favor.	*Sit down, please.*
Vayan a la página...	*Go to page . . .*

■ When the teacher is speaking to one student:

Continúe, por favor.	*Go on, please.*
Lea, por favor.	*Read, please.*
Vaya a la pizarra, por favor.	*Go to the chalkboard, please.*

■ Some other words used in the classroom:

diccionario	*dictionary*	**palabra**	*word*
dictado	*dictation*	**presente**	*present, here*
examen	*exam*	**prueba**	*quiz*
horario de clases	*class schedule*	**tarea**	*homework*

■ Many of the words in these expressions are cognates, words that are the same or similar in two languages. Learning to recognize cognates will be extremely valuable to you in your study of Spanish. Some examples of cognates are **lección, vocabulario,** and **examen.** How many others can you identify?

¿Lo sabía Ud.?[1]

María is a very popular name in Spain and Latin America. It is frequently used in conjunction with other names: **Ana María, María Isabel, María Teresa, María Luisa,** etc. It is also used as a middle name for men, for example, **José María, Luis María,** and **Jesús María.**

---

[1]Did you know?

The alphabet *(El alfabeto)*

Letter	Name	Letter	Name	Letter	Name	Letter	Name
a	a	h	hache	ñ	eñe	u	u
b	be	i	i	o	o	v	ve
c	ce	j	jota	p	pe	w	doble ve
ch	che	k	ka	q	cu	x	equis
d	de	l	ele	r	ere	y	y griega
e	e	ll	elle	rr	erre	z	zeta
f	efe	m	eme	s	ese		
g	ge	n	ene	t	te		

ATENCIÓN **Ch** and **ll** are not treated as separate letters in new dictionaries.

Práctica

A. Spell these well-known acronyms in Spanish.

1. FBI 2. IBM 3. NAACP 4. PTA
5. NBA 6. NHF 7. CIO 8. AFL

B. A Spanish-speaking person may not know how to spell your name. If that person wants to write it, he or she might ask, **¿Cómo se escribe?** *(How do you spell it?)*. Learn how to spell your name in Spanish and ask other members of the class how to spell theirs.

Cardinal numbers 0–30 *(Números cardinales 0–30)*

0 cero	8 ocho	16 dieciséis[1]
1 uno	9 nueve	17 diecisiete
2 dos	10 diez	18 dieciocho
3 tres	11 once	19 diecinueve
4 cuatro	12 doce	20 veinte
5 cinco	13 trece	21 veintiuno
6 seis	14 catorce	30 treinta
7 siete	15 quince	

ATENCIÓN **Uno** changes to **un** before a masculine singular noun: **un profesor** *(one professor)*. **Uno** changes to **una** before a feminine singular noun: **una profesora** *(one professor)*.

---

[1] The numbers 16 to 29 may also be spelled as separate words: **diez y seis…, veinte y uno…,** and so on.

Práctica

A. To ask someone for his or her phone number, say, "**¿Cuál es tu[1] número de teléfono?**" *(What is your phone number?)*. Ask several members of the class for their phone numbers.

B. Complete the following series of numbers.

1. dos, cuatro,... treinta
2. uno, tres, cinco,... veintinueve
3. cero, tres,... dieciocho
4. cero, cuatro,... veintiocho

Colors   *(Colores)*

■   You will see different colors in the classroom. Learn how to say them in Spanish.

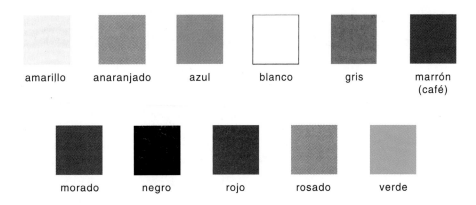

| amarillo | anaranjado | azul | blanco | gris | marrón (café) |

| morado | negro | rojo | rosado | verde |

Práctica

To ask someone whether he or she likes something, you say, "**¿Te gusta...?**"[2] To say that you like something, say, "**Me gusta...**" Conduct a survey of your classmates to find out which color is the most popular in class, following the model.

> MODELO: —¿Qué color te gusta?
> —*Me gusta el color rojo.*

---

[1] **tu**=*your* (when addressing a friend or a very young person). Say, "**¿Cuál es su número de teléfono?**" when addressing someone as **usted.**

[2] When addressing someone as **usted,** use **¿Le gusta...?**

Days of the week   *(Los días de la semana)*

SEPTIEMBRE

LUNES	MARTES	MIÉRCOLES	JUEVES	VIERNES	SÁBADO	DOMINGO
		1	2	3	4	5
6	7	8	9	10	11	12
13	14	15	16	17	18	19
20	21	22	23	24	25	26
27	28	29	30			

—¿Qué día es hoy? **¿Jueves?**   *"What day is today? Thursday?"*
—No, hoy es **viernes.**   *"No, today is Friday."*

◼ In Spanish-speaking countries, the week starts on Monday.

◼ Note that the days of the week are not capitalized in Spanish.

◼ The days of the week are masculine in Spanish. The masculine definite articles **el** and **los** are often used with them to express *on.*

Práctica

The person asking these questions is always a day ahead. Respond, following the model.

MODELO: —¿Hoy es lunes?
—*No, hoy es domingo.*

1. ¿Hoy es miércoles?
2. ¿Hoy es domingo?
3. ¿Hoy es viernes?
4. ¿Hoy es martes?
5. ¿Hoy es sábado?
6. ¿Hoy es jueves?

Months and seasons of the year   *(Los meses y las estaciones del año)*

El invierno

La primavera

El verano

El otoño

- To ask for the date, say:

    —¿Qué fecha es hoy?   *"What's the date today?"*

- When giving the date, always begin with the phrase **"hoy es el..."**

    —Hoy es el veinte de mayo.   *"Today is May twentieth."*

- Begin with the number, followed by the preposition **de** *(of)*, and then the month.

el quince de agosto	*August fifteenth*
el diez de septiembre	*September tenth*

    —¿Qué fecha es hoy?¿**El pri-   *"What's the date today? May
    mero de mayo?**   first?"*
    —No, hoy es **el treinta de abril.** *"No, today is April thirtieth."*

ATENCIÓN   **Primero** *(First)* is the only ordinal number used with dates. Also, the months are not capitalized in Spanish.

Práctica

A. Give the Spanish equivalent of the following dates.

1. July fourth
2. October thirty-first
3. January first
4. May fifth
5. February twelfth
6. December twenty-fifth
7. March twenty-first
8. April second
9. June twentieth
10. September ninth
11. August thirteenth
12. November eleventh

B. Indicate in which season the following months fall in the Northern Hemisphere.

1. febrero
2. agosto
3. mayo
4. enero
5. octubre
6. julio
7. abril
8. noviembre

C. Conduct a survey of your classmates to find out which season is the most popular, following the model. Which one is the least popular?

> **MODELO:** —¿Qué estación te gusta?
> —*Me gusta el (la)* _____ .

¡A VER CUÁNTO APRENDIÓ!

(Let's see how much you learned!)

¡Repase el vocabulario!   *(Review the vocabulary!)*

Match each item in column A with its English equivalent in column B.

A	B
1. Estudien la Lección dos.	a. Open the book, please.
2. Hagan los ejercicios, por favor.	b. Raise your hands.
3. Siéntese, por favor.	c. Repeat, please.
4. Vayan a la página diez.	d. Write the dictation.
5. Abra el libro, por favor.	e. Go to page ten.
6. Repitan, por favor.	f. Sit down, please.
7. Vaya a la pizarra.	g. Study Lesson two.
8. Levanten la mano.	h. Read the exam, please.
9. Escriban el dictado.	i. Go to the chalkboard.
10. Lea el examen, por favor.	j. Do the exercises, please.

Entrevista   *(Interview)*

With a classmate, practice giving appropriate responses to the following statements and questions.

1. Buenos días, ¿cómo estás?
2. Buenas tardes.
3. Buenas noches.
4. Hola, ¿qué tal?
5. ¿Qué hay de nuevo?
6. ¿Qué día es hoy?
7. ¿Qué fecha es hoy?
8. ¿Cuál es tu número de teléfono?
9. Hasta mañana.
10. Hasta luego.

Situaciones   *(Situations)*

What would you say in the following situations? What might the other person say? Act out the scenes with a partner. Take turns playing each role.

1. You encounter your instructor in the morning and ask how he or she is.
2. In the grocery store, you run into a friend you haven't seen for a while.
3. You meet a friend's five-year-old daughter in the park and ask how she is.
4. You leave Dr. María Méndez's office. You have another appointment with her tomorrow.
5. You say good-bye to a friend and add that you will see him or her on Wednesday.
6. You meet an older person and want to know his or her name.
7. Someone tells you he or she is not feeling too well.
8. Someone asks what's new with you.
9. Someone asks how you are. You are not feeling well.
10. You want a classmate to say hello to a friend for you.

Números de teléfono   *(Telephone numbers)*

This is a page from someone's address book. Say the phone number of each of the following people.

1. La doctora Parra
2. José María
3. El señor Pardo
4. Tito
5. La señora Pagán
6. El profesor Paredes
7. La señorita Peña
8. Amanda

NOMBRES	TELÉFONOS
María Luisa Pagán	325-4270
José María Pereyra	476-0389
Teresita Peña	721-4693
Amanda Pidal	396-7548
Ángel Pardo	482-3957
Prof. Benito Paredes	396-1598
Dra. Raquel Parra	476-8539
Tito Paz	721-0653
David Pizarro	482-7986
María Inés Pinto	396-8510

Sumas y restas *(Additions and subtractions)*

Solve these arithmetic problems, using the following mathematical terms.

+ más	− menos	= son
1. 7 + 12 =	4. 14 + 15 =	7. 20 - 16 =
2. 5 + 25 =	5. 11 + 10 =	8. 30 - 13 =
3. 18 + 9 =	6. 22 - 8 =	

En la vida real *(In real life)*

Encuentros *(Encounters)*

Imagine that you and a classmate meet outside of class. How would you greet each other in Spanish? How would you find out each other's complete name and phone number? How would you say good-bye? Act out this situation with a partner. You may want to include these additional phrases:

¿Cómo te va?   *How is it going (for you)?*
Hasta la vista.   *Until I see you again.*

Por teléfono *(By phone)*

You and a classmate are in Madrid, Spain. Take turns reading the telephone numbers you must call according to the following needs.

1. You are having car trouble.
2. You need to cash a check.
3. You need some medicine.
4. You want to send roses to a friend.
5. You want to see a play.
6. You have to travel by plane.
7. You need to have your picture taken.
8. Somebody stole you wallet.

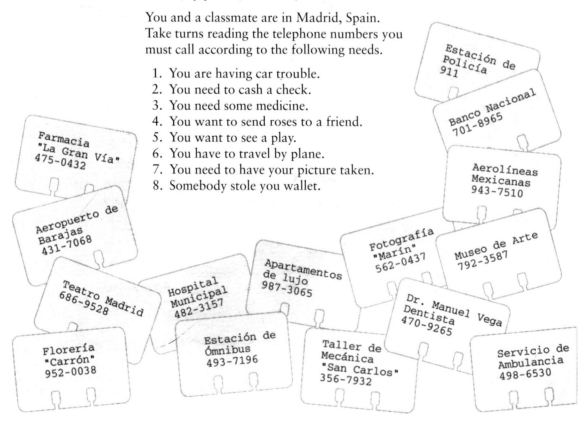

Estación de Policía
911

Banco Nacional
701-8965

Aerolíneas Mexicanas
943-7510

Farmacia "La Gran Vía"
475-0432

Aeropuerto de Barajas
431-7068

Fotografía "Marín"
562-0437

Museo de Arte
792-3587

Teatro Madrid
686-9528

Hospital Municipal
482-3157

Apartamentos de lujo
987-3065

Dr. Manuel Vega Dentista
470-9265

Florería "Carrón"
952-0038

Estación de Ómnibus
493-7196

Taller de Mecánica "San Carlos"
356-7932

Servicio de Ambulancia
498-6530

9. A friend needs to go to the emergency room.
10. You need a place to live.
11. You want to buy a plane ticket to Mexico.
12. You want to see Picasso's paintings.
13. One of your friends has been hospitalized.
14. You want to travel to a nearby city.
15. You have a toothache.

Colores

A splash of color! This is an open-air market in Guatemala. How many colors that you see here can you name in Spanish? You will need to include:

claro   *light*
oscuro   *dark*
(i.e., **azul oscuro** = *dark blue*)

Mercado al aire libre en Guatemala.

EL PRIMER DÍA DE CLASES

OBJECTIVES

■ **Pronunciation**

The Spanish **a** and **e**

■ **Structure**

Gender and number • Definite and indefinite articles • Cardinal numbers 31–100 • Subject pronouns • Present indicative of **ser** • Telling time

■ **Communication**

You will learn vocabulary related to the classroom, useful questions and answers, and some polite expressions

▭ EL PRIMER DÍA DE CLASES

SRTA. ALBA	—*(En la puerta)* Con permiso. Buenos días, profesor.
PROFESOR	—Buenos días. Pase y tome asiento.
SRTA. ALBA	—Muchas gracias.
PROFESOR	—Señorita Alba, el[1] doctor Díaz.
SRTA. ALBA	—Mucho gusto, doctor Díaz.
DR. DÍAZ	—El gusto es mío, señorita Alba.
SRTA. ALBA	—¡Perdón!, profesor, ¿qué hora es?
PROFESOR	—Son las dos.
SRTA. ALBA	—¿A qué hora es la clase hoy?
PROFESOR	—Es a las tres.

MARIO	—¿De dónde son Uds.?
RAÚL	—Nosotros somos de Ecuador. Tú eres de México, ¿verdad?
MARIO	—Sí. Oye, ¿cuántos estudiantes hay en la clase?
RAÚL	—Hay cuarenta estudiantes.
LUISA	—¿Cuál es tu dirección, Mario?
MARIO	—Calle Magnolia, número 98.

ESTUDIANTE	—Profesor, ¿cómo se dice "de nada" en inglés?
PROFESOR	—Se dice *"you're welcome"*.
ESTUDIANTE	—¿Qué quiere decir *"please"*?
PROFESOR	—Quiere decir "por favor".

---

[1]When you are speaking about a third person (indirect address) and use a title with the name, the definite article is required.

LAURA	—Hola. Me llamo Laura Vargas. ¿Cómo te llamas tú?
SILVIA	—Me llamo Silvia Cruz.
LAURA	—¿De dónde eres, Silvia?
SILVIA	—Yo soy de Costa Rica, ¿y tú?
LAURA	—Soy de Chile.
SILVIA	—Adiós, Laura.
LAURA	—Hasta la vista, Silvia.

VOCABULARIO

■ NOMBRES (Nouns)

la calle street
la clase class
el día day

la dirección, el domicilio address
el (la) estudiante student
el inglés English (language)

el número number
la puerta door

■ OTRAS PALABRAS Y EXPRESIONES

¿cómo? how?
¿cuál? what?, which?
¿cuántos(-as)? how many?
de from
¿de dónde? from where?
el primer día de clases the first day
   of classes

en in, at
en inglés in English
hasta la vista until I see you again,
   I'll see you later
hay there is, there are
hoy today

oye listen
sí yes
¿verdad? right?, true?

■ PREGUNTAS Y RESPUESTAS ÚTILES

¿A qué hora...? At what time . . . ?
A la (las)... At . . . (when referring
   to time of day)
¿Cómo se dice...? How do you
   say . . . ?
Se dice... You say . . . ,
   One says . . .
¿Cómo te llamas?[1] What's your
   name?

Me llamo... My name is . . .
¿Cuál es tu dirección?[2] What's
   your address?
Mi dirección es... My address
   is . . .
¿De dónde eres? Where are you
   from?
Soy de... I'm from . . .
¿Qué hora es? What time is it?

Son las... It's . . . (when referring
   to time of day)
¿Qué quiere decir...? What does
   . . . mean?
Quiere decir... It means . . .

---

[1] Use the **tú** form when addressing a child or a very young person.
[2] When addressing someone as **Ud.**, say **¿Cuál es su dirección?**

■ EXPRESIONES DE CORTESÍA *(Polite expressions)*

Mucho gusto. Pleased to meet you.
El gusto es mío. The pleasure is
  mine.
Con permiso. Excuse me.
Perdón. Pardon me.

Pase. Come in.
Tome asiento. Have a seat.
Por favor. Please.

Muchas gracias. Thank you very
  much.
De nada. You're welcome.

VOCABULARIO ADICIONAL

■ EN LA CLASE *(in the class)*

¡CONVERSEMOS! *(Let's talk)*

Team up with a classmate and respond appropriately to the following questions
or statements.

1. Mucho gusto, señor (señora, señorita).
2. Muchas gracias.
3. ¿Cuántos estudiantes hay en la clase?
4. ¿Cómo se dice *"please"* en español *(Spanish)*?
5. ¿Qué quiere decir "con permiso"?
6. ¿Cómo te llamas?
7. ¿Cuál es tu dirección? *(Say street numbers one by one.)*
8. ¿Cuál es tu número de teléfono?

¿Lo sabia Ud.?

- Para los horarios *(schedules)* de aviones *(planes)*, trenes, autobuses, teatros, televisión y algunas *(some)* invitaciones, se usa el sistema de veinticuatro horas. Por ejemplo, las cuatro de la tarde son las dieciséis horas.

- En España y en Latinoamérica, muchas personas estudian inglés en la escuela secundaria *(high school)* y en la universidad.

HORAS XXI

Todos los Martes de 21 a 23 horas RADIO CARITAS en el 680 del dial

PRONUNCIACIÓN

A The Spanish a

The Spanish **a** is pronounced like the *a* in the English word *father*. Listen to your teacher and repeat the following words.

Ana	hora	Rosa
nada	habla	vista
gracias	hasta	asiento

B The Spanish e

The Spanish **e** is pronounced like the *e* in the English word *eight*. Listen to your teacher and repeat the following words.

qué	calle	enero
usted	tome	pase
media	Pepe	Ester

ESTRUCTURAS

1 Gender and number *(Género y número)*

A. Gender, Part I

■ In Spanish, all nouns—including those denoting non-living things—are either masculine or feminine.

Masculine		Feminine	
el hombre	el lápiz	la mujer	la ventana
el profesor	el estudiante	la profesora	la estudiante
el cuaderno	el secretario	la tiza	la secretaria

■ Most nouns that end in **-o** or denote males are masculine: **cuaderno** *(notebook)*; **hombre** *(man)*.

■ Most nouns that end in **-a** or denote females are feminine: **mes**a *(table)*; **profesor**a *(female professor)*; **mujer** *(woman)*.

ATENCIÓN   Some common exceptions include the words **el día** *(day)* and **el mapa** *(map)*, which end in **-a** but are masculine, and the word **la mano** *(hand)*, which ends in **-o** but is feminine.

■ Here are some helpful rules to remember about gender:

■ Some masculine nouns ending in **-o** have a corresponding feminine form ending in **-a**: **el secretario/la secretaria**.

■ When a masculine noun ends in a consonant, the corresponding feminine noun is often formed by adding **-a**: **el profesor/la profesora**.

■ Many nouns that refer to people use the same form for both genders: **el estudiante/la estudiante**. In such cases, gender is indicated by the article **el** (masculine) or **la** (feminine).

Práctica

Indicate whether the following nouns are feminine or masculine.

1. mapa	6. profesora	11. ventana	16. mano
2. tiza	7. pizarra	12. pluma	17. cuaderno
3. escritorio	8. libro	13. hombre	18. doctor
4. señor	9. mujer	14. día	19. silla
5. doctora	10. puerta	15. secretario	20. señora

B. Plural forms

■ The plural of nouns is formed by adding -s to words ending in a vowel and -es to words ending in a consonant.

señora → señoras	reloj → relojes
silla → sillas	borrador → borradores
libro → libros	lección → lecciones

ATENCIÓN Note that the plural form of **lección** does not have a written accent. See Appendix A.

■ When a noun ends in -z, change the -z to c and add -es.

lápiz → lápices   luz *(light)* → luces

■ When the plural is used to refer to two or more nouns of different genders, the masculine form is used.

dos secretarias y un secretario → tres secretarios

Práctica

Give the plural of the following nouns.

1. mapa
2. reloj
3. tiza
4. lápiz
5. ventana
6. puerta
7. lección
8. escritorio
9. borrador
10. día
11. luz
12. profesor

2 Definite and indefinite articles
(Artículos determinados e indeterminados)

A. The definite article

■ Spanish has four forms that are equivalent to the English definite article *the*.

	Masculine	Feminine	English
Singular	el	la	*the*
Plural	los	las	

el profesor	los profesores
la profesora	las profesoras
el lápiz	los lápices

ATENCIÓN It is a good idea to learn new nouns with their corresponding definite articles—this will help you to remember their gender.

B. The indefinite article

The Spanish equivalents of *a (an)* and *some* are as follows.

	Masculine	**Feminine**	**English**
Singular	un	una	*a (an)*
Plural	unos	unas	*some*

un libro   **unos** libros
una silla   **unas** sillas
un profesor   **unos** profesores

Práctica

A. Identify the following objects or people using the appropriate definite article.

1.

2.

3.

4.

5.

6.

B. Identify the following objects or people using the appropriate indefinite article.

1.

2.

3.

4.

5.

6.

3 Cardinal numbers 31–100   *(Números cardinales 31–100)*

31	treinta y uno	70	setenta
32	treinta y dos (and so on)	77	setenta y siete
40	cuarenta	80	ochenta
41	cuarenta y uno (and so on)	84	ochenta y cuatro
50	cincuenta	90	noventa
53	cincuenta y tres	95	noventa y cinco
60	sesenta	100	cien (ciento)
68	sesenta y ocho		

■   Note that **y** appears only in numbers between 16 and 99.

Práctica

When saying phone numbers, people in many Spanish-speaking countries tend to say the first number alone and the rest of the numbers in pairs. Using this system, give the names and phone numbers of the specialists the following people would call for each situation.

1. Your nephew has a bad case of acne.
2. Your best friend thinks she is pregnant.
3. Your grandmother has blurred vision.
4. Your friend's child is sick.
5. Your neighbor has frequent chest pains.

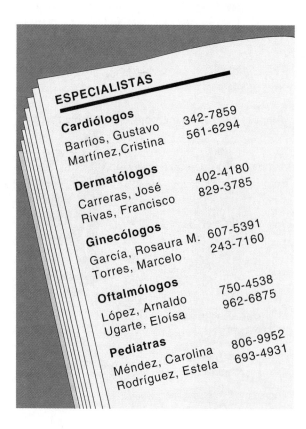

ESPECIALISTAS

Cardiólogos
Barrios, Gustavo   342-7859
Martínez, Cristina   561-6294

Dermatólogos
Carreras, José   402-4180
Rivas, Francisco   829-3785

Ginecólogos
García, Rosaura M.   607-5391
Torres, Marcelo   243-7160

Oftalmólogos
López, Arnaldo   750-4538
Ugarte, Eloísa   962-6875

Pediatras
Méndez, Carolina   806-9952
Rodríguez, Estela   693-4931

4 Subject pronouns *(Pronombres personales usados como sujetos)*

Singular	Plural
yo *I*	nosotros *we* (masc.)
	nosotras *we* (fem.)
tú *you* (informal)	vosotros *you* (masc., informal)
	vosotras *you* (fem., informal)
usted *you* (formal)	ustedes *you* (formal)
él *he*	ellos *they* (masc.)
ella *she*	ellas *they* (fem.)

▪ The **tú** form is used as the equivalent of *you* to address a friend, a coworker, a relative, or a child. The **usted** form is used in general to express deference or respect. In most Spanish-speaking countries today, young people tend to call each other **tú** even if they have just met. If in doubt, use **usted.**

▪ The plural form of **tú** is **vosotros(-as),** which is used only in Spain. In Latin America, the plural form **ustedes** (abbreviated **Uds.**) is used as the plural form of both **usted** (abbreviated **Ud.**) and **tú.**

▪ The masculine plural forms can refer to the masculine gender alone or to both genders together.

Ellos (Luis y Carlos) son de Panamá.	*They (Luis and Carlos) are from Panama.*
Ellos (María, Marta y Raúl) son de España.	*They (María, Marta, and Raúl) are from Spain.*
Nosotros (Ana María, Carlos y yo) somos estudiantes.	*We (Ana María, Carlos, and I) are students.*

Práctica

A. Identify the personal pronoun that corresponds to each picture below.

1. _____   2. _____

3. _____

4. _____

5. _____

6. _____

7. _____

8. _____

9. _____

B. What pronoun would you use to address the following people?

1. the president of the university
2. two strangers
3. your best friend
4. your instructor
5. a new classmate
6. your neighbor's children

5 Present indicative of **ser** *(Presente de indicativo del verbo ser)*

ser *to be*		
Singular		
yo	soy	*I am*
tú	eres	*you are* (inf.)
Ud. ⎫		*you are* (form.)
él ⎬	es	*he is*
ella ⎭		*she is*
Plural		
nosotros(-as)	somos	*we are*
vosotros(-as)	sois	*you are* (inf.)
Uds. ⎫		*you are* (form.)
ellos ⎬	son	*they are* (masc.)
ellas ⎭		*they are* (fem.)

■ The verb **ser,** *to be,* is irregular. Its forms, like the forms of other irregular verbs, must be memorized.

■ The verb ser is commonly used to express identity, place of origin, occupation, and nationality. It is also used to tell time.

—¿Ud. **es** profesor?[1]	*"Are you a teacher?"*
—No, **soy** estudiante.	*"No, I'm a student."*
—¿Carlos Paz **es** mexicano?[1]	*"Is Carlos Paz Mexican?"*
—Sí, **es** de Guadalajara.	*"Yes, he's from Guadalajara."*
—¿Qué hora **es**?	*"What time is it?"*
—**Son** las dos.	*"It's two o'clock."*
—¿Quién **es** él?	*"Who is he?"*
—**Es** Héctor Díaz.	*"He is Héctor Díaz."*
—¿De dónde **es**?	*"Where is he from?"*
—**Es** de Ecuador.	*"He is from Ecuador."*

---

[1]The indefinite article is not used after the verb **ser** when describing profession, nationality, religion, or party affiliation unless an adjective follows the noun: **Ella es católica. Ana es una profesora excelente.**

Práctica

A. Say where these people are from, using the information found in the illustrations. Also, say the capital of each country.

> MODELO: yo
>> *Yo soy de Venezuela. La capital de Venezuela es Caracas.*

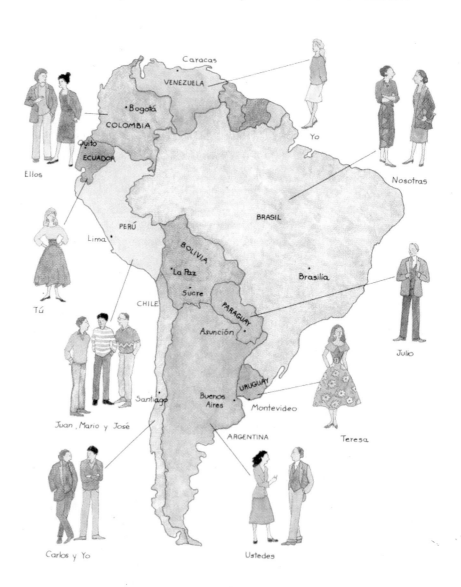

1. Teresa
2. Carlos y yo
3. Juan, Mario y José
4. tú
5. ellos
6. nosotras
7. Uds.
8. Julio

B. Say what nationality everyone is, using the list below. Follow the order used in Exercise A.

> **MODELO:** yo
> *Yo soy venezolana.*

argentino(-a)	chileno(-a)	uruguayo(-a)
boliviano(-a)	ecuatoriano(-a)	venezolano(-a)
brasileño(-a)	paraguayo(-a)	
colombiano(-a)	peruano(-a)	

6 Telling time   *(La hora)*

■ To ask what time it is, say, "**¿Qué hora es?**" To tell the time in Spanish, the following word order is used:

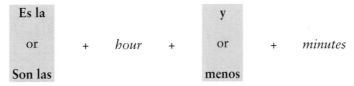

Es la				**y**		
or	+	*hour*	+	or	+	*minutes*
Son las				**menos**		

■ **Es** is used with **una.**

> **Es** la una.

■ **Son** is used with all the other hours.

> **Son** las cuatro.

■ The feminine definite article is always used before the hour, since it refers to *la* **hora.**

> Es **la** una y media.

> Son **las** diez y cuarto.

■ The hour is given first, then the minutes.

> Son las **once** menos **veinte.**

■ The equivalent of *past* or *after* is **y.**

> Es la una **y** veinticinco.

■ The equivalent of *to* or *till* is **menos.** It is used with fractions of time up to a half hour.

> Son las ocho **menos** cinco.

ATENCIÓN The equivalent of *at + time* is **a** + **la(s)** + *time*.

—¿Qué hora es?	*"What time is it?"*
—Son las cinco menos diez.[1]	*"It's ten to five."*
—¿A qué hora es la clase?	*"At what time is the class?"*
—La clase es a las cinco.	*"The class is at five o'clock."*

Práctica

A. With a partner, take turns giving the time indicated on the clocks in the illustration. Start with clock number one.

---

[1]It is becoming increasingly popular to substitute **y quince** for **y cuarto**, **y treinta** for **y media**, and **y treinta y cinco**, **y cuarenta**, etc., for **menos veinticinco, menos veinte**, and so on.

B. With a partner, take turns asking each other what time the programs in the listing are on and what programs are on at different times.

MODELOS: —¿A qué hora es "Telediario"?
—*Es a las seis.*

—¿Qué hay a las seis?
—*"Telediario".*

Programación del Canal 36

Viernes

6:00 Telediario	**9:00** Noticiero Televisa
6:50 Noticias Internacionales	**9:30** Música
7:00 Religión	**10:00** Fútbol
7:30 Música Latina	**11:00** Noticias de última hora
8:00 "María" (Telenovela)	

¡A VER CUÁNTO APRENDIÓ!

¡Repase el vocabulario!

A. Review the words referring to people and objects you see in the classroom, then name the numbered items below, using the definite article.

B. Supply the missing words and read aloud.

1. ¿Qué _____ es? ¿Las nueve?
2. ¿Cómo se _____ "puerta" en _____?
3. Tome _____, por favor.
4. ¿De _____ es Ud.? ¿De México?
5. ¿Cuántos estudiantes _____ en la clase?
6. ¿Qué _____ decir *"the pleasure is mine"*?
7. ¿Dirección? _____ Martí, _____ treinta.
8. ¿A qué _____ es la clase?
9. Hoy es el primer _____ de clases.
10. —Adiós.
    — _____ la vista.

Entrevista

Interview a classmate, using the **tú** form.

Pregúntele a su compañero(-a) de clase...
1. ...cómo se llama.
2. ...cuál es su dirección.
3. ...de dónde es.
4. ...cuántos estudiantes hay en la clase.
5. ...qué hora es.
6. ...qué quiere decir *"come in and have a seat"*.
7. ...cómo se dice "mucho gusto" en inglés.

Situaciones

What would you say in the following situations? What might the other person say? Act out the scenes with a partner. Take turns playing each role.

1. In class, you're not sure how to say "you're welcome" in Spanish.
2. You meet a little girl and want to know her name.
3. You need to know a classmate's address.
4. You can't remember what time your Spanish class meets. Your roommate is also in the class.
5. You are with Dr. Cortés and your teacher, who have never met before.
6. Your elderly neighbor stops by to say hello. You invite him to sit down.
7. You don't know what time it is. The person next to you on the bus is wearing a watch.

Más
que una
Tarjeta

EUROP ASSISTANCE

 **Para escribir**   *(To write)*

Complete the following dialogues.

1. *Julia talks with a classmate.*

JULIA   —_____

ELENA   —Me llamo Elena Martínez.

JULIA   —_____

ELENA   —Soy de Madrid.

JULIA   —_____

ELENA   —486-3497.

JULIA   —_____

ELENA   —Calle Roma, número veintiocho.

2. *Professor Mena and Mr. Roberto Soto are in the classroom. Today is Friday.*

PROF. MENA   —¿Cómo se llama usted, señor?

ROBERTO   —_____

PROF. MENA   —Mucho gusto, señor Soto.

ROBERTO   —_____

PROF. MENA   —¿Qué día es hoy?

ROBERTO   —_____

PROF. MENA   —¿Cómo se dice *"thirty-five"* en español?

ROBERTO   —_____

PROF. MENA   —¿Qué quiere decir *"Until I see you again"*?

ROBERTO   —_____

PROF. MENA   —Muy bien. Hasta luego, señor Soto.

ROBERTO   —_____

3. *A student thanks her teacher.*

MARISA   —_____

PROFESORA   —De nada, señorita García. Hasta luego.

MARISA   —_____

En la vida real

Presentaciones   *(Introductions)*

Form groups of three. After one person introduces the other two, make small talk: find out everybody's address, and talk about what day it is and what time it is. Finally, test each other on the meaning of certain words (¿**Qué quiere decir...?**). You might want to include the following words or phrases:

A sus órdenes.   *At your service.*

Encantado. (If you are male)
Encantada. (If you are female) } *Charmed (It's a pleasure).*

Horario de clases

This is María Elena's schedule. With a classmate, try to figure out when her classes are.

> MODELO: —¿Cuándo es la clase de tenis?
> —*La clase de tenis es los sábados.*
> —¿A qué hora?
> —*A las nueve.*

HORA	LUNES	MARTES	MIÉRCOLES	JUEVES	VIERNES	SÁBADO
8:00-9:00	Psicología		Psicología		Psicología	
9:00-10:00	Biología		Biología		Biología	Tenis
10:00-11:30		Historia		Historia		
12:15-1:00			ALMUERZO[1]			
1:00-2:00	Literatura		Literatura		Literatura	Laboratorio de Biología
5:00-6:30		Educación Física		Educación Física		
7:00-8:30	Arte		Arte			

———
[1]lunch

Mi horario

With the help of a dictionary and/or your instructor, work with a classmate to make up each other's schedules.

Un inventario de la clase

With a classmate, conduct an inventory of everything in your classroom, using **hay**.

Así somos

Vocabulario

Así somos.	This is the way we are.
la avenida	avenue
bastante	quite
bienvenidos	welcome
con acento	with an accent mark
contento	happy
España	Spain
el estado	state
la frontera	border
me encuentro	I feel
me siento	I feel
mi nombre	my name
los países	countries
se llama	is called
un poquito cansado	a little tired
vamos a conocer	we are going to meet
yo vengo de	I come from

Preparación

¿Cuánto saben Uds. ya? *(How much do you already know?)* In this video module, several Spanish-speaking people will say their names, addresses, and phone numbers. They will also describe where they are from and how they feel today. Make a list of the questions you would ask in Spanish to elicit this type of information.

Comprensión

A. ¿Cómo se escribe tu nombre?   Write the letters as each person spells his or her name.

B. Soy de...   Match the people's names with the countries they are from.

	A		B
_____	1. Jaime	a.	Puerto Rico
_____	2. Pedro	b.	Colombia
_____	3. Víctor Manuel	c.	España
_____	4. Leonardo	d.	El Salvador
_____	5. Juan	e.	Paraguay
_____	6. Héctor	f.	Bolivia
_____	7. Gustavo	g.	Ecuador
_____	8. Milka	h.	Estados Unidos
_____	9. Otmara	i.	México
_____	10. Orlando	j.	Panamá

C. ¿Verdadero (*True*) **o falso?**   Read the following statements. After watching the video, circle **V** (**verdadero**) or **F** (**falso**), according to what you understood.

V   F   1. La dirección de Carolina es Avenida El Cortijo 230 en Monte Rico, Lima.

V   F   2. La dirección de Milka es Calle Santa Cruz, número 31.

V   F   3. La dirección de Héctor en Ponce es Las Delicias, Calle 15BB75.

V   F   4. La dirección de Sofía es Andama 130, Interior 1.

D. Números de teléfono.   Write the phone numbers for the following people.

1. Milka   4. Rosalía
2. Pedro   5. Gustavo
3. Juan

Ampliación

¿Quién lo diría? *(Who would say it?)*   Match each statement with the name of the person who would most likely say it.

a. Milka   d. Gustavo
b. Pedro   e. Otmara
c. Jaime   f. Víctor

_____ 1. Yo soy panameña.
_____ 2. Yo soy mexicano.
_____ 3. Yo soy paraguayo.
_____ 4. Yo soy salvadoreño.
_____ 5. Yo soy colombiano.
_____ 6. Yo soy boliviana.

POR TELÉFONO

OBJECTIVES

■ **Pronunciation**
The Spanish **i, o,** and **u**

■ **Structure**
Present indicative of regular **-ar** verbs • Gender, Part II • Negative and interrogative sentences • Possession with **de** • Possessive adjectives • Cardinal numbers 101–1,000

■ **Communication**
You will learn vocabulary used to make and to receive phone calls.

POR TELÉFONO

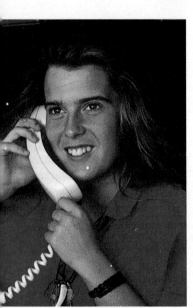

Raquel desea hablar con Marta.

MARISA   —¿Sí?
RAQUEL   —Hola. ¿Está Marta?
MARISA   —No, no está. Lo siento.
RAQUEL   —¿A qué hora regresa?
MARISA   —A las nueve de la noche.
RAQUEL   —Entonces llamo[1] más tarde.
MARISA   —Muy bien. Adiós.

Carmen habla con su amiga María.

MARÍA   —Bueno.
CARMEN   —Hola. ¿Está María?
MARÍA   —Sí, con ella habla… ¿Carmen?
CARMEN   —Sí. ¿Qué tal, María?
MARÍA   —Muy bien, gracias. ¿Qué hay de nuevo?
CARMEN   —Nada. ¡Oye! ¿Cuándo estudiamos[1] inglés?[2] ¿Hoy?
MARÍA   —Sí, y mañana estudiamos[1] francés.
CARMEN   —¿Dónde? ¿En la universidad?
MARÍA   —No, en la casa de Amanda.
CARMEN   —Muy bien. Hasta luego, entonces.

Pedro desea hablar con Ana.

ROSA   —Dígame.
PEDRO   —Hola. ¿Está Ana?
ROSA   —Sí. ¿Quién habla?
PEDRO   —Pedro Morales.
ROSA   —Un momento, por favor.
ANA   —*(A Rosa)* ¿Quién es?
ROSA   —Es tu amigo Pedro.
ANA   —Hola, Pedro. ¿Qué tal?
PEDRO   —Bien, ¿y tú?
ANA   —Más o menos.
PEDRO   —¿Por qué? ¿Problemas sentimentales?
ANA   —No, problemas económicos. ¡Necesito dinero!
PEDRO   —¡Yo también! Oye, ¿tú trabajas en el hospital esta noche?
ANA   —No, hoy no trabajo por la noche. Los lunes mi novio y yo estudiamos
          en la biblioteca.

---

[1] The present indicative is often used in Spanish to express a near future.
[2] Names of languages and nationalities are not capitalized in Spanish.

Vocabulario

◼ Nombres

el (la) **amigo(-a)** friend
la **biblioteca** library
la **casa** house, home

el **dinero** money
el **francés** French (language)
el **hospital** hospital

la **noche** evening, night
la **novia** girlfriend, fiancée, bride
el **novio** boyfriend, fiancé, groom

◼ Verbos

desear to wish, want
estudiar to study
hablar to speak

llamar to call
necesitar to need

regresar to return
trabajar to work

◼ Otras palabras y expresiones

a at, to
bueno, dígame hello (answering the phone)
con with
con ella habla this is she (speaking)
¿cuándo? when?
de of
de la noche in the evening (definite time)
¿dónde? where?
en on
entonces then, in that case

¿Está... + (name)? Is . . . (name) there?
esta noche tonight
mañana tomorrow
más o menos so-so, more or less
más tarde later
no está he *or* she is not (here)
o or
por la noche in the evening, at night (no definite time)
¿por qué? why?
por teléfono on the telephone

problemas económicos financial problems
problemas sentimentales love problems
¿quién? who?
¿quién es? who is it?
¿Quién habla?, ¿De parte de quién? Who is speaking?
su his, her, its, your *(formal)*, their
también also, too
tu your *(inf.)*
un momento one moment

Vocabulario adicional

◼ Los idiomas en Europa *(Languages in Europe)*

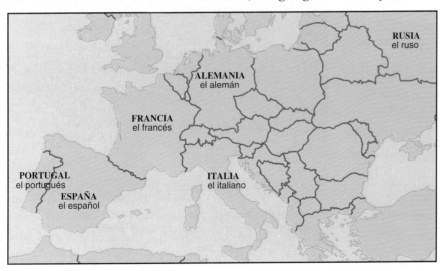

▪ EN ASIA

el chino   Chinese   En Pekín hablan **chino**.
el japonés   Japanese   En Tokio hablan **japonés**.

▪ ¿A QUÉ HORA?   *(What time?)*

de la mañana   in the morning   Estudiamos a las ocho **de la mañana**.
de la tarde   in the afternoon   Regresa a las cinco **de la tarde**.
por la mañana   in the morning   Estudiamos **por la mañana**.
por la tarde   in the afternoon   Regresa **por la tarde**.

ATENCIÓN   Use **de la** when a specific time is mentioned and **por la** when no specific time is mentioned.

¡CONVERSEMOS!

Answer the following questions, basing your answers on the dialogue.

1. ¿Raquel desea hablar con María o con Marta?
2. ¿Marta regresa a las nueve de la mañana o a las nueve de la noche?
3. ¿María habla con Carmen o con Raquel?
4. ¿Carmen y María estudian inglés o francés hoy?
5. ¿Estudian francés o italiano mañana?
6. ¿Estudian en la universidad o en la casa de Amanda?
7. ¿Pedro es el novio o el amigo de Ana?
8. ¿Ana necesita libros o dinero?
9. ¿Pedro necesita un reloj o necesita dinero también?
10. ¿Ana trabaja o estudia en la biblioteca esta noche?

¿Lo sabía Ud.?

- Contestando el teléfono *(Answering the phone)*:
  En España *(Spain):* "Diga", "Dígame", "¿Sí?"
  En Cuba y en otras regiones del Caribe: "Oigo"
  En México: "Bueno"
  En Argentina: "¿Sí?", "Hable", "Hola", "¿Aló?"

- En Latinoamérica y en España los estudiantes frecuentemente estudian juntos *(together)*.

- "Español" y "castellano" son *(are)* equivalentes.

- El español es el idioma nativo de unos *(about)* 400.000.000[1] de personas.

Estudiantes de la Universidad Iberoamericana, Ciudad de México, haciendo investigación en la biblioteca.

---

[1] Note that in Spanish numbers, a period is used instead of a comma to indicate thousands.

PRONUNCIACIÓN

A The Spanish i

The Spanish **i** is pronounced like the double *e* in the English word *see*. Listen to your teacher and repeat the following words.

sí	italiano
dinero	amigo
idioma	necesitar
días	hospital
cinco	

B The Spanish o

The Spanish **o** is a short, pure vowel. It corresponds to the *o* in the English word *no*, but without the glide. Listen to your teacher and repeat the following words.

problema	número
como	noche
momento	ocho
México	teléfono
entonces	

C The Spanish u

The Spanish **u** is shorter in length than the English *u*. It corresponds to the *ue* sound in the English word *Sue*. Listen to your teacher and repeat the following words.

estudiar	Susana
usted	anuncio
computadora	universidad
luz	gusto

ESTRUCTURAS

1 Present indicative of regular -ar verbs
(Presente de indicativo de los verbos regulares terminados en -ar)

■ Spanish verbs are classified in three main patterns of conjugation, according to the infinitive ending. The three infinitive endings are **-ar**, **-er**, and **-ir**.

hablar	*to speak*		
Singular			
yo	hablo	Yo **hablo** español.	*I speak Spanish.*
tú	hablas	Tú **hablas** francés.	*You (inf.) speak French.*
Ud.	habla	Ud. **habla** alemán.	*You (form.) speak German.*
él	habla	Él **habla** italiano.	*He speaks Italian.*
ella	habla	Ella **habla** portugués.	*She speaks Portuguese.*
Plural			
nosotros(-as)	hablamos	Nosotros **hablamos** español.	*We speak Spanish.*
vosotros(-as)	habláis	Vosotros **habláis** francés.	*You (inf.) speak French.*
Uds.	hablan	Uds. **hablan** alemán.	*You (form.) speak German.*
ellos	hablan	Ellos **hablan** italiano.	*They (masc.) speak Italian.*
ellas	hablan	Ellas **hablan** portugués.	*They (fem.) speak Portuguese.*

—¿Qué idioma **hablas**?   *"What language do you speak?"*
—Yo **hablo** español.   *"I speak Spanish."*
—¿Y Pierre?   *"And Pierre?"*
—Él **habla** francés.   *"He speaks French."*

■ Regular verbs ending in **-ar** are all conjugated as **hablar** in the chart above. Some other common **-ar** verbs are:

desear	*to want, wish*	**necesitar**	*to need*
estudiar	*to study*	**regresar**	*to return*
llamar	*to call*	**trabajar**	*to work*

—¿Uds. **estudian** por la noche?   *"Do you study in the evening?"*
—No, nosotros **estudiamos** por la tarde.   *"No, we study in the afternoon."*

—¿Qué **necesitas** tú?   *"What do you need?"*
—Yo **necesito** un libro.   *"I need a book."*

ATENCIÓN   Notice that the verb forms for **Ud., él,** and **ella** are the same. In addition, **Uds., ellos,** and **ellas** share common verb forms. This is true for all verbs in all tenses.

■ The infinitive of Spanish verbs consists of a stem (such as **habl-**) and an ending (such as **-ar**).

■ The stem **habl-** does not change. The endings change with the subject.

■ The Spanish present tense is equivalent to three English forms:

Yo **hablo** inglés.
{ I speak English.
  I do speak English.
  I am speaking English.

■ Because the verb endings indicate who is performing the action, the subject pronouns are frequently omitted.

Necesito dinero.   *I need money.*
Estudiamos inglés.   *We study English.*
Hoy **trabajo.**   *I work today.*

■ Subject pronouns can, however, be used for emphasis or clarification.

—¿**Ellos** hablan inglés?   *"Do they speak English?"*
—**Ella** habla inglés y **él** habla   *"She speaks English, and he*
  alemán.   *speaks German."*

■ In Spanish, as in English, when two verbs are used together, the second verb remains in the infinitive.

—¿Con quién **desea hablar** Ud.?   *"With whom do you wish to speak?"*
—**Deseo hablar** con Roberto.   *"I want to speak with Roberto."*

Práctica

A. Complete the following dialogues, using the present indicative of the verbs given. Then act them out with a partner.

1. estudiar   — ¿Qué _____ Uds.?
               — _____ biología.

2. trabajar   — ¿Tú _____ en el hospital por la noche?
               — No, _____ por la tarde.

3. regresar   — ¿Cuándo _____ Uds.?
               — Yo _____ el lunes y Jorge _____ el miércoles.

4. hablar   — ¿Qué idioma _____ ellos?
               — Carlos _____ español y Michele _____ francés.
               — ¿Cuántos idiomas _____ tú?
               — _____ tres: español, italiano y portugués.

5. desear   — ¿Con quién _____ hablar Ud.?
               — _____ hablar con el profesor Ceballos.
   regresar   — Él no está. _____ a las cinco.
   llamar   — Entonces (yo) _____ más tarde.

6. necesitar   — ¿Qué _____ Uds.?
               — _____ unas tizas.

B. Interview a classmate, using the following questions. When you have finished, switch roles.

1. ¿Dónde trabajas? *(name of city)*
2. ¿Qué idiomas hablas?
3. ¿Qué idioma estudias?
4. ¿Estudias por la mañana, por la tarde o por la noche?
5. ¿Qué necesitas?
6. ¿A qué hora regresas a la clase?

C. Talk about what is going on in these drawings, using the subject pronouns given and the verbs **trabajar, hablar, necesitar, regresar, llamar, estudiar,** and **desear.**

2 Gender, Part II *(Género, Parte II)*

In **Lección 1** you learned that words that end in **-o** in Spanish are generally masculine, and those that end in **-a** are generally feminine. Here are other useful rules to help you determine the gender of nouns that do not end in **-o** or **-a**.

▪ Nouns ending in **-sión, -ción, -tad, -dad,** and **-umbre** are feminine.

la televi**sión**	*television*	la ciu**dad**	*city*
la conversa**ción**	*conversation*	la universi**dad**	*university*
la liber**tad**	*liberty, freedom*	la certid**umbre**	*certainty*

▪ Many words that end in **-ma** are masculine.[1]

el po**ema**	*poem*	el cli**ma**	*climate*
el telegr**ama**	*telegram*	el idi**oma**	*language*
el progr**ama**	*program*	el probl**ema**	*problem*
el sist**ema**	*system*	el t**ema**	*subject, theme*

▪ You must learn the gender of nouns that have other endings and that do not refer to male or female beings. Remember that it is helpful to memorize each noun with its corresponding article.

la pared   **el** lápiz   **el** borrador   **el** reloj   **la** luz

Práctica

A. Read the following words, adding the corresponding definite article (**el, la, los,** or **las**).

1. pared
2. mesa
3. turismo
4. hospital
5. problemas
6. ciudad
7. sociedad
8. borrador
9. mano
10. lumbre *(fire)*
11. libertad
12. idiomas
13. organización
14. día
15. solución
16. conversación
17. universidad
18. muchedumbre *(crowd)*

B. With a partner, take turns asking each other whether or not you need certain items in your classroom.

> **MODELO:** —¿Necesitas un borrador?
> —*Sí, necesito un borrador.*
> —*No, necesito una tiza.*

---

[1] Some feminine words end in **-ma**, such as **la cama** *(bed)* and **la rama** *(branch)*.

3 Negative and interrogative sentences
(Oraciones negativas e interrogativas)

A. Negative sentences

■ To make a sentence negative, simply place the word **no** in front of the verb.

Yo trabajo en el hospital.	*I work at the hospital.*
Yo **no** trabajo en el hospital.	*I don't work at the hospital.*
Ella habla inglés.	*She speaks English.*
Ella **no** habla inglés.	*She doesn't speak English.*

■ If the answer to a question is negative, the word **no** will appear twice: at the beginning of the sentence, as in English, and in front of the verb.

—¿Habla Ud. español?	*"Do you speak Spanish?"*
—**No,** yo **no** hablo español.	*"No, I don't speak Spanish."*

The subject pronoun may be omitted.

—No, no hablo español.	*"No, I don't speak Spanish."*

B. Interrogative sentences

■ In Spanish, there are several ways of asking a question to elicit a *yes* or *no* answer.

¿**Elena** habla español?

¿Habla **Elena** español?   **Sí,** Elena habla español.

¿Habla español **Elena**?

■ These three questions ask for the same information and have the same meaning. The subject may be placed at the beginning of the sentence, after the verb, or at the end of the sentence.

■ Note that written questions in Spanish begin with an inverted question mark.

■ Another common way to ask a question in Spanish is to add tag questions such as ¿**no**? and ¿**verdad**? at the end of a statement.

Elena habla español, ¿**verdad**?	*Elena speaks Spanish, doesn't she?*

■ Questions that ask for information begin with an interrogative word, and the verb, not the subject, is placed after the interrogative word.

¿Dónde **trabajas** tú?	*Where do you work?*
¿Cuándo **regresan** ellos?	*When do they return?*
¿Qué **necesita** Ud.?	*What do you need?*
¿Quién **es** el profesor?	*Who is the professor?*

ATENCIÓN   Spanish does not use an auxiliary verb, such as *do* or *does,* in negative or interrogative sentences.

Práctica

A. The following statements contain the wrong information. Correct them, basing your answers on the dialogues on page 36.

> MODELO: Eva estudia esta noche.
> *Eva no estudia esta noche.*

1. Ana trabaja esta noche.
2. Raquel desea hablar con Pedro.
3. Carmen y María estudian japonés hoy.
4. Ana necesita libros.
5. Marta regresa a las nueve de la mañana.
6. Carmen habla con Raquel.
7. Carmen y María estudian italiano mañana.
8. Carmen y Pablo estudian en la biblioteca.

B. One of your classmates doesn't speak English. How would you ask him or her these questions in Spanish?

1. Do you study in the morning?
2. Are you working tonight?
3. Do you need money?
4. Are you returning to the university tomorrow?
5. Do you want to speak with the teacher?
6. The teacher isn't home. Do you want to call later?

C. Read the following paragraph and prepare a list of comprehension questions to ask your classmates.

El profesor de historia es Carlos Ruiz. Trabaja en la Universidad de Guadalajara. Regresa a la universidad mañana a las diez porque *(because)* necesita tres libros de la biblioteca.

4 Possession with **de** *(El caso posesivo)*

■ The **de** + *noun* construction is used to express possession or relationship. Spanish does *not* use the apostrophe.

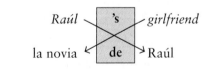

(the girlfriend of Raúl)

la clase **de la Dra. Peña**   *Dr. Peña's class*
el novio **de la muchacha**   *the girl's boyfriend*

ATENCIÓN   Note the use of the definite article before the words **novia, clase,** and **novio.**

—¿Quién es Francisco Acosta?   *"Who is Francisco Acosta?"*
—Es **el profesor de Carmen.**   *"He is Carmen's professor."*

—¿Cuál es **la dirección de Irene?**   *"What is Irene's address?"*
—Calle Magdalena, número seis.   *"Six Magdalena Street."*

Práctica

A. Express possession or relationship as it is shown in each drawing (e.g., the Spanish equivalent of María's professor.)

1.

2.

3.

4.

5.

6.

B. Give the following phrases in Spanish.

1. Miss Vera's students
2. the young lady's phone number
3. the doctor's house
4. the professors' problems
5. Amanda's friends
6. Carmen's maps
7. Javier's chair
8. Marta's notebooks
9. Jorge's clock
10. Mrs. Valle's money

5 Possessive adjectives *(Los adjetivos posesivos)*

Forms of the Possessive Adjectives		
Singular	**Plural**	
mi	mis	*my*
tu	tus	*your* (inf.)
su	sus	*your* (form.) *his* *her* *its* *their*
nuestro(-a)	nuestros(-as)	*our*
vuestro(-a)	vuestros(-as)	*your* (inf.)

—¿**Tu** novio es de Buenos Aires?   *"Is your fiancé from Buenos Aires?"*
—No, **mi** novio es de Asunción.   *"No, my fiancé is from Asuncion."*

■ Possessive adjectives always precede the nouns they introduce. They agree in number with the nouns they modify.

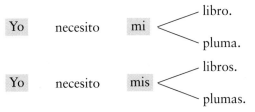

■ **Nuestro** and **vuestro** are the only possessive adjectives that have the feminine endings **-a** and **-as.** The others take the same endings for both genders.

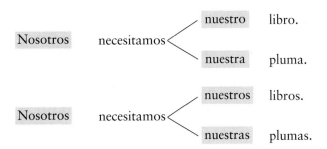

■ Possessive adjectives agree with the thing possessed and *not* with the possessor. For example, two male students referring to their female professor will say *nuestra* **profesora.**

■ Because **su** and **sus** each have several possible meanings, the form **de él** (or **de ella, de ellos, de ellas, de Ud.,** or **de Uds.**) can be substituted to avoid confusion. The "formula" is: *article + noun +* **de** *+ pronoun.*

sus plumas   las plumas **de él** (**ella, Ud.,** etc.)
su libro   el libro **de él** (**ella, Ud.,** etc.)

Práctica

A. Complete the following dialogues, using the Spanish equivalent of the words in parentheses. Then act them out with a partner.

1. —¿A qué hora es la clase _____ ? *(your)*
   —_____ clase es a las ocho. *(Our)*
2. —¿Cuál es _____ dirección, Anita? *(your)*
   —_____ dirección es calle Lima, 230. *(My)*
3. —¿Necesita Ud. _____ libros, señora? *(your)*
   —No, necesito _____ cuadernos. *(my)*
4. —¿Es la casa _____ ? *(his)*
   —No, es la casa _____ . *(her)*
5. —¿De dónde es el profesor _____ ? *(your)*
   —_____ profesor es de Montreal. *(Our)*
6. —¿Con quiénes hablan Teresa y Victoria?
   —Hablan con _____ amigas. *(their)*

B. With a partner, act out the following dialogues in Spanish.

1. "Where does your girlfriend work, Gustavo?"
   "My girlfriend works at the university."
2. "Do your friends need money, Mr. Vera?"
   "Yes, my friends need one hundred pesos."
3. "Do you need your notebooks, Lolita?"
   "Yes, I need my notebooks and my pens."
4. "Do you need her address, Anita?"
   "No, I need his address."
5. "Are your classes in the morning?"
   "No, our classes are in the afternoon."

6 Cardinal numbers 101–1,000 *(Números cardinales 101–1.000)*

101	**ciento uno** (and so on)		600	**seiscientos**
200	**doscientos**		700	**setecientos**
300	**trescientos**		800	**ochocientos**
400	**cuatrocientos**		900	**novecientos**
500	**quinientos**		1.000	**mil**

■ To ask how much a single item costs, say, "**¿Cuánto cuesta?**" For multiple items, use "**¿Cuánto cuestan?**"

—¿Cuánto cuesta el escritorio?   *"How much does the desk cost?"*

—Cuesta ciento cincuenta dólares.   *"It costs a hundred and fifty dollars."*

—¿Cuánto cuestan las ventanas?   *"How much do the windows cost?"*

—Cuestan mil cien dólares.   *"They cost eleven hundred dollars."*

- When counting beyond 100 (101 to 199), **ciento** is used.

- **Y** appears only in numbers between 16 and 99. It is not used to separate thousands, hundreds, and tens from each other: **mil quinientos ochenta y seis.**

- In Spanish, one does not count in hundreds beyond 1,000; thus, 1,100 is expressed as **mil cien.** After 1,000, thousands are counted **dos mil, tres mil,** and so on. Note that Spanish uses a period rather than a comma to indicate thousands.

- When modifying a feminine noun, the feminine form is used: **doscientas sillas.**

Práctica

A. Complete the following series of numbers.

1. cien, doscientos, trescientos,... mil
2. diez mil, veinte mil, treinta mil,... cien mil
3. ciento diez, doscientos veinte, trescientos treinta,... mil cien

B. Look at the following illustration and say how much everything costs.

> MODELO: —¿Cuánto cuesta la silla?
> —*La silla cuesta ciento ochenta dólares.*

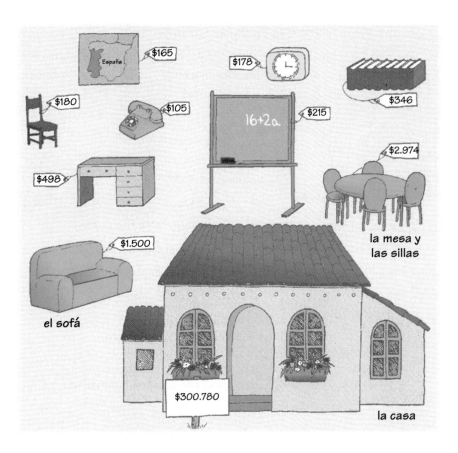

¡A VER CUÁNTO APRENDIÓ!

¡Repase el vocabulario!

Complete the following sentences with the appropriate words; then read them aloud.

1. ¡Oye! ¿ _____ (nosotros) inglés hoy?
2. —¿Qué hay de nuevo?
   — _____ .
3. ¿Problemas sentimentales o _____ ?
4. ¿Nosotros regresamos a las ocho _____
   _____ mañana?
5. ¿No está? Entonces llamo más _____ .
6. Nosotros _____ hablar español con el profesor.
7. ¿ _____ es? ¿Pedro Morales?
8. Jorge necesita dinero y yo _____ .
9. Sí, está. Un _____ , por favor.
10. —¿Qué tal?
    —Más o _____ .
11. En Río de Janeiro hablan _____ y en París hablan _____ .
12. ¿Qué idioma _____ en Roma? ¿Italiano?
13. Ellos estudian en la _____ , no en su casa.
14. —¿Está Marta?
    —Sí, _____ ella _____ .
15. ¿Es tu amigo o tu _____ ?

Entrevista

Interview a classmate, using the **tú** form.

Pregúntele a su compañero(-a) de clase...

1. ...cuántos idiomas habla. ¿Cuál(-es)?
2. ...si *(if)* habla español con el profesor (la profesora).
3. ...dónde estudia.
4. ...si estudia los sábados.
5. ...si necesita dinero. ¿Cuánto?
6. ...si trabaja. ¿Dónde?
7. ...con quién desea hablar.
8. ...si regresa a la universidad mañana. ¿A qué hora?

Situaciones

You are talking on the telephone. What would you say in the following situations? What might the other person say? Act out the scenes with a partner. Take turns playing each role.

1. You want to know whether your friend Carlos is at home.
2. Someone calls and asks for your sister, who is at home.
3. Someone asks to speak to you.
4. You tell someone you'll call later.
5. Someone has asked to talk to you, and you want to know who it is.

Para escribir

Complete the following sentences in your own words, using appropriate verb forms and vocabulary.

1. El Dr. Campos trabaja en el hospital y el profesor...
2. John Wilson estudia español y José García...
3. Yo necesito un lápiz y Teresa...
4. Nosotros trabajamos por la noche y ellos...
5. En México hablan español y en Chicago...
6. Yo deseo hablar con Jorge y tú...
7. Ella regresa a las cuatro de la tarde y yo...
8. En Roma hablan italiano y en Pekín...
9. Yo necesito la dirección de Jorge y ella...
10. Ellos hablan con sus amigos y nosotros...

En la vida real

¡Por teléfono!

With a classmate, act out the following phone conversations in Spanish.

1. Greet each other, and make plans to study together. Find out about each other's work schedule.
2. Call your classmate's roommate or a member of his or her family (your classmate will not be home). Find out when he or she will be back.

Un mensaje telefónico

Based on the information provided in the phone message, complete the statements that follow it.

Hospital El Samaritano

MENSAJE PERSONAL

Para Carlos Vega

De parte de Jorge Ibarra

De la compañía Hotel Plaza

Teléfono 386-4127

Llamó por teléfono a la(s) 10:30

☑ de la mañana ☐ de la tarde ☐ de la noche

MENSAJE

Desea hablar con usted.

ASUNTO

Problemas con las reservaciones del hotel para la convención.

Día Miércoles

1. El mensaje es para _____ .
2. El Sr. Vega trabaja en el _____ .
3. El mensaje es de parte de _____ .
4. El Sr. Ibarra trabaja para el _____ .
5. El número de teléfono del hotel es _____ .
6. El mensaje es _____ .
7. El Sr. Ibarra llamó *(called)* a las _____ de la _____ del día _____ .
8. En el hotel hay problemas con _____ .

Permítame presentarme   *(Allow me to introduce myself)*

Fill out a card with personal information, using the example below as a model; then exchange cards with a classmate. Use the cards to describe each other to the rest of the class, making all necessary changes.

> Yo soy Carlos Bustamante.
>
> Soy de Bogotá, Colombia.
>
> Trabajo en (ciudad) Medellín.
>
> Estudio biología.
>
> Necesito dinero y libros.

MODELO: *Carlos Bustamante es de Bogotá…* and so on.

¡Vamos a leer!

Antes de leer   *(Before reading)*

As you read the photo captions, find the answers to the following questions.

1. ¿De dónde es Alina Rojas? ¿Cuál es su profesión? ¿Qué idiomas habla?
2. ¿De dónde son Ana María y Carlos?
3. ¿De dónde es Francisco Acosta? ¿Cuál es su profesión? ¿Para qué aerolínea trabaja?
4. ¿De dónde es Cristina Vargas Peña? ¿En qué ciudad trabaja?
5. ¿Julio Santacruz es de España? ¿Dónde desea trabajar?
6. ¿De qué parte de Venezuela es Carmen Sandoval? ¿Qué estudia en la universidad?

¡Mucho gusto!

Mucho gusto. Me llamo Alina Rojas y soy de Cuba. Soy profesora de español. Hablo inglés y español.

¿Qué tal? Me llamo Ana María y soy de Buenos Aires, Argentina. Y yo me llamo Carlos y soy de Chile. Somos estudiantes.

¡Buenas tardes! Me llamo Francisco Acosta y soy de México. Soy piloto. Trabajo para *(for)* Aero-México.

¡Mucho gusto! Me llamo Cristina Vargas Peña y soy de Costa Rica. Soy dentista y trabajo en Los Ángeles, California.

¿Cómo están Uds.? Yo soy Julio Santacruz y soy de Madrid. Soy actor de televisión y deseo trabajar en Hollywood.

¡Buenos días! Me llamo Carmen Sandoval y soy de Caracas, Venezuela. Soy secretaria y trabajo para la compañía de teléfonos. Estudio idiomas en la universidad.

Díganos *(Tell us)*

Answer the following questions, based on your own thoughts and experiences.

1. ¿Cómo se llama Ud.?
2. ¿Qué idiomas estudia Ud. en la universidad?
3. ¿Desea Ud. estudiar otros *(other)* idiomas? ¿Cuáles?
4. ¿De dónde es su profesor (profesora)?
5. ¿Dónde desea trabajar Ud.?

EL ESPAÑOL EN LOS ESTADOS UNIDOS Y EN CANADÁ

Estados Unidos

Canadá

■ Más de *(More than)* 26 millones de hispanos viven *(live)* en los Estados Unidos. Los hispanos son el grupo minoritario de mayor crecimiento *(growth)* en la nación. Los estados con la mayor concentración de hispanos son Nuevo México, Tejas, California, Nueva York, New Jersey y la Florida.

■ Los nombres de muchas ciudades, estados y zonas geográficas de los Estados Unidos vienen del español: Arizona, California, Los Ángeles, El Paso, Sierra Nevada y Río Grande, por ejemplo. En Canadá, la gran península al este del país tiene un nombre de origen hispano: Labrador *(Farmer)*.

■ El español es el idioma extranjero *(foreign)* más popular en las escuelas y universidades de los Estados Unidos. Más de 600.000 estudiantes universitarios estudian español cada año *(each year)*.

■ En Canadá hay más de 200.000 habitantes de habla hispana; la mayoría de ellos son de España, Chile, El Salvador y México. La mayor parte vive en Toronto, Montreal y Vancouver.

Durante la época colonial, las órdenes religiosas españolas establecieron misiones en el suroeste de los Estados Unidos, y muchas aún *(still)* existen. La Misión de San Francisco de Asís es la más famosa de Nuevo México. **¿Cuáles son otras atracciones turísticas en el suroeste?**

En muchas partes de los Estados Unidos hay servicios bilingües de tipo social, educativo y legal para los residentes hispanos.
¿Hay muchas personas de habla hispana en su ciudad?

Los programas de educación bilingüe ayudan *(help)* a muchos niños hispanos en sus estudios primarios.
¿La educación bilingüe es una buena idea?

En muchas ciudades norteamericanas hay periódicos *(newspapers)* y revistas *(magazines)* en español. Muchos hispanos los leen *(read them)* porque tienen más información sobre *(about)* la comunidad latina. (Los Ángeles, California)
¿Qué periódicos lee Ud.?

Las emisoras de televisión hispanas son una fuente *(source)* de información importante en ciudades como Nueva York, donde vive *(live)* más de un millón de puertorriqueños, más que en San Juan, la capital de Puerto Rico. En la foto, un grupo musical anima la carroza *(float)* de una estación de televisión hispana de Nueva York.
¿Qué canales de televisión mira Ud.?

En "La Pequeña Habana", un barrio *(neighborhood)* cubano de la ciudad de Miami, las tiendas, los cafés, los restaurantes y los mercados tienen nombres en español, y el español es el idioma más hablado *(spoken)*.
¿Cómo se llama el barrio de Ud.?

La comida *(food)* mexicana es tan *(so)* popular en los Estados Unidos que para muchos norteamericanos la primera clase de español es en un restaurante. **¿Le gusta la comida mexicana? ¿Cuál es su plato favorito?**

En muchas de las grandes ciudades de Canadá hay fiestas y actos interculturales en que se nota *(one notes)* la influencia hispana. La música hispana, especialmente la mexicana, la salsa, el merengue y el tango, son muy populares. En varias ciudades también se celebra el "Cinco de Mayo". **¿Celebran fiestas hispanas en su ciudad? ¿Cuáles?**

Teleinforme

Vocabulario

Anuncios

la mejor decisión	the best decision
le ayudan a embellecerse	help to make you beautiful
¡Qué sabor...!	What flavor . . . !
vale mucho	is worth a lot
vivos	bright

El carnaval de la pequeña Habana

a través	through
al aire libre	open air, outdoors
a lo largo de	along
los bailes folklóricos	folk dances
la carrera	road race
los concursos de belleza	beauty pageants
los conjuntos musicales	musical groups
la cuadra	(city) block
el desfile	parade
disfrutar de	to enjoy
los espectáculos	shows
el hogar	home
no falta	is never absent
las playas	beaches
por supuesto	of course
propio	own
la reina	queen

Preparación

¿Cuánto saben Uds. ya?   After reading Panorama hispánico 1, get together in groups of three or four and complete each statement with the appropriate information.

1. Hay más de _____ millones de hispanos en los Estados Unidos.
2. La mayor concentración de hispanos está en los estados de _____ , _____ , _____ , _____ , _____ y _____ .
3. En muchas ciudades de los Estados Unidos existen programas de _____ y _____ bilingües.
4. Hay _____ , revistas y _____ de televisión en _____ en la mayoría de las grandes ciudades norteamericanas.
5. La Pequeña Habana está en la ciudad de _____ .

Comprensión

A. Anuncios.   Read the following statements and identify the name of the company as you hear or see each slogan on the video.

1. Su dinero vale mucho y muchas cosas más.
2. La mejor decisión.
3. De familia en familia.
4. Colores vivos y reales.
5. ¡Qué momento! ¡Qué sabor...!
6. Los cosméticos que le ayudan a embellecerse.

B. El Carnaval de la Pequeña Habana.   Select the words or phrases that best complete each statement, according to what you understood. More than one answer may be correct.

1. En Miami se celebra (el carnaval "Cinco de Mayo") todos los años.
2. Muchas personas disfrutan del festival (en persona, en la televisión, en la playa).
3. En el festival hay desfiles de (carrozas, mambo, motociclistas).
4. De noche coronan (a la reina, al rey) en un concurso de belleza.
5. La comida para la celebración se prepara (en un restaurante, al aire libre).
6. Hay mucha (comida, música, dirección) durante el carnaval de Miami.

Ampliación

Publicidad.   In groups of three or four, guess what the following words mean. Then brainstorm names of companies that would advertise the following products or services and make a list of them. Take turns reading the names of the products and services out loud.

1. cosméticos	7. refrigeradores
2. desodorantes	8. televisores
3. perfumes	9. computadoras
4. champú	10. relojes
5. aspirinas	11. servicios de hoteles
6. automóviles	12. servicios telefónicos

SUSANA SOLICITA TRABAJO

OBJECTIVES

▪ Pronunciation
Linking

▪ Structure
Descriptive adjectives: Forms, position, and agreement with articles and nouns • Present indicative of regular -er and -ir verbs • Present indicative of the irregular verbs **tener** and **venir** • The personal **a** • Contractions

▪ Communication
You will learn vocabulary related to personal data.

Susana solicita trabajo

Susana y su amigo Quique conversan en la cafetería de la universidad mientras comen sándwiches de jamón y queso y beben café. La muchacha es rubia, bonita y muy inteligente. Quique es alto, moreno, guapo y simpático. Susana lee un anuncio en el periódico y decide solicitar el empleo. Quique cree que ella no debe trabajar.

> La compañía IBM necesita recepcionista. Debe hablar inglés y tener conocimiento de computadoras. Venir, o enviar[1] su solicitud a avenida Simón Bolívar 342, Caracas.

QUIQUE	—Susana, ¡tú tienes cuatro clases! No tienes tiempo para trabajar.
SUSANA	—Todas mis clases son por la mañana. Tengo la tarde libre.
QUIQUE	—Pero tienes que estudiar…
SUSANA	—Bueno, mis clases no son muy difíciles.
QUIQUE	—¡La clase del Dr. Peña no es fácil!
SUSANA	—No es difícil. *(Mira el anuncio.)* Avenida Simón Bolívar… Yo vivo cerca de allí…
QUIQUE	—¿Cerca? Tú vives en la calle Seis.
SUSANA	—No queda lejos. Bueno, me voy.
QUIQUE	—¿A qué hora vienes mañana?
SUSANA	—Vengo a las nueve. Nos vemos.
QUIQUE	—Tenemos examen de francés y debemos estudiar. ¿Por qué no vienes a las ocho?
SUSANA	—No, porque a las ocho llevo a mi hermano al gimnasio.
QUIQUE	—Entonces, hasta mañana ¡y buena suerte!

(En la compañía IBM, Susana llena la solicitud y más tarde llama a Quique por teléfono.)

[1]Spanish frequently uses the infinitive to express instructions.

Vocabulario

Cognados

la **cafetería** cafeteria	el **examen** exam, test	el (la) **recepcionista**[1] receptionist
la **compañía** company	**inteligente** intelligent	el **sándwich**[2] sandwich
la **computadora**, el **computador**, el **ordenador** (*Spain*) computer		

Nombres

el **anuncio** ad	el **hermano** brother	el **periódico**, **diario** newspaper
la **avenida** avenue	el **jamón** ham	el **queso** cheese
el **café** coffee	la **muchacha**, **chica** girl, young woman	la **solicitud** application
el **conocimiento** knowledge	el **muchacho**, **chico** boy, young man	el **tiempo** time
el **gimnasio** gym		el **trabajo**, **empleo** job
la **hermana** sister		

Verbos

beber, **tomar** to drink	**decidir** to decide	**quedar** to be located
comer to eat	**enviar**,[3] **mandar** to send	**solicitar** to apply for
conversar, **charlar**, **platicar** (*Méx.*) to talk, to chat	**leer** to read	**tener** (*irreg.*) to have
creer to think, to believe	**llenar** to fill, to fill out	**venir** (*irreg.*) to come
deber (*+ infinitive*) must, to have to, should	**llevar** to take (*someone or something someplace*)	**vivir** to live
	mirar to look at, to watch (T.V.)	

Adjetivos

alto(-a) tall	**guapo(-a)** handsome	**simpático(-a)** nice, charming
bonito(-a), **lindo(-a)** pretty	**libre** free	**todos(-as)** all
difícil difficult	**moreno(-a)**[4] dark, brunette	
fácil easy	**rubio(-a)**, **güero(-a)** (*Méx.*) blond	

Otras palabras y expresiones

allí there	**lejos (de)** far (from)	**pero** but
buena suerte good luck	**me voy** I'm leaving	**porque** because
bueno well	**mientras** while	**que** that (*relat. pron.*)
cerca (de) close (to), near	**para** to, in order to	

---

[1] Nouns ending in **-ista** change only the article to indicate gender: **el recepcionista** *(masc.)*; **la recepcionista** *(fem.)*.

[2] In addition to **sándwich**, **emparedado** or **bocadillo** is used in Spain.

[3] Present indicative: **envío, envías, envía, enviamos, enviáis, envían.**

[4] **Castaño** is used as the equivalent of *brown* when describing hair or eye color.

VOCABULARIO ADICIONAL

■ CARACTERÍSTICAS

antipático(-a) unpleasant	Antonio no es **antipático**; es muy simpático.
bajo(-a) short	Marcos es **bajo**; no es alto.
delgado(-a) thin, slender	Roberto es alto y **delgado**.
feo(-a) ugly	Martín no es **feo**; es guapo.
gordo(-a) fat	¿María es delgada o **gorda**?
norteamericano(-a) North American	Las chicas son **norteamericanas**.
pelirrojo(-a) red-headed	Teresa no es rubia; es **pelirroja**.

■ DATOS PERSONALES *(Personal data)*

lugar donde trabaja place of employment

nombre del esposo (de la esposa) husband's (wife's) name

nombre y edad de los hijos children's names and ages

número de la licencia de conducir driver's license number

número de seguro social social security number

ocupación occupation

profesión profession

SOLICITUD DE TRABAJO *(Job Application)*

Apellidos y nombre *García López, Susana*
(Surnames and first name)

Fecha de nacimiento
(Date of birth)
Día *7* Mes *12* Año *74*
(Day) *(Month)* *(Year)*

Número de identidad *86407423*
(Identification number)

Edad *24 años*
(Age)

Dirección *Calle 6, 258* Ciudad *Caracas* Zona postal *70-824*
(City) *(Zip Code)*

Teléfono *862-4221*

Nacionalidad *Venezolana* Lugar de nacimiento *Caracas*
(Place of birth)

Estado civil: ☑Soltero(-a) ☐ Casado(-a) ☐ Divorciado(-a) ☐ Viudo(-a)
(Marital status) *(Single)* *(Married)* *(Divorced)* *(Widowed)*

Sexo *(Sex)* ☐ Masculino ☑Femenino

Educación
Institución Años
Universidad de Caracas *1993-1997*
Instituto San Pedro *1989-1993*

Experiencia
Compañía Años
Farmacia Bernardino *1997 (6 meses)*

¡CONVERSEMOS!

Answer the following questions, basing your answers on the dialogue.

1. ¿Dónde conversan Susana y Quique?
2. ¿Qué comen y beben mientras conversan?
3. ¿Susana es rubia o morena?
4. ¿Dónde lee Susana el anuncio?
5. ¿Qué decide solicitar Susana?
6. ¿Qué necesita la compañía IBM?
7. ¿Qué conocimientos debe tener la recepcionista?
8. ¿A qué dirección debe enviar Susana su solicitud?
9. ¿En qué calle vive Susana?
10. ¿Por qué deben estudiar Susana y Quique?
11. ¿Adónde *(Where)* lleva Susana a su hermano?
12. ¿Qué llena Susana en la compañía IBM?

¿Lo sabía Ud.?

• En España y en Latinoamérica, muchas personas tienen sobrenombres *(nicknames)*; por ejemplo *(for example)*: Enrique: **Quique**; Roberto o Alberto: **Beto**; Francisco: **Paco**; María Teresa: **Marité**; Antonia: **Toña**; Dolores: **Lola**; José: **Pepe**; Luis: **Lucho**; Manuel: **Manolo**.

• En los países hispánicos las personas generalmente usan dos apellidos: el apellido del padre y el apellido de la madre. Por ejemplo, los hijos de María **Rivas** y Juan **Pérez** usan los apellidos **Pérez Rivas**.

• En una guía telefónica *(phone book)* en español, alfabetizan *(they alphabetize)* los nombres según *(according to)* los dos apellidos; por ejemplo:
  Peña Aguilar, Rosa
  Peña Aguilar, Sara Luisa
  Peña Gómez, Raúl
  Quesada Álvarez, Javier
  Quesada Álvarez, Octavio
  Quesada Benítez, Ana María

PRONUNCIACIÓN

Linking

- In Spanish, a final consonant is always linked with the next initial vowel sound.

  el‿amigo   ¿Vas‿al baile?   mis‿hermanos[1]

- When two identical consonants are together, they are pronounced as one.

  es‿simpática   Voy con‿Norma.

- When two identical vowels are together, they are pronounced as one long vowel.

  Rodolfo‿Ochoa   ¿Va‿Ana?

- The final vowel of one word is linked with the initial vowel of the following word to form one syllable.

  fin de‿año   la hermana de‿Olga
  hablo‿español

ESTRUCTURAS

1 Descriptive adjectives: Forms, position, and agreement with articles and nouns
(*Adjetivos calificativos: Formas, posición y concordancia con artículos y nombres*)

A. Forms of adjectives

- Descriptive adjectives identify characteristics or qualities such as color, size, and personality. In Spanish, these adjectives agree in gender and number with the nouns they modify. Adjectives ending in -o are made feminine by changing the -o to -a.

  el chico rubio   la chica rubia
  el lápiz rojo   la pluma roja

- Adjectives ending in -e or in a consonant have the same form for the masculine and the feminine.

  el chico inteligente   la chica inteligente
  el esposo feliz *(happy)*   la esposa feliz
  el libro fácil   la clase fácil

---

[1]In Spanish the letter **h** is silent.

■ Adjectives of nationality that end in a consonant add an **-a** in the feminine.

el muchacho español   la muchacha español**a**
el señor inglés   la señora ingles**a**

■ Adjectives ending in **-or, -án, -ón,** or **-ín** add an **-a** in the feminine.

el alumno trabajad**or** ⎤
                        ⎬ *the hard-working student*
la alumna trabajad**ora** ⎦

ATENCIÓN   Adjectives that have an accent in the last syllable of the masculine form drop it in the feminine: **inglés → inglesa**.[1]

■ To form the plural, adjectives follow the same rules as nouns. Adjectives ending in a vowel add **-s**; adjectives ending in a consonant add **-es**; adjectives ending in **-z** change the **-z** to **c** and add **-es**.

norteamericana   norteamericana**s**
español   español**es**
feliz   feli**ces**

B. Position of adjectives

■ Descriptive adjectives generally follow the noun.

Miguel es un chico **inteligente**.   *Miguel is an intelligent boy.*
Necesito dos plumas **rojas**.   *I need two red pens.*

■ Adjectives denoting nationality always follow the noun.

El profesor **mexicano** trabaja en la universidad.

C. Agreement of articles, nouns, and adjectives

■ In Spanish, the article, noun, and adjective agree in gender and number.

un muchacho alto   **una** muchacha alta
los muchachos altos   **las** muchachas altas

■ When an adjective modifies two or more nouns, the plural form is used.

la silla y la mesa **rojas**

■ If two nouns described together are of different genders, the masculine plural form of the adjective is used.

la chica mexicana ⎤
                  ⎬ la chica y el chico mexicanos
el chico mexicano ⎦

---

[1]For rules on accent marks, see Appendix A.

Práctica
....

A. With a partner, take turns asking the following questions. In your answers, contradict what is stated.

> MODELO: —¿Rosaura es alta?
> —*No, es baja.*

1. ¿El novio de Adriana es rubio?
2. ¿Las mujeres son gordas?
3. ¿Los muchachos son bajos?
4. ¿Tu profesora es antipática?
5. ¿La novia de Daniel es fea?
6. ¿Tus clases son fáciles?
7. ¿El hermano de Olga es delgado?
8. ¿Ellas son morenas?

B. Describe the following people, places, or things, using as many descriptive adjectives as possible.

1. Julia Roberts
2. Brad Pitt
3. Roseanne
4. Nueva York
5. su mejor *(best)* amigo
6. el español
7. las chicas de la clase
8. los chicos de la clase
9. el presidente de los Estados Unidos
10. su mejor amiga

2   Present indicative of regular -er and -ir verbs
(Presente de indicativo de los verbos regulares que terminan en -er y en -ir)

comer *to eat*		**vivir** *to live*	
yo	como	yo	vivo
tú	comes	tú	vives
Ud. él ella	come	Ud. él ella	vive
nosotros(-as)	comemos	nosotros(-as)	vivimos
vosotros(-as)	coméis	vosotros(-as)	vivís
Uds. ellos ellas	comen	Uds. ellos ellas	viven

■ Other verbs conjugated like **comer:**

aprender *to learn*   **beber** *to drink*
creer *to believe*   **vender** *to sell*
leer *to read*   **deber** *must, should, ought to*

—¿Qué **comen** Uds.?   *"What are you eating?"*
—Nosotros **comemos** queso y Elsa **come** jamón.   *"We are eating cheese and Elsa is eating ham."*

—¿Qué periódico **lees** tú?   *"What newspaper do you read?"*
—**Leo** *La Prensa.*   *"I read* La Prensa.*"*

■ Other verbs conjugated like **vivir**:

abrir *to open*   **escribir** *to write*
recibir *to receive*   **decidir** *to decide*

—¿Dónde **viven** Uds.?   *"Where do you live?"*
—**Vivimos** en la calle Magnolia.   *"We live on Magnolia Street."*

—¿Tú **escribes** con lápiz o   *"Do you write with a pencil or*
  con pluma?   *with a pen?"*
—**Escribo** con pluma.   *"I write with a pen."*

Práctica

A. Complete the following dialogues, using the present indicative of the verbs given. Then act them out with a partner.

1. comer   – ¿Dónde _____ Uds.?
             – _____ en la cafetería.

2. vivir   – ¿Dónde _____ tú?
             – _____ en la calle Montalvo.

3. recibir   – ¿Cuánto dinero _____ Uds.?
             – Yo _____ quinientos dólares y él _____ cuatrocientos.

4. leer   – ¿Qué periódico _____ ellos?
             – _____ el *Times*.

5. vender   – ¿Dónde _____ (ellos) sándwiches?
    creer   – En la cafetería, pero yo _____ que (ellos) no
    abrir   _____ la cafetería hasta *(until)* las siete.

6. beber   – ¿Qué _____ Uds.?
             – Nosotros _____ café y Ana _____ 7-Up.

7. deber   – ¿Qué _____ llenar (yo)?
             – Ud. _____ llenar la solicitud.

8. escribir   – ¿Uds. _____ en inglés?
             – No, _____ en español.

B. Interview a classmate, using the following questions and two questions of your own. When you have finished, switch roles.

1. ¿Dónde vives?
2. ¿Dónde comes?
3. ¿Comen sándwiches tú y tus amigos?
4. ¿Bebes café o Coca-Cola?
5. ¿Aprendes mucho en la clase de español?
6. En la clase, ¿leen Uds. en español?
7. ¿Lees bien el español?[1]
8. ¿Escribes en español o en inglés?
9. ¿Vendes tus libros?
10. ¿Qué periódico lees tú?
11. ¿Debes trabajar mañana?
12. ¿Reciben mucho dinero tus amigos?

C. Describe what these people do, must do, or decide to do, using **-er** or **-ir** verbs.

1. Yo / café
2. Nosotros / español
3. Uds. / periódico
4. Carlos y Rosa / con una pluma roja
5. Tú / la puerta
6. Las chicas / en un apartamento
7. Ud. / jamón y queso
8. Nosotros / estudiar hoy
9. Susana / solicitar el empleo

3 Present indicative of the irregular verbs **tener** and **venir**
*(Presente de indicativo de los verbos irregulares **tener** y **venir**)*

tener *to have*		**venir** *to come*	
yo	tengo	yo	vengo
tú	tienes	tú	vienes
Ud. ⎫		Ud. ⎫	
él ⎬	tiene	él ⎬	viene
ella ⎭		ella ⎭	
nosotros(-as)	tenemos	nosotros(-as)	venimos
vosotros(-as)	tenéis	vosotros(-as)	venís
Uds. ⎫		Uds. ⎫	
ellos ⎬	tienen	ellos ⎬	vienen
ellas ⎭		ellas ⎭	

—¿Cuántas clases **tienen** Uds.?　　"How many classes do you have?"
—**Tenemos** dos. ¿Cuántas　　　　　"We have two. How many do you
　tienes tú?　　　　　　　　　　　have?"
—Yo **tengo** cuatro.　　　　　　　　"I have four."

---

[1]The definite article is used with names of languages except after the prepositions **en** and **de**, or after the verbs **hablar** and usually **estudiar**.

—¿A qué hora **vienen** Uds.?	*"What time are you coming?"*
—Sergio y yo **venimos** a las dos, y Olga **viene** a la una.	*"Sergio and I are coming at two and Olga is coming at one."*
—¿Tú **tienes que** venir a la universidad mañana?	*"Do you have to come to the university tomorrow?"*
—No.	*"No."*

ATENCIÓN **Tener que** means *to have to,* and it is followed by an infinitive. Olga **tiene que trabajar** hoy. *Olga has to work today.*

Práctica

A. Give each of the following sentences a logical ending.

1. Yo tengo un examen de español y ella…
2. Uds. vienen los sábados y nosotros…
3. Ella tiene veinte dólares y nosotros…
4. Ana viene con Roberto y tú…
5. Ellos vienen a las seis y yo…
6. Nosotros tenemos dos hijos y ellos…

B. Interview a classmate, using the following questions.

1. ¿Tienes mi número de teléfono?
2. ¿Tienes mi dirección?
3. ¿Tiene la profesora tu número de seguro social?
4. ¿Vienen Uds. a la universidad por la noche o por la mañana?
5. ¿A qué hora vienen Uds. a la clase de español?
6. ¿Vienes a la clase con tus amigos?
7. ¿Vienes a clase los sábados?
8. ¿Vienen todos los estudiantes a clase?
9. ¿Tienen Uds. mucho trabajo en la clase de español?
10. ¿Tú tienes la tarde libre mañana?

C. Say what the following people have to do, using **tener que** + *infinitive.*

1. Silvia tiene un examen mañana.
2. John tiene una amiga de Madrid que no habla inglés.
3. Nosotros necesitamos dinero.
4. Yo solicito un empleo.
5. Necesito escribir y no tengo pluma.
6. Necesito hablar por teléfono con Marta, y ella no está.

D. Make a list of tasks or errands for the week; then, with one or two classmates, take turns asking each other what you have to do (**¿Qué tienes que hacer?**) each day.

> MODELO: el lunes: leer un libro
> —¿Qué tienes que hacer el lunes?
> —*Tengo que leer un libro.*

4 The personal a *(La a personal)*

■ The preposition **a** is used in Spanish before a direct object[1] referring to a specific person or persons. It is called the "personal **a**" and has no equivalent in English.

Yo llevo **a mi hermana.**	Nosotros llamamos **a los estudiantes.**
D.O.	D.O.
I take my sister.	*We call the students.*
D.O.	D.O.

■ The personal **a** is *not* used when the direct object is not a person.

Yo llevo **la computadora.**
D.O.

I take the computer.
D.O.

■ The verb **tener** generally does not take the personal **a**, even if the direct object is a person.

No tengo **hijos.**	Tenemos **dos hermanas.**
D.O.	D.O.
I don't have children.	*We have two sisters.*
D.O.	D.O.

—¿Llevas **a** tus hermanos a la universidad?
—Yo no tengo hermanos. Llevo **a** Jorge y **a** Luis.

"Do you take your brothers to the university?"
"I don't have (any) brothers. I take Jorge and Luis."

ATENCIÓN When there is a series of direct object nouns referring to people, the personal **a** is repeated: **Llevo *a Jorge* y *a Luis.***

Práctica

Use the personal **a** when needed to complete the following dialogues. Then act them out with a partner.

1. —¿Cuántos hijos tienes?
   —Tengo _____ dos hijos y una hija.
2. —¿Llama Ud. _____ Carmen o _____ Elena?
   —Llamo _____ Carmen.
3. —¿Tu amigo lleva _____ Rosa a la biblioteca?
   —No, lleva _____ su novia.
4. —¿Adónde lleva Ud. _____ los libros?
   —A la clase.
5. —¿Tienes _____ muchos hermanos?
   —No, no tengo _____ hermanos.
6. —¿Qué lees?
   —Leo _____ el periódico.

---

[1] See **Lección 6** for further explanation of the direct object.

5 Contractions *(Contracciones)*

■ There are only two contractions in Spanish: **al** and **del**. Both the preposition **a** *(to, toward)* and the personal **a** followed by the article **el** contract to **al**.

Llevo	a	+	el	profesor.

Llevo	al	profesor.

■ The preposition **de** *(of, from)* followed by the article **el** contracts to **del**.

Tiene los libros	de	+	el	profesor.

Tiene los libros	del	profesor.

—¿Llevas **al** hermano de Ana?	*"Are you taking Ana's brother?"*
—No, llevo **a las** hermanas de Eva.	*"No, I'm taking Eva's sisters."*

—¿La casa es **de la** Sra. Vega?	*"Is it Mrs. Vega's house?"*
—No, es **del** Sr. Parra.	*"No, it's Mr. Parra's."*

ATENCIÓN **A** + **el** and **de** + **el** must always be contracted to **al** and **del**. None of the other combinations (**de la, de las, de los, a la, a las, a los**) is contracted: **Llaman *a los* hijos *de los* profesores.**

Práctica

A. Complete the following dialogues, using **de la, de las, del, de los, a la, a las, al,** or **a los.** Then act them out with a partner.

1. —¿De dónde vienes?
   —Vengo _____ gimnasio _____ universidad. ¿Y tú?
   —Yo vengo _____ hospital.
2. —¿A qué hora llamas _____ chicas?
   — _____ dos.
3. —¿Los mapas son _____ Sr. Vega?
   —No, son _____ Srta. Ruiz.
4. —¿Tienes que ir *(go)* _____ club?
   —No, tengo que ir _____ biblioteca.
5. —¿Adónde llevas _____ chicos?
   — _____ clase _____ Sr. Peña.

B. With a partner, take turns asking and answering the following questions, using the cues provided.

1. ¿De quién *(Whose)* son los libros?   (profesor)
2. ¿De quién es el escritorio?   (Srta. Paz)
3. ¿A quiénes llevas a la universidad?   (chicos)
4. ¿Adónde envías la solicitud?   (universidad)
5. ¿A quiénes llaman los chicos?   (muchachas)
6. ¿Adónde llevan a las muchachas?   (gimnasio)
7. ¿A quién miran?   (hermana de Jorge)
8. ¿Los sándwiches son de los muchachos?   (no / muchachas)

¡A VER CUÁNTO APRENDIÓ!

¡Repase el vocabulario!

A. Match each question in column A with the best response in column B.

A	B
1. ¿Con quién charla Anita?	a. No, es difícil.
2. ¿Dónde viven Uds.?	b. No, es mi hermano.
3. ¿Ella es casada?	c. En la avenida Olmos.
4. ¿La clase es fácil?	d. Café.
5. ¿Uds. trabajan hoy?	e. De la cafetería.
6. ¿De dónde vienes?	f. El número de seguro social.
7. ¿Qué beben ellos?	g. A mi novia.
8. ¿Qué necesita Ud.?	h. Con Roberto.
9. ¿Qué leen?	i. No, tenemos el día libre.
10. ¿Qué decide Elena?	j. No, soltera.
11. ¿Qué comen Uds.?	k. El anuncio.
12. ¿Paco es feo?	l. Jamón y queso.
13. ¿Es tu novio?	m. Solicitar el empleo.
14. ¿A quién llevas?	n. No, es muy guapo.

B. By combining the words or phrases in the three columns (one from each column, starting with A), you can form many different sentences. Write five affirmative and five negative sentences.

A	B	C
Yo	venir	en español
La chica	escribir	del hospital
Uds.	trabajar	bien
Ud.	comer	dos hijos
Ana y Luisa	solicitar	para la compañía Ford
Nosotros	llenar	café
El Dr. Jiménez	aprender	la solicitud
Tú	vivir	las preguntas
	beber	inglés
	tener	en Madrid
	leer	trabajar
		jamón y queso
		el periódico
		en la calle Roma
		empleo

Entrevista

Interview a classmate using the **tú** form.

Pregúntele a su compañero(-a) de clase...

1. ...si *(if)* su mejor *(best)* amigo(-a) es rubio(-a), moreno(-a) o pelirrojo(-a).
2. ...qué días tiene la clase de español.
3. ...cuántas clases tiene.
4. ...a qué hora viene a la universidad.
5. ...cuándo tiene la tarde libre.
6. ...si vive cerca o lejos de la universidad.
7. ...si vive en una calle o en una avenida.
8. ...si por la noche estudia o mira televisión.
9. ...si tiene hermanos. (¿Cuántos?)
10. ...si tiene amigos mexicanos.

Situaciones

What would you say in the following situations? What might the other person say? Act out the scenes with a partner. Take turns playing each role.

1. You are helping a Spanish-speaking person to fill out a form. You need to know his or her name and surname, address, place of origin, age, marital status, and whether he or she has children.
2. A friend drops by, and all you have to offer is a ham and cheese sandwich. Ask if he or she wishes to eat one.
3. You are trying to convince your friend to go on a blind date. Describe the young woman or the young man to him or her.

Para escribir

What information would you put in a cover letter to a potential employer? Write a brief description of yourself, including information about your schedule and your activities.

SECRETARIA BILINGUE

Compañía multinacional requiere secretaria bilingüe español-inglés, con responsabilidad para manejo oficina mediano tamaño. Favor enviar hoja de vida con foto reciente al apartado aéreo 094890 de Bogotá.

En la vida real

Los amigos

With a classmate, discuss and compare your best friends. Ask each other as many questions as you can to learn what the person being described is like (**cómo es él/ella**), where he or she is from, and so on. Here are some additional words you may want to include:

trabajador(-a) *hard-working*
haragán(-ana), perezoso(-a) *lazy*
optimista *optimistic*
pesimista *pessimistic*
tímido(-a) *shy*

rico(-a) *rich*
pobre *poor*
responsable *responsible*
irresponsable *irresponsible*

Necesitamos trabajo...

Some friends of yours are looking for jobs. Help them by answering their questions about the following classified ads.

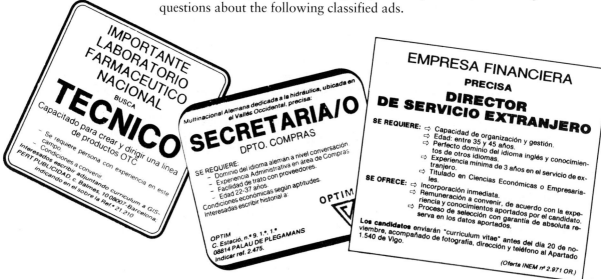

1. ¿Qué empresa necesita secretario(-a)?
2. Si deseo trabajar de secretario(-a) en la compañía Optim, ¿qué idioma necesito hablar?
3. ¿En qué ciudad está el laboratorio farmacéutico?
4. ¿Qué experiencia mínima debo tener si solicito el puesto de director de servicio extranjero?
5. ¿Para solicitar qué empleos necesito mandar una foto?
6. ¿Qué edad debo tener para trabajar en la empresa financiera?
7. ¿Qué debo enviar a la empresa financiera antes del *(before)* día 20 de noviembre?

La solicitud

Imagine that you are applying for a job. Fill out the application with your own personal data.

SOLICITUD DE TRABAJO

Apellidos y nombre

_____

| Fecha de nacimiento |
| Día   Mes   Año |

Número de identidad   Edad

_____   _____

Dirección   Ciudad   Zona postal

_____   _____   _____

_____

Teléfono

_____

Nacionalidad   Lugar de nacimiento

_____   _____

Estado civil: ❑ Soltero(-a)   ❑ Casado(-a)   ❑ Divorciado(-a)   ❑ Viudo(-a)

Sexo ❑ Masculino   ❑ Femenino

Educación
Institución   Años

_____   _____

_____   _____

Experiencia
Compañía   Años

_____   _____

_____   _____

Así somos

Vocabulario

a la vez	at the same time
actual	present
la agencia de carros	car dealership
ahora mismo	right now
alegre	happy
la anfitriona	hostess
los bienes raíces	real estate
el chiquito	the youngest
deportista	keen on sports
¿Dónde naciste?	Where were you born?
la equitación	horseback riding
la empresa	company, business
la estatura	height
los familiares	relatives
el/la gerente	manager
el ingeniero	engineer
la más pequeña	the youngest
largo	long
la librería	bookstore
mejor	better
mayor	older
menor	younger
el médico cirujano	surgeon
muy a gusto	very comfortably
muy buena gente	a good person
los ojos	eyes
las pecas	freckles
el pelo	hair
el periodismo	journalism
la piel	skin
la secundaria	high school
el/la subgerente de ventas	buyer
trabajador	hard working
Vamos a ver qué dicen.	Let's see what they say.

Preparación

¿Las reconoce? *(Do you recognize them?)*   Guess the meaning of the following words. While watching the video, circle each one as you hear the person say it.

administración	especialidad	serio
administrativo	opción	sincero
alternativa	piloto	turismo
dinámico	robusto	

Comprensión

A. Profesiones.   Match the people's names with their professions or occupations.

_____ 1. Manuel   a. Es gerente de la Librería de Cuba.
_____ 2. Ricardo   b. Es estudiante.
_____ 3. José   c. Es ingeniero.
_____ 4. Rosalía   d. Es piloto.
_____ 5. Héctor   e. Es médico cirujano.

B. ¿Verdadero o falso?   Read the following statements. After watching the video, circle **V** (**Verdadero**) or **F** (**falso**), according to what you understood.

V   F   1. Yolanda no es casada.
V   F   2. Carolina no tiene novio.
V   F   3. Orlando es casado.

C. ¿Cómo es?   Complete the following statements with the appropriate adjectives.

1. El novio de Paula es _____ y _____ .
2. El novio de Milka es _____ y _____ .
3. La novia de Juan es _____ y _____ .

D. ¿Verdadero o falso?   Read the following statements and circle **V** (**Verdadero**) or **F** (**falso**), according to what you understood.

V   F   1. Ivonne tiene dos hermanos y dos hermanas.
V   F   2. Carolina tiene tres hermanos.
V   F   3. La mejor amiga de Carolina es delgada y estudia periodismo.
V   F   4. La mejor amiga de Milka tiene ojos azules y pelo rubio.

E. Entrevista.   Select the word or phrase that best completes each statement, according to what you understood from the interview.

1. La señorita Guzmán Robles es de (Guadalajara, Oaxaca).
2. Es (soltera, casada).
3. Estudió (*She studied*) en la (Universidad Autónoma de México, Universidad Autónoma de Guadalajara).
4. Su título (*degree*) es en administración de (bienes raíces, empresas).

Ampliación

Necesito trabajo.   You are interviewing a student who wants a part-time job at your employment agency. What questions would you ask to elicit the following responses?

Supervisor(-a)   —_____
Estudiante   —Me llamo Martín Mena.
Supervisor(-a)   —_____
Estudiante   —Deseo trabajar diez horas por semana (*a week*).
Supervisor(-a)   —_____
Estudiante   —Tengo libres los martes, jueves y sábados.
Supervisor(-a)   —_____
Estudiante   —Estudio administración de empresas.

Take this test. When you have finished, check your answers in the answer key provided in Appendix E. Then use a red pen to correct any mistakes you may have made. Are you ready?

SELF TEST

Lección 1

A. Gender and number, Part I; Definite and indefinite articles

Give the correct form of the definite (**el** or **la**) and indefinite (**un** or **una**) articles for each of the following nouns.

1. puerta
2. libro
3. mapa
4. mujer
5. borrador
6. secretario
7. mano
8. hombre
9. día
10. silla

B. Plural forms

Make the following words plural.

1. el señor y la señorita
2. un reloj
3. la doctora y el profesor
4. un lápiz
5. la lección
6. una mujer
7. la ventana
8. la pluma y el cuaderno

C. Cardinal numbers 31–100

Write out the following numbers in Spanish.

32   55   43   69   86   92   71   100

D. Subject pronouns and the present indicative of the verb *ser*

Complete the following dialogue, using the present indicative of the verb **ser.**

—¿De dónde _____ tú, Anita?
—Yo _____ de Caracas. ¿De dónde _____ ustedes?
—_____ de Santiago.
—¿Y Elena?
—Ella _____ de Lima.

E. Telling time

Write the following times in Spanish.

1. It's one-thirty.
2. It's a quarter to three.
3. It's ten after four.
4. It's twelve o'clock.
5. It's two-fifteen.

F. Just words . . .

Match each question or statement in column A with the best response in column B. Use each response once.

<table>
<tr><td align="center">A</td><td align="center">B</td></tr>
<tr><td>1. Mucho gusto.</td><td>a. *"Desk"*.</td></tr>
<tr><td>2. ¿De dónde eres?</td><td>b. Cincuenta.</td></tr>
<tr><td>3. ¿Cómo se dice *"chalk"* en español?</td><td>c. José Luis Peña</td></tr>
<tr><td></td><td>d. Somos de Montevideo.</td></tr>
<tr><td>4. ¿Qué quiere decir "escritorio"?</td><td>e. A las nueve.</td></tr>
<tr><td>5. ¿Cómo te llamas?</td><td>f. El gusto es mío.</td></tr>
<tr><td>6. ¿A qué hora es la clase?</td><td>g. Tiza.</td></tr>
<tr><td>7. Muchas gracias.</td><td>h. De nada.</td></tr>
<tr><td>8. ¿Cómo se dice *"chalkboard"* en español?</td><td>i. Soy de Santiago.</td></tr>
<tr><td></td><td>j. Gracias.</td></tr>
<tr><td>9. ¿Cuál es tu dirección?</td><td>k. Pizarra.</td></tr>
<tr><td>10. ¿Qué hora es?</td><td>l. Las cinco y veinte.</td></tr>
<tr><td>11. ¿De dónde son ustedes?</td><td>m. Calle Palma, número treinta.</td></tr>
<tr><td>12. Tome asiento.</td><td></td></tr>
<tr><td>13. ¿Cuántos estudiantes hay en la clase?</td><td></td></tr>
</table>

G. Culture

Answer the following questions based on the **¿Lo sabía Ud.?** section.

1. ¿Qué estudian muchas personas en España y en Latinoamérica?
2. ¿Qué hora es si *(if)* son las veinte horas?

Lección 2

A. Present indicative of regular -*ar* verbs

Rewrite each pair of sentences to form one sentence. Use the plural forms of the subject pronouns to include both subjects.

1. Ella habla inglés y español.
   Yo *(f.)* hablo inglés y español.
2. Él trabaja en el hospital.
   Ud. trabaja en el hospital.
3. Ella llama más tarde.
   Ella llama más tarde.
4. Ella estudia ruso y chino.
   Él estudia ruso y chino.
5. Tú *(m.)* necesitas dinero.
   Yo *(f.)* necesito dinero.
6. Él desea hablar con Eva.
   Yo *(m.)* deseo hablar con Eva.

B. Gender, Part II

Use the appropriate form of the definite article (**el, la, los,** or **las**) with each of the following nouns.

1. televisión
2. ciudades
3. libertad
4. programas
5. lección
6. problema
7. certidumbre
8. universidades
9. idioma
10. sistema
11. conversaciones
12. telegramas

C. Negative and interrogative sentences

Write the following dialogues in Spanish.

1. "Do you speak French, Miss Peña?"
   "No, I don't speak French."
2. "Does he need the money?"
   "No, he doesn't need the money."
3. "Are they calling later?"
   "No, they are not calling later."
4. "Do you work at the university, Miss Rojas?"
   "No, I don't work at the university."

D. Possession with *de*

Write the following sentences in Spanish.

1. What is Javier's address?
2. What is Rosa's phone number?
3. I need Teresa's books.

E. Possessive adjectives

Complete the following sentences, using possessive adjectives that correspond to the subjects.

1. Yo hablo con _____ amigos y tú hablas con _____ amigos.
2. Nosotros hablamos con _____ profesora.
3. David necesita hablar con _____ novia.
4. Los estudiantes desean hablar con _____ profesor.
5. Nosotros necesitamos _____ sillas.

F. Cardinal numbers 101–1,000

In Spanish, write out the following dates and house numbers.

1. El año *(year)* 1492
2. El año 1776
3. El año 1865
4. El año 1998
5. Calle Paz, número 2552
6. Calle Bolívar, número 5123

G. Just words . . .

Match each question or statement in column A with the best response in column B. Use each response once.

A	B
1. Hola. ¿Está Raúl?	a. Yo también.
2. ¿Por qué? ¿Problemas económicos?	b. Habla Pedro Morales.
	c. Un momento, por favor.
3. ¿Qué idioma hablan en París?	d. No, problemas sentimentales…
4. Nosotros estudiamos japonés.	e. Dinero.
5. Deseo hablar con Ana.	f. Estudiamos italiano y
6. ¿A qué hora regresa?	portugués.
7. ¿Quién habla?	g. Soy María Gómez.
8. ¿Quién es Ud.?	h. No, en la universidad.
9. ¿Estudiamos esta noche?	i. Con él habla.
10. ¿Qué idiomas estudian Uds.?	j. No, mañana.
11. ¿Qué necesitan Uds.?	k. A las nueve y media.
12. ¿Trabaja en el hospital?	l. Hablan francés.

H. Culture

Answer the following questions based on the **¿Lo sabía Ud.?** section.

1. ¿Cómo contestan el teléfono en México?
2. ¿Cuál es el equivalente de "español"?

Lección 3

A. Agreement of adjectives, articles, and nouns

Rewrite the following sentences, making all of the nouns feminine. Change the adjectives and articles accordingly.

1. El chico es alto.
2. El doctor es español.
3. Los señores son ingleses.
4. El profesor es mexicano.
5. Los hijos de ella no son felices.

B. Present indicative of regular -er and -ir verbs

Complete the following sentences, using the appropriate form of the verbs in the list.

vivir	escribir	decidir	leer	comer
creer	beber	aprender	recibir	deber

1. Yo no _____ sándwiches.
2. Adriana _____ en la calle Magnolia.
3. Ellos _____ el inglés, no el español.
4. ¿_____ Uds. café?
5. ¿Tú no _____ en Santa Claus?

6. Ud. _____ el anuncio en el periódico.
7. Juan y yo _____ en alemán.
8. Paco no _____ mucho dinero.
9. Yo _____ solicitar el empleo.
10. Ud. _____ escribir la lección.

C. Present indicative of the irregular verbs *tener* and *venir*

Complete the following sentences, using the correct forms of **venir** or **tener,** as appropriate.

1. ¿Cuántos hijos _____ Uds.?
2. Ella _____ a la universidad para estudiar.
3. Nosotros no _____ el número de teléfono de Ana.
4. El señor Rojas _____ más tarde.
5. Yo _____ dos hijos. Ellos _____ a la universidad con mi esposa.
6. Yo no _____ a solicitar trabajo.

D. The personal *a*

Form sentences, using the elements provided. Include the personal **a** when necessary.

1. yo / llevar / mis hermanos / a / la universidad
2. nosotros / llevar / los papeles / a / la clase
3. ellos / llevan / Julio / y / su novia
4. nosotros / tener / cuatro hijos

E. Contractions

Complete the following sentences, using the Spanish equivalent of the words in parentheses.

1. Necesito llamar _____ . *(Mr. Varela)*
2. Yo vengo _____ . *(from the gym)*
3. ¿Tú vienes _____ ? *(from the library)*
4. Ellos llevan _____ a las cuatro. *(the girls)*
5. Los mapas son _____ . *(Mr. Soto's)*

F. Just words . . . (Part I)

Complete the following sentences, using appropriate words or phrases from the vocabulary list in **Lección 3.**

1. Para trabajar en la compañía, debe tener _____ de computadoras.
2. No es moreno; es _____ .
3. Tiene que llenar la _____ para el empleo.
4. La clase de la Dra. Vargas no es fácil; es muy _____ .
5. Ellos beben _____ y _____ sándwiches de _____ y queso.
6. Él _____ el anuncio en el _____ .
7. Trabajo por la mañana, pero tengo la tarde _____ .
8. Ellos no viven _____ ; viven cerca de aquí.

G. Just words . . . (Part II)

Supply the missing categories from a job application, according to the information provided.

1. _____ : Marisa Cortés
2. _____ : Calle Lima, 432
3. _____ : Veinticinco años
4. _____ : Caracas, Venezuela
5. _____ : Casada
6. _____ : Profesora
7. _____ : Femenino

H. Culture

Answer the following questions based on the **¿Lo sabía Ud.?** section.

1. Si el nombre de una mujer es María Teresa, ¿cuál es su sobrenombre?
2. Luis Miguel es el hijo de María Isabel Peña y Marcos Antonio Vargas. ¿Cuál es el nombre completo de Luis Miguel?

EN UNA FIESTA

OBJECTIVES

Pronunciation

The Spanish **b**, **v**, **d**, and **g** (before **a**, **o**, or **u**)

Structure

Expressions with **tener** • Present indicative of the irregular verbs **ir**, **dar**, and **estar** • **Ir a** + *infinitive* • Uses of **ser** and **estar** • Present indicative of e:ie stem-changing verbs

Communication

You will learn vocabulary related to party activities, foods, and beverages.

EN UNA FIESTA **87**

EN UNA FIESTA

Adela, una chica uruguaya, da una fiesta de fin de año en su casa e[1] invita a muchos de sus compañeros de la universidad. En la fiesta, Humberto y Adela conversan mientras bailan.

ADELA	—Humberto, ¿dónde está tu prima?
HUMBERTO	—Va a venir más tarde. Tiene que traer a mi mamá.
ADELA	—También va a traer unos discos compactos. Oye, ¿dónde vamos a celebrar el año nuevo?[2]
HUMBERTO	—Vamos a ir al baile del Club Náutico.
ADELA	—¡Tienes razón! La fiesta es allí. Julio y su novia van a ir también.
HUMBERTO	—¡Magnífico! Ellos son muy simpáticos. Además, mañana es el cumpleaños de Julio.
ADELA	—¿Ah sí? ¿Cuántos años tiene Julio?
HUMBERTO	—Creo que tiene veintidós.
ADELA	—Oye, ¿tienes hambre? ¿Quieres pollo, entremeses, ensalada...? El pollo está delicioso.
HUMBERTO	—No, gracias. No tengo mucha hambre, pero tengo sed.
ADELA	—¿Quieres un coctel, sidra,[3] champán, cerveza, sangría[4]...?
HUMBERTO	—Prefiero un refresco.
ADELA	—¿A qué hora empieza el baile en el club?
HUMBERTO	—A las diez y media. Voy a llamar a Julio y a Teresa.
ADELA	—Y Silvia, ¿también piensa ir con nosotros?
HUMBERTO	—No, ella no va porque está enferma.

Más tarde, en el Club Náutico, todos celebran el año nuevo.

ADELA	—La orquesta es magnífica. ¿Bailamos, Humberto?
HUMBERTO	—Sí.
JULIO	—*(A su novia)* ¿Estás cansada, Teresa?
TERESA	—No, tengo calor.[5] ¿Por qué no vamos todos a la terraza ahora?
JULIO	—Buena idea. ¿Llevamos las bebidas?
TERESA	—Sí, tengo mucha sed.
JAVIER	—¿No tienen uvas? En España siempre comemos doce uvas a la medianoche.
MARISA	—Aquí en Montevideo brindamos con sidra.
ADELA	—¡Son las doce! ¡Feliz año nuevo!
TODOS	—¡Feliz año nuevo! ¡Feliz año nuevo...!
HUMBERTO	—Y, ¡feliz cumpleaños, Julio!

---

[1] Note that before a word beginning with **i** or **hi**, the equivalent of *and* is **e**.

[2] In Hispanic countries, it is common for people to celebrate the New Year by attending a party in a private home early in the evening, then moving to a club before midnight.

[3] It is an alcoholic drink in Hispanic countries.

[4] It is a drink prepared with red wine and fruit.

[5] In the Southern Hemisphere the seasons are reversed.

VOCABULARIO

COGNADOS

el champán champagne	**la ensalada** salad	**la sidra** cider
el coctel cocktail	**la idea** idea	**la terraza** terrace
delicioso(-a) delicious	**mucho(-a)** much, a lot of	**uruguayo(-a)** Uruguayan
el disco compacto compact disk (CD)	**la orquesta** orchestra, group	
	la sangría sangría	

■ NOMBRES

el baile dance
la bebida drink, beverage
la cerveza beer
el (la) compañero(-a) de clase classmate
el cumpleaños birthday

los entremeses hors d'oeuvres
la fiesta party
la mamá, madre Mom, mother
la medianoche midnight
el pollo chicken
el (la) primo(-a) cousin

el refresco soft drink, soda pop
las uvas grapes

■ VERBOS

bailar to dance
brindar to toast
celebrar to celebrate
dar (*irreg.*) to give
empezar, comenzar (e:ie) to begin, to start

estar (*irreg.*) to be
invitar to invite
ir (*irreg.*) to go
pensar (e:ie) to think
preferir (e:ie) to prefer

querer (e:ie) to want, to wish
traer (yo traigo) to bring

■ ADJETIVOS

bueno(-a)[1] good
cansado(-a) tired
enfermo(-a) sick

feliz happy
magnífico(-a) great

muchos(-as) many
nuevo(-a) new

■ OTRAS PALABRAS Y EXPRESIONES

a la medianoche at midnight
además besides
ah oh
ahora now
aquí here
¿Bailamos? Shall we dance?

fiesta de fin de año New Year's Eve party
siempre always
tener... años to be . . . years old
tener razón to be right
tengo calor I'm hot

tengo hambre I'm hungry
tengo sed I'm thirsty
todos(-as) everybody, all

---

[1] **Bueno** drops the -o when placed before a masculine singular noun: **un** *buen* **profesor.**

Vocabulario adicional

La fiesta de Navidad *(Christmas)*

- el árbol de Navidad
- Ellos cantan.
- el brindis
- la mesa
- el ponche
- el tocadiscos compactos
- el equipo estereofónico
- la cinta, el casete
- el vino

Para describir *(to describe)*

contento(-a) happy		Estoy **contenta** porque voy a la fiesta.
enojado(-a), enfadado(-a) angry		Él no está contento. Está **enojado**.
malo(-a)[1] bad		La orquesta es **mala**.
ocupado(-a) busy		Hoy estoy muy **ocupado**.
triste sad		No está contento. Está **triste**.

Para aclarar *(to clarify)*

¿adónde? where? (destination)	**¿Adónde** vamos hoy?
al mediodía at noon	Aurora viene **al mediodía**.
¿cuánto(-a)? how much?	**¿Cuánta** ensalada quieres?
¿de quién? whose?	**¿De quién** es la cinta? ¿De Raúl?

---

[1] **Malo** drops the -o when placed before a masculine singular noun: **un *mal*** hombre.

¡CONVERSEMOS!

Answer the following questions, basing your answers on the dialogues.

1. ¿A quiénes invita Adela?
2. ¿Quién tiene que traer a la mamá de Humberto?
3. ¿Quiénes son muy simpáticos?
4. ¿Cuántos años tiene Julio?
5. ¿Qué prefiere beber Humberto?
6. ¿Dónde van a celebrar el año nuevo?
7. ¿A qué hora empieza el baile en el Club Náutico?
8. ¿Por qué no va Silvia a la fiesta?
9. ¿Está cansada Teresa?
10. ¿Qué llevan a la terraza?
11. ¿Es uruguayo Javier?
12. ¿Con qué brindan a la medianoche?

 # ¿Lo sabía Ud.?

- En España y en Latinoamérica, no existe tanta *(as much)* separación entre *(among)* generaciones como en los Estados Unidos. Los niños, los padres y los abuelos frecuentemente van juntos a fiestas y a celebraciones.

- En los países *(countries)* hispanos, las chicas y los muchachos generalmente van en grupos a fiestas, al teatro y a conciertos.

- Los hispanos generalmente celebran el cumpleaños y también el día de su "santo", que corresponde al santo de su nombre en el calendario católico. Por ejemplo, si un niño nace *(is born)* en junio y sus padres lo llaman Miguel, celebra su cumpleaños en junio y celebra el día de su "santo" el 29 de septiembre, que es el día de San Miguel.

- En algunos *(some)* países hispanos no existe una edad mínima para comprar *(buy)* o tomar bebidas alcohólicas.

- En español se dice "¡Salud!" *(Cheers!)* al brindar. En España, también dicen "Salud, amor y pesetas" *(Health, love, and pesetas)*.

Una familia argentina, celebrando un cumpleaños.

PRONUNCIACIÓN

A The Spanish b and v

The Spanish **b** and **v** are pronounced exactly alike. Both sound like a weak English *b*, as in the word *Abe*. In Spanish, they are even weaker when pronounced between vowels. The lips don't quite touch. Never pronounce these consonants like English *v*. Listen to your instructor and repeat the following words.

veinte	bien
venir	baile
Viviana	rubio
uva	sobrina

B The Spanish d

The Spanish **d** is slightly softer than the *d* in the English word *day*. When pronounced between two vowels or at the end of a word, it is similar to the *th* in the English word *they*. Listen to your instructor and repeat the following words.

delgado	universidad
de	sábado
debe	bebida
dos	adiós

C The Spanish g (before a, o, or u)

■ When followed by **a, o,** or **u**, the Spanish **g** is similar to the *g* in the English word *guy*. Listen to your instructor and repeat the following words.

delgado	guapo	gordo

■ When pronounced between vowels, the Spanish **g** is much softer. Repeat after your instructor.

amigo	pregunta	uruguaya

■ In the combinations **gue** and **gui**, the **u** is silent. Repeat after your instructor.

Guevara	Guillermo	alguien

ESTRUCTURAS

1 Expressions with **tener** *(Expresiones con **tener**)*

■ Many useful idiomatic expressions that use *to be + adjective* in English are formed with **tener** *+ noun* in Spanish.

tener (mucho) frío	*to be (very) cold*
tener (mucha) sed	*to be (very) thirsty*
tener (mucha) hambre	*to be (very) hungry*
tener (mucho) calor	*to be (very) hot*
tener (mucho) sueño	*to be (very) sleepy*
tener (mucha) prisa	*to be in a (great) hurry*
tener (mucho) miedo	*to be (quite) afraid, scared*
tener cuidado	*to be careful*
tener razón	*to be right*
no tener razón[1]	*to be wrong*
tener... años de edad	*to be . . . years old*

—¿**Tienes** calor?   *"Are you hot?"*
—Sí, y también **tengo** mucha **sed.**   *"Yes, and I'm also very thirsty."*

—¿Deseas comer pollo?   *"Do you want to eat chicken?"*
—No, gracias, no **tengo hambre.**   *"No, thank you, I'm not hungry."*

—¿Cuántos **años tienes?**   *"How old are you?"*
—**Tengo** diecinueve **años.**   *"I'm nineteen years old."*

ATENCIÓN Note that Spanish uses **mucho(-a)** *(adjective) + noun* (as in **mucha hambre**) the way English uses *very + adjective* (as in *very hungry*).

Práctica

A. ¿Qué tienen?

1. Jorge

2. Yo

---
[1] Incorrectness is also conveyed by the expression **estar equivocado(-a).**

3. Tú

4. *La profesora*

5. Ud.

6. Felipe

7. Marisa y Elena

8. Ella

B. Interview a classmate, using the following questions. When you have finished, switch roles.

1. ¿Qué bebes cuando tienes sed? ¿Y cuando tienes frío?
2. ¿Qué comes cuando tienes hambre?
3. ¿Cuántos años tienes?
4. ¿Cuántos años tiene tu mamá? ¿Y tu papá *(Dad)*?
5. En tu familia, ¿quién tiene razón siempre? ¿Y en la clase?
6. ¿Tienes miedo a veces *(sometimes)*?

C. With a partner, act out the following dialogues in Spanish.

1. "I'm very thirsty."
   "What do you want to drink?"
   "A soft drink, please."
   "Do you want a sandwich?"
   "No, I'm not hungry."
2. "Are you sleepy?"
   "Yes, it's midnight!"

3. "Delia is twenty years old."
   "No, I think that she is nineteen."
   "You are right."
4. "Are you in a hurry, Miss Peña?"
   "No, why?"
   "Because I have to speak with you."
5. "I need to open the window. I'm hot."
   "You're hot? I'm cold."

D. Which expression with **tener** would you use in each of the following situations?

1. You are in the Sahara desert in the middle of summer.
2. A big dog is chasing you.
3. You have only a minute to get to your next class.
4. You are in Alaska in the middle of winter.
5. You haven't eaten for an entire day.
6. You got up at four A.M. and it is now midnight.
7. You just ran for two hours in the sun.
8. You are blowing out thirty candles on your birthday cake.

2 Present indicative of the irregular verbs **ir, dar,** and **estar**
*(Presente de indicativo de los verbos irregulares **ir, dar** y **estar**)*

	ir *to go*	**dar** *to give*	**estar** *to be*
yo	voy	doy	estoy
tú	vas	das	estás
Ud. / él / ella	va	da	está
nosotros(-as)	vamos	damos	estamos
vosotros(-as)	vais	dais	estáis
Uds. / ellos / ellas	van	dan	están

—Susana **da** una fiesta hoy. ¿Tú **vas**?

—No, no **voy** porque **estoy** muy cansada.

—Entonces invito a tu hermana. ¿Dónde **está**?

—**Está** en la universidad. Viene a las tres.

"Susana is giving a party today. Are you going?"

"No, I'm not going because I am very tired."

"Then I'm inviting your sister. Where is she?"

"She is at the university. She is coming at three o'clock."

■ The verb **estar,** *to be,* is used here to indicate current condition (**Estoy muy cansada.**) and location (**Está en la universidad.**). **Ser,** another equivalent of the English verb *to be,* has been used up to now to refer to origin (**Él es de Chile.**), nationality (**Ellas son mexicanas.**), characteristics (**Jorge es rubio.**), profession (**Elsa es profesora.**), and time (**Son las doce.**).

■ Other frequent uses of **dar** are **dar un examen, dar una conferencia** *(lecture),* and **dar una orden** *(order).*

Práctica

A. Complete the following conversation, using the appropriate forms of the verbs **ir, dar,** and **estar.** Then act out the dialogue with a partner.

JOSÉ —Rosa, ¿tú _____ a la fiesta que _____ Estrella el sábado?

ROSA —Sí, _____ con Inés. ¿Tú _____ también?

JOSÉ —Sí. Oye, ¿estudiamos esta noche? El Dr. Vargas y la Dra. Soto _____ exámenes mañana.

ROSA —Ay, José, _____ muy cansada.

JOSÉ —Pero, Rosa, ¡tú siempre _____ cansada!

ROSA —No siempre. ¿Por qué no estudias con Jorge y Raúl? Ellos no _____ al club esta noche.

JOSÉ —Buena idea. ¿Dónde _____ ellos ahora?

ROSA — _____ en la universidad.

B. Interview a classmate, using the following questions. When you have finished, switch roles.

1. ¿Cómo estás?
2. ¿Estás contento(-a) o triste hoy?
3. ¿Quién no está en clase hoy?
4. ¿Está muy ocupado(-a) el profesor (la profesora)?
5. ¿Da el profesor (la profesora) exámenes difíciles o fáciles?
6. ¿Adónde vas los sábados por la noche con tus amigos?
7. ¿Van Uds. a un club? (¿A cuál?)
8. ¿Con quién vas a las fiestas?
9. ¿Das muchas fiestas en tu casa?
10. ¿Das una fiesta de fin de año? ¿De Navidad?
11. ¿Adónde van Uds. mañana? ¿Por qué?
12. ¿Dónde están tus amigos ahora? ¿Por qué?

C. Complete the following sentences in a logical manner.

1. Roberto está allí y nosotros...
2. Yo doy una fiesta esta noche y tú...
3. Tú vas a la universidad y yo...
4. Yo estoy muy enojado(-a) y ellos...
5. Nosotros damos una fiesta de Navidad y él...
6. Ellos van hoy y nosotros...

3 Ir a + *infinitive* (*Ir a + infinitivo*)

■ **Ir a** + *infinitive* is used to express future action. It is equivalent to the English expression *to be going (to)* + *infinitive*. The "formula" is as follows:

ir (conjugated)	+ a +	infinitive
Voy	**a**	**trabajar.**
I am going		*to work.*

—¿En qué universidad **van a estudiar** Uds.? "*At what university are you going to study?*"
—**Vamos a estudiar** en la Universidad de Costa Rica. "*We're going to study at the University of Costa Rica.*"

—¿Ud. **va a dar** una conferencia? "*Are you going to give a lecture?*"
—Sí, **voy a dar** una conferencia el viernes. "*Yes, I'm going to give a lecture on Friday.*"

—¿Tú **vas a cantar**? "*Are you going to sing?*"
— No, **voy a bailar.** "*No, I'm going to dance.*"

Práctica

A. What do you think these people are going to do? Consider where they are and what time of day it is.

MODELO: —José / en el hospital / por la tarde
—*José va a trabajar en el hospital por la tarde.*

1. Yo / en mi casa / por la noche
2. Los estudiantes / en la clase / por la mañana
3. Nosotros / en el club / por la noche
4. Tú / en la cafetería / a las doce
5. El profesor / en la universidad / por la tarde
6. Julio y Teresa / en la terraza / a las diez de la noche
7. Susana / en la compañía IBM / por la mañana
8. Uds. / en la fiesta / por la noche

B. What are these people going to do? With a partner, take turns asking and answering questions, using the information in the illustrations.

MODELO: —¿Con quién va a bailar Marisol?
—*Va a bailar con Tito.*

Tito

1. Roberto

2. Elisa

3. Julio y Estrella

4. Daniel

5. Eduardo

6. Graciela

C. Interview a classmate, using the following questions. When you have finished, switch roles.

1. ¿Dónde vas a comer hoy?
2. ¿Con quién vas a comer?
3. ¿A qué hora van a comer Uds.?
4. ¿Qué van a comer?
5. ¿Qué van a tomar Uds.?
6. ¿Qué vas a hacer *(to do)* mañana por la tarde?
7. ¿Qué van a estudiar Ud. y sus amigos?
8. ¿Qué van a hacer Uds. por la noche?
9. ¿Dónde vas a trabajar mañana?
10. ¿Tu amigo(-a) va a trabajar también?

4   Uses of **ser** and **estar**   *(Usos de ser y estar)*

The English verb *to be* has two Spanish equivalents, **ser** and **estar.** As a general rule, **ser** expresses *who* or *what* the subject is *essentially,* and **estar** indicates *state* or *condition.* **Ser** and **estar** are *not* interchangeable.

A. Uses of *ser*

Ser expresses a fundamental quality and identifies the essence of a person or thing.

▪ It describes the basic nature or character of a person or thing. It is also used with expressions of age that do not refer to a specific number of years.

> La orquesta **es** buena.
> Yo **soy** joven *(young).*

▪ It describes the material that things are made of.

> Las mesas **son** de metal.

▪ It is used to denote nationality, origin, and profession or trade.

> Sandra **es** norteamericana.
> Yo **soy** de Caracas.
> Mi mamá **es** profesora.

▪ It is used with expressions of time and with dates.

> Hoy **es** miércoles, cuatro de abril.
> **Son** las cuatro y cuarto de la tarde.

▪ It is used with events as the equivalent of *taking place.*

> La fiesta **es** en el club Los Violines.

▪ It is used to indicate possession or relationship.

> Los discos compactos **son** de Julia.
> Antonio **es** el hermano de Raúl.

Práctica

Interview a classmate, using the following questions and two of your own. When you have finished, switch roles.

1. ¿Eres norteamericano(-a)? ¿De dónde eres?
2. ¿De qué ciudad eres?
3. ¿Cómo es tu mamá?
4. ¿Quién es tu mejor amigo(-a)?
5. ¿Es alto(-a) o bajo(-a)?
6. ¿Eres feliz?
7. ¿Dónde son tus clases?
8. ¿Qué día es hoy?
9. ¿Qué fecha es hoy?
10. ¿Qué hora es?

B. Uses of estar

Estar is used to express more transitory qualities and often implies the possibility of change.

▪ It indicates place or location.

> Mi prima no **está** aquí. ¿Dónde **está**?

▪ It is used to indicate condition.

> Mis amigos **están** muy cansados.
> Sara **está** enferma.

▪ With personal reactions, it describes what is perceived through the senses—that is, how a person or thing seems, looks, tastes, or feels.

> El ponche **está** delicioso.

Práctica

A. Imagine that you and a friend are at a party at the Club Náutico, and answer the following questions.

1. ¿En qué calle está el club?
2. ¿Los amigos de Uds. están en el club?
3. ¿Sus amigos están contentos o tristes?
4. ¿Cómo están los entremeses? ¿Deliciosos?
5. ¿Quiénes están en la terraza?
6. ¿Tu mamá está en la fiesta?

B. Complete the following dialogues, using the appropriate forms of **ser** or **estar.** Then act them out with a partner.

1. —¿De dónde _____ tu mamá? ¿ _____ mexicana?
   —Sí, pero ahora _____ en California.
   —¿Tu mamá _____ profesora?
   —No, _____ doctora.
2. —¿Olga _____ tu prima?
   —No, _____ mi hermana.
   —¿Cómo _____ ella?
   —_____ alta, morena y delgada. _____ muy bonita.
   —¿Dónde _____ ella ahora?
   —_____ en su casa.
3. —¿ Qué hora _____ ?
   —_____ las siete.
   —¿Dónde _____ la fiesta de Navidad?
   —_____ en el Club Náutico. ¿Tú vas a ir?
   —No, _____ muy cansada.
4. —¿Qué comes?
   —Arroz con pollo.
   —¿_____ rico *(tasty)*?
   —Sí, _____ delicioso.

5. —¿Ése *(That)* _____ tu escritorio?
   —Sí, _____ mi escritorio.
   —¿ _____ de metal?
   —No, _____ de madera *(wood)*.
6. —¡Oye! ¿Qué día _____ hoy?
   —Hoy _____ jueves.

C. With a partner, act out the following dialogues in Spanish.

1. "Are you (an) American, Mr. Cortés?"
   "No, I am (a) Spaniard. I am from Madrid."
2. "How is the salad?"
   "It's delicious."
3. "What's the date today?"
   "It's September third. Is it your birthday?"
   "No, it's my mother's birthday."
4. "Where are the CDs?"
   "They are at my house."

D. With two or three other students, prepare a description of a famous person. Include as much information as possible (nationality, profession, physical characteristics, etc.). Read your description to the rest of the class and see who can identify your subject.

5 Present indicative of **e:ie** stem-changing verbs
*(Presente de indicativo de los verbos que cambian en la raíz **e:ie**)*

■ Some Spanish verbs undergo a stem change in the present indicative. For these verbs, when **e** is the last stem vowel and it is stressed, it changes to **ie** as follows.

preferir *to prefer*			
yo	prefiero	nosotros(-as)	preferimos
tú	prefieres	vosotros(-as)	preferís
Ud.		Uds.	
él }	prefiere	ellos }	prefieren
ella		ellas	

—¿A qué hora **piensas** ir a la fiesta?   "What time are you planning to go to the party?"
—**Prefiero** ir a las diez. ¿Y tú?   "I prefer to go at ten. And you?"
—Yo **no quiero** ir. Estoy cansado.   "I don't want to go. I'm tired."

—¿A qué hora **empiezan** a[1] estudiar Uds.?   "What time do you start to study?"
—**Empezamos** a las tres.   "We start at three."

■ Note that the stem vowel is not stressed in the verb forms used with **nosotros(-as)** and **vosotros(-as)**; therefore, the **e** does not change to **ie**.

---

[1] The preposition **a** is used after **empezar** and **comenzar** when they are followed by an infinitive.

■ Stem-changing verbs have the same endings as regular -ar, -er, and -ir verbs.

■ Some verbs that undergo this change:

cerrar   *to close*
comenzar   *to begin, to start*
empezar   *to begin, to start*
entender   *to understand*
pensar   *to think*

pensar (+ *infinitive*)   *to plan*
   (to do something)
perder   *to lose*
querer   *to want, to wish, to*
   love

Práctica

A. Complete the following dialogues, using the verbs given. Then act them out with a partner, expanding each dialogue by adding one or two sentences.

1. preferir
   – ¿Dónde _____ comer Uds.? ¿En la cafetería o en su casa?
   – _____ comer en nuestra casa.

2. querer
   – ¿Qué _____ comer Uds.?
   – Rosa _____ comer pollo y Oscar y yo _____ comer entremeses.

3. pensar
   – ¿Adónde _____ ir Uds. el domingo?
   – _____ ir al club.

4. cerrar
   – ¿No _____ (ellos) la cafetería los sábados?
   – No, creo que no _____ la cafetería los sábados.

5. perder
   – Cuando Uds. van a Las Vegas, ¿ _____ mucho dinero?
   – Sí, _____ mucho.

6. empezar
   – ¿A qué hora _____ Uds. a trabajar?
   – Nosotros _____ a las ocho y Luis _____ a las nueve.

B. You have just enrolled at a new university, and some current students are helping to orient you. Compare their routines and preferences with your own.

1. Comenzamos las clases a las nueve.
2. No entendemos inglés.
3. Pensamos trabajar mañana.
4. Queremos ir al club.
5. Preferimos beber refrescos.
6. No cerramos las ventanas por la noche.

C. Interview a classmate, using the following questions. When you have finished, switch roles.

1. ¿Entienden tú y tus amigos inglés?
2. ¿Entiendes una conversación en español?
3. ¿Entiendes la lección?
4. ¿Quieres tomar un refresco?
5. ¿Prefieres Coca-Cola o Sprite?
6. ¿Quieren Uds. comer en su casa o en la cafetería?
7. ¿Piensas ir a un baile el sábado?
8. Para bailar, ¿prefieres una orquesta o discos compactos?

D. With a classmate, prepare four questions to ask your instructor, using stem-changing verbs.

¡A VER CUÁNTO APRENDIÓ!

¡Repase el vocabulario!

Complete the following sentences with the appropriate words; then read them aloud.

1. ¿ _____ son los discos compactos? ¿De Rosa?
2. En las fiestas de _____ de año en España, comen doce _____ a la _____ .
3. La orquesta es muy, muy buena. ¡Es _____ !
4. Julio Iglesias _____ muy bien.
5. ¿ _____ vas? ¿Al club?
6. ¡Feliz año _____ !
7. Marta está _____ porque va al baile del club.
8. ¿Tienes refrescos? Tengo mucha _____ .
9. No tengo _____ , pero tengo discos compactos.
10. No quiero bailar ahora porque estoy muy _____ .
11. ¿ _____ dinero tiene Ud.? ¿Mil pesos?
12. ¿Quién va a traer el _____ de Navidad?
13. Un _____ . Vamos a brindar con sidra.
14. Hoy vamos a celebrar el _____ de Julio.
15. ¿Estudiamos esta noche o vas a estar _____ ?
16. Tengo un equipo _____ , pero es muy malo.

Entrevista

Interview a classmate, using the **tú** form.

Pregúntele a su compañero(-a) de clase...

1. ...cuántos años tiene.
2. ...si va a estar ocupado(-a) mañana.
3. ...si da muchas fiestas en su casa.
4. ...si va a dar una fiesta el sábado.
5. ...si baila muy bien.
6. ...si prefiere beber vino, cerveza o refrescos.
7. ...si es una buena idea tener una fiesta hoy.
8. ...adónde va a ir esta noche.
9. ...si tiene cintas o discos compactos.
10. ...si tiene hambre.
11. ...si quiere comer pollo o entremeses.
12. ...si va a comer en la cafetería mañana.

Situaciones

What would you say in the following situations? What might the other person say? Act out the scenes with a partner. Take turns playing each role.

1. You want to ask someone to dance with you.
2. You are having a party. Offer one of your guests a selection of beverages.
3. Your friend is hungry. You have plenty of food in the house.
4. You call a friend to say that you are going to bring the drinks for a party.
5. It's 12:00 A.M. on January 1.
6. It's your best friend's birthday.

Para escribir

Look at the photo and make up a story about the people you see. Give their names, describe them, and say how they are related. Say who is giving the party, the occasion for the party, what they are doing, and so on.

En la vida real

Una visita

With a classmate, plan activities you would have in your hometown to entertain a visitor from a Spanish-speaking country. Give your visitor a name and decide which country he or she is from. In your plans include a party, visits to places of interest, and outdoor activities. Decide who is going to do what, and include food and drinks you are going to offer your visitor.

Some additional words or phrases you may want to include are:

la hamburguesa *hamburger*		**la montaña** *mountain*	
el perro caliente *hot dog*		**el picnic** *picnic*	
el pollo frito *fried chicken*		**la playa** *beach*	
el cine *movie theater*			
la discoteca *disco*			**béisbol**
el museo *museum*		**el partido** *(game)* de	**básquetbol**
el teatro *theater*			**fútbol** *(soccer)*
			fútbol americano

Un espectáculo

In Spain, you and a classmate come across this ad about a show and decide to go see it. What information can you get from the ad? After reading the ad, take turns answering the questions that follow.

MADRID ABIERTO

«Holiday on Ice», en el Palacio de Deportes

❈❈❈❈❈❈

Música y acrobacias en una fiesta sobre hielo

Setenta artistas del patinaje, de diversas nacionalidades, participan en el espectáculo musical «Holiday on Ice», que se presenta en Madrid solamente hasta el 2 de agosto, antes de continuar hacia Valladolid y Bilbao.

El "show" ofrece dos horas de números musicales, bailes y acrobacias dedicadas a México y a Rusia. La "danza de los platillos" y las acrobacias de los hermanos Ribelli son lo mejor.

El espectáculo se presenta a las 21,30 horas. Hay entradas desde 500 a 1.400 pesetas, con precios especiales para los niños menores de doce años. Venta anticipada por las tardes, de 18 a 21 horas, en el **Palacio de Deportes de la Comunidad** (avenida Felipe II, 19).

Zdenek Pazdirek, doble campeón checoslovaco.

1. ¿Cómo se llama el espectáculo?
2. ¿Dónde presentan el espectáculo?
3. ¿Hasta *(Until)* cuándo va a estar en Madrid el grupo?
4. De Madrid, ¿adónde va el grupo?
5. ¿Cuántos artistas hay en el grupo?
6. ¿Son todos mexicanos?
7. ¿A qué países dedican los artistas el espectáculo?
8. ¿El espectáculo es a las nueve y media de la mañana o de la noche?
9. En España no usan dólares; usan pesetas. ¿Cuánto dinero necesitan Uds. para comprar las entradas *(buy the tickets)*?
10. ¿En qué calle está el Palacio de Deportes de la Comunidad?

¡Damos una fiesta!

Get together with two or three students and plan a party. Discuss the following:

1. how much money you have
2. when you are going to have the party
3. where you are going to have the party
4. whom you are going to invite
5. what you are going to eat and who is going to bring the food
6. what you are going to drink and who is going to bring the drinks
7. what you are going to do
8. who is going to bring the CDs and tapes
9. what kinds of music you want

¡Vamos a leer!

Antes de leer

As you read the following dialogue, find the answers to these questions.

1. ¿Cuál es el apellido de Ana María?
2. ¿De dónde es?
3. ¿Dónde está su familia?
4. ¿Qué estudia Ana María en la universidad?
5. ¿Por qué no son fáciles las clases para ella?
6. ¿La muchacha trabaja? ¿Dónde?
7. ¿Ud. cree que Ana María va mucho a la playa?
8. ¿Con quiénes piensa ir a Disney World?
9. ¿Cuánto tiempo va a estar ella en Miami?
10. ¿Cuándo piensa regresar a Chile?

Una entrevista°

Ana María Estévez estudia en la Universidad Internacional de la Florida. Ella es de Chile, pero ahora su familia y ella viven en Miami. Hoy la entrevistamos° para el periódico de la universidad.

PERIODISTA	—¿Qué clases tomas en la universidad, Ana María?
ANA MARÍA	—Matemáticas, historia del arte, inglés y sociología. Las clases son muy difíciles para mí porque no hablo muy bien el inglés.
PERIODISTA	—¿Trabajas también?
ANA MARÍA	—Sí, trabajo en el laboratorio de lenguas.°
PERIODISTA	—¿Te gusta Miami?
ANA MARÍA	—Sí, especialmente la playa.°
PERIODISTA	—¿Piensas ir a Disney World?
ANA MARÍA	—Sí, pienso ir con unos amigos cubanos. Son unos chicos muy simpáticos y divertidos.°
PERIODISTA	—¿Cuánto tiempo° vas a estar en Miami?
ANA MARÍA	—Unos cuatro años.
PERIODISTA	—¿Piensas regresar a Chile?
ANA MARÍA	—Algún° día...

interview

la... we are interviewing her

languages

beach

entertaining
¿Cuánto...? How long

Some

Díganos

Answer the following questions, based on your own thoughts and experiences.

1. ¿Cuál es su apellido?
2. ¿Dónde vive y estudia Ud.?
3. ¿Dónde vive su familia?
4. ¿Cuántas clases toma Ud.? ¿Son fáciles o difíciles?
5. ¿Va Ud. a la playa? ¿Con quién?
6. ¿Son divertidos sus amigos?

ESPAÑA (1)

España

- España forma, con Portugal, la Península Ibérica. Su capital es Madrid y su sistema de gobierno es una monarquía constitucional. El actual rey *(king)* de España es Juan Carlos de Borbón.

- El turismo tiene una gran importancia para la economía de España. Más de 63 millones de personas visitan España cada *(each)* año para disfrutar de *(enjoy)* su clima y de su rica historia.

- Los moros *(Moors)*, del norte de África, dominaron España por más de 700 años. Su influencia es evidente en la arquitectura de Toledo, Córdoba, Granada, Sevilla y otras ciudades.

Una de las grandes atracciones turísticas de Madrid es la Plaza de España, donde se encuentra un monumento a Cervantes. Frente a la estatua del escritor están Don Quijote y Sancho Panza, los personajes *(characters)* centrales de su inmortal novela *Don Quijote de la Mancha.*
¿Cuáles son las principales atracciones turísticas de su estado?

PANORAMA HISPÁNICO

La ciudad de Ávila, situada al noroeste de Madrid, está completamente rodeada de murallas románicas *(Romanesque walls)*. Aunque las murallas tienen casi *(almost)* 1.000 años, están muy bien conservadas. **¿Hay ciudades como Ávila en su país?**

Vista parcial del puerto de San Sebastián en el País Vasco *(Basque Country)*. Situado sobre el Mar Cantábrico y muy cerca de la frontera francesa, San Sebastián es un centro pesquero *(fishing)* importante. La ciudad también es conocida *(known)* por su hermosa *(beautiful)* playa, "La Concha". **¿Vive Ud. cerca del mar *(sea)*?**

El Templo de la Sagrada Familia, del arquitecto catalán Antonio Gaudí, es un símbolo de la ciudad de Barcelona. Gaudí murió en 1926 sin terminar la construcción de la iglesia, que todavía no está acabada *(finished)*. **¿Cómo se llaman algunos arquitectos norteamericanos famosos?**

El pueblo de Alcázar de San Juan, en la región de La Mancha. Esta región, una extensa llanura *(plain)*, y sus molinos de viento *(windmills)* son famosos en todo el mundo gracias a la novela *Don Quijote de la Mancha,* de Miguel de Cervantes.
¿Qué sabe Ud. de Don Quijote?

El Monasterio de Montserrat, situado en la montaña del mismo *(same)* nombre, cerca de Barcelona, es famoso por la estatua de la Virgen María y el Niño. La Virgen de Montserrat, a la que los catalanes llaman "la Moreneta", por su color negro, es la patrona de Cataluña. En el monasterio hay varios museos y una de las bibliotecas más importantes de España.
¿Hay algún museo importante en su ciudad? ¿Cuál?

Las ferias *(fairs)* son muy populares en toda España. La feria de abril de Sevilla, que se celebra después de la Semana Santa *(Holy Week)*, es una de las más famosas del país.
¿Dónde hay ferias en su país?

El Patio de los Leones de la Alhambra de Granada. La Alhambra es un palacio inmenso, construído por los árabes en los siglos XIII y XIV. Los salones y jardines del palacio forman una especie *(sort)* de laberinto.
¿Dónde está su edificio favorito?

Mallorca, Menorca e Ibiza, las Islas Baleares, están situadas en el Mar Mediterráneo y pertenecen a España. Más de cinco millones de turistas visitan estas islas todos los años. Sin embargo, las islas aún conservan muchas de sus típicas aldeas *(small towns)* de pescadores, como la que vemos en la foto.
¿Qué islas pertenecen a los Estados Unidos?

Teleinforme

Vocabulario

Madrid

a la vez	at the same time
los aficionados	fans
antigua, vieja	old
la corrida de toros	bullfight
el deporte	sport
la diosa	goddess
la fuente	fountain
grande	big, large
hermosa	beautiful
los jardines	gardens
el lago	lake
el país	country

Antonio Gaudí

a principios de	at the beginning of
creó	created
los edificios	buildings
entre	among
el genio	genius
la gruta	grotto
hoy día	today
la iglesia	church
la obra	work
ondulantes	undulating, wavy

Granada

los arcos	arches
los diseños	designs
era	was
la fortaleza	fortress
el sur	south

Preparación

¿Cuánto saben Uds. ya?   After reading the information in **Panorama hispánico 2**, get together in groups of three or four and complete each statement with the appropriate information.

1. _____ es la capital de España.
2. En la Plaza de España hay un monumento a _____ .
3. Antonio Gaudí es un _____ catalán.

4. El Templo de la Sagrada Familia está en _____ .
5. Los _____ dominaron España por más de _____ años.
6. La influencia árabe se observa en la arquitectura de ciudades como Toledo, _____ , _____ y _____ .
7. El _____ de los Leones está en la Alhambra.
8. La Alhambra es un _____ inmenso, construido por los _____ en los siglos XIII y XIV.

Comprensión

A. Madrid.   Read the following statements. After watching the video, circle **V** (**Verdadero**) or **F** (**Falso**), according to what you understood.

V F   1. La Plaza Mayor es muy grande.
V F   2. La Puerta del Sol es un monumento.
V F   3. En la Plaza de la Cibeles hay un monumento a Cervantes.
V F   4. Hay un lago en el Parque del Buen Retiro.
V F   5. El fútbol es el deporte más popular entre los madrileños.

B. Antonio Gaudí.   Complete the following statements with the appropriate words.

1. Antonio Gaudí creó un estilo _____ de arquitectura.
2. La Casa Milá es una casa de _____ .
3. El Parque Güell tiene mosaicos y una _____ .
4. El Templo de la Sagrada Familia es la obra más _____ y más original de Gaudí.
5. La construcción de la _____ continúa hasta hoy día.

C. Granada.   Select the word or phrase that best completes each statement, according to what you understood.

1. La Alhambra era una (fortaleza militar, fuente).
2. Las paredes de la Alhambra están decoradas con (complicados, simples) diseños geométricos.
3. En el Patio de los Leones, la fuente está rodeada de (diez, doce) leones.
4. En el Generalife hay (palacios, jardines) muy bonitos.

Ampliación

Dos culturas.   With a partner, make a list of counterparts you can find in your city, state, or country for each of the following items.

1. Madrid
2. El monumento a La Cibeles
3. La Plaza Mayor
4. El Parque de Buen Retiro
5. El Templo de la Sagrada Familia
6. La Casa Milá
7. El Generalife

PLANES PARA UN FIN DE SEMANA

OBJECTIVES

■ **Pronunciation**

The Spanish **p, t, c,** and **q**

■ **Structure**

Verbs with irregular first-person forms • **Saber** vs. **conocer** • Comparative forms • Irregular comparative forms • Present indicative of **o:ue** stem-changing verbs

■ **Communication**

You will learn vocabulary related to family relationships and personal characteristics.

PLANES PARA UN FIN DE SEMANA

Carol, una estudiante de los Estados Unidos, está en España. Asiste a la universidad de Salamanca y vive en una pensión cerca de la Plaza Mayor. Quiere aprender a[1] hablar español perfectamente y por eso nunca pierde la oportunidad de practicar el idioma. Ahora está en un café con dos amigos españoles.

LUIS — Oye, Carol, ¿puedes ir con nosotros a Madrid este fin de semana?

CAROL — No sé... Tengo que escribir muchas cartas: a mi abuela, a mi tío, a mi hermano...

LUIS — Tú echas de menos a tu familia, ¿no?

CAROL — Sí, ...especialmente a mi hermano mayor.

CARMEN — ¿Cómo es tu hermano? ¿Rubio? ¿Moreno?

CAROL — Es rubio, delgado y de estatura mediana. Estudia medicina.

CARMEN — ¡Muy interesante! ¿Cuándo viene a España? ¿En el verano?

CAROL — No, va a viajar a México con su esposa y sus dos hijas.

CARMEN — ¡Bah! Es casado... ¡Qué lástima! ¿No tienes otro hermano?

CAROL — No, lo siento. ¿Quieren ver una fotografía de mis sobrinas?

CARMEN — Sí. *(Mira la foto.)* ¡Son muy bonitas!

CAROL — Empiezan a[1] asistir a la escuela el quince de septiembre.

LUIS — ¡Oye! ¿Por qué no vas a Madrid con nosotros? Es más interesante que escribir cartas...

CAROL — ¿Van en coche?

LUIS — No, preferimos ir en autobús. Es tan cómodo como el coche, no cuesta mucho y no tenemos que conducir.

CAROL — ¡Buena idea! Yo nunca conduzco en Madrid. ¿Y adónde piensan ir?

CARMEN — Al Museo del Prado. Allí están algunos de los cuadros más famosos del mundo.

LUIS — ¡Es muy interesante! ¡Y Madrid tiene unos restaurantes muy buenos! Nosotros siempre almorzamos en Casa Botín.

CAROL — Vale. ¡Vamos a Madrid! ...¡Si no llueve! Porque si llueve no salgo de mi casa.

CARMEN — No, hija, no va a llover.

CAROL — ¿Cuándo volvemos?

LUIS — El sábado por la noche o el domingo.

---

[1]The preposition **a** is used after **aprender** and **empezar** when they are followed by a verb in the infinitive.

Vocabulario

Cognados

¡Bah! Bah!
el café café
especialmente especially
la familia family
famoso(-a) famous
la fotografía, la foto
  photograph, photo

interesante interesting
la medicina medicine
el museo museum
la oportunidad opportunity

perfectamente perfectly
el plan plan
el restaurante restaurant

Nombres

la abuela grandmother
el autobús, el ómnibus, el camión
  de pasajeros *(Mex.)* bus
la carta letter
el coche, el carro, el automóvil, el
  auto car, automobile
el cuadro, la pintura painting,
  picture

la escuela school
los Estados Unidos United States
el fin de semana weekend
el mundo world

la pensión boarding house
la plaza town square
la sobrina niece
el tío uncle

Verbos

almorzar (o:ue) to have lunch
asistir (a) to attend
conducir (yo conduzco), manejar
  to drive
costar (o:ue) to cost

echar de menos, extrañar to miss
  (feel homesick for)
llover (o:ue) to rain
poder (o:ue) to be able to, can
practicar to practice

saber (yo sé) to know
salir (yo salgo) to leave, to go out
ver (yo veo) to see
viajar to travel
volver (o:ue) to return

Adjetivos

cómodo(-a) comfortable
este this *(m.)*

mayor older
otro(-a) other, another

Otras palabras y expresiones

algunos(-as) some
de estatura mediana of medium
  height
nunca never
por eso that is why

¡qué lástima! what a pity!
si if
tan... como... as . . . as . . .

vale okay *(Spain)*
vamos let's go

Vocabulario adicional

La familia

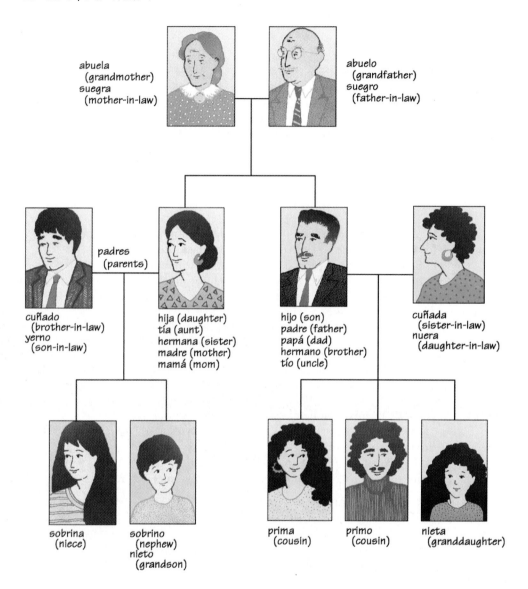

abuela
(grandmother)
suegra
(mother-in-law)

abuelo
(grandfather)
suegro
(father-in-law)

cuñado
(brother-in-law)
yerno
(son-in-law)

padres
(parents)

hija (daughter)
tía (aunt)
hermana (sister)
madre (mother)
mamá (mom)

hijo (son)
padre (father)
papá (dad)
hermano (brother)
tío (uncle)

cuñada
(sister-in-law)
nuera
(daughter-in-law)

sobrina
(niece)

sobrino
(nephew)
nieto
(grandson)

prima
(cousin)

primo
(cousin)

nieta
(granddaughter)

Otros miembros de la familia

la **hijastra**	stepdaughter	Elena es mi **hijastra.**
el **hijastro**	stepson	Julio es el **hijastro** de María.
la **madrastra**	stepmother	Mi **madrastra** se llama Dolores.
la **media hermana**	half sister	Yo tengo dos **medias hermanas.**
el **medio hermano**	half brother	Pedro es mi **medio hermano.**
el **padrastro**	stepfather	No es mi padre; es mi **padrastro.**

¡CONVERSEMOS!

Answer the following questions, basing your answers on the dialogue.

1. ¿De dónde es Carol y dónde vive ahora?
2. ¿Dónde estudia?
3. ¿Cómo es el hermano de Carol?
4. ¿Con quién va a viajar a México?
5. ¿Cuándo empiezan a asistir a la escuela las sobrinas de Carol?
6. ¿Por qué cree Luis que es mejor viajar en autobús?
7. ¿Dónde están algunos de los cuadros más famosos del mundo?
8. En Madrid, ¿dónde comen Luis y Carmen?
9. Si llueve, ¿va a ir Carol a Madrid? ¿Por qué?
10. ¿Cuándo vuelven los chicos a Salamanca?

¿Lo sabia Ud.?

- La Universidad de Salamanca es una de las universidades más antiguas y famosas del mundo. Además de los cursos regulares para españoles, ofrece muchas clases para estudiantes extranjeros *(foreign)*.

- El Museo del Prado es uno de los museos más importantes del mundo. Tiene una colección de más de 2.000 cuadros y más de 300 esculturas. Allí están representados los grandes pintores españoles —Goya, Murillo, Velázquez, El Greco y otros. También hay cuadros de otros pintores europeos famosos.

- En la mayoría de los países hispánicos, las universidades no tienen residencias universitarias *(dorms)*. Los estudiantes viven con su familia o en pensiones, donde el precio incluye el cuarto y la comida *(room and board)*.

La Universidad de Salamanca, la más antigua de España.

- El café al aire libre es una parte importante de la cultura hispánica, donde la gente *(people)* conversa mientras come y toma algo *(something)*.

- En los países de habla hispana, la fecha *(date)* se escribe con el día antes del mes: 2-5-98 equivale al dos de mayo de 1998.

PRONUNCIACIÓN

A The Spanish **p**

The Spanish **p** is pronounced like the English *p* as in the word *sparks,* but with no expulsion of air. Listen to your instructor and repeat the following words.

perfectamente	tiempo	oportunidad
pintura	papá	septiembre
pensión	primo	poder

B The Spanish **t**

The Spanish **t** is pronounced by placing the tongue against the upper teeth, as in the English word *stop.* Listen to your instructor and repeat the following words.

nieta	restaurante	practicar
tío	carta	auto
otro	este	foto

C The Spanish **c**

The Spanish sound for the letter **c** in the combinations **ca, co,** and **cu** is /k/, pronounced as in the English word *scar,* but with no expulsion of air. Listen to your instructor and repeat the following words.

café	coche	cuñado
nunca	cómodo	cuánto
calle	simpático	cuándo

D The Spanish **q**

The Spanish **q** is always followed by a **u**; it is pronounced like the *c* in the English word *come,* but without any expulsion of air. Listen to your instructor and repeat the following words.

Quintana	Roque	quien
que	quiere	orquesta
aquí	queso	Quevedo

ESTRUCTURAS

1 Verbs with irregular first-person forms
(Verbos irregulares en la primera persona)

■ The following verbs are irregular in the first-person singular of the present tense.

Verb	yo form	Regular forms
salir *(to go out)*	salgo	sales, sale, salimos, salís, salen
hacer *(to do, make)*	hago	haces, hace, hacemos, hacéis, hacen
poner *(to put, place)*	pongo	pones, pone, ponemos, ponéis, ponen
traer *(to bring)*	traigo	traes, trae, traemos traéis, traen
conducir *(to drive; to conduct)*	conduzco	conduces, conduce, conducimos, conducís, conducen
traducir *(to translate)*	traduzco	traduces, traduce, traducimos, traducís, traducen
conocer *(to know)*	conozco	conoces, conoce, conocemos, conocéis, conocen
caber *(to fit)*	quepo	cabes, cabe, cabemos, cabéis, caben
ver *(to see)*	veo	ves, ve, vemos, veis, ven
saber *(to know)*	sé	sabes, sabe, sabemos, sabéis, saben

Práctica

A. Interview a classmate, using the following questions. When you have finished, switch roles.

1. ¿Sabes español?
2. ¿Ves al profesor (a la profesora) todos los días?
3. ¿Dónde pones tus libros?
4. ¿Conoces a la familia del profesor (de la profesora)?
5. ¿Traes fotos de tu familia?
6. ¿Haces la tarea los domingos?
7. ¿Traduces la lección al inglés?
8. ¿A qué hora sales de tu casa?
9. ¿Conduces el coche a la universidad?
10. Hay seis personas en el coche. ¿Cabes tú también?

B. Read this paragraph about Lucía's day and then rewrite it as if you were Lucía, starting with **Yo...**

Lucía sale de su casa a las siete de la mañana. Va a la universidad en carro; ella conduce muy bien. Su clase de francés es a las ocho, pero ella sale a las siete porque sabe que hay mucho tráfico. Siempre trae dinero para almorzar en la cafetería, donde ve a muchos de sus amigos. Por la tarde vuelve a su casa y hace la tarea; generalmente traduce del inglés al francés.

2 Saber vs. conocer

Spanish has two verbs that mean *to know,* **saber** and **conocer.**

■ When *to know* means *to know something by heart, to know how to do something,* or *to know a fact,* **saber** is used.

No sé los verbos irregulares.	*I don't know the irregular verbs.*
Juan **sabe** hablar ruso.	*Juan knows how to speak Russian.*
Ellos **saben** que ella es profesora.	*They know that she's a professor.*

■ When *to know* means *to be familiar with* or *to be acquainted with a person, a thing,* or *a place,* it is translated as **conocer.**

Nosotros **conocemos** a tu tía.	*We know your aunt.*
Elisa **conoce** las novelas de García Márquez.	*Elisa knows (is acquainted with) García Márquez's novels.*
¿Conoces Canadá?	*Do you know (have you been to) Canada?*

Práctica

A. Complete the following dialogues, using **saber** or **conocer** as appropriate. Then act them out with a partner.

1. — ¿ _____ tú al abuelo de Olga?
   — Sí, lo _____ , pero no _____ dónde vive.
2. — Tú _____ Brasil, ¿no?
   — Sí, pero no _____ hablar portugués.
3. — ¿Tú _____ el poema *"The Raven"*?
   — ¡Lo _____ de memoria *(by heart)*!
4. — ¿ _____ tú qué hora es?
   — Sí, son las ocho.
5. — Jorge conduce muy mal.
   — Sí, no _____ conducir muy bien.

B. Interview a classmate, using the following questions. When you have finished, switch roles.

1. ¿Cuántos idiomas sabes hablar? ¿Cuáles son?
2. ¿Conoces a los padres de tu mejor amigo(-a)?
3. ¿Sabes dónde viven?
4. ¿Qué sabes hacer?

5. ¿Sabes tocar *(play)* el piano?
6. ¿Sabes preparar sangría?
7. ¿Conoces un buen restaurante por aquí? ¿Dónde está?
8. ¿Conoces a un actor famoso? ¿Quién es? ¿Cómo es?

3 Comparative forms *(Formas comparativas)*

A. Comparisons of inequality

▪ In Spanish, the comparative of inequality of most adjectives, adverbs, and nouns is formed by placing **más** *(more)* or **menos** *(less)* before the adjective, the adverb, or the noun and **que** *(than)* after it.

más *(more)*		*adjective*	
	+	or *adverb* +	**que** *(than)*
menos *(less)*		or *noun*	

— ¿Tú eres **más alta que** Ana? "*Are you taller than Ana?*"
— Sí, ella es mucho **más baja que** yo. "*Yes, she is much shorter than I.*"

ATENCIÓN **De** is used instead of **que** before a numerical expression of quantity or amount.

Luis tiene **más de** treinta años. *Luis is over thirty years old.*
Hay **menos de** veinte estudiantes aquí. *There are fewer than twenty students here.*

B. Comparisons of equality

▪ To form comparisons of equality with adjectives, adverbs, and nouns in Spanish, use the adjectives **tanto, -a, -os, -as,** or the adverb **tan... como.**

When comparing adjectives or adverbs:	**When comparing nouns:**
tan *(as)* ⟨ bonita / tarde + **como**	**tanto** *(as much)* dinero **tanta** plata *(money)* **tantos** *(as many)* libros + **como** **tantas** plumas

— ¿Vas en autobús? "*Are you going by bus?*"
— Sí, es **tan** cómodo **como** el coche. "*Yes, it's as comfortable as the car.*"

— Tengo mucho trabajo. "*I have a lot of work.*"
— Yo tengo **tanto** trabajo **como** tú. "*I have as much work as you (do).*"

C. The superlative

■ The superlative construction is similar to the comparative. It is formed by placing the definite article before the person or thing being compared.

definite article	+	(noun)	+	más or menos	+	adjective	+	de

— ¿Quieres ir al Museo del Prado?
— Sí, allí están **los cuadros más famosos** de España.

"Do you want to go to the Prado Museum?"
"Yes, the most famous paintings in Spain are there."

— Juan no es muy inteligente.
— No, es el[1] **menos inteligente** de la familia.

"Juan is not very intelligent."
"No, he is the least intelligent (one) in the family."

ATENCIÓN   Note that the Spanish **de** translates to the English *in* after a superlative.

Son los cuadros más famosos **de** España.
Es la chica más bonita **de** la clase.

They are the most famous paintings in Spain.
She is the prettiest girl in the class.

Práctica

A. Complete the following sentences, using the Spanish equivalent of the words in parentheses.

1. Tu primo es _____ tú. *(fatter than)*
   Tú eres _____ que él. *(much thinner)*
2. Mi cuñado es _____ que ella, pero estudia mucho. *(less intelligent)*
3. Mi suegra tiene _____ años, pero mi suegro tiene _____. *(less than fifty / more than seventy)*
4. Mi abuela tiene _____ mis padres. *(as much money as)*
5. Carlos tiene _____ yo. *(as many CDs as)*
6. Mi sobrina es _____ su mamá. *(as tall as)*
7. Tu tía habla español _____ mi padre. *(as well as)*
8. Aquí hay _____ allí. *(as many girls as)*

---
[1]As in English, the noun may be omitted.

B. Compare the people in the picture below with each other.

1. María es _____ Rosa.
2. Rosa es _____ María.
3. Carlos es _____ Rosa y que María.
4. Carlos es _____ Juan.
5. Juan es _____ Carlos.
6. Juan es _____ María.
7. Juan es el _____ de todos.
8. Carlos es el _____ de todos.

C. Establish comparisons between the following people and things, using the adjectives provided and adding any necessary words.

1. Michael Jordan / Danny De Vito (alto)
2. Cuba / Canadá (pequeño)
3. la clase de español / la clase de ruso (difícil)
4. coche / ómnibus (cómodo)
5. Puerto Rico / Argentina (grande)

Now find a partner. Take turns comparing more people and things.

D. With a partner, act out the following dialogues in Spanish.

1. "I do not have as many opportunities as he (does) to practice Spanish."
   "You are right, Ana, he has more opportunities than you."
2. "Are you taller than your sister, Miss Rojas?"
   "Yes, I am the tallest woman in the family."
3. "You are the most intelligent girl in the world."
   "No, you are as intelligent as I."
4. "I live very far from the university."
   "I live as far as you, Paco."

4 Irregular comparative forms *(Formas comparativas irregulares)*

■ The following adjectives and adverbs have irregular comparative and superlative forms in Spanish.

Adjective	Adverb	Comparative	Superlative
bueno	bien	mejor	el (la) mejor
malo	mal	peor	el (la) peor
grande		mayor	el (la) mayor
pequeño		menor	el (la) menor

— El restaurante El Dorado es muy **malo.**
"The El Dorado Restaurant is very bad."

— Sí, pero la cafetería de la universidad es **peor.**
"Yes, but the university's cafeteria is worse."

— Eva es una **buena** estudiante.
"Eva is a good student."

— Sí, es **la mejor** de la clase.
"Yes, she's the best in the class."

■ When the adjectives **grande** and **pequeño** refer to size, the regular forms are generally used.

Tu casa es **más grande** que la de Carolina.
Your house is bigger than Carolina's.

■ When these adjectives refer to age, the irregular forms are used.

Ella es **mucho mayor** que yo.
She is much older than I.

Teresa es **menor** que Carlos.
Teresa is younger than Carlos.

Ella es **la menor** de todos.
She is the youngest of all.

Práctica

A. Answer the following questions with complete sentences.

1. Mi sobrina tiene siete años y mi sobrino tiene cinco. ¿Quién es mayor? ¿Quién es menor?
2. Mi tío tiene cuarenta años y mi tía tiene treinta y ocho. ¿Quién es menor? ¿Quién es mayor?
3. ¿Quién habla mejor el español, tú o el profesor (la profesora)?
4. Pedro tiene una "B" en inglés; Antonio tiene una "C"; y José tiene una "F". ¿Quién es el peor estudiante? ¿Quién es el mejor estudiante?

Now write three original comparative situations, using the ones you have just completed as models. When you have finished, take turns giving and responding to situations with a partner.

B. Interview a classmate, using the following questions. When you have finished, switch roles.

1. ¿Tú eres mayor o menor que tu mejor amigo(-a)?
2. ¿Tu mamá es menor que tu papá?
3. ¿Quién cocina *(cooks)* mejor, tú o tu mamá?
4. ¿Quién crees tú que es el (la) mejor estudiante de la clase?
5. ¿Cuál crees que es la mejor universidad de los Estados Unidos?
6. ¿Cuál crees tú que es la mejor película *(film)* del año? ¿Y la peor?
7. De los restaurantes que tú conoces, ¿cuál es el mejor? ¿Y el peor?
8. ¿Quiénes crees tú que conducen mejor: los hombres o las mujeres?

5 Present indicative of **o:ue** stem-changing verbs
*(Presente de indicativo de los verbos que cambian en la raíz **o:ue**)*

poder *to be able*	
puedo	podemos
puedes	podéis
puede	pueden

■ Some verbs undergo a stem change in the present indicative. For these verbs, when **o** is the last stem vowel and it is stressed, it changes to **ue**.

— ¿A qué hora **vuelven** Uds.? *"At what time are you returning?"*

— **Volvemos** a las doce. *"We'll return at twelve o'clock."*

— Entonces comemos a las doce y media. *"Then we'll have lunch (eat) at twelve-thirty."*

■ Note that the stem vowel is not stressed in the verb forms used with **nosotros(-as)** and **vosotros(-as)**; therefore, the **o** does not change to **ue**.

■ Other verbs that undergo this change:[1]

almorzar	*to have lunch*	**llover** (impersonal)	*to rain*
contar	*to tell, to count*	**morir**	*to die*
costar	*to cost*	**recordar**	*to remember*
dormir	*to sleep*	**volar**	*to fly*
encontrar	*to find*	**volver**	*to return*

Práctica

A. Interview a classmate, using the following questions. When you have finished, switch roles.

1. ¿Almuerzas en la cafetería o en tu casa?
2. ¿Cuánto cuestan los sándwiches en la cafetería?

---

[1] For a complete list of stem-changing verbs, see Appendix B.

3. ¿Cuántas horas duermes?
4. ¿Cuentas ovejas *(sheep)* para dormir?
5. ¿Hasta *(Up to)* qué número puedes contar en español?
6. ¿Encuentras difícil o fácil la clase de español?
7. ¿Cuándo vuelves a tu casa?
8. ¿Llueve mucho en tu ciudad?

B. Marité is talking to her roommate, who is sound asleep. Complete the story, supplying the missing (**o:ue**) verbs. Then read it aloud.

MARITÉ —¡Teresa, me voy! No _____ mis libros. ¿Dónde están? No
_____ ir a mi clase sin *(without)* mis libros. ¡Oye! Hoy _____
con Pedro en la cafetería; no tengo dinero y los sándwiches en la
cafetería _____ tres dólares. ¡Ay, Teresa!, hoy tengo que llamar a
Marta y no _____ su número de teléfono. ¡Teresa!, ¿tú _____
el número de Marta? ¡Oye! ¿Roberto _____ a San Francisco hoy?
¿Vas al aeropuerto con él? *(Mira por la ventana.)* ¡Ay, cómo _____!
Necesito tu impermeable *(raincoat)*. ¡Ah!, hoy _____ a casa a las
cinco. *(Abre la puerta de Teresa.)* ¡Teresa! ¡Teresa! ¿Por qué no
contestas *(answer)*?

TERESA —*(Mmm...)* Nunca _____ dormir cuando tú estás en casa.

MARITÉ —Tú _____ mucho. No necesitas dormir más. Me voy. Nos vemos.

C. Arnaldo is very nosy and is always asking questions. Here are the answers. What are his questions?

1. ¿ _____ ? Mi equipo estereofónico cuesta $1.000.
2. ¿ _____ ? Nosotros almorzamos en el restaurante.
3. ¿ _____ ? Volvemos a casa a las cinco.
4. ¿ _____ ? No, yo no duermo mucho.
5. ¿ _____ ? No, no recuerdo el número de teléfono de Ana.
6. ¿ _____ ? Vuelo a Los Ángeles los domingos.
7. ¿ _____ ? No, no puedo ir a tu casa esta noche.

D. With a classmate, prepare four or five questions to ask your instructor, using stem-changing (**o:ue**) verbs.

REAL BALLET
NACIONAL DE ESPAÑA

¡A VER CUÁNTO APRENDIÓ!

¡Repase el vocabulario!

Match each question in column A with the best response in column B; then read them aloud.

A	B
1. ¿Dónde está tu familia?	a. No, es de estatura mediana.
2. ¿Qué estudias?	b. Sí, es mi cuñada.
3. ¿Estás incómoda?	c. El 3 de septiembre.
4. ¿Vamos al museo mañana?	d. Medicina.
5. ¿Practicas el español?	e. Pienso ir a Salamanca.
6. ¿Pedro es menor que Juan?	f. No, es mi sobrina.
7. ¿No tienen dinero para ir a un hotel?	g. Sí, ¡qué lástima!
8. ¿Es la hermana de tu esposo?	h. ¡Vale!
9. ¿Es tu prima?	i. Sí, es el hijo de mi hija.
10. ¿Van en ómnibus?	j. En Canadá.
11. ¿Cuándo es tu cumpleaños?	k. No, por eso van a una pensión.
12. ¿Qué planes tienes para el fin de semana?	l. No, vamos en coche.
13. ¿Es tu nieto?	m. Sí, mi silla es muy pequeña.
14. ¿Van a perder la oportunidad de ir a México?	n. Sí, nunca pierdo la oportunidad.
15. ¿Es alta?	o. No, es mayor.

Entrevista

Interview a classmate, using the **tú** form.

Pregúntele a su compañero(-a) de clase...

1. ...si es más bajo(-a) que su papá.
2. ...si su mamá es alta, baja o de estatura mediana.
3. ...si es mayor o menor que el profesor (la profesora).
4. ...si la clase de español es la más interesante que tiene.
5. ...si habla español perfectamente.
6. ...a qué hora vuelve a su casa.
7. ...dónde almuerza generalmente.
8. ...dónde piensa ir este fin de semana y qué piensa hacer.
9. ...si este verano va a viajar o piensa estudiar o trabajar. ¿Por qué?
10. ...cuál cree que es la ciudad más bonita del mundo. ¿Por qué?

Situaciones

What would you say in the following situations? What might the other person say? Act out the scenes with a partner. Take turns playing each role.

1. A Spanish exchange student is visiting your home, and you don't want to miss the opportunity to speak Spanish.
2. Someone asks about your weekend plans.
3. You are with a friend who has never seen pictures of your family, and you just happen to have some in your wallet.
4. You are trying to get a reluctant friend to go with you somewhere.

Para escribir

Write a composition describing two members of your family. Include the following information for each person:

> color of hair and eyes (**pelo y ojos**)
> age
> current residence
> place of employment or study
> marital status and number of children
> other personal characteristics (Establish comparisons between the other members of your family and yourself.)

En la vida real

Objetivos

You and a classmate have a goal: to someday speak Spanish like native speakers and to learn as much as possible about the culture of Spanish-speaking countries. Come up with a list of things you are going to do to reach that goal.

Here are some additional words and phrases you may want to include:

escuchar *(to listen to)* {
canciones *(songs)*
las cintas del laboratorio de lenguas
programas de radio
}

gente *people*
películas españolas y latinoamericanas *Spanish and Latin American movies*
revistas *magazines*
tener correspondencia *to correspond*
visitar países de habla hispana *to visit Spanish-speaking countries*

Árbol genealógico *(Family tree)*

Prepare your family tree, following the model on page 116. Call it **"Mi árbol genealógico"**. Be sure to include each family member's relationship to you.

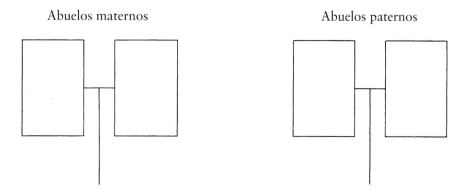

Abuelos maternos   Abuelos paternos

¿Quieres ver mis fotos?

Bring pictures of your relatives to class and tell a classmate who they are, giving information about each one. Ask each other any pertinent questions.

¿A qué museo vamos?

You and a friend want to go to a museum. Read the following ads and answer the questions.

Museo de Arte Contemporáneo

Avda. de Herrera Oria, s/n.
Metro Moncloa. Autobús 62

Teléfono 449-5071

Abierto: de 10:00 a 18:00
Cerrado los lunes.

■

Pintura y escultura española
y extranjera de los últimos años:

*Chillida, Botero, Miró, Stella,
Warhol, Gris, Dalí.*

■

Precio: 450 pesetas.
Con carné de estudiante entrada libre.

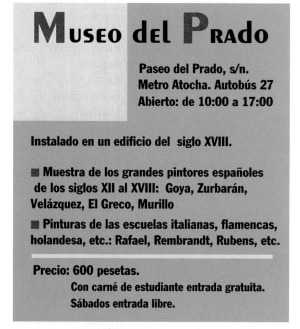

MUSEO DEL PRADO

**Paseo del Prado, s/n.
Metro Atocha. Autobús 27
Abierto: de 10:00 a 17:00**

Instalado en un edificio del siglo XVIII.

■ **Muestra de los grandes pintores españoles de los siglos XII al XVIII: Goya, Zurbarán, Velázquez, El Greco, Murillo**

■ **Pinturas de las escuelas italianas, flamencas, holandesa, etc.: Rafael, Rembrandt, Rubens, etc.**

**Precio: 600 pesetas.
Con carné de estudiante entrada gratuita.
Sábados entrada libre.**

1. ¿En qué calle está el Museo de Arte Contemporáneo?
2. ¿Pueden Uds. ir al Museo de Arte Contemporáneo el lunes? ¿Por qué?
3. ¿Cuánto cuesta la entrada *(ticket)* al Museo de Arte Contemporáneo?

4. ¿Cuánto pagan *(pay)* los estudiantes para visitar el Museo de Arte Contemporáneo?
5. ¿Qué metro *(subway)* deben Uds. tomar *(take)* para ir al Museo del Prado?
6. ¿Pueden ir en autobús también? ¿En cuál?
7. El Museo del Prado, ¿es antiguo *(old)* o moderno?
8. ¿En cuál de los dos museos es más barata *(cheap)* la entrada?
9. En el Museo del Prado, ¿encuentran Uds. solamente *(only)* cuadros de pintores españoles?
10. ¿En qué museo no es necesario pagar los sábados?

Así somos

Vocabulario

el abogado	lawyer
los ahijados	godchildren
así que	consequently
cada quien	each person
la calva	bald patch
casi	almost
compartir	to share
de vez en cuando	from time to time
el descanso	rest
el empresario	director of a business
entre	between, among
espero	I hope
Estoy apenas acabando de estudiar.	I am just finishing my studies.
la gente	people
juntos	together
la más chica	the youngest
la reina	queen
les	(to) them
la médica	doctor
los niños	children
la playa	beach
plenamente	fully
por lo general	generally
el prep	a type of high school
la psicóloga	psychologist
la vida	life

Preparación

¿Cuánto saben Uds. ya?   In this video module, several people will describe their families and what they do during the weekends. Make a list of the words and phrases that you think they will use. Circle the ones you hear as you watch the video.

Comprensión

A. Mi familia.   Select the word or phrase that best completes each statement, according to what you understood.

1. La mamá de Jaime es (médica, secretaria).
2. El papá de Carolina es (muy alto, bajito).
3. La abuelita de Juan (vive, no vive) con Juan y su familia.
4. El papá de Otmara es (empresario, ingeniero electricista).
5. Otmara tiene (treinta y cinco, veintiún) años.
6. Tamara tiene dos hermanas (mayores, menores).
7. La familia de Frank es muy (numerosa, pequeña).

B. Los fines de semana.   Read the following statements. After watching the video, circle **V** (**Verdadero**) or **F** (**Falso**), according to what you understood.

V   F   1. Por lo general Yolanda sale a comer con su esposo.
V   F   2. Héctor pasa *(spends)* los fines de semana en un club.
V   F   3. Olga pasa los domingos con sus hijos.

C. ¿Quién lo dice?   Match the people's names with their weekend plans.

     a. Pedro   b. Carolina   c. Tamara   d. Héctor

_____ 1. Voy a salir a comer con los amigos.
_____ 2. Tengo que estudiar.
_____ 3. Voy a la fiesta de los latinoamericanos.
_____ 4. Hay planes para ir a la playa.

Ampliación

Entrevista.   Imagine that you are going to interview two people from the video. Make a list of questions you would want to ask them.

UN VIAJE A PERÚ

LECCIÓN
6

OBJECTIVES

Pronunciation

The Spanish **j**, **g** (before **e** or **i**), and **h**

Structure

Present indicative of **e:i** stem-changing verbs • Pronouns as objects of prepositions • Affirmative and negative expressions • Present progressive • Direct object pronouns

Communication

You will learn vocabulary related to travel: going through customs, obtaining information, and getting a room at a hotel.

Un viaje a Perú

Teresa, una profesora mexicana, va a pasar sus vacaciones en Perú. Ella acaba de llegar a Lima, donde piensa pasar unos días antes de ir a Machu Picchu para visitar las famosas ruinas de los incas. Ahora está en el aeropuerto, que es grande y muy moderno. Teresa muestra su pasaporte y luego pasa por la aduana.

En la aduana, Teresa está hablando con el inspector.

INSPECTOR	—Debe abrir sus maletas. ¿Tiene Ud. algo que declarar?
TERESA	—Tengo una cámara fotográfica y una grabadora. Nada más.
INSPECTOR	—No es necesario declararlas. Todo está en regla.
TERESA	—¿Hay alguna oficina de turismo por aquí?
INSPECTOR	—Sí, está allí, a la izquierda.

En el aeropuerto venden objetos de oro y de plata, y Teresa compra algunos para su familia.

En la oficina de turismo, Teresa pide información.

TERESA	—Buenos días, señor. ¿Tiene Ud. una lista de hoteles y pensiones?
EMPLEADO	—Sí, señorita. También tenemos una lista de restaurantes y lugares de interés. Aquí las tiene.
TERESA	—Gracias. ¿Dónde puedo tomar un taxi?
EMPLEADO	—La segunda puerta a la derecha. También hay un autobús que la lleva al centro.

Teresa toma el autobús y va a un hotel del centro, donde pide una habitación.

TERESA	—Necesito una habitación sencilla con baño privado, por favor. No tengo reservación.
EMPLEADO	—Tenemos una con vista a la calle que cuesta 208 soles[1] por día. También hay otra interior en el segundo piso por 130 soles.
TERESA	—Son muy caras para mí. ¿No tiene alguna habitación más barata?
EMPLEADO	—No, no hay ninguna. Ahora hay pocos cuartos libres.
TERESA	—Prefiero el cuarto interior. ¿Aceptan cheques de viajero?
EMPLEADO	—Sí, los aceptamos, y también aceptamos tarjetas de crédito.
TERESA	—¿A cómo está el cambio de moneda?
EMPLEADO	—Está a 3 soles el dólar.[2]

Teresa firma el registro y pregunta si tienen servicio de habitación.

TERESA	—Quiero cenar en mi habitación. ¿Hasta qué hora sirven la cena?
EMPLEADO	—La sirven hasta las once.
TERESA	—¿Puede alguien llevar mis maletas al cuarto, por favor?
EMPLEADO	—Sí, en seguida viene el botones a llevarlas. Aquí tiene la llave.

---

[1] Peruvian currency
[2] This exchange rate is subject to change.

VOCABULARIO

COGNADOS

el **aeropuerto** airport
el **dólar** dollar
el **hotel** hotel
la **información** information
el (la) **inspector(-a)** inspector
el **interés** interest
interior interior
la **lista** list

mexicano(-a) Mexican
moderno(-a) modern
necesario(-a) necessary
el **objeto** object
la **oficina** office
el **pasaporte** passport
privado(-a) private
el **registro** register

la **reservación**, la **reserva** reservation
las **ruinas** ruins
el **taxi** taxi
el **turismo** tourism
las **vacaciones**[1] vacation

◼ NOMBRES

la **aduana** customs
el **baño**, el **cuarto de baño** bathroom
el **botones** bellhop
la **cámara fotográfica** camera
la **cena** dinner, supper
el **centro** downtown (area)
el **cheque de viajero** traveler's check

el **cuarto**, la **habitación** room
el (la) **empleado(-a)** clerk
la **grabadora** tape recorder
la **llave** key
el **lugar** place
la **maleta**, la **valija** suitcase
la **oficina de turismo** tourist office
el **oro** gold

el **piso** floor
la **plata** silver
el **servicio de habitación (cuarto)** room service
la **tarjeta de crédito** credit card
el **viaje** trip, journey

◼ VERBOS

aceptar to accept
cenar to have dinner, supper
comprar to buy
declarar to declare
firmar to sign

llegar to arrive
mostrar (o:ue), enseñar to show
pasar to spend (time), to pass
pasar (por) to go through, by
pedir (e:i) to ask for, to request

preguntar to ask (a question)
servir (e:i) to serve
tomar to take
visitar to visit

◼ ADJETIVOS

alguno(-a) some, any
barato(-a) inexpensive, cheap *costoso*
caro(-a) expensive
libre vacant

pocos(-as) few
segundo(-a) second
sencillo(-a) single, simple
unos(-as) a few

---

[1] **Vacaciones** is always used in the plural in Spanish.

OTRAS PALABRAS Y EXPRESIONES

¿A cómo está el cambio de moneda? What is the exchange rate?

a la derecha to the right

a la izquierda to the left

acabar de + *infinitive* to have just + *past participle*

algo something, anything

alguien someone, somebody

antes (de) before

Aquí las tiene. Here they are. (Here you have them.)

con vista a overlooking

en seguida right away

hasta until

luego then, afterwards

lugares de interés places of interest

mí me

nada más nothing else

ninguno(-a) none, not any

para for

por per, for

por aquí around here

que which

tener algo que declarar to have something to declare

Todo está en regla. Everything is in order.

VOCABULARIO ADICIONAL

EN EL HOTEL

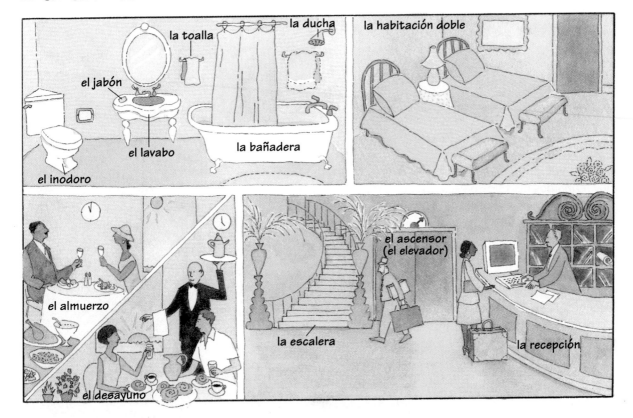

la toalla · la ducha · la habitación doble · el jabón · el lavabo · la bañadera · el inodoro · el almuerzo · el desayuno · el ascensor (el elevador) · la escalera · la recepción

PARA EL TURISMO

la cámara de video video camera

cancelar to cancel

confirmar to confirm

la embajada embassy

la lista de espera waiting list

la tarjeta de turista tourist card

¿Tiene Ud. una **cámara de video**?

Voy a **cancelar** la reservación.

Deseo **confirmar** la reservación.

¿Dónde queda la **embajada** norteamericana?

Estoy en la **lista de espera**.

Los norteamericanos necesitan una **tarjeta de turista** para visitar México.

¡CONVERSEMOS!

Answer the following questions, basing your answers on the dialogues.

1. ¿Qué ruinas famosas hay en Perú?
2. ¿Dónde piensa Teresa pasar unos días antes de ir a Machu Picchu?
3. ¿Qué compra Teresa en el aeropuerto?
4. ¿Tiene Teresa algo que declarar?
5. ¿Qué pide Teresa en la oficina de turismo?
6. ¿Qué toma para ir al centro?
7. ¿Pide Teresa una habitación sencilla o doble?
8. ¿Qué cuarto prefiere Teresa? ¿Por qué?
9. ¿Cómo puede Teresa pagar el hotel?
10. ¿A cómo está el cambio de moneda?
11. ¿Quién lleva las maletas de Teresa al cuarto?
12. ¿Hasta qué hora sirven la cena?

 ## ¿Lo sabía Ud.?

- Lima, la capital de Perú, es una ciudad de contrastes. Junto a *(Next to)* edificios *(buildings)* muy modernos hay otros de arquitectura colonial. El 25% de la población es de origen indígena.

- La moneda *(currency)* que utilizan con más frecuencia los latinoamericanos cuando viajan fuera de su país es el dólar norteamericano. Esto se debe a que *(is due to the fact that)* es fácil cambiar dólares en la mayoría de los principales bancos de los países hispano-americanos.

Fachada de uno de los edificios que rodean la Plaza de San Martín en Lima, Perú.

PRONUNCIACIÓN

A The Spanish j

The Spanish j sounds somewhat like the *h* in the English word *hit*. It is never pronounced like the English *j* in *John* or *James*. Listen to your instructor and repeat the following words.

Julia	dejar	embajada
pasaje	jabón	viajero
tarjeta	objeto	jueves

B The Spanish g (before e or i)

When followed by e or i, the Spanish g sounds like the Spanish j mentioned above. Listen to your instructor and repeat the following words.

Gerardo	inteligente	agente
agencia	general	Genaro
registro	Argentina	ingeniero

C The Spanish h

The Spanish h is always silent. Listen to your instructor and repeat the following words.

hay	Hilda	habitación
Honduras	hermano	hasta
ahora	hotel	hija

familia®

En calidad y economia lo tiene todo.

ESTRUCTURAS

1 Present indicative of e:i stem-changing verbs
(Presente de indicativo de los verbos que cambian en la raíz e:i)

servir *to serve*	
sirvo	servimos
sirves	servís
sirve	sirven

■ Some -**ir** verbs undergo a special stem change in the present indicative. For these verbs, when **e** is the last stem vowel and it is stressed, it changes to **i**.

—¿Qué **sirven** Uds. en sus fiestas?   *"What do you serve at your parties?*

—**Servimos** champán.   *"We serve champagne."*

■ Note that the stem vowel is not stressed in the **nosotros(-as)** and **vosotros(-as)** verb forms; therefore, the **e** does not change to **i**.

■ Other verbs that undergo this change:[1]

conseguir *to get, to obtain*   **pedir** *to ask for, to request, to order*
decir *to say, to tell*   **seguir** *to follow, to continue*

■ The verb **decir** undergoes the same change, but in addition it has an irregular first-person singular form: **yo digo.**

■ Note that in the present tense **seguir** and **conseguir** drop the **u** before **a** or **o**: **yo sigo, yo consigo.**

Práctica

A. Form complete sentences by combining the words in the three columns in sequence, starting with A. Use each subject and each verb at least once.

A	B	C
yo	decir	el desayuno
el inspector	servir	habitaciones
nosotros	pedir	que necesitamos cheques de
Ana y Eva	conseguir	viajero
mis padres	seguir	la solicitud
tú		que debo abrir las maletas
el empleado		jabón y toalla
		al botones
		un cuarto con baño privado
		la llave del cuarto
		pollo y refrescos

---
[1] For a complete list of stem-changing verbs, see Appendix B.

B. Complete the following dialogues, using the verbs given. Then act them out with a partner, adding a sentence or two to each dialogue.

1. decir
   - ¿Tú _____ que Roberto es simpático?
   - Sí, yo _____ que es simpático, pero Carmen _____ que es antipático.

2. servir
   - ¿Qué _____ Uds. en sus fiestas?
   - _____ entremeses y refrescos. ¿Qué _____ tú?
   - Yo _____ sándwiches y cerveza.

3. pedir
   - ¿Qué _____ Uds. cuando van a un restaurante mexicano?
   - Yo _____ tacos y Ernesto _____ enchiladas.

4. conseguir
   - Yo no _____ trabajo.
   - Tú no _____ trabajo porque no hablas dos idiomas.

SUMMARY OF THE PRESENT INDICATIVE OF STEM-CHANGING VERBS

e:ie	o:ue		e:i
cerrar	almorzar	morir	conseguir
comenzar	contar	mostrar	decir
empezar	costar	poder	pedir
entender	dormir	recordar	seguir
pensar	encontrar	volar	servir
perder	llover	volver	
preferir			
querer			

2 Pronouns as objects of prepositions
(Pronombres usados como objetos de preposición)

■ The object of a preposition is the noun or pronoun that immediately follows it: **La fiesta es *para María (ella)*. Ellos van *con nosotros*.**

Singular		*Plural*	
mí	*me*	**nosotros(-as)**	*us*
ti	*you* (inf.)	**vosotros(-as)**	*you* (inf.)
Ud.	*you* (form.)	**Uds.**	*you* (form.)
él	*him*	**ellos**	*them* (masc.)
ella	*her*	**ellas**	*them* (fem.)

— ¿Hablan de **mí**?   *"Are you talking about me?"*
— No, no hablamos de **ti**;   *"No, we are not talking about*
   hablamos de **ella**.   *you; we're talking about her."*

— ¿Vas **conmigo** o con Carlos?   *"Are you going with me or with*
                                          Carlos?"

— No voy **contigo**; voy **con él**.   *"I'm not going with you; I'm*
                                          going with him."

■ Only the first- and second-persons singular, **mí** and **ti**, are different from regular subject pronouns.

■ **Mí** and **ti** combine with **con** to become **conmigo** *(with me)* and **contigo** *(with you)*, respectively.

Práctica

A. Complete the following dialogues, using the Spanish equivalent of the words in parentheses. Then act them out with a partner, adding a sentence or two to each dialogue.

1. —¿Carlos va _____ ? *(with me)*
   —No, no va _____ ; va _____ . *(with you / with her)*
2. —¿Para quién son los discos compactos, Paquito?
   ¿ _____ o _____ ? *(For him / for her)*
   —Son _____ . *(for me)*
   —¿ _____ ? *(For you)*
   —Sí, señor.
   —¿La cámara de video es _____ ? *(for you, pl.)*
   —No, es _____ . *(for them, fem.)*

B. Interview a classmate, using the following questions and two questions of your own. When you have finished, switch roles. Use the appropriate prepositions and pronouns in your responses.

1. ¿Hablas con tus amigos en la clase?
2. ¿Puedes estudiar español conmigo?
3. ¿Trabajas para tus padres?
4. ¿Vives cerca de tus abuelos?
5. ¿Hablas mucho con tus amigos por teléfono?
6. ¿Puedo ir contigo a la biblioteca?

3 Affirmative and negative expressions
(Expresiones afirmativas y negativas)

Affirmative		Negative	
algo	*something, anything*	**nada**	*nothing, not anything*
alguien	*someone, somebody, anyone*	**nadie**	*nobody, no one, not anyone*
alguno(-a), algún	*any, some*	**ninguno(-a), ningún**	*no, none, not any*
siempre	*always*	**nunca, jamás**	*never*
también	*also, too*	**tampoco**	*neither, not either*
o... o	*either . . . or*	**ni... ni**	*neither . . . nor*

— ¿Tiene **algo** que declarar?	*"Do you have anything to declare?"*
— No, no tengo **nada**.	*"No, I don't have anything."*
— ¿Tienes **algunos** amigos peruanos?	*"Do you have any Peruvian friends?"*
— No, no tengo **ningún** amigo peruano.	*"No, I don't have any Peruvian friends."*

ATENCIÓN   **No** is never used as an adjective, as it sometimes is in English *(No person could do all that.).*

■ **Alguno** and **ninguno** drop the -o before a masculine singular noun: *algún niño, ningún niño;* but *alguna niña, ninguna niña.*

ATENCIÓN   Note that **alguno(-a)** may be used in the plural forms, but **ninguno(-a)** is not pluralized.

■ Spanish sentences frequently use a double negative form to express a degree of negation: the adverb **no** is placed before the verb and the second negative word either follows the verb or appears at the end of the sentence. If, however, the negative word precedes the verb, **no** is never used.

No hablo español **nunca.**
or: **Nunca** hablo español. } *I never speak Spanish.*

No compro **nada nunca.**
or: **Nunca** compro **nada.** } *I never buy anything*

■ Note that Spanish often uses several negatives in one sentence.

Yo **no** quiero **nada tampoco.**   *I don't want anything either.*

Práctica

A. Your friend Oscar always gets the facts wrong when he talks about other people. Set him straight!

MODELO: Ana necesita algo.
Ana no necesita nada.

1. Raquel siempre viaja en el verano.
2. Ana va con Raquel, y Jorge va con ella también.
3. Siempre piden habitaciones dobles.
4. Siempre compran algo cuando viajan.
5. Siempre compran algunos objetos de oro.
6. Cenan en la pensión o en una cafetería.
7. Siempre hay alguien en su casa.
8. El esposo de Luisa nunca habla con nadie.

B. Answer these personal questions negatively, using the expressions you have just learned.

1. ¿Quiere Ud. viajar a Bolivia o a Perú?
2. ¿Tiene Ud. algunos amigos en Perú?
3. Yo no hablo portugués. ¿Y Ud.?
4. ¿Siempre viaja Ud. en invierno?
5. ¿Siempre viaja Ud. con alguien?
6. ¿Compra Ud. algo cuando viaja?

C. With a partner, act out the following dialogues in Spanish.

1. "Do you need anything else?"
   "No, I do not need anything else."
2. "There aren't any vacant rooms in the hotel."
   "Yes, there are some, but they are very expensive."
3. "Are there any Spanish employees at the American embassy?"
   "Yes, there are some."
4. "I never serve wine."
   "I never serve wine, either. I always serve soda or coffee."
5. "I don't have a camera or a video camera."
   "Neither do I."

D. With a partner, write a list of complaints frequently heard on campus. Use the expressions you have just learned.

MODELO: *Nunca podemos comer nada en la cafetería.*

4 Present progressive *(Estar + gerundio)*

■ The present progressive describes an action that is in progress. It is formed with the present tense of **estar** and the **gerundio**, which is equivalent to the English present participle (the *-ing* form of the verb.)

Gerundio		
hablar	**comer**	**escribir**
habl -ando	com -iendo	escrib -iendo
speaking	*eating*	*writing*
	Yo estoy comiendo.	
	I am eating.	

—¿**Estás estudiando?**   "*Are you studying?*"
—No, **estoy escribiendo** una   "*No, I am writing a letter.*"
carta.

■ The following forms are irregular:

pedir: **pidiendo**	dormir: **durmiendo**
decir: **diciendo**	traer: **trayendo**
servir: **sirviendo**	leer: **leyendo**

—¿Daniel **está leyendo?**　　　*"Is Daniel reading?"*
—No, **está durmiendo.**　　　*"No, he's sleeping."*

■ Note that as shown with **traer** and **leer,** the **i** of **-iendo** becomes **y** between vowels.

ATENCIÓN　In Spanish, the present progressive is *never* used to indicate a future action. The present tense is used in future expressions that would require the present progressive in English.

　　　Trabajo mañana.　　　　　　I'm working tomorrow.

■ Some verbs, such as **ser, estar, ir,** and **venir,** are rarely used in the progressive construction.

Práctica

A. Describe what the following people are doing.

1. Tú...

2. Yo...

3. Ellos...

4. Eva...

5. La profesora...

6. Nosotros... y el chico...

B. Complete the following dialogues, using the present progressive of the verbs given. Then act them out with a partner, adding a sentence or two to each dialogue.

1. comer   – ¿Qué _____ tú?
                – Yo _____ ensalada.

2. leer   – ¿Qué libro _____ Uds.?
                – _____ *Don Quijote.*

3. servir   – ¿Qué _____ Uds.?
                – Yo _____ refrescos y Luisa _____ vino.

4. decir   – ¿Qué _____ Juan Carlos?
                – No _____ nada.

5. estudiar   – ¿José _____ ?
    dormir   – No, _____ .

C. With a partner, discuss what you think these people are doing. Give two or three possibilities for each situation.

1. la secretaria / en la oficina
2. los estudiantes / en la clase
3. los chicos / en la cafetería
4. el botones / en el hotel
5. los muchachos y las muchachas / en la fiesta
6. el Sr. Vega / en su cuarto
7. el camarero *(waiter)* / en el restaurante
8. la Srta. Barrios / en la oficina de turismo

5   Direct object pronouns
(Pronombres usados como complemento directo)

A. The direct object

■ In addition to a subject, most sentences have an object that directly receives the action of the verb.

     Ellos compran el libro.

      S.   V.   D.O.

In the preceding sentence, the subject (**Ellos**) performs the action, while **el libro,** the direct object, directly receives the action of the verb. The direct object of a sentence may be either a person or a thing.

■ The direct object can be easily identified as the answer to the questions *whom?* and *what?* about what the subject is doing.

     Ellos compran **el libro.**   (What are they buying?)
     Pepe llama **a su primo.**   (Whom is he calling?)

■ Direct object pronouns may be used in place of the direct object.

B. Forms of the direct object pronouns

	Singular			Plural	
me	*me*		nos	*us*	
te	*you* (inf.)		os	*you* (inf.)	
lo	*you* (form., masc.) *him, it* (masc.)		los	*you* (form., masc.) *them* (masc.)	
la	*you* (form., fem.) *her, it* (fem.)		las	*you* (form., fem.) *them* (fem.)	

—¿Tiene **la llave?**   *"Do you have the key?"*
—Sí,   la   tengo.   *"Yes, I have it."*

—¿Compra Ud. **los pasajes?**   *"Are you buying the tickets?"*
—Sí,   los   compro.   *"Yes, I'm buying them."*

C. Position of direct object pronouns

▪ In Spanish, object pronouns are normally placed before a conjugated verb.

      D.O.   D.O.
  Ellos sirven **la cena.**   *They serve dinner.*
  Ellos   **la**   sirven.   *They serve it.*

▪ In negative sentences, the **no** must precede the object pronoun.

      D.O.   D.O.
  Ellos sirven **la cena.**   *They serve dinner.*
  Ellos   **la**   sirven.   *They serve it.*
  Ellos   **no**   **la**   sirven.   *They don't serve it.*

▪ When an infinitive is used with a conjugated verb, the direct object pronoun may either be attached to the infinitive or be placed before the conjugated verb. The same principle applies with the present participle in progressive constructions.

   Puedo firmar**lo.** ⎫
          ⎬   *I can sign it.*
   Lo puedo firmar. ⎭

   Estoy leyéndo**lo.** ⎫
          ⎬   *I am reading it.*
   Lo estoy leyendo. ⎭

ATENCIÓN   When a direct object pronoun is attached to a present participle (**leyéndolo, firmándola**), an accent mark is added to maintain the correct stress.

LA LINEA AEREA DE VENEZUELA

Práctica

A. Complete the following dialogue, using the appropriate direct object pronouns. Then act it out with a partner.

JULIO —¿Tú me puedes llevar a casa hoy?

DELIA —Sí, puedo llevar_____ a las tres.

JULIO —¡Ah! Necesito la maleta de mamá. ¿Tú _____ tienes?

DELIA —Sí, yo _____ tengo. ¿Tú quieres llevar_____ a México?

JULIO —Sí. También necesito comprar cheques de viajero...

DELIA —Podemos comprar_____ esta tarde.

JULIO —Rosa y yo tenemos que estar en el aeropuerto a las ocho de la noche. ¿Tú _____ puedes llevar?

DELIA —Sí, yo _____ puedo llevar...

JULIO —¡Ah! Las sobrinas de Rosa quieren ir al aeropuerto con nosotros. ¿ Tú _____ puedes traer a mi casa a las siete?

DELIA —¡No! ¡Yo no tengo un servicio de taxi!

B. You and your friends are planning a party. Volunteer to do the following tasks yourself.

> MODELO: ¿Quién invita a las chicas?
> *Yo las invito.*

1. ¿Quién llama a los muchachos?
2. ¿Quién compra las bebidas?
3. ¿Quién va a traer los discos compactos?
4. ¿Quién consigue el equipo estereofónico?
5. ¿Quién trae a mi compañera?
6. ¿Quién prepara *(is preparing)* los entremeses?
7. ¿Quién va a traer a Luis?
8. ¿Quién lleva a las chicas a su casa?

C. You and some friends will be traveling in Mexico shortly. Answer another friend's questions about your arrangements. Use direct object pronouns in your answers.

1. ¿Tus amigos te van a llamar esta noche?
2. ¿Tienen Uds. reservaciones para el hotel?
3. ¿Vas a comprar cheques de viajero?
4. ¿Tienes tu tarjeta de crédito?
5. ¿Llevas tu cámara fotográfica?
6. ¿Van a visitar Uds. las ruinas de Teotihuacán?
7. ¿Quién los va a llevar a Uds.[1] al aeropuerto?
8. ¿Me llevan con Uds. a México?

D. With a partner, act out the following dialogues in Spanish.

1. "Do you love me?"
   "Yes, I love you."
2. "Are you going to sign the register?"
   "No, I'm not going to sign it."

---

[1] A **Uds.** is needed for clarification because **los** could also be *them*.

3. "Do I have to show my passport?"
   "Yes, you have to show it, sir."
4. "Do your cousins visit you?"
   "Yes, they visit us on Sundays."
5. "Are you going to buy the suitcases?"
   "Yes, I'm going to buy them today."

¡A VER CUÁNTO APRENDIÓ!

¡Repase el vocabulario!

Choose the word or phrase that best completes each sentence.

1. En el aeropuerto debo mostrar...
   a. la llave.   b. el baño.   c. el pasaporte.
2. Quiero una habitación...
   a. en la oficina de turismo.   b. con vista a la calle.   c. en el autobús.
3. No tiene que declarar...
   a. la reservación.   b. esta cámara fotográfica.   c. la lista de hoteles.
4. Debes pasar por la aduana...
   a. con el restaurante.   b. con el piso.   c. con las maletas.
5. Voy a comprar algo para...
   a. mis padres.   b. la aduana.   c. la llave.
6. El botones va a llevar...
   a. el interés.   b. la plata.   c. las maletas.
7. ¿Dónde puedo tomar...
   a. el jabón?   b. el ascensor?   c. la tarjeta de turista?
8. Sirven la cena...
   a. a las nueve de la mañana.   b. a las tres de la tarde.
   c. a las nueve de la noche.
9. En el verano hay pocos cuartos...
   a. libres.   b. modernos.   c. casados.
10. En el Hilton una habitación con vista a la calle cuesta ciento cincuenta dólares...
    a. por año.   b. por mes.   c. por día.
11. No tengo reservación, pero estoy en...
    a. el centro.   b. la lista de espera.   c. el cuarto.
12. La habitación no es barata; es...
    a. cara.   b. libre.   c. sencilla.
13. Ada pregunta si el hotel tiene...
    a. lugares de interés.   b. servicio de habitación.   c. algo que declarar.
14. El baño tiene ducha y...
    a. elevador.   b. escalera.   c. bañadera.
15. El inspector trabaja en...
    a. la recepción.   b. la aduana.   c. el lavabo.

Entrevista

Interview a classmate, using the **tú** form.

Pregúntele a su compañero(-a) de clase...

1. ...cuántas maletas lleva cuando viaja.
2. ...si lleva cheques de viajero cuando viaja.
3. ...si siempre lleva su cámara fotográfica cuando viaja.
4. ...qué lugares de interés hay en la ciudad donde vive.
5. ...a qué hora sirven el desayuno en la cafetería de la universidad.
6. ...si quiere llevarlo(la) a Ud. a almorzar.
7. ...si quiere comprar una grabadora.
8. ...si prefiere objetos de oro o de plata.
9. ...si hay alguien en su cuarto ahora.
10. ...si su cuarto tiene baño privado.

Situaciones

What would you say in the following situations? What might the other person say? Act out the scenes with a partner. Take turns playing each role.

1. You have just checked into a hotel. You want to know what time they serve breakfast and whether they have room service.
2. You are going through customs at the airport. You have nothing to declare to the inspector, but you want to make sure that everything is in order.
3. You are talking to the clerk at a tourist office. You need a list of hotels and boarding houses and a list of places of interest right away.
4. You work at an airport tourist office. Some tourists want to get downtown, and you know that they can take either a taxi or a bus.
5. You are a hotel clerk. Someone calls to reserve a single room with a private bathroom, but it is July, and you don't have any. Tell the person you can put his or her name on the waiting list.

¿Qué pasa aquí?   *(What is happening here?)*

In groups of three or four, look at the photo on page 160 and make up a story about the people you see. Give them names and say where they are coming from and where they are going. Where are they going to stay? What places of interest are they going to visit?

Para escribir

Complete the following dialogues.

1. *Carlos va a Tijuana.*

CARLOS —¿Dónde está tu pasaporte?
ROBERTO — _____
CARLOS —¡Sí, lo necesitas! ¿No vas a ir a México?
ROBERTO — _____
CARLOS —¿Tijuana? ¿Y para eso *(that)* necesitas todas esas maletas?
ROBERTO — _____
CARLOS —¡No! ¡No puedo llevarlas al coche!

2. *En el hotel*

TURISTA	—¿Tienen habitaciones?
HOTELERO	— _____
TURISTA	—No, interior.
HOTELERO	— _____
TURISTA	—¡Cien dólares por día! ¿Aceptan cheques de viajero?
HOTELERO	— _____

En la vida real

Discusión

Four or five students (or more, according to class size) will pretend to own hotels and will make up signs describing accommodations and prices. The rest of the class will discuss the similarities and differences and will decide in pairs or individually where they would like to stay. At the end of this activity each student will explain his or her choice.

A follow-up activity: After staying at the hotel people will have encountered one or more of the following problems:

(no) hay
- **agua caliente**   *hot water*
- **cucarachas**   *cockroaches*
- **frazadas, cobijas**   *blankets*
- **sábanas limpias**   *clean sheets*

no funciona
(it's not working)
- **el aire acondicionado**   *air conditioning*
- **el ascensor, el elevador**   *elevator*
- **la calefacción**   *heater*

Prepare a list of complaints on a card and drop it in the "suggestion box" (the instructor's desk).

Plaza Las Glorias
Puerto Vallarta

Plaza Las Glorias
Cancún

Plaza Las Glorias
Cozumel

¿Dónde hospedarse?   *(Where shall we stay?)*

Imagine it's the month of August. Say whether these people are going to stay at the **Aloha Puerto Sol** hotel or at the **Atlanterra Sol** hotel. Give reasons for your choice, according to the information provided in the following ads. You should also indicate how much each group will have to pay. Start out by saying, "**Se van a hospedar en... porque...**"

ESTANCIAS EN EL HOTEL ALOHA PUERTO SOL****

LE OFRECEMOS:
- Alojamiento en régimen de habitación y desayuno.
- Todas las habitaciones son mini-suites.
- Mini-bar.
- Cesta de fruta en la habitación.
- Botella de vino en la habitación.
- Entrada al Aquapark con 50% de descuento.
- Entrada gratis al Zoo de Fuengirola.
- Programa completo de deportes y animación para adultos y niños (Mini-Club).
- Espectáculos - actuaciones.

ALOHA PUERTO SOL H.D.

Precio por persona y día en habitación doble-habitación y desayuno						
01/05 - 15/07 01/10 - 31.10	01.09 - 30/09	16/07 - 31/06	SUPL. M.P.	SUPL. P.C SOBRE M.P.	SUPL. INDIV.	DESCUENT 3ª PERSON
3.165	4.060	4.455	1.340	610	1.310	15%
Código 048			IVA NO INCLUIDO			

ESTANCIAS EN EL HOTEL ATLANTERRA SOL****

LE OFRECEMOS:
- Régimen de habitación y desayuno. Habitación doble.
- Cesta de fruta en la habitación.
- Botella de vino en la habitación.
- 1 hora de tenis gratis.
- 1 copa gratis en la discoteca.
- Programa completo de deportes y animación para niños (Mini-Club) y adultos.
- Espectáculos - actuaciones.
- Salida de la habitación a las 14 horas.
- Condiciones especiales en nuestro restaurante grill «Oasis»
- Oferta novios 10%.

ATLANTERRA SOL H.D.

Precio por persona y día en habitación doble-habitación y desayuno						
	01/10 - 31/10	16/07 al 30/09	SUPL. M.P.	SUPL. PC. SOBRE M/P.	SUPL. INDIV.	DESCUENT 3ª PERSON
	4.970	6.495	1.490	1.320	2.295	15%
Desc. niños 2 - 15 años	1º 50% 2º 35%	1º 35% 2º 35%	IVA NO INCLUIDO			
Código 054						

---

1. La familia Salcedo: el papá, la mamá y dos niños. Jorgito tiene diez años y Alicia tiene ocho. No tienen mucho dinero.
2. Gustavo y Carolina, que son recién casados *(newlyweds)*. Desean ver un espectáculo y bailar. Tienen mucho dinero.
3. Teresa, Raquel y Rebeca, tres muchachas españolas que están viajando juntas. Les gusta jugar *(They like to play)* al tenis y bailar.

De viaje   *(Traveling)*

Get together with a couple of your classmates and plan a trip to a Spanish-speaking country. Visit a travel agency to obtain brochures of the country you are going to visit. Find out about hotels, rates of exchange, places of interest, and so on. Discuss how and when you will be leaving, how much spending money you'll bring, what cities and special sites you intend to visit, and what you will need to take with you.

¡Vamos a leer!

Antes de leer

As you read about Mark and Craig, find the answers to the following questions.

1. ¿De dónde son Mark y Craig?
2. ¿Qué van a estudiar?
3. ¿A qué universidad van a asistir?
4. ¿Cuánto tiempo duran las clases?
5. ¿Qué van a hacer por las mañanas?
6. ¿Adónde van a ir los fines de semana?
7. ¿Qué museos van a visitar?
8. ¿Qué ruinas quieren ver?
9. ¿Qué piensan comprar?

Un curso de verano

Mark y Craig son dos estudiantes norteamericanos que van a tomar clases de arqueología y de antropología en la Universidad Nacional de San Marcos, en Lima, la capital de Perú.

last / according to / advisor

Las clases duran° ocho semanas y, según° su consejero,° los chicos van a estar muy ocupados todo el tiempo. De lunes a viernes tienen clases en la universidad por la mañana y, por las tardes, los profesores van a llevarlos a visitar la ciudad y sus museos. Además, van a ir de excursión los fines de semana a varios lugares de interés cerca de Lima.

During / course

old / church

Durante° el curso° van a visitar, entre otros, el Museo Nacional de Arqueología y Antropología y el Museo Nacional de Historia. Mark quiere visitar, además, los edificios antiguos° de Lima, especialmente la famosa iglesia° de San Francisco, y Craig quiere pasar mucho tiempo en el Museo del Oro.

to stay

handicraft

Los dos quieren ver también las ruinas de Machu Picchu. Piensan ir en autobús hasta Cuzco, y allí tomar un tren para llegar a las ruinas. Van a quedarse° unos días en Cuzco, y ya tienen reservaciones para un hotel. Los dos muchachos piensan comprar objetos típicos de artesanía° para sus amigos y para sus familias.

Díganos

Answer the following questions, based on your own thoughts and experiences.

1. ¿Cuánto tiempo duran sus clases?
2. ¿Tiene Ud. clases por la mañana o por la tarde?
3. ¿Hay algunos edificios antiguos en la ciudad donde Ud. vive? ¿Cuáles?
4. ¿Hay algún museo en su ciudad? ¿Cuál es?
5. ¿Qué lugares de interés hay en la ciudad donde Ud. vive?

Take this test. When you have finished, check your answers in the answer key provided in Appendix E. Then use a red pen to correct any mistakes you may have made. Are you ready?

Lección 4

A. Expressions with *tener*

Write the following sentences in Spanish.

1. My classmates are in a hurry.
2. I'm not hungry, but I'm very thirsty.
3. Are you hot? I'm cold!
4. My friends are sleepy.
5. We are not scared.
6. You are right, Miss Peña. Mary is thirty years old.

B. Present indicative of the irregular verbs *ir, dar,* and *estar*

Complete the following sentences, using the present indicative of **ir, dar,** or **estar,** as appropriate.

1. Yo no _____ al baile con mis compañeros.
2. Nosotros _____ una fiesta aquí esta noche.
3. Mi hermana _____ en su casa.
4. ¿Dónde _____ el champán?
5. Las chicas _____ a la fiesta con sus amigos.
6. Tus primos no _____ mucho dinero.
7. Yo _____ cansado.
8. ¿Adónde _____ tus primos?
9. ¿Dónde _____ tú?
10. Yo no _____ mi número de teléfono.

C. *Ir a* + infinitive

Form sentences that tell what *is* or *is not* going to happen. Use the given elements.

MODELO: mi prima / dar / fiesta / el domingo
Mi prima va a dar una fiesta el domingo.

1. yo / no hablar / con mi mamá / hoy
2. mis hijos / estudiar / en España
3. mi amiga / leer / el anuncio
4. Uds. / bailar / en la fiesta
5. tú / no vivir / cerca / de la universidad
6. nosotros / brindar / con sidra

D. Uses of *ser* and *estar*

Form sentences, using the elements provided and the appropriate forms of **ser** or **estar.** Add the necessary connectors.

1. ella / mamá / María
2. Club Náutico / calle Siete
3. ¡Mmmm! / el pollo / delicioso

4. Roberto / de España / ahora / en California
5. cerveza / fría
6. escritorio / metal
7. hoy / martes / mañana / miércoles
8. Elsa / profesora
9. fiesta / casa / Lucía
10. orquesta / magnífica
11. ellos / enfermos
12. María Laura / uruguaya

E. Present indicative of *e:ie* stem-changing verbs

Complete the following sentences, using the present indicative of the verbs in the list, as necessary.

entender   cerrar   empezar   preferir
pensar   querer   perder   comenzar

1. Mi primo no _____ beber café.
2. Nosotros no _____ la Lección 2.
3. Ella siempre _____ mucho dinero en Las Vegas.
4. ¿ _____ tú la ventana?
5. Las clases _____ hoy.
6. Nosotros _____ a bailar ahora.
7. Yo no _____ trabajar el domingo.
8. Luis y yo _____ beber refrescos.

F. Just words . . .

Choose the word or phrase in parentheses that best completes each sentence.

1. (Invitamos, Brindamos, Bailamos) a nuestros compañeros a la fiesta.
2. Siempre (comemos, empezamos, estamos) doce uvas a la medianoche el día de fin de año.
3. Aquí no beben (sidra, entremeses, pollo).
4. Esta orquesta es muy buena. ¡Es (magnífica, antipática, feliz)!
5. ¡Feliz año (simpático, nuevo, guapo)!
6. No bebo (cocteles, refresco, Coca-Cola) porque yo no tomo bebidas alcohólicas.
7. Aquí todos (bailamos, brindamos, estamos) con vino.
8. Tengo todos los (primos, pollos, discos compactos) de Julio Iglesias.

G. Culture

Circle the correct answer, based on the **¿Lo sabía Ud.?** section.

1. En España y en Latinoamérica (existe, no existe) mucha separación entre las generaciones.
2. Además del cumpleaños muchos hispanos celebran su (baile, santo).
3. En algunos países hispanos (existe, no existe) edad mínima para comprar bebidas.
4. En español se dice (“¡Salud!”, “¡Santo!”) al brindar.

Lección 5

A. Irregular first-person verb forms

Complete the following sentences with the present indicative of the verbs in the list, as needed.

traducir	hacer	conocer	saber	salir
poner	caber	ver	traer	conducir

1. Yo _____ un Ford modelo 1989.
2. Yo no _____ dónde está el museo.
3. Yo no _____ en este coche. ¡Hay ocho personas!
4. Yo siempre _____ de casa a las siete y media.
5. Yo _____ las lecciones del inglés al portugués.
6. Yo no _____ las cartas. ¿Dónde están?
7. Yo no _____ nada los domingos.
8. Yo no _____ las fotografías allí.
9. Yo no _____ al tío de Fernando.
10. Yo _____ a mis sobrinas a la universidad.

B. *Saber* vs. *conocer*

Complete the following sentences with **saber** or **conocer**.

1. Yo _____ que él no quiere ir.
2. Ester no _____ a mi sobrina, pero ella _____ dónde vive.
3. Peter _____ España, pero él no _____ hablar español.
4. Ellos no _____ los poemas de memoria *(by heart)*.

C. Comparative forms

Form sentences, using the elements provided. Use the comparative or the superlative, as necessary.

1. Alfredo / estudiante / más / inteligente / clase
2. la Lección 2 / menos / interesante / la Lección 7
3. mi novia / más / bonita / tu novia
4. Roberto / más / guapo / familia
5. el profesor / tener / menos / veinte estudiantes
6. Ana / tan / alta / Roberto

D. Irregular comparative forms

Complete the following sentences, using regular or irregular comparative forms, as necessary.

1. California es _____ que Maine.
2. El profesor de español habla español _____ que los estudiantes.
3. Eva tiene "A" en español, Roberto tiene "B" y Marisa tiene "F". Eva es la _____ estudiante. Marisa es la _____ estudiante.
4. Yo tengo veinte años y Raquel tiene catorce años. Yo soy _____ que Raquel.
5. Rhode Island es _____ que California.

E. Present indicative of *o:ue* stem-changing verbs

Complete the following sentences, using the present indicative of the verbs in the list, as necessary.

recordar	almorzar	costar
contar	volver	poder

1. ¿Cuánto _____ el libro?
2. Ellos no _____ ir hoy.
3. ¿ _____ Ud. cuál es su número de teléfono?
4. Yo _____ de uno a veinte en español.
5. Tengo hambre. ¿A qué hora _____ (nosotros)?
6. ¿Cuándo _____ tú a España?

F. Just words . . .

Choose the word or phrase in parentheses that best completes each sentence.

1. El hijo de mi hija es mi (yerno, nieto, cuñado).
2. Vamos a ver (los cumpleaños, las pinturas, a la abuela) de Picasso en el museo.
3. Tengo que escribir muchas (medicinas, cartas, pensiones) este fin de semana.
4. ¿Quieres (extrañar, llover, almorzar) con él hoy?
5. ¿Tú (asistes, echas de menos, viajas) mucho a tu familia?
6. ¿No vamos a tener oportunidad de practicar el español? (¡Qué famoso!, ¡Qué lástima!, ¡Qué pequeño!)
7. Ellos quieren viajar en ómnibus; nunca (conducen su auto, comen en este restaurante, hablan francés).
8. ¿Quieres ver algunas (bebidas, fotos, cintas) de mi novia? ¡Es la chica más bonita del mundo!
9. Ellos no (saben, conocen, vuelven) Madrid.
10. No es alto. Es de estatura (mayor, interesante, mediana).

G. Culture

Read the following statements and circle **V** (Verdadero) or **F** (Falso), based on the **¿Lo sabía Ud.?** section.

1. V F La Universidad de Salamanca es una de las más famosas del mundo.
2. V F Sólo (Only) los españoles pueden estudiar en la Universidad de Salamanca.
3. V F En el Museo del Prado sólo hay cuadros de pintores españoles.
4. V F La mayoría de las universidades de los países hispanos no tienen residencias universitarias.
5. V F En los países hispanos la fecha se escribe con el día antes del mes.

Lección 6

A. Present indicative of *e:i* stem-changing verbs

Give the Spanish equivalent of the following.

1. At the Mexico Restaurant they serve dinner at nine.
2. She requests a room overlooking the street.

3. We follow the bellhop to the room.
4. Are you *(pl.)* getting reservations in December?
5. I'm saying (I say) that he must sign the register now.

B. Pronouns as objects of prepositions

Complete the following sentences, using the Spanish equivalent of the words in parentheses.

1. La maleta es para _____ . *(me)*
2. Los empleados están hablando de _____ . *(you,* inf.)
3. Hay dos valijas para _____ . *(them)*
4. La cámara fotográfica es para _____ . *(us)*
5. ¿Quieres almorzar _____ ? *(with me)*
6. Bueno. Voy a dejar *(to leave)* la grabadora _____ . *(with you,* inf.)

C. Affirmative and negative expressions

Change the following sentences to the affirmative.

1. Ellos no van a querer nada.
2. No hay nadie en el baño.
3. No tengo ningún objeto de oro y plata.
4. Ellos nunca pasan por la aduana.
5. Yo tampoco ceno a las nueve.
6. Jamás tiene las listas de los hoteles.
7. No puedes ir ni a la derecha ni a la izquierda.
8. Ellos nunca quieren nada tampoco.

D. Present progressive

Complete the following sentences, using the present progressive of the verbs in the list, as necessary.

pedir	comer	hablar
leer	decir	dormir

1. Ella _____ que nosotros necesitamos más dinero.
2. Yo _____ con el empleado.
3. Nosotros _____ una novela de Cervantes.
4. ¿Qué _____ tú? ¿Entremeses?
5. Luis _____ en su cuarto.
6. ¿Uds. _____ una habitación con vista a la calle?

E. Direct object pronouns

Complete the following sentences with the Spanish equivalent of the words in parentheses.

1. ¿El libro? No quiero _____ . Es muy caro.   *(to buy it)*
2. Yo _____ más tarde, Anita.   *(call you)*
3. ¿La cena? Ellos _____ a las siete.   *(serve it)*
4. Ella tiene una grabadora, pero no va a _____ .   *(to declare it)*
5. Mamá no _____ al baile.   *(take me)*
6. ¿Las toallas? Yo no _____ .   *(need them)*

7. Yo tengo cheques de viajero, pero ellos no _____ . *(accept them)*
8. Yo no puedo _____ , Sr. Vega. *(to take you)*
9. Ellos quieren las cámaras fotográficas pero yo no _____ . *(have them)*
10. Nosotros no podemos _____ , Srta. Roca. *(to call you)*

F. Just words . . .

Choose the correct response to each question or statement.
1. ¿Son caras las habitaciones en los hoteles del centro?
   a. No, son de oro y de plata.   b. No, son baratas.
   c. No, están en el segundo piso.
2. ¿Dónde vas a conseguir la lista de hoteles?
   a. En la oficina de turismo.   b. En el baño.   c. En un restaurante.
3. ¿Qué documentos debo mostrar?
   a. Veinte dólares.   b. El pasaporte.   c. El ascensor.
4. ¿A cómo está el cambio de moneda?
   a. Aquí tiene la llave.   b. Nada más.   c. Está a 3 soles por dólar.
5. ¿Tengo que declarar mi cámara fotográfica?
   a. Necesito una lista de lugares de interés.   b. No, no es necesario
   declararla.   c. Sí, van a declararla.
6. Necesitamos una habitación doble y dos habitaciones sencillas.
   a. No tenemos ningún cuarto libre.
   b. Hay pocas habitaciones modernas.   c. Todo está en regla.
7. ¿Dónde trabaja el inspector?
   a. En el autobús.   b. En la aduana.   c. En el viaje.
8. El cuarto con vista a la calle es muy caro.
   a. ¿Quiere una habitación interior?   b. El ascensor está a la izquierda.
   c. No hay muchas oficinas de turismo por aquí.
9. ¿Qué desea, señorita?
   a. Una habitación sencilla con baño privado.
   b. El autobús está a la derecha.   c. No tengo nada que declarar.
10. ¿No puedes ir a México?
    a. No, voy a confirmar la información.
    b. No, voy a cancelar las reservaciones.
    c. No soy de México; soy de Guatemala.
11. ¿Tienen jabón?
    a. Están en la embajada norteamericana.
    b. Sí, tenemos uno con vista a la calle.   c. Sí, pero no tenemos toallas.
12. ¿Están Uds. en la lista de espera?
    a. Tengo una lista de los lugares de interés.
    b. El botones tiene la lista.   c. No, nosotros tenemos reservaciones.

G. Culture

Circle the correct answer, based on the **¿Lo sabía Ud.?** section.

1. Lima, la capital de (Chile, Perú), es una ciudad de contrastes.
2. El (35%, 25%) de la población de Lima es de origen indígena.
3. La moneda más usada por los latinoamericanos cuando viajan es el (dólar, peso).
4. Es (fácil, difícil) cambiar dólares en los bancos hispanoamericanos.

★ 3 ESPAÑA (II)

España

■ España es un país que se distingue en la pintura y en la música. Algunos de los pintores más famosos del mundo son españoles: el Greco, Velázquez, Picasso, Miró y Dalí. En la música Andrés Segovia y Pablo Casals, entre otros, tienen fama internacional.

■ Entre los deportes *(sports)* más populares de España están el fútbol, el ciclismo, el baloncesto *(basketball)* y, en el País Vasco, el jai alai.

■ El día siete de julio se celebra en Pamplona la fiesta de San Fermín. Ese día sueltan los toros *(turn the bulls loose)* y la gente corre delante de *(in front of)* ellos hasta llegar a la plaza de toros para la corrida.

Saboreando *(tasting)* unas tapas en un bar de Málaga. Las tapas son pequeñas porciones de diferentes comidas *(foods)* típicas de España. Generalmente las tapas se sirven en los bares por la tarde.
¿Cuáles son algunas comidas típicas de su país?

Juan Carlos I de Borbón, rey *(king)* de España,
aparece aquí con la Reina Sofía y con el
primer ministro de gobierno, el líder José
María Aznar.
**¿Quién es el presidente (o primer ministro)
de su país?**

La Fundación Joan Miró está en el Parque de Montjuïc de Barcelona, junto a un edificio
diseñado por el arquitecto catalán Josep Lluís Sert. Aquí está el Centro de Estudio de Artes
Contemporáneas, establecido por Miró. La fundación contiene muchas de las pinturas y
esculturas del gran artista.
¿Quiénes son sus pintores favoritos?

Julio Iglesias es uno de los cantantes españoles más famosos del mundo. Iglesias ha vendido *(has sold)* más de cien millones de discos, y ha recibido el premio Grammy como el mejor cantante de música popular en español.
¿Conoce Ud. alguna canción en español? ¿Cuál es?

La procesión de la Semana Santa, en Sevilla, es la más famosa de las procesiones religiosas en España. Todos los años, mientras miles de españoles caminan por las calles detrás de la imagen de Jesucristo, turistas de todo el mundo contemplan el espectáculo.
¿Qué fiestas religiosas se celebran en su país?

Una pareja come paella, un plato típico de España, preparado con arroz *(rice)* y mariscos *(shellfish)* u otras carnes. La preparación de la paella varía de región a región, pero la más famosa es la paella valenciana.
¿Cuáles son sus platos favoritos?

El Ballet Real aparece aquí en los jardines del Generalife, en Granada. El repertorio del Ballet Real incluye bailes clásicos y folklóricos. Aquí vemos una representación del baile flamenco, típico del sur de España.
¿Qué tipo de baile prefiere Ud.: clásico, moderno o folklórico?

La corrida de toros tiene orígenes antiquísimos y es uno de los espectáculos más populares de España. Las corridas generalmente tienen lugar *(take place)* los domingos por la tarde en estadios especiales llamados plazas de toros, de las cuales hay más de 400 en España.
¿Quiere Ud. ver una corrida de toros algún día?

Teleinforme

Vocabulario

España y el arte de comer

el ajo	garlic
las carnes	meats
el cochinillo	suckling pig
la cocina	cooking, cuisine
la comida	meal
las especias	spices
las hojas de laurel	bay leaves
mundial	worldwide
el pescado	fish
la sartén	frying pan
se reúne	get together
la sopa	soup
las verduras	vegetables

Sevilla

a través de	throughout
las amantes	lovers
desarrolló	developed
después de	after
el Día de Pascua	Easter Sunday
el Domingo de Ramos	Palm Sunday
el encarcelamiento	imprisonment
los gitanos	Gypsies
ha llegado a ser	has become
la madrugada	dawn
el orgullo	pride
las raíces	roots, origins
los trajes	costumes
el placer	delight, pleasure
las velas	candles

Preparación

¿Cuánto saben Uds. ya?   After reading the information in **Panorama hispánico 3**, get together in groups of three or four and answer the following questions.

1. ¿Qué baile es típico del sur de España?
2. ¿Durante la primavera, qué fiesta religiosa se celebra en España con procesiones?
3. ¿Cuál es un plato típico de España?
4. ¿Cuál es uno de los espectáculos más populares de España?

Comprensión

A. España y el arte de comer.   Complete the following statements with the appropriate words.

1. Los españoles se reúnen en cafés y restaurantes para tener largas conversaciones informales que se llaman _____ .
2. Los españoles toman _____ en el desayuno.
3. En Madrid, uno de los platos más populares es el _____ .
4. El plato español más famoso es la _____ .
5. El gazpacho es una _____ fría de tomate y verduras.
6. Dos ingredientes muy importantes en la cocina española son el _____ y los _____ .

B. Sevilla.   Read the following statements. After watching the video, circle **V** (**Verdadero**) or **F** (**Falso**), according to what you understood.

V   F   1. Miguel de Cervantes fue *(was)* un político español.
V   F   2. Sevilla inspiró *(inspired)* cuatro óperas famosas.
V   F   3. Los indios trajeron *(brought)* el flamenco a España.
V   F   4. En Sevilla celebran la Feria de Abril antes de la Semana Santa.
V   F   5. Los pasos representan escenas religiosas.
V   F   6. Durante la Feria de Abril las personas no llevan trajes típicos.

Ampliación

A. Entrevista.   You are going to interview some Spaniards about their customs and traditions. In groups of three, prepare two or three questions for each of the following topics.

- la comida española
- la Semana Santa
- la Feria de Abril

B. Dos culturas.   With a partner, compare your eating habits and the foods you eat with those of the Spaniards.

HABLANDO DE LAS VACACIONES

OBJECTIVES

Pronunciation
The Spanish ll and ñ

Structure
Demonstrative adjectives and pronouns • Indirect object pronouns •
Constructions with **gustar** • Time expressions with **hacer** • Preterit of
regular verbs

Communication
You will learn vocabulary related to travel.

HABLANDO DE LAS VACACIONES

Teresa llegó ayer de su viaje a Perú y ahora está hablando por teléfono con su amiga Silvia. Hace media hora que las chicas están charlando y Teresa le está contando de su viaje.

TERESA —Me gustó mucho la capital, pero me gustó más Machu Picchu.

SILVIA —¡Y no me mandaste una tarjeta postal!

TERESA —Te compré dos, pero no las mandé. Oye, tengo que devolverte la maleta y el bolso de mano que me prestaste.

SILVIA —No hay apuro. ¿Llevaste mucho equipaje?

TERESA —Sí, llevé tres maletas. Pagué exceso de equipaje.

SILVIA —¿Cuánto te costó el pasaje? ¿Viajaste en primera clase?

TERESA —¿Estás loca? Viajé en clase turista. ¡Y me costó tres mil quinientos pesos![1] Ida y vuelta, claro…

SILVIA —¿Qué tal el vuelo?

TERESA —Un poco largo… Y como el avión salió con dos horas de retraso, llegamos muy tarde.

SILVIA —¿Te pasó algo interesante en Lima?

TERESA —Bueno… en la agencia de viajes donde compré el pasaje para Machu Picchu, conocí a un muchacho[2] muy simpático.

SILVIA —¿Viajó contigo? Tienes que contarme todo lo que pasó.

TERESA —Sí, viajé con él en avión a Cuzco, donde almorzamos juntos. Después, conversamos durante todo el viaje en tren a Machu Picchu.

SILVIA —No sé por qué tus vacaciones siempre son magníficas y mis vacaciones son tan aburridas.

TERESA —Pues la próxima vez tenemos que viajar juntas.

SILVIA —Bueno, pero sólo si vamos en tren o en barco. A mí no me gusta viajar en avión.

TERESA —Bueno, viajamos en tren. Oye, este sábado voy al cine con Cecilia, ¿quieres ir con nosotras?

SILVIA —¿Quién es Cecilia?

TERESA —Es la chica que te presenté en la biblioteca el mes pasado.

SILVIA —Ah, ésa… ya recuerdo. Sí, vamos juntas.

TERESA —¿Quieres ir a almorzar conmigo ahora?

SILVIA —No, gracias, ya almorcé.

TERESA —Bueno, entonces nos vemos mañana.

---

[1]Mexican currency.
[2]Note that **muchacho(-a)** can be used familiarly to refer to men and women under thirty.

Vocabulario

Cognados

la capital   capital (city)   **el exceso**   excess

■ Nombres

la agencia de viajes   travel
  agency
el avión   plane
el barco   boat, ship
el bolso de mano   carry-on bag
el cine   movie theater, movies
la clase turista   tourist class
el equipaje   luggage

la hora   hour
el pasaje, el billete (*Spain*)   ticket
  (for plane, train, or bus)
   _____ de ida   one-way ticket
   _____ de ida y vuelta   round-trip
  ticket
   _____ de primera clase   first-
  class ticket

el retraso, atraso   delay
la tarjeta   card
   _____ postal   postcard
el tren   train
la vez   time (occasion)
el vuelo   flight

■ Verbos

conocer   to meet (for the first time)
contar (o:ue)   to tell
devolver (o:ue)   to return
  (something)

gustar   to like, to be pleasing
  to
pagar   to pay
pasar   to happen

presentar   to introduce
prestar   to lend

■ Adjetivos

aburrido(-a)   boring
ése(-a)   that one
juntos(-as)   together

largo(-a)   long
loco(-a)   crazy
pasado(-a)   last

próximo(-a)   next

■ Otras palabras y expresiones

ayer   yesterday
bueno, bien   okay, fine
claro, por supuesto   of course
como   since
de   about
después   then
durante   during
el mes pasado   last month
exceso de equipaje   excess
  baggage

la próxima vez   next time
llegar tarde[1]   to be late
media hora   half an hour
No hay apuro., No hay prisa.
   There's no hurry.
primera clase   first class
pues   then
¿Qué tal...?   How was (is) . . . ?
sólo   only
tarde   late

todo   all
todo el viaje   the whole trip
todo lo que pasó   everything that
  happened
un poco + *adjetivo*   a little +
  adjective
ya   now, already

---

[1]**llegar temprano**   to be early

Vocabulario adicional

En el aeropuerto

la puerta de salida

la tarjeta de embarque

el turista

la viajera

la sección de fumar

la sección de no fumar

el asiento de ventanilla

el asiento de pasillo

el auxiliar de vuelo

la azafata

De viaje (traveling)

el (la) **agente de viajes** travel agent	El **agente de viajes** me vendió los pasajes.
¡Buen viaje! Have a nice trip!	¡Adiós, Marisa! **¡Buen viaje!**
la **entrada** entrance	¿Dónde está la **entrada** al aeropuerto?
la **salida** exit	Aquella puerta no es la entrada; es la **salida**.
tener... de retraso (atraso) to be . . . behind schedule	El avión **tiene dos horas de retraso**.

¡Conversemos!

Answer the following questions, basing your answers on the dialogue.

1. ¿Hace una hora que Teresa y Silvia hablan por teléfono?
2. ¿De qué le está contando Teresa a su amiga?
3. ¿Qué le gustó más a Teresa, Machu Picchu o Lima?
4. ¿Qué le prestó Silvia a Teresa para el viaje?
5. ¿Pagó Teresa exceso de equipaje? ¿Por qué?
6. ¿Cuánto le costó a Teresa el pasaje?
7. ¿Viajó Teresa a Cuzco en avión o en tren?

8. ¿Con cuántas horas de retraso salió el avión?
9. ¿Las vacaciones de Teresa son magníficas o aburridas?
10. ¿Cómo van a viajar Teresa y Silvia la próxima vez?
11. ¿Adónde va Teresa este sábado? ¿Con quiénes va?
12. ¿Cuál de las chicas ya almorzó?

¿Lo sabía Ud.?

- **Cuzco**, situado a más de diez mil pies de altura en los Andes peruanos, es la antigua capital del imperio de los incas. Hoy día, la ciudad es un gran centro turístico y artístico.

- **Machu Picchu**, conocida también como "la ciudad perdida de los incas", está situada en la cordillera de los Andes a unos ciento diez kilómetros al noroeste *(northwest)* de Cuzco. El imperio de los incas se extendió desde el sur *(south)* de Colombia hasta el norte de Chile y Argentina.

Mercado de artesanías cerca de Cuzco, Perú.

PRONUNCIACIÓN

A The Spanish ll

In most countries, the Spanish **ll** has a sound similar to the *y* in the English word *yes*. Listen to your instructor and repeat the following words.

calle	cuchillo	llave	botella
llevar	llegar	pollo	platillo

B The Spanish ñ

The Spanish **ñ** is similar to the *ny* in the English word *canyon*. Listen to your instructor and repeat the following words.

español	niño	mañana	España
señor	señorita	otoño	año

ESTRUCTURAS

1 Demonstrative adjectives and pronouns
(Los adjetivos y los pronombres demostrativos)

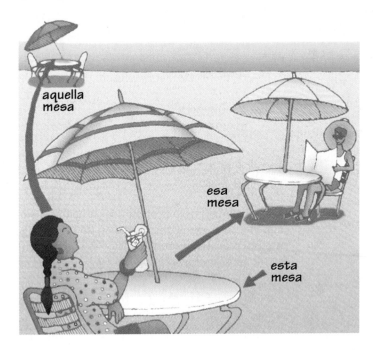

A. Demonstrative adjectives

■ Demonstrative adjectives point out persons or things. Like all other adjectives, they agree in gender and number with the nouns they modify. The forms of the demonstrative adjectives are as follows.

Masculine		Feminine		
Singular	*Plural*	*Singular*	*Plural*	
este	estos	esta	estas	*this, these*
ese	esos	esa	esas	*that, those*
aquel	aquellos	aquella	aquellas	*that, those* (at a distance in space or time)

—¿Qué necesitas?　　　　　　　　　*"What do you need?"*
—Necesito **esta** pluma, **ese**　　　*"I need this pen, that notebook,*
　cuaderno y **aquellos** libros.　　　　*and those books* (over there).*"

B. Demonstrative pronouns

■ The forms of the demonstrative pronouns are as follows.

Masculine		Feminine		Neuter	
Singular	*Plural*	*Singular*	*Plural*		
éste	éstos	ésta	éstas	esto	*this* (one), *these*
ése	ésos	ésa	ésas	eso	*that* (one), *those*
aquél	aquéllos	aquélla	aquéllas	aquello	*that* (one), *those* (at a distance)

—¿Quieres este jabón o **ése**?	*"Do you want this soap or that one?"*
—No quiero ni **éste** ni **ése**; quiero **aquél**.	*"I don't want this one or that one; I want that one over there."*

■ The masculine and feminine demonstrative pronouns are the same as the demonstrative adjectives, except that they have a written accent.

■ Each demonstrative pronoun has a neuter form. They are **esto, eso,** and **aquello**. The neuter forms, which do not change in number or gender, are used to refer to situations, ideas, and nonspecific objects or things, equivalent to the English *this, that matter; this, that business;* and *this, that stuff.*

—¿Entiendes **eso**?	*"Do you understand that?"*
—No, no lo entiendo.	*"No, I don't understand it."*
—¿Qué es **esto**?	*"What's this?"*
—No sé…	*"I don't know . . ."*

Práctica

A. Change the demonstrative adjectives according to the gender and number of the nouns.

1. *esta* lista de espera, _____ terrazas, _____ elevador, _____ cuadros
2. *ese* empleado, _____ orquesta, _____ hoteles, _____ ruinas
3. *aquella* señora, _____ billete, _____ toallas, _____ agentes de viaje

B. Complete the following sentences according to the cue given.

1. Firmo este registro y _____ *(that one over there).*
2. Quiero estos lápices y _____ *(those).*
3. Necesito esta llave y _____ *(that one over there).*
4. Voy a comprar esta toalla y _____ *(those).*
5. No quiero esas maletas; quiero _____ *(these).*
6. No voy a comer en ese restaurante. Voy a comer en _____ *(this one).*

C. With a partner, use demonstrative adjectives to describe people or objects that are at varying distances from you.

1. sus cuadernos
2. la pizarra
3. las ventanas
4. la puerta
5. los coches en la calle
6. las chicas que están en la cafetería
7. los libros del profesor
8. su pluma (o lápiz)

2 Indirect object pronouns
(Pronombres usados como complemento indirecto)

▪ In addition to a subject and a direct object, a sentence may have an indirect object.

Él le da el libro a María.   *He gives the book to María.*

D.O.   I.O.   D.O.   I.O.

▪ An indirect object describes *to whom* or *for whom* an action is done. An indirect object pronoun can be used in place of an indirect object. In Spanish, the indirect object pronoun includes the meaning *to* or *for*: **Yo *les* mando los libros (a los estudiantes).**

▪ The forms of the indirect object pronouns are as follows. Notice that the indirect object pronouns are the same as the direct object pronouns, except in the third person.

Singular		Plural	
me	*(to, for) me*	nos	*(to, for) us*
te	*(to, for) you* (inf.)	os	*(to, for) you* (inf.)
le	*(to, for) you* (form.) *(to, for) him* *(to, for) her*	les	*(to, for) you* (form.) *(to, for) them* (masc., fem.)

▪ Indirect object pronouns are usually placed in front of the conjugated verb.

—¿Qué **te** dice tu papá en la tarjeta?   *"What does your Dad say to you in the postcard?"*

—**Me** dice que viene por unos días.   *"He tells me (says to me) that he is coming for a few days."*

▪ In sentences with a conjugated verb followed by an infinitive, the indirect object pronoun may either be placed in front of the conjugated verb or be attached to the infinitive.

Le quiero dar dinero.
 Quiero dar**le** dinero. }   *I want to give him money.*

■ When used in sentences with the present progressive, an indirect object pronoun may either be placed in front of the conjugated verb or be attached to the present participle.

Nos está diciendo   que viene hoy. ⎫ *He is telling us that*
Está diciéndo**nos**[1] que viene hoy. ⎭ *he is coming today.*

ATENCIÓN   The indirect object pronouns **le** and **les** sometimes require clarification when the person to whom they refer is not specified. Spanish provides clarification (or emphasis) by using the preposition **a** + *personal pronoun or noun.*

Le doy el pasaje.   *I am giving the ticket . . .*
                                                          (to him? to her? to you?)
but: **Le** doy el pasaje **a ella.**   *I am giving the ticket to her.*

Note, however, that the prepositional phrase is optional, while the indirect object pronoun must always be used.

Le traigo un libro **a Roberto.**   *I am bringing a book to Roberto.*
¿Les vas a dar el dinero **a ellas?**   *Are you going to give the money to
                                                           them?*

Práctica

A. You are in an airport waiting for a friend to arrive and you overhear some people making the following comments. Complete their sentences with the appropriate indirect object pronoun.

1. _____ dan los billetes. (a nosotros)
2. _____ doy el bolso de mano. (a ellos)
3. _____ doy la maleta. (a él)
4. _____ doy los cheques de viajero. (a ella)
5. _____ traigo la tarjeta de embarque. (a Uds.)
6. _____ piden el pasaporte. (a ella)
7. _____ traigo el equipaje. (a ti)
8. _____ traen el periódico. (a él)
9. _____ decimos "gracias". (a ellos)
10. _____ dan las bebidas. (a mí)

---

[1]When an indirect object pronoun is attached to a present participle, an accent mark is added to maintain the correct stress.

B. The following people are going on a trip and need certain items. Say who is going to give, bring, or buy the things they need.

> MODELO: Oscar necesita un mapa.
> *El papá de Oscar le va a traer (comprar, dar) el mapa.*

tu mamá	el amigo de…	mi hermano
nuestros amigos	el papá de…	la abuela de…
los chicos	el novio de…	su esposo(-a)

1. Yo necesito las maletas.
2. Teresa necesita cheques de viajero.
3. Tú necesitas un bolso de mano.
4. Ana y yo necesitamos una tarjeta de crédito.
5. Carlos necesita una cámara de video.
6. Los chicos necesitan una cámara fotográfica.
7. Olga y Pedro necesitan dinero.
8. Ud. necesita una grabadora.

C. You are going on a trip to Miami to visit your aunt and uncle. Discuss with a classmate what you are doing now and what you are going to do once you get there.

1. ¿Les estás escribiendo a tus tíos de la Florida?
2. ¿Qué les estás diciendo?
3. ¿Qué les vas a llevar a tus tíos?
4. ¿Tu papá te va a dar su cámara fotográfica?
5. ¿Nos vas a escribir desde *(from)* Miami?
6. ¿Me vas a dejar la llave de tu casa?
7. ¿Qué les vas a traer a tus padres?
8. ¿Qué me vas a traer a mí?

D. With a partner, act out the following dialogues in Spanish.

1. "Are you going to lend David your suitcases?"
   "No, because he never returns anything to me."
2. "Are you going to write to your parents, Rosita?"
   "Yes, I'm going to send them a postcard."
3. "What are you going to tell your sister, Mr. Varela?"
   "I'm going to tell her that the plane leaves at six."
4. "What are you going to bring us, aunt Isabel?"
   "I'm going to bring you a tape recorder."

E. You are going on a trip. Say what you are going to bring the following people as souvenirs.

1. a tu mamá
2. a tus hermanos
3. a mí (*use* tú *form*)
4. a tu mejor amigo(-a)
5. a Carlos y a mí

3 Constructions with **gustar** *(Construcciones con **gustar**)*

- The verb **gustar** means *to like* (literally, *to be pleasing to*). **Gustar** is always used with an indirect object pronoun (**me** in the following example).

Me gusta tu casa.		*I like your house.*
I.O. V. S.		S. V. D.O.
		Your house is pleasing to me.
		S. V. I.O.

- The two most commonly used forms of **gustar** are the third-person singular form, **gusta**, used if the subject is singular or if **gustar** is followed by one or more infinitives; and the third-person plural form, **gustan**, used if the subject is plural.

Indirect object pronouns

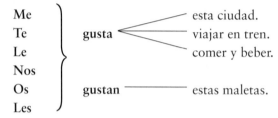

- Note that the verb **gustar** agrees with the *subject* of the sentence—that is, with the person or thing being liked.

Me gust**a** **Lima.**	*I like Lima.*
No me gust**an** **los vuelos** largos.	*I don't like long flights.*

ATENCIÓN When what is liked is an activity, **gustar** is followed by the infinitive.

Me gust**a** **hablar** por teléfono.	*I like to talk (talking) on the phone.*

- The person who does the liking is the indirect object.

Me gustan los cuadros de Picasso.

I.O.

—¿Te gusta San Diego?	*"Do you like San Diego?"*
—Sí, me gusta mucho San Diego, pero me gusta más San Francisco.	*"Yes, I like San Diego very much, but I like San Francisco better."*
—A Eva le gusta Santa Bárbara.	*"Eva likes Santa Barbara."*

ATENCIÓN Note that the words **mucho** and **más** *(better)* immediately follow **gustar**.

- The preposition **a** + *noun or pronoun* may be used to emphasize or specify the name of the person referred to by the indirect object pronoun.

A Eva (A ella) le gusta el pollo y **a mí** me gusta la ensalada.	*Eva (She) likes chicken and I like salad.*

Práctica

A. Interview a classmate to find out what the following members of his or her family like and don't like to do on weekends. When you have finished, switch roles.

> MODELO: —A tu hermana, ¿qué (no) le gusta hacer?
> —*A mi hermana le gusta ir a bailar. No le gusta trabajar.*

1. A ti
2. A tus hermanos
3. A tu padre
4. A Uds.
5. A tus primos

B. Interview a classmate, using the following questions. When you have finished, switch roles.

1. ¿Adónde te gusta ir de vacaciones?
2. ¿Te gustan más las ciudades grandes o las ciudades pequeñas?
3. ¿Te gusta más viajar en tren o en avión?
4. ¿Qué les gusta hacer a tus amigos los fines de semana?
5. ¿A Uds. les gusta bailar? ¿cantar?
6. ¿A tu mejor amiga le gusta Julio Iglesias?
7. ¿Qué estación del año te gusta más?
8. ¿Qué te gusta hacer cuando llueve?

C. Compare your likes and dislikes with those of two classmates. Consider your tastes in food, music, classes, and travel.

D. Be an interpreter. What are these people saying?

1. "Do you like this carry-on bag, Lolita?"
   "No . . . I like that one better."
2. "Do your parents like to travel by ship, Mr. Vega?"
   "Yes, they like (to) very much."
3. "Do you like this seat, sir?"
   "No, I don't like window seats."
4. "What do you like to do, ladies?"
   "We like to read and to travel."
5. "Do you like that hotel, Miss Rojas?"
   "No, I like this one better."

E. With a classmate, prepare four questions to ask your instructor about his or her likes and dislikes.

4 Time expressions with **hacer**
*(Expresiones de tiempo con el verbo **hacer**)*

■ English uses the present perfect progressive or the present perfect tense to express how long something has been going on.

> ***I have been living*** *here **for** twenty years.*

■ Spanish uses the following construction.

> **Hace +** *length of time* **+ que +** *verb* (in the present tense)
> Hace   veinte años   que   vivo aquí.

—**¿Cuánto tiempo hace que** Ud. estudia español?	*"How long have you been studying Spanish?"*
—**Hace** tres meses **que** estudio español.	*"I have been studying Spanish for three months."*
—¿Tienes mucha hambre?	*"Are you very hungry?"*
—¡Sí! **Hace** ocho horas **que** no como.	*"Yes! I haven't eaten for eight hours."*

ATENCIÓN   To ask how long something has been going on, use the expression **¿Cuánto tiempo hace que…?**

Práctica

A. Tell how long each action depicted below has been going on. Use **hace… que** and the length of time specified.

1. veinte minutos

2. tres años

3. una hora

4. dos horas

5. siete horas

6. quince días

B. Interview a classmate, using the following questions and two questions of your own. When you have finished, switch roles.

1. ¿Cuánto tiempo hace que vives en esta ciudad?
2. ¿Cuánto tiempo hace que estudias aquí?
3. ¿Cuánto tiempo hace que trabajas en esta ciudad?
4. ¿Cuánto tiempo hace que hablas español?
5. ¿Cuánto tiempo hace que no comes?
6. ¿Cuánto tiempo hace que no ves a tus padres?

C. With a partner, act out the following dialogues in Spanish.

1. "How long have you been studying Spanish?"
   "I have been studying it for six months."
2. "How long has he been working at the travel agency?"
   "Five years."
3. "How long have you known your professor?"
   "I have known her for two weeks."
4. "Are you still (**todavía**) working?"
   "Yes, I've been working for two hours."

D. In groups of three, prepare six questions to ask your instructor, using time expressions with **hacer**. You may want to use the verb **enseñar** *(to teach)* in your questions.

5 Preterit of regular verbs *(Pretérito de verbos regulares)*

■ Spanish has two simple past tenses: the preterit and the imperfect. (The imperfect tense will be studied in **Lección 10**.) The preterit tense is used to refer to actions or states that the speaker views as completed in the past.

■ The preterit of regular verbs is formed as follows. Note that the endings for the -**er** and -**ir** verbs are the same.

-ar *verbs*	-er *verbs*	-ir *verbs*
tomar *to take*	**comer** *to eat*	**escribir** *to write*
tomé	comí	escribí
tomaste	comiste	escribiste
tomó	comió	escribió
tomamos	comimos	escribimos
tomasteis	comisteis	escribisteis
tomaron	comieron	escribieron

—¿**Hablaste** con Silvia ayer?

—Sí, **comimos** juntas en la cafetería.

"Did you speak with Silvia yesterday?"

"Yes, we ate together in the cafeteria."

—¿Le **escribió** Roberto?

—Sí, **recibió** una tarjeta de él ayer.

"Did Roberto write to her?"

"Yes, she received a card from him yesterday."

■ The first-person plural of -ar and -ir verbs is identical to the present tense forms.

—¿A qué hora salieron Uds.?   *"What time did you leave?"*
—**Salimos** de casa a las seis y   *"We left home at six, and we*
     no **llegamos** hasta las siete.   *didn't arrive until seven."*

■ Verbs ending in -gar, -car, and -zar change g to gu, c to qu, and z to c before é in the first-person singular of the preterit: **pagar** → **pagué**; **buscar** *(to look for)* → **busqué**; **empezar** → **empecé.**

—¿A qué hora **llegaste** al   *"What time did you arrive*
     hospital?   *at the hospital?"*
—**Llegué** a las ocho y **empecé**   *"I arrived at eight and I started to*
     a trabajar.   *work."*

■ Certain -er and -ir verbs with the stem ending in a vowel change i to y in the third-person singular and plural endings: leer → **leyó, leyeron**; creer → **creyó, creyeron.**

Él lo **leyó** en el periódico, pero no lo **creyó.**

■ Verbs of the -ar and -er groups that are stem-changing in the present indicative are regular in the preterit.

Rosa **volvió** a las seis y **cerró**   *Rosa returned at six o'clock*
     las puertas.   *and closed the doors.*

■ Spanish has no equivalent for the English word *did* used as an auxiliary verb in questions and negative sentences.

—¿Encontraste el billete?   *"Did you find the ticket?"*
—No lo busqué.   *"I didn't look for it."*

Práctica

A. Complete the following dialogues, using the verbs given. Then act them out with a partner.

1. hablar / hablar /   —¿Tú _____ por teléfono con tus suegros ayer?
     llamar / charlar   —Sí, _____ con ellos. Los _____ por la mañana.
             _____ hasta las once.

2. volver / volver /   —¿A qué hora _____ Uds.?
     volver   —Yo _____ a las cuatro y Mario _____ a las
             seis.

3. recibir / mandar /   —¿ _____ (tú) las tarjetas que yo te _____ ?
     recibir   —No, no las _____ .

4. llegar / llegar /   —¿A qué hora _____ Ud., señorita?
     comenzar   —_____ a las nueve y _____ a trabajar a las
             nueve y media.

5. cerrar / cerrar /   —¿ _____ Uds. las puertas?
     abrir   —Sí, _____ las puertas y _____ las ventanas.

B. Say what you and your friends did yesterday.

1. ¿Qué comió Ud. ayer?
2. ¿Qué bebió Ud.?
3. ¿Estudiaron Uds. español anoche *(last night)*?
4. ¿A qué hora salió Ud. de su casa?
5. ¿A qué hora llegó Ud. a su primera clase?
6. ¿Trabajaron ayer sus amigos?
7. ¿Dónde almorzó su mejor amigo(-a)?
8. ¿A qué hora volvió Ud. a su casa?
9. ¿Leyó el periódico?
10. ¿A qué hora cenó Ud.?

C. With a partner, use the verbs listed to ask each other what you did yesterday and last night (**anoche**).

MODELO: —¿Dónde almorzaste ayer?
—Almorcé en la cafetería.

almorzar	devolver	mandar	salir
cenar	escribir	mirar	trabajar
cerrar	leer	pagar	ver
conversar	llegar	practicar	buscar

¡A VER CUÁNTO APRENDIÓ!

¡Repase el vocabulario!

Complete the following sentences with words from the lesson vocabulary.

1. No me gusta viajar en la _____ de fumar.
2. No es la entrada; es la _____ .
3. Le voy a _____ a Teresa las maletas que me prestó.
4. ¿Quiere un _____ de ventanilla o de pasillo?
5. Le tengo que dar la tarjeta de _____ a la _____ de vuelo.
6. Si vas a tomar el _____ a las ocho, tienes que estar en el aeropuerto a las siete.
7. Como Ana y Elsa viajan _____ , conversan durante _____ el viaje.
8. —¿Qué _____ el vuelo?
   —Un _____ largo.
9. Los viajeros llegaron tarde; llegaron con dos horas de _____ .
10. —Roberto, ¿le vas a prestar mil dólares para ir a Las Vegas?
    —¡¿Estás _____ ?!
11. Yo les deseé _____ viaje a los turistas.
12. Compré un pasaje de ida y _____ .
13. Le voy a enviar una _____ postal.
14. —¿Tienes seis maletas? ¡Vas a pagar exceso de _____ !
15. Elsa, te quiero _____ a mi amigo Roberto Fuentes.

Entrevista

Interview a classmate, using the **tú** form.

Pregúntele a su compañero(-a)…

1. …adónde le gusta ir cuando tiene vacaciones.
2. …si le gusta más viajar en avión o en tren.
3. …si viaja en primera clase o en clase turista.
4. …si cuando viaja les manda tarjetas postales a sus amigos.
5. …si lleva mucho equipaje cuando viaja.
6. …si conoció a alguien interesante en sus vacaciones. (¿A quién?)
7. …si sus vacaciones son magníficas o aburridas.
8. …adónde va a ir de vacaciones la próxima vez.

Situaciones

What would you say in the following situations? What might the other person say? Act out the scenes with a partner. Take turns playing each role.

1. You are checking in for a flight at the airport. The airline representative wants to know how many suitcases you have. You are not sure whether you can take your carry-on bag on the plane.
2. You are seeing a friend off at the airport.
3. A friend has borrowed your suitcase. You want to know when he or she plans to return it to you, because you are going on a trip. Arrange to see your friend tomorrow at noon.
4. You are in a travel agency. You want to buy a round-trip ticket to Bogotá. Ask for a seat assignment.

Para escribir

Write a short composition about the people in the photo. Tell who they are, what their relationship to each other is, where they went last summer, what they did, and also what they plan to do next summer. Here are some words you might want to use: **pintar** *(to paint)*, **dibujar** *(to sketch)*.

En la vida real

En una agencia de viajes

You and a classmate will play the roles of a travel agent and a tourist. Discuss the following.

- ticket prices according to destination and different kinds of transportation
- prices for first class or tourist class, one-way or round-trip
- flight schedules
- seat reservations
- how much luggage can be taken

Planes para un viaje

You are helping some friends plan a trip. With a classmate, study the ad and answer your friends' questions.

Caribe Asómese al paraíso . . . *República Dominicana*

SALIDAS EN AVION LINEA REGULAR DE IBERIA, DIRECTO A SANTO DOMINGO, TODOS LOS JUEVES Y VIERNES		
PRECIOS POR PERSONA EN HABITACION DOBLE Y REGIMEN DE MEDIA PENSION		
TEMPORADAS	7 NOCHES	14 NOCHES
Mayo y 1 al 21 de Junio	**114.900**	**137.800**
22 al 30 de Junio	**125.900**	**148.800**
Julio y Septiembre	**137.500**	**165.000**
Agosto	**142.900**	**176.400**
Octubre	**131.500**	**159.000**
Noviembre y Diciembre (1 al 12)	**132.900**	**161.800**

Suplemento Habitación Individual: Consultar al efectuar la reserva.
LOS PRECIOS INCLUYEN: Avión línea regular clase turista ida y vuelta. Traslados aeropuerto/hotel/aeropuerto. Estancia en habitación doble en régimen de Media Pensión (Hotel Bávaro Casino).
OFERTA VALIDA PARA SALIDAS Y REGRESOS DESDE MADRID.

1. ¿A qué país vamos a viajar?
2. ¿En qué clase viajamos?
3. ¿En qué hotel vamos a estar?
4. Queremos viajar en julio. ¿Cuánto tenemos que pagar (en pesetas) por una semana? ¿Y por dos semanas?
5. ¿El precio incluye el traslado (*transportation*) del aeropuerto al hotel y del hotel al aeropuerto?
6. ¿De qué ciudad salen los vuelos?
7. ¿Qué días de la semana salen los vuelos?

¿Adónde vamos?

You and a friend have won a radio contest. The prize is $5,000 to spend on a dream vacation. With a classmate, decide where you will go, how long you will be away, where you will stay, and what you will need to take with you.

 # Así somos

Vocabulario

ahí	there
al día siguiente	the next day
al extranjero	abroad
antigua	old
convivimos	we share our lives
disfruto	I enjoy
el encanto	charm
espero	I hope
fui	I went
he viajado	I have traveled
hemos estado trabajando	we have been working
la iglesia	church
lo que	what
Marruecos	Morocco
me encanta	I love
me fascinó	it fascinated me
el Medio Oriente	Middle East
el mío	mine
muchísimo	very much
no había ido	I had not gone
no he tenido	I have not had
los parientes	relatives
los pasajeros	passengers
varios	several, various

Preparación

¿Las reconoce?   Guess the meaning of the following words. While watching the video, circle each one as you hear the person say it.

costumbre	ideología	normales	semestre
familiar	increíble	reunión	Suiza
Grecia	Irlanda	rutina	Turquía

Comprensión

A. ¿Qué países conoces?   Select the word or phrase that best completes each statement, according to what you understood.

1. Ángela conoce (Europa, Asia).
2. Gustavo vivió en (Brasil, los Estados Unidos).
3. Leonardo (viaja, no viaja) mucho.
4. Tamara (conoce, no conoce) muchos países.

B. ¿Quién lo dice?   Match each statement with the name of the person who said it.

a. Pablo   b. Leonardo   c. Ángela   d. Gustavo

_____ 1. Buenos Aires es una ciudad increíble.
_____ 2. Me fascinó el Medio Oriente.
_____ 3. Me gustaron los Estados Unidos y Canadá.
_____ 4. Me gusta el mío—España.

C. Las vacaciones.   Read the following statements. After watching the video, circle **V** (**Verdadero**) or **F** (**Falso**), according to what you understood.

V F   1. Tamara pasó sus vacaciones en Puerto Rico.
V F   2. John visitó a sus parientes en Guatemala.
V F   3. La casa de Zaida está en Bogotá.
V F   4. Pablo pasó sus vacaciones en México.

D. Entrevista.   Answer the following questions, according to what you understood from the interview.

1. ¿Qué profesión tiene Manuel Ticó?
2. ¿Qué oportunidades tiene él en su trabajo?
3. ¿Conoce Manuel un país de Centro América? ¿Cuál?
4. ¿Le gusta a Manuel su trabajo?
5. ¿Tiene él una rutina en su trabajo?

Ampliación

Vamos a viajar.   With a partner, discuss the countries that you want to visit and the reasons why you want to go there.

EN UN RESTAURANTE CUBANO

OBJECTIVES

Pronunciation
The Spanish **l, r, rr,** and **z**

Structure
Direct and indirect object pronouns used together • Preterit of **ser, ir,** and **dar** • Preterit of **e:i** and **o:u** stem-changing verbs • Weather expressions • Uses of **por** and **para**

Communication
You will learn vocabulary related to restaurant menus, ordering meals at a restaurant, and paying the bill.

EN UN RESTAURANTE CUBANO

Hoy es el 15 de diciembre. Es el aniversario de bodas de Lidia y Jorge Torres. Van a cenar en uno de los mejores restaurantes de Miami para celebrarlo. Llegan al restaurante El Caribe.

LIDIA —¡Qué sorpresa! ¡Éste es un restaurante muy elegante!

JORGE —Y la comida es excelente.

MOZO —Por aquí, por favor. Aquí está el menú.

LIDIA —Gracias. *(Lee el menú.)* Bistec, cordero asado con puré de papas, pavo relleno, camarones…

JORGE —¿Por qué no pides un filete? Aquí preparan unos filetes muy ricos. ¿O langosta?

LIDIA —No, anoche fui a la cena de los Ruiz y sirvieron langosta.

MOZO —Les recomiendo la especialidad de la casa: lechón asado y arroz con frijoles negros. De postre, helado, flan o torta helada.

JORGE —Yo quiero lechón asado y arroz con frijoles negros. ¿Y tú?

LIDIA —Yo quiero sopa, camarones y arroz.

MOZO —¿Y para tomar?

JORGE —Primero un vermut y después media botella de vino tinto.

MOZO —Muy bien, señor. *(Anota el pedido.)*

Antes de cenar, Lidia y Jorge toman vermut y conversan.

LIDIA —¿Tus padres fueron a la fiesta que dio Eva ayer?

JORGE —Sí. Fue en el club Los Violines.

LIDIA —¿Le dieron la pulsera que compraron para ella en México?

JORGE —Sí, se la dieron. Le encantó.

LIDIA —¿Te la enseñaron antes de dársela?

JORGE —Sí, me la enseñaron cuando fui por ellos anteayer por la tarde.

LIDIA —La consiguieron a muy buen precio en una tienda muy elegante.

El mozo trae la comida. Después de comer, Lidia y Jorge beben café. Ya son las nueve. Jorge pide la cuenta, la paga, le deja una buena propina al camarero y salen. Tienen entradas para el teatro para ver una comedia. Como llueve a cántaros, toman un taxi.

JORGE —Feliz aniversario, mi amor. *(Le da un beso.)*

LIDIA —*(Lo abraza.)* Feliz aniversario, querido.

Vocabulario

Cognados

el aniversario anniversary	**la especialidad** specialty	**el teatro** theater
la comedia comedy	**excelente** excellent	**el vermut** vermouth
cubano(-a) Cuban *la lista de platos*	**el menú** menu	
elegante elegant	**la sorpresa** surprise	

Nombres

el amor love	**el filete** tenderloin steak	**el pedido** order
el arroz rice	**el flan** caramel custard	**el postre** dessert
el beso kiss	**los frijoles** beans	**el precio** price
el bistec steak	**el helado** ice cream[1]	**la propina** tip
la botella bottle	**la langosta** lobster	**la pulsera** bracelet
los camarones shrimp	**el lechón** suckling pig (pork)	**la sopa** soup[1]
la comida food, meal	**el mozo, camarero, mesero** *(Mex.)* waiter[2]	**la tienda** store
el cordero lamb	**la papa, la patata** *(Sp.)* potato	**la torta helada** ice cream cake
la cuenta bill	**el pavo** turkey	
la entrada, el boleto ticket (i.e., for a show)		

Verbos

abrazar to hug	**encantar**[3] to love, to like very much	**preparar** to prepare
anotar to write down	**pedir (e:i)** to order	**recomendar (e:ie)** to recommend
dejar to leave (behind)		

Adjetivos

asado(-a) roasted	**relleno(-a)** stuffed	**tinto** red (wine)
helado(-a) iced, ice cold	**rico(-a), sabroso(-a)** tasty, delicious	
medio(-a) half		

Otras palabras y expresiones

aniversario de bodas wedding anniversary	**de postre** for dessert	**mi amor** my love, my darling
anoche last night	**después de** after	**por aquí** this way
anteayer the day before yesterday	**llover (o:ue) a cántaros** to rain cats and dogs, to pour down raining	**puré de papas** mashed potatoes
cuando when		**¡Qué sorpresa!** What a surprise!
		querido(-a) dear, darling

---

[1]In Spanish, the verb **tomar** is used with **sopa** and often with **helado**.
[2]*waitress:* **la camarera, mesera**
[3]**Encantar** has the same structure as **gustar**.

VOCABULARIO ADICIONAL

RESTAURANTE EL CARIBE
ESPECIALIDAD EN CARNES Y MARISCOS

Menú

PARA EL ALMUERZO

Sándwich de pollo	$3.50	Tortilla a la española *huevos*	$2.50
Sándwich de jamón y queso	$2.50	*(Omelette)*	
Sándwich de huevo *(egg)*	$1.50	Tortilla mexicana	$ .50
Sopa del día	$2.00	Frijoles	$1.75
Ensalada	$3.50	Arroz	$1.80
Hamburguesa[1]	$2.50	Arroz con frijoles negros	$2.00
Papas fritas *(French fries)*	$1.00		

PARA LA CENA
(Todos los platos de la lista se sirven[2] con la sopa del día y ensalada.)

Pescados y mariscos (Fish and shellfish)

Langosta	$18.00	Trucha *(Trout)*	$11.50
Salmón[1]	$14.50	Camarones	$11.00

Carne (Meat)

Albóndigas *(Meatballs)*	$ 6.00	Pavo relleno	$10.00
Bistec	$12.00	Pollo frito	$ 8.50
Cordero	$13.00	Arroz con pollo	$ 6.00
Lechón asado	$17.00	*(Chicken and rice)*	

POSTRES

Arroz con leche	$2.00	Helado	$1.50
(Rice pudding)		Frutas[1]	$1.25
Torta de chocolate[1]	$2.50	Queso	$3.00
Flan con crema	$2.50		

BEBIDAS

Agua mineral	$1.00	Café	$ .80
(Mineral water)		Té[1]	$ .80
Cerveza	$3.00	Chocolate caliente	$1.20
Champán	$6.00	*(Hot chocolate)*	
Vino blanco	$3.50	Jugo de frutas	$1.50
Vino tinto	$3.50	*(Fruit juice)*	
Vermut	$3.50	Leche fría *(Cold milk)*	$1.20

---

[1]These words are cognates, so you can guess what they mean.
[2]**se sirven** = *are served*

■ PARA PONER LA MESA (TO SET THE TABLE)

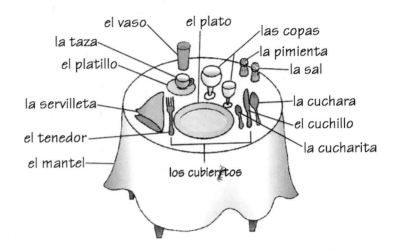

la taza
el vaso
el plato
las copas
la pimienta
el platillo
la sal
la servilleta
la cuchara
el tenedor
el cuchillo
el mantel
la cucharita
los cubiertos

¡CONVERSEMOS!

Answer the following questions, basing your answers on the dialogue.

1. ¿Cuándo es el aniversario de bodas de Lidia y Jorge?
2. ¿Qué dice Lidia del restaurante?
3. ¿Cuál es la especialidad de la casa?
4. ¿Qué pide Lidia?
5. ¿Qué pide Jorge?
6. ¿Qué beben Lidia y Jorge?
7. ¿Adónde fueron los padres de Jorge ayer?
8. ¿Qué compraron para Eva?
9. ¿Cuándo le enseñaron la pulsera a Jorge?
10. ¿Qué deja Jorge para el mozo?
11. ¿Qué dicen Jorge y Lidia al salir del restaurante?
12. ¿Por qué tienen que tomar un taxi para ir al teatro?

El Restaurant de la Familia

Lila's Restaurant

**EL BISTEC
CON PAPITAS FRITAS
MAS DELICIOSO DE MIAMI**

¿Lo sabía Ud.?

- La ciudad de Miami en el estado de la Florida es uno de los centros turísticos más importantes del mundo. Cientos de miles de turistas latinoamericanos la visitan todos los años. Más de un millón de hispanos viven en Miami, en su mayoría cubanos. El español se usa tanto en Miami que en muchos lugares hay letreros *(signs)* que dicen *"English spoken here"*.

- En los países de habla hispana, el café se sirve después del postre, nunca durante la comida. Generalmente es café tipo expreso, y se sirve en tazas muy pequeñas.

- Después de comer, los hispanos generalmente se quedan sentados *(remain seated)* alrededor de la mesa y conversan. A esto se le llama "hacer la sobremesa".

- En los países de habla hispana, la propina que generalmente se ofrece en los restaurantes es del 10%, pero hay variación según el país y el tipo de restaurante. Con frecuencia la propina está incluída en la cuenta.

Cubanos en un café de la Pequeña Habana en Miami, Florida.

PRONUNCIACIÓN

A The Spanish l

The Spanish l is pronounced like the *l* in the English word *lean*. The tip of the tongue must touch the palate. Listen to your instructor and repeat the following words.

langosta	Silvia	sólo
loco	helado	filete
capital	él	plato

B The Spanish r

The Spanish r sounds something like the *dd* in the English word *ladder*. Listen to your instructor and repeat the following words.

teatro	hora	tarde
dejar	Teresa	cordero
frijoles	primero	postre

C The Spanish **rr** (spelled **r** at the beginning of words and **rr** between vowels)

The Spanish **rr** is a strong trill. Listen to your instructor and pronounce the following words.

aburrido	Rosa	Reyes
rico	arroz	Roberto
recomendar	Raúl	relleno

D The Spanish **z**

In Latin America the Spanish **z** is pronounced like the *ss* in the English word *pressing*. In Spain it is pronounced like the *th* in the English word *think*. Avoid using the buzzing sound of the English *z* in the words *zoo* and *zebra*. Listen to your instructor and repeat the following words.

pizarra	vez	Pérez
Zulema	zoológico	taza
lápiz	mozo	azul

ESTRUCTURAS

1 Direct and indirect object pronouns used together
(Pronombres de complemento directo e indirecto usados juntos)

■ When an indirect object pronoun and a direct object pronoun are used together, the indirect object pronoun always comes first.

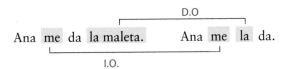

D.O

Ana me da la maleta.   Ana me la da.

I.O.

■ With an infinitive, the pronouns can either be placed before the conjugated verb or be attached to the infinitive.

      I.O. D.O.

Ana me la va a dar.

Ana va a dármela.[1]

■ With the present progressive, the pronouns can either be placed before the conjugated verb or be attached to the gerund.

      I.O. D.O.

Ella te lo está diciendo.

Ella está diciéndotelo.[1]

---

[1]Note the use of the written accent, which follows the rules for accentuation. See Appendix A.

■ If both pronouns begin with **l**, the indirect object pronoun (**le** or **les**) is changed to **se**.

$$
\underset{\text{I.O.}}{\underbrace{\text{Ana le da}}}\ \underset{\text{D.O}}{\overbrace{\text{la cuenta.}}}\qquad \text{Ana se la da.}
$$

For clarification, it is sometimes necessary to add **a él, a ella, a Ud., a Uds., a ellos,** or **a ellas**.

— ¿A quién le da la cuenta Ana?
— **Se la da a él.**

Práctica

A. Complete the following dialogues, using direct and indirect object pronouns. Then act them out with a partner, adding a sentence or two to each dialogue.

1. —¿*Le* dejaste *la propina* al mozo?
   —Sí, _____ _____ dejé en la mesa.
2. —¿*Me* compraste *las entradas* para el teatro?
   —No, no _____ _____ compré. Lo siento.
3. —¿El mozo *te* sirvió *el café*?
   —Sí, _____ _____ sirvió.
4. —¿*Le* vas a dar *la pulsera* a tu madre?
   —Sí, _____ _____ voy a dar mañana.
5. —¿*Nos* va a traer *los postres* ahora?
   —Sí, _____ _____ voy a traer ahora.
6. —¿El mozo *les* va a traer a Uds. *la cuenta*?
   —Sí, va a traér_____ en seguida.

B. You have a friend who is always willing to help others. Explain how, using the information provided.

> MODELO: Yo necesito *una maleta.* (comprar)
> *Mi amigo **me la** compra.*

1. Yo necesito *dos tarjetas postales.* (comprar)
2. Tú necesitas *los discos compactos.* (traer)
3. Nosotros queremos *frutas.* (servir)
4. Elsa necesita *un bolso de mano.* (prestar)
5. Mis hermanos necesitan *dinero.* (dar)
6. Mi prima necesita *las maletas.* (traer)
7. Ud. necesita *la cinta.* (enviar)
8. Yo quiero *los periódicos.* (dar)

C. You are in a bad mood, and people keep asking you to do things you don't want to do. Tell them you can't do the favors they are requesting.

> MODELO: —¿Puedes traer*me el menú?*
> —*No, no puedo traértelo.*

1. —¿Puedes traer*me las servilletas?*
2. —¿Puedes dar*le el mantel* a Julio?
3. —¿Puedes comprar*le la pulsera* a mamá?
4. —¿Puedes prestar*me los cubiertos?*
5. —¿Puedes traer*nos el helado?*
6. —¿Puedes dar*le las cucharas* a Luisa?

D. Now repeat Exercise C, following the model below.

> MODELO: — ¿Puedes traer*me el menú?*
> — *No, no **te lo** puedo traer.*

E. Interview a classmate, using the following questions and two questions of your own. When you have finished, switch roles.

1. Cuando tú necesitas dinero, ¿a quién se lo pides?
2. Cuando tú les pides dinero a tus padres, ¿te lo dan?
3. Si yo necesito tu libro de español, ¿me lo prestas?
4. Si Uds. no entienden algo, ¿se lo preguntan a su profesor(-a)?
5. Si tú y yo somos amigos y yo necesito tu coche, ¿tú me lo prestas?
6. Necesito tu pluma. ¿Puedes prestármela?

F. With a partner, act out the following dialogues in Spanish.

1. "Are you going to give me the tickets for the theater?"
   "Yes, I'm going to give them to you tonight, Miss Peña."
2. "When did you send him the postcards, Paquito?"
   "I sent them to him yesterday."
3. "And the suitcase? Can you lend it to me?"
   "Yes, Anita, I am going to lend it to you."
4. "Did your grandmother send you the cake, Mr. Vega?"
   "Yes, she sent it to us yesterday."
5. "Are they going to give us the bill?"
   "Yes, they're going to give it to us."

2 Preterit of **ser**, **ir**, and **dar** *(Pretérito de los verbos ser, ir y dar)*

■ The preterit forms of **ser**, **ir**, and **dar** are irregular.

ser *to be*	**ir** *to go*	**dar** *to give*
fui	fui	di
fuiste	fuiste	diste
fue	fue	dio
fuimos	fuimos	dimos
fuisteis	fuisteis	disteis
fueron	fueron	dieron

■ Note that **ser** and **ir** have identical forms in the preterit.

—Ayer **fue** el cumpleaños de
　Lucía, ¿no?

—Sí, Ana y yo **fuimos** a su casa y
　le **dimos** el reloj.

—¿**Fuiste** a la fiesta que **dio**
　Sara?

—Sí, **fui**. **Fue** la mejor fiesta del
　año.

"Yesterday was Lucía's birthday,
　right?"

"Yes, Ana and I went to her house
　and gave her the clock."

"Did you go to the party that Sara
　gave?"

"Yes, I went. It was the best party
　of the year."

Práctica

A. Complete the following dialogues, using the preterit of **ser**, **ir**, or **dar** as appropriate. Then act them out with a partner, adding a sentence or two to each dialogue.

1. —¿Adónde _____ tú ayer?
   —_____ a la tienda. Compré una pulsera de oro y se la _____ a mi esposa.
2. —¿ _____ Uds. a casa de tía Eva ayer?
   —Sí, _____ y le _____ el libro que tú mandaste para ella.
3. —¿Uds. _____ estudiantes del Dr. Paz?
   —Carlos _____ su estudiante, pero Raquel y yo _____ estudiantes de la Dra. Guerra.
4. —¿A quién le _____ (tú) la botella de vino tinto?
   —Se la _____ a Jorge.
5. —¿Adónde _____ Uds. anoche?
   —_____ al teatro. Los padres de Dora nos _____ las entradas.

B. Interview a classmate, using the following questions. When you have finished, switch roles.

1. ¿Quién fue tu profesor(-a) favorito(-a) el año pasado?
2. ¿Fuiste a la cafetería ayer? ¿A qué hora?
3. ¿Adónde fuiste el sábado pasado?
4. ¿Tus amigos fueron también?
5. ¿Dieron tus amigos una fiesta para celebrar tu cumpleaños?
6. ¿Diste una fiesta el viernes pasado?

3 Preterit of **e:i** and **o:u** stem-changing verbs
*(Pretérito de los verbos que cambian en la raíz: **e:i** y **o:u**)*

■ Verbs of the -**ir** conjugation that have a stem change in the present tense change e to i and o to u in the third-person singular and plural of the preterit.[1]

preferir *to prefer*		**dormir** *to sleep*	
preferí	preferimos	dormí	dormimos
preferiste	preferisteis	dormiste	dormisteis
prefirió	prefirieron	durmió	durmieron

■ Other verbs that follow the same pattern:

pedir	seguir
mentir *(to lie)*	conseguir
servir	morir
repetir *(to repeat)*	

—Ella dice que no **durmió** anoche.   *"She says she didn't sleep last night."*
—Te **mintió**.   *"She lied to you."*

—¿Qué **pidieron** ellos?   *"What did they order?"*
—Raúl **pidió** camarones y Rosa **pidió** langosta.   *"Raúl ordered shrimp and Rosa ordered lobster."*

Práctica

A. Find out what Andrés did yesterday by adding the correct form of the missing verbs.

1. Yo _____ (ir) a visitar a mi padre y le _____ (pedir) dinero.
2. _____ (Conseguir) entradas para el teatro.
3. _____ (Salir) con otra chica y le _____ (mentir) a mi novia.
4. Nosotros _____ (ir) a un restaurante y yo _____ (pedir) cordero asado; ella _____ (pedir) langosta.
5. Yo _____ (volver) a mi casa y _____ (dormir) dos horas.
6. Mis padres me _____ (invitar) a una fiesta pero yo _____ (preferir) no ir.
7. Por la noche, yo _____ (dar) una fiesta y _____ (servir) ponche.

B. Now, using the information above, prepare questions to ask your classmates.

---

[1]Remember that the -**ar** and -**er** stem-changing verbs are regular in the preterit: **él cerró, ellos volvieron.** Exceptions are **poder** and **querer,** which are explained in **Lección 9.**

4 Weather expressions   *(Expresiones para describir el tiempo)*

■ In the following expressions, Spanish uses the verb **hacer,** *to make,* followed by a noun.

Hace (mucho) **frío.**	*It is (very) cold.*
Hace (mucho) **calor.**	*It is (very) hot.*
Hace (mucho) **viento.**	*It is (very) windy.*
Hace sol.	*It is sunny.*

■ To ask about the weather, say, "**¿Qué tiempo hace?**" *(What's the weather like?).*

—¿**Qué tiempo hace** hoy?   *"What's the weather like today?"*

—**Hace** buen (mal) **tiempo.**   *"The weather is good (bad)."*

■ The following words used to describe the weather do not combine with **hacer;** they are impersonal verbs used only in the infinitive, present participle, past participle, and third-person singular forms of all tenses.

llover (o:ue) *to rain*	**Llueve.** *It is raining (It rains).*
lloviznar *to drizzle*	**Llovizna.** *It is drizzling (It drizzles).*
nevar (e:ie) *to snow*	**Nieva.** *It is snowing (It snows).*

■ Other weather-related words are **lluvia** *(rain)* and **niebla** *(fog).*

—¿**Hace** mucho **frío** en Buenos   *"Is it very cold in Buenos*
  Aires?   *Aires?"*

—Sí, pero nunca **nieva.**   *"Yes, but it never snows."*

—¿Vas a volar hoy a San   *"Are you going to fly to San*
  Francisco?   *Francisco today?"*

—No, porque **hay niebla.**   *"No, because it's foggy.[1]"*

Práctica

A. Study the words in the following list, then complete the dialogues.

el paraguas *umbrella*		**el abrigo** *coat*	
el impermeable *raincoat*		**el suéter** *sweater*	
el sombrero *hat*			

1. —¿Necesitas un paraguas?
   —Sí, porque en Oregón _____ mucho.
2. —¿No necesitas un abrigo?
   —No, porque _____ .
3. —¿Quieres un impermeable?
   —No, gracias, apenas *(hardly)* _____ .

---

[1]**hay niebla** = *it's foggy*

4. —¿Por qué no quieres llevar el suéter?
  —¡Porque _____ !
5. —¿Vas a llevar el sombrero?
  —Sí, porque _____ .
6. —¿Necesitas un suéter y un abrigo?
  —Sí, porque _____ .
7. —¿Un impermeable? ¿Por qué? ¿Llueve? ¿Llovizna?
  —No, pero _____ .
8. —¡Qué lluvia! Necesito un _____ y un _____ .

B. Say what the weather will be like in different locations at different times of the year.

1. Portland, Oregón–el 2 de enero
2. Anchorage, Alaska–el 25 de diciembre
3. Phoenix, Arizona–el 13 de agosto
4. Londres *(London)*–el 5 de febrero
5. Chicago–el 6 de marzo

C. A visiting professor from a Hispanic country is planning a weekend visit to your hometown. What questions is he or she likely to ask about the weather there and what clothes to bring? How will you respond? Act out the scene with a partner. Say at least five lines each.

D. You and a classmate are in charge of preparing the weather report for a local T.V. station. Discuss the weather in your area today.

| Sol | Nublado | Cubierto | Posibilidad de lluvia | Lluvia | Tormenta | Nieve |

5 Uses of **por** and **para**   *(Usos de por y para)*

A. Uses of por

The preposition **por** is used to express the following concepts.

■ motion or approximate location *(through, around, along, by)*

Luis salió **por** la ventana.	*Luis went out through the window.*
Enrique va **por** la calle Juárez.	*Enrique is going down Juárez Street.*
Gustavo pasó **por** el hotel.	*Gustavo went by the hotel.*

■ cause or motive of an action *(because of, on account of, on behalf of)*

| Llegamos tarde **por** la lluvia. | *We were late because of the rain.* |
| Lo hago **por** ellos. | *I do it on their behalf.* |

■ means, manner, unit of measure *(by, for, per)*

Siempre viajamos **por** tren.	*We always travel by train.*
Van a 100 kilómetros **por** hora.	*They're going 100 kilometers per hour.*

■ *in exchange for*

Te doy veinte dólares **por** esa grabadora.	*I'll give you twenty dollars for that tape recorder.*

■ period of time during which an action takes place *(during, in, for)*

Ella prepara la comida **por** la mañana.	*She prepares the meal in the morning.*
Va a estar aquí **por** dos meses.	*He's going to be here for two months.*

■ *in search of, for*

Voy a venir **por** ti a las siete.	*I'll come by for you at seven.*

Práctica

Interview a classmate, using the following questions. When you have finished, switch roles.

1. ¿Tienes una clase por la mañana?
2. Antes de ir a clase, ¿vas por tus amigos?
3. ¿Cuánto pagaste por tu libro de español?
4. ¿Pasaste por mi casa anoche?
5. Si tú pierdes la llave de tu casa, ¿entras por la ventana?
6. ¿Tus padres hacen mucho por ti?
7. ¿Tú les escribes a tus padres o prefieres llamarlos por teléfono?
8. ¿Prefieres viajar por tren o por avión? ¿Por qué?

B. Uses of para

The preposition **para** is used to express the following concepts.

■ destination

Quiero un pasaje **para** Montevideo.	*I want a ticket for Montevideo.*
¿A qué hora hay vuelos **para** Buenos Aires?	*What time are the flights to Buenos Aires?*

■ goal for a point in the future *(by or for a certain time)*

Quiero el dinero **para** el sábado.	*I want the money for Saturday.*
Debo estar allí **para** el mes de noviembre.	*I must be there by the month of November.*

■ whom or what something is for

Compré una mesa **para** mi cuarto.	*I bought a table for my room.*
Compramos los libros **para** Fernando.	*We bought the books for Fernando.*

■ *in order to*

Necesito mil dólares **para** pagar el viaje.	*I need a thousand dollars in order to pay for the trip.*
Vamos al teatro **para** celebrar nuestro aniversario de bodas.	*We are going to the theater (in order) to celebrate our wedding anniversary.*

■ objective or goal

Mi novio estudia **para** profesor.	*My boyfriend is studying to be a professor.*

Práctica

A. Look at the illustrations and describe what is happening, using **por** or **para**.

1. Fuimos _____ a Miami.

2. Daniel salió _____ .

3. La torta es _____ .

4. Luisa va a estar en Orlando _____ .

5. Jorge pagó _____ el vino.

6. Eva sale mañana _____ .

B. Imagine that you and your best friend are planning a trip to Spain. Answer the following questions.

1. ¿Cuánto dinero necesitan Uds. para pagar el viaje?
2. ¿Van a pedirles dinero a sus padres para el viaje?
3. ¿Para qué día quieren los pasajes?
4. ¿A qué hora sale el avión para Madrid?
5. ¿Van a traer regalos *(gifts)* para su familia?
6. ¿Van Uds. a España para practicar el español?
7. John estudia para profesor de español y quiere visitar Madrid. ¿Puede ir con Uds.?

C. Complete the following description of a trip to Paraguay, using **por** or **para**.

Robert y yo salimos _____ Asunción la semana próxima. Vamos a viajar _____ avión. Tenemos pasajes _____ el sábado _____ la mañana. Pagamos tres mil dólares _____ los billetes, pero como pensamos pasar _____ Caracas y _____ Lima, donde vamos a estar _____ unos días, no es muy caro. Mañana _____ la tarde vamos a Bloomingdale's _____ comprar algunos regalos _____ nuestros amigos paraguayos. Desde Lima, vamos a llamar _____ teléfono a nuestros amigos en Asunción, y ellos van a ir al aeropuerto _____ nosotros.

D. Plan a trip to a Hispanic country with a classmate. Using the paragraph in Exercise C as a model, describe your travel plans.

¡A VER CUÁNTO APRENDIÓ!

¡Repase el vocabulario!

Match each question in column A with the answers in column B, and then read them aloud.

A
1. ¿Qué celebran hoy?
2. ¿Está rico el pavo relleno?
3. ¿Cuál es la especialidad de la casa?
4. ¿Qué bebidas prefieres?
5. ¿Qué quieres de postre?
6. ¿Vas a pedir agua mineral?
7. ¿Qué está anotando el mozo?
8. ¿Quieres bistec?
9. ¿Adónde vamos esta noche?
10. ¿Está lloviendo?
11. ¿No quieres camarones?
12. ¿Cuánto vas a dejar de propina?
13. ¿Qué venden en McDonald's?
14. ¿Quién paga la cuenta?
15. ¿Quieres café?
16. ¿Te gusta la pulsera?

B
a. Flan con helado.
b. Sí, quiero pedirlos, pero son muy caros.
c. El pedido.
d. Lechón asado con arroz y frijoles negros.
e. Sí, a cántaros.
f. Hamburguesas.
g. Sí, me encanta.
h. Ocho dólares.
i. Sí, está muy sabroso.
j. Ana.
k. Sí, una botella.
l. No, prefiero té.
m. Al teatro.
n. Su aniversario de bodas.
o. Sí, quiero comer carne.
p. Vermut o vino tinto.

Entrevista

You and a classmate are at the El Caribe Restaurant. Look at the menu on page 188 and ask the following questions, using the **tú** form.

Pregúntele a su compañero(-a) de clase…

1. …qué va a pedir.
2. …qué le recomienda para comer.

3. …qué prefiere tomar: vino blanco, champán o agua mineral.
4. …qué quiere de postre: arroz con leche, torta o flan con crema.
5. …cuánto es la cuenta.
6. …cuánto va a dejar de propina.
7. …qué van a hacer después de cenar.
8. …si sabe peparar algún postre sabroso. ¿Cuál?

Situaciones

What would you say in the following situations? What might the other person say? Act out the scenes with a partner. Take turns playing each role.

1. You are at a restaurant, and you are very hungry. Ask to see the menu; order a first and second course and something to drink while you wait for your food. Then tell the waiter what you want for dessert.
2. You are a waiter or waitress. Recommend two or three main dishes and a dessert to your customers. Ask them if they want coffee or tea.
3. You are cooking a gourmet dinner. Ask your roommate to set the table. Name the utensils and other items you want.
4. You are hosting a party at your home. Some of your guests have brought children. Offer a selection of beverages.

Para escribir

Write a dialogue between a waiter or waitress and a customer. Include the following exchanges.

■ asking for a menu

■ ordering the food, drink(s), and dessert

■ asking for the check

En la vida real

¿Qué les servimos?

You and a classmate are hosting a special weekend for some foreign students. Discuss the breakfast, lunch, and dinner menus you will be preparing, taking into account your guests' different peculiarities.

- María Inés Soto is a vegetarian.

- Juan Carlos Reyes loves meat and dairy products.

- Isabel Peña is on a diet.

- Francisco Rojas is extremely thin and wants to gain weight.

- Raquel Arias loves seafood.

Some additional words and phrases that you might include:

el chorizo *sausage* ⎫ **con huevos** **el pan** *bread*
el tocino *bacon* ⎭ *with eggs* **el panqueque** *pancake*
el cereal *cereal* **el yogur** *yogurt*
la mantequilla *butter* **las zanahorias** *carrots*
la mermelada *jam*

¡Vamos a cenar!

You and a classmate have received a $40.00 gift coupon to eat dinner at the El Caribe Restaurant. Select what you are going to have, including drinks and dessert. And don't forget to leave a tip!

¡Buen provecho!

You and a friend have decided to go out to dinner tonight. Read the following ads for Hispanic restaurants in Miami, and answer the questions that follow.

1. Ud. y un amigo quieren comer pescado. ¿A qué restaurante pueden ir?
2. Si quieren hacer reservaciones en ese restaurante, ¿a qué número deben llamar?
3. ¿Cuál es la especialidad del restaurante Las Redes?
4. ¿Por qué es famoso el restaurante Segovia?
5. ¿Cuándo hay música en el restaurante Segovia?
6. ¿Cuánto cuesta el almuerzo allí?
7. ¿Qué comidas típicas cubanas sirven en el restaurante La Carreta?
8. Si quieren dar un banquete, ¿a qué restaurante deben ir?
9. ¿En qué calle está El Bodegón Castilla?
10. ¿Cree Ud. que en El Bodegón Castilla sirven comida cubana o española?

¡Vamos a leer!

Antes de leer

As you read Teresa's letter, find the answers to the following questions.

1. ¿Son buenas amigas Teresa y Ángela? ¿Cómo lo sabe Ud.?
2. ¿Teresa está de vacaciones todavía?
3. ¿Qué dice Teresa de las ruinas de Machu Picchu?
4. ¿A quién le mandó Teresa tarjetas postales?
5. ¿Cómo se llama el muchacho a quien Teresa conoció en Lima? ¿De dónde es?
6. ¿De qué conversaron Teresa y el muchacho?
7. ¿Qué dice Teresa de los peruanos?
8. ¿Adónde la llevaron los amigos de su padre?
9. ¿Qué le recomienda Teresa a Ángela?
10. ¿Adónde va a ir Teresa? ¿Por qué?

Una carta de Teresa

12 de septiembre de 1998

Querida Ángela:

Hace mucho tiempo que no te escribo, pero siempre pienso en ti. Ya estoy de vuelta° de mi viaje a Perú. Me gustó todo, pero especialmente Machu Picchu, las famosas ruinas de los incas, que son muy interesantes. Ya sé que no te mandé tarjetas postales, pero tampoco le mandé ninguna a nadie.

estoy... I'm back

En Lima conocí a un muchacho argentino muy simpático y muy educado. Se llama José Luis Vera Vierci. Conversamos mucho, de todo tema° imaginable. Me mandó una tarjeta desde Buenos Aires, donde él vive.

topic

Los peruanos son encantadores.° Me trataron° muy bien. Los amigos de mi padre me llevaron a muchos lugares, especialmente al teatro, al cine y... ¡a restaurantes! La comida es muy buena, tan buena que aumenté° dos kilos.

charming / they treated

I gained

Bueno, para tus próximas vacaciones, te recomiendo una visita a Perú. Y ahora te dejo porque voy a ir a cenar con mis padres. Hoy es su aniversario de bodas. Hace treinta y cinco años que están casados.

Te extraño mucho. Saludos a Sandra y a Marcelo.

Un abrazo,

Teresa

Díganos

Answer the following questions, based on your own thoughts and feelings.

1. ¿Cuánto tiempo hace que Ud. no le escribe a su mejor amigo(-a)?
2. ¿A quién le manda Ud. tarjetas postales cuando va de vacaciones?
3. ¿Qué lugares interesantes visitó Ud. el verano pasado?
4. ¿Conoció Ud. a alguien simpático(-a) durante sus vacaciones?
5. Cuando Ud. conversa con sus amigos, ¿de qué temas hablan Uds.?
6. Cuando Ud. visita a sus amigos, ¿adónde lo (la) llevan?
7. ¿Qué me recomienda Ud. para mis próximas vacaciones?
8. ¿Cuándo es el aniversario de bodas de sus padres?

MÉXICO

México

- Con más de veintitrés millones de habitantes en el área metropolitana, la Ciudad de México es el centro urbano más grande del mundo. Fundada por los aztecas en el año 1325, es también la capital más antigua de América.

- El turismo es una de las principales fuentes de ingresos *(sources of income)* de la economía mexicana. Cancún, Acapulco, Puerto Vallarta, Ixtapa, Mazatlán y otros centros turísticos reciben millones de visitantes todos los años, principalmente de los Estados Unidos.

- La comida mexicana es muy conocida *(well known)* en los Estados Unidos. Muchos de los alimentos típicos mexicanos, como los frijoles y las tortillas de maíz, son de origen indígena. Los platos más populares son las enchiladas, el guacamole, los tamales y los tacos.

- Antes de la conquista de México por parte de los españoles, existían allí numerosas culturas indígenas, las de los aztecas, los mayas, los toltecas y los mixtecas, entre otras. Aún hoy existen grandes concentraciones de indígenas en las regiones de Yucatán, Chiapas y Oaxaca.

En muchos lugares de México es posible visitar ruinas muy bien conservadas, como por ejemplo las pirámides, que son un elemento muy importante de la arquitectura prehispánica. Ésta es la Pirámide del Mago en Uxmal, una antigua ciudad maya en la península de Yucatán. Está formada por cinco templos construídos uno encima *(on top)* del otro.
¿Qué culturas indígenas existen en su país?

La península de Yucatán es famosa no sólo por sus ruinas mayas sino *(but)* también por sus playas *(beaches)* de aguas cálidas *(warm)* y cristalinas. A cien kilómetros de Cancún está Akumal, un centro turístico de belleza *(beauty)* inigualable. **¿Qué centros turísticos hay en el estado donde Ud. vive?**

El mercado del pueblo de Tlacolula, en el estado de Oaxaca, es uno de los más famosos de México. Allí los indígenas de la región venden productos agrícolas y también objetos de artesanía, como vasijas de barro *(clay pots)* y sarapes. Lo más popular de la artesanía de Oaxaca es la cerámica negra. **¿Le gustan a Ud. los objetos de artesanía?**

Este mural del famoso artista mexicano Diego Rivera
presenta la historia y las costumbres de la civilización
totoneca. El mural está en el Palacio Nacional,
construído en el lugar donde antes estaba el palacio del
emperador azteca Moctezuma. Otros murales famosos
de Rivera están en el Ministerio de Educación y en la
Universidad Nacional Autónoma de México, ambos
(both) en la Ciudad de México.
¿Conoce Ud. otros pintores mexicanos? ¿Cuáles?

Guadalajara, capital del estado de Jalisco, con más de cinco
millones de habitantes, es la segunda ciudad de México en
población. La ciudad tiene una rica tradición cultural. En ella
se mezclan magníficos ejemplos de la arquitectura y el arte
español coloniales con modernas avenidas y edificios
contemporáneos. Aquí vemos el patio del Museo del
Estado, famoso por sus magníficas pinturas de José
Clemente Orozco.
¿Cuál es la capital del estado donde Ud. vive?

El Ballet Folklórico de México le ofrece al público espectáculos llenos *(full)* de arte y color. El ballet actúa *(performs)* los miércoles y los domingos en el Palacio de Bellas Artes de la Ciudad de México. Sus danzas y trajes típicos son de una gran belleza *(beauty)*.
¿A Ud. le gusta bailar? ¿Por qué o por qué no?

El primero y el dos de noviembre se celebra en México el Día de los Muertos *(Dead)*. En la foto, una mujer reza *(prays)* en el Cementerio de Patzcuaro, en el estado de Michoacán. Los habitantes del pueblo llevan comida a las tumbas de sus familiares y se quedan *(they stay)* allí toda la noche. Miles de velas *(candles)* y flores de papel adornan el cementerio, creando un espectáculo inolvidable.
¿Existe un equivalente al Día de los Muertos en su país?

Estatua de Cuauhtémoc, último emperador azteca, que fue vencido *(defeated)* por Hernán Cortés en 1521. Cuauhtémoc simboliza el orgullo *(pride)* del pueblo *(people, nation)* mexicano.
¿Qué estatuas importantes hay en su ciudad?

El Paseo de la Reforma en la Ciudad de México. En este paseo hay numerosos monumentos impresionantes, entre ellos la estatua del rey Carlos IV de España, el espléndido monumento a Cristóbal Colón *(Christopher Columbus)* y el del Ángel de la Independencia, que vemos en la foto.
¿Qué monumentos históricos hay en la ciudad de Washington, D.C.?

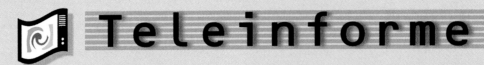

Teleinforme

Vocabulario

La Ciudad de México y Teotihuacán

la altivez	arrogance
el comienzo	beginning
el descubrimiento	discovery
fue tallada	was carved
la gran urbe	the big city
los ladrillos secados al sol	sun-dried bricks
el peso	weight
la piedra	stone
proporciona	offers
los restos	remains
vencido	defeated

Cancún

la altura	height
los costados	sides
de primera categoría	first-class
los escalones	steps
el mar	sea
los rincones	corners
rodeada de murallas	surrounded by walls
se halla	is found
una de las pocas	one of the few

Guadalajara

apuntando hacia el cielo	pointing to the sky
la ayuda	help
el corazón	heart, center
corre libremente	runs freely
doradas	golden
se acerca a	approaches
se arrodillaron	knelt down
la tierra	land
los viejos muros	old walls

El Día de los Muertos

el ánima *(f.)*	spirit, soul
bullanguera	noisy
las costumbres	customs
los deudos	the relatives of the deceased
el día siguiente	the following day
los dulces	sweets
hoy en día	nowadays
los juguetes	toys
La Pelona	*(Mex.)* Death (colloquial; literally, the bald one)
velan	keep watch over

Preparación

¿Cuánto saben Uds. ya?   After reading the information in **Panorama hispánico 4**, get together in groups of three or four and answer the following questions.

1. ¿Cuál es el centro urbano más grande del mundo?
2. ¿Cuántos millones de habitantes tiene la Ciudad de México?
3. ¿Por quiénes fue fundada la Ciudad de México?
4. ¿Cuáles son algunos de los centros turísticos de México?
5. ¿Cómo es la arquitectura de Guadalajara?
6. ¿Cuándo se celebra el Día de los Muertos?
7. ¿Qué llevan ese día los familiares a las tumbas de sus muertos?
8. ¿Con qué adornan el cementerio el Día de los Muertos?

Comprensión

A. La Ciudad de México y Teotihuacán.   Complete the following statements with the appropriate words.

1. La Ciudad de México comenzó a construirse en el siglo _____ .
2. El Paseo de la _____ es la principal arteria de la gran urbe mexicana.
3. El _____ de América fue en 1492.
4. Cuauhtémoc fue el último emperador _____ .
5. A la entrada del Museo Antropológico está la _____ del dios de la lluvia. Esta estatua tiene 170 toneladas *(tons)* de _____ .
6. La Pirámide del _____ está en Teotihuacán.
7. Se usaron _____ secados al sol para construir la gran pirámide.

B. Guadalajara.   Select the word or phrase that best completes each statement.

1. En Guadalajara, la música (de salsa, de mariachis) corre libremente por la ciudad.
2. (Guadalajara, Guanajuato) es la capital del estado de Jalisco.
3. La población de Guadalajara es de unos (tres, cinco) millones de habitantes.
4. Guadalajara es la (segunda, tercera) ciudad en importancia en México.

C. Cancún.   Read the following statements and circle **V** (**Verdadero**) or **F** (**Falso**), according to what you understood.

V F   1. Hay ruinas mayas cerca de Cancún.
V F   2. En Cancún no hay playas.
V F   3. En Cancún hay muchos hoteles de primera categoría.
V F   4. Solamente los mexicanos visitan Cancún.
V F   5. La pirámide de Cobá es la más alta de la península de Yucatán.

D. El Día de los Muertos.   Complete the following statements with the appropriate words.

1. El Día de los Muertos es una festividad _____ y _____ .
2. En México llaman a la muerte "La _____ ".
3. Flores, pan de muerto, _____ para los niños, _____ y velas dan ambiente *(atmosphere)* a esta celebración.
4. Los deudos velan las ofrendas *(offerings)* toda la _____ y todo el día _____ .

Ampliación

Planes de vacaciones.   In groups of three or four, discuss which places you want to visit in Mexico City, Teotihuacán, Guadalajara, and Cancún and what you want to do and see while you are there.

UN DÍA MUY OCUPADO

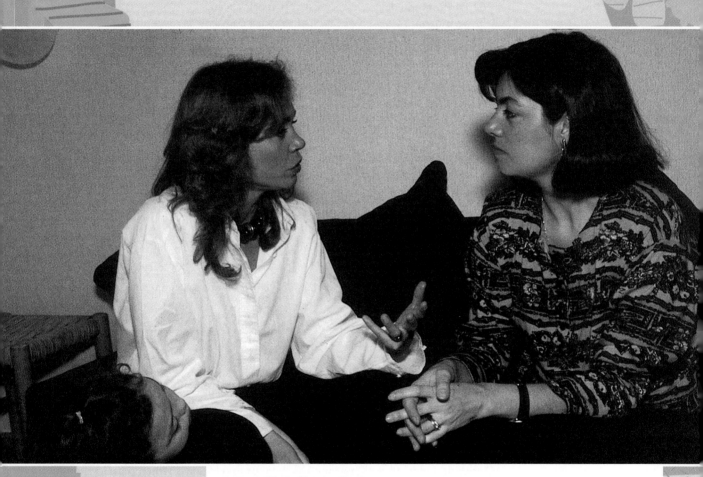

OBJECTIVES

Pronunciation
La entonación

Structure
Reflexive constructions • Some uses of the definite article • Possessive pronouns • Irregular preterits • Ordinal numbers

Communication
You will learn vocabulary related to household chores and the hairdresser.

Un día muy ocupado

Aunque hoy es sábado, Mirta e Isabel se levantaron temprano para terminar de limpiar el apartamento. Esta noche, las dos chicas están invitadas a un concierto en la Casa de Cultura Paraguaya. Isabel está un poco cansada porque anoche se acostó tarde.

MIRTA —¿Por qué viniste tan tarde anoche? ¿Dónde estuviste?

ISABEL —En la tienda. Tuve que comprar un regalo para Eva porque mañana es su cumpleaños. Bueno, ¿empezamos a limpiar?

MIRTA —Sí, yo voy a barrer la cocina y le voy a pasar la aspiradora a la alfombra.

ISABEL —Entonces yo voy a limpiar el baño. Después voy a cocinar y a planchar mi vestido rojo. Me lo voy a poner esta noche.

MIRTA —Yo no sé qué ponerme.

ISABEL —¿Por qué no te pones el vestido azul? Es muy bonito.

MIRTA —No, me lo probé ayer y no me queda bien. ¡Ah! ¿Dónde está la palita?

ISABEL —En la terraza. ¡Ay! Necesito bañar al perro, ducharme y vestirme... ¡y tengo turno en la peluquería a las tres!

MIRTA —Yo quiero lavarme la cabeza y no me acordé de comprar champú. ¿Puedo usar el tuyo?

ISABEL —Sí, está en el botiquín.

MIRTA —Gracias. Yo no pude ir a la farmacia ayer.

Cuando llegó a la peluquería, Isabel le pidió una revista al peluquero y se sentó a esperar su turno.

ISABEL —*(Al peluquero)* Quiero corte, lavado y peinado.

PELUQUERO —Tiene el pelo muy lacio. ¿No quiere una permanente?

ISABEL —No, cuando quiero rizos, uso el rizador. ¡Ay, tengo el pelo muy largo!

PELUQUERO —Ahora está de moda el pelo corto. *(Le corta el pelo y, cuando termina, Isabel se mira en el espejo.)*

ISABEL —¡Muy bien! Ahora quiero pedir turno para mi amiga para la semana próxima.

PELUQUERO —¿El miércoles, primero de febrero, a las nueve y media? Generalmente hay menos gente por la mañana.

ISABEL —Está bien. Mi amiga se llama Mirta Ortega.

Isabel deja la cartera en el mostrador. El peluquero la llama.

PELUQUERO —¡Señorita! ¿Esta cartera es suya?

ISABEL —Sí, es mía. Gracias.

VOCABULARIO

NOMBRES

la alfombra rug, carpet	**el lavado** shampoo, wash	**el perro** dog
la aspiradora vacuum cleaner	**el mostrador** counter	**el regalo** present
el botiquín medicine cabinet	**la palita, el recogedor** dustpan	**la revista** magazine
la cartera, el bolso, la bolsa (*Méx.*) purse, handbag	**el peinado** hairdo, hairstyle	**el rizador** curling iron
la cocina kitchen	**el pelo** hair	**el rizo** curl
el corte haircut, cut	**la peluquería, el salón de belleza** salon, beauty parlor	**la semana** week
el espejo mirror	**el (la) peluquero(-a)** hairdresser, beautician	**el turno, la cita** appointment
la gente[2] people		**el vestido** dress

VERBOS

acordarse (o:ue)[3] to remember	**esperar** to wait (for)	**probarse (o:ue)** to try on
acostarse (o:ue) to go to bed	**lavar(se)** to wash (oneself)	**quedar** to fit
bañar(se) to bathe (oneself)	**levantarse** to get up	**sentarse (e:ie)** to sit down
barrer to sweep	**limpiar(se)** to clean (oneself)	**terminar** to finish
cocinar to cook	**llamarse** to be called	**usar** to use, to wear
cortar(se) to cut (oneself)	**planchar** to iron	**vestirse (e:i)** to get dressed
ducharse to take a shower	**ponerse** to put on	

ADJETIVOS

corto(-a)   short
lacio   straight (hair)

OTRAS PALABRAS Y EXPRESIONES

aunque although	**lavarse la cabeza** to wash one's hair	**pedir (e:i) turno, cita** to make an appointment
cortarse el pelo to get a haircut	**pasar la aspiradora** to vacuum	**temprano** early
estar de moda to be in style		
estar invitado(-a) to be invited		

---

[1]In many countries, *la* **permanente** is used.
[2]**Gente** is used in the singular in Spanish.
[3]**Acordarse** is always used with a reflexive pronoun.

VOCABULARIO ADICIONAL

■ EN LA BARBERÍA

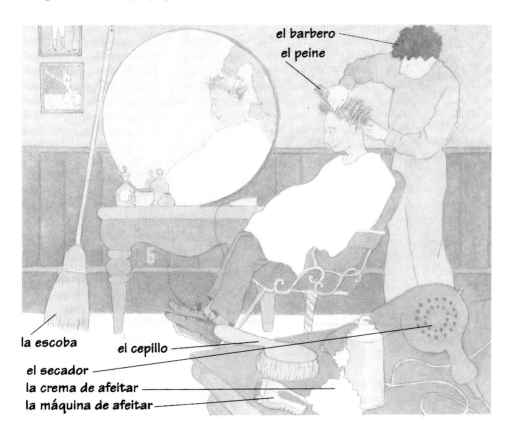

el barbero
el peine
la escoba
el cepillo
el secador
la crema de afeitar
la máquina de afeitar

■ VERBOS ÚTILES

ensuciar(se) to get (oneself) dirty	El niño **se ensució** las manos.
olvidarse (de) to forget	**Me olvidé de** pedir turno en la peluquería.
peinar(se) to comb or style one's hair	**Me voy a peinar** antes de salir.
regalar to give (as a gift)	María me **regaló** un vestido verde.

¡CONVERSEMOS!

Answer the following questions, basing your answers on the dialogues.

1. ¿Para qué se levantaron temprano hoy Mirta e Isabel?
2. ¿Qué van a hacer las chicas esta noche?
3. ¿Quién le va a pasar la aspiradora a la alfombra?
4. ¿Qué va a planchar Isabel? ¿Para qué?
5. ¿Quién celebra su cumpleaños mañana?
6. ¿Sabe Mirta qué ponerse esta noche?
7. ¿Por qué no se pone Mirta el vestido azul?

8. ¿Qué tiene que hacer Isabel antes de ir a la peluquería?
9. ¿Por qué no quiere Isabel una permanente?
10. ¿Dónde dejó Isabel la cartera?
11. ¿Qué le pregunta el peluquero a Isabel?
12. ¿Por qué es mejor ir a la peluquería por la mañana?

 # ¿Lo sabia Ud.?

• **Asunción** es la capital de Paraguay. La ciudad fue fundada en el año 1537. Allí se ve un contraste muy grande entre los edificios muy modernos y las casas coloniales. No muchos turistas visitan esta encantadora *(charming)* ciudad, pero los que lo hacen hablan muy bien de la hospitalidad de los paraguayos.

• **Paraguay** tiene más o menos el tamaño *(size)* de California. Su moneda es el **guaraní,** que es de valor bastante estable. El idioma oficial es el español, pero los paraguayos hablan también el guaraní, un idioma indígena que aún se conserva y que se enseña en las escuelas. Alrededor *(Around)* del ochenta y uno por ciento de la población sabe leer y escribir.

Edificios modernos junto a casas viejas en Asunción, Paraguay.

PRONUNCIACIÓN

La entonación

Intonation refers to the variations in the pitch of your voice when you are talking. Intonation patterns in Spanish are different from those in English. Note the following regarding Spanish intonation.

1. For normal statements, the pitch generally rises on the first stressed syllable.

Yo compré el regalo para Elena.

2. For questions eliciting information, the pitch is highest on the stressed syllable of the interrogative pronoun.

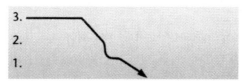

¿Cómo está tu mamá?

3. For questions that can be answered with **sí** or **no,** the pitch is generally highest on the last stressed syllable.

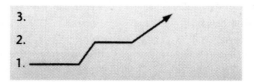

¿Fuiste al mercado ayer?

4. In exclamations, the pitch is highest on the first stressed syllable.

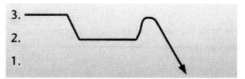

¡Qué bonita es esa alfombra!

Listen to your instructor and repeat the following sentences, imitating closely your instructor's intonation.

1. Marta no trabajó anoche.
2. ¿Dónde vive tu hermano?
3. ¿Le diste el dinero a Ramona?
4. ¡Qué delgado es ese muchacho!
5. ¿Vas a ir a la peluquería?
6. ¿Quién puede llevarte?

ESTRUCTURAS

1 Reflexive constructions *(Construcciones reflexivas)*

A. Reflexive pronouns

Subjects	Reflexive pronouns	
yo	**me**	*myself, to (for) myself*
tú	**te**	*yourself, to (for) yourself* (**tú** form)
nosotros(-as)	**nos**	*ourselves, to (for) ourselves*
vosotros(-as)	**os**	*yourselves, to (for) yourselves* (**vosotros** form)
Ud.		*yourself, to (for) yourself* (**Ud.** form)
Uds.		*yourselves, to (for) yourselves* (**Uds.** form)
él	**se**	*himself, to (for) himself*
ella		*herself, to (for) herself*
		itself, to (for) itself
ellos, ellas		*themselves, to (for) themselves*

■ Reflexive pronouns are used whenever the direct or indirect object is the same as the subject of the sentence.

■ Note that except for **se**, the reflexive pronouns have the same forms as the direct and indirect object pronouns.

■ The third-person singular and plural **se** is invariable.

■ Reflexive pronouns are positioned in the sentence in the same manner as object pronouns. They are placed in front of a conjugated verb: **Yo *me* levanto;** or they may be attached to an infinitive or to a present participle: **Yo voy a levantar*me*. Yo estoy levantánd*ome*.**

B. Reflexive verbs

■ Many verbs can be made reflexive in Spanish, that is, they can be made to act upon the subject, by the use of a reflexive pronoun.

lavarse *to wash oneself*	
Yo **me lavo**	*I wash (myself)*
Tú **te lavas**	*You wash (yourself)* (**tú** form)
Ud. **se lava**	*You wash (yourself)* (**Ud.** form)
Él **se lava**	*He washes (himself)*
Ella **se lava**	*She washes (herself)*
Nosotros(-as) **nos lavamos**	*We wash (ourselves)*
Vosotros(-as) **os laváis**	*You wash (yourselves)* (**vosotros** form)
Uds. **se lavan**	*You wash (yourselves)* (**Uds.** form)
Ellos **se lavan**	*They (masc.) wash (themselves)*
Ellas **se lavan**	*They (fem.) wash (themselves)*

Julia baña al perro.

Julia se baña.

Elsa acuesta a su hijo a las siete.

Elsa se acuesta a las diez.

■ In addition to the verbs included in the vocabulary list, the following verbs are commonly used in reflexive constructions.

afeitarse *to shave*
despertarse (e:ie) *to wake up*
desvestirse (e:i) *to get undressed*
preocuparse (por) *to worry (about)*
sentirse (e:ie) *to feel* (mood or physical condition)

—¿A qué hora **se acuestan** Uds.?   *"What time do you go to bed?"*

—Yo **me acuesto** a las diez y Ana **se acuesta** a las doce.   *"I go to bed at ten and Ana goes to bed at twelve."*

ATENCIÓN The Spanish reflexives are seldom translated using the reflexive pronouns in English: **Yo me acuesto** = *I go to bed.*

■ The following verbs have different meanings when they are used with reflexive pronouns.

acostar (o:ue) *to put to bed*	**acostarse** *to go to bed*
dormir (o:ue) *to sleep*	**dormirse** *to fall asleep*
ir *to go*	**irse** *to go away, leave*
levantar *to raise, lift*	**levantarse** *to get up*
llamar *to call*	**llamarse** *to be called*
poner *to put, place*	**ponerse** *to put on*
probar (o:ue) *to try; to taste*	**probarse** *to try on*
quitar *to take away*	**quitarse** *to take off*

—¿Te vas a **acostar**?
—Sí, pero primero voy a
   acostar a los niños.

"Are you going to go to bed?"
"Yes, but first, I'm going
   to put the children to bed."

Práctica

A. Say what you and your relatives normally do by adding the correct form of the missing verbs.

1. Mi tía siempre _____ (despertarse) tarde.
2. Yo _____ (levantarse) muy temprano.
3. Mi padre _____ (afeitarse) en el baño.
4. Nosotros _____ (bañarse) por la mañana.
5. Mi hermana _____ (lavarse) la cabeza todos los días.
6. Mis primos _____ (vestirse) en diez minutos.
7. Yo _____ (desvestirse) y _____ (acostarse).
8. Mi mamá _____ (preocuparse) mucho cuando yo llego tarde.

B. Say what these people are doing.

1. María _____ bien.

2. Los estudiantes _____ en la clase.

3. Juan le _____ el dinero al niño.

4. Pepito _____ el suéter.

5. Yo _____ la _____ en la clase.

6. Yo _____ a las seis.

7. Rosa _____ el _____ en la _____ .

8. Rosa _____ el _____ .

9. Sergio _____ a Eva.

10. El muchacho _____ Sergio _____ .

C. Interview a classmate, using the following questions and two questions of your own. When you have finished, switch roles.

1. ¿A qué hora te levantas tú generalmente?
2. ¿A qué hora te levantaste hoy?
3. ¿A qué hora te acuestas?
4. ¿A qué hora te acostaste anoche?
5. ¿Puedes bañarte y vestirte en diez minutos?
6. ¿Te lavas la cabeza cuando te bañas?
7. ¿Te miras en el espejo para peinarte?
8. ¿Te acordaste de traer el libro de español?
9. ¿Cómo se llama tu mejor amigo(-a)?
10. ¿Se preocupan tus padres por ti?

D. With a partner, act out the following conversation between two roommates in Spanish.

"What are you doing?"
"I'm putting on your yellow sweater."
"But I lent you the red one!"
"Yes, I tried it on, but I didn't like it."
"I still have to shower and wash my hair. Where's the shampoo?"
"It's in the bathroom. I always put it there."
"I like Anita's parties, but I want to go to bed early tonight."
"Me, too. I didn't sleep well last night."

Summary of Personal Pronouns

Subject	Direct object	Indirect object	Reflexive	Object of prepositions
yo	me	me	me	mí
tú	te	te	te	ti
usted *(fem.)*	la			usted
usted *(masc.)*	lo	le	se	usted
él	lo			él
ella	la			ella
nosotros(-as)	nos	nos	nos	nosotros(-as)
vosotros(-as)	os	os	os	vosotros(-as)
ustedes *(fem.)*	las			ustedes
ustedes *(masc.)*	los	les	se	ustedes
ellos	los			ellos
ellas	las			ellas

2 Some uses of the definite article   *(Algunos usos del artículo definido)*

The definite article has the following uses in Spanish.

▪ The possessive adjective is often replaced by the definite article. An indirect object pronoun or a reflexive pronoun (if the subject performs the action upon himself or herself) usually indicates who the possessor is. Note the use of the definite article in Spanish in the following specific situations indicating possession.

■ With parts of the body

Voy a cortar**le el pelo.**	*I'm going to cut his hair.*
Me lavé **las manos.**	*I washed my hands.*

■ With articles of clothing and personal belongings

¿**Te** quitaste **el vestido?**	*Did you take off your dress?*
Ellos **se** quitaron **el suéter.**	*They took off their sweaters.*

ATENCIÓN   The number of the subject and verb generally does not affect the number of the thing possessed. Spanish uses the singular to indicate that each person has only one of any particular object.

Ellas se quitaron **el vestido.**	*They took off their dresses.*
(Each one has one dress.)	
but: Ellas se quitaron **los zapatos.**	*They took off their shoes.*
(Each one has two shoes.)	

▦   The definite article is used with abstract and generic nouns.

Me gusta **el té,** pero prefiero **el café.**	*I like tea, but I prefer coffee.*
Las madres siempre se preocupan por sus hijos.	*Mothers always worry about their children.*
La educación es muy importante.	*Education is very important.*

▦   The definite article is used with certain nouns, including **cárcel** *(jail)*, **iglesia** *(church)*, and **escuela** when they are preceded by a preposition.

—¿Vas a **la iglesia** los viernes?	*"Do you go to church on Fridays?"*
—No, voy a **la escuela.**	*"No, I go to school."*

▦   Remember that the definite article is also used with days of the week, when indicating titles in indirect address, and when telling time.

El Sr. Vega viene **el sábado** a **las tres** de la tarde.	*Mr. Vega is coming on Saturday at three o'clock in the afternoon.*

Práctica

A. Interview a classmate, using the following questions. When you have finished, switch roles.

1. ¿Qué te gusta más, el pavo relleno o el arroz con pollo?
2. ¿Qué les gusta más a tus padres, el café o el té?
3. ¿Te gustan los rizos o prefieres el pelo lacio?
4. ¿Quién te corta el pelo?
5. ¿Con qué champú te lavas la cabeza?
6. ¿Te quitas los zapatos cuando llegas a tu casa?
7. ¿Te gustan los idiomas extranjeros *(foreign)*?
8. ¿Te gusta más el francés o el español?
9. ¿Vas a la iglesia los domingos?
10. ¿Qué es más importante para ti, el amor o el dinero?

B. With a partner, act out the following dialogues in Spanish.

1. "What are the girls doing?"
   "They are putting on their dresses."
2. "Did you get your hands dirty, Paquito?"
   "Yes, but I washed them."
3. "Women are more intelligent than men."
   "Women always say that."
4. "Is he in school?"
   "No, he is in jail."
5. "I don't want to go to college."
   "But education is very important!"

3 Possessive pronouns *(Pronombres posesivos)*

Singular		Plural		
Masculine	**Feminine**	**Masculine**	**Feminine**	
el mío	la mía	los míos	las mías	*mine*
el tuyo	la tuya	los tuyos	las tuyas	*yours* (inf.)
el suyo	la suya	los suyos	las suyas	{ *yours* (form.) *his* *hers*
el nuestro	la nuestra	los nuestros	las nuestras	*ours*
el vuestro	la vuestra	los vuestros	las vuestras	*yours* (inf.)
el suyo	la suya	los suyos	las suyas	{ *yours* (form.) *theirs*

▨ In Spanish, possessive pronouns agree in gender and number with the thing possessed. They are generally used with the definite article.

—Aquí están **mis maletas.**   *"Here are my suitcases. Where*
¿Dónde están **las tuyas?**   *are yours?"*
—**Las mías** están en mi cuarto.   *"Mine are in my room."*

—**Nuestro profesor** es de   *"Our professor is from*
Colombia.   *Colombia."*
—**El nuestro** es de Venezuela.   *"Ours is from Venezuela."*

ATENCIÓN After the verb **ser,** the definite article is frequently omitted.

—¿Estos billetes son **suyos,** señor?   *"Are these tickets yours, sir?"*
—No, no son **míos**.   *"No, they're not mine."*

▨ Because the third-person forms of the possessive pronouns (**el suyo, la suya, los suyos, las suyas**) can be ambiguous, they can be replaced by the following for clarification.

| el de
la de
los de
las de | { Ud.
él
ella
Uds.
ellos
ellas | el [libro] de él
el   de él

Es **suyo.** *(unclarified)*
Es **el de él.** *(clarified)* |

—Estas maletas son de Eva y
de Jorge, ¿no?
—Bueno, la maleta azul es **de
ella** y la maleta marrón es
de él.

*"These suitcases are Eva's and
Jorge's, aren't they?"*
*"Well, the blue suitcase is hers,
and the brown suitcase is
his."*

Práctica

A. Provide the correct possessive pronoun for each subject.

> **MODELO:** Yo tengo una tarjeta postal. Es…
> *Yo tengo una tarjeta postal. Es mía.*

1. Mario tiene una revista. Es…
2. Nosotros tenemos dos entradas. Son…
3. Tú tienes un espejo. Es…
4. Inés tiene dos pinturas. Son…
5. Yo tengo dos casas. Son…
6. Ud. tiene un perro. Es…
7. Ellos tienen los regalos. Son…
8. Paco tiene una botella de vino. Es…

B. With a partner, make comparisons between the objects and people described
and those in your own experience. Use appropriate possessive pronouns when
asking each other questions.

> **MODELO:** —El hermano de Teresa tiene quince años. ¿Y el tuyo?
> —*El mío tiene dieciocho.*

1. Los mejores amigos de Rosa son de Cuba.
2. El apartamento de Ana tiene cuatro cuartos.
3. Los padres de Ramiro viven en San Diego.
4. El cumpleaños de Jorge es en septiembre.
5. Las maletas de Alina son verdes.
6. La hermana de Rafael es muy bonita.
7. El idioma de Hans es alemán.
8. Las primas de Enrique son uruguayas.

Now, with your partner, compare other aspects of your lives, such as your room
or apartment, relatives, classes, car, tapes, jobs, and so on.

C. With a partner, act out in Spanish the following dialogue between two tourists.

"My tickets are here. Where are yours, Anita?"
"Mine are here, too, but Pedro doesn't have his."
"I don't have suitcases, but Teresa is going to lend me one of hers."
"Or I can lend you one of mine..."
"But you are going to need yours!"
"I have three suitcases."

4 Irregular preterits *(Pretéritos irregulares)*

The following Spanish verbs are irregular in the preterit.

tener:	tuve, tuviste, tuvo, tuvimos, tuvisteis, tuvieron
estar:	estuve, estuviste, estuvo, estuvimos, estuvisteis, estuvieron
poder:	pude, pudiste, pudo, pudimos, pudisteis, pudieron
poner:	puse, pusiste, puso, pusimos, pusisteis, pusieron
saber:	supe, supiste, supo, supimos, supisteis, supieron
hacer:	hice, hiciste, hizo,[1] hicimos, hicisteis, hicieron
venir:	vine, viniste, vino, vinimos, vinisteis, vinieron
querer:	quise, quisiste, quiso, quisimos, quisisteis, quisieron
decir:	dije, dijiste, dijo, dijimos, dijisteis, dijeron[2]
traer:	traje, trajiste, trajo, trajimos, trajisteis, trajeron[2]
conducir:	conduje, condujiste, condujo, condujimos, condujisteis, condujeron[2]
traducir:	traduje, tradujiste, tradujo, tradujimos, tradujisteis, tradujeron[2]

—¿Por qué no **viniste** anoche?　　*"Why didn't you come last night?"*

—No **pude; tuve** que trabajar. Y tú, ¿qué **hiciste**?　　*"I wasn't able to; I had to work. And you, what did you do?"*

—Yo **estuve** en casa toda la noche.　　*"I was home all night."*

ATENCIÓN The preterit of **hay** (impersonal form of **haber**) is **hubo** *(there was, there were)*.

Anoche **hubo** un concierto.　　*Last night there was a concert.*

---

[1]Note that in the third-person singular form, c changes to z in order to maintain the soft sound.
[2]Note that in the third-person plural ending of these verbs, the i is omitted.

Práctica

A. Elsa and David are arguing. Complete their dialogue, using the preterit of the verbs given. Then act it out with a partner.

ELSA —¿Dónde _____ (estar) (tú) anoche?
¡ _____ (Venir) muy tarde!

DAVID —¡Te lo _____ (decir)! _____ (Estar) en casa de mamá. _____ (Tener) que hablar con papá. No te llamé porque no _____ (poder).

ELSA —¿No _____ (poder) o no _____ (querer)?

DAVID —Bueno. ¿Dónde _____ (poner) tú las cartas que yo _____ (traducir) ayer en la oficina?

ELSA —¡Tú no _____ (traer) ninguna carta!

DAVID —No… los empleados las _____ (traer) cuando _____ (venir) ayer.

ELSA —Ellos no me _____ (decir) nada. ¡Son unos idiotas!

B. Answer the following questions about yourself and your friends.

1. ¿Qué tuvo que hacer ayer?
2. ¿Qué hicieron sus amigos ayer?
3. ¿Dónde estuvieron Uds. anoche?
4. ¿Hubo una fiesta en su casa ayer?
5. ¿Uds. tuvieron que limpiar la casa?
6. ¿Vino a clase la semana pasada?
7. ¿Pudo venir Ud. temprano a la universidad ayer?
8. ¿Condujo su coche ayer?

C. Read what the following people typically do. Then, using your imagination, say what everyone did differently yesterday.

1. Yo estoy en mi casa por la mañana.
2. Tú vienes a la universidad a las diez de la mañana.
3. Paquito hace la tarea por la tarde.
4. Julio tiene que trabajar en el hospital.
5. Nosotros traemos a nuestros hijos a la escuela.
6. Ellos traducen las lecciones al inglés.
7. María se pone el vestido azul.
8. Yo conduzco mi coche.

D. In groups of three, prepare some questions for your instructor about what he or she did yesterday, last night, or last week. Use irregular preterit forms in your questions.

5 Ordinal numbers *(Números ordinales)*

primero(-a)[1]	*first*	sexto(-a)	*sixth*
segundo(-a)[1]	*second*	séptimo(-a)	*seventh*
tercero(-a)[1]	*third*	octavo(-a)	*eighth*
cuarto(-a)	*fourth*	noveno(-a)	*ninth*
quinto(-a)	*fifth*	décimo(-a)	*tenth*

■ Ordinal numbers agree in gender and number with the nouns they modify.

el segundo **chico**   la segunda **chica**
los primeros **días**   las primeras **semanas**

■ Ordinal numbers are seldom used after **décimo** *(tenth)*.

ATENCIÓN   The ordinal numbers **primero** and **tercero** drop the final **-o** before masculine singular nouns.

el **primer**[2] día   el **tercer**[3] año

Práctica

Supply the ordinal numbers that correspond to the following cardinal numbers.

1. cuatro
2. diez
3. uno
4. siete
5. dos

6. ocho
7. tres
8. nueve
9. cinco
10. seis

¡A VER CUÁNTO APRENDIÓ!

¡Repase el vocabulario!

Say whether the following statements are logical or not. If they're not logical, give a statement that is.

1. El perro limpió el apartamento.
2. No puedo afeitarme porque no tengo escoba.
3. Elvira lee una revista en la peluquería.

---

[1] abbreviated 1º, 2º, 3º, and so on
[2] abbreviated 1er
[3] abbreviated 3er

4. Tengo el pelo muy lacio. Necesito un rizador.
5. Generalmente pongo el recogedor en el botiquín.
6. Tengo que ir a la tienda porque necesito corte, lavado y peinado.
7. No estoy haciendo nada. Estoy muy ocupado.
8. Ahora podemos comer porque yo ya cociné. Preparé cordero y arroz.
9. No quiero una permanente porque no me gustan los rizos.
10. Una semana tiene diez días.
11. Me voy. El peluquero no terminó de cortarme el pelo.
12. Nunca me olvido de nada. Siempre me acuerdo de todo.
13. El peluquero me cortó el pelo.
14. Necesito el secador para planchar mi vestido.
15. Generalmente hay menos gente en la peluquería por la mañana.

Entrevista

Interview a classmate, using the **tú** form.

Pregúntele a su compañero(-a) de clase…

1. …si le gustan los rizos o el pelo lacio.
2. …si va a pedir turno en la peluquería y para cuándo.
3. …si se lava la cabeza todos los días.
4. …si cree que está de moda el pelo corto o el pelo largo.
5. …si está invitado(-a) a alguna fiesta el sábado.
6. …si tiene algo que ponerse para ir a una fiesta.
7. …qué le va a regalar a su mejor amigo(-a) para su cumpleaños.
8. …si barre la cocina o le pasa la aspiradora.
9. …si sabe cocinar.
10. …si siempre limpia la cocina cuando la ensucia.

Situaciones

What would you say in the following situations? What might the other person say?

1. You are at home. Ask your younger brother if he bathed and combed his hair. Also ask if he cleaned his room. Tell him he has to sweep the kitchen.
2. Someone asks about your schedule. Tell him or her what time you generally go to bed and get up. Also say how long it takes you to bathe and get dressed.
3. You are at the beauty parlor (barbershop). Tell the hairdresser (barber) what you want done. Then make an appointment for next month.

Para escribir

Write a composition about your daily routine. Say what you do from the time you wake up until the time you go to bed.

En la vida real

¡Vamos a la peluquería!

Carefully read the following ads for two hair salons, and then answer the questions that follow.

PELUQUERÍA ANABEL

Especiales de esta semana
Permanentes de . . . .$35 a $50
Tinte $15
Manicura $7
Corte $8
Corte, lavado y peinado $20

Abierto de martes a sábado
Martes a viernes de 9 a 5
Sábados de 8 a 6

Avenida Paz #28 Teléfono 287–3574

Si presenta este anuncio Ud. recibe un 10% de descuento.

Salón de belleza La Época

- Expertos peluqueros y barberos
- Especialidad en permanentes
- Tenemos los mejores equipos y los precios más bajos para hombres y mujeres.

Abierto de lunes a sábado de 9 a 5
Calle Bolívar No. 439

Para pedir su turno llame al teléfono 287–2308

Martes precios especiales para mayores de 50 años.

1. En la peluquería Anabel, ¿cuál es el precio mínimo de una permanente?
2. Si Ud. quiere cortarse el pelo el lunes, ¿a qué peluquería puede ir?
3. Su hermano desea afeitarse y cortarse el pelo. ¿Puede ir a la peluquería Anabel? ¿Por qué sí o por qué no?
4. ¿Adónde puede ir? ¿Por qué?
5. ¿Por qué es importante tener el anuncio de la peluquería Anabel?

6. ¿Cuánto hay que pagar por un tinte y por un corte de pelo?
7. Mi abuela tiene 58 años. ¿Por qué debe ir a la peluquería La Época y qué día debe ir?
8. ¿A qué teléfono debe llamar ella para pedir turno?
9. ¿Cuál es la especialidad del salón de belleza La Época?
10. ¿Cuál es la dirección de la peluquería Anabel?

Una visita importante

With a classmate, act out a scene involving two roommates who are expecting a visitor. Discuss what you have to do in order to get the house (apartment) and yourselves ready for your guest, and divide up the chores that must be done.

¿Qué es?

The class will be divided into two teams. Your instructor will give each student an item from the vocabulary list in this lesson to draw on the board. The other members of the team must try to guess what is being drawn. If they guess within one minute, they get a point.

Así somos

Vocabulario

al revés	the other way around
ayudar	to help
el colegio	school
el comedor	dining room
los cubiertos	silverware
cuida	she takes care of
de acuerdo a	according to
jugar futbolito o billar	to play soccer or billiards
la limpieza	cleaning
el mantenimiento	maintenance
me quedo	I stay
nos reunimos	we get together
nos turnamos	we take turns
la película	movie, film
pesado	hard, tiresome
ponerse a	to start (to do something)
por ahí	there
por lo regular	as a rule
la sala	living room
la siestecita	little nap
tempranito	nice and early
transcurre mi día	my day is spent
trapear	to mop
los trastes	dishes
un rato	a while

Preparación

¿Cuánto saben Uds. ya?   This video module focuses on daily routines and household chores. With a partner, brainstorm possible words and phrases that the people in the video might use in these contexts. Make a list of them and then circle the ones you hear as you watch the video.

Comprensión

A. La rutina diaria.   Read the following statements. After watching the video, circle **V** (**Verdadero**) and **F** (**Falso**), according to what you understood.

V   F   1. Por lo general, Pedro hace ejercicio por la mañana.
V   F   2. Pedro almuerza con sus amigos.
V   F   3. Pedro y sus amigos juegan futbolito o billar.
V   F   4. Zaida se levanta muy tarde.
V   F   5. Zaida tiene clases sólo por la mañana.
V   F   6. Zaida va al gimnasio por la tarde.

V F   7. Juan se levanta temprano.
V F   8. Juan duerme una siestita.
V F   9. Juan sale con su novia o con sus amigos después de cenar.
V F   10. Anselmo no tiene hijos.
V F   11. Anselmo llega a la oficina a las nueve.
V F   12. El día de Anselmo transcurre en atender clientes.

B. ¿Quién lo dice?   Match the people's names with what they say in the video.

a. Zaida   b. Gustavo   c. Tamara   d. Juan

_____ 1. Una vez a la semana hacemos la limpieza general de toda la casa.
_____ 2. Una señora y mi madre hacen los trabajos de la casa.
_____ 3. Mis compañeras y yo nos turnamos para limpiar los cuartos de la casa.
_____ 4. Tengo una señora que nos limpia la casa.

Ampliación

A. Los quehaceres de la casa.   Make a list of the chores you have to do this weekend. Then, with a partner, compare your lists.

B. Dos culturas.   In groups of three or four, compare your daily routines with those described by the people on the video.

SELF TEST

Take this test. When you have finished, check your answers in the answer key provided in Appendix E. Then use a red pen to correct any mistakes you may have made. Are you ready?

Lección 7

A. Demonstrative adjectives and pronouns

Give the Spanish equivalent of the following.

1. these cards and those (over there)
2. that suitcase and this one
3. these travel agencies and those (over there)
4. this plane and that one (over there)
5. this boat and that one
6. these letters and those

B. Indirect object pronouns

Rewrite the following sentences, using indirect object pronouns to replace the words in italics.

1. Ella trae la lista *para ellos.*
2. Yo voy a preparar un sándwich *para ti.*
3. Él trae el equipaje *para Ud.*
4. Ana va a comprar las tarjetas *para mí.*
5. El agente de viajes trae los pasajes *para nosotros.*
6. Traen los cheques de viajeros *para ellas.*

C. Constructions with gustar

Write the following sentences in Spanish.

1. I don't like that travel agency.
2. He likes the aisle seat.
3. Do you like this carry-on bag?
4. We don't like to travel by plane.
5. Do they like their hotel?

D. Time expressions with *hacer*

Form sentences with the elements provided, using the expression **hace... que** to report how long an event has been going on. Follow the model.

MODELO: una hora / nosotros / trabajar
        Hace una hora que nosotros trabajamos.

1. dos días / yo / no dormir
2. un mes / tú / no llamarme
3. media hora / nosotros / estar aquí
4. un año / ellos / vivir / España
5. doce horas / mi hija / no comer

E. Preterit of regular verbs

Rewrite the following sentences so that instead of describing things that *are going to happen*, they describe things that *have already happened*.

1. Mañana Luisa y yo vamos a comprar los billetes. (ayer)
2. La semana próxima yo voy a viajar. (la semana pasada)
3. Hoy ella va a presentarme a sus padres. (ayer)
4. ¿No van a pagar Uds. los pasajes hoy? (ayer)
5. Esta tarde ellos van a abrir las ventanas. (al mediodía)
6. Nosotros vamos a comer en la cafetería. (el lunes)
7. ¿Vas a empezar a estudiar mañana? (esta mañana)
8. Yo voy a prestarle las maletas. (ayer)

F. Just words . . .

Complete the following sentences, using appropriate words or phrases from the vocabulary list in **Lección 7.**

1. Voy a la agencia de _____ para comprar el pasaje.
2. ¿Uds. van a volar a México mañana? ¡ _____ !
3. No puedo comprar un pasaje de primera clase. Tengo que viajar en clase _____ .
4. Voy a Buenos Aires, pero no vuelvo. Quiero un pasaje de _____ .
5. ¡Son las cuatro! El avión tiene tres horas de _____ .
6. Mañana te voy a _____ el bolso de mano que me prestaste.
7. La _____ vez tenemos que viajar juntas.
8. Aquí está la entrada y ahí está la _____ .
9. No tengo valijas; sólo un bolso de _____ .
10. Tus vacaciones son siempre magníficas. Mis vacaciones son muy _____ .
11. Llevé cinco maletas y pagué _____ de equipaje.
12. Puedo ir de California a Arizona en avión, en coche, en tren o en ómnibus, pero no en _____ .

G. Culture

Answer the following questions, based on the **¿Lo sabía Ud.?** section.

1. ¿A qué altura está situada Cuzco?
2. ¿De qué civilización es Cuzco la antigua capital?
3. ¿Qué es la ciudad de Cuzco hoy día?
4. ¿Cómo se conoce a Machu Picchu?
5. ¿Cuánto se extendió el imperio de los incas?

Lección 8

A. Direct and indirect object pronouns used together

Answer the following questions, using the cues provided, substituting direct object pronouns for the italicized words, and making any necessary changes.

1. ¿Cuándo le van a mandar *el pasaje* a Jorge? (mañana)
2. ¿Quién te va a comprar *las entradas*? (Elsa)
3. ¿Quién les va a traducir *las cartas* a Uds.? (Luis)

4. ¿Cuándo me vas a traer *el lechón?* (esta tarde)
5. ¿Quién le va a dar *la pulsera* a Ud.? (la profesora)

B. Preterit of *ir, ser,* and *dar*

Change the following sentences according to the new subjects.

1. Yo fui al restaurante y comí pavo asado. (Nosotros)
2. Ud. no fue mi profesor el año pasado. (Él)
3. ¿Ud. le dio la botella, señora? (Tú, querido)
4. ¿Quién pidió el bistec? ¿Fuiste tú, Tere? (Ud., señorita)
5. Ella no le dio el flan a Pedro. (Nosotras)
6. Ellos fueron al teatro. (Yo)
7. Nosotros no le dimos la cuenta. (Yo)
8. ¿Fueron ellos al restaurante anoche? (tú)
9. Carlos y yo fuimos a la fiesta la semana pasada. (Ellos)
10. ¿Fueron Uds. sus estudiantes el año pasado? (Raúl y Eva)
11. Nosotros te dimos la propina. (Yo)
12. Ella nos dio una torta helada. (Ellos)

C. Preterit of *e:i* and *o:u* stem-changing verbs

Complete the following sentences, using the preterit tense of the verbs listed below, as needed.

mentir   pedir   dormir   repetir
seguir   morir   conseguir   servir

1. ¿_____ ellos en el hotel el jueves?
2. Los chicos _____ a sus padres a la tienda.
3. Nosotros _____ sándwiches de jamón y queso.
4. Ella me _____ . No tiene veinte años; tiene diez y siete.
5. ¿No _____ Ud. el dinero para ir de vacaciones?
6. ¿Qué le _____ los niños a Santa Claus?
7. El hombre _____ en un accidente.
8. Ella me _____ la pregunta.

D. Weather expressions

Complete the following sentences appropriately.

1. Necesito un paraguas. _____ mucho.
2. ¿No te vas a poner el abrigo? ¡Brrr! ¡ _____ _____ _____ !
3. ¡No necesito abrigo! ¡Hace _____ !
4. En Alaska _____ mucho en el invierno.
5. Necesitas el sombrero. Hoy _____ _____ _____ .
6. No quiero vivir en Oregón porque allí llueve mucho, y no me gusta la _____ .

E. Uses of *por* and *para*

Complete the following sentences with **por** or **para**, as needed.

Ayer fui a la agencia de viajes _____ comprar un pasaje _____ Madrid.
Pagué setecientos dólares _____ el pasaje, pero eso no es demasido caro.

Quería *(I wanted)* el pasaje _____ el sábado, pero no pude conseguirlo. El avión sale el domingo _____ la mañana. _____ la tarde fui otra vez al centro _____ comprar un regalo _____ mi hermano, porque mañana es su aniversario de bodas. Llamé a mi padre _____ teléfono _____ decirle que no podía *(I wasn't able)* ir _____ él hasta las siete. Caminé *(I walked)* _____ el centro y pasé _____ la casa de Julia, que estudia _____ dentista. Julia me deseó buen viaje.

F. Just words . . .

Match each question in column A with the best response in column B. Use each response once.

A	B
1. ¿Qué quieres de postre?	a. No, prefiero cordero.
2. ¿Quieres café?	b. Sí, con champán.
3. ¿Quieres albóndigas?	c. No, agua mineral.
4. ¿Cuánto vas a dejar de propina?	d. Los frijoles son muy buenos aquí.
5. ¿Qué vas a pedir?	e. Es una sorpresa…
6. ¿Cómo está la comida?	f. No, prefiero jugo de frutas. Hace mucho calor.
7. ¿Qué vas a anotar?	g. No, no me gusta el pescado.
8. ¿Qué me recomiendas?	h. No sé. ¿Quieres ver el menú?
9. ¿Quieres salmón?	i. Sí, con crema, por favor.
10. ¿Qué sirven en este restaurante?	j. No, la pimienta.
11. ¿Vas a beber cerveza?	k. Sí, traigan las copas.
12. ¿Quieres chocolate caliente?	l. Sí, ¿dónde están las tazas, los platitos y las cucharitas?
13. ¿Vamos a celebrar nuestro aniversario?	m. Cinco dólares.
14. ¿Van al teatro?	n. Creo que es pescado y mariscos.
15. ¿Qué me vas a traer?	o. El pedido.
16. ¿Vamos a tomar vermut?	p. Sí, porque voy a poner la mesa.
17. ¿Cuál es la especialidad de la casa?	q. La cuenta.
18. ¿Quieres la sal?	r. No, al cine.
19. ¿No vas a servir el té?	s. Arroz con leche o flan.
20. ¿Necesitas el mantel y las servilletas?	t. Está rica.

G. Culture

Circle the correct answer, based on the **¿Lo sabía Ud.?** section.

1. Cientos de miles de turistas (franceses, latinoamericanos, españoles) visitan Miami todos los años.
2. Más de un millón de hispanos viven en Miami, en su mayoría (cubanos, mexicanos, uruguayos).
3. En los países de habla hispana, el café se sirve (después del, antes del, durante el) postre.
4. Después de comer, los hispanos generalmente "hacen la (comida, cena, sobremesa)".
5. En los restaurantes hispanos, la propina es del (10%, 25%, 15%).

Lección 9

A. Reflexive constructions

Rewrite each sentence according to the new cue. Follow the model.

MODELO: Yo *me despierto* a las nueve. (levantarse)
    Yo me levanto a las nueve.

1. *La gente* se viste muy bien. (Tú)
2. Ellos *se bañan* todos los días. (afeitarse)
3. *Nosotros* nos acostamos a las once. (Ellos)
4. ¿*Tú* no te preocupas por tus hijos? (Ud.)
5. Yo *me pruebo* el vestido. (ponerse)
6. *Nosotros* nos sentamos aquí. (Juan)
7. *Ella* se lava la cabeza todos los días. (Tú)
8. Yo no *me peiné.* (cortarse el pelo)
9. *Ellos* no se acordaron de eso. (Yo)
10. *Yo* me fui. (Uds.)
11. ¿Cómo se llama *ella?* (tú)
12. *Los niños* no se despertaron hasta las diez. (Daniel)

B. Some uses of the definite article

Form sentences with the elements given, adding the necessary connectors. Use verbs in the present tense. Follow the model.

MODELO: yo / ponerse / vestido
    Yo me pongo el vestido.

1. ¿ / tú / quitarse / suéter / ?
2. el barbero / cortarme / pelo
3. la peluquera / lavarme / cabeza
4. Uds. / no lavarse / manos
5. nosotros / preferir / té
6. madres / preocuparse / por / sus hijos
7. comunicación / ser / lo más importante

C. Possessive pronouns

Give the Spanish equivalent of the pronouns in parentheses.

1. El espejo de Nora está en la mesa. _____ está en mi cuarto. *(Mine)*
2. Mis revistas están aquí. ¿Dónde están _____ , Sr. Vega? *(yours)*
3. Ellos van a enviar sus cartas hoy. ¿Cuándo vamos a enviar _____ ? *(ours)*
4. No tengo maletas. ¿Puedes prestarme _____ , Anita? *(yours)*
5. Aquí están los regalos de Jorge. ¿Dónde están _____ ? *(ours)*
6. Enrique necesita tu cuaderno, Eva. _____ está en la universidad. *(His)*

D. Irregular preterits

Give the Spanish equivalent of the verbs in parentheses.

1. Ellos _____ que ir al teatro. *(had)*
2. ¿Dónde _____ Uds. anoche? *(were)*
3. Yo lo _____ al italiano. *(translated)*
4. Yo no _____ ir a la peluquería. *(was able)*
5. ¿Dónde _____ tú la aspiradora? *(put)*
6. Anoche _____ una fiesta. *(there was)*
7. Él no _____ las maletas. *(packed)*
8. Mi abuelo no _____ ayer. *(came)*
9. Ellos _____ nada. *(didn't say)*
10. Ella me _____ un secador. *(brought)*

E. Ordinal numbers

Complete the following sentences.

1. Marzo es el _____ mes del año.
2. Mayo es el _____ mes del año.
3. Abril es el _____ mes del año.
4. El _____ mes del año es octubre.
5. Agosto es el _____ mes del año.
6. Enero es el _____ mes del año.

F. Just words . . .

Complete the following sentences, using the appropriate words and phrases from the vocabulary list in **Lección 9.**

1. Necesito la _____ para barrer la cocina.
2. Voy a pedir turno en la peluquería para corte, _____ y _____ .
3. Prefiero el pelo largo porque el pelo corto no está de _____ .
4. ¿Por qué no le pasas la _____ a la alfombra?
5. Siempre como en restaurantes porque no me gusta _____ .
6. Tengo que comprar _____ para lavarme la cabeza.
7. No tiene rizos; tiene el pelo muy _____ .
8. No le di el dinero para comprar la _____ *Time.*
9. No puedo peinarme porque no tengo _____ .
10. Voy a afeitarme. ¿Dónde está la _____ de _____ ?
11. Es el cumpleaños de Jorge. Tengo que comprarle un _____ .

G. Culture

Read the following statements and circle **V** (**Verdadero**) or **F** (**Falso**), based on the **¿Lo sabía Ud.?** section.

V F   1. Montevideo es la capital de Paraguay.

V F   2. Paraguay es más o menos del tamaño *(size)* de California.

V F   3. Muchos turistas visitan Paraguay.

V F   4. En Paraguay hablan dos idiomas: el español y el italiano.

V F   5. La mayoría de los paraguayos saben leer y escribir.

LECCIÓN 10

PLANES DE VACACIONES

OBJECTIVES

■ Structure

• Formation of adverbs • The imperfect • The preterit contrasted with the imperfect • Verbs that change meaning in the preterit

■ Communication

You will learn vocabulary related to leisure activities.

Planes de vacaciones

Marisa y Nora, dos chicas chilenas que viven en Buenos Aires, están sentadas en un café de la Avenida de Mayo. Están planeando sus vacaciones de verano, pero no pueden ponerse de acuerdo porque a Nora le gustan las actividades al aire libre pero Marisa las odia.

MARISA —Traje unos folletos turísticos sobre excursiones a Punta del Este para mostrártelos.

NORA —Yo estuve allí el año pasado. Me gustó mucho la playa, pero había demasiada gente.

MARISA —Cuando yo era niña mi familia y yo siempre íbamos de vacaciones a Montevideo o a Río de Janeiro.

NORA —Nosotros generalmente íbamos al campo o a las montañas. Acampábamos, montábamos a caballo y en bicicleta, pescábamos truchas en un lago...

MARISA —¡Qué horrible! Para mí, dormir en una tienda de campaña en un saco de dormir es como un castigo.

NORA —¿Pues sabes lo que yo hice ayer? Compré una caña de pescar para ir de pesca contigo.

MARISA —Tengo una idea. Podemos hospedarnos en el Hotel del Lago y tú puedes pescar mientras yo nado en la piscina.

NORA —¿Por qué no alquilamos una cabaña en las montañas por unos días? Te vas a divertir...

MARISA —El año pasado me quedé en una cabaña con mi familia y me aburrí horriblemente. Mi mamá me dijo que yo no sabía apreciar la naturaleza.

NORA —*(Bromeando)* Eso pasó porque yo no estaba allí para enseñarte a pescar.

MARISA —¡Por suerte! Oye, en serio, tenemos que ir a la playa porque mi traje de baño me costó un ojo de la cara.

NORA —Yo también quería comprarme uno, pero desafortunadamente no pude ir a la tienda.

MARISA —Voy contigo a comprarlo si salimos para Punta del Este el sábado.

NORA —Está bien, pero en julio vamos a Bariloche a esquiar.

MARISA —Yo no sabía que te gustaba esquiar...

NORA —Sí, aprendí a esquiar el año pasado. Allí conocí a Gustavo, que era uno de los instructores.

MARISA —¡Con razón quieres volver! Bueno, vamos a la tienda y luego hacemos las maletas.

Las chicas fueron de compras y cuando por fin llegaron a su casa ya eran las ocho de la noche.

Vocabulario

Cognados

la actividad activity	**la excursión** excursion	**el (la) instructor(-a)** instructor
la bicicleta bicycle	**horriblemente** horribly	**la montaña** mountain
chileno(-a) Chilean		

Nombres

el caballo horse
la cabaña cabin
el campo country
la caña de pescar fishing rod
el castigo punishment
el folleto turístico tourist brochure

el lago lake
la naturaleza nature
el (la) niño(-a) child
la piscina, la alberca (Mex.) swimming pool
la playa beach

el saco (la bolsa) de dormir sleeping bag
la tienda de campaña tent
el traje de baño bathing suit

Verbos

aburrirse to be bored
acampar to camp, to go camping
alquilar to rent
apreciar to appreciate
bromear to kid, to joke

divertirse (e:ie) to have a good time, to enjoy oneself
enseñar[1] to teach
esquiar to ski
hospedarse (en) to stay (at a hotel)

nadar to swim
odiar to hate
pescar to fish, to catch (a fish)
planear to plan
quedarse to stay, remain

Adjetivos

sentado(-a) sitting, seated
turístico(-a) tourist

Otras palabras y expresiones

al aire libre outdoors
con razón no wonder
costar un ojo de la cara to cost an arm and a leg
demasiada gente too many people
desafortunadamente unfortunately
en serio seriously
está bien fine, all right

hacer las maletas to pack
ir de compras to go shopping
ir de pesca to go fishing
ir de vacaciones to go on vacation
lo que what
montar a caballo to ride a horse

montar en bicicleta to ride a bicycle
ponerse de acuerdo to agree
por fin finally
por suerte luckily
pues well
¡Qué horrible! How horrible!
sobre about

---

[1] **Enseñar** takes the preposition **a** when followed by an infinitive: **Mi hermano me enseñó a esquiar.**

VOCABULARIO ADICIONAL

■ LOS PASATIEMPOS *(Pastimes)*

la mochila

escalar

jugar [1] al tenis

jugar al golf

cazar

el salvavidas

el mar

tomar el sol

---

[1] Present tense: **juego, juegas, juega, jugamos, jugáis, juegan**

◼ TÉRMINOS GEOGRÁFICOS

el desierto

la nieve

el río

Océano Atlántico

Portugal

España

el país

Mar Mediterráneo

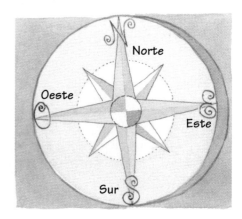

Norte

Oeste

Este

Sur

¡CONVERSEMOS!

Answer the following questions, basing your answers on the dialogue.

1. ¿Quiénes están sentadas en un café de la Avenida de Mayo?
2. ¿Por qué no pueden ponerse de acuerdo las chicas?
3. ¿Para qué trajo Marisa los folletos turísticos?
4. ¿Cree Ud. que Punta del Este es un lugar popular? ¿Por qué?
5. ¿A qué países iban de vacaciones Marisa y su familia?
6. ¿Qué es un castigo para Marisa?
7. ¿Qué compró Nora ayer? ¿Para qué?
8. ¿Qué idea tiene Marisa?
9. ¿Se divirtió Marisa en sus vacaciones el año pasado?
10. ¿Es caro el traje de baño de Marisa? ¿Cómo lo sabe Ud.?
11. ¿A quién conoció Nora en Bariloche?
12. ¿Qué hora era cuando las chicas llegaron a su casa?

¿Lo sabía Ud.?

- Mar del Plata (Argentina), Viña del Mar (Chile) y Punta del Este (Uruguay) están entre *(among)* las playas más hermosas e importantes de la América del Sur. Estas ciudades son centros turísticos internacionales.

- Mucha gente va a Chile y al sur de Argentina (Bariloche) para esquiar durante junio, julio y agosto, que son los meses de invierno en el hemisferio sur *(southern)*.

Vista de Mar del Plata y del océano Atlántico. Mar del Plata está a unos 400 kilómetros de Buenos Aires.

ESTRUCTURAS

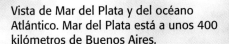

1 Formation of adverbs   *(La formación de los adverbios)*

- Most Spanish adverbs are formed by adding **-mente** (the equivalent of the English *-ly*) to the adjective.

especial	*special*	especial**mente**	*especially*
reciente	*recent*	reciente**mente**	*recently*
general	*general*	general**mente**	*generally*

- Adjectives ending in **-o** change the **-o** to **-a** before adding **-mente**.

lento	*slow*	lent**amente**	*slowly*
rápido	*rapid*	rápid**amente**	*rapidly*
desafortunado	*unfortunate*	desafortunad**amente** *unfortunately*	

- If two or more adverbs are used together, both change the **-o** to **-a**, but only the last adverb takes the **-mente** ending.

Habló clara y **lentamente**.   *He spoke clearly and slowly.*

- If the adjective has an accent, the adverb retains it.

fácil   **fácilmente**

Práctica

A. Change the following adjectives to adverbs.

1. fácil
2. feliz
3. claro *(clear)*
4. raro *(rare)*
5. necesario

6. frecuente *(frequent)*
7. triste
8. trágico *(tragic)*
9. alegre *(merry)*
10. desgraciado

B. Complete the following sentences with appropriate adverbs.

1. Ellos hablaron _____ y _____ .
2. Mis padres vienen a verme _____ .
3. Jaime llegó _____ .
4. El muchacho me habló _____ .
5. _____ me levanto a las siete.
6. Los muchachos bailan _____ .
7. _____ no tengo dinero.
8. Compré esa caña de pescar _____ para ti.
9. _____ no pude ir de vacaciones con ellos.

C. Interview a classmate, using the following questions and two of your own. Include adverbs in your responses. When you have finished, switch roles.

1. ¿A qué hora te levantas tú?
2. ¿Tú y tu familia van de compras juntos?
3. ¿Tú ves a tus abuelos a menudo *(often)*?
4. ¿Vas al teatro a menudo?
5. ¿Tú tienes mucho dinero?

2 The imperfect *(El imperfecto de indicativo)*

There are two simple past tenses in the Spanish indicative: the preterit, which you studied in **Lecciones 7, 8,** and **9,** and the imperfect.

A. Regular forms

▪ To form the regular imperfect, add the following endings to the verb stem.

-ar *verbs*		-er *and* -ir *verbs*			
hablar		**comer**		**vivir**	
habl-	**aba**	com-	**ía**	viv-	**ía**
habl-	**abas**	com-	**ías**	viv-	**ías**
habl-	**aba**	com-	**ía**	viv-	**ía**
habl-	**ábamos**	com-	**íamos**	viv-	**íamos**
habl-	**abais**	com-	**íais**	viv-	**íais**
habl-	**aban**	com-	**ían**	viv-	**ían**

▓ Note that the endings of the **-er** and **-ir** verbs are the same, and that there is a written accent on the first í of the endings of the **-er** and **-ir** verbs.

▓ The Spanish imperfect tense is equivalent to three English forms.

Yo **vivía** en Santiago.
$\begin{cases} \textit{I used to live in Santiago.} \\ \textit{I was living in Santiago.} \\ \textit{I lived in Santiago.} \end{cases}$

▓ The imperfect is used to refer to habitual or repeated actions in the past, with no reference to when they began or ended.

—¿Tú **asistías** a la universidad cuando **vivías** en Cuba?
"Did you attend the university when you were living in Cuba?"

—No, **trabajaba** cuando **vivía** en Cuba.
"No, I worked when I was living in Cuba."

▓ The imperfect is also used to refer to actions, events, or conditions that the speaker views as *in the process of* happening in the past, again with no reference to when they began or ended.

Veníamos para casa cuando vimos a Raúl.
We were coming home when we saw Raúl.

B. Irregular forms

▓ Only three verbs are irregular in the imperfect tense: **ser, ver,** and **ir.**

ser	ver	ir
era	veía	iba
eras	veías	ibas
era	veía	iba
éramos	veíamos	íbamos
erais	veíais	ibais
eran	veían	iban

—¿**Ibas** mucho a casa de tus abuelos cuando **eras** niño?
"Did you often go to your grandparents' house when you were a child?"

—Sí, los **veía** todos los sábados.
"Yes, I used to see them every Saturday."

—¿Adónde **iban** Uds. de vacaciones cuando eran niños?
"Where did you go on vacation when you were children?"

—**Íbamos** a la playa o a las montañas.
"We used to go to the beach or to the mountains."

Práctica

A. Ten years ago María wrote this composition about herself and her family. Rewrite her composition, using the imperfect tense.

Mi familia y yo vivimos en Buenos Aires. Mi padre trabaja para la compañía Sandoval y mi madre enseña en la universidad. Es una profesora excelente. Mis hermanos y yo asistimos a la escuela. Generalmente pasamos las vacaciones en Mar del Plata. Allí nadamos, pescamos y tomamos el sol. Como a mi padre le gusta ir a las montañas para esquiar, en invierno vamos a Bariloche. Mis abuelos viven en Rosario y no los vemos mucho, pero siempre les escribimos.

B. Now write a paragraph about your own childhood, using Exercise A as a model.

C. Interview a classmate, using the following questions and two of your own. When you have finished, switch roles.

1. ¿Dónde vivías tú cuando eras niño(-a)?
2. ¿A qué escuela asistías?
3. ¿Odiabas estudiar o te gustaba?
4. ¿Eras buen estudiante?
5. ¿Adónde iban tú y tu familia de vacaciones?
6. ¿Qué les gustaba hacer?
7. ¿Preferías pasar las vacaciones en el campo o en la ciudad?
8. ¿Te divertías mucho o te aburrías?
9. ¿Veías mucho a tus abuelos?
10. ¿Vivías cerca o lejos de tus abuelos?

D. Compare your teenage years with those of a classmate by taking turns completing the following sentences.

1. Cuando yo era adolescente...
2. Mi familia y yo siempre...
3. Mis abuelos...
4. Mi mejor amigo(-a)...
5. Frecuentemente nosotros...
6. Cuando yo tenía dieciséis años...
7. En la escuela yo...
8. Todos los fines de semana, mis amigos y yo...
9. En el verano...
10. Cuando yo quería salir con mis amigos, mis padres...

3 The preterit contrasted with the imperfect
(El pretérito contrastado con el imperfecto)

■ The difference between the preterit and the imperfect can be visualized in the following way.

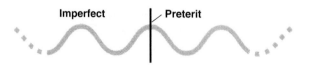

The wavy line representing the imperfect shows an action or event taking place over a period of time in the past. There is no reference to when the action began or ended. The vertical line representing the preterit shows an action or event as completed in the past.

In many instances, the choice between the preterit and the imperfect depends on how the speaker views the action or event. The following table summarizes some of the most important uses of both tenses.

Preterit	Imperfect
1. Reports past actions that the speaker views as finished and completed. Yo **estuve** allí el año pasado. Ayer **compré** una caña de pescar.	1. Describes past actions in the process of happening, with no reference to their beginning or end. **Iba** a la biblioteca cuando lo vi.
2. Sums up a condition or state viewed as a whole (and no longer in effect). Me **sentí** mal todo el día.	2. Refers to repeated or habitual actions or events: *used to . . .* Cuando **era** niña **iba**[1] de vacaciones a Montevideo.
	3. Describes a physical, mental, or emotional state or condition in the past. Me **sentía** muy mal.
	4. Expresses time in the past. **Eran** las ocho de la noche cuando llegaron a su casa.
	5. Is generally used in indirect discourse. Me dijo que no **sabía** apreciar la naturaleza.
	6. Describes age in the past. Cuando **tenía** veinte años, vivía en Chile.
	7. Describes or sets the stage in the past. **Hacía** frío y **llovía**.

—¿Qué **te dijo** Nora anoche?
"*What did Nora tell you last night?*"

—**Me dijo** que le **gustaba** esquiar.
"*She told me that she liked to ski.*"

—¿Qué hora **era** cuando **llegaste** a tu casa?
"*What time was it when you got home?*"
—**Eran** las cuatro.
"*It was four o'clock.*"
—¿Por qué no te **quedaste** en el club?
"*Why didn't you stay at the club?*"
—Porque no me **sentía** bien.
"*Because I wasn't feeling well.*"

---

[1] Note that this use of the imperfect also corresponds to the English *would* used to describe a repeated action in the past: *When I was a child, I used to go to Montevideo on vacation.* = *When I was a child, I would go to Montevideo on vacation.*

Práctica

A. Write the Spanish equivalent of the following sentences, paying special attention to the use of the preterit or the imperfect in each situation.

Preterit	*Imperfect*
1. I *went* to the lake last year. *(Narrates an action as a completed whole.)*	1. I *was going* to the lake when I saw Mary. *(Describes an action in progress.)*
2. I *was* sick all day long. *(Sums up a condition or state viewed as a whole.)*	2. I always *used to be* sick. *(Describes what used to happen.)*
	3. I *was* cold. They *were* very happy here. *(A physical, mental, or emotional state or condition in the past.)*
	4. He said he *wanted* a sleeping bag. *(Indirect discourse.)*
	5. It *was* six o'clock in the morning. *(Time in the past.)*
	6. My niece *was* five years old. *(Age in the past.)*
	7. My boyfriend *was* tall and handsome. *(Description in the past.)*

B. Complete the following dialogues. Then act them out with a partner.

1. —¿Cuántos años _____ (tener) tú cuando _____ (venir) a vivir a Caracas?
   —_____ (Tener) doce años.
2. —¿Qué te _____ (decir) el instructor ayer?
   —Me _____ (decir) que yo _____ (necesitar) practicar más.
3. —¿Qué tiempo _____ (hacer) cuando Uds. _____ (salir) de casa esta mañana?
   —_____ (Hacer) frío y _____ (nevar).
4. —¿Adónde _____ (ir) Uds. de vacaciones cuando _____ (ser) niños?
   —Siempre _____ (ir) a la playa, pero un verano mis padres _____ (decidir) alquilar una cabaña en las montañas y ésas _____ (ser) nuestras mejores vacaciones.
5. —¿Qué hora _____ (ser) cuando tú _____ (llegar) a casa ayer?
   —_____ (Ser) las ocho.
   —¿ _____ (Ir) a la tienda?
   —Sí, _____ (ir) con Nora. Cuando nosotras _____ (ir) a la tienda, _____ (ver) un accidente en la calle.
   —¿ _____ (Morir) alguien?
   —No, por suerte no _____ (morir) nadie.

C. This interview takes place in Buenos Aires. Play the role of a reporter interviewing a famous star.

— _____

—Yo nací (*I was born*)[1] en Sevilla, y no le digo cuándo.

_____
[1] **Nacer** is a regular verb in the preterit.

—
——————————————————

—Yo tenía diez años cuando nos fuimos a vivir a Madrid.
——————————————————

—¿Cuando era niña? Era fea y un poco gorda.
——————————————————

—Sí, tenía un perro que se llamaba Chispita.
——————————————————

—Cuando era niña me gustaba la vida al aire libre. Me gustaba nadar y montar a caballo.
——————————————————

—Estudié en la Escuela de Arte Dramático.
——————————————————

—Empecé a trabajar en televisión en 1980.
——————————————————

—Vine a Buenos Aires en el año 1997.
——————————————————

—Sí, el año pasado estuve en París y trabajé en un club nocturno.
——————————————————

—Estuve allí por tres meses.
——————————————————

—No, no pienso volver a España por ahora.

D. Interview a classmate, using the following questions and two of your own. When you have finished, switch roles.

1. ¿Cuántos años tenías cuando aprendiste a nadar?
2. ¿Adónde ibas de vacaciones?
3. ¿Te divertías durante el verano?
4. ¿Te gustaba acampar?
5. ¿Qué te gustaba hacer cuando eras niño(-a)?
6. ¿Cómo era tu primer(-a) novio(-a)?
7. ¿Qué hiciste ayer?
8. ¿A qué hora te levantaste esta mañana?
9. ¿Qué tiempo hacía cuando saliste de tu casa?
10. ¿Qué hora era cuando llegaste a la universidad?
11. ¿Tomaste una clase de inglés el año pasado?
12. ¿Quién fue tu profesor(-a)?

E. In groups of four or five, prepare 8 to 10 questions to ask your instructor about his or her life as a teenager.

4 Verbs that change meaning in the preterit
(Verbos que cambian de significado en el pretérito)

■ Some Spanish verbs change meaning when they are used in the preterit. Note the usage of the verbs in the following examples.

| conocer: | conocí (preterit) | *I met* |
| | conocía (imperfect) | *I knew (was acquainted or familiar with)* |

Anoche **conocí** a una chica muy simpática. *(met her for the first time)*
Yo no **conocía** la ciudad. *(I wasn't familiar with the city.)*

| saber: | supe (preterit) | *I found out, I learned* |
| | sabía (imperfect) | *I knew* |

Lo **supe** cuando él me lo dijo. *(I found it out.)*
Yo no **sabía** que te gustaba esquiar. *(I wasn't aware of it.)*

| no querer: | no quise (preterit) | *I refused* |
| | no quería (imperfect) | *I didn't want* |

Raúl **no quiso** ir. *(didn't want to and refused)*
Rita **no quería** ir, pero después decidió ir. *(didn't want to at the time)*

—¿Tú **conocías** al cuñado de Carmen?
—No, lo **conocí** anoche.

"*Did you know Carmen's brother-in-law?*"
"*No, I met him last night.*"

—¿**Sabías** que teníamos una fiesta?
—No, lo **supe** esta mañana.

"*Did you know that we were having a party?*"
"*No, I found (it) out this morning.*"

—¿Y Roberto? ¿No vino?
—No, **no quiso** venir.

"*And Roberto? Didn't he come?*"
"*No, he refused to come.*"

Práctica

A. Interview a classmate, using the following questions and at least two of your own.

1. ¿Conocías tú al profesor (a la profesora) antes de empezar esta clase?
2. ¿Cuándo lo (la) conociste?
3. ¿Sabías tú la nacionalidad del profesor (de la profesora)?
4. ¿Cuándo la supiste?
5. Yo no quería venir a clase hoy. ¿Y tú?
6. Tú no viniste al concierto anoche. ¿No pudiste o no quisiste?

B. Act out the following scene from a soap opera (**telenovela**) with a partner, providing the missing verbs.

ADRIÁN   —¿Tú _____ que Rosaura estaba embarazada *(pregnant)*?

SARA   —No, lo _____ anoche.

ADRIÁN   —¡Qué horrible! Dicen que su esposo es un idiota. Los padres de ella no _____ ir a la boda *(wedding)*. Ese día se fueron a Europa.

SARA   —Pero, ¿dónde _____ Rosaura a Lorenzo?

ADRIÁN   —En una fiesta. Rosaura no _____ ir, pero Olga la llevó.

SARA   —¿Olga _____ a Lorenzo?

ADRIÁN   —Sí, Olga es la ex esposa de Lorenzo...

¡AVER CUÁNTO APRENDIÓ!

¡Repase el vocabulario!

Choose the correct word or phrase to complete each statement.

1. Rosa nada en (el desierto, el mar, la nieve).
2. Ya hice (la propina, la playa, las maletas).
3. Los muchachos montaron (en el pasaje, a caballo, en la excursión).
4. El instructor es de Santiago; es (argentino, uruguayo, chileno).
5. Está bien. No vamos a comprar la cabaña. Vamos a (apreciarla, alquilarla, bañarla).
6. ¿No sabes nadar? Pues voy a (enseñarte, afeitarte, vestirte).
7. Por suerte los chicos se (aburrieron, quedaron, divirtieron) mucho.
8. No te lo digo en serio. Estoy (planeando, bromeando, acampando).
9. El Misisipí es un (lago, río, mar).
10. Desafortunadamente no todos podemos dormir en (la tienda de campaña, la trucha, la mochila).
11. Mis vacaciones fueron magníficas. (Me aburrí horriblemente., No hice nada interesante., Me divertí mucho.)
12. Pagué cien dólares por ese traje de baño. (Fui de pesca., Pedí turno., Me costó un ojo de la cara.)
13. Fuimos de pesca y por supuesto llevamos la (naturaleza, caña de pescar, cabaña) nueva.
14. Hay demasiada gente en (el desierto, el océano, las ciudades grandes).
15. No pudimos (hospedarnos, acampar, esquiar) en el hotel.

Entrevista

Interview a classmate, using the **tú** form.

Pregúntele a su compañero(-a) de clase...

1. ...si acampó este fin de semana.
2. ...si le gustaba ir a las montañas cuando era niño(-a).
3. ...si prefería montar a caballo o en bicicleta.

4. ...si quiere ir a cazar con Ud. la próxima vez.
5. ...si quiere ir de pesca al lago.
6. ...si pescó alguna vez una trucha enorme.
7. ...si vive cerca del océano Pacífico o del océano Atlántico.
8. ...si fue de compras ayer.
9. ...si bromea mucho con el profesor (la profesora).
10. ...si le costó un ojo de la cara el libro de español.

Situaciones

What would you say in the following situations? What might the other person say? Act out the scenes with a partner. Take turns playing each role.

1. On your vacation, you learned how to swim and ride a horse, and you caught a trout. Someone asks whether you had a good time. Say what you did.
2. A friend invites you to go camping. You don't have a tent or a sleeping bag, and you want to know what else you will need.
3. You are trying to convince a friend to go camping. Tell him or her how much fun it can be.

¿Qué pasa aquí?

In groups of three or four, look at the following photo and make up a story about the people you see. Say who they are, their professions, how long they have been on vacation, what they did yesterday, and so on.

Para escribir

Tomás and Víctor are very good friends, but their tastes differ: Tomás likes the outdoors, while Víctor prefers city life. Using your imagination, write an account of how each of them spent his vacation last summer.

En la vida real

Nuestras vacaciones

You and a classmate are going on a vacation. Make plans for the trip, including activities and things you might need to take with you. Then tell a group of classmates about your plans.

Viajes a México

Ángela and Elena went to Ixtapa on vacation, and Alberto and Julio went to Playa Blanca on the Pacific coast of Mexico. The four went with Club Mediterranée. Read the ad below and answer the following questions.

Conozca el nuevo y sensacional modo
de disfrutar las vacaciones
"al estilo de CLUB MEDITERRANEE" con

Dos fabulosas excursiones especiales para viajeros
sofisticados y exigentes, amantes del sol, el mar
¡y la buena vida!

IT3AM1VB770 CLUB MEDITERRANEE	IT3AM1VB771 CLUB MEDITERRANEE
Ixtapa	**Playa Blanca**
ZIHUATANEJO	(COSTA CAREYES)
PLAN 1 - 4 días/3 noches	**PLAN 1** - 4 días/3 noches
Salidas: los Jueves	Salidas: los Domingos
ADULTO MENOR	ADULTO MENOR
$ 16,300.00 $ 12,100.00	$ 19,550.00 $ 15,500.00
NOCHE ADICIONAL $ 1,640.00	NOCHE ADICIONAL $ 1,150.00
PLAN 2 - 5 días/4 noches	**PLAN 2** - 5 días/4 noches
Salidas: los Domingos	Salidas: los Jueves
ADULTO MENOR	ADULTO MENOR
$ 20,250.00 $ 13,250.00	$ 24,650.00 $ 16,850.00
NOCHE ADICIONAL $ 1,640.00	NOCHE ADICIONAL $ 1,150.00

NOTA: Estos precios incluyen tarifa aérea especial saliendo desde México, D.F. también operamos con tarifa especial saliendo desde Guadalajara, Monterrey y otros destinos. Favor de consultar estas tarifas en cualquiera de nuestras oficinas.

Utilice la Tarjeta American Express y disfrute los siguientes beneficios:

● Membresía por un año del Club Mediterranée.
● Seguro de vida contra accidentes por $ 1,000,000.00 durante el transporte aéreo.

1. ¿Cómo son las excursiones en los Viajes Bojorquez?
2. ¿Para qué tipo de viajeros son?
3. Las chicas viajaron con el plan 1 a Ixtapa. ¿Qué día salieron y cuántas noches estuvieron en Ixtapa?

4. ¿Cuánto pagaron por el viaje?
5. Las chicas usaron la tarjeta American Express para pagar el viaje. ¿Qué beneficios recibieron?
6. Los muchachos viajaron con el plan 2 y estuvieron en Playa Blanca por cinco noches. ¿Cuánto les costó el viaje?

El viaje de fin de curso

Imagine that your class is planning a field trip. One group of students would like to do outdoor activities such as camping, fishing, and swimming. Another group would prefer a visit to a large city and stay in hotels, visit museums, see films, etc. After preparing for a discussion, each group must try to convince the other to agree to its plan.

¡Vamos a leer!

Antes de leer

A. Before you read the fable of the hare and the tortoise (**la liebre y la tortuga**), think about things you already know that may be useful to you as you read. For example, what characteristics are typically associated with hares and tortoises? What is the purpose of a fable? With the answers to these questions in mind, make a brief list of vocabulary you might expect to encounter in the reading.

B. As you read the fable, find the answers to the following questions.

1. ¿Por qué se burlaba continuamente la liebre de la tortuga?
2. ¿Qué le hizo la tortuga a la liebre en presencia de los otros animales?
3. ¿Cómo respondió la liebre?
4. ¿A quién nombraron juez de la carrera?
5. Durante la carrera, ¿qué hizo la liebre? ¿Y la tortuga?
6. ¿Cómo terminó la carrera?
7. ¿Cuál es la moraleja (moral) de la fábula?

La liebre y la tortuga
(FÁBULA DE ESOPO°)

Aesop

hare / made fun / tortoise

Una liebre° se burlaba° continuamente de una tortuga,° porque la pobre tortuga era muy lenta.

hacer... to pay attention to
fed up / to challenge
race

La tortuga no quería hacer caso de° las burlas de la liebre, pero un día, harta° de oírlas, decidió desafiar° a la liebre, en presencia de los otros animales, a tener una carrera.°

win

—¡Qué idea! —dijo la liebre—. Tú sabes muy bien que no puedes ganar° esa carrera...

ready

—¡Ésa es tu opinión! ¿Estás lista° para comenzar?

judge / fox

Los animales nombraron juez° al zorro° y empezó la carrera. En dos segundos, la liebre desapareció. La tortuga empezó a

to walk

caminar° con su lentitud de siempre.

stopped

nap

grass

Mientras...   *Meanwhile /*
  sin...   *without stopping*

ashamed
were applauding

a...   *sometimes*

Al rato, la liebre se detuvo° para esperar a la tortuga. Esperó y esperó hasta que empezó a tener sueño.

—Puedo dormir una siesta° y continuar la carrera más tarde —pensó la liebre. Y durmió, tranquila y feliz, en la verde hierba.°

Mientras tanto,° la tortuga seguía caminando lentamente pero sin parar° y pasó a la liebre, que continuaba durmiendo.

Lenta y paciente, la tortuga ganó la carrera. La liebre, avergonzada,° se quedó donde estaba, sin mirar a los animales que aclamaban° a la tortuga victoriosa.

Moraleja: *Con perseverancia se gana
                    a veces° la carrera.*

Díganos

Answer the following questions, based on your own thoughts and experiences.

1. ¿Alguien se burlaba de Ud. cuando era niño(-a)? ¿Ud. se burlaba de alguien? Explique.
2. ¿De qué o de quién está harto(-a) Ud.?
3. ¿Ud. se identifica con la liebre o con la tortuga? ¿Por qué?

Costa Rica

El Salvador

Guatemala

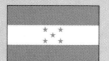
Honduras

Nicaragua

Panamá

■ Costa Rica es el país con el mayor ingreso *(income)* por persona, y con el más alto nivel de educación de Centroamérica. Es un país democrático y no tiene ejército *(army)*. A Costa Rica la llaman "la Suiza *(Switzerland)* de América" por su tradición pacifista. Uno de sus presidentes, Oscar Arias, recibió el Premio Nóbel de la Paz.

■ El Salvador es el país más pequeño de Centroamérica, pero es el más densamente poblado. Más de cinco millones de habitantes viven en un área aproximadamente del tamaño del estado de Massachusetts. Nicaragua, en comparación, es cinco veces más grande que El Salvador, pero tiene una población de sólo unos cuatro millones de habitantes.

■ El canal de Panamá es actualmente la única vía de comunicación que conecta los dos grandes océanos. Ahorra *(It saves)* 16.000 kilómetros de travesía *(voyage)* para los barcos que ya no *(no longer)* tienen que pasar por el Cabo de Hornos.

Nicaragua se siente orgullosa *(proud)* de su poeta nacional Rubén Darío, creador y líder del modernismo, un movimiento literario que comenzó a fines del siglo XIX. En la foto aparece una de las muchas estatuas del gran poeta que hay en Managua, la capital del país.
¿Qué poetas norteamericanos puede nombrar Ud.?

Tikal, situada en un bosque *(forest)* tropical al noroeste de Guatemala, es la ciudad más grande y más antigua de la civilización maya. En esta ciudad vivían unas 80.000 personas. Aquí se ve el Templo del Gran Jaguar, el edificio más alto y más importante de Tikal.
¿Cuáles son algunas de las ciudades más antiguas de su país?

El cultivo del banano *(banana tree)* es una de las principales fuentes *(sources)* de ingreso de los países centroamericanos. El banano se cultiva en Panamá, Costa Rica, El Salvador, Honduras, Nicaragua y Guatemala. En la foto, un agricultor verifica el tamaño de las bananas en una hacienda de El Salvador.
¿Qué frutas se cultivan en la región donde Ud. vive?

Estudiantes de la Universidad Nacional Autónoma de Honduras se dirigen a sus clases. Esta universidad, que está en Tegucigalpa, la capital de Honduras, es el centro educativo más importante del país.
¿Cuál es la universidad más importante del estado donde Ud. vive?

Guatemala es la ciudad más grande y más importante del país centroamericano del mismo nombre. La mayor parte de la ciudad es moderna, pues fue reconstruída después de una serie de terremotos (*earthquakes*) ocurridos en 1917–1918. En sus calles se mezclan las construcciones antiguas, como la Universidad de San Carlos, la Catedral y el Conservatorio Nacional de Música, y edificios modernos como la Ciudad Olímpica y el Palacio Nacional.
¿Cuáles son los edificios más antiguos de su ciudad?

Costa Rica es el país centroamericano que más se preocupa por proteger la naturaleza y la ecología. Son famosos sus parques nacionales y algunos de sus jardines, como el Jardín Botánico de Lankester, que aparece en la foto. Este jardín contiene numerosas especies de orquídeas y otras plantas tropicales.
¿Cuáles son los principales parques nacionales de su país?

La construcción del canal de Panamá por parte de los Estados Unidos duró *(lasted)* siete años y se terminó en el año 1914.
¿Puede Ud. identificar otros canales famosos?

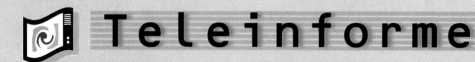

Teleinforme

Vocabulario

Panamá

a poca distancia	at a short distance
el bastimento	supplies
los bosques pluviosos	rain forests
el casco viejo	old part
el centro bancario	financial center
cubre	covers
los fuertes	forts
ha mantenido	has kept
ha sido ignorado	has been ignored
las joyas	jewels
el puerto marítimo	seaport
el siglo	century
los tesoros	treasures

Las carretas costarricenses

la bocina	hubcap (Costa Rica)
el campesino	farmer
la caoba	mahogany
las carretas	oxcarts
en principio	at first
el fango	mud
la finca	farm
las flores	flowers
el hierro	iron
la intemperie	inclemency (of the weather)
llamativo	bright
la madera	wood
la rueda	wheel

El Jardín Botánico de Lankester

cultivar	to grow (plants)
da la bienvenida	welcomes
los géneros	types, kinds
los jardines	gardens
los pájaros	birds
sin embargo	however

Preparación

¿Cuánto saben Uds. ya?   After reading the information in **Panorama hispánico 5**, get together in groups of three or four and answer the following questions.

1. ¿Cuál es la única vía de comunicación que conecta el Pacífico con el Atlántico?
2. ¿Dónde está Costa Rica?
3. ¿Cómo llaman a Costa Rica y por qué?
4. ¿Qué protegen en Costa Rica?

Comprensión

A. Panamá.   Read the following statements. After watching the video, circle **V** (**Verdadero**) or **F** (**Falso**), according to what you understood.

V F   1. Todo el mundo conoce las bellezas de Panamá.
V F   2. Hay bosques pluviosos en Panamá.
V F   3. Algunas civilizaciones indígenas precolombinas todavía *(still)* viven en Panamá.
V F   4. La ciudad de Panamá es un centro comercial.
V F   5. La ciudad de Panamá fue por siglos el centro del imperio español en América.
V F   6. La ciudad de Panamá tiene muchos ejemplos de arquitectura colonial española.

B. Las carretas costarricenses.   Complete the following statements with the appropriate word or phrase.

1. Se usan las carretas en las _____ de Costa Rica.
2. Las carretas están hechas *(made)* de _____ .
3. Las carretas tienen dos _____ grandes.
4. Lo más típico de las carretas es el _____ que tienen.

C. El Jardín Botánico de Lankester.   Select the word or phrase that best completes each statement, according to what you understood.

1. La orquídea es (un pájaro, una flor) tropical.
2. En el Jardín Botánico de Lankester hay más de (80.800) variedades de orquídeas.
3. En los jardines de Lankester hay más de (100.150) géneros de pájaros.
4. El hombre que fundó *(founded)* el Jardín de Lankester era de (Inglaterra, Costa Rica, los Estados Unidos).
5. (La Universidad, El presidente) de Costa Rica mantiene el jardín.

Ampliación

Una entrevista.   You and a partner are going to conduct a series of interviews. Make a list of three questions for each of the following people:

1. a un panameño
2. al artesano costarricense que pinta las carretas
3. al administrador del Jardín Botánico de Lankester

HACIENDO DILIGENCIAS

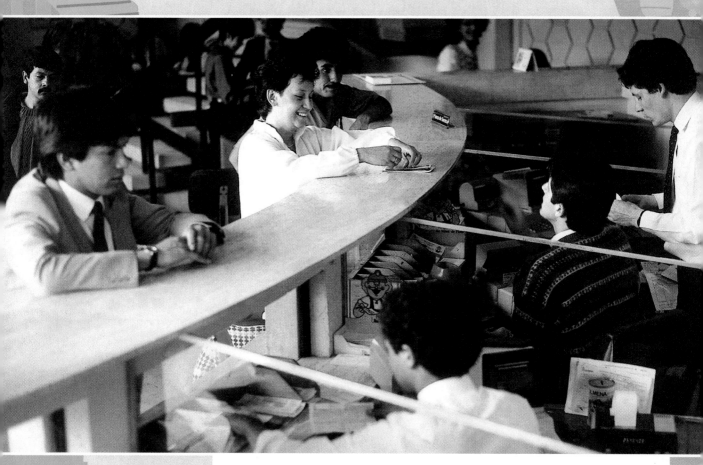

OBJECTIVES

■ Structure

• **Hace...** meaning *ago* • The subjunctive mood • The subjunctive with verbs of volition • The subjunctive with verbs of emotion

■ Communication

You will learn vocabulary related to everyday activities and running errands.

Haciendo Diligencias

En una casa de la calle Ponce en San Juan, Puerto Rico, vive la familia Vargas. Sergio está muy cansado hoy y quiere quedarse en la cama hasta tarde. Su mamá quiere que haga varias diligencias, de modo que el pobre muchacho tiene que levantarse en cuanto suena el despertador a las siete de la mañana.

A las nueve, llega a la tintorería.

SERGIO —Vengo a recoger esta ropa. Aquí está el comprobante. *(Piensa)* Ojalá que estén listos mis pantalones.

EMPLEADO —*(Lee)* Un abrigo de mujer y un pantalón. *(A Sergio)* Un momento, por favor. *(Al rato vuelve.)* Los pantalones son rosados, ¿verdad?

SERGIO —¡Eran blancos cuando los traje...!

A las diez, Sergio está en el departamento de fotografía de la tienda La Francia.

SERGIO —Hace una semana que traje un rollo de película en colores. Espero que esté listo.

EMPLEADO —A ver... ¿Sergio Vargas...? Sí, las fotos salieron muy bien.

SERGIO —¿Y cuánto cobran por revelar un rollo de película?

EMPLEADO —Seis dólares, señor.

SERGIO —Muy bien. *(Mira las fotografías.)* ¿Quién es esta señora? ¡Estas fotos no son mías!

A las once, Sergio estaciona su motocicleta frente al banco.

SERGIO —Quiero depositar este cheque, que está a nombre de mi madre. ¿Es necesario que lo firme ella?

EMPLEADO —Si lo va a depositar en la cuenta corriente de ella, no.

SERGIO —Muy bien, eso es lo que quiero hacer. También quiero sacar doscientos dólares de mi cuenta de ahorros.

EMPLEADO —Tiene que llenar esta tarjeta.

SERGIO —Necesito que me dé el saldo de mi cuenta de ahorros.

EMPLEADO —Sólo tiene veinte dólares. Lo siento, señor Vargas, pero no tiene suficiente dinero.

Cuando Sergio sale del banco, no encuentra su motocicleta.

SERGIO —*(Grita)* ¡Ay, no! ¡Alguien me robó la motocicleta!

SEÑORA —El muchacho que se llevó su motocicleta dijo que Ud. era su hermano...

SERGIO —¡Yo soy hijo único!

SEÑORA —*(Piensa)* Se parecen mucho. Me sorprende que no sean hermanos.

SERGIO —*(Mientras camina hacia la estación de policía)* ¡El próximo martes trece no salgo de casa!

VOCABULARIO

COGNADOS

el banco   bank
el cheque   check
el departamento   department, section

la motocicleta, la moto   motorcycle
suficiente   sufficient, enough

◾ NOMBRES

la cama   bed
el comprobante   claim check
la cuenta   account
la cuenta corriente   checking account
la cuenta de ahorros   savings account

el despertador   alarm clock
la diligencia   errand
la estación de policía   police station
el pantalón, los pantalones   pants, trousers
el rollo de película   roll of film

la ropa[1]   clothes, clothing
el saldo   balance
la tintorería   dry cleaner's

◾ VERBOS

caminar   to walk
cobrar   to charge
depositar   to deposit
esperar   to hope
estacionar, aparcar, parquear   to park

gritar   to scream
llevarse   to take (away)
parecerse (yo me parezco)   to look like
recoger   to pick up
revelar   to develop (film)

robar   to steal
sacar   to take out, to withdraw
sonar (o:ue)   to ring
sorprender   to surprise

◾ ADJETIVOS

listo(-a)   ready
pobre   poor

varios(-as)   several, various

◾ OTRAS PALABRAS Y EXPRESIONES

a ver   let's see
al rato   a while later
de modo que, de manera que   so
en cuanto, tan pronto como   as soon as
frente a   in front of
hacer diligencias   to run errands

hacia   toward
hijo(-a) único(-a)   only child
ojalá   I hope, God grant
quedarse en la cama hasta tarde   to sleep late
suena el despertador   the alarm goes off

---

[1]**Ropa** is always used in the singular.

Vocabulario adicional

■ En el banco

el cajero automático

en efectivo

la libreta de ahorros

el talonario de cheques,
la chequera

la firma

a plazos on installments	Compré el coche **a plazos**.	
ahorrar to save	Tienes que **ahorrar** más dinero.	
al contado in cash	No voy a comprarlo a plazos; voy a comprarlo **al contado**.	
fechar to date (a check, a letter, etc.)	Tiene que firmar y **fechar** el cheque.	
gratis free of charge	No cuesta nada; es **gratis**.	
pedir prestado(-a) to borrow	Voy a **pedirle prestados** doscientos dólares a Juan.	
pedir un préstamo to apply for a loan	Voy al banco para **pedir un préstamo** de cinco mil dólares.	

¡CONVERSEMOS!

Answer the following questions, basing your answers on the dialogues.

1. ¿Qué quiere hacer Sergio hoy? ¿Por qué?
2. ¿Qué pasa en cuanto suena el despertador?
3. ¿Por qué no puede quedarse en la cama hoy?
4. ¿Dónde estaban los pantalones de Sergio?
5. ¿De qué color eran los pantalones de Sergio? Y ahora, ¿de qué color son?
6. ¿A qué departamento de la tienda La Francia va Sergio?
7. Las fotos que él quería revelar, ¿son en colores o en blanco y negro?
8. ¿Puede sacar Sergio doscientos dólares de su cuenta de ahorros? ¿Por qué o por qué no?
9. ¿Cuál es el saldo de su cuenta de ahorros?
10. ¿Por qué grita Sergio "¡Ay, no!"?
11. ¿Sergio tiene hermanos? ¿Cómo lo sabe Ud.?
12. ¿Qué dice Sergio mientras camina a la estación de policía?

 # ¿Lo sabía Ud.?

- Puerto Rico es una de las Antillas Mayores. Es un Estado Libre Asociado a los Estados Unidos, y sus lenguas oficiales son el español y el inglés. Su capital es San Juan.

  Los indios llamaban a la isla de Puerto Rico "Boriquén", y hoy en día muchos de sus habitantes todavía usan el nombre "Borinquen". En vez de *(Instead of)* decir que son "puertorriqueños" dicen que son "boricuas" o "borinqueños".

- Cada nación latinoamericana tiene un banco central encargado de *(in charge of)* emitir el dinero y de controlar la actividad de los bancos comerciales. En algunos países hay también sucursales *(branches)* de bancos extranjeros. El uso del cheque no es tan común en América Latina como en los Estados Unidos, pero muchos bancos tienen sus propias *(own)* tarjetas de crédito.

La Puerta de San Juan, en el Viejo San Juan, parte antigua de la capital de Puerto Rico.

ESTRUCTURAS

1 Hace... meaning *ago*   (*Hace... como equivalente de* ago)

- In sentences using the preterit and in some cases the imperfect, **hace** + *period of time* is the equivalent of the English *ago*. When **hace** is placed at the beginning of the sentence, the construction is as follows.

> **Hace** + *period of time* + **que**
> **Hace** + *dos años*   + **que** la conocí.[1]

—¿Cuánto tiempo hace que conociste a tu novia?   *"How long ago did you meet your girlfriend?"*
—**Hace tres años que** la conocí.   *"I met her three years ago."*

Práctica

A. With a partner, take turns asking each other how long ago you did each of the following things.

1. ir al cine
2. ir al dentista
3. comprar tu coche
4. ir al banco
5. ir al teatro
6. empezar a estudiar español
7. ver a tus padres
8. ir de vacaciones
9. llamar a tu mejor amigo(-a)
10. levantarte

---

[1]Note that it is also possible to say: **La conocí** *hace dos años.*

B. With a partner, act out the following dialogues in Spanish.

1. "How long ago did you open your savings account, Mr. Aranda?"
   "Two months ago."
2. "I picked up my pants three days ago."
   "Did you pick up my overcoat too, Gustavo?"
   "Yes, I brought it to your house two days ago."
3. "Where is your car, Anita?"
   "I parked it ten minutes ago and now I don't remember where it is."
4. "How long ago did you take the roll of film to be developed, Tere?"
   "A week ago."

2 The subjunctive mood   *(El modo subjuntivo)*

A. Introduction to the subjunctive

Until now, you have been using verbs in the indicative mood. The indicative is used to express factual, definite events. By contrast, the subjunctive is used to reflect the speaker's feelings or attitudes toward events, or when the speaker views events as uncertain, unreal, or hypothetical.

■ The Spanish subjunctive is most often used in subordinate or dependent clauses.

■ The subjunctive is also used in English, although not as often as in Spanish. Consider the following sentence:

   *I suggest that he **arrive** tomorrow.*

The expression that requires the use of the subjunctive is in the main clause, *I suggest.* The subjunctive appears in the subordinate clause, *that he **arrive** tomorrow.* The subjunctive is used because the action of arriving is not real; it is only what is *suggested* that he do.

B. Present subjunctive forms of regular verbs

■ To form the present subjunctive, add the following endings to the stem of the first-person singular of the present indicative after dropping the **o**.

-ar *verbs*	-er *verbs*	-ir *verbs*
habl -e	com -a	viv -a
habl -es	com -as	viv -as
habl -e	com -a	viv -a
habl -emos	com -amos	viv -amos
habl -éis	com -áis	viv -áis
habl -en	com -an	viv -an

■ Note that the endings for **-er** and **-ir** verbs are identical.

■ The following table shows how to form the first-person singular of the present subjunctive. The stem is the same for all persons.

Verb	First-person singular present indicative	Subjunctive stem	First-person singular present subjunctive
caminar	camino	camin-	camine
aprender	aprendo	aprend-	aprenda
escribir	escribo	escrib-	escriba
decir	digo	dig-	diga
hacer	hago	hag-	haga
traer	traigo	traig-	traiga
sacar	saco	sac-	saque[1]
llegar	llego	lleg-	llegue[1]
empezar	empiezo	empiez-	empiece[1]

Práctica

Give the present subjunctive of the following verbs.

1. *yo:* solicitar, recibir, traer, decir, caminar, comer, ver
2. *tú:* escribir, cobrar, decidir, regresar, venir, barrer, aparcar
3. *él:* gritar, hacer, mandar, salir, anotar, esperar
4. *nosotros:* cocinar, depositar, leer, poner, pagar
5. *ellos:* caminar, deber, robar, conocer, vender, salir, empezar

C. Subjunctive forms of stem-changing verbs

◼ Verbs that end in -ar and -er undergo the same stem changes in the present subjunctive as in the present indicative.

recomendar (e:ie) *to recommend*	
recomiende	recomendemos
recomiendes	recomendéis
recomiende	recomienden

recordar (o:ue) *to remember*	
recuerde	recordemos
recuerdes	recordéis
recuerde	recuerden

entender (e:ie) *to understand*	
entienda	entendamos
entiendas	entendáis
entienda	entiendan

devolver (o:ue) *to return (something)*	
devuelva	devolvamos
devuelvas	devolváis
devuelva	devuelvan

---

[1]Remember that in verbs ending in -**gar**, -**car**, and -**zar**, **g** changes to **gu**, **c** changes to **qu**, and **z** changes to **c** before **e**.

◼ In stem-changing verbs that end in **-ir,** the unstressed **e** changes to **i** and the unstressed **o** changes to **u** in the first- and second-persons plural (**nosotros** and **vosotros**) forms. The other persons follow the same pattern as the indicative.

mentir (e:ie) *to lie*		**dormir (o:ue)** *to sleep*	
mienta	mintamos	duerma	durmamos
mientas	mintáis	duermas	durmáis
mienta	mientan	duerma	duerman

D. Verbs that are irregular in the subjunctive

◼ The following verbs are irregular in the subjunctive.

dar	**estar**	**saber**	**ser**	**ir**
dé	esté	sepa	sea	vaya
des	estés	sepas	seas	vayas
dé	esté	sepa	sea	vaya
demos	estemos	sepamos	seamos	vayamos
deis	estéis	sepáis	seáis	vayáis
den	estén	sepan	sean	vayan

ATENCIÓN The subjunctive of **hay** (impersonal form of **haber**) is **haya**.

Práctica

Give the present subjunctive of the following verbs.

1. *yo:* dormir, mentir, recomendar, dar, pensar, ir
2. *tú:* volver, estar, ser, preferir, recordar, morir, ver, pedir
3. *él:* cerrar, saber, perder, probar, dar, servir, seguir
4. *nosotros:* sentir, ir, dar, dormir, perder, cerrar, saber, ser
5. *ellos:* estar, ser, recordar, saber, encontrar, repetir

E. Uses of the subjunctive

There are four main concepts that call for the use of the subjunctive in Spanish:

◼ Volition: demands, wishes, advice, persuasion, and other attempts to impose will

Ella **quiere** que yo **solicite** el trabajo.	*She wants me to apply for the job.*
Te **aconsejo** que no **vayas** a ese banco.	*I advise you not to go to that bank.*
Les **ruego** que no se **vayan.**	*I beg you not to leave.*

▓ Emotion: pity, joy, fear, surprise, hope, and so on

Espero que **lleguen** temprano.	*I hope they arrive early.*
Siento que no **puedas** venir a clase.	*I'm sorry you can't come to class.*
Me **sorprende** que no **vayas** al concierto.	*It surprises me that you're not going to the concert.*

▓ Doubt, disbelief, denial, uncertainty, and negated facts

Dudo que **paguen** la cuenta.	*I doubt they'll pay the bill.*
No creo que ella **sea** una idiota.	*I don't think she's an idiot.*
No es verdad que Antonio **sea** instructor de tenis.	*It isn't true that Antonio is a tennis instructor.*

▓ Unreality, indefiniteness, and nonexistence

¿**Hay alguien** que **esté** libre hoy?	*Is there anyone who's free today?*
No hay nadie que **tenga** el comprobante.	*There's nobody that has his or her claim check.*

3 The subjunctive with verbs of volition
(El subjuntivo con verbos que indican voluntad o deseo)

▓ All impositions of will, as well as indirect or implied commands, require the subjunctive in subordinate clauses. The subject in the main clause must be different from the subject in the subordinate clause.

▓ Note the sentence structure for this use of the subjunctive in Spanish.

Él **quiere** que yo **estudie.**	
He wants	*me to study.*
main clause	subordinate clause

—¿Quiere que le **dé** el número de mi cuenta?	*"Do you want me to give you my account number?"*
—Sí, y también necesito que **firme** la solicitud.	*"Yes, and I also need you to sign the application."*
—Roberto quiere que tú **vayas** a la fiesta.	*"Robert wants you to go to the party."*
—Sí, pero yo no quiero ir.	*"Yes, but I don't want to go."*

ATENCIÓN   Notice that the infinitive is used after a verb of volition if there is no change of subject: **Yo no quiero *ir*.**

■ Some verbs of volition are:

aconsejar *to advise*	**querer** (e:ie) *to want*
desear *to want*	**recomendar** (e:ie) *to recommend*
mandar *to order*	**rogar** (o:ue) *to beg, plead*
necesitar *to need*	**sugerir** (e:ie) *to suggest*
pedir (e:i) *to ask for, request*	

Práctica

A. Tell the following people that you want them to do something other than what they'd like to do.

> **MODELO:** Yo quiero lavarme la cabeza ahora. (más tarde)
> Yo *te sugiero que te laves la cabeza más tarde.*

1. Nosotros necesitamos comprar una motocicleta. (un coche)
2. Yo quiero probarme el vestido aquí. (tu cuarto)
3. Ella quiere abrir una cuenta corriente. (una cuenta de ahorros)
4. Ellos quieren ir al banco hoy. (mañana)
5. Esteban quiere dar una fiesta el viernes. (el sábado)
6. Mi hermano quiere ser profesor de francés. (de inglés)
7. Anita y yo queremos venir mañana. (el lunes)
8. Uds. necesitan ir al campo en bicicleta. (en auto)
9. Alicia quiere pagar la cuenta este mes. (el mes próximo)
10. Nosotros queremos hacer la sopa. (ensalada)

B. Describe what the following people want each person to do, using the present subjunctive.

¡Tienes que estudiar!

Sí, mamá.

MODELO: *La mamá de Anita quiere que ella **estudie.***

1. Tito

2. Julia

3. Beto

4. Los estudiantes

5. Hugo

C. Your friends are always coming to you with their problems. Tell them what you suggest, recommend, or advise for each situation.

> MODELO: Mañana tengo un examen. ¿Qué me aconsejas que haga?
> *Te aconsejo que estudies mucho.*

1. Yo no puedo lavar mis pantalones en casa. ¿Adónde me sugieres que los lleve?
2. Un Porsche es muy caro para mí. ¿Qué coche me recomiendas que compre?
3. A mi hermano le regalaron mil dólares. ¿Qué le sugieres que haga con el dinero?
4. Mi prima no tiene suficiente dinero para ir al teatro. ¿Le aconsejas que se lo pida prestado a su papá o a su novio?
5. Alguien nos robó las maletas. ¿Adónde nos aconsejas que vayamos?
6. Tengo hambre. ¿Qué me recomiendas que coma?
7. Mi tía está enferma. ¿Qué le aconsejas que haga?
8. Los chicos ensuciaron la alfombra. ¿Qué les sugieres que hagan?
9. A mi hermana no le gusta cocinar. ¿Qué le sugieres que haga?
10. Mañana es el cumpleaños de mi padre. ¿Qué me sugieres que le regale?

D. With a partner, act out the following dialogues in Spanish.

1. "Where can I park, Ana?"
   "I suggest that you park in front of the bank."
2. "Do I need to fill out this card?"
   "Yes, and I need you to sign it and date it."
3. "I always sleep late, and now I have a job . . ."
   "Well . . . I advise you to buy an alarm clock."
4. "My mother wants me to run errands tomorrow."
   "Then I suggest that you get up early, Lupita."

E. Discuss with a classmate things that important people in your lives (parents, relatives, friends, professors, etc.) want you to do. List at least five things, and then compare your results with the rest of the class.

F. Write two or three problems on a slip of paper. Then, form a small group with two or three classmates. Switch slips within the group and take turns offering solutions to each other's problems.

4 The subjunctive with verbs of emotion
(El subjuntivo con verbos de emoción)

■ In Spanish, the subjunctive is always used in subordinate clauses when the verb in the main clause expresses any kind of emotion, such as fear, joy, pity, hope, pleasure, surprise, anger, regret, sorrow, likes and dislikes, and so forth.

—**Siento** que Julia no **venga** hoy.	*"I'm sorry that Julia is not coming today."*
—**Espero** que **pueda** venir mañana.	*"I hope she can come tomorrow."*
—Ramón no tiene dinero para comprar un coche.	*"Ramón doesn't have money to buy a car."*
—Ojalá que **consiga** un préstamo.	*"I hope that he obtains a loan."*

ATENCIÓN   **Ojalá** is always followed by the subjunctive.

■ If there is no change of subject, the infinitive is used instead of the subjunctive.

Me alegro de estar aquí.
(**Yo** me alegro—**yo** estoy aquí.) ⎱ *I'm glad to be here.*

■ Some verbs and expressions that express emotion are:

alegrarse (de) *to be glad*	**es una lástima** *it's a pity*
esperar *to hope*	**ojalá** *I hope*
sentir (e:ie) *to be sorry, to regret*	
sorprender *to surprise*	
temer *to fear*	

Práctica

A. You are talking to a classmate. Say whether you are glad (**Me alegro de que...**) or sorry (**Siento que...**) about what is happening to your classmate and his or her family.

> MODELO: Estoy enferma.
> *Siento que estés enferma.*

1. Yo quiero salir, pero tengo que quedarme en casa.
2. Mi hermano y yo no podemos ponernos de acuerdo.
3. Mi mamá estaba enferma, pero ahora está mejor.
4. Mi hijo es muy inteligente.
5. Mi hermana sabe cocinar muy bien.
6. No hay suficiente dinero en mi cuenta corriente.
7. Mis padres van a Buenos Aires.
8. Mis profesores me dan muchos problemas.

Now, tell your classmate about three things that are going on in your life. He or she should react appropriately.

B. With a partner, act out the following dialogues in Spanish.

1. "I'm going to go to bed."
   "I hope the bed is comfortable."
2. "I'm afraid she doesn't have much money in her checking account."
   "I hope she has money in her savings account."
3. "I'm glad you are here, ladies."
   "We're glad to be here."
4. "I'm afraid your pants aren't ready, sir."
   "I hope they're ready tomorrow."
5. "It's a pity that your brother isn't here."
   "I hope he comes back tomorrow."

C. Complete the following sentences to express how you feel, using the infinitive or the subjunctive as appropriate.

1. Yo me alegro mucho de...
2. Yo me alegro mucho de que mis amigos...
3. Yo temo no...
4. Yo temo que mi papá [mamá, hijo(-a)] no...
5. Yo siento...
6. Yo siento que el profesor (la profesora, los profesores)...
7. Yo espero...
8. Yo espero que mis padres (Ud.)...
9. Ojalá que...
10. Es una lástima que...

¡A VER CUÁNTO APRENDIÓ!

¡Repase el vocabulario!

Complete the following sentences with the appropriate words; then read them aloud.

1. Quiero comprar _____ nueva, especialmente unos pantalones.
2. ¿Cuánto _____ Uds. por _____ un rollo de película en colores?
3. Voy a _____ mil dólares de mi cuenta de ahorros y los voy a _____ en mi cuenta corriente.
4. Necesita el _____ para recoger los pantalones.
5. ¡_____ Julio! ¡Los muchachos se llevaron su motocicleta y nunca se la devolvieron!
6. A ver... No puedo verte esta semana, de _____ que tienes que venir la semana próxima.
7. Llegó Antonio y al _____ llegó Luis.
8. Anita caminó _____ mí y me dio un beso.
9. ¿Lo vas a comprar al _____ o a plazos?

10. Tengo mi _____ de cheques, pero no quiero pagar con un cheque; quiero pagar en _____ .
11. Si quieres asistir a la universidad, tienes que empezar a _____ dinero.
12. Tienes tu libreta de _____ contigo, ¿verdad? ¿O la dejaste en casa?
13. Para sacar dinero, siempre uso el _____ automático.
14. No me desperté porque no sonó el _____ .
15. Mi hermano es alto y de ojos azules, como tú. Uds. se _____ mucho.

Entrevista

Interview a classmate, using the **tú** form.

Pregúntele a su compañero(-a) de clase...

1. ...en qué calle y en qué ciudad vive.
2. ...si tiene hermanos o es hijo(-a) único(-a).
3. ...si se parece más a su mamá o a su papá.
4. ...si le gusta levantarse temprano o quedarse en la cama hasta tarde.
5. ...si hizo alguna diligencia ayer.
6. ...si lava su ropa o la lleva a la tintorería.
7. ...si está ahorrando dinero para comprar algo especial. (¿Qué?)
8. ...si prefiere que le regalen un coche o una motocicleta.
9. ...si prefiere que le tomen fotografías en colores o en blanco y negro.
10. ...si la última *(last)* vez que tomó fotos, las fotos salieron bien.

Situaciones

What would you say in the following situations? What might the other person say? Act out the scenes with a partner. Take turns playing each role.

1. You are at the dry cleaner's and you want to pick up your pants. You are upset because they are not ready. You want to know when they are going to be ready.
2. You are in the photo section of a large department store. Find out how much they charge to develop black and white and color film. Ask about the rolls of film you brought in last week for developing.
3. You are at the bank. You want to withdraw money from your savings account and deposit it in your checking account, but you're not sure what you have to do.

Para escribir

Write a short composition about the people in the photo on page 264. Describe what the employees and the customers do and want to do. Include as many banking transactions as possible.

En la vida real

Mis diligencias

Have a conversation with a classmate about the errands you have run lately, including those that did not go as planned.

Here are some words and expressions you may want to include:

mala suerte   *bad luck*
todo me fue mal   *everything went wrong (for me)*

todo el día   *all day long*
el taller de mecánica   *mechanic's shop*

Cosas por hacer

With a classmate, look at the list of errands that must be done tomorrow. Then take turns saying what you want each other to do, and give different reasons why you can't do it.

MODELO: Yo quiero que tú compres la medicina para Ernesto.
Yo *no puedo comprarla porque tengo que estudiar.*

Cosas que debemos hacer

1. Llevar los pantalones a la tintorería.
2. Llevar a revelar el rollo de película.
3. Depositar el cheque en el banco.
4. Llevar la motocicleta al taller de mecánica.
5. Comprar las bebidas para la fiesta.
6. Llevar los discos compactos a casa de Ana.
7. Alquilar un video.
8. Comprar los billetes para la excursión.
9. Recoger las entradas para el concierto.
10. Comprar la medicina para Ernesto.
11. Pedirle prestada la grabadora a Rosita.
12. Ir a la oficina de turismo para pedir la lista de hoteles.
13. Comprar el regalo para Eva.
14. Devolverle las maletas a Luis.

¿Qué dice tu horóscopo?

Read the following horoscopes, and then compare your own horoscope with those of your classmates. Try to find a classmate for each sign of the zodiac by asking, **¿De qué signo eres?** *(What's your sign?).* Offer each other suggestions on how to fulfill your horoscopes.

CAPRICORNIO (21 de diciembre–20 de enero)

Tú eres, como siempre, ¡superpráctico! Debes recordar, sin embargo *(however)*, que a veces es bueno ser impulsivo. Si recibes una invitación interesante... ¿por qué no aceptarla?

ACUARIO (21 de enero–19 de febrero)

Si quieres progresar en tus estudios o en tu profesión, no debes dejar para mañana lo que puedes hacer hoy. Alguien muy importante te está observando.

PISCIS (20 de febrero–20 de marzo)

Más que nunca, Cupido va a ser parte de tu vida *(life)* este año. Probablemente va a querer que estés preparado para cualquier cosa *(anything)*, incluso una boda.

ARIES (21 de marzo–20 de abril)

¡Siempre empiezas proyectos con mucho entusiasmo pero casi nunca los terminas! Tienes que hacer lo posible por aprender a ser perseverante. Este año va a ser muy importante para ti.

TAURO (21 de abril–20 de mayo)

Buena oportunidad para mejorar *(improve)* las finanzas. Un nuevo empleo... una beca *(scholarship)*... Pero tienes que hacer tu parte y aceptar nuevas responsabilidades.

GÉMINIS (21 de mayo–20 de junio)

¡Tienes que salir de la rutina! ¿Por qué no tomas una clase o das una fiesta? Hay muchas personas que quieren ser tus amigos... pero tú no les das la oportunidad.

CÁNCER (21 de junio–20 de julio)

Muy pronto vas a tener que tomar una decisión muy importante. Debes pensar en todas las posibilidades antes de decidir lo que vas a hacer. Hay alguien que está esperando ansiosamente *(anxiously)* tu decisión.

LEO (21 de julio–20 de agosto)

Pronto vas a recibir noticias *(news)* de alguien que hace mucho que no ves. También debes tratar de llamar o de escribirles a aquellas personas que son parte de tu pasado.

VIRGO
(21 de agosto–20 de septiembre)
Como siempre, estás trabajando demasiado. No debes sentirte culpable *(guilty)* si decides tomarte unas vacaciones o simplemente ir al cine o al teatro con tus amigos. Esta semana vas a tener muchas oportunidades de divertirte y debes aprovecharlas *(take advantage of them)*.

LIBRA
(21 de septiembre–20 de octubre)
Tú eres generalmente una persona muy equilibrada, pero últimamente *(lately)* le estás dando más importancia a tu trabajo y a tus proyectos que a tu familia. Tienes que pasar más tiempo con tu familia.

ESCORPIÓN
(21 de octubre–20 de noviembre)
Éstos son los momentos indicados para tomar decisiones importantes. Es muy posible que hagas un viaje muy largo, probablemente al extranjero *(abroad)*.

SAGITARIO
(21 de noviembre–20 de diciembre)
Hay una persona que está secretamente enamorada de *(in love with)* ti. Muy pronto vas a saber quién es. Debes aceptar las invitaciones de tus amigos porque vas a conocer a esa persona en una fiesta o en un picnic.

Tenemos algunas quejas... *(We have some complaints)*

Get ready to complain and to respond to complaints about different commercial establishments. The class will be divided into two groups owning different businesses. Group A owns a restaurant, a hotel, and a travel agency. Group B owns a bank, a beauty salon, and a maid service. Before the two groups express their complaints to each other about bad service, each group should decide on the types of concerns and problems that they'll present.

As í s o m o s

Vocabulario

aguantar	to hold back
ayudar	to help
la cantidad	sum
cargar	to carry
compartir	to share
la compra	purchase
con bastante frecuencia	quite frequently
cualquier	whatever
cuidar	to take care of
gastaría	I would spend
los gastos	expenses
el historial	record
el hogar	home, house
me encargo	I am in charge of, I look after
obtener	to obtain
los pagos	payments
los quehaceres	chores, tasks
repartir	to distribute, to divide
los retiros	withdrawls
se rebase	exceeds
segura	safe
solamente	only
sobre todo	especially
sucede	occurs

Preparación

¿Cuánto saben Uds. ya?   This video module focuses on certain aspects related to running errands, banking, and forms of payment. With a partner, brainstorm possible words and phrases that people might use in these contexts. Make a list of them and circle the ones you hear as you watch the video.

Comprensión

A. Las diligencias.   Select the word or phrase that best completes each statement, according to what you understood.

1. El papá de Juan se ocupa de *(takes charge of)* (los aspectos financieros, las compras diarias).
2. (Olga, Roberto) lleva a los niños a la escuela.
3. Los padres de Tamara comparten (los pagos de la luz, las tareas del hogar).

B. El banco y el cajero automático.   Answer the following questions.

1. ¿Cuándo va Víctor al banco?
2. ¿Va Tamara al banco con mucha frecuencia?
3. ¿Por qué no usa Juan el cajero automático?
4. ¿Quién usa el cajero automático sólo para emergencias?

C. Maneras de pagar.   Read the following statements. After watching the video, circle **V** (**Verdadero**) and **F** (**Falso**), according to what you understood.

V F 1. Víctor nunca usa tarjeta de crédito.
V F 2. Cuando va de compras, Juan siempre paga en efectivo.
V F 3. Gustavo dice que las tarjetas de crédito no son seguras.
V F 4. Paula prefiere usar la tarjeta de crédito porque sus papás pagan la cuenta.
V F 5. Gustavo tiene cuatro tarjetas de crédito.
V F 6. Tamara tiene muchas tarjetas de crédito.

Ampliación

A. Mis gastos.   Make a list of your weekly expenses. Then in groups of three or four, compare your lists.

B. Entrevista.   Interview a classmate about his or her banking habits.

LECCIÓN 12

PIDIENDO INFORMACIÓN

OBJECTIVES

■ **Structure**

The **Ud.** and **Uds.** commands • The relative pronouns **que** and **quien** • The subjunctive to express doubt, disbelief, and denial • Constructions with **se**

■ **Communication**

You will learn vocabulary related to asking for directions and postal services.

PIDIENDO INFORMACIÓN

Julia, una chica de Honduras, llegó a Madrid hace una semana. Con sus amigos españoles visitó el Parque del Retiro, el Palacio Real y las antiguas ciudades de Segovia, Ávila y Toledo. En cada lugar compró un montón de tarjetas postales para enviárselas a sus padres y a sus amigos. Hoy decidió ir al correo para enviar las tarjetas, y recoger un paquete y un giro postal.

JULIA —*(Piensa)* Dudo que el correo esté abierto a esta hora. Creo que se abre a las nueve. *(A un señor que está parado en la esquina)* Dígame, señor, ¿dónde queda la oficina de correos?

SR. GÓMEZ —Está a cinco manzanas de aquí, en la Plaza de La Cibeles.

JULIA —Es que… soy extranjera y no conozco las calles. ¿Puede decirme cómo llegar allí?

SR. GÓMEZ —¡Ah!, siga derecho por esta calle hasta llegar a la Plaza de Colón.

JULIA —¿Cuántas cuadras?

SR. GÓMEZ —Dos. Después doble a la derecha al llegar al semáforo, en la calle Alcalá.

JULIA —¿La oficina de correos está en esa calle?

SR. GÓMEZ —Sí, allí mismo. Es un edificio antiguo y está frente a la estación del metro.

En el correo, Julia habla con el empleado que está en la ventanilla de información.

JULIA —Vengo a recoger un paquete y un giro postal. Me llamo Julia Reyes.

EMPLEADO —¿Tiene un documento de identidad?

JULIA —Mi pasaporte… pero lo dejé en el hotel.

EMPLEADO —No creo que se los den sin identificación.

JULIA —Bueno, vuelvo esta tarde. ¿Dónde puedo comprar sellos?

EMPLEADO —Vaya a la ventanilla número dos, a la izquierda.

En la ventanilla número dos, Julia le pide al empleado los sellos que necesita.

JULIA —Quiero enviar estas tarjetas postales por vía aérea y una carta certificada a Honduras.

EMPLEADO —Son mil quinientas pesetas,[1] señorita.

JULIA —¿Puede decirme cómo llegar desde aquí a El[2] Corte Inglés?

EMPLEADO —Salga por la puerta principal, cruce la Plaza de La Cibeles y camine por la Gran Vía hasta llegar a la Plaza Callao. El Corte Inglés está al lado de la plaza.

En El Corte Inglés, Julia se encuentra con su amiga Pilar, con quien va a ir de compras.

JULIA —Creía que no ibas a estar aquí.

PILAR —Oye, guapa, no es cierto que los españoles siempre lleguemos tarde. A veces somos puntuales.

Las chicas suben al tercer piso, donde está el departamento de ropa para señoras.

---

[1] Spanish currency
[2] Note that **a** and **el** do not contract to form **al** since **El** is part of the store name.

Vocabulario

Cognados

el documento document
la estación station
el palacio palace

el parque park
puntual punctual

▪ Nombres

el departamento de (ropa para) señoras (damas) women's department
el documento de identidad (identificación) I.D.
el edificio building
el (la) español(-a) Spaniard
la esquina corner

el (la) extranjero(-a) foreigner
el giro postal money order
la manzana[1] *(Spain)*, **la cuadra** *(Sp. Am.)* city block
el metro, el subterráneo subway
la oficina de correos, el correo post office
el paquete package, parcel

la puerta principal main exit (door)
el sello, la estampilla, el timbre *(Mex.)* stamp
el semáforo traffic light
la ventanilla window (of a car or booth, as in a bank or post office)

▪ Verbos

cruzar to cross
doblar to turn, to bend
dudar to doubt

encontrarse (con) (o:ue) to meet
subir to go up, to climb

▪ Adjetivos

abierto(-a) open
antiguo(-a), viejo(-a)[2] old
certificado(-a) registered, certified

parado(-a) standing
real royal

▪ Otras palabras y expresiones

a veces sometimes
al lado de next to
allí mismo right there
cada each
derecho straight (ahead)
desde from

es que... the fact is . . .
está a... de aquí it is . . . from here
frente a across from
hasta llegar until you get
No es cierto. (No es verdad.) It's not true.

por vía aérea by airmail
que that, which, who
quien(-es) who, whom
sin without
un montón de a pile of

---

[1]In Spanish America, **manzana** is used to refer to a block of buildings, not to the distance between streets.
[2]When referring to people, use **viejo**, not **antiguo**.

Vocabulario adicional

El correo

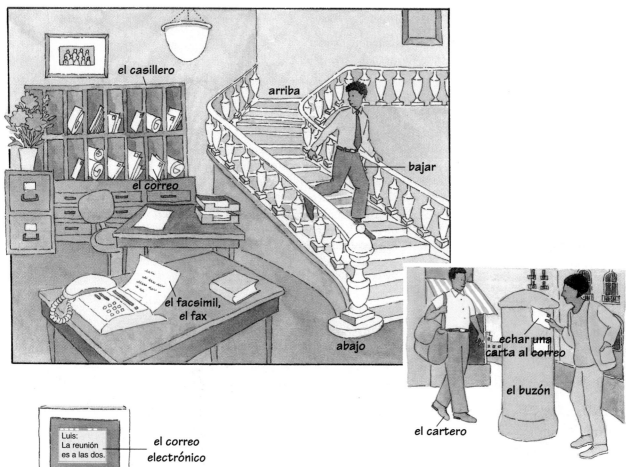

el casillero

arriba

el correo

bajar

el facsimil,
el fax

abajo

echar una
carta al correo

el buzón

el cartero

Luis:
La reunión
es a las dos.

el correo
electrónico

el giro postal

CORREOS DE ESPAÑA
Oficina de Correos de Atocha
Madrid

Giro Postal No._____
Oficina expedidora No.
Fecha: _____

Remitente: _____
(Nombre y apellidos, en letra de molde)
Dirección: **Calle y número:** _____
Ciudad y zona postal: _____
Beneficiario: _____
Dirección: **Calle y número:** _____
Ciudad y zona postal: _____
Valor del giro: _____ (_____)
(En letra de molde) **(En cifras)**

Firma del Remitente: _____

¡CONVERSEMOS!

Answer the following questions, basing your answers on the dialogues.

1. ¿Cuánto tiempo hace que Julia está en Madrid?
2. ¿Qué lugares visitó con sus amigos españoles?
3. ¿A quién le pregunta dónde queda la oficina
4. En la calle Alcalá, ¿Julia debe doblar a la i
5. ¿Cómo es el edificio de correos y dónde est
6. ¿Por qué no puede Julia recoger el paquete
7. ¿En qué ventanilla puede comprar sellos?
8. ¿Cómo va a enviar las tarjetas postales Julia?
9. ¿Por dónde sale Julia del correo y qué cruza?
10. ¿A qué tienda va Julia y con quién se encuentra
11. ¿Qué dice Pilar de los españoles?
12. ¿En qué piso está el departamento de ropa para se

 # ¿Lo sabía Ud.?

- Situada en la parte central de la península Ibérica, Madrid es la capital de España. Su población de más de seis millones de habitantes y su importancia cultural y económica la hacen la principal ciudad española.

  Una de las calles principales de la ciudad es la Gran Vía, donde hay muchas tiendas elegantes y cafés al aire libre.

- El correo de Madrid, o el Palacio de Comunicaciones, es un edificio monumental. Está frente a la hermosa fuente *(fountain)* de La Cibeles, que, para muchos, es el símbolo de Madrid.

- El Palacio Real, situado frente a la Plaza de Oriente, fue la antigua residencia de los reyes de España. Está considerado uno de los mejores edificios de su tipo en Europa.

- El metro de Madrid es un sistema de transporte muy eficiente y barato. Es el medio *(means)* de transportación que usa la mayoría de los madrileños. También hay un metro en Barcelona.

- Segovia es un punto de atracción turístico. Entre sus muchos lugares de interés están el Alcázar, un castillo fortaleza *(fortress)*, y el famoso acueducto romano.

- El uso del "Internet" o la "Red", como se llama en español, es cada día más popular en el mundo hispano, y muchos países tienen su propia página *(home page)*.

Entrada del metro en La Puerta del Sol, Madrid, España.

ESTRUCTURAS

1 The **Ud.** and **Uds.** commands *(Formas del imperativo para **Ud.** y **Uds.**)*

The command forms for **Ud.** and **Uds.**[1] are identical to the corresponding present subjunctive forms.

A. Regular forms

Endings of the Formal Commands			
		Ud.	**Uds.**
-ar verbs	cantar	cant **-e**	cant **-en**
-er verbs	beber	beb **-a**	beb **-an**
-ir verbs	vivir	viv **-a**	viv **-an**

—¿Sigo derecho? *"Do I keep going straight ahead?"*
—No, no **siga** derecho. **Doble** *"No, don't keep going straight*
a la izquierda. *ahead. Turn left."*

ATENCIÓN To give a negative **Ud./Uds.** command, place **no** in front of the verb:
No siga derecho.

B. Irregular forms

■ The command forms of the following verbs are irregular.

	dar	**estar**	**ser**	**ir**
Ud.	dé	esté	sea	vaya
Uds.	den	estén	sean	vayan

—¿Adónde tengo que ir? *"Where do I have to go?"*
—**Vaya** a la ventanilla número *"Go to window number two."*
dos.

Práctica

A. What commands would these people give?

1. *El profesor a los estudiantes:*

   venir a clase temprano   cerrar el libro
   abrir el libro   hablar solamente español
   ir a la pizarra   no hablar inglés en la clase
   hacer los ejercicios

---

[1] **Tú** commands will be studied in **Lección 13.**

2. *La directora a la secretaria:*

estar en la oficina a las ocho
traer las cartas
traducir los documentos
llevar las cartas al correo
comprar estampillas

llamar por teléfono al Sr. Paz
conseguir la dirección del Banco
   de Ponce
no volver hasta las tres

B. After spending a few weeks in Madrid, Julia has decided to visit Granada. She would like to visit many places, but doesn't know how to get to them. Using the map below, can you help her?

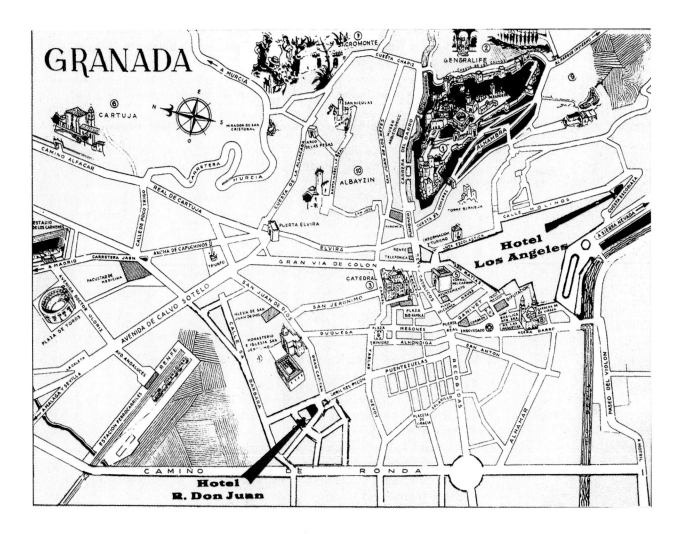

¿Cómo se puede ir...

1. del hotel Don Juan a la Puerta Elvira?
2. de la Puerta Elvira a la Catedral?
3. del Albayzín al Sacromonte?
4. del Sacromonte a la Alhambra?
5. de la Alhambra al Generalife?
6. de la estación de trenes a la Plaza de Toros?

C. Position of object pronouns with direct commands

■ In all direct *affirmative* commands, the object pronouns are placed *after* the verb and attached to it.

Ud. *form*		Uds. *form*	
Hágalo.	*Do it.*	Cómprenlo.	*Buy it.*
Dígales.	*Tell them.*	Díganle.	*Tell him/her.*
Tráiganosla.	*Bring it to us.*	Tráiganselo.	*Bring it to him/her.*
Quédese.	*Stay.*	Quédense.	*Stay.*

ATENCIÓN Note the use of the written accent, which follows the rules for accentuation. See Appendix A.

■ In all *negative* commands, the pronouns are placed *in front of the verb*.

Ud. *form*		Uds. *form*	
No **lo** haga.	*Don't do it.*	No **lo** hagan.	*Don't do it.*
No **le** hable.	*Don't speak to him/her.*	No **le** hablen.	*Don't speak to him/her.*
No **se lo** dé.	*Don't give it to him/her.*	No **se lo** den.	*Don't give it to him/her.*

■ Remember that when an indirect and a direct object pronoun are used together in the same sentence, the indirect object always precedes the direct object.

Práctica

A. Using the direct commands, tell your younger brothers to do the following.

1. Levantarse a las siete, bañarse y vestirse.
2. Preparar unos sándwiches y ponerlos en el refrigerador.
3. Escribirle una carta a la abuela y echarla al correo.
4. Mandarle un paquete a Teresa.
5. Llamar a la Dra. Peña, pero no llamarla antes de las tres.
6. Comprarle el regalo a mamá, pero no dárselo hoy.
7. Decirle a Marta que la fiesta es mañana, pero no decírselo a Raúl.
8. No acostarse muy tarde.

B. You are having dinner at a fancy restaurant. Tell the waiter what you want or don't want him to do.

> MODELO: ¿Le traigo el menú?
> *Sí, tráigamelo, por favor. (No, no me lo traiga.)*

1. ¿Le traigo la lista de vinos?
2. ¿Le sirvo la ensalada primero?
3. ¿Le pongo pimienta a la ensalada?
4. ¿Abro la botella de vino ahora?
5. ¿Le traigo una tortilla a la española?

6. ¿Le sirvo el café ahora?
7. ¿Le traigo la cuenta ahora?

C. With a partner, take turns playing the roles of a tourist who is planning a trip to an exotic location and a travel agent. The tourist should name a destination and ask whether he or she should bring along certain items. The agent should say whether each article would or would not be appropriate. List five or six items each. Follow the models.

> MODELO: —¿Debo llevar tarjetas postales?
> —*No, no las lleve. Cómprelas allí.*
>
> —¿Debo llevar mi tienda de campaña?
> —*Sí, llévela. No hay hoteles.*

2 The relative pronouns **que** and **quien**
(Los pronombres relativos que y quien)

Relative pronouns are used to combine two sentences that have a common element, usually a noun or a pronoun.

A. The relative pronoun *que*

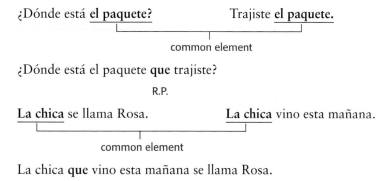

¿Dónde está **el paquete?**   Trajiste **el paquete.**

common element

¿Dónde está el paquete **que** trajiste?

R.P.

La chica se llama Rosa.   **La chica** vino esta mañana.

common element

La chica **que** vino esta mañana se llama Rosa.

R.P.

■ Note that the relative pronoun **que** not only helps to combine the two sentences in each example, but also replaces the nouns **el paquete** and **la chica** in the second sentences.

■ The relative pronoun **que** is invariable and is used for both persons and things. It is the Spanish equivalent of *that*, *which*, and *who*. Unlike its English equivalent, the Spanish **que** is never omitted.

—¿Para quién es el libro **que** compraste?	*"For whom is the book that you bought?"*
—Es para la señora **que** enseña español.	*"It is for the woman who teaches Spanish."*

B. The relative pronoun *quien*

—¿La muchacha **con quien** hablabas es americana?	*"Is the girl with whom you were talking an American?"*
—No, es extranjera.	*"No, she's a foreigner."*
—¿Quiénes son esos señores?	*"Who are those gentlemen?"*
—Son los señores **de quienes** te habló José.	*"They are the gentlemen about whom José spoke to you."*

▇ The relative pronoun **quien** is used only with persons.

▇ The plural of **quien** is **quienes**. **Quien** does not change for gender.

▇ **Quien** is generally used after prepositions, i.e., **con quien**, **de quienes**.

▇ **Quien** is the Spanish equivalent of *whom* and *that*.

Práctica

A. Complete the following dialogues, using **que**, **quien**, or **quienes**. Then act them out with a partner.

1. —¿Quién es el señor _____ trajo las cartas?
   —Es el papá de Marisa, la chica con _____ trabajo.
2. —¿Dónde están las estampillas _____ compré ayer?
   —En tu escritorio.
3. —Las chicas con _____ salimos anoche llamaron esta mañana.
   —¿Qué dijeron?
   —Que nos van a traer los libros _____ necesitamos.
4. —¿Con quién vas al museo?
   —Con María Luisa, la chica de _____ te hablé.
5. —¿Ella es la muchacha _____ trabaja contigo?
   —No, es la chica con _____ estudio.

B. Interview a classmate, using the following questions. When you have finished, switch roles.

1. ¿Cómo se llama la persona a quien más admiras?
2. ¿Cómo se llama el profesor o la profesora que enseña tu clase favorita?
3. ¿Quiénes son las personas que viven contigo?
4. ¿Cómo se llaman las personas con quienes vas a salir el sábado?
5. ¿Quién es la persona que más te quiere?
6. ¿Cuál es la comida que más te gusta?
7. ¿Cuál es el color que más te gusta?
8. ¿Dónde está el banco en el que tienes tu cuenta corriente? (¿Y tu cuenta de ahorros?)

3 The subjunctive to express doubt, disbelief, and denial
(Uso del subjuntivo para expresar duda, incredulidad y negación)

A. Doubt

■ In Spanish, the subjunctive is always used in a subordinate clause when the verb of the main clause expresses doubt or uncertainty.

—Vamos al correo.	*"Let's go to the post office."*
—**Dudo** que **esté** abierto a esta hora.	*"I doubt that it's open at this time."*
—Estoy seguro de que abren a las ocho.	*"I'm sure that they open at eight."*

ATENCIÓN When *no doubt* is expressed and the speaker is certain of the reality (**Estoy seguro[-a], No dudo**), the indicative is used: **Estoy seguro** de que **abren** a las ocho.

B. Disbelief

■ The verb **creer** is followed by the subjunctive in negative sentences, where it expresses disbelief.

—¿Uds. van a ir de compras hoy?	*"Are you going to go shopping today?"*
—No..., **no creo** que **tengamos** tiempo...	*"No..., I don't think we'll have time..."*
—Yo creo que pueden ir, si salen temprano.	*"I think you can go if you leave early."*

ATENCIÓN **Creer** is followed by the indicative, when it expresses belief or conviction: **Yo creo** que **pueden** ir.

C. Denial

■ When the main clause expresses denial of what is said in the subordinate clause, the subjunctive is used.

—¡Tú siempre llegas tarde!	*"You always arrive late!"*
—**No es verdad** que siempre **llegue** tarde. No niego que a veces llego un poco tarde, pero a veces soy puntual.	*"It's not true that I always arrive late. I don't deny that sometimes I arrive a little late, but sometimes I'm punctual."*

ATENCIÓN When the main clause does *not* deny, but rather confirms what is said in the subordinate clause, the indicative is used: **No niego** que a veces **llego** un poco tarde.

Práctica

A. Say whether the following statements are true or not. If a statement is false, correct it.

> MODELO: Nosotros celebramos la independencia de Chile.
> *No es verdad que nosotros celebremos la independencia de Chile; celebramos la independencia de los Estados Unidos.*

1. Texas es más grande que Maine.
2. Hace más calor en Alaska que en Arizona.
3. Buenos Aires es la capital de Chile.
4. México está al norte de los Estados Unidos.
5. El 25 de diciembre celebramos la independencia de nuestro país.
6. El presidente del país puede ser extranjero.
7. Necesitamos un documento de identidad para comprar estampillas.
8. Revelan rollos de película en el correo.
9. Echamos las cartas en el buzón.
10. Podemos comprar un giro postal en el correo.

B. You and a friend are spending the weekend in a very small town. Your friend wants to know about things to do, places to go, and so on. Answer, expressing belief or disbelief, doubt or certainty.

1. ¿Tú crees que hay habitaciones libres en el hotel?
2. ¿Tú crees que un cuarto cuesta menos de cien dólares la noche?
3. ¿Tú crees que aceptan cheques de viajero en el hotel?
4. ¿Tú crees que hay un aeropuerto aquí?
5. ¿Podemos alquilar un coche?
6. Son las siete; ¿tú crees que el correo está abierto?
7. Vamos al centro. Quiero ir a una tienda elegante.
8. Tengo el pelo muy largo. Dicen que aquí hay peluquerías excelentes.
9. Quiero ir a cenar a un restaurante francés.
10. ¿Tú crees que vamos a volver aquí algún día?

C. Complete the following sentences logically, using the subjunctive or the indicative as appropriate.

1. Yo dudo que en mi cuenta de ahorros…
2. Estoy seguro(-a) de que el banco…
3. No creo que la oficina de correos…
4. Estoy seguro(-a) de que la estación del metro…
5. No es verdad que yo…
6. Yo no niego que mis padres…
7. Creo que los sellos…
8. No dudo que allí mismo…

4 Constructions with **se** *(Construcciones con se)*

■ In Spanish the pronoun **se** + *the third-person singular or plural form of the verb* is used as an impersonal construction. It is equivalent to the English passive voice, in which the person doing the action is not specified. It is also equivalent to English constructions that use the impersonal subjects *one, they, people,* and *you* (indefinite). The impersonal construction is widely used in Spanish.

| | Spanish is spoken in Chile. |
| Se habla español en Chile. { | They speak Spanish in Chile. |

—¿A qué hora **se abren** los bancos?

"*What time do the banks open?*"

—**Se abren** a las nueve de la mañana.

"*They open at nine A.M.*"

—**Se dice** que los españoles no son puntuales.

"*It's said that Spaniards aren't punctual.*"

—Sí, **se dice,** pero no es verdad.

"*Yes, it's said, but it's not true.*"

■ The impersonal **se** is often used in ads, instructions, or directions.

FOR SALE

NO SMOKING

EXIT TO THE RIGHT

Práctica

A. In groups of three, draw signs with the following information on them.

1. No parking
2. Exit to the left
3. Spanish spoken here
4. No littering (*to litter*: **tirar basura**)
5. No crossing
6. No swimming
7. Cars for sale

B. With a classmate, act out a scene between a tourist in Madrid and a resident of the city who responds to the tourist's questions about the city. Use constructions with **se** in your conversation.

El turista necesita saber…

1. …el horario *(schedule)* de los bancos, del correo y de las tiendas.
2. …qué idiomas habla la gente.
3. …qué y dónde comen.
4. …si venden objetos de oro y de plata.
5. …dónde alquilan coches.

¡A VER CUÁNTO APRENDIÓ!

¡Repase el vocabulario!

Complete the following sentences with words from the lesson vocabulary.

1. Tengo que bajar porque el departamento de señoras no está _____ ; está _____ .
2. No estamos sentados; estamos _____ .
3. Hoy vamos a visitar el _____ del Retiro y el _____ Real.
4. Dígame, ¿la _____ del metro está en la calle Alcalá?
5. Mis padres me van a mandar un _____ postal porque necesito dinero.
6. Recibí un _____ de tarjetas de Navidad el año pasado.
7. Le voy a decir al secretario que ponga las cartas certificadas en mi _____ .
8. Mandé el paquete por vía _____ y _____ .
9. Está allí _____ , en la esquina. Va a _____ la calle.
10. Los colores del _____ son rojo, amarillo y verde.
11. Primero voy a estudiar y después voy a _____ con Carlos en la tienda.
12. En _____ lugar que visitamos, compramos tarjetas.
13. La oficina está arriba. Dudo que ellos puedan _____ hasta el décimo piso.
14. Elsa le va a preguntar al cartero dónde queda la _____ de correos.
15. Para ir al banco no debe seguir derecho. Debe _____ a la izquierda.

Entrevista

Interview a classmate, using the **tú** form.

Pregúntele a su compañero(-a) de clase...

1. ...si sabe dónde queda la oficina de correos.
2. ...si es verdad que el correo se abre a las siete de la mañana.
3. ...a cuántas cuadras de su casa queda el correo.
4. ...qué queda frente a su casa. (¿Al lado de su casa?)
5. ...si prefiere los edificios antiguos o modernos.
6. ...si para ir a la cafetería debe seguir derecho o doblar a la izquierda o a la derecha.
7. ...si hay metro en la ciudad donde vive.
8. ...si hay muchos extranjeros en la ciudad donde vive.
9. ...si tiene pasaporte.
10. ...si cree que los norteamericanos son puntuales.

Situaciones

What would you say in the following situations? What might the other person say? Act out the scenes with a partner. Take turns playing each role.

1. You are in Madrid, and you want to know where the post office is located. You are a foreigner and you don't know your way around. Ask someone on the street for help.
2. A foreigner asks you for directions to a post office in your town. Explain to him or her how to get to the nearest one.
3. You are at the post office. You want to send some letters by airmail, buy some stamps, and find out how much it costs to send a registered letter to the United States. You also want to know if there is a package for you.

Para escribir

You are an advice columnist for a Spanish newspaper. How would you respond to the following letters? Use command forms to give your advice in writing.

1. Tengo 18 años y quiero vivir sola *(alone)* en un apartamento, pero mis padres no quieren que me vaya de la casa. ¿Qué me sugiere que haga?

   Ansiosa de libertad

2. Pienso viajar a París este verano y tengo un amigo que quiere ir conmigo. Yo no quiero ofenderlo, pero no deseo ir con él porque es muy aburrido y siempre está cansado. ¿Qué puedo hacer?

   Un viajero

3. Tengo un novio que es muy bueno, pero no es muy interesante. El sábado pasado fui a una fiesta y conocí a un hombre extraordinario y muy guapo que me invitó a salir. ¿Debo aceptar su invitación o no? ¿Qué me aconseja que haga?

   Indecisa

4. Tenemos unos vecinos *(neighbors)* que tienen cinco hijos; los niños son terribles y todo lo rompen *(break)*. Planeamos dar una fiesta muy elegante para celebrar el fin de año y queremos invitarlos pero ellos siempre llevan a sus hijos a todas partes *(everywhere)*. ¿Cómo les pedimos que no traigan a sus hijos a la fiesta?

   Entre la espada y la pared[1]

En la vida real

¿Cómo se llega...?

With a classmate, figure out how to give a new student the following directions:

Within the university	***Outside the university***
¿Cómo voy de la clase de español...	¿Cómo voy de la universidad...
1. a la biblioteca?	1. al restaurante McDonald's?
2. al edificio de administración?	2. a la oficina de correos?
3. a la cafetería?	3. a la gasolinera *(gas station)*?
4. al baño?	4. a tu casa o apartamento?

---

[1]*Between a rock and a hard place (lit., between the sword and the wall)*

Señales de tráfico *(Traffic signs)*

You are traveling in Spain and see the following signs. What do they mean?

1.

2.

3.

4.

5.

a. Yield
b. No parking
c. Stop

d. One way
e. Pedestrian crossing

Nuestra casa es su casa

You and your roommate are going away for a couple of weeks and are letting friends from out of town stay in your apartment. With your roommate (a classmate), prepare a list of 1) recommendations of fun things to do in town, including instructions for how to get to them; 2) household chores or errands they should do in your absence.

¡Vamos a leer!

Antes de leer

A. Before you read *La señorita Julia* in detail, skim it quickly to get the gist of the story, without stopping to look up unfamiliar vocabulary. What is the setting for the story? Who are the main characters? What important events take place? Identifying these points will help you understand the story better the second time through.

B. As you read the story, answer the following questions.

1. ¿Qué problema tiene Alberto y cómo lo soluciona?
2. ¿En qué consiste el trabajo de Alberto?
3. ¿Cómo es el cuarto donde está el cuadro? ¿Cómo es el cuadro?
4. ¿Qué diferencias hay entre la muchacha del cuadro y la señorita Julia?
5. ¿Qué le hace Alberto a la señorita Julia? ¿Por qué?
6. ¿Qué cree la criada que pasó?
7. ¿Qué ven los policías cuando miran el cuadro? ¿Por qué les parece *(seem)* raro?

La señorita Julia

ANA CORTESI-JARVIS

Ana Cortesi-Jarvis nació en Paraguay y se educó en Argentina. Es autora de varios libros de texto para la enseñanza del español. Ha publicado también varios cuentos y poemas. Vive y enseña en los Estados Unidos.

Alberto Aguirre necesita ganar algún dinero para poder asistir a la universidad. Solicita y obtiene un trabajo en casa de la señorita Julia Ocampos, anciana° de ochenta años, que tiene muchísimo dinero y vive sola, con una criada.°

    El trabajo de Alberto consiste en hacer un inventario completo de todas las posesiones de la señorita Julia.

    Un día, Alberto sube a un cuarto pequeño, con cortinas° de encaje° blanco y olor° a jazmines. Es entonces que nota el cuadro enorme colgado° en la pared. Es el retrato° de una muchacha de belleza espléndida, sentada bajo un árbol grande, con margaritas° en el regazo.°

    Alberto pasa horas en el cuarto, contemplando el cuadro. Allí trabaja, come, sueña°, vive…

old lady
maid

curtains / lace
smell / hung
portrait
daisies / lap

dreams

steps

pointing to / mixture

Un día oye los pasos° de la señorita Julia, que viene hacia el cuarto.

—¿Quién es? —pregunta Alberto, señalando° el cuadro con una mezcla° de admiración, respeto y delirio.

—Soy yo… —responde la señorita Julia—, yo a los dieciocho años.

Alberto mira el cuadro y mira a la señorita Julia, alternativamente. En su

heart / hatred
wrinkled

corazón° nace un profundo odio° por la señorita Julia, que es vieja y arrugada° y tiene el pelo blanco.

Cada día que pasa, Alberto está más pálido y nervioso. Casi no trabaja. Cada día está más enamorado de la muchacha del cuadro, y cada día odia más a la señorita Julia.

Una noche, cuando está listo para regresar a su casa, oye pasos que vienen hacia el cuarto. Es la señorita Julia.

—Su trabajo está terminado —dice—; no necesita regresar mañana…

kills
feet
she discovers

Alberto mata° a la señorita Julia y pone el cadáver de la anciana a los pies° de la muchacha.

Pasan dos días. La criada llama a la policía cuando descubre° el cuerpo de la señorita Julia en el cuarto de arriba.

robber / weeps
Falta… *Is anything of value missing? / detailed*
handwriting / cramped

—Estoy segura de que fue un ladrón°—solloza° la criada.

—¿Falta algo de valor?° —pregunta uno de los policías.

La criada tiene una idea. Va a buscar el inventario detallado,° escrito por Alberto con su letra° pequeña y apretada.° Los dos policías leen el inventario, van por toda la casa y ven que no falta nada.

Regresan al cuarto.

Parados al lado de la ventana con cortinas de encaje blanco y olor a jazmines, leen la descripción del cuadro que tienen frente a ellos: "retrato de una muchacha de belleza espléndida, sentada bajo un árbol grande, con margaritas en el regazo".

odd / frunciendo… frowning
couple

—¡Qué raro!° —exclama uno de los policías, frunciendo el ceño.°

—Según este inventario, es el retrato de una muchacha, no de una pareja…°

Díganos

Answer the following questions based on your own thoughts and experiences.

1. ¿Qué tipo de cuento considera Ud. *La señorita Julia*: divertido, serio, romántico, realista, de suspenso…? ¿Por qué?
2. ¿Qué tipo de cuentos prefiere Ud.?
3. ¿Quiénes son sus escritores favoritos?
4. ¿Qué novelas famosas conoce Ud.?

Take this test. When you have finished, check your answers in the answer key provided for this section in Appendix E. Then use a red pen to correct any mistakes you may have made. Are you ready?

Lección 10

A. Formation of adverbs

Give the Spanish equivalent of the adverbs in parentheses.

1. Me gustan estos trajes de baño, _____ el azul. *(especially)*
2. Yo _____ voy a la playa. *(frequently)*
3. El profesor habló _____ . *(slowly and clearly)*
4. Vino a verme _____ . *(recently)*
5. _____ ellos se van de vacaciones a California. *(Generally)*
6. _____ no voy al teatro. *(Unfortunately)*

B. The imperfect

Complete the following sentences with the imperfect tense of the verbs in the list. Use each verb once.

montar	acampar	servir	divertirse	asistir	ser
pescar	vivir	trabajar	gustar	ver	ir

1. Nosotros nunca _____ porque no nos _____ el campo.
2. Yo siempre _____ a caballo y _____ truchas en mis vacaciones.
3. Ellos siempre _____ mucho en las fiestas.
4. Nosotros nunca _____ a nuestros abuelos en el verano.
5. Cuando yo _____ chica siempre _____ a la playa con mis amigos.
6. Cuando nosotros _____ en Chile, yo _____ a la universidad.
7. Nosotros no _____ en el hospital.
8. ¿Tú siempre _____ vino con la cena?

C. The preterit contrasted with the imperfect

Give the Spanish equivalent of the words in parentheses.

1. Mi hermano _____ a verme ayer. (Nosotros) _____ por dos horas. *(came / conversed)*
2. La semana pasada, ellos _____ a la playa. *(went)*
3. _____ las nueve de la mañana cuando yo _____ a casa ayer. *(It was / arrived)*
4. Ayer Elsa me _____ que ella _____ ir al campo. *(told / wanted)*
5. Cuando ella _____ chica, _____ en Caracas. *(was / she lived)*
6. Ana _____ que el niño _____ muy cansado. *(said / was)*
7. Anoche _____ una fiesta en mi casa. *(there was)*
8. Ayer nosotros _____ muy ocupados todo el día. *(were)*
9. Pedro y yo _____ a la piscina cuando _____ a Marcela. *(were going / we saw)*
10. ¿Qué hora _____ cuando Uds. _____ a trabajar? *(was it / started)*

D. Verbs that change meaning in the preterit

Write sentences using the preterit or the imperfect of **saber, conocer,** or **querer** and the elements given. Add the necessary connectors.

1. yo / conocer / mi esposo / en 1995
2. Ana / no querer / ir / la fiesta / anoche / quedarse / casa
3. Carlos / no saber / ella / ser / casada

E. Just words . . .

Match the questions in column A with the appropriate responses in column B.

A	B
1. ¿Van a comprar la cabaña?	a. No, es un río.
2. ¿Te aburriste?	b. Blanca.
3. ¿No quieres ir de pesca?	c. Sí, en la piscina.
4. ¿El Amazonas es un lago?	d. No, no les gusta el mar.
5. ¿Qué es el Pacífico?	e. Mi novia.
6. ¿De qué color es la nieve?	f. No, a caballo.
7. ¿No van a la playa ellos?	g. En el Hotel del Lago.
8. ¿Compraste la caña de pescar?	h. No, me divertí mucho.
9. ¿Vas a nadar?	i. No, Carlos me va a enseñar.
10. ¿Qué pescaste?	j. Un océano.
11. ¿Quién te enseñó a nadar?	k. Ayer por la noche.
12. ¿Montaron en bicicleta?	l. No, la vamos a alquilar.
13. ¿Sabes nadar?	m. Una trucha.
14. ¿Dónde van a hospedarse?	n. Sí, y me costó un ojo de la cara.
15. ¿Cuándo hiciste las maletas?	o. No, prefiero cazar.
16. ¿Se divirtieron mucho?	p. Sí, fue una fiesta magnífica.

F. Culture

Answer the following questions, based on the **¿Lo sabía Ud.?** section.

1. ¿En qué países están Mar del Plata, Viña del Mar y Punta del Este?
2. ¿Durante qué meses esquían en Bariloche?

Lección 11

A. *Hace...* meaning *ago*

Write statements or questions using the elements provided and the expression **hace... que.** Follow the model.

MODELO: ¿ / cuánto tiempo / ella / venir / esta ciudad / ?
¿Cuánto tiempo hace que ella vino a esta ciudad?

1. dos días / ellos / depositar / dinero
2. tres meses / él / revelar / esos rollos
3. una semana / mi perro / morir
4. ¿ / cuánto tiempo / Ud. / ver / su padre / ?
5. ¿ / cuánto tiempo / ellos / robar / motocicleta / ?

B. The subjunctive with verbs of volition

Give the Spanish equivalent of the words in parentheses.

1. Yo te sugiero que _____ al banco mañana.   *(you go)*
2. Mis padres quieren _____ una cuenta de ahorros.   *(to open)*
3. Elena quiere _____ un cheque.   *(to deposit)*
4. El empleado nos sugiere que _____ a plazos.   *(we buy it [masc.])*
5. Dígales a ellos que _____ y _____ la solicitud.   *(to date / to sign)*
6. Ella quiere que _____ al contado.   *(I pay her)*
7. Deseo _____ con un billete de cien dólares.   *(to pay him)*
8. Yo les recomiendo a Uds. que _____ el dinero en el banco.   *(you deposit)*
9. Nosotros necesitamos _____ más.   *(to save)*
10. Yo le sugiero que _____ su talonario de cheques.   *(you bring)*
11. Mi esposo quiere que _____ sus pantalones a la tintorería.   *(I take)*
12. Ella me sugiere que _____ aquí.   *(I park)*
13. Ella quiere _____ por lo menos cincuenta dólares.   *(to charge them)*
14. Ellos quieren que tú _____ todo el dinero en el banco.   *(leave)*
15. ¿Qué cuenta quieren _____ Uds.?   *(to open)*
16. Mis padres quieren que _____ temprano.   *(I leave)*
17. Yo les sugiero que _____ cien dólares todos los meses.   *(you save)*
18. Mi hermano quiere que su hijo _____ con nosotros por seis meses.   *(live)*

C. The subjunctive with verbs of emotion

Write the Spanish equivalent of the following sentences.

1. "I hope you have the claim check, Mr. Vega."
2. "I'm sorry that they can't stay."
3. "We're afraid that Juana isn't coming."
4. "I'm glad you don't have to borrow money, dear."
5. "I hope the photos are ready."

D. Just words . . .

Complete the following sentences with vocabulary learned in **Lección 11**, as appropriate.

1. No me desperté porque el _____ no sonó.
2. Si quiero pagar con cheques, debo tener una cuenta _____ .
3. Necesito que ponga su _____ y la fecha en la solicitud.
4. No tengo mucho tiempo porque hoy tengo que hacer muchas _____ .
5. Tenía mil dólares en mi cuenta corriente. Escribí un cheque por doscientos. El _____ es de ochocientos dólares.
6. Hoy es domingo y el banco está cerrado. Voy a sacar dinero del _____ .
7. Quiero _____ este rollo de fotografías.
8. No voy a pagarlo al contado sino a _____ .
9. El banco está _____ al cine.
10. Es una lástima que él no se _____ a su padre.
11. Llamé a la policía porque me _____ el coche.
12. Voy a _____ mi coche aquí.
13. Estoy muy cansada. Voy a _____ en la cama hasta tarde.

E. Culture

Answer the following questions, based on the **¿Lo sabía Ud.?** section.

1. ¿Cómo llamaban los indios a la isla de Puerto Rico?
2. ¿Cuáles son los idiomas oficiales de Puerto Rico?
3. En las naciones latinoamericanas, ¿de qué están encargados los bancos centrales?

Lección 12

A. The *Ud.* and *Uds.* commands

Complete the following sentences with the command form of the verbs in parentheses.

1. Señorita, _____ (mandar) las cartas por vía aérea y certificadas.
2. _____ (Estar) aquí a las siete, señores.
3. _____ (Ir) a la oficina de correos ahora, señor.
4. Señora, _____ (caminar) dos cuadras y _____ (doblar) a la derecha.
5. No _____ (ser) impacientes, señoras.
6. _____ (Caminar) Uds. hasta la esquina.
7. _____ (Comprar) los sellos hoy, Sr. Torres.
8. _____ (Cerrar) las puertas, señoritas. Hace mucho frío.
9. No _____ (Dar) su dirección, señoras.
10. No _____ (Dejar) los paquetes aquí, señorita.

B. Position of object pronouns with direct commands

Give the Spanish equivalent of the words in parentheses.

1. Necesito las estampillas. _____ , señorita. *(Bring them to me)*
2. El señor quiere la cuenta. _____ , mozo. *(Give it to him)*
3. ¿Las cartas? _____ después, señoritas. *(Write them to him)*
4. La señora quiere leche fría. _____ , camarero. *(Take it to her)*
5. _____ que ellos son extranjeros, señor. *(Tell him)*
6. Necesito el periódico. _____ aquí, señora. *(Leave it)*
7. Éste es el más caro pero _____ , señora. *(don't tell it to him)*
8. Yo no quiero los camarones. _____ , mozo. *(Don't bring them to me)*

C. The relative pronouns *que* and *quien*

Combine the following pairs of sentences, using **que, quien,** or **quienes,** as needed. Follow the model on the facing page.

MODELO: Ayer hablé con el señor.
          El señor quería tomar mi clase.
          Ayer hablé con el señor que quería tomar mi clase.

1. Ésta es la señorita.
   La señorita le va a dar los pantalones.
2. Éstos son los vestidos.
   Los vestidos están de moda.
3. Ayer vi a las profesoras.
   Ellos nos hablaron de las profesoras.
4. Ésta es la señora.
   Yo le mostré las fotos a la señora.
5. Él compró una maleta.
   La maleta es cara.

D. The subjunctive to express doubt, disbelief, and denial

Rewrite the following sentences with the new beginnings.

1. Creo que el correo queda en la esquina.
   No creo que…
2. No es verdad que ella esté en la oficina de correos.
   Es verdad que…
3. No dudo que tenemos que subir.
   Dudo que…
4. No niego que él maneja muy bien.
   Niego que…
5. Estoy seguro de que Luis sabe dónde está el paquete.
   No estoy seguro de que…
6. Es verdad que necesitamos un documento de identidad.
   No es verdad que…

E. Constructions with *se*

Form questions with the elements given, adding the necessary connectors. Follow the model.

MODELO: a qué hora / abrir / las tiendas
          ¿A qué hora se abren las tiendas?

1. qué idioma / hablar / Chile
2. a qué hora / cerrar / los bancos
3. a qué hora / abrir / el correo
4. dónde / vender / sellos
5. por dónde / subir / segundo piso

F. Just words . . .

Match the questions in column A with the appropriate responses in column B.
Use each response once.

A	B
1. ¿Dónde queda la oficina?	a. No, está abajo.
2. ¿Vas a caminar?	b. Sí, hasta llegar al semáforo.
3. ¿Dónde puedo comprar sellos?	c. Sí, necesito comprar estampillas.
4. ¿Es puntual?	d. No, son extranjeros.
5. ¿Vas a la oficina de correos?	e. No, tiene treinta años.
6. ¿Está arriba?	f. No, hacia la estación.
7. ¿Van a subir?	g. No, voy a tomar el metro.
8. ¿Es viejo?	h. No, el correo no llega hasta las diez.
9. ¿Sigo derecho?	i. No, siempre llega tarde.
10. ¿Son norteamericanos?	j. No, un giro postal.
11. ¿Está lejos?	k. No, vamos a bajar.
12. ¿Tienes la carta de Juan?	l. En Cuatro Caminos, a dos cuadras de aquí.
13. ¿Va hacia el aeropuerto?	m. No, queda allí mismo.
14. ¿Le van a mandar dinero?	n. No, todavía está parado.
15. ¿Está sentado el señor?	o. En la ventanilla número dos.
16. ¿Es un edificio moderno?	p. No, es muy antiguo.

G. Culture

Answer the following questions, based on the **¿Lo sabía Ud.?** section.

1. ¿Cuál es, para muchos, el símbolo de Madrid?
2. ¿Cuál es el medio de transportación que usa la mayoría de los madrileños?
3. ¿Cómo se llama la antigua residencia de los reyes españoles?
4. ¿Dónde se encuentra un famoso acueducto romano en España?

EL CARIBE

Cuba

Rep. Dominicana

Puerto Rico

■ El Viejo San Juan, fundado en 1521, es uno de los barrios coloniales mejor conservados de las Américas. El barrio está casi totalmente rodeado de murallas de piedra *(stone walls)* construídas por los españoles.

■ Puerto Rico es una de las áreas más densamente pobladas del mundo. Con una extensión de unos nueve mil kilómetros cuadrados, tiene una población de más de tres millones y medio de habitantes.

■ La isla donde se encuentra la República Dominicana fue descubierta en 1492 durante el primer viaje de Colón al Nuevo Mundo. Colón le dio a la isla el nombre de La Española. La parte occidental *(western)* está ocupada por la República de Haití, donde se hablan francés y francés criollo *(creole)*.

■ La Habana, capital de Cuba, con sus dos millones de habitantes, es la ciudad más grande del Caribe. Antes de la revolución de Castro en 1958, era uno de los mayores centros de atracción turística del Caribe para los norteamericanos. Hoy el gobierno cubano trata de atraer a turistas de Europa y de Latinoamérica.

Puerto Rico tiene numerosas playas de arena *(sand)* blanca y fina como la Playa de las Croabas. Miles de turistas visitan estas playas todos los años, especialmente en el invierno.
¿A Ud. le gusta ir a la playa?

La sección antigua de La Habana, Cuba, se distingue por los numerosos edificios coloniales que aún conserva. "La Habana Vieja", como se conoce la parte antigua de la ciudad, fue declarada por la UNESCO *Monumento de la humanidad*, y se caracteriza por sus calles estrechas *(narrow)*, sus casas de tipo colonial y sus monumentos históricos. La Catedral de La Habana, que aparece en la foto, es uno de los edificios más característicos de la arquitectura colonial española. **¿Hay edificios de tipo colonial en la ciudad donde Ud. vive?**

La fortaleza *(fortress)* del Morro está situada a la entrada de la bahía *(Bay)* de San Juan, en Puerto Rico. Los españoles la construyeron en el siglo XVI para defender la isla de los ataques de los piratas. Hoy el Morro es un monumento nacional y constituye una importante atracción turística. **¿Qué monumentos históricos se encuentran donde Ud. vive?**

El béisbol es el deporte más popular en los países del Caribe. De sus equipos *(teams)* locales, como éste de Puerto Rico, han salido algunos de los mejores jugadores *(players)* de las Grandes Ligas de los Estados Unidos. El béisbol es también un deporte popular en Nicaragua, Panamá, Venezuela y México.
¿Puede Ud. nombrar algunos jugadores de béisbol hispanos de las Grandes Ligas?

La Catedral de Santa María la Menor en Santo Domingo, capital de la República Dominicana, fue la primera catedral fundada en América. Diego Colón, hijo de Cristóbal Colón, inició su construcción en 1514. La catedral se terminó de construir en 1540. Se dice que aquí están enterrados *(buried)* los restos de Cristóbal Colón.
¿En qué fecha se conmemora la llegada *(arrival)* de Colón al Nuevo Mundo?

La Universidad de La Habana, la más antigua de la isla de Cuba, fue establecida en 1728. La universidad tiene dos sedes *(campuses)*: la antigua está en el centro de la ciudad, y la moderna se encuentra en las afueras *(outskirts)* de la ciudad. La universidad fue autónoma hasta poco después de la llegada de Fidel Castro al poder.
¿Cuál es la universidad más antigua de su país?

El clima tropical del Caribe ofrece condiciones ideales para el cultivo de una gran variedad de frutas: el mango, la papaya, la banana y la guayaba, entre muchas otras. En la foto, un puesto de frutas en el Viejo San Juan muestra esta gran variedad.
¿Puede Ud. identificar las frutas que aparecen en la foto?

Teleinforme

Vocabulario

San Juan, Puerto Rico

a través de	through
el adoquín	paving stone
amanece	it dawns
el arco iris	rainbow
una calurosa bienvenida	a warm welcome
cristalina	clear
la herencia mundial	world heritage
las huellas	footprints, marks
luce	it shines
los peces	fish

La Habana, Cuba

a lo largo	along
barroco	baroque
las bellas artes	humanities
casi	almost
las flotas	fleets
el puerto	port
las riquezas	riches, wealth

Santo Domingo, República Dominicana

a orillas	on the banks
el alcázar	palace
el barrio	district
el desembarco	landing
se reúne	assemble

Preparación

¿Cuánto saben Uds. ya?   After reading the information in **Panorama hispánico 6**, get together in groups of three or four and answer the following questions.

1. ¿Por qué van muchos turistas a Puerto Rico?
2. ¿Quiénes construyeron la fortaleza del Morro y para qué?
3. ¿Cuál es la ciudad más grande del Caribe?
4. ¿Cómo se llama la parte antigua de la ciudad de La Habana?
5. ¿Cuál es la universidad más antigua de la isla de Cuba y cuántas sedes tiene?
6. ¿Qué nombre le dio Colón a la isla donde se encuentra la República Dominicana?
7. ¿Qué otro país es parte de la isla?
8. ¿Cuál fue la primera catedral fundada en América?

Comprensión

A. San Juan, Puerto Rico. Complete the following statements with the appropriate words.

1. Puerto Rico es una _____ del _____ . Fue descubierta por _____ .
2. San Juan fue _____ por los españoles hace _____ siglos.
3. El Viejo San Juan ha sido declarado Distrito _____ Nacional.
4. En Puerto Rico hay majestuosos _____ y _____ de aguas cristalinas.
5. Hay _____ de especies de peces _____ en el Mar Caribe.

B. La Habana, Cuba. Select the word or phrase that best completes each statement, according to what you understood.

1. Cuba está situada a la entrada del (Mar Caribe, Golfo de México).
2. Una (quinta, tercera) parte de la población cubana vive en La Habana.
3. A Cuba la llaman "(el Oro, la Perla) de las (Antillas, Bahamas)".
4. Los (españoles, ingleses, franceses) construyeron fortalezas en La Habana.
5. La Catedral queda en (Centro Habana, la Habana Vieja, la Habana del Este).
6. (Muchos, Muy pocos) estudiantes toman clases en la Universidad de la Habana.

C. Santo Domingo, República Dominicana. Read the following statements. After watching the video, circle **V** (**Verdadero**) or **F** (**Falso**), according to what you understood.

V   F   1. La capital de la República Dominicana es Santo Domingo.
V   F   2. Santo Domingo es la ciudad más antigua de Latinoamérica.
V   F   3. Cristóbal Colón vivió en el Alcázar de Colón.
V   F   4. Cada doce de agosto celebran en Santo Domingo el Día de Colón.
V   F   5. Santa María la Menor es una catedral muy moderna.

Ampliación

Dos culturas. With a partner, prepare some questions that you would like to ask a Cuban, a Puerto Rican, or a Dominican living in the U.S. about how he or she has adapted to life in this country.

SE ALQUILA UN APARTAMENTO

OBJECTIVES

Structure

The familiar command (**tú**) • **¿Qué?** and **¿cuál?** used with **ser** • The subjunctive to express indefiniteness and nonexistence

Communication

You will learn vocabulary related to renting an apartment, the various parts of a house, and home furnishings.

SE ALQUILA UN APARTAMENTO

Irene y Lucía, dos chicas colombianas que estudian en la Universidad Nacional Autónoma de México y viven en una pensión, quieren mudarse porque necesitan un apartamento que esté más cerca de la universidad.

LUCÍA —¡Irene! En el periódico anuncian un apartamento que tiene dos dormitorios y está en un buen barrio.[1]

IRENE —¡A ver! Dame el periódico. *(Lee el anuncio.)*

Anuncios Clasificados

Se alquila: apartamento amueblado: dos recámaras, sala, comedor, cocina y cuarto de baño. Calefacción central, aire acondicionado, Colonia 1. Llamar al teléfono 481–3520 de 1 a 5 de la tarde. Alquiler: $1200.[2]

LUCÍA —Podemos llamar para ir a verlo.

IRENE —No sé… Es muy caro para nosotras, Lucía. Además, necesitamos un apartamento que tenga garaje…

Al día siguiente, en cuanto vuelven de la universidad, las chicas van a ver el apartamento.

LUCÍA —¡Me encantan los muebles y las cortinas!

IRENE —Con el sueldo que nosotras ganamos no vamos a poder pagar el alquiler.

LUCÍA —Entonces en vez de trabajar medio día podemos trabajar tiempo completo.

IRENE —¡Estás loca! No hay nadie que pueda trabajar tiempo completo y al mismo tiempo estudiar en la universidad.

LUCÍA —¡No seas tan pesimista, Irene!

IRENE —No soy pesimista; soy realista. Además, vamos a necesitar dinero para comprar mantas, sábanas, fundas y utensilios de cocina.

LUCÍA —*(No le hace caso y va a la cocina.)* Irene, ven a la cocina. Mira, tiene refrigerador, microondas, lavaplatos, una cocina nueva… y un fregadero grande.

---

[1] The word **colonia** is also used in Mexico.
[2] Based on a currency exchange rate of eight Mexican pesos to one U.S. dollar.

IRENE	—No podemos tomar una decisión hasta ver otros apartamentos.
LUCÍA	—Pero, Irene, no vamos a encontrar ningún apartamento que sea tan bueno como éste.
IRENE	—Tal vez, pero no podemos pagar el alquiler de este apartamento.
LUCÍA	—Oye, ¿y si ganamos la lotería?
IRENE	—Hazme un favor, no digas tonterías. ¡Vámonos!
LUCÍA	—*(Enojada)* ¡Aguafiestas!

Vocabulario

Cognados

clasificado(-a) classified	**el garaje** garage	**el refrigerador** refrigerator
colombiano(-a) Colombian	**la lotería** lottery	**el utensilio** utensil
la decisión decision	**pesimista** pessimistic	
el favor favor	**realista** realistic	

Nombres

el (la) aguafiestas spoilsport
el aire acondicionado[1] air conditioning
el alquiler rent
el barrio neighborhood
la calefacción central[1] central heating
la cocina stove, kitchen
el comedor dining room

la cortina curtain
el dormitorio, la recámara *(Mex.)* bedroom
el fregadero kitchen sink
la funda pillowcase
el lavaplatos dishwasher
la manta, la frazada, la cobija blanket

el (horno de) microondas microwave (oven)
los muebles furniture
la sábana sheet
la sala living room
el sueldo, el salario salary

Verbos

anunciar to advertise
ganar to earn, to win

mudarse to move (from one house or place to another)

Adjetivos

amueblado(-a) furnished

mismo(-a) same

Otras palabras y expresiones

al día siguiente the following day
al mismo tiempo at the same time
decir tonterías to talk nonsense
en vez de instead of

hacer caso to pay attention
medio día half a day, part-time
se alquila for rent
tal vez maybe, perhaps

tiempo completo full time
tomar una decisión to make a decision
¡Vámonos! Let's go!

---

[1] **Poner el aire acondicionado (la calefacción)** = To turn on the air conditioning (the heat).

Vocabulario adicional

■ El salón de estar

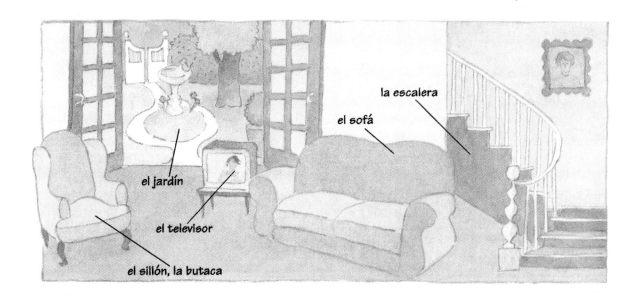

■ El dormitorio

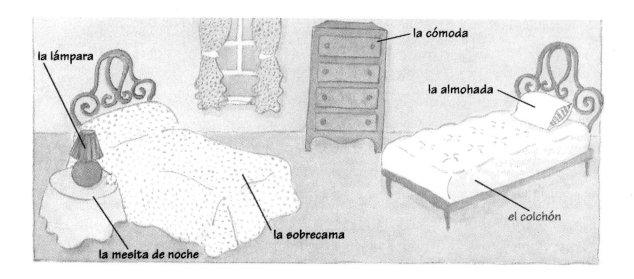

■ APARATOS ELECTRODOMÉSTICOS Y BATERÍA DE COCINA
(Home appliances and cookware)

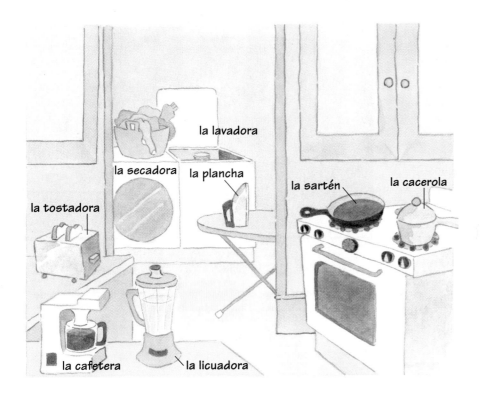

la lavadora

la secadora

la plancha

la sartén

la cacerola

la tostadora

la cafetera

la licuadora

¡CONVERSEMOS!

Answer the following questions, basing your answers on the dialogue.

1. ¿Irene y Lucía estudian en su país?
2. ¿Por qué quieren mudarse?
3. Si las chicas alquilan el apartamento que anuncian en el periódico, ¿van a tener que comprar muebles? ¿Por qué o por qué no?
4. ¿Cómo describen el apartamento en el anuncio?
5. ¿Qué quiere Lucía que haga Irene?
6. ¿Cree Ud. que las chicas tienen automóvil? ¿Cómo lo sabe Ud.?
7. ¿Qué hacen al día siguiente en cuanto vuelven de la universidad?
8. ¿Le gustan a Lucía los muebles y las cortinas del apartamento?
9. ¿Por qué le dice Irene a Lucía que está loca?
10. ¿Qué tiene la cocina del apartamento?

¿Lo sabía Ud.?

- En las grandes ciudades españolas y latinoamericanas, la mayoría de la gente vive en apartamentos, que en España se llaman "pisos". Los apartamentos se alquilan o se compran. Muchos edificios tienen oficinas o tiendas en la planta baja y apartamentos en los otros pisos.

- La palabra "barrio" tiene una connotación negativa en muchos lugares de los Estados Unidos, pero en los países hispanos equivale simplemente al inglés *neighborhood*.

- La Universidad Nacional Autónoma de México está situada en la parte sur de la Ciudad de México. Es la principal universidad del país, y es una de las más grandes del mundo. Unos 400.000 estudiantes asisten a la UNAM.

Mural del pintor mexicano David Alfaro Siqueiros en el edificio de la Administración de la Universidad de México.

ESTRUCTURAS

1 The familiar commands (tú) *(Las formas imperativas de tú)*

Unlike other commands in Spanish, the familiar affirmative command does not use the subjunctive.

A. *Tú* commands[1]

■ The affirmative command form for **tú** has exactly the same form as the third-person singular form of the present indicative.

Verb	Present Indicative	Familiar command (tú)[1]
hablar	él habla	**habla** (tú)
comer	él come	**come** (tú)
abrir	él abre	**abre** (tú)
cerrar	él cierra	**cierra** (tú)
volver	él vuelve	**vuelve** (tú)

---

[1] The affirmative command form for **vosotros** is formed by changing the final **r** of the infinitive to **d**: hablar → **hablad**, comer → **comed**, vivir → **vivid**.

—Teresa, **trae** las frazadas.	*"Teresa, bring the blankets."*
—**Espera** un momento. Estoy ocupada.	*"Wait a moment. I'm busy."*
—Me voy.	*"I'm leaving."*
—**Vuelve** temprano y **cierra** la puerta.	*"Return early and close the door."*

◼ Spanish has eight irregular **tú** command forms.

decir	**di**	poner	**pon**	tener	**ten**
hacer	**haz**	salir	**sal**	venir	**ven**
ir	**ve**	ser	**sé**		

—Carlitos, **ven** aquí; **hazme** un favor. **Ve** a la casa de Rita y **dile** que la fiesta es hoy.	*"Carlitos, come here. Do me a favor. Go to Rita's house and tell her the party is today."*
—¿Dónde pongo los libros?	*"Where shall I put the books?"*
—**Ponlos** en la mesa.	*"Put them on the table."*

B. Negative forms

◼ The negative **tú**[1] commands use the corresponding forms of the present subjunctive.

hablar	no **hables** tú
vender	no **vendas** tú
decir	no **digas** tú

—¿Voy con Julia?	*"Shall I go with Julia?"*
—No, no **vayas** con ella.	*"No, don't go with her."*
—¿Pongo las sábanas aquí?	*"Do I put the sheets here?"*
—No, no las **pongas** aquí.	*"No, don't put them here."*

ATENCIÓN Object and reflexive pronouns are positioned with familiar commands just as they are with the formal commands.

Pon**lo** aquí.	*Put it here.*
No **lo** pongas allí.	*Don't put it there.*
Vénde**nosla**.	*Sell it to us.*
No **nos la** vendas.	*Don't sell it to us.*

Práctica

A. Play the role of an older sibling giving instructions to a younger brother or sister, using the cues provided.

1. levantarse temprano
2. estudiar y no hablar por teléfono con sus amigos
3. hacer la tarea y no mirar televisión

---

[1] The negative **vosotros** commands also use the present subjunctive: **no habléis.**

4. escribirle una carta a la abuela
5. bañar al perro
6. ir al mercado *(market)* y comprar frutas
7. recoger la ropa de la tintorería
8. llamar por teléfono a Carlos y decirle que traiga los discos compactos
9. lavar el mantel y las servilletas pero no lavar las sábanas
10. limpiar su cuarto
11. poner la mesa
12. barrer la cocina pero no pasarle la aspiradora a la alfombra

B. Juana always has a hard time deciding what to do. Give her some suggestions, using the cues provided.

> **MODELO:** No sé qué clase tomar.   (francés)
> *Toma una clase de francés.*

1. No sé adónde ir esta noche.   (cine)
2. No sé con quién salir.   (Mauricio)
3. No sé qué hacer mañana.   (ir de compras)
4. No sé qué comprar.   (un traje de baño)
5. No sé qué regalarle a papá.   (una cámara fotográfica)
6. No sé qué comprarle a mamá   (un vestido)
7. No sé qué hacer para comer.   (sopa y pollo)
8. No sé qué decirle a Jorge.   (que te lleve al baile)
9. No sé en qué banco poner mi dinero.   (en el Banco de América)
10. No sé qué hacer con mi pelo.   (cortártelo)

C. Say two commands, one affirmative and one negative, that the following people would be likely to give.

1. una madre a su hijo de quince años
2. un(-a) estudiante a su compañero(-a) de cuarto
3. una muchacha a su novio
4. una médica *(doctor)* a una niña
5. un profesor a un estudiante

D. Lucía is moving into her new apartment and some friends are helping her. Based on the illustration, what does she tell each person to do? Use familiar commands.

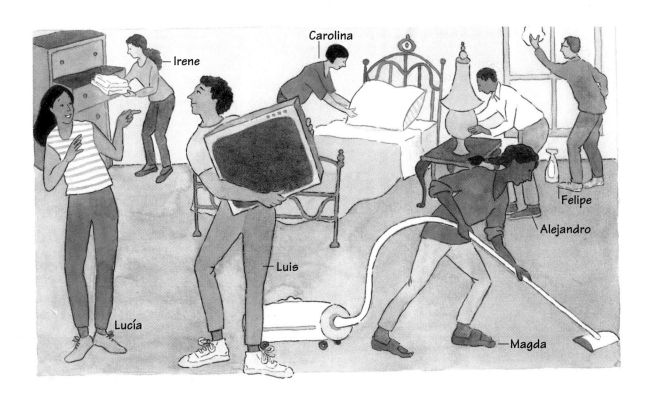

2 ¿Qué? and ¿cuál? used with **ser** *(Qué y cuál usados con el verbo ser)*

- *What* translates as **¿qué?** when it is used as the subject of the verb and it asks for a definition.

  —¿**Qué** es una enchilada?   *"What is an enchilada?"*
  —Es un plato mexicano.   *"It's a Mexican dish."*

- *What* translates as **¿cuál?** when it is used as the subject of a verb and it asks for a choice. **Cuál** conveys the idea of selection from among several or many available objects, ideas, and so on.

  —¿**Cuál** es su número de   *"What is your phone number?"*
    teléfono?
  —792–4856.   *"792–4856."*

Práctica

Write the questions you would ask to get the following information. Use **qué** or **cuál**, as needed.

1. — _____
   — Mi apellido es Velázquez.
   — _____
   — Calle Rosales, número 420.
   — _____
   — 835–2192.

2. — ¿Quiere una sangría?
   — _____
   — Es una bebida que se hace con frutas y vino tinto. ¿Quiere comer una paella?
   — _____
   — Es un plato español que se prepara con arroz, pollo y mariscos.

3 The subjunctive to express indefiniteness and nonexistence
(El subjuntivo para expresar lo indefinido y lo inexistente)

■ The subjunctive is always used when the subordinate clause refers to someone or something that is indefinite, unspecified, or nonexistent.

Necesitan **un apartamento** que **esté** cerca de la universidad.	*They need an apartment that is close to the university.*
En la oficina necesitan a **alguien** que **sepa** español.	*At the office they need someone who knows Spanish.*
Busco **un empleado** que **hable** inglés.	*I'm looking for an employee who speaks English.*
¡No hay **nadie** que **pueda** trabajar tiempo completo!	*There's nobody who can work full time!*

■ If the subordinate clause refers to existent, definite, or specific persons or things, the indicative is used instead of the subjunctive.

Viven en **un apartamento** que **está** cerca de la universidad.	*They live in an apartment that is near the university.*
En la oficina hay **alguien** que **sabe** español.	*At the office there is someone who knows Spanish.*
Busco **al empleado** que **habla** inglés.	*I'm looking for the employee who speaks English.*
Hay **alguien** que **puede** trabajar tiempo completo.	*There's someone who can work full time.*

Práctica

A. With a partner, play the roles of a newcomer to Mexico City and a helpful long-time resident who is able to offer solutions to all of the newcomer's needs. Follow the model.

> MODELO: una casa – tener piscina
> —*Quiero (Necesito, Busco) una casa que tenga piscina.*
> —*En mi barrio hay una casa que tiene piscina.*

1. una casa – tener tres dormitorios
2. una casa – estar cerca de la universidad
3. una casa – no costar un ojo de la cara
4. un coche – tener aire acondicionado
5. muebles – ser baratos
6. un empleo – pagar bien
7. alguien – ayudarme a mudarme
8. un restaurante – servir hamburguesas

B. A friend of yours is planning to move to your city or town and wants some information about it. Answer his or her questions as completely as possible.

1. ¿Hay alguna casa en un buen barrio que sea barata?
2. ¿Hay alguna casa que tenga piscina?
3. ¿Hay algún apartamento que esté cerca del centro?
4. Yo necesito una secretaria. ¿Conoces a alguien que sepa hablar alemán y japonés?
5. A mí me gusta la comida argentina. ¿Hay algún restaurante que sirva comida argentina?
6. A mis padres les gusta la comida mexicana. ¿Hay algún restaurante que sirva comida mexicana?

C. With a partner, act out the following dialogues in Spanish.

1. "I'm looking for a receptionist who can work full time."
   "I'm sorry. I only know students who can work part-time."
2. "We want a hotel that has air conditioning."
   "There is a hotel that is near here and that has air conditioning."
3. "Is there anyone who can tell me the weather forecast *(el pronóstico del tiempo)* for tomorrow?"
   "Yes, I know it. It's going to rain cats and dogs."
4. "Do you know anyone who can teach Japanese?"
   "I know many people who speak Japanese, but I don't know anyone who can teach it."

D. Complete the following sentences logically, using the subjunctive or indicative as appropriate.

1. Necesitamos un apartamento que…
2. En mi barrio no hay ninguna casa que…
3. Alquilan un apartamento que…
4. Rosa tiene una criada *(maid)* que…
5. Busco a alguien que…
6. En esta clase no hay nadie que…
7. Mi novio(-a) necesita un empleo que…
8. ¿Hay alguien aquí que…

¡A VER CUÁNTO APRENDIÓ!

¡Repase el vocabulario!

Choose the best answer for each of the following questions.

1. ¿Es de Bogotá?
   a. Sí, es uruguayo.
   b. Sí, es chileno.
   c. Sí, es colombiano.
2. ¿Dónde vas a poner el sofá?
   a. En el comedor.
   b. En la sala.
   c. En la secadora.
3. ¿Por qué estás enojado con tu hermano?
   a. Porque no me hace caso.
   b. Porque es de estatura mediana.
   c. Porque tiene refrigerador.
4. ¿Para qué quieres la frazada?
   a. Para ponerla en la cacerola.
   b. Para ponerla en la cama.
   c. Para decir tonterías.
5. ¿Por qué no puedes alquilar ese apartamento?
   a. Porque no gano suficiente dinero.
   b. Porque se alquila.
   c. Porque tengo que pagar exceso de equipaje.
6. ¿Para dónde son las cortinas?
   a. Para aquella butaca.
   b. Para aquella ventana.
   c. Para aquel jardín.
7. ¿Por qué no te gusta Emilio?
   a. Porque es muy simpático.
   b. Porque trabaja tiempo completo.
   c. Porque es muy pesimista.

8. ¿Qué vas a poner en la sala en vez del sofá?
   a. Un asiento de ventanilla.
   b. Una cacerola.
   c. Una butaca.
9. ¿Es un apartamento amueblado?
   a. Sí, pero no tiene lavaplatos.
   b. Sí, pero no tiene tienda de campaña.
   c. Sí, pero no tiene barrio.
10. ¿Qué necesitas para el dormitorio?
    a. Una caña de pescar.
    b. Un rizador y un secador.
    c. Una cama y una mesita de noche.
11. ¿Qué aparatos electrodomésticos necesitas para la cocina?
    a. Una licuadora y una tostadora.
    b. Una lavadora y una secadora.
    c. Una butaca y una cómoda.
12. ¿Qué necesitas para freír *(fry)* el pollo?
    a. La cafetera.
    b. La sartén.
    c. La plancha.

Entrevista

Interview a partner, using the **tú** form.

Pregúntele a su compañero(-a) de clase...

1. ...si su casa tiene calefacción central y aire acondicionado.
2. ...qué muebles tiene en su dormitorio.
3. ...si se va a mudar a otra ciudad.
4. ...si prefiere alquilar un apartamento o comprar una casa.
5. ...si prefiere una casa que tenga garaje para tres coches o una casa que tenga piscina.
6. ...si trabaja tiempo completo o medio día.
7. ...si dice tonterías a veces.
8. ...si juega a la lotería.
9. ...si es pesimista, optimista o realista.
10. ...si es un(-a) aguafiestas.

Situaciones

What would you say in the following situations? What might the other person say? Act out the scenes with a partner. Take turns playing each role.

1. You are talking to a real estate agent. You are looking for a house that is in a good neighborhood, with at least five bedrooms, air conditioning, and a three-car garage.
2. You are describing the house or apartment where you live to a friend.
3. You and your friend are going to share an apartment. Describe one you have just seen, telling him or her why you should take the apartment. Your friend doesn't think it's a good idea.

Para escribir

Write a composition describing the house of your dreams *(sueños)*. Include the following information:

■ location

■ kind of neighborhood

■ what type of rooms you want

■ number of bedrooms and bathrooms

■ backyard (patio)

■ color scheme

■ furniture you would have in each room

■ conveniences

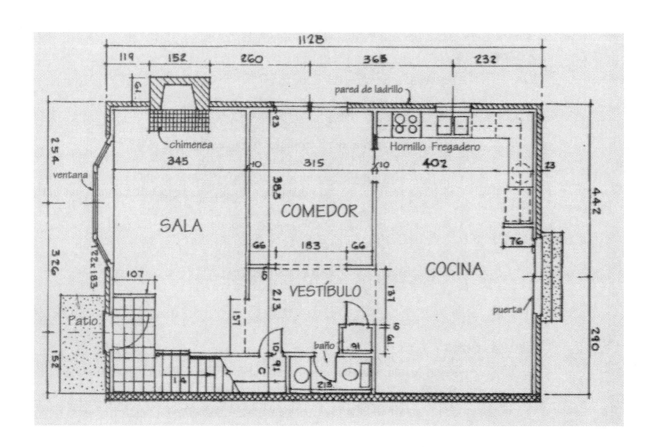

En la vida real

Mi pareja ideal

Pair up with a classmate to write personal ads designed to help you find your ideal mate. Your description of the type of person you are looking for (use **Busco…** or **Quiero conocer a…**) should include physical characteristics, personality, age, economic status, and favorite activities. Don't forget to describe yourselves, as well.

Casas y apartamentos

Imagine that you and several classmates own a real estate agency. Prepare ads for the following types of houses.

1. A very expensive house in a good neighborhood.
2. A small house in a student neighborhood.
3. Two different types of apartment for rent.

En busca de apartamento

Some friends of yours want to buy an apartment in or near Barcelona. Help them by using the information provided in the ads below to answer their questions.

VIVA EN EL CENTRO
DE BLANES
A 5 minutos de la playa
APARTAMENTOS
Con Plazas de Parking, 1 y 2 hab. Salón - Comedor – Cocina equipada – Baño completo - Acabados
ALTO STANDING. Información: **FINCAS VERA.**
*C. Muralla, n.° 3. BLANES. Tels.: (972) 33-53-74
y (972) 33-70-47*

Veranee todo el año en Barcelona. Vista panoramica, por encima capa polución ciudad, 135 m. sobre el nivel del mar
APARTAMENTOS
(JUNTO AL PARQUE GUINARDO)
Calle Dr. Cadevall, 1-3 Barcelona (entrada por Avda. V.de Montserrat y calle Fco. Alegre)
Gran calidad, estar-comedor, 2 ó 3 dorm., cocina, baño, calef. ind., terraza, antena colectiva, y parabólica, 70 a 90 m². A partir de ptas. 7.000.000

*Información: MANSUR, S.A. De 5.30 a 8.30 h. tarde
Tel. 257-53-45. Con financiación de Caja Postal*

CONJUNTO RESIDENCIAL DE **TIANA**

Con participación en Club Social Piscina, tenis, squash, y zona ajardinada de recreo.

Vivir todo el año a 8 Km. de Barcelona.

ALTING
Tel. 321 32 36

4 dormitorios (1 suite) • cocina office • salón con chimenea • 3 baños • 1 aseo • 1 estudio • 1 solarium y terraza • garaje 3 coches.
Acabados de calidad. 225 m² + jardín individual.

TORREDEMBARRA
Apartamentos 2 habitaciones, salón comedor, cocina, baño completo con instalación para lavadora. Situados en el centro del pueblo.
Avda. Catalunya. 11.
Precio: 4.000.000 pesetas
Vd. puede ser propietario con 1 millón de pesetas más 3 millones de hipoteca (a 15 años)
Vea apartamento de muestra y compruebe su calidad.

Información en la misma obra laborable de 10 a 14 h. y de 16.30 a 20 hs. Excepto lunes y martes

1. ¿Hay algún apartamento que esté cerca de la ciudad de Barcelona? ¿Cuál? ¿Cuántos dormitorios tiene? ¿Tiene piscina? ¿Cuál es el número de teléfono?
2. ¿Hay algún apartamento que quede cerca de la playa? ¿Cuál es la dirección? ¿Los apartamentos son grandes o pequeños? ¿Se puede estacionar allí?
3. ¿Hay algún apartamento que quede cerca de un parque? ¿Qué parque? ¿A qué hora se puede ver? ¿Cuánto cuesta el más barato?
4. ¿Hay algún apartamento donde se pueda poner una lavadora? ¿Cuánto tiempo hay para pagar la hipoteca *(mortgage)*? ¿Se puede ver cualquier *(any)* día de la semana? ¿Cuánto cuesta?

Así somos

Vocabulario

a la vez	at the same time
a pesar de que	in spite of the fact that
al nivel	at the level
alegre	happy, cheerful
amable	kind, amiable
amigable	friendly
los bienes raíces	real estate
la bodega	cellar
Casi no me enojo.	I hardly ever get mad.
chica	small
la cochera	garage
con buena cara	with a good outlook
el departamento	apartment
los negocios	business transactions
las plantas	stories *(of a house)*
el promedio	average
las propiedades	properties
el pueblo	town
la renta	rent
sacar mi carrera	to finish school
el sentido	sense
superior	upper
tranquilo	tranquil, laid back
la ubicación	location
ver hacia adelante	to look ahead
la vida	life

Preparación

A. ¿Cuánto saben Uds. ya?   In this video module, several people will describe their homes and their personalities. With a partner, brainstorm possible words and phrases they might use in these contexts and make a list of them.

B. ¿Las reconoce?   Guess the meaning of the following words. While watching the video, circle each as you hear the person say it.

canadiense	optimista	tímido
decoración	positivo	típico
futuro	privilegiada	vegetación
individual	rústico	zona
nacional	servicio	

Comprensión

A. ¿Dónde viven? As the people in the video describe where they live, write their names under the appropriate category.

En un departamento   **En una casa**

_____   _____

_____   _____

_____   _____

B. ¿Quién lo dice? Match each statement with the name of the person who said it.

a. Alejandro   c. María   e. Yolanda
b. Jaime   d. Pedro   f. Leonardo

_____ 1. Mi casa tiene seis habitaciones, una mini-alberca y una cochera para seis coches.
_____ 2. Tenemos sala-comedor pequeñita, cocinita, dos recámaras, y un baño y medio.
_____ 3. Mi casa es un "chalet".
_____ 4. Mi casa tiene cinco salas, tres comedores, una piscina y cinco garajes.
_____ 5. Mi apartamento tiene dos pisos y un altillo.
_____ 6. En el primer piso se encuentran la cocina, el salón, la habitación de mis padres y un baño.

C. Mi personalidad. Answer the following questions, according to what you understood.

1. ¿Es Milka optimista, pesimista o realista?
2. ¿Leonardo ve lo negativo o lo positivo de la vida?
3. ¿Pedro es nervioso o es muy tranquilo?
4. ¿Alejandro es una persona alegre o triste?
5. ¿Cómo es Jaime?
6. Según *(According to)* Otmara, ¿cómo hay que ver la vida?

D. Entrevista. Read the following statements. After watching the video, circle **V** (**Verdadero**) or **F** (**Falso**), according to what you understood.

V F   1. El señor Velasco Pérez trabaja en bienes raíces.
V F   2. En la oficina del señor Velasco Pérez administran propiedades.
V F   3. En la oficina hacen negocios sólo con mexicanos.
V F   4. La oficina está en un área privilegiada.
V F   5. Las propiedades que venden allí son las más baratas de la ciudad.
V F   6. Los apartamentos de esa zona son muy pequeños.

Ampliación

Dos culturas. In groups of three or four, compare your homes or apartments with those described by the people on the video.

PLANEANDO UNA CENA

OBJECTIVES

■ Structure
The subjunctive or indicative after certain conjunctions • Uses of **sino** and **pero** • First-person plural commands

■ Communication
You will learn vocabulary related to shopping for groceries and typical weekend activities.

▣ PLANEANDO UNA CENA

Oscar y Jorge, dos estudiantes cubanos que viven in Miami, deciden ir al mercado para hacer las compras de la semana. Por la noche piensan salir con dos chicas, Elsa y Adela. Tienen una cita para ir al cine, pero primero van a cocinar una cena para ellas en su apartamento. El supermercado se abre a las nueve y los muchachos son los primeros en llegar.

OSCAR —Necesitamos muchas cosas: mantequilla, leche, una docena de huevos, pan, azúcar...

JORGE —¿No vamos a comprar carne?

OSCAR —Sí, compremos carne, pescado y pollo. También aceite, dos latas de frijoles y seis de salsa de tomate.

JORGE —No hombre, no compremos tanta salsa de tomate, a menos que quieras comer comida italiana por el resto del mes.

OSCAR —Tienes razón. A ver... necesitamos manzanas, uvas, naranjas, melón, toronjas y peras para la ensalada de frutas...

JORGE —¿Dónde están las verduras? Tenemos que comprar lechuga, papas, zanahorias, cebollas y tomates.

OSCAR —El tomate no es una verdura sino una fruta... ¡Caramba! Ahora que lo pienso esto va a costar una fortuna. Vamos a tener que ponernos a dieta.

JORGE —Buena idea. Pongámonos a dieta, con tal que podamos comer perros calientes y hamburguesas de vez en cuando.

OSCAR —Oye, apurémonos porque tenemos que limpiar el apartamento antes de que lleguen las chicas.

Después de cenar, Oscar, Elsa, Jorge y Adela van al cine. Ahora están haciendo cola para comprar las entradas.

ADELA —Esta película ganó el premio como la mejor película del año.

ELSA —Es un drama, ¿verdad? Yo prefiero las comedias.

JORGE —El próximo sábado, cuando vayamos al cine, podemos ver una película musical.

OSCAR —No, no vayamos al cine otra vez. Vamos a un club a bailar.

ADELA —Tengo ganas de tomar algo. ¿Por qué no vamos a la cafetería Versailles cuando termine la película? Yo invito.

JORGE —Ésta es la última función, ¿no? ¿A qué hora termina la película?

OSCAR —A eso de las doce.

Tan pronto como termina la película, los chicos van a la cafetería a tomar algo y a charlar un rato.

ELSA —Como mañana es feriado, ¿por qué no vamos a la playa?

OSCAR —Sí, y llevemos algo para comer.

ADELA —¡Perfecto! En cuanto me levante voy a preparar una tortilla a la española.

Vocabulario

Cognados

la **dieta** diet
la **docena** dozen
el **drama** drama, play
la **fortuna** fortune

el **melón** melon
musical musical
perfecto(-a) perfect

el **resto** rest
el **supermercado** supermarket
el **tomate** tomato

■ Nombres

el **aceite** oil
el **azúcar** sugar
la **cebolla** onion
la **cita** date
la **cosa** thing
el **feriado, el día de fiesta** holiday
la **función** show
la **lata, el bote** *(Mex.)* can

la **lechuga** lettuce
la **mantequilla** butter
la **manzana** apple
el **mercado** market
la **naranja** orange
el **pan** bread
la **película** movie
la **pera** pear

el **perro caliente** hot dog
el **premio** prize
la **salsa** sauce
la **toronja, el pomelo** grapefruit
la **verdura, el vegetal** vegetable
la **zanahoria** carrot

■ Verbos

apurarse, darse prisa to hurry
  (up)

■ Adjetivos

tanto(-a) so much

último(-a) last

■ Otras palabras y expresiones

a eso de at about
a menos que unless
ahora que lo pienso now that I
  think about it
antes de que before
con tal (de) que provided that
de vez en cuando from time to
  time
hacer cola to stand in line
hacer (las) compras to shop, do
  the shopping

otra vez again
ponerse a dieta to go on a diet
sino but
tener ganas de to feel like (doing
  something)
tomar algo[1] to have something to
  drink
un rato a while
¡Yo invito! My treat!

---

[1] **comer algo** = to have something to eat

■ Cosas del supermercado

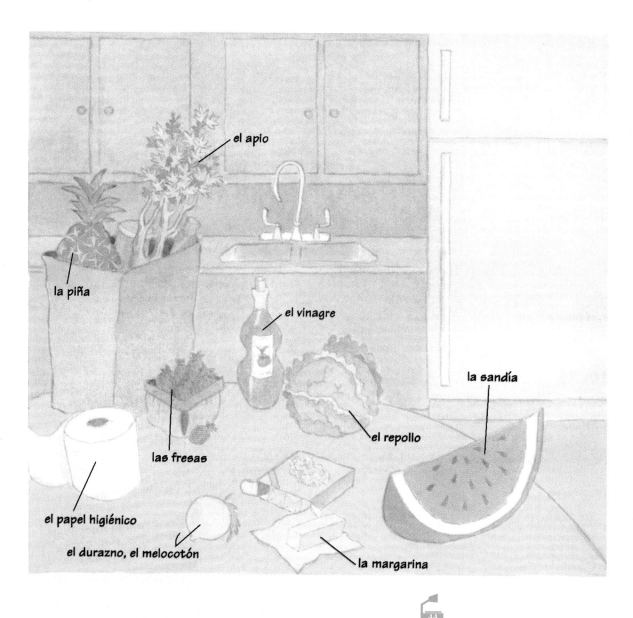

el apio

la piña

el vinagre

la sandía

las fresas

el repollo

el papel higiénico

el durazno, el melocotón

la margarina

44

■ Las diversiones

el circo circus
la montaña rusa roller coaster
el parque de diversiones
  amusement park
el zoológico zoo

Los niños querían ir al **circo** pero no tenían dinero.
La **montaña rusa** de Disneylandia es la mejor de todas.
Six Flags es mi **parque de diversiones** favorito.

En ese **zoológico** hay muchos animales de África.

¡Conversemos!

Answer the following questions, basing your answers on the dialogue.

1. ¿Adónde van Jorge y Oscar para hacer las compras de la semana?
2. ¿Qué piensan hacer por la noche?
3. ¿A qué hora se abre el supermercado?
4. Según Oscar, ¿qué necesitan comprar?
5. ¿Cuántas latas de frijoles compran los muchachos?
6. ¿Qué frutas necesitan para la ensalada?
7. ¿Por qué dice Oscar que van a tener que ponerse a dieta?
8. ¿Por qué tienen que apurarse los muchachos?
9. ¿Para qué tienen que hacer cola los muchachos?
10. ¿Qué premio ganó la película que van a ver?
11. ¿Adónde van a ir después de ver la película? ¿Para qué?
12. ¿Qué va a hacer Adela en cuanto se levante? ¿Por qué?

 ## ¿Lo sabía Ud.?

- Aunque hoy en día hay un gran número de supermercados en los países hispanos, muchas personas prefieren comprar en los mercados al aire libre o en las tiendas pequeñas que generalmente se especializan en uno o dos productos. Por ejemplo, se vende **carne** en la **carnicería, frutas** en la **frutería, verduras** en la **verdulería** y **pan** en la **panadería.**

- En España, México y Argentina, entre otros países, la producción de películas tiene gran importancia. Las películas hispanas, muchas de ellas de tipo sociopolítico, se conocen en Europa y en los Estados Unidos.

- Las películas norteamericanas son muy populares en el mundo hispánico. Generalmente tienen subtítulos en español o están dobladas (*dubbed*). Muchos de los títulos en español son completamente diferentes a los del inglés. Por ejemplo, la película *Primal Fear* se llama ***Las dos caras de la verdad;*** *Babe* se llama ***El puerquito valiente.***

Una panadería en la Ciudad de México.

ESTRUCTURAS

1 The subjunctive or indicative after certain conjunctions
(El subjuntivo o el indicativo después de ciertas conjunciones)

A. Conjunctions that are always followed by the subjunctive

■ Some conjunctions, by their very meaning, imply uncertainty or condition. They are, therefore, always followed by the subjunctive. Here are some of them.

en caso de que *in case*	**a menos que** *unless*
sin que *without*	**para que** *in order that*
con tal (de) que *provided that*	**antes de que** *before*

—Voy a ir al cine **con tal que** los chicos **vayan** conmigo.
"I'm going to go to the movies provided the boys go with me."

—Llámelos **antes de que salgan.**
"Call them before they leave."

—No me van a dar el préstamo **a menos que** ella **firme** la carta.
"They're not going to give me the loan unless she signs the letter."

—Yo puedo firmarla **en caso de que** ella no **quiera** hacerlo.
"I can sign it in case she doesn't want to do it."

—Te voy a dar dinero **para que vayas** al mercado.
"I'm going to give you money so that you can go to the market."

—Voy a salir **sin que** los chicos me **vean,** porque siempre quieren ir conmigo.
"I'm going to leave without the boys seeing me, because they always want to go with me."

B. Conjunctions that are followed by the subjunctive or indicative

■ The subjunctive follows certain conjunctions when the main clause refers to the future or is a command. Some of these conjunctions are:

cuando *when*	**tan pronto como, en**
hasta que *until*	**cuanto** *as soon as*

—¿Lo van a esperar?
"Are you going to wait for him?"

—Sí, **hasta que llegue.**
"Yes, until he arrives."

—**En cuanto llegue,** díganle que me llame.
"As soon as he arrives, tell him to call me."

■ If there is no indication of a future action, the conjunction of time is followed by the indicative.

—¿Siempre lo esperan?
"Do you always wait for him?"

—Sí, **hasta que llega.**
"Yes, until he arrives."

Práctica

A. Complete the following dialogue between two friends who are expecting a houseguest, using **con tal que, sin que, en caso de que, a menos que, para que,** and **antes de que** and the verbs given. Then act it out with a partner adding two original lines.

—Tenemos que limpiar el apartamento _____ _____ (llegar) él.

—Yo voy a preparar unos sándwiches _____ _____ (tener) hambre.

—Sí, ¿y por qué no compras unos refrescos _____ _____ (poder) tomar algo en cuanto llegue?

—Bueno, pero yo no puedo ir al mercado _____ tú me _____ (dar) el dinero.

—Está bien. Yo te voy a dar el dinero _____ tú me lo _____ (devolver) mañana.

—Vale. Voy ahora mismo. Voy a salir _____ me _____ (ver) Paquito porque va a querer ir conmigo.

— _____

— _____

B. Compare what the people mentioned usually do to what they are going to do.

1. Todos los días yo llamo a mi amiga en cuanto llego a casa.
   Mañana,...
2. Generalmente esperamos al profesor hasta que llega.
   El próximo viernes,...
3. Todos los meses, tan pronto como recibimos el sueldo, lo depositamos en el banco.
   El mes próximo,...
4. Cuando Uds. van a verla, siempre le llevan un regalo.
   La semana próxima,...
5. Ud. se lo dice a ellos cuando los ve.
   Dígaselo a ellos...

C. With a partner, act out the following dialogues in Spanish.

1. "We are going to have lunch as soon as they arrive."
   "I'm going to prepare the salad so that we can eat right away."
2. "I always give my son a kiss when I see him."
   "I don't see mine very frequently."
3. "We have to leave the house without the children seeing us."
   "We can't do that unless we leave through the window!"
4. "I have to clean the apartment before my friends arrive."
   "Why don't you wait until I come back?"
   "I can wait for you provided that you be here before two."

2 Uses of **sino** and **pero**   *(Usos de* **sino** *y* **pero***)*

▨ **Sino,** meaning *but* in the sense of *rather* or *on the contrary,* is used only when the second part of a sentence negates or contradicts the first part.

No van al circo **sino** al zoológico.	*They aren't going to the circus, but rather to the zoo.*
No quiero una cuenta corriente **sino** una cuenta de ahorros.	*I don't want a checking account, but a savings account.*

▨ **Pero** is used for *but* in all other cases.

La casa es pequeña **pero** cómoda.	*The house is small but comfortable.*
A Juan no le gustaba el apartamento, **pero** lo alquiló.	*Juan didn't like the apartment, but he rented it.*

Práctica

Complete the following sentences, using **sino** or **pero** as needed.

1. Trabaja, _____ no gana mucho dinero.
2. No vive en una casa _____ en un apartamento.
3. No es rubia _____ pelirroja.
4. Tengo manzanas, _____ no tengo peras.
5. No es una comedia _____ un drama.
6. No está en el salón _____ en la sala.
7. No me gusta mucho el apartamento, _____ lo voy a alquilar.
8. No vienen todos los días _____ de vez en cuando.
9. Fueron al supermercado, _____ no había tomates.
10. No necesitan naranjas _____ toronjas.

3 First-person plural commands
(El imperativo de la primera persona del plural)

▨ The first-person plural of an affirmative command *(let's + verb)* may be expressed in two different ways:

■ by using the first-person plural of the present subjunctive

Compremos carne y pescado.	*Let's buy meat and fish.*

■ by using the expression **vamos a** + *infinitive*

Vamos a comprar carne y pescado.	*Let's buy meat and fish.*

▨ The verb **ir** does not use the subjunctive for the first-person plural affirmative command.

Vamos a la playa.	*Let's go to the beach.*

▨ For the negative command, the subjunctive is used.

No vayamos a la playa.	*Let's not go to the beach.*

■ In all direct affirmative commands, the object pronouns are attached to the verb. An accent must be used to maintain the original stress.

Llamémos**lo**.	*Let's call him.*
Escribámos**les**.	*Let's write to them.*

■ If the pronouns **nos** or **se** are attached to the verb, the final **-s** of the verb is dropped before adding the pronoun.

Vámo**nos**.	*Let's leave.*
Sentémo**nos** aquí.	*Let's sit here.*
Vistámo**nos** ahora.	*Let's get dressed now.*
Démo**selo** a los niños.	*Let's give it to the children.*
Digámo**selo** a ella.	*Let's tell (it to) her.*

■ In direct negative commands, the object pronouns are placed in front of the verb.

No **lo** hagamos.	*Let's not do it.*
No **nos** vistamos ahora.	*Let's not get dressed now.*
No **nos** vayamos todavía.	*Let's not leave yet.*

Práctica

A. You and a classmate are going to a restaurant. Take turns asking each other what you should do and responding with first-person plural commands.

Antes de ir:

1. ¿A qué restaurante vamos?
2. ¿Hacemos reservaciones?
3. ¿Llevamos el coche o tomamos un taxi?

En el restaurante:

1. ¿Dónde nos sentamos?
2. ¿Qué pedimos para comer?
3. ¿Qué tomamos?
4. ¿Qué comemos de postre?
5. ¿Pedimos algo más?
6. ¿Cuánto le dejamos de propina al mozo?
7. ¿Adónde vamos ahora?
8. ¿Invitamos a alguien?

B. With a partner, act out the following dialogues in Spanish.

1. "Let's do the shopping today."
   "Yes, let's go to the supermarket."
2. "Let's buy butter."
   "No, let's not buy it. I want to go on a diet."
3. "Where do you want to sit?"
   "Let's sit near the window."
4. "Let's go to bed early tonight."
   "Why?"
   "Because we have to get up at six o'clock."

¡A VER CUÁNTO APRENDIÓ!

¡Repase el vocabulario!

Select the response that best answers each question.

1. ¿Vas a hacer una ensalada de frutas?
   a. Sí, necesito una lata de frijoles.
   b. Sí, necesito dos latas de salsa de tomate.   c. Sí, necesito naranjas.
2. ¿Qué te gustó más en el parque de diversiones?
   a. El supermercado.   b. La montaña rusa.   c. El feriado.
3. ¿Hay mucha gente que quiere comprar entradas?
   a. Sí, tenemos que hacer cola.   b. Sí, tenemos que ganar.
   c. Sí, tenemos que darles un premio.
4. A ver… ¿qué verduras necesitamos?
   a. Agua y vinagre.   b. Pescado y pollo.
   c. Lechuga, repollo y zanahorias.
5. ¿Vas a ponerle mantequilla al pan?
   a. No, azúcar.   b. No, margarina.   c. No, repollo.
6. ¿Adónde vas a llevar a los niños para que se diviertan?
   a. Al mercado.   b. A la biblioteca.   c. Al circo.
7. ¿No tienes una cita con Juan Carlos?
   a. Sí, pero no puedo ir porque él es famoso.
   b. Sí, pero no tengo ganas de ir.
   c. Sí, pero no puedo ir porque hay mucha gente en el supermercado.
8. ¿Qué vas a usar para hacer el jugo?
   a. Huevos.   b. Toronjas.   c. Aceite.
9. ¿Ves a tus amigos?
   a. Sí, tengo que apurarme.   b. Sí, de vez en cuando.
   c. Sí, tengo que darme prisa.
10. Dicen que esa película es fantástica.
    a. Sí, ganó el primer premio.   b. Sí, ganó la licencia para conducir.
    c. Sí, a mí tampoco me gustó.
11. Mi hermano quiere ver los elefantes.
    a. Llévalo al parque de diversiones.   b. Llévalo al zoológico.
    c. Llévalo a la playa.
12. ¿Tienes ganas de tomar algo?
    a. Sí, pescado.   b. Sí, carne.   c. Sí, una copa de vino blanco.

Entrevista

Interview a classmate, using the **tú** form.

Pregúntele a su compañero(-a) de clase…

1. …si prefiere ver una comedia musical o un drama.
2. …si acepta una cita con una persona a quien no conoce.
3. …qué hace cuando es feriado.
4. …si se preocupa cuando alguien viene a comer a su casa, y por qué
   o por qué no.

5. ...cuántas docenas de huevos compra para una semana.
6. ...qué frutas y qué verduras le gustan.
7. ...si prefiere comer carne, pescado o pollo.
8. ...si sabe a qué hora se abre y se cierra el mercado.

Situaciones

What would you say in the following situations? What would the other person say? Act out the scenes with a partner. Take turns playing each role.

1. Tell a group of friends you are going to meet them at the amusement park.
2. You and your roommate are having a party tonight, and he or she is about to go to the grocery store. Discuss the items you will need for a fruit salad.
3. Invite a friend to go see a movie with you this weekend and tell her or him it's your treat. Discuss possible movies and times, and make plans to do something afterwards.
4. Tell a friend what you are going to do as soon as you get home.

Para escribir

Write a dialogue in which you and a friend make plans for the weekend.

En la vida real

Discusión

With a classmate, discuss a movie or a T.V. show you have both seen and summarize the plot. Say whether you liked it or not and why.

Here are some words and phrases you might want to use:

actor *actor*
actriz *actress*

(la) película
- de acción
- de ciencia-ficción
- cómica
- dramática
- de guerra
- de horror
- de misterio
- policíaca

De la cocina a la mesa

You and a classmate are planning a dinner party. One of you has found a recipe (**receta**) for enchiladas, and the other, a recipe for flan. Read your recipe silently, and then tell your partner how to prepare the dish, without looking at the recipe. After your classmate does the same, read each other's recipes to see if your descriptions left out any of the steps. Here are some words you might want to use:

calentar (e:ie) to heat up, warm up
cubrir to cover
derretir (e:i) to melt
enfriar to cool (down)

freír (e:í) to fry
mojar to dip
rallado(-a) grated
revolver (o:ue) to mix

ENCHILADAS
Ingredientes:
1 docena de tortillas de maíz
1 lata de salsa de enchilada
1/4 taza de aceite
1 libra de queso rallado
1 cebolla grande, rallada

Preparación:
Caliente la salsa en una sartén. En otra sartén caliente las tortillas en el aceite, sin freírlas. Sáquelas del aceite y mójelas en la salsa. Póngalas en un plato, y cúbralas con queso y cebolla. Enrolle las tortillas como tubos y cúbralas con el resto del queso. Póngalas en el horno a 325 grados por cinco minutos.

FLAN

Ingredientes:

Para el flan
2 tazas de leche evaporada
4 huevos
8 cucharadas de azúcar
1 cucharadita de vainilla

Para el caramelo
3 cucharadas de azúcar

Preparación: En el molde donde va a hacer el flan, ponga a derretir al fuego tres cucharadas de azúcar. Después de unos minutos el azúcar va a tener un color dorado. Mueva el molde para cubrirlo todo con el caramelo y déjelo enfriar.

Bata los huevos. Añada el azúcar, la leche y la vainilla y revuélvalo bien. Póngalo todo en el molde y cocínelo a Baño María en el horno a 350 grados por una hora. (Para saber si ya está cocinado, introduzca un cuchillo en el flan y si sale limpio, ya está listo.)

Sáquelo del horno y déjelo enfriar. Póngalo en el refrigerador. Antes de servirlo, voltee el molde en un plato.

¡Vamos a leer!

Antes de leer

A. Before you read the fable of the fox and the grapes (**la zorra y las uvas**), think about things you already know that may be useful to you as you read. For example, what characteristics are typically associated with foxes? How would grapes figure in the story? What is their purpose? What human vice, folly, or virtue do you think this story will illustrate?

B. As you read the fable, find the answers to the following questions.

1. ¿Qué tiempo hace? ¿Cuál es la estación del año?
2. ¿Qué descubrió la zorra mientras paseaba por un huerto?
3. ¿Dónde estaban las uvas?
4. ¿La zorra tenía sed o tenía hambre?
5. ¿Qué método usó la zorra para alcanzar las uvas?
6. ¿Alcanzó la zorra las uvas?
7. ¿Qué hizo finalmente?
8. ¿Cuál es la moraleja de la fábula?

---

[1] Double boiler.

La zorra y las uvas
(Fábula de Esopo)

orchard

bunch / ripe / vine / was growing

to quench

steps / he ran / he leaped

strength

to reach

darse... *to give up*

to disdain it

En un caluroso día de verano, paseaba la zorra por un huerto.° De pronto descubrió un racimo° de uvas que estaban casi maduras° en una vid° que crecía° enrollada a una rama muy alta. —Precisamente lo que necesito para apagar° la sed— exclamó la zorra.

Retrocedió unos pasos,° corrió° y saltó° pero perdió el racimo por un pelo.

Retrocedió de nuevo, reunió todas sus fuerzas° y diciendo: —¡Uno, dos y tres!— dio un tremendo salto, pero no fue mejor el resultado.

Una y otra vez trató de alcanzar° las uvas que estaban en la vid, pero finalmente tuvo que darse por vencida° y marchándose del huerto comentó: —¡Están verdes!

Moraleja: *Cuando no se puede conseguir algo, es fácil desdeñarlo.°*

Díganos

Answer the following questions, based on your own thoughts and experiences.

1. ¿Qué le gusta tomar para apagar la sed?
2. ¿Qué le gustaba hacer en el verano cuando Ud. era pequeño(-a)?
3. ¿Había un huerto en su casa o iba a un huerto para recoger frutas? ¿Qué tipos de frutas crecían en el huerto?
4. ¿Persevera Ud. cuando quiere algo o se da por vencido(-a) fácilmente? ¿Por que o por qué no?
5. Cuando Ud. era niño(-a), ¿le gustaba leer fábulas? ¿Cuáles?

Bolivia

Colombia

Ecuador

Perú

Venezuela

- La cuenca *(basin)* del Amazonas, que ocupa partes de Perú, Ecuador, Colombia, Brasil y Venezuela, es la más grande del mundo. El río Amazonas tiene más de 1.000 tributarios.

- Bolivia tiene dos capitales. Sucre es la capital histórica y sede *(seat)* del poder *(power)* judicial. La Paz es la capital administrativa y está situada a más de diez mil pies de altura. La ciudad se encuentra al pie del nevado *(snow-covered)* Illimani, que alcanza *(reaches)* una altura de más de veinte mil pies.

- Las islas Galápagos, situadas en el océano Pacífico frente a las costas de Ecuador, se consideran una de las zonas ecológicas mejor conservadas. Las distintas especies de plantas y animales que allí se encuentran son exclusivas de las islas y no tienen similaridad con las especies del continente.

- Caracas, la capital de Venezuela, es el lugar de nacimiento de Simón Bolívar, el Libertador de América. Bolívar luchó *(fought)* por la independencia de Colombia, Venezuela, Ecuador, Perú y Bolivia.

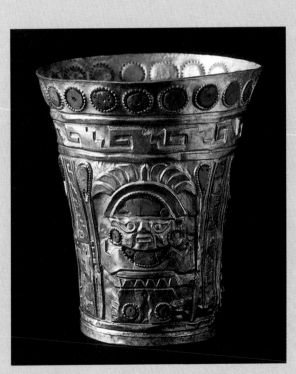

Este brazalete de oro, usado en ritos funerarios preincaicos, se encuentra en el Museo del Oro en Lima, Perú. En el museo existe una gran variedad de piezas precolombinas de oro y de plata con piedras preciosas. Esta colección es un ejemplo del talento artístico y de los conocimientos técnicos de las culturas indígenas que habitaban el continente antes de la llegada de Colón. **¿Cuáles son algunos museos famosos de su país? ¿Dónde están?**

La Avenida Doce de Octubre es una de las principales de Quito, la capital de Ecuador. Esta ciudad, situada al pie del volcán Pichincha, goza de *(enjoys)* un clima primaveral todo el año por estar a una altura de 9.250 pies sobre el nivel del mar.
¿Dónde hay volcanes en su país?

En los llanos orientales *(eastern plains)* de Colombia, la ganadería *(livestock)* es la principal fuente de ingresos. Estos "llaneros" llevan una manada *(herd)* de caballos a los corrales de una hacienda en el departamento de Meta, situado al sureste de Colombia.
¿Qué región de su país es conocida por la importancia de la ganadería?

El Salto Ángel *(Angel Falls)*, localizado en el Parque Nacional de Canaima en Venezuela, es el más alto del mundo, con una altura de unos 3.200 pies. Las cataratas *(falls)* se llaman Ángel en honor al piloto norte-americano Jimmy Angel, que fue el primero en aterrizar *(land)* allí en 1937.
¿Qué cataratas de los Estados Unidos y Canadá son famosas en todo el mundo?

Entrada del metro en la estación de Sabana Grande en Caracas, Venezuela. Se comenzó a construir el metro de Caracas en los años 70.
¿Hay un metro en la ciudad donde Ud. vive?

Esta vista es de una de las típicas calles coloniales de Cartagena de Indias en la costa norte de Colombia. Durante la conquista y el período colonial, la parte antigua de la ciudad estaba completamente amurallada *(walled in)* para dar protección contra los ataques de piratas ingleses y franceses. **¿En qué ciudades de su país se ve la influencia de otras culturas?**

En el centro de Lima hay dos grandes plazas: la Plaza de Armas y la Plaza de San Martín. La Plaza de San Martín, que aparece en la foto, se llama así en honor a José de San Martín, considerado héroe nacional por haber liberado Perú, además de Argentina y Chile, del dominio español. **¿Cuáles son algunos lugares o monumentos norte-americanos nombrados en honor a héroes nacionales?**

Las islas Galápagos deben su nombre a sus tortugas gigantes, llamadas galápagos, que pesan unos 280 kilos y viven unos 250 años. Las Galápagos se hicieron famosas por los estudios sobre la evolución de las especies que hizo en ellas el naturalista británico Charles Darwin. El gobierno ecuatoriano estableció el Parque Nacional de las Islas Galápagos en 1959. **¿Cuáles son algunos de los lugares de Norteamérica que tienen interés especial para los naturalistas?**

Una manada de alpacas pace *(grazes)* en las montañas de Bolivia. La alpaca pertenece a la familia de las llamas, especie relacionada con los camellos, que habita la región de los Andes. La llama se usa principalmente como animal de transporte mientras que la lana *(wool)* de la alpaca se utiliza para hacer alfombras y diferentes artículos de ropa. **¿En qué países de Sudamérica se pueden encontrar llamas y alpacas?**

Teleinforme

Vocabulario

Santafé de Bogotá, Colombia

a medida que	as
la artesanía	handicrafts
Atenas	Athens
el cerro	peak
de primera línea	first class
las mercancías	merchandise
el nivel	level
los rascacielos	skyscrapers
la sabana	plain, savannah
los techos de tejas	tiled roofs
los tejidos	woven fabrics, weavings

El sombrero de panamá

el barco de vapor	steamboat
los comerciantes	merchants, shopkeepers
duraba	lasted
por aquel entonces	at that time
recorren	go around
sacaban las producciones	took shipments
se enamoraban de	fell in love with
se realizaba	it was made
las tocas, las toquillas	straw hats

Ecoturismo en Venezuela

cálidas	warm, hot
la cordillera	mountain range
de suma importancia	of utmost importance
el ganado	cattle
los manglares	mangrove swamps
por ciento	percent
los vaqueros	cowboys

Lima, Perú

los aconteceres	events
añadiendo	adding
celosamente	jealously
en medio de	in the center of
hecha por	made by
la herencia	inheritance, legacy
los limeños	natives of Lima
majestuosa	majestic
quizás	perhaps
el ritmo	rhythm
se destacan	stand out
se esconden	are hidden
se hallaba	was found
señorial	elegant
el testigo	witness
los virreyes	the viceroys

Preparación

¿Cuánto saben Uds. ya?   After reading the information in **Panorama hispánico** 7, get together in groups of three or four and answer the following questions.

1. ¿Cuál es la capital de Ecuador? ¿Y de Venezuela?
2. ¿Cuál es una de las zonas ecológicas mejor conservadas?
3. ¿Cuál es la principal fuente de ingresos de los llanos orientales de Colombia?
4. ¿Cuál es un museo importante en Lima, Perú?
5. ¿Cómo se llaman dos plazas importantes en el centro de Lima?
6. ¿Qué países liberó Simón Bolívar?

Comprensión

A. Santafé de Bogotá, Colombia.   Select the word or phrase that best completes each statement, according to what you understood.

1. En la zona de la Candelaria hay muchas casas lindas de estilo (moderno, colonial español).
2. La ciudad fue construída en una (montaña, sabana).
3. Santafé de Bogotá ofrece (tiendas, mercados) donde se pueden comprar vegetales y frutas.
4. Los tejidos y las máscaras son ejemplos de la (cerámica, artesanía) colombiana.
5. La mejor vista de Bogotá se puede ver desde (el cerro, los rascacielos) de Monserrate.
6. Una de las razones por las cuales llaman a Bogotá "la Atenas de la América del Sur" es porque tiene muchas (artesanías, universidades).

B. Ecoturismo en Venezuela.   Read the following statements. After watching the video, circle **V** (**Verdadero**) or **F** (**Falso**), according to what you understood.

V F   1. Hay mucha variedad en las tierras de Venezuela.
V F   2. Venezuela queda muy lejos de Miami, Florida, a más de seis horas por avión.
V F   3. En los llanos de Maracaibo trabajan vaqueros con su ganado.
V F   4. El ecoturismo no trae muchos turistas a Venezuela.
V F   5. El dieciséis por ciento de las tierras nacionales ya son parques nacionales en Venezuela.

C. El sombrero de panamá.   Answer the following questions.

1. ¿Qué otro nombre tienen las tocas?
2. ¿Dónde se originaron las tocas?
3. ¿Quiénes compraban las tocas?
4. ¿Qué tipo de transporte usaban en el pasado para llevar las tocas a la ciudad de Panamá?

D. Lima, Perú.   Read the following statements. After watching the video, circle **V** (**Verdadero**) or **F** (**Falso**), according to what you understood.

V F   1. Lima es una ciudad totalmente moderna.
V F   2. Lima fue llamada "la ciudad de los virreyes".
V F   3. Lima fue fundada por Cristóbal Colón.
V F   4. La población de Lima es de menos de un millón de habitantes.
V F   5. La Plaza de Armas es el centro de la Lima antigua.
V F   6. En el centro de la plaza hay una hermosa fuente de bronce.
V F   7. Uno de los lugares preferidos por los limeños es la Plaza de San Martín.

Ampliación

¿Adónde vamos?   The class will be divided into three groups: one group prefers to spend a semester studying in Colombia, the second group prefers to go to Venezuela, and the third group prefers Peru. Each group will list the reasons for their choice.

DE COMPRAS

OBJECTIVES

Structure
The past participle • The present perfect • The past perfect (pluperfect)

Communication
You will learn vocabulary related to clothing and shopping.

DE COMPRAS

Anita y su esposo Hugo han abierto el armario y han dicho, casi al mismo tiempo, "¡No tengo nada que ponerme!" Han decidido, pues, ir de compras a El Corte Inglés, una tienda por departamentos que está en el centro de Madrid.

Cuando llegan, la tienda no está abierta todavía, pero ya hay mucha gente porque hoy hay una gran rebaja. A las nueve entran en la tienda. Anita sube por la escalera mecánica hasta el primer piso, donde está el departamento de ropa para señoras. Hugo se queda en el departamento de ropa para caballeros, que está en la planta baja.

En el departamento de ropa para señoras, Anita se encuentra con su amiga Tere.[1]

ANITA —¿Qué tal? Aprovechando las rebajas, ¿no? Dime Tere, ¿cuánto cuesta esa blusa de seda?

TERE —Dos mil ochocientas pesetas. ¿Qué talla usas?

ANITA —Uso talla treinta y ocho.[2] Voy a probármela.

TERE —Espera, ¿no te gusta esta falda? Combina muy bien con la blusa y es talla mediana. Pruébatela. El probador está a la izquierda.

ANITA —*(Desde el probador)* Tere, hazme un favor. Tráeme una falda talla treinta y seis.

TERE —Espera… Lo siento, no hay tallas más pequeñas. ¿Por qué no te pruebas este suéter?

ANITA —No… no me gusta…

Anita compró la blusa, pero no compró la falda porque le quedaba grande y era demasiado cara. Después fue a la zapatería porque necesitaba comprar un par de zapatos rojos para combinar con un bolso rojo que Hugo le había regalado.

ANITA —¿Tiene zapatos rojos?

DEPENDIENTE —Lo siento, señora, pero en rojo solamente tengo estas sandalias.

ANITA —Son bonitas. Yo calzo el treinta y seis.[3] ¿Las tiene en mi número? *(A Tere)* Hacen juego con mi bolso.

DEPENDIENTE —Sí, en seguida vuelvo.

El dependiente le prueba las sandalias.

ANITA —Me aprietan… Son un poco estrechas… pero me las llevo.

DEPENDIENTE —¿Se las envuelvo o quiere llevárselas puestas?

ANITA —Envuélvamelas, por favor. *(A Tere)* ¡Son una ganga!

---

[1] nickname for Teresa
[2] equivalent to an American size 10
[3] equivalent to an American size 6

En el departamento de ropa para caballeros, Hugo ha comprado un traje de lana, tres camisas de algodón, dos camisetas, un chaleco y una chaqueta de lino. También ha cambiado un par de botas que había comprado, porque eran muy anchas. Hugo, Anita y Tere se encuentran a la salida.

ANITA —Hugo, llévanos a comer algo. ¡Estamos muertas de hambre!
HUGO —¡Yo también! Esperadme[1] aquí. Yo voy por el coche.
ANITA —¿Has estado en el restaurante Villa Alegre alguna vez?
TERE —Sí, es muy bueno. Vamos a ése.

VOCABULARIO

COGNADOS

el **centro**   center
el **par**   pair

la **sandalia**   sandal
el **suéter**   sweater

NOMBRES

el **algodón**   cotton
el **armario**, el **ropero**   wardrobe, closet
la **blusa**   blouse
la **bota**   boot
la **camisa**   shirt
la **camiseta**   T-shirt
el **chaleco**   vest
la **chaqueta**   jacket
el **departamento de (ropa para) caballeros**   men's department

el (la) **dependiente(-a)**   store clerk
la **escalera mecánica**   escalator
la **falda**   skirt
la **ganga**   bargain
la **lana**   wool
el **lino**, el **hilo**   linen
el **número**   size (of shoes)
la **planta baja**   ground floor
el **probador**   fitting room
la **rebaja**, la **liquidación**   sale
la **seda**   silk

la **talla**, la **medida**   size
la **tienda por departamentos**, el **almacén**   department store
el **traje**   suit
la **zapatería**   shoe department, shoe store
el **zapato**   shoe

VERBOS

apretar (e:ie)   to be tight
aprovechar   to take advantage of
calzar   to take (a certain size in shoes)
cambiar   to exchange, change

entrar (en)   to go in, enter
envolver (o:ue)   to wrap
llevar   to wear, use
llevarse   to take (buy)

---

[1] Hugo is a Spaniard, so he uses the **vosotros** form here.

■ ADJETIVOS

ancho(-a) wide

estrecho(-a) narrow

mediano(-a) medium

■ OTRAS PALABRAS Y EXPRESIONES

alguna vez ever
casi almost
de compras shopping
En seguida vuelvo. I'll be right back.
estar muerto(-a) de hambre to be starving

hacer juego, combinar to match, go together
llevar puesto(-a) to wear, have on
me aprietan they feel tight (on me)
no tener nada que ponerse not to have anything to wear

pues therefore
quedarle grande (chico) a uno to be too big (small) on someone
solamente only
todavía yet, still

VOCABULARIO ADICIONAL

■ MIRANDO VIDRIERAS *(window shopping)*

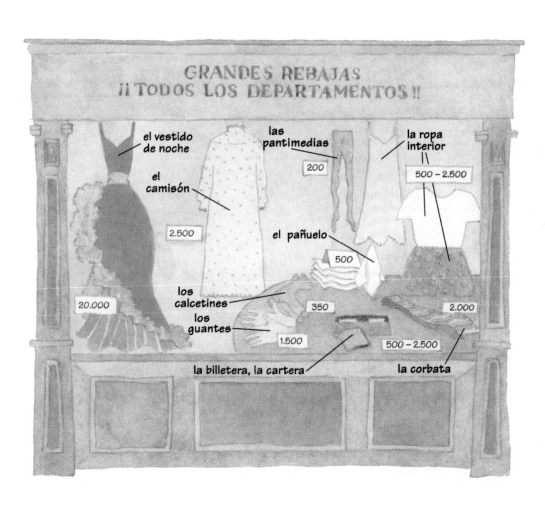

■ DISEÑOS (designs)

de rayas

de cuadros

estampado(-a)

de lunares

¡CONVERSEMOS!

Answer the following questions, basing your answers on the dialogues.

1. ¿Por qué han decidido ir de compras Anita y Hugo?
2. ¿Está cerrado El Corte Inglés cuando llegan Anita y Hugo?
3. ¿Cómo va Anita al primer piso?
4. ¿Tiene Hugo que subir para ir al departamento de caballeros? ¿Por qué o por qué no?
5. ¿Es gorda Anita? ¿Cómo lo sabe Ud.?
6. ¿Qué no compra Anita y por qué?
7. ¿Por qué quiere Anita comprar unos zapatos rojos?
8. ¿Tiene Anita los pies (feet) grandes?

9. ¿Le quedan bien las sandalias?
10. ¿Qué ha comprado Hugo? ¿Dónde?
11. ¿Por qué ha cambiado Hugo las botas que había comprado?
12. ¿Adónde van Hugo, Anita y Tere? ¿Por qué?

¿Lo sabia Ud.?

- Lo que en los Estados Unidos es el primer piso es la planta baja en los países hispanos. Entonces el primer piso en España, por ejemplo, corresponde al segundo piso en los Estados Unidos.

- En las ciudades hispanas hay excelentes tiendas donde se puede comprar ropa hecha *(ready-to-wear)*, pero muchas personas prefieren utilizar los servicios de un sastre *(tailor)* o de una modista *(dressmaker)*.

- Aunque ahora hay muchos grandes almacenes, todavía existen en los países hispanos muchas tiendas pequeñas especializadas en un solo producto. Por ejemplo, se vende **perfume** en la **perfumería, joyas** *(jewelry)* en la **joyería** y **relojes** en la **relojería**.

- Actualmente *(Nowadays)*, los dependientes de las tiendas a menudo tutean *(use the **tú** form of address)* a los clientes en España.

Una joyería elegante en la Ciudad de México.

ESTRUCTURAS

1 The past participle *(El participio pasado)*

A. Forms of the past participle

Past Participle Endings		
-ar verbs	**-er verbs**	**-ir verbs**
habl-**ado** *(spoken)*	com-**ido** *(eaten)*	decid-**ido** *(decided)*

■ The following verbs have irregular past participles.

abrir	**abierto**	*opened*
cubrir	**cubierto**	*covered*
decir	**dicho**	*said*
hacer	**hecho**	*done*
escribir	**escrito**	*written*
morir	**muerto**	*died*
poner	**puesto**	*put*
romper	**roto**	*broken*
ver	**visto**	*seen*
volver	**vuelto**	*returned* (somewhere)
devolver	**devuelto**	*returned* (something)
envolver	**envuelto**	*wrapped*

ATENCIÓN   Verbs ending in **-er** and **-ir** whose stem ends in a strong vowel require an accent mark on **i** of the **-ido** ending.

creer	**creído**	*believed*
leer	**leído**	*read*
oír[1]	**oído**	*heard*
traer	**traído**	*brought*

Práctica

Supply the past participle of each of the following verbs.

1. tener
2. traer
3. cerrar
4. decir
5. aprovechar
6. apretar
7. cortar
8. volver
9. romper
10. cubrir
11. cambiar
12. sentir
13. entrar
14. salir
15. hacer
16. poner
17. abrir
18. escribir
19. ver
20. aceptar
21. devolver
22. leer
23. dar
24. sacar

---

[1] Present tense: **oigo, oyes, oye, oímos, oís, oyen.**

B. Past participles used as adjectives

In Spanish, most past participles may be used as adjectives. As such, they agree in number and gender with the nouns they modify.

La peluquería está **abierta** hoy. — *The beauty parlor is open today.*
El restaurante está **abierto** hoy. — *The restaurant is open today.*
Las peluquerías están **abiertas** hoy. — *The beauty parlors are open today.*
Le mandé dos cartas **escritas** en inglés. — *I sent him two letters written in English.*
No dejen los libros **abiertos**. — *Don't leave the books open.*

Práctica

A. You are very efficient. When a friend asks whether you did something, you say it is already done.

MODELO: ¿Ya pusiste la mesa?
Sí, ya está puesta.

1. ¿Ya cerraste la puerta?
2. ¿Ya abriste las ventanas?
3. ¿Ya hiciste la ensalada?
4. ¿Ya envolviste el regalo?
5. ¿Ya escribiste las cartas?
6. ¿Ya pagaste la cuenta?
7. ¿Ya cubriste los muebles?
8. ¿Ya lavaste la blusa?

B. Act out the following dialogues with a partner, providing the missing adjectives (past participle form) of the verbs listed.

abrir   hacer   traducir
cerrar   poner   usar
escribir servir

1. —¿Dónde fueron _____ las sandalias?
   —En México.
2. —Oye, ¿está _____ la puerta?
   —Sí, pero las ventanas están _____ .
   —Pues ábrelas, porque hace mucho calor.
3. —¿Ya podemos comer?
   —Sí, la mesa ya está _____ y la comida está _____ .
4. —¿Aquí se vende ropa _____ ?
   —Sí, este vestido de noche es _____ .
5. —¿Esos libros están _____ en español?
   —Sí, pero también están _____ al inglés y al francés.

2 The present perfect *(El pretérito perfecto)*

■ The present perfect tense is formed by using the present indicative of the auxiliary verb **haber** with the past participle of the verb that expresses the action or state. This tense is equivalent to the English present perfect *(have + past participle, as in I have spoken.).*

Present indicative of **haber**	
he	hemos
has	habéis
ha	han

Formation of the Present Perfect Tense			
	hablar	**tener**	**venir**
yo	**he** hablado	**he** tenido	**he** venido
tú	**has** hablado	**has** tenido	**has** venido
Ud. él ella	**ha** hablado	**ha** tenido	**ha** venido
nosotros(-as)	**hemos** hablado	**hemos** tenido	**hemos** venido
vosotros(-as)	**habéis** hablado	**habéis** tenido	**habéis** venido
Uds. ellos ellas	**han** hablado	**han** tenido	**han** venido

—¿**Has pagado** más de cien dólares por una blusa alguna vez?
—No, nunca **he pagado** tanto dinero.

"Have you ever paid more than one hundred dollars for a blouse?"
"No, I've never paid that much money."

—¿**Has visto** a Teresa?
—No, no la **he visto.**

"Have you seen Teresa?"
"No, I haven't seen her."

■ Note that when the past participle is part of a perfect tense, it is invariable. The past participle only changes in form when it is used as an adjective.

Ella ha escrit**o** la carta.
La carta está escrit**a**.

She has written the letter.
The letter is written.

■ In the Spanish present perfect tense the auxiliary verb **haber** can never be separated from the past participle as it can in English.

Yo nunca **he estado** en Lima.

I have never been in Lima.

■ Remember that when reflexive or object pronouns are used with compound tenses, the pronouns are placed immediately before the auxiliary verb.

Le ha dado mucho dinero a su hijo.
María y José **se** han ido.

He has given a lot of money to his son.
María and José have left.

Práctica

A. Look at the following illustrations and describe what these people have done today, using the present perfect.

1. Tú

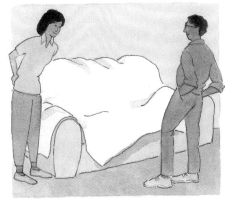

2. Tú y yo

3. Los chicos

4. Yo

5. Mi mamá

6. Uds.

B. With a partner, discuss five things that you or your family and friends have never done. Compare your own experiences with those of your partner.

> MODELO: —Yo *nunca he estado en España.*
> —Yo *tampoco he estado en España.*
> (Yo *he estado en España dos veces.*)

3 The past perfect (pluperfect) *(El pluscuamperfecto)*

■ The past perfect tense is formed by using the imperfect tense of the auxiliary verb **haber** with the past participle of the verb that expresses the action or state.

■ This tense is equivalent to the English past perfect *(had + past participle,* as in *I had spoken.).* Generally, the past perfect tense expresses an action that has taken place before another action in the past.

Imperfect of **haber**	
había	habíamos
habías	habíais
había	habían

Formation of the Past Perfect Tense			
	estudiar	**beber**	**ir**
yo	**había** estudiado	**había** bebido	**había** ido
tú	**habías** estudiado	**habías** bebido	**habías** ido
Ud. / él / ella	**había** estudiado	**había** bebido	**había** ido
nosotros(-as)	**habíamos** estudiado	**habíamos** bebido	**habíamos** ido
vosotros(-as)	**habíais** estudiado	**habíais** bebido	**habíais** ido
Uds. / ellos / ellas	**habían** estudiado	**habían** bebido	**habían** ido

—¿No hablaste con Teresa?	*"Didn't you speak with Teresa?"*
—No, cuando yo llegué, ella ya **se había ido.**	*"No, when I arrived, she had already left."*

Práctica

A. One of your roommates is never around when there is work to be done. Say what had already been done by the time he or she got home last night.

> MODELO: nosotros / lavar los platos
> *Cuando él (ella) llegó, nosotros ya habíamos lavado los platos.*

1. yo / barrer la cocina
2. los chicos / pasarle la aspiradora a la alfombra

3. Roberto y yo / hacer la comida
4. Elsa / planchar la ropa
5. tú / limpiar el refrigerador
6. Carmen y Elena / bañar al perro
7. Anita / poner la mesa
8. Raúl y Carlos / comprar la comida

B. Interview a classmate, using the following questions. When you have finished, switch roles.

1. Cuando llegaste a tu casa anoche, ¿las otras personas ya habían cenado?
2. A las once de la noche, ¿ya te habías acostado?
3. Cuando te levantaste esta mañana, ¿alguien te había preparado el desayuno?
4. Cuando yo llegué a clase, ¿ya habías llegado tú?
5. Cuando llegaste a clase hoy, ¿ya habías hecho todos los ejercicios de esta lección?
6. ¿Ya habías tomado español antes de tomar esta clase?

C. With a partner, act out the following dialogues in Spanish.

1. "Did you talk with Carlos, Paquito?"
   "No, when I left he hadn't returned yet."
2. "Didn't you write the letter, Anita?"
   "No, Olga had already written it."
3. "I didn't know that the dog had died."
   "I thought that the children had told you (about it)."
4. "Did you have a good time in Barcelona?"
   "Yes, we saw many things that we had never seen before."

D. Complete the following sentences logically, using the pluperfect tense.

1. Antes de venir a esta universidad, yo nunca…
2. Antes de tomar esta clase, mis compañeros y yo nunca…
3. Hasta el año pasado, mis amigos y yo siempre…
4. Hasta el semestre pasado, los estudiantes de esta clase nunca…
5. Hasta que yo cumplí *(turned)* dieciséis años, yo nunca…

¡A VER CUÁNTO APRENDIÓ!

¡Repase el vocabulario!

Choose the correct word or phrase to complete each statement.

1. Puede probarse (la ganga, el chaleco, el armario) en el probador.
2. Mi bolso (hace juego, está muerto de hambre, va de compras) con mis zapatos.
3. Yo calzo el número siete y estos zapatos son número diez. (Me aprietan mucho. Me quedan grandes. Me quedan bien.)
4. Necesito un par de (calcetines, tallas, escaleras mecánicas).
5. Pagué solamente treinta dólares por el vestido de lino. Hoy hubo una gran (bota, liquidación, billetera) en la tienda París.

6. Estos pantalones me quedan un poco chicos, pero no los he devuelto todavía porque (me gustan mucho, son muy estrechos, no me quedan bien).
7. Hace frío. Ponte (la chaqueta, las sandalias, el pañuelo) de lana.
8. ¿Quiere llevar las sandalias puestas o se las (aprieto, aprovecho, envuelvo)?
9. ¿Qué medida (usa, vuela, camina) Ud.?
10. El traje tiene que hacer juego con (la corbata, la ropa interior, el camisón).
11. Puse el dinero en (la billetera, la lana, el algodón).
12. No hay ropa en mi ropero. No tengo nada que (ponerme, bañarme, afeitarme).
13. ¿Usa Ud. talla grande, chica o (abierta, ancha, mediana)?
14. Pues yo me quedo en la (seda, taza, planta baja).
15. Compré una falda estampada y una falda (a lunares, muy sabrosa, enfadada).

Entrevista

Interview a classmate, using the **tú** form.

Pregúntele a su compañero(-a) de clase...

1. ...si prefiere camisas (blusas) a rayas o a cuadros.
2. ...qué talla de camisa (blusa) usa.
3. ...qué número calza.
4. ...si le aprietan los zapatos que lleva puestos.
5. ...si cuando compra un par de zapatos se los lleva puestos.
6. ...dónde ha comprado esa falda (chaqueta, camisa).
7. ...si su camisa (blusa) y sus pantalones siempre hacen juego.
8. ...cuál es la tienda que más le gusta.
9. ...si prefiere comprar cuando hay una liquidación y por qué.
10. ...si prefiere usar la escalera o la escalera mecánica.

Situaciones

What would you say in the following situations? What would the other person say? Act out the scenes with a partner. Take turns playing each role.

1. You are shopping in a large department store. You need a pair of gloves, a white shirt, and a blue tie. You also saw a brown suit in the window that you liked, and you want to know how much it costs.
2. You are a clerk. A customer is admiring a pink blouse. Ask her what size she wears, and tell her the fitting room is on the left.
3. A clerk at a shoe store wants to sell you a pair of boots. The ones he is showing you are too expensive and too tight on you.
4. Tell your friend that you haven't eaten yet, that you are starving, and that you want to have something to eat.

Para escribir

Write a dialogue between yourself and a clerk at a department store. You should mention what size you wear, what colors you like, and whether or not something fits you. Describe different things you want to buy.

En la vida real

Haciendo las maletas

You and a classmate are going on vacation. You are going to Hawaii in August and she or he is going to Colorado in December. Help each other select the type of clothes you will need for the trip, according to the different activities you are planning.

Here are some other words and phrases you may want to use in addition to the lesson vocabulary:

los bluejeans, los vaqueros *jeans*   **de rayón** *made of rayon*
la bufanda *scarf*   **los pantalones cortos** *shorts*

¡De compras!

Help a friend of yours who is shopping at El Corte Inglés in Madrid. Answer her questions, using the information provided in the ad.

En Agosto MAS VENTAJAS

Ahora en El Corte Inglés, Rebajas sobre Rebajas. Todo cuesta mucho menos.

SEÑORAS
- Vestidos lisos y estampados, en poliéster-algodón **2.995**
- Pareos estampados, en distintos dibujos y colores **995**

CABALLEROS
- Pantalones de sport y de vestir, lisos y fantasía, en poliéster-lana y poliéster-algodón **2.595**
- Mocasines en piel de búfalo, con piso de suela **3.995**

JÓVENES
- Para ellas, bañadores y bikinis, lisos y fantasía **1.595**
- Para ellos, bañadores, lisos y estampados **1.495**

NIÑOS
- Camisetas para niños y niñas, lisas y estampadas **595**
- Playeros en distintos colores, todas las tallas **695**

MENAJE
- Batería de cocina ocho piezas, en acero vitrificado, tres colores **4.495**

TEXTILES
- Mantelería de seis servicios estampada, acabada en festón **2.795**

MUEBLES
- Sillón cromado, con asiento y respaldo en piel **8.160**

LAS REBAJAS DE EL CORTE INGLÉS

1. ¿En qué mes son las rebajas?
2. Tengo una hija de nueve años. ¿Qué puedo comprarle?
3. Mi esposo necesita zapatos. ¿Qué tipo de zapatos venden y cuánto cuestan?
4. No tengo nada que ponerme. ¿Qué puedo comprar para mí?
5. Pensamos ir a la playa. ¿Qué puedo comprar para mí y para mis hijos?
6. Es el cumpleaños de mi padre. ¿Qué puedo regalarle? ¿Cuánto me va a costar?
7. ¿Para cuántas personas son los manteles?
8. ¿Cuánto cuesta el sillón?

La última moda

Stage a fashion show in class. A few students will play the role of runway models, and other students will describe the clothes and shoes the models are wearing. The rest of the class will be customers and will ask the price and size of the clothes and shoes the models are wearing.

Así somos

Vocabulario

el ambiente	environment
amplias	full
aparte	besides
atrasado	behind *(the times)*
bastante arregladas	rather well dressed
la calidad	quality
de manga larga	long sleeved
embolados	shined, polished
gruesas	heavy
la guerra	war
hace uno amistad	one makes friends
igual	the same
elegir	to choose
manejamos	we handle
las marcas	brands
la mezclilla	jeans, material used for jeans
la playera	T-shirt
presionando	pressuring
el saco	jacket, coat
suave	soft, light
la tela	material, cloth
los zapatos altos	high-heel shoes

Preparación

¿Cuánto saben Uds. ya?   This video module focuses on clothing and how Hispanics dress for a date. Make a list of the words and expressions that you think they will use. Circle the ones you hear as you watch the video.

Comprensión

A. **¿Qué se ponen?**   After watching the video, answer the following questions, according to what you understood.

1. Para ir a clase, ¿Paula se pone falda o jeans?
2. ¿Usa Leonardo camisas o camisetas?
3. ¿Se viste María de una manera *(manner)* informal o formal?
4. ¿Lleva Juan uniforme o ropa casual a clase?
5. A Miriam, ¿le gusta más usar jeans o usar faldas?

B. **¿Quién lo dice?**   Match each statement with the name of the person who said it.

   a. Juan   b. Paula   c. Otmara   d. Jaime   e. Leonardo

_____ 1. Utilizo traje, corbata, una buena colonia y los zapatos bien embolados.

_____ 2. Uso pantalón y camisa y a veces corbata.
_____ 3. No me gusta vestirme muy sofisticado.
_____ 4. Uso pantalones de tela, los saquitos o una falda.
_____ 5. Casi siempre me gusta ponerme minifaldas, zapatos altos y blusas.

C. La moda. Read the following statements. After watching the video, circle **V** (**Verdadero**) or **F** (**Falso**), according to what you understood.

V   F   1. En Bogotá usan camisas de lana o sacos.
V   F   2. En España la gente va bien arreglada para ir a una cita o a una fiesta.
V   F   3. Alejandro dice que los jeans y las playeras están de moda.
V   F   4. Otmara dice que en su país usan telas gruesas y faldas largas.

D. De compras. Answer the following questions, according to what you understood.

1. ¿Hay muchos almacenes grandes en Nicaragua?
2. ¿Miriam prefiere comprar ropa en un almacén o en una boutique?
3. ¿En Colombia hay muchos o pocos centros comerciales?
4. Para una ocasión especial, ¿Otmara compra en un almacén o en una boutique?
5. Para Alejandro, ¿es importante el precio de la ropa?

E. Entrevista. Read the following statements. After watching the video, circle **V** (**Verdadero**) or **F** (**Falso**), according to what you understood.

V   F   1. En la tienda venden sólo jeans.
V   F   2. Venden sólo una marca de jeans.
V   F   3. A Jorge le gusta trabajar en la tienda.
V   F   4. A Jorge no le gusta el ambiente de la tienda.
V   F   5. Jorge hace amistad con algunos clientes.

Ampliación

A. Vamos de compras. You and a classmate are going on a shopping spree. Discuss what you are going to buy and where you are going to shop.

B. Dos culturas. In groups of three or four, compare your clothing styles and shopping habits with those described by the people on the video.

Take this test. When you have finished, check your answers in the answer key provided for this section in Appendix E. Then use a red pen to correct any mistakes you may have made. Are you ready?

Lección 13

A. The familiar commands (*tú*)

Give the Spanish equivalent of the words in parentheses.

1. _____ , Paco. ¿Pusiste los platos en el fregadero?   *(Tell me)*
2. _____ el trabajo y luego _____ la cocina, Ana.   *(Do / clean)*
3. _____ de mi recámara, Carlos.   *(Leave)*
4. _____ con ella y _____ las cortinas para el cuarto, Pepe.
   (Go / buy)
5. ¿Los libros? _____ en la mesa, querida.   *(Put them)*
6. _____ conmigo.   *(Come)*
7. _____ buena y _____ las sábanas y la frazada, Anita.   *(Be / bring me)*
8. _____ paciencia. _____ unos minutos más.   *(Have / Wait for me)*
9. _____ la casa si no tiene aire acondicionado, Luis.   *(Don't buy)*
10. ¿El té? _____ todavía *(yet)*, Petrona.   *(Don't serve it.)*
11. _____ , querido.   *(Don't go away)*
12. _____ a las seis y _____ hasta las once.   *(Get up / work)*

SELF TEST

B. *Qué* and *cuál* used with *ser*

Supply the questions that elicited the following responses, beginning with **qué** or **cuál**, as needed.

1. Mi número de teléfono es 862–4031.
2. El apellido de mi madre es Lovera.
3. Un pasaporte es un documento que necesitamos para viajar a un país extranjero.
4. Las lecciones que necesitamos son la once y la doce.
5. Su dirección es calle Universidad, número treinta.
6. La paella es un plato hecho *(made)* con pollo, arroz y mariscos.

C. The subjunctive to express indefiniteness and nonexistence

Give the Spanish equivalent of the following sentences.

1. Is there anybody here who knows how to speak Spanish?
2. We have a house that has five bedrooms.
3. I don't know anybody who is from Spain.
4. Do you want a house that has a swimming pool?
5. I need an armchair that is comfortable.
6. There is a girl who speaks French, but there is no one who speaks Russian.

D. Just words . . .

Match the questions in column A with the appropriate responses in column B.
Use each response once.

A	B
1. ¿Tienes calor?	a. No, pero tiene terraza.
2. ¿Por qué es tan cara la casa?	b. No, uso el fregadero.
3. ¿Por qué necesitas un garaje tan grande?	c. No, necesito una cafetera.
4. ¿Cuánto va a costar el refrigerador?	d. Porque era más cómodo.
5. ¿La casa tiene jardín?	e. La semana próxima.
6. ¿Es optimista?	f. Está en un buen barrio.
7. ¿Necesitas una tostadora?	g. Una cómoda y una butaca.
8. ¿Tienes lavaplatos?	h. No, tiempo completo.
9. ¿Cuándo se mudan?	i. No, muy pesimista.
10. ¿Tienen dinero?	j. Sí, pero no tenemos fundas.
11. ¿Por qué compraste este sofá en vez del otro?	k. ¡Tengo tres coches!
12. ¿Vas a trabajar medio día?	l. Póngalo en la sala.
13. ¿Qué muebles necesitas?	m. Sí, pon el aire acondicionado, por favor.
14. ¿Dónde pongo el sofá?	n. Sí, ganaron la lotería.
15. ¿Tienen almohadas?	o. Quinientos dólares.
16. ¿Dónde vas a poner el pollo?	p. En el microondas.

E. Culture

Read the following statements and circle **V (Verdadero)** or **F (Falso)** based on the
¿Lo sabía Ud.? section.

V   F   1. En España llaman "pisos" a los apartamentos.

V   F   2. En los países latinos muchos edificios tienen oficinas o tiendas en la planta baja.

V   F   3. La palabra "barrio" tiene una connotación negativa en los países de habla hispana.

V   F   4. La Universidad Nacional Autónoma de México es la menos importante del país.

V   F   5. Unos 400.000 estudiantes asisten a la UNAM.

Lección 14

A. The subjunctive or indicative after certain conjunctions

Give the Spanish equivalent of the verbs in parentheses.

1. Tan pronto como Marta _____ a casa, le voy a dar las entradas. *(arrives)*

2. Voy a esperarlos hasta que _____ . *(they return)*

3. Cuando ellos _____ a trabajar, siempre dejan las ventanas abiertas. *(go)*

4. Cuando lo _____ , dile que somos seis. *(see)*

5. Vamos antes de que _____ la lámpara que te gusta. *(they sell)*
6. Ella va a ir al parque con tal que tú _____ con ella. *(go)*
7. No puedo sacar el sillón de la casa sin que ellos me _____ . *(see)*
8. En caso de que ella _____ otras frutas, yo puedo traérselas. *(needs)*
9. No puedo comprar las verduras a menos que tú me _____ el dinero. *(give)*
10. Voy a hacer todo lo posible para que él _____ el premio. *(wins)*

B. Uses of *sino* and *pero*

Complete the following, using **sino** or **pero** as needed.

1. No quiero ensalada de tomates _____ de lechuga.
2. Ellos van al circo, _____ yo prefiero ir al cine.
3. No voy a comprar naranjas _____ manzanas.
4. Fueron al supermercado, _____ no trajeron el pan.
5. No es un drama _____ una comedia.
6. No tengo ganas de comer nada _____ de tomar algo.

C. First-person plural commands

Answer the following questions, using appropriate command forms and the cues provided.

1. ¿Adónde vamos?   (al supermercado)
2. ¿A qué hora vamos?   (a las dos)
3. ¿Qué compramos?   (frutas y vegetales)
4. ¿A quién le pedimos el dinero?   (a mamá)
5. ¿Adónde vamos después? ¿Al teatro?   (no, al cine)
6. ¿A qué hora volvemos a casa?   (a las siete)
7. ¿A qué hora nos acostamos esta noche?   (a las once)
8. ¿A qué hora nos levantamos mañana?   (a las seis)

D. Just words . . .

Complete the following sentences, using words learned in **Lección 14.**

1. ¿Tú le pones crema y _____ al café?
2. Quiero una _____ de salsa de tomate y una de frijoles.
3. ¿Compraste mantequilla o _____ ? A mí me gusta el pan con mantequilla.
4. No quiero zanahorias; no me gustan las _____ .
5. ¿Te vas a _____ a dieta?
6. Tengo una _____ con Rosalía. Vamos a ir al cine.
7. ¿Qué _____ ponen en el cine Rex?
8. El 4 de julio es _____ ; no tenemos que trabajar.
9. Voy a comprar una _____ de huevos.
10. Necesitamos papel _____ para el baño.
11. Fuimos al parque de _____ el sábado pasado.
12. A él le gustan mucho los animales. Lo voy a llevar al _____ .

E. Culture

Read the following statements and circle **V** (**Verdadero**) or **F** (**Falso**) based on the **¿Lo sabía Ud.?** section.

V F   1. En los países hispanos no existen los supermercados.

V F   2. En los países hispanos muchas personas prefieren comprar en tiendas pequeñas especializadas, como carnicerías y panaderías.

V F   3. Las películas hispanas son desconocidas en Europa y en los Estados Unidos.

V F   4. Las películas norteamericanas no son populares en el mundo hispano.

V F   5. Las películas norteamericanas que se ven en el mundo hispano generalmente están dobladas o tienen subtítulos en español.

Lección 15

A. The past participle

Give the Spanish equivalent of the following past participles.

1. written
2. opened
3. seen
4. done
5. broken

6. gone
7. spoken
8. eaten
9. drunk
10. received

B. Past participles used as adjectives

Give the Spanish equivalent of the words in parentheses.

1. Los espejos están _____ . *(broken)*
2. ¿Están _____ las puertas de la tienda? *(open)*
3. El hombre estaba _____ . *(dead)*
4. El departamento de señoras está _____ . *(closed)*
5. Estas sandalias fueron _____ aquí. *(made)*

C. The present perfect

Complete the sentences with the present perfect tense of the verbs in the list, as needed.

decir   usar   comer
quedarse   hacer   envolver

1. ¿Tú nunca _____ esa falda?
2. Él me _____ los zapatos. No voy a llevarlos puestos.
3. Ellos me _____ que no tienen nada que hacer.
4. Nosotros _____ demasiado.
5. Yo _____ en la planta baja.
6. ¿Uds. no _____ el trabajo todavía?

D. The past perfect (pluperfect)

Complete the following sentences with the past perfect tense of the verbs in parentheses.

1. Cuando yo llegué, la liquidación ya _____ (terminar).
2. Elsa dijo que ellos _____ (ir) al departamento de ropa para caballeros.
3. El dependiente me _____ (decir) que la cartera costaba cincuenta dólares.
4. Yo ya _____ (abrir) el probador.
5. Nosotros todavía no _____ (comprar) la camisa.
6. ¿Tú le _____ (preguntar) qué talla usaba?

E. Just words . . .

Choose the appropriate answer to each of the following questions.

1. ¿Qué número calza Ud.?
   a. Talla mediana.
   b. El treinta y seis.
   c. No tengo pantimedias.

2. ¿Quiere las botas negras y el bolso azul?
   a. No, no hacen juego.
   b. Casi al mismo tiempo.
   c. No, me gusta la ropa interior.

3. ¿Puedo probarme estos zapatos?
   a. Sí, pero antes tiene que ponerse calcetines.
   b. Sí, pero necesita esta corbata.
   c. Sí, pero necesita ponerse estos guantes.

4. ¿Va a llevar este par de zapatos?
   a. No, me quedan muy bien.
   b. No, están en la zapatería.
   c. No, me aprietan un poco.

5. ¿Dónde pusiste el traje?
   a. ¡En la billetera, por supuesto!
   b. ¡En el ropero, por supuesto!
   c. ¡En la escalera, por supuesto!

6. ¿Tiene frío, señora?
   a. Sí, tráigame el pañuelo.
   b. Sí, tráigame las sandalias.
   c. Sí, tráigame la chaqueta.

7. ¿Quieres comer algo?
   a. Sí, estoy muerta de hambre.
   b. Sí, me gusta este vestido.
   c. Sí, quiero esa camisa y esa blusa.

8. ¿Cómo subieron al tercer piso?
   a. Nos encontramos en la planta baja.
   b. Por la escalera mecánica.
   c. Compramos ropa.

F. Culture

Circle the correct answer, based on the **¿Lo sabía Ud.?** section.

1. El primer piso en España corresponde (a la planta baja, al segundo piso) en los Estados Unidos.
2. En las ciudades hispanas muchas mujeres prefieren (comprar ropa hecha, utilizar los servicios de una modista).
3. En los países hispanos (existen, no existen) grandes almacenes de ropa.
4. En España los dependientes de las tiendas (a veces, nunca) tutean a los clientes.

LAS CARRERAS

OBJECTIVES

Structure
The future • The conditional • The future perfect and the conditional perfect

Communication
You will learn vocabulary related to college activities and careers.

LAS CARRERAS

Alina y Daniel son dos jóvenes latinoamericanos que están estudiando en la Universidad de California en Los Ángeles. Alina es cubana y Daniel es argentino. Los dos están tomando una clase de administración de empresas.

ALINA —Tendré que matricularme en la clase de sociología de la Dra. Saldívar. No podré tomar la clase del professor Wilson porque a esa hora tengo que tomar física.

DANIEL —Yo tomaría esa clase contigo, pero necesito tomar otras asignaturas. Mi consejero me ha sugerido que tome química, cálculo y geología.

ALINA —Tu especialización es química, ¿no? ¿Siempre te han gustado las ciencias?

DANIEL —Sí, mi padre quiere que sea abogado, como él, pero yo asistí a la Facultad de Derecho en Buenos Aires y no me gustó.

ALINA —De haber seguido los consejos de mis padres, yo habría estudiado ingeniería o contabilidad, pero yo decidí estudiar periodismo.

DANIEL —¡Y serás una periodista magnífica!

ALINA —Gracias. Oye, tú te habrás graduado para el año próximo, ¿verdad? ¿Qué harás después?

DANIEL —Quiero trabajar en un laboratorio, porque me gusta mucho la investigación. ¿Y tú? ¿Cuáles son tus planes?

ALINA —Probablemente trabajaré para un periódico… Sé que tendré que preocuparme por eso más tarde, pero por el momento mis planes son terminar el informe que estoy preparando para mi clase de literatura y sacar una "A" en el examen de psicología.

DANIEL —¡Pero, Alina, lo único importante no son las notas! Tienes que divertirte un poco. ¿Te gustaría ir conmigo al estadio esta noche? Hay un partido de fútbol americano[1] y juega nuestro equipo.

ALINA —No puedo. Tengo una beca y necesito mantener un buen promedio. Si saco una mala nota, perderé la beca. Además, no me gustan los deportes.

DANIEL —Hablando de notas… ahora me acuerdo de que tengo un examen parcial en mi clase de matemáticas mañana.

ALINA —Supongo que quieres que te preste mi calculadora, como siempre.

DANIEL —Gracias, flaca.[2] Me voy, porque David quiere que lo ayude con su informe de biología y ya es tarde. ¡Chau!

ALINA —Hasta mañana. ¿Almorzamos juntos al mediodía?

DANIEL —Sí, para esa hora habré terminado el examen y estaré libre.

---

[1] **fútbol americano** = *football*

[2] **Flaca** literally means "skinny," but is also used affectionately in many Hispanic countries to address close friends regardless of the person's physical characteristics. Comparable expressions in English are "kid," "pal," and "buddy."

Vocabulario

COGNADOS

argentino(-a) Argentinian
la **biología** biology
la **calculadora** calculator
el **cálculo** calculus
la **ciencia** science
el **estadio** stadium

la **física** physics
la **geología** geology
importante important
el **laboratorio** laboratory
latinoamericano(-a) Latin
American

la **literatura** literature
las **matemáticas** mathematics
probablemente probably
la **psicología** psychology
la **sociología** sociology

NOMBRES

el (la) **abogado(-a)** lawyer
la **administración de empresas**
business administration
la **asignatura**, la **materia** subject
la **beca** scholarship
la **carrera** university studies,
career
el (la) **consejero(-a)** advisor
el **consejo** advice
la **contabilidad** accounting

el **deporte** sport
el **equipo** team
la **especialización** major (field of
study)
el **examen parcial, examen de
mitad de curso** midterm exam
la **facultad de derecho** law school
el **fútbol** soccer
el **informe** report, paper
la **ingeniería** engineering

la **investigación** research
el (la) **joven (los jóvenes)** young
person(s)
la **nota** grade
el **partido** game
el **periodismo** journalism
el (la) **periodista** journalist
el **promedio** grade point average
la **química** chemistry

VERBOS

ayudar (a) to help
graduarse[1] to graduate
mantener to maintain (*conj. like*
tener)

matricularse to register
sacar to get, receive (a grade)
suponer to suppose (*conj. like*
poner)

OTRAS PALABRAS Y EXPRESIONES

como siempre as usual
de haber seguido had I followed
lo único[2] the only thing

---

[1] Present tense: **me gradúo, te gradúas, se gradúa, nos graduamos, os graduáis, se gradúan**
[2] **Lo** + *adjective* is the equivalent of *the* + *adjective* + *thing:* **Lo importante,** *the important thing;* **lo
bueno,** *the good thing.*

VOCABULARIO ADICIONAL

■ PROFESIONES Y OFICIOS *(trades)*[1]

el (la) bibliotecario(-a) librarian

el (la) carpintero(-a) carpenter

el (la) cocinero(-a) cook, chef

el (la) contador(-a) accountant

el (la) electricista electrician

el hombre (la mujer) de negocios
businessman (woman)

el (la) ingeniero(-a) engineer

el (la) plomero(-a) plumber

el (la) programador(-a)
programmer

---

[1] For an extensive list of professions and trades, see Appendix F.

el (la) psicólogo(-a) psychologist

el (la) vendedor(-a) salesperson

■ PARA HABLAR DE LOS ESTUDIOS

aprobar (o:ue) to pass (an exam or course)	**Aprobé** el examen de química ayer.
entregar to turn in, deliver	Le **entregué** la tarea al profesor.
el horario schedule	Este semestre tengo un **horario** muy bueno.
la matrícula registration, tuition	No tengo dinero para pagar la **matrícula**.
quedar suspendido(-a) to fail (an exam or course)	**Quedé suspendida** en el examen parcial.
el requisito requirement	He tomado todos los **requisitos** generales.
el semestre semester	El próximo **semestre** tomaré física.
el trimestre quarter	Este **trimestre** tengo una clase de matemáticas.

¡CONVERSEMOS!

Answer the following questions, basing your answers on the dialogue.

1. ¿Qué clase están tomando juntos Alina y Daniel?
2. ¿En qué clase tendrá que matricularse Alina?
3. ¿Qué le ha sugerido el consejero a Daniel?
4. ¿Cuál es la especialización de Daniel?
5. ¿Cuál es la profesión del padre de Daniel?
6. De haber seguido los consejos de sus padres, ¿qué habría estudiado Alina?
7. ¿Qué habrá hecho Daniel para el año próximo?
8. Por el momento, ¿cuáles son los planes de Alina?
9. ¿Por qué no quiere ir Alina al partido de fútbol?
10. ¿Por qué dice Daniel que estará libre al mediodía?

¿Lo sabía Ud.?

- En la mayoría de las universidades hispanas no existe el concepto de "*major*" usado en los Estados Unidos. Los estudiantes españoles y latinoamericanos toman muy pocas clases optativas (*electives*), ya que la mayoría comienza a especializarse a partir de su primer año en la universidad.

- En España y en Latinoamérica, las universidades se dividen en "facultades", donde los estudiantes toman clases directamente relacionadas con su especialización (por ejemplo, la Facultad de Medicina, la Facultad de Ingeniería, la Facultad de Arquitectura, etc.). No existen requisitos generales, pues éstos se toman en la escuela secundaria.

- En lugar de letras, el sistema de calificaciones (*grading system*) en las universidades hispanas usa números. Por lo general, se califica asignando notas de 1 a 5 en Hispanoamérica y de 1 a 10 en España. Una nota de 3 o 6 es normalmente la nota mínima para aprobar una clase o un examen.

Estudiantes de la Facultad de Derecho en Lima, Peru.

ESTRUCTURAS

1 The future *(El futuro)*

Most Spanish verbs are regular in the future tense. The infinitive serves as the stem of almost all of them, and the endings are the same for all three conjugations.

The Future Tense					
Infinitive			*Stem*	*Ending*	
trabajar	yo		trabajar-	é	trabajaré
aprender	tú		aprender-	ás	aprenderás
escribir	Ud.		escribir-	á	escribirá
hablar	él		hablar-	á	hablará
decidir	ella		decidir-	á	decidirá
dar	nosotros(-as)		dar-	emos	daremos
ir	vosotros(-as)		ir-	éis	iréis
caminar	Uds.		caminar-	án	caminarán
perder	ellos		perder-	án	perderán
recibir	ellas		recibir-	án	recibirán

ATENCIÓN   Note that all the endings, except the one for the **nosotros** form, have written accents.

—¿Qué clases **tomarás** el año próximo?	*"What classes will you take next year?"*
—No sé. Lo **decidiré** cuando hable con mi consejero.	*"I don't know. I'll decide when I talk with my advisor."*

◼ The English equivalent of the Spanish future is *will* or *shall* + *a verb*. As you have already learned, Spanish also uses the construction **ir a** + *infinitive* or *the present tense with a time expression* to express future action, very much like the English present tense or the expression *going to*.

Vamos a ir al cine esta noche.	*We're going (We'll go) to the movies tonight.*
or: **Iremos** al cine esta noche.	

Anita **toma** el examen mañana.	*Anita is taking (will take) the exam tomorrow.*
or: Anita **tomará** el examen mañana.	

ATENCIÓN   The Spanish future is *not* used to express willingness, as is the English future. In Spanish this is expressed with the verb **querer.**

¿Quieres llamar a Tomás?	*Will you call Tomás?*

■ A small number of verbs are irregular in the future. These verbs use a modified form of the infinitive as a stem, but have the same endings as the regular verbs.

Irregular Future Stems		
Infinitive	*Modified form (Stem)*	*First-person singular*
decir	dir-	diré
hacer	har-	haré
querer	querr-	querré
saber	sabr-	sabré
poder	podr-	podré
caber	cabr-	cabré
poner	pondr-	pondré
venir	vendr-	vendré
tener	tendr-	tendré
salir	saldr-	saldré
valer[1]	valdr-	valdré

—¿Qué les **dirás** a tus padres?
—Les **diré** que no **podremos** venir en enero y que **vendremos** en febrero.

"What will you tell your parents?"
"I will tell them that we won't be able to come in January and that we will come in February."

ATENCIÓN The future of **hay** (impersonal form of **haber**) is **habrá**.

¿Habrá una fiesta?

Will there be a party?

Práctica

A. Say what the following people will do after classes are over, using the future tense.

1. Jorge / ir de vacaciones / México
2. Marta y yo / salir para Colombia / julio
3. Mis padres / venir / a visitarme / agosto
4. Ana / tener que / trabajar / verano
5. Yo / tomar / una clase / francés
6. Uds. / poner / alfombra nueva / casa
7. Tú / viajar / por Latinoamérica
8. Ud. / pasar / dos semanas / Sevilla

B. You and a friend will be traveling to Spain next year. Answer these questions about your trip.

1. ¿Adónde irán?
2. ¿Cuándo saldrán de viaje?
3. ¿Viajarán en barco o en avión?

---

[1] *to be worth*

4. ¿Cuánto tiempo estarán viajando?
5. ¿Podrán visitar muchas ciudades?
6. ¿Qué lugares visitarán?
7. ¿Les enviarán tarjetas postales a sus amigos?
8. ¿Cuánto dinero necesitarán para el viaje?
9. ¿Se lo pedirán a sus padres?
10. ¿Cuándo volverán?

C. Now, use the questions in Exercise B as a model to ask a classmate about his or her upcoming vacation plans.

D. Say what the following people will do in each situation.

1. Los estudiantes tienen que escribir un informe para su clase de sociología.
2. Jorge no tiene dinero para pagar la matrícula.
3. Ud. y yo tenemos un examen mañana.
4. Antonio y Luis no saben qué clases pueden tomar.
5. Yo tengo un examen de matemáticas y no tengo calculadora.
6. Los muchachos tienen mucha hambre.

E. Write predictions about five of your classmates and what will happen to them in the future.

> **MODELO:** *Dentro de cinco años, Alina será periodista y trabajará para el periódico* Los Angeles Times.

2 The conditional *(El condicional)*

The conditional tense in Spanish is equivalent to the conditional in English, expressed by *should* or *would + a verb*.[1] Like the future tense, the conditional uses the infinitive as the stem and has only one set of endings for all three conjugations.

The Conditional Tense				
Infinitive		**Stem**	**Ending**	
trabajar	yo	trabajar-	ía	trabajaría
aprender	tú	aprender-	ías	aprenderías
escribir	Ud.	escribir-	ía	escribiría
ir	él	ir-	ía	iría
ser	ella	ser-	ía	sería
dar	nosotros(-as)	dar-	íamos	daríamos
hablar	vosotros(-as)	hablar-	íais	hablaríais
servir	Uds.	servir-	ían	servirían
estar	ellos	estar-	ían	estarían
preferir	ellas	preferir-	ían	preferirían

---

[1] The conditional is never used in Spanish as an equivalent of *used to.*
Cuando era pequeño siempre **iba a la playa.** *When I was little I would always go to the beach.*

■ All of the conditional endings have written accents.

—Él dijo que **tomaría** esta clase.	*"He said that he would take this class."*
—Sí, y también dijo que **hablaría** con una consejera.	*"Yes, and he also said that he would speak with an advisor."*

■ The conditional is also used as the future of a past action. The future states what *will* happen; the conditional states what *would* happen.

Future (states what *will* happen)	*Conditional* (states what *would* happen)
Él **dice** que **estará** aquí mañana.	Él **dijo** que **estaría** aquí mañana.
He says that he will be here tomorrow.	*He said that he would be here tomorrow.*

■ The verbs that have irregular stems in the future tense are also irregular in the conditional. The endings are the same as those for regular verbs.

Irregular Conditional Stems		
Infinitive	*Modified form (Stem)*	*First-person singular*
decir	dir-	diría
hacer	har-	haría
querer	querr-	querría
saber	sabr-	sabría
poder	podr-	podría
caber	cabr-	cabría
poner	pondr-	pondría
venir	vendr-	vendría
tener	tendr-	tendría
salir	saldr-	saldría
valer	valdr-	valdría

—¿A qué hora te dijo que **vendría**?	*"What time did he tell you he would come?"*
—Dijo que **saldría** de casa a las dos.	*"He said he would leave home at two."*

ATENCIÓN The conditional of **hay** (impersonal form of **haber**) is **habría**.

Dijo que **habría** un examen mañana.	*He said there would be an exam tomorrow.*

Práctica

A. Nobody would do the things that Carlos does. Say what the following people would do instead, using the conditional tense.

> MODELO: Carlos come en la cafetería. (yo)
> *Yo no comería en la cafetería; comería en mi casa.*

Carlos...

1. se levanta a las cinco. (Uds.)
2. estudia por la mañana. (Ana y Luis)
3. viene a la universidad en ómnibus. (nosotros)
4. toma clases de alemán. (yo)
5. se baña por la noche. (Elsa)
6. se acuesta a las nueve de la noche. (Ud.)
7. va a las montañas los fines de semana. (ellos)
8. sale con Margarita. (tú)

B. Interview a classmate, using the following questions.

1. ¿Qué harías con mil dólares?
2. ¿Adónde irías de vacaciones? ¿En qué mes saldrías de vacaciones? ¿Por qué?
3. ¿Qué te gustaría hacer hoy?
4. ¿Dónde te gustaría almorzar mañana?
5. ¿Preferirías ver un partido de fútbol o un partido de fútbol americano?
6. ¿Qué asignaturas te gustaría tomar el semestre (trimestre) próximo?
7. ¿Preferirías un apartamento en la planta baja o en el séptimo piso? ¿Por qué?
8. Vamos a tener una fiesta. ¿Qué podrías traer?

C. Describe what you would do in the following situations, using the conditional.

1. Su hijo(-a) le pide consejos sobre la carrera que debe seguir.
2. Su equipo de fútbol americano favorito juega hoy.
3. Un compañero quiere que Ud. lo ayude con su informe.
4. Sus amigos lo (la) invitan a ir al cine y Ud. tiene que trabajar mañana.
5. Una persona muy antipática lo (la) invita a salir.

D. With a partner, take turns telling each other what you would do if you won a million dollars in the lottery. Say at least five things each, and then compare your responses with those of other classmates.

3 The future perfect and the conditional perfect
(El futuro perfecto y el condicional perfecto)

A. The future perfect

■ The future perfect in Spanish corresponds closely in formation and meaning to the same tense in English. The Spanish future perfect is formed with the future tense of the auxiliary verb **haber** + *the past participle* of the main verb.

Future tense of **haber**	
habré	habremos
habrás	habréis
habrá	habrán

Formation of the Future Perfect Tense		
yo	**habré terminado**	*I will have finished*
tú	**habrás vuelto**	*you will have returned*
Ud.		
él	**habrá comido**	*you (he, she) will have eaten*
ella		
nosotros(-as)	**habremos escrito**	*we will have written*
vosotros(-as)	**habréis dicho**	*you (inf.) will have said*
Uds.		
ellos	**habrán salido**	*you (they) will have left*
ellas		

■ Like its English equivalent, the future perfect is used to indicate an action that will have taken place by a certain time in the future.

—¿Tus padres estarán aquí para el dos de junio?

—Sí, para esa fecha ya **habrán vuelto** de Madrid.

"Will your parents be here by June second?"

"Yes, by that date they will have returned from Madrid."

Práctica
. . . .

A. Complete the following dialogues, using the future perfect forms of the verbs listed. Then act them out with a partner.

acostarse   limpiar   terminar
cenar   salir   volver

1. —Esta noche a las once voy a llamar a Quique.
   —¿Estás loco(-a)? Para esa hora él ya _____ . Llámalo mañana a las siete.
   —Para esa hora ya _____ de su casa.
2. —¿Uds. _____ de México para el 4 de julio?
   —No, no _____ todavía. Vamos a estar allí hasta agosto.

3. —Tú y yo podemos salir para España el 12 de diciembre porque ya
   estaremos de vacaciones.
   —Bueno, tú _____ las clases para entonces, pero yo no las _____
   todavía.
4. —No podemos traer a mis amigos esta noche porque la casa está muy sucia
   (dirty).
   —No te preocupes. Para cuando Uds. vengan, las chicas ya la _____ .
5. —¿Quieres cenar con nosotros hoy?
   —Gracias, pero para cuando yo vuelva, Uds. ya _____ .

B. With your partner, discuss things that you will or will not have done by the
following times.

1. para las once de la noche
2. para mañana a las cinco de la mañana
3. para mañana a las seis de la tarde
4. para el sábado próximo
5. para junio del año próximo
6. para el año 2004

B. The conditional perfect

■ The conditional perfect is formed with the conditional tense of the auxiliary
verb **haber** + *the past participle* of the main verb.

Conditional tense of **haber**	
habría	habríamos
habrías	habríais
habría	habrían

Formation of the Conditional Perfect Tense		
yo	**habría vuelto**	*I would have returned*
tú	**habrías comido**	*you would have eaten*
Ud. él ella	**habría salido**	*you (he, she) would have left*
nosotros(-as)	**habríamos estudiado**	*we would have studied*
vosotros(-as)	**habríais hecho**	*you (inf.) would have done*
Uds. ellos ellas	**habrían muerto**	*you (they) would have died*

■ Like the English conditional perfect, the Spanish conditional perfect is used
to indicate an action that would have taken place but didn't.

—Yo me matriculé ayer. *"I registered yesterday."*
—Yo **me habría matriculado** la *"I would have registered last*
   semana pasada. *week."*

Práctica

A. Last summer, my family, a friend, and I took a trip to New York. Based on what I tell you about our trip, say what you and each member of your family would have done differently, if anything.

> MODELO: Mi padre llevó tres maletas.
> *Mi padre habría llevado una maleta.*

1. Nosotros fuimos a Nueva York.
2. Viajamos en tren.
3. Yo me senté en la sección de no fumar.
4. Mi mamá preparó sándwiches para el viaje.
5. Mi amigo y yo bebimos refrescos en el café del tren.
6. En Nueva York, mi amigo se quedó en casa de su abuelo.
7. Nosotros nos quedamos en un hotel.
8. Mis padres fueron a ver una comedia musical.
9. Yo fui a bailar.
10. Nosotros visitamos el Museo de Arte Moderno.
11. Mi amigo visitó la Estatua de la Libertad.
12. Estuvimos en Nueva York por dos semanas.

B. With a partner, act out the following dialogues in Spanish.

1. "I took my nephew to the soccer game."
   "I would have taken him to the beach."
2. "They went to the movies last Saturday."
   "I would have gone to the theater."
3. "I'm very tired. I had to clean my apartment."
   "Why didn't you call me? I would have helped you."
4. "Do you like my jacket? It cost me a fortune!"
   "I wouldn't have spent ten dollars on that jacket."
5. "She said that she was starving, and I made her a sandwich."
   "We would have taken her to a restaurant."

Summary of the Tenses of the Indicative

Simple Tenses

	-ar	-er	-ir
Presente	hablo	como	vivo
Pretérito	hablé	comí	viví
Imperfecto	hablaba	comía	vivía
Futuro	hablaré	comeré	viviré
Condicional	hablaría	comería	viviría

Compound Tenses

	-ar	-er	-ir
Presente perfecto	he hablado	he comido	he vivido
Pretérito plus-cuamperfecto	había hablado	había comido	había vivido
Futuro perfecto	habré hablado	habré comido	habré vivido
Condicional perfecto	habría hablado	habría comido	habría vivido

¡A VER CUÁNTO APRENDIÓ!

¡Repase el vocabulario!

Complete the following sentences with the missing words; then read them aloud.

1. Como Fernando sacó una "F" en física, quedó _____ en esa asignatura.
2. Estoy tomando una clase de administración de _____ .
3. El golf es el _____ que menos me gusta.
4. Quiere ser abogado. Estudia en la Facultad de _____ .
5. Tengo que preparar un _____ para mi clase de literatura.
6. Fue elegido *(chosen)* el mejor _____ porque vendió cien casas en un año.
7. Voy a hablar con mi _____ para que me diga qué clases debo tomar.
8. ¿Quieres jugar al _____ esta tarde?
9. Tengo que _____ un promedio alto o pierdo la beca.
10. Para Juan, lo _____ importante es el fútbol.
11. Escribe para la revista *Time*. Es _____ .
12. Para ser ingeniero tienes que estudiar en la Facultad de _____ .
13. ¿Cuál es tu _____ ? ¿Matemáticas o contabilidad?
14. Son _____ . Pedro es de Chile y Ana es de México.
15. Mi papá es un hombre de _____ .
16. El _____ de ese restaurante cocina muy bien.

Entrevista

Interview a classmate, using the **tú** form.

Pregúntele a su compañero(-a) de clase...

1. ...si conoce a algún (alguna) estudiante latinoamericano(-a). (¿De qué país?)
2. ...cuál es la materia que más le gusta. (¿Y el deporte?)
3. ...qué quería ser cuando era pequeño(-a).
4. ...si ha tomado todos los requisitos generales.
5. ...cuándo espera graduarse.
6. ...si le gustaría tomar una clase de psicología.
7. ...cuándo tiene exámenes parciales (finales).
8. ...qué clases tomará el próximo trimestre (semestre).
9. ...qué nota espera sacar en esta clase.
10. ...si preferiría ser contador(-a), vendedor(-a) o periodista, y por qué.

Situaciones

What would you say in the following situations? What might the other person say? Act out the scenes with a partner. Take turns playing each role.

1. A freshman asks you what courses to take. Find out something about his or her interests and plans, and make some appropriate course recommendations. Be sure to mention some of your school's requirements.
2. You are talking with a friend about classes you like, classes you don't like, and the reasons why.

3. You have just graduated, and one of your parents has taken you out for a celebration dinner. You haven't done everything they had hoped you would do in college, but you are pleased with your decisions. Discuss your plans for the future.

¿Qué pasa aquí?

In groups of three or four, make up a story about the people in the photo. Say who they are, what subjects they are taking, their majors, their grade point averages, when they will graduate, and so forth.

 **Para escribir**

Write a composition about your college activities. Include the following information:

■ your major

■ classes you are taking this semester

■ classes you took last semester

■ classes you like and classes you don't like

■ your extracurricular activities

■ your career plans

En la vida real

El primer empleo

With a classmate, play the roles of a recent college graduate who is applying for a job and a prospective employer. The interviewer wants to know about the applicant's college courses and activities and how they are relevant to the job.

Here is a list that might help you answer the interviewer's questions:

Lista de materias

Administración de empresas	Ciencias políticas	Humanidades
Alemán	Contabilidad	Inglés
Álgebra	Drama	Literatura
Antropología	Educación física	Matemáticas
Arte	Electrónica	Música
Astronomía	Español	Química
Biología	Estadística	Relaciones públicas
Cálculo	Física	Ruso
Cibernética (*Computer Science*)	Francés	Sociología
Ciencias económicas	Geología	Telecomunicaciones
	Geometría	
	Historia	

Ahora Ud. es profesor(-a)

Imagine that you are an instructor at one of the schools in the ads. Study the ads carefully, noting all of the features that are described. Then try to convince a classmate why he or she should take a course there. Your classmate should ask questions after you have finished.

¡Vamos a leer!

Antes de leer

A. What images or ideas do you associate with the colors green, red, and white? Scan the two poems and make a list of the words associated with nature.

B. As you read the introduction to Martí and the poems, answer the following questions.

1. ¿En qué año nació *(was born)* el poeta?
2. ¿Dónde y en qué año murió?
3. ¿Cuáles son los temas principales de la poesía de Martí?
4. ¿Cómo se describe el poeta en el primer poema?
5. ¿Qué quiere hacer Martí antes de morirse?
6. ¿Qué imágenes usa Martí para describir sus versos?
7. ¿Con quiénes quiere echar su suerte el poeta?
8. ¿Qué flor *(flower)* cultiva el poeta?
9. ¿Cultiva el poeta la rosa solamente para sus amigos o también para sus enemigos?
10. ¿Qué simboliza la rosa blanca?
11. Según este poema, ¿el poeta odia a sus enemigos?

Versos sencillos
José Martí

campo... battlefield

José Martí (Cuba: 1853–1895) dedicó su vida y su obra a la independencia de Cuba, donde murió en el campo de batalla° en 1895. Es famoso no sólo como poeta y ensayista, sino también como orador.

oppressed

Los poemas de Martí se caracterizan por la melodía, el ritmo y el uso de frases cortas, con las que expresa ideas muy profundas. Sus temas principales son la libertad, la justicia, la independencia de su patria y la defensa de los pobres y los oprimidos.°

De *Versos sencillos*[1]

I

grows

to pour out / soul

Yo soy un hombre sincero
de donde crece° la palma
y antes de morirme quiero
echar° mis versos del alma.°

V

light
carmín... bright red
ciervo... wounded deer
shelter

Mi verso es de un verde claro,°
y de un carmín encendido°
mi verso es un ciervo herido°
que busca en el monte amparo.°

---

[1] Este poema es la letra de la canción "La Guantanamera".

III

earth, land   Con los pobres de la tierra,°
mi... *to share my destiny* quiero yo mi suerte echar;°
brook   el arroyo° de la sierra
pleases   me complace° más que el mar.

XXXIX

 Cultivo una rosa blanca,
en julio como en enero,
para el amigo sincero
open   que me da su mano franca.°

tears out   Y para el cruel que me arranca°
heart   el corazón° con que vivo,
thistle / nettle   cardo° ni ortiga° cultivo:
cultivo la rosa blanca.

Díganos

Answer the following questions based on your own thoughts and experiences.

1. ¿Le gusta a Ud. la poesía?
2. ¿Quién es su poeta favorito(-a)?
3. ¿Conoce Ud. a otros poetas hispanos? ¿Cuáles?
4. ¿Ha oído Ud. la canción "La Guantanamera"?
5. Al final del segundo poema, el poeta perdona *(forgives)* las ofensas de sus enemigos. ¿Haría Ud. lo mismo?

PANORAMA HISPÁNICO

Argentina

Chile

Paraguay

Uruguay

■ Buenos Aires, la capital de Argentina, tiene una población de más de diez millones de habitantes, y su área metropolitana es una de las más extensas del mundo. Su sistema de metro, "el subterráneo", es el más antiguo de Latinoamérica.

■ Uruguay es el país de habla hispana más pequeño de la América del Sur. El 45% de la población del país está concentrado en Montevideo, la capital. Muy cerca de esta ciudad está la playa de Punta del Este, de fama internacional.

■ La represa *(dam)* de Itaipú, entre Brasil y Paraguay, es la represa hidroeléctrica más grande del mundo y fue construída por los gobiernos de Brasil y Paraguay.

■ Paraguay es conocido por sus joyas de oro y de plata, sus objetos de madera tallada *(carved wood)* y sus encajes *(laces)* de "ñandutí". Estos encajes son hechos a mano, y para hacerlos, se utilizan más de cien diseños diferentes.

■ La isla de Pascua, situada en el océano Pacífico, pertenece a Chile y es famosa por las gigantescas estatuas de piedra que se encuentran allí.

El centro de Santiago, capital de Chile, se distingue por el contraste de modernos rascacielos y edificios coloniales como la Casa Colorada, residencia del primer presidente de la República; el Palacio de la Moneda, palacio presidencial actual, y la catedral, construída en 1780. **¿Cómo se llama, en español, la residencia del presidente de los Estados Unidos?**

Una pareja baila el tango, el baile típico de Argentina. El tango se hizo *(became)* popular en Latinoamérica a principios del siglo XX y fue introducido en los Estados Unidos alrededor de 1912. **¿Conoce Ud. algunos otros bailes típicos latinoamericanos? ¿Cuáles?**

El gaucho argentino, inmortalizado en la literatura y en la música popular argentinas, es hoy día más una leyenda que un personaje real. Una de las costumbres de los gauchos que persiste es la del rodeo, como se ve en la foto. **¿En qué son similares los vaqueros norteamericanos y los gauchos argentinos?**

Vista panorámica del puerto de Asunción, la capital de Paraguay. En esta ciudad se mezclan armoniosamente la arquitectura colonial y la moderna. Aquí se ve la Plaza de los Héroes y, al fondo, el río Paraguay, que sirve como vía de comunicación con el océano Atlántico. **¿Cuáles son algunos de los puertos principales de su país?**

Vista del Obelisco y la avenida Nueve de Julio, en Buenos Aires. La avenida Nueve de Julio es una de las más anchas del mundo y lleva este nombre para conmemorar la fecha de la independencia de Argentina. **¿Le gusta a Ud. la idea de vivir en una gran ciudad como Buenos Aires? ¿Por qué o por qué no?**

Las cataratas *(falls)* de Iguazú, formadas por los ríos Iguazú y Paraná, están situadas en el punto de unión entre Argentina, Brasil y Paraguay. Se consideran las cataratas más anchas y caudalosas *(abundant)* del mundo, y de ahí su nombre, que en el idioma guaraní significa "agua grande". **¿Son exclusivamente de los Estados Unidos las cataratas del Niágara?**

El polo es un deporte popular en Argentina, especialmente en Buenos Aires. Los jugadores *(players)* argentinos de polo se encuentran entre los mejores del mundo. **¿Qué deporte es muy popular en la ciudad donde Ud. vive?**

Teleinforme

Vocabulario

Buenos Aires, Argentina

la casualidad	coincidence
como gran remate	as a great finishing touch
los griegos	Greeks
levantar edificaciones	to construct buildings
no descansa	doesn't rest
el (la) porteño(-a)	native of Buenos Aires
el sabor europeo	European flavor
se rinde homenaje	homage is paid
sobre todo	above all
un sinnúmero	a great number
vivos	bright

Paraguay

atravesar	to cross
corren	run
de punta a punta	from one end to the other
la fuente	source
el gigante dormido	sleeping giant
la labor conjunta	joint effort
el límite, la frontera	border
la paz	peace
el recorrido	journey
el tratado	treaty

Isla de Pascua

alejado	removed
los antepasados	ancestors
las canteras	quarries
cotidianamente	every day
los cuerpos	bodies
esculpidos	sculptured
el globo terráqueo	earth
nacer	to be born
el ombligo	navel, center
Rapa Nui	Easter Island
el rincón	corner
los rostros	faces
se destacan	stand out
se traspasará	it will be transferred
surge	appears, emerges
los tamaños	sizes
la ubicación	position

Preparación

¿Cuánto saben Uds. ya?   After reading the information in **Panorama hispánico 8,** get together in groups of three or four and answer the following questions.

1. ¿Cuál es la capital de Argentina?
2. ¿Cuál es la población de Buenos Aires?
3. ¿Qué monumento importante está en la avenida Nueve de Julio?
4. ¿Dónde está situada la represa de Itaipú?
5. ¿Qué ríos forman las cataratas de Iguazú?
6. ¿Qué significa la palabra "Iguazú" en guaraní?
7. ¿Cuál es la capital de Chile?
8. ¿Por qué es famosa la Isla de Pascua?

Comprensión

A. Buenos Aires, Argentina.   Complete the following statements.

1. Buenos Aires ha sido llamada "la _____ sudamericana".
2. En Buenos Aires hay inmigrantes griegos, _____ , franceses y _____ .
3. La avenida Nueve de Julio es una de las más _____ del mundo.
4. El río de la _____ es el mar de Argentina.
5. En el barrio de La Boca se concentró la inmigración _____ .
6. Las casas de La Boca se caracterizan por sus _____ .
7. El porteño es de carácter _____ y _____ .
8. La ciudad de Buenos Aires no _____ en ningún momento del día.
9. El género musical más conocido del país es el _____ .

B. Paraguay.   Read the following statements. After watching the video, circle **V (Verdadero)** or **F (Falso),** according to what you understood.

V F   1. La película *La Misión* fue filmada en Paraguay.
V F   2. La capital de Paraguay es Montevideo.
V F   3. El nombre "Paraguay" significa "aguas que corren hacia el mar".
V F   4. El río Paraguay divide el país en cuatro regiones.
V F   5. Paraguay tiene varias salidas al mar.
V F   6. Itaipú es la planta hidroeléctrica más grande del mundo.
V F   7. Las cataratas de Iguazú están a pocos kilómetros de la frontera entre Paraguay y Brasil.

C. Isla de Pascua.   Select the word or phrase that best completes each sentence, according to what you understood.

1. La Isla de Pascua está situada en el océano (Pacífico, Atlántico).
2. Hay varios (mares, volcanes) en la Isla de Pascua.
3. Los *(ahus, moais)* son estatuas grandes de piedra.
4. Hay (muchas, pocas) estatuas en la Isla de Pascua.
5. Algunas estatuas llevan (sombreros, abrigos).

Ampliación

Otros países, otras culturas.   With a partner, discuss in Spanish what aspect of each place appealed to you and why.

PROBLEMAS MÉDICOS

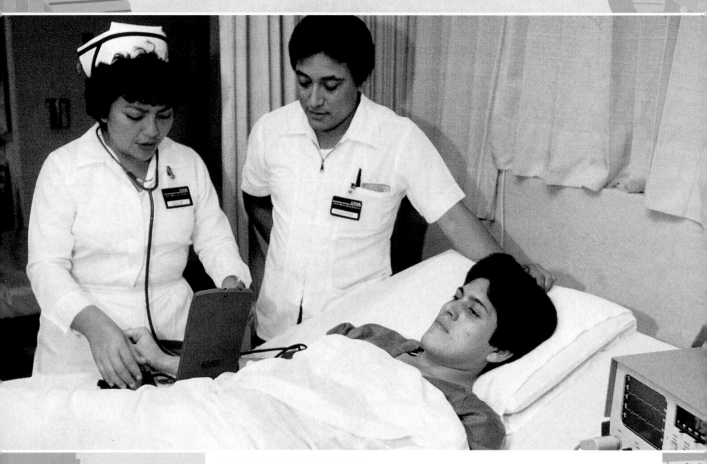

OBJECTIVES

■ Structure
Reciprocal reflexives • The imperfect subjunctive • Special uses of some prepositions

■ Communication
You will learn vocabulary related to medical emergencies and visits to the doctor's office.

PROBLEMAS MÉDICOS

Mirta y su esposo se encuentran en un restaurante para almorzar. Ella no se siente muy bien hoy.

MIRTA — No sé qué me pasa. Tengo fiebre y me duele mucho la cabeza.[1] Ya tomé cuatro aspirinas.

HÉCTOR — Te dije que fueras al médico para que te hiciera un buen chequeo…

MIRTA — Teresa me sugirió que viera a la doctora Vargas. Tengo una cita para esta tarde.

Más tarde, en el consultorio de la doctora Vargas.

DOCTORA — Tiene una temperatura de ciento dos grados. ¿Cuánto tiempo hace que tiene esos dolores de cabeza?

MIRTA — Una semana. Tengo tos y me duele la garganta. ¿Cree que tengo catarro o gripe?

DOCTORA — Tiene gripe. Voy a recetarle un antibiótico. ¿Es Ud. alérgica a alguna medicina?

MIRTA — Sí. Soy alérgica a la penicilina.

DOCTORA — ¿Está Ud. embarazada?

MIRTA — No, doctora.

DOCTORA — Tome estas pastillas cuatro veces al día. Empiece a tomarlas hoy mismo. Aquí tiene la receta.

En la sala de emergencia del mismo hospital. Oscar tuvo un accidente y lo trajeron al hospital en una ambulancia. Ahora está hablando con un médico.

MÉDICO — ¿Qué le pasó?

OSCAR — Me atropelló un coche. Me duele mucho la pierna. Creo que me la rompí.

MÉDICO — Vamos a hacerle unas radiografías. Veo que también tiene una herida en el brazo. Voy a llamar a la enfermera.

Con la enfermera.

ENFERMERA — El doctor me dijo que le desinfectara y le vendara la herida para evitar una infección. ¿Cuándo fue la última vez que le pusieron una inyección antitetánica?

OSCAR — Hace dos años.

La enfermera lleva a Oscar a la sala de rayos X.

---

[1] Note that definite articles, rather than possessive adjectives, are used in Spanish with parts of the body.

VOCABULARIO

COGNADOS

el accidente accident	**la aspirina** aspirin	**la penicilina** penicillin
alérgico(-a) allergic	**la emergencia** emergency	**la temperatura** temperature
la ambulancia ambulance	**la infección** infection	
el antibiótico antibiotic	**la inyección** injection, shot	

NOMBRES

el brazo arm
la cabeza head
el catarro, resfriado, resfrío cold
el chequeo, examen checkup, examination
el consultorio doctor's office
el dolor pain
— de cabeza headache
el (la) enfermero(-a) nurse

la fiebre fever
la garganta throat
el grado degree
la gripe flu
la herida wound
la inyección antitetánica tetanus shot
el (la) médico(-a) doctor
la pastilla pill

la pierna leg
la radiografía X-ray
la receta prescription
la sala de emergencia emergency room
la sala de rayos X X-ray room
la tos cough

VERBOS

atropellar to run over, hit someone (i.e., with a car)
desinfectar to disinfect
doler[1] **(o:ue)** to hurt, ache
evitar to avoid

recetar to prescribe
romper(se), quebrar(se) (e:ie) to break
vendar to bandage

ADJETIVOS

embarazada pregnant

médico(-a) medical

OTRAS PALABRAS Y EXPRESIONES

al día a day
hacer una radiografía to take an X-ray
hoy mismo this very day

poner una inyección to give an injection, a shot
la última vez the last time

---

[1] **Doler** has the same structure as **gustar: Me duele la cabeza.**

Vocabulario adicional

EL CUERPO

1. el pelo, el cabello
2. el ojo
3. la nariz
4. los dientes
5. la lengua
6. la boca
7. la oreja
8. el oído

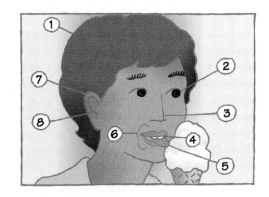

9. la cabeza
10. la cara
11. el pecho
12. el estómago
13. la mano
14. la rodilla
15. el tobillo
16. el dedo del pie
17. el pie

18. el cuello
19. la espalda
20. el dedo

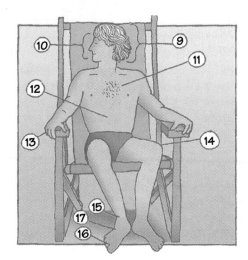

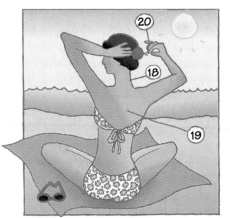

¡Conversemos!

Answer the following questions, basing your answers on the dialogues.

1. ¿Dónde se encuentran Mirta y su esposo, y por qué están allí?
2. ¿Qué problemas tiene Mirta?
3. ¿Qué le sugirió Teresa a Mirta?
4. ¿Por qué no le receta la doctora penicilina a Mirta?
5. ¿Cuántas veces al día tiene que tomar Mirta las pastillas?
6. ¿Qué le pasó a Oscar y dónde está ahora?
7. ¿Qué clase *(kind)* de accidente tuvo Oscar?
8. ¿Qué le dijo el médico a la enfermera?
9. ¿Cree Ud. que la enfermera le va a poner una inyección antitetánica a Oscar? ¿Por qué o por qué no?
10. ¿Adónde lleva la enfermera a Oscar y para qué?

¿Lo sabia Ud.?

- En la mayoría de los países de habla hispana, los hospitales son gratis *(free)* y subvencionados *(subsidized)* por el gobierno. Hay clínicas privadas para la gente de mejor posición económica que no quiere ir a un hospital público.

- Especialmente en las grandes ciudades hispanas, la medicina está muy adelantada *(advanced)*, pero en muchos pueblos *(towns)* remotos no hay médicos ni hospitales. En ese caso, mucha gente recurre a *(turn to)* los servicios de un curandero *(healer)*. Muchas mujeres tienen sus bebés con la ayuda de una partera *(midwife)*.

- En España y en algunos países latinoamericanos, las farmacias venden principalmente medicinas. En algunos países hispanos es posible comprar medicinas como la penicilina sin tener receta médica.

Comprando medicinas en una farmacia de Humacao, Puerto Rico.

ESTRUCTURAS

1 Reciprocal reflexives *(Pronombres reflexivos en función recíproca)*

As you have already learned in **Lección 9,** the reflexive pronouns are used whenever the subject does the action to itself. The reflexive pronouns may also be used in the plural form (**nos, os, se**) to express a mutual or reciprocal relationship. The reflexive then translates as the expressions *(to) each other* or *(to) one another.*

Nos queremos mucho.	*We love **each other** very much.*
Los amigos **se** escriben.	*(The) friends write **to each other.***
Ustedes **se** ven.	*You see **each other.***

Práctica

A. Interview a classmate, using the following questions.

1. ¿Tú y tu amigo(-a) se escriben por correo electrónico o se llaman por teléfono?
2. ¿Dónde y cuándo se encuentran tú y tus amigos?
3. ¿En qué idioma se hablan tú y tus amigos?
4. ¿En qué idioma nos hablamos en esta clase?
5. Nuestros compañeros de clase ¿se ayudan a veces?
6. ¿Cuántas veces a la semana nos vemos en la clase?
7. ¿Cuándo se ven tú y tus padres?
8. ¿Tú y tu novio(-a) se quieren mucho?

B. Describe the relationship or activities shared between the following people, using reciprocal reflexives.

> MODELO: Marta dice que Daniel es tonto y él dice que Marta es antipática.
> *Ellos se odian.*

1. Miguel y Elisa son novios.
2. A Teresa y a Eva les gusta mucho hablar por teléfono.
3. Ana y yo vivimos en la misma calle.
4. Fernando y Tomás van al mismo barbero.
5. Hace veinte años que nosotros somos amigos.

2 The imperfect subjunctive (*El imperfecto de subjuntivo*)

A. Forms

■ To form the imperfect subjunctive of all Spanish verbs—regular and irregular—drop the **-ron** ending of the third-person plural of the preterit and add the following endings to the stem.[1]

Imperfect Subjunctive Endings	
-ra *form*	
-ra	-ramos
-ras	-rais
-ra	-ran

---

[1] A second form of the imperfect subjunctive ends in **-se** rather than **-ra: hablase, hablases, hablase, hablásemos, hablaseis, hablasen.** The two forms are interchangeable, but the **-ra** form is more commonly used.

	Forms of the Imperfect Subjunctive		
Verb	*Third-person plural preterit*	*Stem*	*First-person singular imperfect subjunctive*
hablar	hablaron	habla-	hablara
aprender	aprendieron	aprendie-	aprendiera
vivir	vivieron	vivie-	viviera
dejar	dejaron	deja-	dejara
ir	fueron	fue-	fuera
saber	supieron	supie-	supiera
decir	dijeron	dije-	dijera
poner	pusieron	pusie-	pusiera
pedir	pidieron	pidie-	pidiera
estar	estuvieron	estuvie-	estuviera

ATENCIÓN The **nosotros** form of the imperfect subjunctive always takes an accent on the vowel that precedes the **-ra** ending.

Práctica

Give the imperfect subjunctive forms of the following verbs.

1. yo: ganar, volver, pedir, decir, recibir
2. tú: ser, dormir, querer, dar, conocer
3. él: ir, estar, poner, conducir, servir
4. nosotros: saber, poder, regresar, conseguir, hacer
5. ellos: tener, recetar, comenzar, seguir, mentir

B. Uses

▪ The imperfect subjunctive is used in a subordinate clause when the verb of the main clause is in the past and calls for the subjunctive.

—¿Qué te dijo el médico?   *"What did the doctor tell you?"*

—Me dijo que **comiera** menos.   *"He told me to eat less."*

—Yo esperaba que el profesor me **diera** una "A".   *"I was hoping that the professor would give me an A."*

—Bueno, yo te sugerí que **estudiaras** más.   *"Well, I suggested that you study more."*

▪ When the verb of the main clause is in the present, but the subordinate clause refers to the past, the imperfect subjunctive is used.

—Es una lástima que no **fueras** al teatro ayer.   *"It's a pity that you didn't go to the theater yesterday."*

—No me sentía bien.   *"I wasn't feeling well."*

Práctica

A. Complete the following dialogues, using the imperfect subjunctive of the verbs given. Then act them out with a partner.

1. —¿Qué te dijo Roberto?
   —Me dijo que _____ (ir) al médico para que me _____ (hacer) un chequeo y me recomendó que _____ (ver) al Dr. Salgado.
2. —No fui al hospital porque no tenía coche.
   —¿Por qué no le pediste a alguien que te _____ (llevar)?
   —No había nadie que _____ (poder) llevarme a esa hora.
   —Pues yo te dije que me _____ (llamar) si me necesitabas.
3. —¿Fuiste al médico?
   —Sí, y me dijo que _____ (tomar) estas pastillas para el dolor de garganta y me sugirió que no _____ (hablar) mucho.
4. —¿Le dieron el trabajo a Sandra?
   —No, porque necesitaban una enfermera que _____ (saber) español.
   —Yo le dije que _____ (estudiar) español, pero no me hizo caso.
5. —Siento que tú no _____ (poder) venir a mi casa ayer.
   —No me sentía bien... Yo le pedí a Ramón que te _____ (llamar) por teléfono y te _____ (decir) que yo estaba enferma.
   —Pues yo esperaba que tú _____ (venir) con los niños.

B. Describe all the things your parents did and did not want you to do at college, using the cues provided and the imperfect subjunctive.

Mis padres querían que yo...

1. *escribirles* todas las semanas
2. *llamarlos* por teléfono los domingos
3. *tomar* varias clases el primer semestre
4. *estudiar* mucho
5. *abrir* una cuenta corriente en el banco
6. *hacer* la tarea todos los días
7. *levantarme* temprano
8. *visitarlos* en las vacaciones

Mis padres no querían que yo...

1. *vivir* lejos de la universidad
2. *ir* a muchas fiestas
3. *comer* hamburguesas todos los días
4. *pedirles* dinero extra todos los meses
5. *conducir* muy rápido
6. *olvidarme* de tomar la medicina
7. *acostarme* muy tarde

C. Compare your childhood and adolescence to those of a classmate by completing the following sentences.

1. Cuando yo era chico(-a), mis padres esperaban que yo...
2. Cuando yo era niño(-a), mi mamá no me permitía que...

3. Cuando yo estaba en la escuela primaria, mis maestros *(teachers)* querían que yo...
4. Cuando yo tenía diez años, quería que mis amigos...
5. Cuando yo estaba en la escuela secundaria, no quería que mi papá...
6. Cuando yo tenía dieciséis años, esperaba que mis padres...

3 Special uses of some prepositions
(Usos especiales de algunas preposiciones)

In Spanish, some verbs are used with prepositions that have no equivalent to or are different from the ones used in English. The prepositions used most often are **a, de, con,** and **en.**

■ The preposition **a**

aprender a *to learn (how)*	**enseñar a** *to teach*
asistir a *to attend*	**invitar a** *to invite*
ayudar a *to help*	**ir a** *to go*
empezar (comenzar) a *to begin, to start*	**venir a** *to come*

—¿**Fuiste a** estudiar con Rafael?   *"Did you go to study with Rafael?"*

—Sí, **empezamos a** estudiar para el examen final.   *"Yes, we started to study for the final exam."*

—Yo quiero **aprender a** bailar bailes latinoamericanos.   *"I want to learn how to dance Latin American dances."*

—Yo te puedo **enseñar a** bailar.   *"I can teach you how to dance."*

■ The preposition **de**

acordarse de *to remember*	**enamorarse de** *to fall in love with*
alegrarse de *to be glad*	**olvidarse de** *to forget*

—No te **olvides de** llamar al médico.   *"Don't forget to call the doctor."*

—Bueno..., y tú, **acuérdate de** tomar las pastillas.   *"Okay . . . , and you, remember to take your pills."*

■ The preposition **con**

casarse con *to marry, to get married to*	
comprometerse con *to get engaged to*	
soñar (o:ue) con *to dream about (of)*	

—Teresa **se comprometió con** Antonio.   *"Teresa got engaged to Antonio."*

—Debe estar muy contenta. Siempre **soñó con casarse con** él.   *"She must be very happy. She always dreamed of marrying him."*

■ The preposition **en**

> **fijarse en**   *to notice*
> **insistir en**   *to insist on*
> **pensar en**   *to think about*

—¿**En** que estás **pensando**?   *"What are you thinking about?"*
—Estoy **pensando en** la fiesta de   *"I am thinking about Beatriz's*
Beatriz. Ella **insistió en** invitar a   *party. She insisted on inviting*
Pablo y él siempre causa   *Pablo and he always causes*
problemas…   *problems . . ."*

Práctica

A. Complete the following dialogues with the Spanish equivalent of the words in parentheses. Then act them out with a partner.

1. —¿_____ pedir la receta, Anita?   *(Did you remember)*
   —Sí, pero _____ dejarla en la farmacia.   *(I forgot)*
2. —¿Ángel te dijo que le dolía el estómago?
   —Sí, e _____ que lo llevara a la sala de emergencia.   *(he insisted on)*
3. —¿Dónde _____ poner inyecciones tu mamá?   *(did learn)*
   —En Cuba. Y también le _____ hacer radiografías.   *(they taught)*
4. —Luis _____ Raquel, pero ella nunca _____ él.
   (fell in love with / noticed)
   —No, ella _____ Ernesto.   *(married)*
5. —¡Hola, Luisa! _____ verte.   *(I'm glad)*
   —¡Hola! Vengo a _____ ir al cine.   *(to invite you)*
   —Ay, no puedo porque tengo que _____ la conferencia *(lecture)* de la Dra.
   Ruiz.   *(to attend)*

B. With a partner, take turns asking and answering questions about the people in the following situations.

1.

2.

3.

4.

5.

6.

¡A VER CUÁNTO APRENDIÓ!

¡Repase el vocabulario!

A. Say whether the following statements are logical or not. If a statement is not logical, give one that is.

1. En serio, los muchachos vinieron a esquiar en una ambulancia.
2. Cuando tengo dolor de estómago voy al médico.
3. Si necesito una radiografía voy al aeropuerto.
4. Me vendaron la herida.
5. Tiene fiebre. Tiene una temperatura de ciento tres grados.
6. Algunas personas son alérgicas a la penicilina.
7. Las orejas sirven para planchar.
8. La aspirina es un antibiótico.
9. La lengua está en la boca.
10. La rodilla es parte de la cara.
11. Tenemos treinta dedos.

12. Necesitamos la nariz para caminar.
13. Para hacerle una radiografía, debemos ir a la sala de rayos X.
14. Roberto está embarazado.
15. Está enferma. Debe ir al consultorio del médico.
16. Cada vez que tengo dolor de cabeza tomo dos aspirinas.
17. Lo atropelló una bolsa de dormir en el mar.
18. Fuimos de pesca a la sala de emergencia y nos divertimos mucho.

B. Name all the parts of the body numbered below.

Entrevista

Interview a classmate, using the **tú** form.

Pregúntele a su compañero(-a) de clase...

1. ...cómo se siente hoy.
2. ...si le duelen los oídos.
3. ...qué hace cuando le duele la cabeza.
4. ...cuándo fue la última vez que le hicieron un chequeo.
5. ...si es alérgico(-a) a alguna medicina.
6. ...si le hicieron radiografías del pecho alguna vez.
7. ...si le han puesto alguna vez una inyección antitetánica.
8. ...qué medicina toma cuando tiene tos.

Situaciones

What would you say in the following situations? What might the other person say? Act out the scenes with a partner. Take turns playing each role.

1. A friend wants you to go to the store with him or her. You can't go, for the following reasons: you've just taken two aspirins because you have a headache, your little brother cut his hand and you have to disinfect the wound.
2. You have had an accident and are in the emergency room, talking to the doctor. You need something for the pain.
3. You are at the doctor's office because you started having headaches three days ago. The doctor wants to know whether you are allergic to any medications.

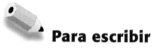

Para escribir

Write a note to your instructor, explaining that you cannot take an exam because you are sick. Describe your symptoms.

En la vida real

Llenando una hoja clínica

With a partner, play the role of a health care worker who is taking the history of a new patient. Refer to the list of words and phrases on pages 404–5. Be as thorough as possible in obtaining both personal information (such as date of birth, family history, childhood experiences, education, and marital status) and medical data (including illnesses, accidents, and surgeries, and how long ago the patient had them; allergies; and any general pains the patient is currently suffering) for the patient's permanent file. Write down his or her responses. When you have finished, switch roles with your partner.

Here are some words and phrases you might want to use:

la amigdalitis *tonsilitis*	**nacer** *to be born*
la apendicitis *appendicitis*	**la operación** *surgery*
el asma *asthma*	**las paperas** *mumps*
la bronquitis *bronchitis*	**la presión arterial** *blood pressure*
las enfermedades de la niñez	**la pulmonía** *pneumonia*
childhood diseases	**el sarampión** *measles*
el mareo *dizziness, dizzy spell*	**la varicela** *chicken pox*

Buenos consejos

What advice from this list would you give to the people below?

Buenos consejos para conservar la salud[1]

Debe	No debe
✔ comer más vegetales y frutas	✗ fumar
✔ dormir lo suficiente	✗ consumir mucho alcohol
✔ visitar al médico periódicamente	✗ consumir mucha sal o azúcar
✔ hacer ejercicio	✗ usar drogas
✔ consumir menos calorías	✗ comer mucha grasa
✔ aprender a relajarse	✗ trabajar en exceso
✔ evitar la tensión (*stress*)	
✔ pensar positivamente	
✔ tener una dieta balanceada	
✔ controlar su peso (*weight*)	

---

1. El Sr. Vega toma diez cervezas todos los días.
2. La Srta. Díaz está siempre sentada, mirando la televisión.
3. Elsa come muchos dulces (*sweets*).
4. El Dr. Álvarez trabaja catorce horas cada día.
5. La Sra. Carreras duerme sólo cuatro horas cada noche.
6. Estela se preocupa constantemente por todo.
7. Adela siempre come papas fritas, hamburguesas, mantequilla, pollo frito, etc.
8. Hace cinco años que Carlos no va a ver a su médico.
9. La dieta de Eduardo es de 5.000 calorías al día.
10. Raúl pesa (*weighs*) 300 libras (*pounds*).
11. Raquel solamente come carne y pastas.
12. A Jorge le gustan mucho los cigarrillos.

---

[1] *health*

Así somos

Vocabulario

el abastecimiento	supply
acudir	to go
algo así	something like that
alimentarse	to eat
la amigadalitis	tonsilitis
asegurar	to insure
las carencias	shortages
como tal	as such
la ficha	(insurance) card
el gabinete	room
la gordura	fat
el hecho	act
inscrito	enrolled
los lentes, los anteojos, los espejuelos	glasses
más bien	rather
me cayó mal	it made me sick
me cuido	I worry about
me mido	I moderate
mente sana en cuerpo sano	healthy mind in a healthy body
opinar	to think
la otorrinolaringología	medical specialty concerned with the ear, nose, and throat
por medio de	through
las reglas	rules
el reposo	rest
los riesgos	risks
se le atiende	he or she is tended to
el tratamiento	treatment
tratar de	to try to
la vista	vision

Preparación

A. ¿Cuánto saben Uds. ya?   This video module focuses on health and medical care. With a partner, brainstorm possible words and phrases the people in the video might use in these contexts and make a list of them.

B. ¿Las reconoce?   Guess the meaning of the following words. While watching the video, circle each as you hear the person say it.

cardiología	ginecología	psiquiatría
clínica	neurología	traumatología
dermatología	ortopedia	ultrasonido
endocrinología	pediatría	urología
estudios endoscópicos		

Comprensión

A. Para conservar la salud. Read the following statements. After watching the video, circle **V** (**Verdadero**) or **F** (**Falso**), according to what you understood.

V F 1. Alejandro opina que, para conservar la salud, lo básico es alimentarse bien y hacer ejercicio.

V F 2. Otmara no come muchas carnes rojas.

V F 3. Juan trata de no consumir drogas.

V F 4. A Miriam no le gusta caminar.

V F 5. El doctor dice que el autocontrol no es muy importante.

B. ¿Quién lo dice? Match each statement with the name of the person who said it.

a. Miriam   b. Jaime   c. Otmara   d. Alejandro

_____ 1. Tuve hepatitis A.   _____ 3. Tuve una infección del estómago.
_____ 2. Me pusieron lentes.   _____ 4. Tuve amigdalitis.

C. La asistencia médica. Read the following statements and circle **V** (**Verdadero**) or **F** (**Falso**), according to what you understood.

V F 1. La gente trabajadora no recibe asistencia médica en El Salvador.

V F 2. Según Otmara, en su país, el seguro social incluye las medicinas.

V F 3. Según María, en su país, sólo algunas personas están inscritas en la seguridad social.

D. Los servicios médicos. Select the word or phrase that best completes each statement.

1. Según Leonardo, los hospitales del Ecuador son (buenos, malos).
2. Según Juan, la gente pobre necesita (comida, asistencia médica) en Nicaragua.
3. Según la doctora, la preparación de los médicos en su país es (mala, buena).
4. En la clínica donde trabaja la doctora, hay cierta carencia de (médicos, medicinas).

E. Entrevista. Complete the following statements with the appropriate words.

1. En la clínica ofrecen _____ servicios.
2. Tienen servicios por especialidades como la _____ , la _____ y la

_____ .

3. El _____ clínico es importante en la evaluación de los pacientes.
4. En la clínica tienen un gabinete de _____ _____ y _____ .

Ampliación

La hipocondría. With a partner, roleplay the situation of two hypochondriacs who try to outdo each other talking about their illnesses.

¡Este coche no sirve!

OBJECTIVES

Structure
The present perfect subjunctive • The pluperfect subjunctive • *If* clauses

Communication
You will learn vocabulary related to automobiles, including going to a
service station and dealing with road emergencies.

¡ESTE COCHE NO SIRVE!

Gloria y Julio, una pareja de recién casados, están de vacaciones en Costa Rica. Ahora están en la carretera, camino a San José.

GLORIA —Julio, ¡estás manejando muy rápido! La velocidad máxima es de noventa kilómetros por hora. ¡Si te ve un policía, te va a poner una multa!

JULIO —No te preocupes. ¿Dónde estamos? ¿Tú tienes el mapa?

GLORIA —Está en el portaguantes pero, según ese letrero, estamos a cuarenta kilómetros de San José.

JULIO —¿Hay una gasolinera cerca? El tanque está casi vacío.

GLORIA —Es una lástima que no hayas llenado el tanque antes…

JULIO —Si me lo hubieras dicho antes, lo habría hecho.

GLORIA —¡Hablas como si yo tuviera la culpa!

JULIO —*(Bromeando)* ¿Y a quién voy a culpar? Mira, allí hay una estación de servicio…

Julio para en la estación de servicio para comprar gasolina.

JULIO —*(Al empleado)* Llene el tanque, por favor. Además, ¿podría revisar el aceite y las llantas?

EMPLEADO —Sí, señor.

JULIO —Ayer tuve un pinchazo y cuando fui al taller, el mecánico me dijo que necesitaba neumáticos nuevos.

EMPLEADO —Sí, si yo fuera usted, los cambiaría… y también compraría un acumulador nuevo.

GLORIA —¡Caramba! También te dijo que arreglaras los frenos e instalaras una bomba de agua nueva.

JULIO —Haremos todo eso en San José, si es necesario.

GLORIA —¿No dijiste que también cambiarías el filtro del aceite y que comprarías limpiaparabrisas nuevos?

JULIO —Si yo hubiera sabido que íbamos a tener tantos problemas, habría comprado un coche nuevo antes de salir de viaje.

GLORIA —Sí, porque vamos a gastar una fortuna en arreglos.

JULIO —¡Y ayer el motor estaba haciendo un ruido extraño…!

Cuando Julio trata de arrancar, el coche no funciona.

JULIO —¡Ay, no! Tendremos que llamar una grúa para remolcar el coche hasta San José.

GLORIA —No vale la pena. Yo lo dejaría aquí.

JULIO —¡Estoy de acuerdo contigo! Si yo pudiera, compraría un coche nuevo ahora mismo.

VOCABULARIO

COGNADOS

el filtro filter	**el kilómetro** kilometer	**el motor** motor, engine
la gasolina gasoline	**el mecánico** mechanic	**el tanque** tank

NOMBRES

el acumulador, la batería battery
el arreglo repair
la bomba de agua water pump
el camino road
la carretera highway
la culpa blame, fault
el freno brake
la gasolinera, la estación de servicio gas (service) station

la grúa, el remolcador tow truck
el letrero sign
el limpiaparabrisas windshield wiper
la multa fine, ticket
el neumático, la llanta, la goma tire
la pareja couple (people)
el policía police officer

el portaguantes, la guantera glove compartment
los recién casados newlyweds
el ruido noise
el taller (de mecánica) repair shop
la velocidad speed

VERBOS

arrancar to start (a car)
arreglar to repair, to fix
culpar to blame
funcionar to work, to function

gastar to spend (money)
instalar to install
parar to stop
remolcar to tow

revisar, chequear to check
tratar (de) to try

ADJETIVOS

extraño(-a) strange

vacío(-a) empty

OTRAS PALABRAS Y EXPRESIONES

ahora mismo right now
camino a… on the way to…
como si as if
estar de acuerdo to agree
no sirve it's no good
(no) vale la pena it's (not) worth the trouble

poner (dar) una multa to give a ticket (fine)
rápido fast, rapidly
salir de viaje to leave on a trip
según according to
tener la culpa to be one's fault

tener un pinchazo to have a flat tire
velocidad máxima speed limit

Vocabulario adicional

■ En el taller de mecánica

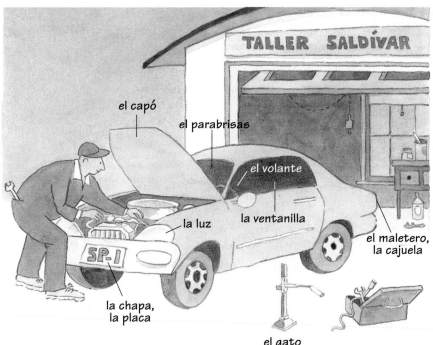

el capó

el parabrisas

el volante

la luz

la ventanilla

el maletero, la cajuela

la chapa, la placa

el gato

■ Para hablar del coche

la **autopista** freeway, highway	En California hay muchas **autopistas**.
el **carburador** carburetor	El mecánico revisó el **carburador**.
descompuesto(-a) out of order, not working	No pude usar el coche porque estaba **descompuesto**.
lleno(-a) full	El tanque está **lleno**.
la **milla** mile	La velocidad máxima es de 65 **millas** por hora.
la **pieza de repuesto** spare part	¿Se venden **piezas de repuesto** aquí?

¡Conversemos!

Answer the following questions, basing your answers on the dialogue.

1. ¿Quiénes están en la carretera y adónde van?
2. ¿Cuál es la velocidad máxima en la carretera?
3. Julio está manejando muy rápido. ¿Qué va a pasar si un policía lo ve?
4. Según el letrero, ¿a qué distancia están Julio y Gloria de San José?

5. ¿Por qué necesitan ir a una gasolinera?
6. ¿Tiene el tanque mucha gasolina?
7. ¿Qué cosas hace el empleado de la gasolinera?
8. ¿Qué le pasó al coche de Julio ayer y qué le dijo el mecánico que necesitaba?
9. ¿Está de acuerdo el empleado con el mecánico?
10. ¿Qué otros problemas tiene el coche?
11. ¿Cree Gloria que va a costar mucho dinero arreglar el coche?
12. ¿Qué haría Julio si pudiera?

 ## ¿Lo sabia Ud.?

- En las grandes ciudades como Madrid, Caracas, la Ciudad de México y Buenos Aires, hay muchísimos automóviles y autobuses, lo cual *(which)* está causando graves problemas de contaminación del aire *(smog)*. Sin embargo, en muchas zonas rurales de los países hispanos, particularmente en Hispanoamérica, hay muy pocos automóviles, ya que no hay carreteras, o las que existen están en muy malas condiciones.

- En la mayoría de los países hispanos, la gasolina y los automóviles son mucho más caros que en los Estados Unidos. Por esta razón es muy popular la motocicleta, especialmente entre la gente joven.

- En los países hispanos, se usa el sistema métrico decimal. Un kilómetro equivale a 0,6 millas; un galón equivale a 3,8 litros.

Congestión de tráfico en la Ciudad de México.

ESTRUCTURAS

1 The present perfect subjunctive *(El pretérito perfecto de subjuntivo)*

■ The present perfect subjunctive is formed with the present subjunctive of the auxiliary verb **haber** + *the past participle* of the main verb.

Present subjunctive of **haber**	
haya	hayamos
hayas	hayáis
haya	hayan

Formation of the Present Perfect Subjunctive

yo	haya cambiado
tú	hayas temido
Ud. / él / ella	haya salido
nosotros(-as)	hayamos hecho
vosotros(-as)	hayáis puesto
Uds. / ellos / ellas	hayan visto

■ The present perfect subjunctive is used in the same way as the present perfect tense in English, but only in sentences that require the subjunctive in the subordinate clause. It is used to describe events that have ended prior to the time indicated in the main clause.

—Me alegro de que **hayas venido.**

"I'm glad you have come."

—Es una lástima que papá no **haya podido** venir conmigo.

"It is a pity that Dad has not been able to come with me."

Práctica

A. Complete the following dialogues, using the present perfect subjunctive forms of the verbs listed. Then act them out with a partner.

gastar	poder	poner	conseguir	valer
decir	llegar	llamar	hacer	

1. —Es una lástima que el mecánico no _____ arreglar el coche.
   —Ojalá que ya _____ la pieza de repuesto que necesita.
   —Dudo que la pieza _____ porque la pidió ayer.
2. —El coche no arranca.
   —Ya lo sé. Espero que Pablo _____ a la Triple A para que manden una grúa.
   —Dudo que él _____ nada.
3. —Los mecánicos del taller han dicho que este coche no sirve.
   —No es verdad que ellos _____ eso.
4. —Pagamos quinientos dólares por el arreglo del coche.
   —Espero que _____ la pena.
5. —Ellos no creen que nosotros _____ tanto dinero en nuestro viaje.
   —¡Porque ellos nunca han viajado!
6. —Espero que (tú) _____ los mapas en el portaguantes.
   —No, pero voy a ponerlos ahora mismo.

B. Express your own feelings and those of the people mentioned, using the present perfect subjunctive.

1. Yo espero que el mecánico…
2. Ojalá que mis padres…
3. Es una lástima que los recién casados…
4. Mis padres no creen que yo…
5. No es verdad que mis amigos…
6. Me alegro mucho de que Ud…
7. Mi amigo teme que su novia…
8. Mi profesor siente que los estudiantes…

C. With a partner, act out the following dialogues in Spanish.

1. "I want to speak with the mechanic."
   "I doubt that he has returned."
2. "What is David saying?"
   "That he doesn't believe that we have changed the tire."
3. "You are driving very fast, Rosita."
   "You're right. I hope that the police officer hasn't seen us."
4. "Is there anybody who has traveled to Costa Rica?"
   "I know that Sandra has been to (in) Panama, but I don't think she has been to (in) Costa Rica."

2 The pluperfect subjunctive *(El pluscuamperfecto de subjuntivo)*

The pluperfect subjunctive is formed with the imperfect subjunctive of the auxiliary verb **haber** + *the past participle* of the main verb. It is used in the same way that the past perfect is used in English, but only in sentences in which the main clause calls for the subjunctive.

Imperfect subjunctive of haber

hubiera	hubiéramos
hubieras	hubierais
hubiera	hubieran

Formation of the Present Perfect Subjunctive

yo	hubiera hablado
tú	hubieras comido
Ud. / él / ella	hubiera vivido
nosotros(-as)	hubiéramos visto
vosotros(-as)	hubierais hecho
Uds. / ellos / ellas	hubieran vuelto

—¿No había nadie que **hubiera
visto** esa película?
—Sí, Eva la había visto ya.

*"Wasn't there anybody who
had seen that movie?"*
"Yes, Eva had already seen it."

Práctica

A. Say what your mother had expected everyone in the family to do by the time
she got home yesterday.

> MODELO: Aída / planchar la ropa
> *Mamá esperaba que Aída **hubiera planchado** la ropa.*

Mamá esperaba que...

1. yo / hacer la comida
2. Quique / lavar el coche
3. nosotros / llevar a Raulito a la escuela
4. tú / escribirle a tío Carlos
5. Uds. / devolver los libros a la biblioteca
6. Eva y Luis / comprar la batería
7. Irma / poner la mesa
8. Eva y yo / pasarle la aspiradora a la alfombra
9. Daniel / llevar el coche al taller
10. Jorge y yo / cambiar las llantas

B. Say that you doubted that the following things had occurred.

> MODELO: Carlos / venir muy tarde
> *Yo dudaba que Carlos hubiera venido muy tarde.*

1. Pepe / arreglar los frenos
2. tú / salir de viaje
3. mis amigos / poder cambiar el filtro
4. el policía / ponerles una multa
5. nosotros / tener la culpa
6. el mecánico / conseguir las piezas de repuesto
7. Uds. / venir ayer
8. Irma / dejar todas las puertas abiertas

3 If clauses *(Cláusulas con si)*

- In Spanish, the imperfect subjunctive is used in *if* clauses when a contrary-to-
fact statement is made.

> —Si **tuviera** dinero, compraría
> la batería hoy.
> —Usa tu tarjeta de crédito...

*"If I had money, I would buy
the battery today."*
"Use your credit card..."

■ Note that the imperfect subjunctive is used in the *if* clause and the conditional is used in the main clause. When a statement expresses a contrary-to-fact situation in the past, the pluperfect subjunctive is used in the *if* clause and the conditional perfect is used in the main clause.

—No pude comprar el coche. / "I wasn't able to buy the car."
—**Si hubieras ahorrado** tu dinero, habrías podido comprarlo. / "If you had saved your money, you would have been able to buy it."

■ The imperfect subjunctive is also used in *if* clauses that express an unlikely fact, or simply the Spanish equivalent of the English *if . . . were to . . .*

—**Si** Raúl me **invitara** a salir con él, aceptaría. / "If Raúl were to ask me to go out with him, I would accept."
—No creo que te invite... / "I don't think he'll ask you . . . "

■ The imperfect subjunctive is also used after the expression **como si** *(as if).*

—Pepe se compró otro coche. / "Pepe bought himself another car."
—Ese hombre gasta dinero **como si fuera** millonario. / "That man spends money as if he were a millionaire."

■ When an *if* clause refers to something that is possible or likely to happen, the indicative is used.

—¿Me vas a comprar los zapatos? / "Are you going to buy me the shoes?"
—Si **tengo** dinero, te los compro. / "If I have money, I'll buy them for you."

ATENCIÓN The present subjunctive is *never* used in an *if* clause.

Práctica

A. Interview a classmate, using the following questions.

1. Si tuvieras un pinchazo, ¿tratarías de cambiar la llanta?
2. ¿Qué harías si los frenos de tu coche no funcionaran?
3. ¿Qué haces si tu coche no arranca?
4. Si tu coche hubiera estado descompuesto, ¿cómo habrías venido a la universidad hoy?
5. Si el tanque de tu coche estuviera casi vacío, ¿a qué gasolinera irías?
6. Si no quieres que te pongan una multa, ¿a qué velocidad debes manejar en la autopista?
7. Si el arreglo de tu coche costara mil dólares, ¿podrías pagarlo?
8. ¿Qué harías si alguien te dejara una fortuna?
9. ¿Qué harías si tuvieras que comprar un coche nuevo?
10. Si tu mejor amigo quiere usar tu coche, ¿se lo prestas?

B. Say what the following people are going to do, would do, or would have done according to each situation.

MODELO: María quiere comprar ropa, pero no tiene dinero.
Si María tuviera dinero compraría ropa.

1. Yo no estudié mucho el semestre pasado y mi promedio fue de "C".
2. Teresa quiere ir al cine, pero no tiene tiempo.
3. Nosotros necesitamos comprar un coche nuevo. Es posible que tengamos suficiente dinero.
4. Juan quiere que yo le dé la dirección de Pedro, pero yo no la sé.
5. Mi madre quería que yo fuera contador, pero no me gustaban las matemáticas.
6. Tú quieres estudiar para programador(-a), pero no tienes computadora. Es posible que tus padres te regalen una.
7. Yo habría llevado a Marta al estadio, pero tuve que trabajar.
8. Nosotros habríamos hablado con el profesor, pero él no estaba en la universidad hoy.

El Subjuntivo: Resumen General

- Use the subjunctive . . .

  a. After verbs of volition (when there is change of subject).

  Yo quiero que **él salga.**

  b. After verbs of emotion (when there is change of subject).

  Me alegro de que **tú estés** aquí.

- Use the subjunctive . . .

  a. To express doubt and denial.

  Dudo que **pueda** venir.
  Niego que él **esté** aquí.

  b. To refer to the indefinite or non-existent.

  Busco una casa que **sea** cómoda.
  No había nadie que lo **supiera.**

  c. With certain conjunctions when referring to a future action.[1]

  Lo llamaré cuando **llegue.**

  d. In an *if* clause, to refer to something contrary-to-fact or to something impossible or very improbable.

  Si **pudiera,** iría.
  Si el presidente me **invitara** a la Casa Blanca, yo aceptaría.

- Use the infinitive . . .

  a. After verbs of volition (when there is no change of subject).

  Yo quiero **salir.**

  b. After verbs of emotion (when there is no change of subject).

  Me alegro de **estar** aquí.

- Use the indicative . . .

  a. When there is no doubt or denial.

  No dudo que **puede** venir.
  No niego que él **está** aquí.

  b. To refer to something specific.

  Tengo una casa que **es** cómoda.
  Había alguien que lo **sabía.**

  c. With certain conjunctions when there is no indication of future action.

  Lo llamo cuando **llego.**

  d. In an *if* clause, when not referring to anything that is contrary-to-fact, impossible, or very improbable.

  Si **puedo,** iré.
  Si Juan me **invita** a su casa, aceptaré.

---

[1] The subjunctive is always used after the conjunctions **con tal que, sin que, en caso de que, a menos que, para que,** and **antes de que,** which by their very meaning imply uncertainty or condition: **Puedo salir sin que los chicos me vean, a menos que estén en la sala.**

¡A VER CUÁNTO APRENDIÓ!

¡Repase el vocabulario!

Circle the word or phrase that best completes each sentence.

1. Tuve un pinchazo. Tendré que cambiar (el acumulador, el neumático, la bomba de agua).
2. Voy a llevar el coche al taller porque está (sabroso, sentado, descompuesto).
3. Tendrá que llenar el tanque porque está casi (preocupado, extraño, vacío).
4. Te van a poner una multa porque estás (manejando muy rápido, mirando las luces, abriendo el maletero).
5. No pude parar porque (los frenos no funcionaban, no tenía limpiaparabrisas, tenía las manos en el volante).
6. Iba (autopista, carretera, camino) a Quito cuando tuvimos un accidente.
7. Vino (una ambulancia, una chapa, una grúa) para remolcar el coche.
8. Los recién (cansados, casados, cazados) salieron de viaje ayer.
9. Según (ese letrero, esa ventanilla, ese gato), estamos a cien kilómetros de San José.
10. Pondré los mapas en el (arreglo, aceite, portaguantes).
11. Gasté una fortuna en el (ruido, arreglo, taller) del coche.
12. No vale la (pareja, chapa, pena) arreglar el coche.
13. Cuando él tiene problemas con el coche, siempre (gasta, para, culpa) al mecánico.
14. Ella dice que necesitamos un coche nuevo porque el nuestro no sirve, pero yo no estoy de (extraño, acuerdo, ruido).
15. Levantó (el maletero, el capó, la ventanilla) para revisar el motor.

Entrevista

Interview a classmate, using the **tú** form.

Pregúntele a su compañero(-a) de clase…

1. …si tendrá que ir a la gasolinera mañana.
2. …si está lleno o vacío el tanque de su coche.
3. …si su coche necesita un acumulador nuevo.
4. …cuándo piensa comprar neumáticos para su coche.
5. …si tiene que cambiar el filtro de aceite de su coche.
6. …cuál es el número de la chapa de su coche.
7. …cuántas millas hay de su casa a la universidad.
8. …a qué velocidad maneja generalmente en la autopista.
9. …si le gustaría manejar un Mercedes Benz.
10. …qué haría si su coche no funcionara bien.

*Los Mapas y las Guías Michelin
se complementan…¡Utilícelos juntos!*

Situaciones

What would you say in the following situations? What might the other person say? Act out the scenes with a partner. Take turns playing each role.

1. You have a flat tire, and you think the brakes on your car are out of order. You want your mechanic to check them.
2. Tell a tourist that he or she can buy gasoline at the service station located at the next corner.
3. You are a police officer, and you have stopped a motorist. The car doesn't have a license plate, and the lights aren't working. Ask to see the motorist's driver's license.
4. Your car won't start, and you're going to need a tow truck. Someone passes by as you fiddle with the ignition.
5. Your friend bought a car that was a lemon, and then spent three thousand dollars to have it fixed. Say what you would have done in this situation.

¿Qué pasa aquí?

In groups of three or four, look at the cartoon and write a dialogue between the mechanic and the driver.

Para escribir

What if **Romeo** and **Julieta** were living now? Write an account of what their circumstances would be and what they would be doing. In our story, of course, they *don't* die! Start out with: **Romeo y Julieta vivirían en...**

En la vida real

¡Nos vamos!

You and a classmate are planning to drive to Mexico. Working together, make a list of everything you need to do before you leave. Make sure you include things you need to do to get the car and yourselves ready.

Comprando coche

What questions would you ask before buying a car? Carefully read the following brochure and identify the questions that would cover these topics:

- la condición del coche (dos preguntas)
- la garantía
- las reparaciones (dos preguntas)
- la inspección del estado
- el precio de reventa (resale)

Cuando vaya a comprar un automóvil, ¡pregunte!

Ciertas preguntas le ahorrarán dinero.
Determine primero qué automóvil necesita y cuánto dinero puede invertir.
Consulte por lo menos con tres comerciantes de automóviles antes de decidir a cuál le comprará.

Pregunte a cada comerciante:
—¿Qué garantía tiene el automóvil?
—Si el automóvil se descompone, ¿quién va a componerlo?
—¿El automóvil será aprobado en la inspección del Estado?
—¿Qué precio de reventa tendrá el automóvil cuando Ud. quiera venderlo?
—¿Está el automóvil en perfectas condiciones?
—¿Le dejarán probar el automóvil antes de entregárselo?
—Si el automóvil necesita ser reparado, ¿quién pagará la reparación?
Recuerde hacer estas preguntas y ahorrará mucho dinero.
Asegúrese de que el vendedor no lo engañe. Muchos vendedores tratarán de engañarlo para hacer la venta.

¡PREGUNTE EL PRECIO!

Hágale saber al vendedor que Ud. ya conoce los precios de otros competidores.
Recuerde que los vendedores a veces pueden cambiar el precio. No cierre el trato si el precio que le ofrecen no le parece correcto o justo.

RECUERDE, ES SU DINERO.

En la agencia de seguros

With a classmate, play the roles of an insurance agent and a student who wants to purchase an auto insurance policy (**un seguro de automóvil**). The agent wants to determine the overall condition of the car, whether the student is a conscientious driver, and how much the car is worth. The student is anxious to make a good impression.

¡Vamos a leer!

Antes de leer

A. Before you read the fable, look at the illustration. Is the milkmaid happy or sad? What is she thinking about? Why? Now make a list of situations in which the saying "Don't count your chickens before they hatch" would apply.

B. As you read the fable, find the answers to the following questions.

1. ¿Adónde iba la lechera?
2. ¿Qué llevaba en la cabeza?
3. ¿En qué iba pensando?
4. ¿Qué es lo primero que comprará con el dinero que obtenga?
5. ¿En qué se convertirán los huevos?
6. ¿Qué hará con el dinero que obtenga de la venta de los pollitos?
7. Cuando venda el cochino, ¿qué comprará con el dinero de la venta?
8. ¿Qué pasó cuando la lechera tropezó?
9. ¿Por qué perdió lo único que realmente tenía?
10. ¿Cuál es la moraleja de la fábula?

La lechera
(Fábula de origen oriental)

milkmaid / jug   Una lechera° iba al mercado, llevando un cántaro° en la cabeza. Iba muy
sale   contenta, pensando en el dinero que ganaría con la venta° de la leche.
basket   "Con el dinero que obtenga, podré comprar un canasto° de huevos que, en el
se... will turn into /   verano, se convertirán en° pollitos que me rodearán° cantando *pío, pío.*"
will surround
enough / pig   Entusiasmada con esta idea, la lechera piensa que, cuando venda los pollos
                      tendrá bastante° dinero para comprar un cochino.°
cow / calf   "En cuanto el cochino engorde, lo llevaré al mercado para venderlo y, con el
thoughts   dinero que me den, compraré una vaca° y un ternero.°"
stone / she tripped / fell   Tan contenta iba la lechera con estos pensamientos° que no se fijó en una
spilling   piedra° que había en el camino y tropezó.° El cántaro se le cayó° de la cabeza y se
                      rompió, derramando° toda la leche. ¡Adiós leche, dinero, pollos, cochino, vaca y
                      ternero!

                          ¡Pobre lechera! Si no hubiera estado haciendo castillos en el aire, no habría
                      perdido lo único que realmente tenía.

reader / No... Don't yearn   Recuerde el lector° esta moraleja: "No anheles° impaciente el bien futuro;
                      mira que ni el presente está seguro".

Díganos

Answer the following questions, based on your own thoughts and experiences.

1. ¿Ha hecho Ud. "castillos en el aire" alguna vez?
2. ¿Qué animales domésticos tenía Ud. cuando era niño(-a)?
3. ¿Recuerda Ud. una circunstancia en que Ud. sufrió una desilusión *(disappointment)*?
4. ¿Qué significado tiene para Ud. la moraleja de esta fábula?

Take this test. When you have finished, check your answers in the answer key provided for this section in Appendix E. Then use a red pen to correct any mistakes you have made. Are you ready?

Lección 16

A. The future

Rewrite the following sentences using the future tense.

1. Le *vamos a decir* la verdad.
2. ¿Qué *van a hacer* Uds.?
3. No *van a querer* ir.
4. Lo *voy a saber* mañana.
5. No *van a poder* venir.
6. ¿Adónde *vamos a ir?*
7. ¿Dónde lo *vas a poner?*
8. Nosotros *vamos a venir* con él.
9. *Voy a tener* que trabajar.
10. *Vamos a salir* mañana.

SELF TEST

B. The conditional

Rewrite the following sentences to say what the people named *would* do, using the conditional tense.

1. Yo *voy* a México.
2. Nosotros les *escribimos.*
3. ¿Tú se lo *dices?*
4. Ellos *hablan* con Ana.
5. ¿Ud. lo *pone* en el banco?
6. ¿Uds. *vienen* el domingo?
7. Julio *pide* ensalada.
8. Nosotros lo *hacemos* hoy.
9. Tú no *sales* con ella.
10. Ella *no camina, va* en coche.

C. The future perfect

Complete the following sentences, using the future perfect of the verbs listed.

comer   terminar   escribir   volver   decir

1. Para mañana, el consejero me _____ qué clases tomar.
2. Para las cuatro de la tarde, ellos _____ a casa.
3. Para junio, yo _____ las clases.
4. Para las dos, nosotros ya _____ el postre.
5. ¿Tú _____ todas las cartas para las cinco de la tarde?

D. The conditional perfect

Write the following sentences in Spanish.

1. I would have studied and would have passed the test.
2. Julio would have helped me with the report.
3. Luis and I would have gone to the game.
4. Had they known I didn't have the money, my parents would have paid the tuition.
5. What would you have done, Anita?

E. Just words . . .

Match the questions in column A with the answers in column B.

A	B
1. ¿Es argentino?	a. Sí, porque juega nuestro equipo.
2. ¿Qué materias estás tomando?	b. El año próximo.
3. ¿Quién es tu consejero?	c. No, es plomero.
4. ¿Asiste a la Facultad de Derecho?	d. Sí, es de Buenos Aires.
5. ¿Qué tienes que escribir?	e. Sí. Hoy tengo examen de matemáticas.
6. ¿Qué nota sacaste?	f. Física, química y geología.
7. ¿Es periodista?	g. No, quedé suspendido.
8. ¿Necesitas la calculadora?	h. El Dr. Peña.
9. ¿Aprobaste el examen?	i. Un informe para mi clase de biología.
10. ¿Es carpintero?	j. Sí, quiere ser abogado.
11. ¿Vamos al estadio hoy?	k. Una "B".
12. ¿Cuándo te gradúas?	l. Sí, trabaja para el *Times*.

F. Culture

Circle the correct answer, based on the **¿Lo sabía Ud.?** section.

1. En las universidades hispanas no (entrega, existe, queda) el concepto de *"major"* usado en los Estados Unidos.
2. La mayoría de los estudiantes comienzan a (matricularse, graduarse, especializarse) a partir de su primer año en la universidad.
3. En España, las universidades se dividen en (facultades, carreras, administraciones).
4. Los estudiantes toman clases relacionadas con su (consejero, equipo, especialización).
5. Una nota de (1 a 4, 3 a 6, 2 a 5) es la mínima para aprobar una clase.

Lección 17

A. Reciprocal reflexives

Write the following sentences in Spanish.

1. My friend Marta and I write to each other frequently and sometimes we call each other on the phone.
2. Olga and my brother see each other on Sundays but they never talk to each other.
3. Do you and your friends help each other on weekends?

B. The imperfect subjunctive

Rewrite the following sentences with the new beginnings.

1. Quiere que vaya con ellos.
   Quería…
2. Les digo que no se preocupen.
   Les dije…
3. Me alegro de que el doctor te vea hoy.
   Me alegré…
4. Temo que me ponga una inyección.
   Temí…
5. Necesito una enfermera que sepa español.
   Necesitaba…
6. No creo que tengan que desinfectarme la herida.
   No creí…
7. ¿Hay alguien que pueda recetar penicilina?
   ¿Había…?
8. Me alegro de que te sientas bien.
   Me alegré…
9. No es verdad que necesitemos una ambulancia.
   No era verdad…
10. No creo que esté embarazada.
    No creía…

C. Verbs and prepositions

Complete the following sentences, using the verbs listed and the appropriate prepositions.

insistir   comprometerse   olvidarse   venir   enamorarse   soñar

1. Yo nunca _____ traer mis libros a clase.
2. Julio y Estrella _____ casarse el año que viene.
3. El profesor _____ que todos los estudiantes hagan los ejercicios.
4. Nosotros _____ verla cinco días a la semana.
5. Adela _____ Pepe en la fiesta de anoche.
6. Yo _____ mi novia la primera vez que la vi.

D. Just words . . .

Choose the word or phrase in parentheses that best completes each of the following sentences.

1. Ella es alérgica a la (radiografía, penicilina, clase).
2. Comemos con (los oídos, los dientes, el pecho).
3. Hablamos con (la espalda, los dedos, la lengua).
4. Vemos con (los ojos, la boca, las orejas).
5. Caminamos con (las manos, el cuello, los pies).
6. Me desinfectaron (el dolor, la herida, la receta).
7. ¿Te (rompiste, atropellaste, evitaste) el brazo alguna vez?
8. Me dolía mucho (la pierna, el pelo, el consultorio).
9. Le vendé (el tobillo, el pelo, el catarro).
10. Tenía ciento tres (fiebre, gripe, grados) de temperatura.
11. ¿Cuándo fue la última vez que le (cortaron, quebraron, pusieron) una inyección antitetánica?
12. ¿Por qué tomaste aspirinas? ¿Tenías (dolor de cabeza, tos, frío)?
13. ¿Tienes Alka Seltzer? Es para (el pecho, el estómago, los dedos de los pies).
14. Va a tener un niño. Está (cansada, enferma, embarazada).
15. Raúl no se siente bien. El médico dice que tiene (pastillas, gripe, recetas).

E. Culture

Answer the following questions, based on the **¿Lo sabía Ud.?** section.

1. ¿Quién subvenciona *(subsidizes)* los hospitales en los países de habla hispana?
2. ¿Adónde va la gente que no quiere ir a un hospital público?
3. ¿Qué clase de medicina hay en muchos pueblos remotos?
4. ¿Quién ayuda a algunas mujeres hispanas cuando van a tener un bebé?
5. ¿Es posible comprar medicinas en algunos países hispanos sin tener receta?

Lección 18

A. The present perfect subjunctive

Write the following sentences in Spanish.

1. It's a pity that they haven't found the car.
2. I'm glad you have installed new brakes, Pedro.
3. Is there anyone who has checked the tires?
4. He hopes we have not spent all the money.
5. I don't think you have fixed the engine, Luis.

B. The pluperfect subjunctive

Give the Spanish equivalent of the words in parentheses.

1. No había nadie que _____ el accidente. *(had seen)*
2. Yo me alegré de que ellos no _____ un pinchazo. *(had had)*

3. Ellos no creían que nosotros _____ la gasolina. *(had paid)*
4. Yo temía que _____ la pierna, Anita. *(you had broken)*
5. Ellos se alegraron de que yo _____ . *(had returned)*

C. *If clauses*

Complete the following sentences, using the present indicative, the imperfect subjunctive, or the pluperfect subjunctive, as needed.

1. Si yo _____ (tener) tiempo, iré a buscarte.
2. Nosotros iríamos con ellos si _____ (poder).
3. Si ellos _____ (ir) a la biblioteca, habrían encontrado el libro.
4. Si Uds. _____ (querer) ir con nosotros, podemos llevarlos.
5. Tú habrías hablado con ella si la _____ (ver).
6. Antonio gasta dinero como si _____ (ser) rico.

D. Summary of the uses of the subjunctive

Write the following sentences in Spanish.

1. I wanted them to install a new battery.
2. I hope they can talk with the mechanic.
3. Tell her to call me if she wants to go, Paquito.
4. I don't think we can go to the game, but I think we can go to the movies.
5. Is there anyone who has taken business administration?
6. I am going to help my mother when I get home.
7. I gave her money so that she could pay the fine.
8. It isn't true that this car is no good.

E. Just words . . .

Complete the following sentences, using words learned in **Lección 18**.

1. ¿Cuál es la _____ máxima en la carretera?
2. Adela y Fernando están _____ casados.
3. No pude parar porque los _____ estaban descompuestos.
4. ¿Tienes tu licencia de _____ ?
5. Fuimos a la estación de _____ .
6. Está lloviendo, y el _____ de mi coche no funciona. ¡No veo nada!
7. ¿Está lleno o _____ el tanque?
8. Voy a poner las maletas en el _____ .
9. Mi coche no arranca; la grúa lo va a _____ .
10. Un sinónimo de "batería" es _____ .
11. Yo pongo los mapas en la _____ del coche.
12. No es mi _____ que el coche no tenga gasolina.
13. Yo no arreglaría el coche. ¡No _____ la pena!
14. Mis padres van a salir de _____ el 15 de junio.
15. Cuando él va de compras, siempre _____ mucho dinero.

F. Culture

Circle the correct answer, based on the **¿Lo sabía Ud.?** section.

1. Madrid, Buenos Aires y México tienen graves problemas de (asimilación, contaminación, introducción) del aire.
2. En zonas rurales de Hispanoamérica, las carreteras están en muy (buenas, medianas, malas) condiciones.
3. La gasolina es más (cara, barata, libre) en la mayoría de los países hispanos.
4. La gente joven usa más (el camión, la motocicleta, la bicicleta).
5. Un kilómetro equivale a (0,7; 0,6; 0,5) millas.

LAS MINORÍAS HISPANAS EN LOS ESTADOS UNIDOS

Estados Unidos

- Muchas de las estrellas *(stars)* de cine y de televisión en los Estados Unidos son de ascendencia hispana: Rita Moreno, Ricardo Montalbán, Charlie Sheen, Emilio Estévez, Edward James Olmos, María Conchita Alonso, Linda Ronstadt, Andy García y Rosie Pérez, entre muchos otros.

- En la ciudad de Nueva York hay más de dos millones de hispanos, la mayoría de los cuales son puertorriqueños. Otros grupos hispanos concentrados en Nueva York son los dominicanos, los centroamericanos y los cubanos.

- La minoría hispana más numerosa en los Estados Unidos es la de origen mexicano, que se concentra principalmente en los estados de Tejas, Colorado, Nuevo México, Arizona y California.

- Más de medio millón de cubanos viven en Miami, donde ejercen una gran influencia cultural y económica. Hace poco más de tres décadas, cuando los cubanos empezaron a llegar a Miami, la ciudad era fundamentalmente un centro turístico. Hoy Miami es un centro industrial y comercial de primer orden, y el puente que une la economía de los Estados Unidos con la de América Latina y aun la de España.

Para las muchachas latinoamericanas, tiene mucha importancia la celebración de los quince años. En México la fiesta recibe el nombre de "quinceañera"; en otros países se llama la celebración de "los quince". Las familias latinas en los Estados Unidos, generalmente siguen la tradición con un baile y una comida especial.
¿Qué cumpleaños es muy importante para muchas chicas norteamericanas?

La calle Olvera, con sus aceras adoquinadas *(tiled sidewalks)*, sus piñatas, sus mariachis y sus puestos de artesanía mexicana es un trozo *(piece)* del viejo México en el corazón de Los Ángeles. Aquí se ve el edificio Ávila, construído de adobe y considerado el más antiguo de los edificios existentes en Los Ángeles.
¿Puede Ud. describir lo que ve en esta foto?

Uno de los grupos minoritarios más numerosos en la ciudad de Nueva York es el de los puertorriqueños. Aquí se ve un festival hispano en la calle 14 de Manhattan, el centro de Nueva York.
¿Cuál es el grupo minoritario más numeroso en su ciudad?

La cantante cubana Gloria Estefan es una de las más populares de los Estados Unidos. Gloria canta y compone canciones en español y en inglés. Recientemente su nombre fue añadido *(was added)* al famoso *Walk of Fame* de Hollywood.
¿Cuál es su cantante favorito?

La actriz Jennifer López, de origen puertorriqueño, se ha convertido en una de las actrices latinas más populares al interpretar el papel *(role)* de *Selena*, la trágicamente desaparecida cantante de la música "*Tex-Mex*", en la película del mismo nombre. Jennifer López ya había participado en varias películas, entre ellas *My Family*, *U Turn* y *Money Train*.
¿Cuál es su actriz favorita?

Edward James Olmos, nacido en Los Ángeles, de padres mexicanos, es uno de los actores hispanos más conocidos en los Estados Unidos. Entre sus películas están *Stand and Deliver*, *My Family* y *Selena*, donde representa el papel del padre de la famosa cantante de origen mexicano.
¿Cuál es su actor favorito?

No hay duda de que en la ciudad de San Antonio, Tejas, la cultura mexicana es la predominante. En la foto, una familia come en el restaurante mexicano "Mi tierra". **¿Cuál es su restaurante mexicano favorito?**

Ileana Ros-Lehtinen, cubana de nacimiento, es una muestra del poder político de los hispanos en los Estados Unidos. Educadora de profesión, y ya con una maestría de Ciencias en Lideratura Educacional y una candidatura al doctorado, se decidió por la política. Fue Representante a la Cámara y Senadora de la Florida y, desde 1989, es Representante al Congreso de los Estados Unidos. Ileana Ros fue la primera mujer hispana elegida para esta posición. **¿Puede Ud. nombrar otros políticos hispanos? ¿Cuáles?**

Teleinforme

Vocabulario

La calle Olvera, Los Ángeles

las arepas	round maize loaves
las carnitas	fried chunks of pork
el condado	county
los espectadores	spectators, audience
la harina	flour
el juez	judge
lucir	to display
las mercancías	goods
saborear	to taste

El desfile puertorriqueño de Nueva York

la bandera	flag
el desfile	parade
Estado Libre Asociado	Free Associated State (Commonwealth)
la fuerza	power, strength
ondeó	wove
orgullosamente	proudly
promueve	promotes, fosters
reúne	unites

Preparación

¿Cuánto saben Uds. ya?   After reading the information in **Panorama hispánico 9**, get together in groups of three or four and answer the following questions.

1. ¿En qué estados se concentra el mayor número de personas de origen mexicano?
2. ¿De dónde son la mayoría de los hispanos que viven en Nueva York?
3. ¿Qué otros grupos hispanos se concentran en Nueva York?
4. ¿Dónde vive la mayor parte de los cubanos?
5. ¿En qué ciudad se encuentra la calle Olvera?
6. ¿Cuál es uno de los edificios más antiguos de la ciudad de Los Ángeles?

Comprensión

A. La calle Olvera, Los Ángeles.   Complete the following statements with the appropriate words.

1. La calle Olvera es una de las calles más _____ de Los Ángeles.
2. La calle Olvera fue nombrada así por el juez _____ .
3. En el mercado mexicano venden _____ típicas.

4. "El cinco de mayo" es una _____ mexicana.
5. Algunos ejemplos de la comida mexicana son _____ , _____ y _____ .

B. El desfile puertorriqueño de Nueva York.   Read the following statements and circle **V** (**Verdadero**) or **F** (**Falso**), according to what you understood.

V F   1. La bandera puertorriqueña fue creada en Puerto Rico.

V F   2. La bandera puertorriqueña ondeó por primera vez en Puerto Rico en el año 1902.

V F   3. Puerto Rico es un Estado Libre Asociado a los Estados Unidos.

V F   4. Muy pocas personas asisten al desfile puertorriqueño en la Quinta avenida de Nueva York.

V F   5. Los representantes de los pueblos de Puerto Rico participan en el desfile puertorriqueño en Nueva York.

V F   6. Las empresas que sirven a la comunidad colaboran para crear un ambiente de solidaridad y de celebración.

Ampliación

A. Celebraciones hispanas.   With a partner, discuss in Spanish what you would like to see and do if you went to a festival on Olvera Street in Los Angeles or the Puerto Rican Day celebration in New York City.

B. Dos culturas.   Now that you have seen all the video modules, what preconceived ideas that you might have had about the Hispanic world and its people have changed? Which ones haven't? With a partner, discuss this in Spanish.

APPENDIX A

SPANISH SOUNDS

Vowels

There are five distinct vowels in Spanish: **a, e, i, o,** and **u.** Each vowel has only one basic, constant sound. The pronunciation of each vowel is constant, clear, and brief. The length of the sound is practically the same whether it is produced in a stressed or unstressed syllable.[1]

While producing the sounds of the English stressed vowels that most closely resemble the Spanish ones, the speaker changes the position of the tongue, lips, and lower jaw, so that the vowel actually starts as one sound and then glides into another. In Spanish, however, the tongue, lips, and jaw keep a constant position during the production of the sound.

> **English:** ban*a*na   **Spanish:** ban*a*na

The stress falls on the same vowel and syllable in both Spanish and English, but the English stressed *a* is longer than the Spanish stressed **a.**

> **English:** ban*a*na   **Spanish:** ban*a*na

Note also that the English stressed *a* has a sound different from the other a's in the word, while the Spanish a sound remains constant.

a The Spanish **a** sounds similar to the English *a* in the word *father.*

alta	casa	palma	Ana
cama	Panamá	alma	apagar

e The Spanish **e** is pronounced like the English *e* in the word *eight.*

mes	entre	este	deje
ese	encender	teme	prender

i The Spanish **i** has a sound similar to the English *ee* in the word *see.*

fin	ir	sí	sin	dividir	Trini	difícil

o The Spanish **o** is similar to the English *o* in the word *no,* but without the glide.

toco	como	poco	roto
corto	corro	solo	loco

u The Spanish **u** is pronounced like the English *oo* sound in the word *shoot* or the *ue* sound in the word *Sue.*

su	Lulú	Úrsula	cultura
un	luna	sucursal	Uruguay

Diphthongs and Triphthongs

When unstressed **i** or **u** falls next to another vowel in a syllable, it unites with that vowel to form what is called a *diphthong.* Both vowels are pronounced as one syllable. Their

---

[1]In a stressed syllable, the prominence of the vowel is indicated by its loudness.

445

sounds do not change; they are only pronounced more rapidly and with a glide. For example:

traiga	Lidia	treinta	siete	oigo	adiós
Aurora	agua	bueno	antiguo	ciudad	Luis

A triphthong is the union of three vowels: a stressed vowel between two unstressed ones (**i** or **u**) in the same syllable. For example: Paraguay, estudiéis.

NOTE: Stressed **i** and **u** do not form diphthongs with other vowels, except in the combinations **iu** and **ui.** For example: **rí**-o, sa-**bí**-ais.

In syllabication, diphthongs and triphthongs are considered a single vowel; their components cannot be separated.

Consonants

p Spanish **p** is pronounced in a manner similar to the English *p* sound, but without the puff of air that follows after the English sound is produced.

pesca	pude	puedo	parte	papá
postre	piña	puente	Paco	

k The Spanish **k** sound, represented by the letters **k, c** before **a, o, u** or a consonant, and **qu,** is similar to the English *k* sound, but without the puff of air.

casa	comer	cuna	clima	acción	que
quinto	queso	aunque	kiosko	kilómetro	

t Spanish **t** is produced by touching the back of the upper front teeth with the tip of the tongue. It has no puff of air as in the English *t*.

todo	antes	corto	Guatemala	diente
resto	tonto	roto	tanque	

d The Spanish consonant **d** has two different sounds depending on its position. At the beginning of an utterance and after **n** or **l,** the tip of the tongue presses the back of the upper front teeth.

día	doma	dice	dolor	dar
anda	Aldo	caldo	el deseo	un domicilio

In all other positions the sound of **d** is similar to the *th* sound in the English word *they*, but softer.

medida	todo	nada	nadie	medio
puedo	moda	queda	nudo	

g The Spanish consonant **g** is similar to the English *g* sound in the word *guy* except before **e** or **i.**

goma	glotón	gallo	gloria	lago	alga
gorrión	garra	guerra	angustia	algo	Dagoberto

j The Spanish sound **j** (or **g** before **e** and **i**) is similar to a strongly exaggerated English *h* sound.

gemir	juez	jarro	gitano	agente
juego	giro	bajo	gente	

b, v There is no difference in sound between Spanish **b** and **v.** Both letters are pronounced alike. At the beginning of an utterance or after **m** or **n, b** and **v** have a sound identical to the English *b* sound in the word *boy*.

vivir	beber	vamos	barco	enviar
hambre	batea	bueno	vestido	

When pronounced between vowels, the Spanish **b** and **v** sound is produced by bringing the lips together but not closing them, so that some air may pass through.

sábado	autobús	yo voy	su barco

y, ll In most countries, Spanish **ll** and **y** have a sound similar to the English *y* sound in the word *yes*.

el llavero	trayecto	su yunta	milla
oye	el yeso	mayo	yema
un yelmo	trayectoria	llama	bella

NOTE: When it stands alone or is at the end of a word, Spanish **y** is pronounced like the vowel **i**.

rey	hoy	y	doy	buey
muy	voy	estoy	soy	

r The sound of Spanish **r** is similar to the English *dd* sound in the word *ladder*.

crema	aroma	cara	arena	aro
harina	toro	oro	eres	portero

rr Spanish **rr** and also **r** in an initial position and after **n, l,** or **s** are pronounced with a very strong trill. This trill is produced by bringing the tip of the tongue near the alveolar ridge and letting it vibrate freely while the air passes through the mouth.

rama	carro	Israel	cierra	roto
perro	alrededor	rizo	corre	Enrique

s Spanish **s** is represented in most of the Spanish world by the letters **s, z,** and **c** before **e** or **i**. The sound is very similar to the English sibilant *s* in the word *sink*.

sale	sitio	presidente	signo
salsa	seda	suma	vaso
sobrino	ciudad	cima	canción
zapato	zarza	cerveza	centro

h The letter **h** is silent in Spanish.

hoy	hora	hilo	ahora
humor	huevo	horror	almohada

ch Spanish **ch** is pronounced like the English *ch* in the word *chief*.

hecho	chico	coche	Chile
mucho	muchacho	salchicha	

f Spanish **f** is identical in sound to the English *f*.

difícil	feo	fuego	forma
fácil	fecha	foto	fueron

l Spanish **l** is similar to the English *l* in the word *let*.

dolor	lata	ángel	lago	sueldo
los	pelo	lana	general	fácil

m Spanish **m** is pronounced like the English *m* in the word *mother*.

mano	moda	mucho	muy
mismo	tampoco	multa	cómoda

n In most cases, Spanish **n** has a sound similar to the English *n*.

nada	nunca	ninguno	norte
entra	tiene	sienta	

The sound of Spanish **n** is often affected by the sounds that occur around it. When it appears before **b, v,** or **p,** it is pronounced like an **m.**

tan bueno	toman vino	sin poder
un pobre	comen peras	siguen bebiendo

ñ Spanish **ñ** is similar to the English *ny* sound in the word *canyon.*

señor	otoño	ñoño	uña
leña	dueño	niños	años

x Spanish **x** has two pronunciations depending on its position. Between vowels the sound is similar to English *ks.*

examen	exacto	boxeo	éxito
oxidar	oxígeno	existencia	

When it occurs before a consonant, Spanish **x** sounds like *s.*

expresión	explicar	extraer	excusa
expreso	exquisito	extremo	

NOTE: When **x** appears in **México** or in other words of Mexican origin, it is pronounced like the Spanish letter **j.**

Rhythm

Rhythm is the variation of sound intensity that we usually associate with music. Spanish and English each regulate these variations in speech differently, because they have different patterns of syllable length. In Spanish the length of the stressed and unstressed syllables remains almost the same, while the English stressed syllables are considerably longer than unstressed ones. Pronounce the following Spanish words, enunciating each syllable clearly.

es-tu-dian-te	bue-no	Úr-su-la
com-po-si-ción	di-fí-cil	ki-ló-me-tro
po-li-cí-a	Pa-ra-guay	

Because the length of the Spanish syllables remains constant, the greater the number of syllables in a given word or phrase, the longer the phrase will be.

Linking

In spoken Spanish, the different words in a phrase or a sentence are not pronounced as isolated elements but are combined together. This is called *linking.*

Pepe come pan.	→	Pe-pe-co-me-pan
Tomás toma leche.		To-más-to-ma-le-che
Luis tiene la llave.		Luis-tie-ne-la-lla-ve
La mano de Roberto.		La-ma-no-de-Ro-ber-to

■ The final consonant of a word is pronounced together with the initial vowel of the following word.

Carlos anda	→	Car-lo-san-da
un ángel		u-nán-gel
el otoño		e-lo-to-ño
unos estudios interesantes		u-no-ses-tu-dio-sin-te-re-san-tes

■ A diphthong is formed between the final vowel of a word and the initial vowel of the following word. A triphthong is formed when there is a combination of three vowels (see rules for the formation of diphthongs and triphthongs on pages 445–446).

su hermana	suher-ma-na
tu escopeta	tues-co-pe-ta
Roberto y Luis	Ro-ber-toy-Luis
negocio importante	ne-go-cioim-por-tan-te
lluvia y nieve	llu-viay-nie-ve
ardua empresa	ar-duaem-pre-sa

■ When the final vowel of a word and the initial vowel of the following word are identical, they are pronounced slightly longer than one vowel.

Ana alcanza	A-n*a*l-can-za
lo olvido	l*o*l-vi-do
tiene eso	tie-n*e*-so
Ada atiende	Ad*a*-tien-de

The same rule applies when two identical vowels appear within a word.

crees	cr*e*s
Teherán	T*e*-rán
coordinación	cor-di-na-ción

■ When the final consonant of a word and the initial consonant of the following word are the same, they are pronounced as one consonant with slightly longer than normal duration.

el lado	e-*l*a-do
Carlos salta	Car-lo-*s*al-ta
tienes sed	tie-ne-*s*ed

Intonation

Intonation is the rise and fall of pitch in the delivery of a phrase or a sentence. In general, Spanish pitch tends to change less than English, giving the impression that the language is less emphatic.

As a rule, the intonation for normal statements in Spanish starts in a low tone, rises to a higher one on the first stressed syllable, maintains that tone until the last stressed syllable, and then goes back to the initial low tone, with still another drop at the very end.

Tu amigo viene mañana.	José come pan.
Ada está en casa.	Carlos toma café.

Syllable Formation in Spanish

General rules for dividing words into syllables:

Vowels

■ A vowel or a vowel combination can constitute a syllable.

a-lum-no   a-bue-la   Eu-ro-pa

■ Diphthongs and triphthongs are considered single vowels and cannot be divided.

bai-le   puen-te   Dia-na   es-tu-diáis   an-ti-guo

■ Two strong vowels (**a, e, o**) do not form a diphthong and are separated into two syllables.

    em-ple-ar   vol-te-ar   lo-a

■ A written accent on a weak vowel (**i** or **u**) breaks the diphthong, separating the vowels into two syllables.

    trí-o   dú-o   Ma-rí-a

Consonants

■ A single consonant forms a syllable with the vowel that follows it.

    po-der   ma-no   mi-nu-to

NOTE: Spanish **ch, ll,** and **rr** are considered single consonants: **a-ma-ri-llo, co-che, pe-rro.**

■ When two consonants appear between two vowels, they are separated into two syllables.

    al-fa-be-to   cam-pe-ón   me-ter-se   mo-les-tia

EXCEPTION: When a consonant cluster composed of **b, c, d, f, g, p,** or **t** with **l** or **r** appears between two vowels, the cluster joins the following vowel: **so-bre, o-tros, ca-ble, te-lé-gra-fo.**

■ When three consonants appear between two vowels, only the last one goes with the following vowel.

    ins-pec-tor   trans-por-te   trans-for-mar

EXCEPTION: When there is a cluster of three consonants in the combinations described in rule 2, the first consonant joins the preceding vowel and the cluster joins the following vowel: **es-cri-bir, ex-tran-je-ro, im-plo-rar, es-tre-cho.**

Accentuation

In Spanish, all words are stressed according to specific rules. Words that do not follow the rules must have a written accent to indicate the change of stress. The basic rules for accentuation are as follows.

■ Words ending in a vowel, **n,** or **s** are stressed on the next-to-last syllable.

    hi-jo   **ca**-lle   **me**-sa   fa-**mo**-sos
    flo-**re**-cen   **pla**-ya   **ve**-ces

■ Words ending in a consonant, except **n** or **s,** are stressed on the last syllable.

    ma-**yor**   a-**mor**   tro-pi-**cal**   na-**riz**   re-**loj**   co-rre-**dor**

■ All words that do not follow these rules must have the written accent.

    ca-**fé**   **lá**-piz   **mú**-si-ca   sa-**lón**
    án-gel   **lí**-qui-do   fran-**cés**   **Víc**-tor
    sim-**pá**-ti-co   rin-**cón**   a-**zú**-car   de-**mó**-cra-ta
    sa-**lió**   **dé**-bil   e-**xá**-me-nes

■ Pronouns and adverbs of interrogation and exclamation have a written accent to distinguish them from relative pronouns.

    ¿Qué comes?   *What are you eating?*
    La pera que él no comió.   *The pear that he did not eat.*

¿Quién está ahí?	*Who is there?*
El hombre a quien tú llamaste.	*The man whom you called.*
¿Dónde está él?	*Where is he?*
En el lugar donde trabaja.	*At the place where he works.*

■ Words that have the same spelling but different meanings take a written accent to differentiate one from the other.

el	*the*	él	*he, him*		te	*you*	té	*tea*
mi	*my*	mí	*me*		si	*if*	sí	*yes*
tu	*your*	tú	*you*		mas	*but*	más	*more*

Regular Verbs

Model **-ar, -er, -ir** verbs

INFINITIVE

amar *(to love)*   comer *(to eat)*   vivir *(to live)*

PRESENT PARTICIPLE

amando *(loving)*   comiendo *(eating)*   viviendo *(living)*

PAST PARTICIPLE

amado *(loved)*   comido *(eaten)*   vivido *(lived)*

SIMPLE TENSES

Indicative Mood

PRESENT

(I love)		*(I eat)*		*(I live)*	
amo	amamos	como	comemos	vivo	vivimos
amas	amáis	comes	coméis	vives	vivís
ama	aman	come	comen	vive	viven

IMPERFECT

(I used to love)		*(I used to eat)*		*(I used to live)*	
amaba	amábamos	comía	comíamos	vivía	vivíamos
amabas	amabais	comías	comíais	vivías	vivíais
amaba	amaban	comía	comían	vivía	vivían

PRETERIT

(I loved)		*(I ate)*		*(I lived)*	
amé	amamos	comí	comimos	viví	vivimos
amaste	amasteis	comiste	comisteis	viviste	vivisteis
amó	amaron	comió	comieron	vivió	vivieron

FUTURE

(I will love)		*(I will eat)*		*(I will live)*	
amaré	amaremos	comeré	comeremos	viviré	viviremos
amarás	amaréis	comerás	comeréis	vivirás	viviréis
amará	amarán	comerá	comerán	vivirá	vivirán

CONDITIONAL

(I would love)		*(I would eat)*		*(I would live)*	
amaría	amaríamos	comería	comeríamos	viviría	viviríamos
amarías	amaríais	comerías	comeríais	vivirías	viviríais
amaría	amarían	comería	comerían	viviría	vivirían

Subjunctive Mood

PRESENT

([that] I [may] love)		*([that] I [may] eat)*		*([that] I [may] live)*	
ame	amemos	coma	comamos	viva	vivamos
ames	améis	comas	comáis	vivas	viváis
ame	amen	coma	coman	viva	vivan

IMPERFECT (two forms: -ra, -se)

([that] I [might] love)	*([that] I [might] eat)*	*([that] I [might] live)*
amara(-ase)	comiera(-iese)	viviera(-iese)
amaras(-ases)	comieras(-ieses)	vivieras(-ieses)
amara(-ase)	comiera(-iese)	viviera(-iese)
amáramos(-ásemos)	comiéramos(-iésemos)	viviéramos(-iésemos)
amarais(-aseis)	comierais(-ieseis)	vivierais(-ieseis)
amaran(-asen)	comieran(-iesen)	vivieran(-iesen)

Imperative Mood

(love)	*(eat)*	*(live)*
ama (tú)	come (tú)	vive (tú)
ame (Ud.)	coma (Ud.)	viva (Ud.)
amemos (nosotros)	comamos (nosotros)	vivamos (nosotros)
amad (vosotros)	comed (vosotros)	vivid (vosotros)
amen (Uds.)	coman (Uds.)	vivan (Uds.)

COMPOUND TENSES

PERFECT INFINITIVE

haber amado	haber comido	haber vivido

PERFECT PARTICIPLE

habiendo amado	habiendo comido	habiendo vivido

Indicative Mood

PRESENT PERFECT

(I have loved)	*(I have eaten)*	*(I have lived)*
he amado	he comido	he vivido
has amado	has comido	has vivido
ha amado	ha comido	ha vivido
hemos amado	hemos comido	hemos vivido
habéis amado	habéis comido	habéis vivido
han amado	han comido	han vivido

PLUPERFECT

(I had loved)	*(I had eaten)*	*(I had lived)*
había amado	había comido	había vivido
habías amado	habías comido	habías vivido
había amado	había comido	había vivido
habíamos amado	habíamos comido	habíamos vivido
habíais amado	habíais comido	habíais vivido
habían amado	habían comido	habían vivido

FUTURE PERFECT

(I will have loved)	*(I will have eaten)*	*(I will have lived)*
habré amado	habré comido	habré vivido
habrás amado	habrás comido	habrás vivido
habrá amado	habrá comido	habrá vivido
habremos amado	habremos comido	habremos vivido
habréis amado	habréis comido	habréis vivido
habrán amado	habrán comido	habrán vivido

CONDITIONAL PERFECT

(I would have loved)	*(I would have eaten)*	*(I would have lived)*
habría amado	habría comido	habría vivido
habrías amado	habrías comido	habrías vivido
habría amado	habría comido	habría vivido
habríamos amado	habríamos comido	habríamos vivido
habríais amado	habríais comido	habríais vivido
habrían amado	habrían comido	habrían vivido

Subjunctive Mood

PRESENT PERFECT

([that] I [may] have loved)	*([that] I [may] have eaten)*	*([that] I [may] have lived)*
haya amado	haya comido	haya vivido
hayas amado	hayas comido	hayas vivido
haya amado	haya comido	haya vivido
hayamos amado	hayamos comido	hayamos vivido
hayáis amado	hayáis comido	hayáis vivido
hayan amado	hayan comido	hayan vivido

PLUPERFECT (two forms: -ra, -se)

([that] I [might] have loved)	*([that] I {might} have eaten)*	*([that] I {might} have lived)*
hubiera(-iese) amado	hubiera(-iese) comido	hubiera(-iese) vivido
hubieras(-ieses) amado	hubieras(-ieses) comido	hubieras(-ieses) vivido
hubiera(-iese) amado	hubiera(-iese) comido	hubiera(-iese) vivido
hubiéramos(-iésemos) amado	hubiéramos(-iésemos) comido	hubiéramos(-iésemos) vivido
hubierais(-ieseis) amado	hubierais(-ieseis) comido	hubierais(-ieseis) vivido
hubieran(-iesen) amado	hubieran(-iesen) comido	hubieran(-iesen) vivido

Stem-Changing Verbs

The -ar and -er stem-changing verbs

Stem-changing verbs are those that have a spelling change in the root of the verb. Stem-changing verbs that end in -ar and -er change the stressed vowel e to ie, and the stressed o to ue. These changes occur in all persons, except the first- and second-persons plural, of the present indicative, present subjunctive, and imperative.

Infinitive	Indicative	Imperative	Subjunctive
cerrar	cierro	——	cierre
(to close)	cierras	cierra	cierres
	cierra	cierre	cierre
	cerramos	cerremos	cerremos
	cerráis	cerrad	cerréis
	cierran	cierren	cierren
perder	pierdo	——	pierda
(to lose)	pierdes	pierde	pierdas
	pierde	pierda	pierda
	perdemos	perdamos	perdamos
	perdéis	perded	perdáis
	pierden	pierdan	pierdan
contar	cuento	——	cuente
(to count;	cuentas	cuenta	cuentes
to tell)	cuenta	cuente	cuente
	contamos	contemos	contemos
	contáis	contad	contéis
	cuentan	cuenten	cuenten
volver	vuelvo	——	vuelva
(to return)	vuelves	vuelve	vuelvas
	vuelve	vuelva	vuelva
	volvemos	volvamos	volvamos
	volvéis	volved	volváis
	vuelven	vuelvan	vuelvan

Verbs that follow the same pattern:

acordarse	*to remember*	entender	*to understand*
acostar(se)	*to go to bed*	extender	*to stretch*
almorzar	*to have lunch*	llover	*to rain*
atravesar	*to go through*	mover	*to move*
cocer	*to cook*	mostrar	*to show*
colgar	*to hang*	negar	*to deny*
comenzar	*to begin*	nevar	*to snow*
confesar	*to confess*	pensar	*to think; to plan*
costar	*to cost*	probar	*to prove; to taste*
demostrar	*to demonstrate, show*	recordar	*to remember*
		rogar	*to beg*
despertar(se)	*to wake up*	sentar(se)	*to sit down*
empezar	*to begin*	soler	*to be in the habit of*
encender	*to light; to turn on*	soñar	*to dream*
encontrar	*to find*	torcer	*to twist*

The **-ir** stem-changing verbs

There are two types of stem-changing verbs that end in **-ir**: one type changes stressed **e** to **ie** in some tenses and to **i** in others, and stressed **o** to **ue** or **u**; the second type changes stressed **e** to **i** only in all the irregular tenses.

Type I: **-ir**: e > ie or i / o > ue or u

These changes occur as follows.

Present Indicative: All persons except the first- and second-persons plural change **e** to **ie** and **o** to **ue**. *Preterit:* Third-person singular and plural changes **e** to **i** and **o** to **u**. *Present Subjunctive:* All persons change **e** to **i** and **o** to **u**. *Imperfect Subjunctive:* All persons change **e** to **i** and **o** to **u**. *Imperative:* All persons except the first- and second-persons plural change **e** to **ie** and **o** to **ue**; first-person plural changes **e** to **i** and **o** to **u**. *Present Participle:* This form changes **e** to **i** and **o** to **u**.

Infinitive	Indicative		Imperative	Subjunctive	
sentir (to feel)	**PRESENT**	**PRETERIT**		**PRESENT**	**IMPERFECT**
	siento	sentí		sienta	sintiera(-iese)
	sientes	sentiste	siente	sientas	sintieras
PRESENT PARTICIPLE	siente	sintió	sienta	sienta	sintiera
sintiendo	sentimos	sentimos	sintamos	sintamos	sintiéramos
	sentís	sentisteis	sentid	sintáis	sintierais
	sienten	sintieron	sientan	sientan	sintieran
dormir (to sleep)	duermo	dormí		duerma	durmiera(-iese)
	duermes	dormiste	duerme	duermas	durmieras
PRESENT PARTICIPLE	duerme	durmió	duerma	duerma	durmiera
durmiendo	dormimos	dormimos	durmamos	durmamos	durmiéramos
	dormís	dormisteis	dormid	durmáis	durmierais
	duermen	durmieron	duerman	duerman	durmieran

Other verbs that follow the same pattern:

advertir	*to warm*	herir	*to wound, hurt*
arrepentirse	*to repent*	mentir	*to lie*
consentir	*to consent; to pamper*	morir	*to die*
convertir(se)	*to turn into*	preferir	*to prefer*
discernir	*to discern*	referir	*to refer*
divertir(se)	*to amuse oneself*	sugerir	*to suggest*

Type II: **-ir**: e > i

The verbs in the second category are irregular in the same tenses as those of the first type. The only difference is that they have only one change: **e** > **i** in all irregular persons.

Infinitive	Indicative		Imperative	Subjunctive	
pedir *(to ask for, request)*	**PRESENT**	**PRETERIT**		**PRESENT**	**IMPERFECT**
	pido	pedí		pida	pidiera(-iese)
PRESENT	pides	pediste	pide	pidas	pidieras
PARTICIPLE	pide	pidió	pida	pida	pidiera
p*i*diendo	pedimos	pedimos	pidamos	pidamos	pidiéramos
	pedís	pedisteis	pedid	pidáis	pidierais
	piden	pidieron	pidan	pidan	pidieran

Verbs that follow this pattern:

concebir	*to conceive*	repetir	*to repeat*
competir	*to compete*	reñir	*to fight*
despedir(se)	*to say good-bye*	seguir	*to follow*
elegir	*to choose*	servir	*to serve*
impedir	*to prevent*	vestir(se)	*to dress*
perseguir	*to pursue*		

Orthographic-Changing Verbs

Some verbs undergo a change in the spelling of the stem in some tenses in order to maintain the sound of the final consonant. The most common ones are those with the consonants **g** and **c**. Remember that **g** and **c** in front of **e** or **i** have a soft sound, and in front of **a, o,** or **u** have a hard sound. In order to keep the soft sound in front of **a, o,** or **u, g** and **c** change to **j** and **z**, respectively. In order to keep the hard sound of **g** or **c** in front of **e** and **i, u** is added to the **g** (**gu**) and the **c** changes to **qu**. The most important verbs that are regular in all the tenses but change in spelling are the following.

1. Verbs ending in **-gar** change **g** to **gu** before **e** in the first person of the preterit and in all persons of the present subjunctive.

   pagar *to pay*
   Preterit: pa**gu**é, pagaste, pagó, etc.
   Pres. Subj.: pa**gu**e, pa**gu**es, pa**gu**e, pa**gu**emos, pa**gu**éis, pa**gu**en
   Verbs that follow the same pattern: **colgar, llegar, navegar, negar, regar, rogar, jugar.**

2. Verbs ending in **-ger** or **-gir** change **g** to **j** before **o** and **a** in the first person of the present indicative and in all the persons of the present subjunctive.

   proteger *to protect*
   Pres. Ind.: prote**j**o, proteges, protege, etc.
   Pres. Subj.: prote**j**a, prote**j**as, prote**j**a, prote**j**amos, prote**j**áis, prote**j**an
   Verbs that follow the same pattern: **coger, corregir, dirigir, elegir, escoger, exigir, recoger.**

3. Verbs ending in **-guar** change **gu** to **gü** before **e** in the first person of the preterit and in all persons of the present subjunctive.

   averiguar *to find out*
   Preterit: averi**gü**é, averiguaste, averiguó, etc.
   Pres. Subj.: averi**gü**e, averi**gü**es, averi**gü**e, averi**gü**emos, averi**gü**éis, averi**gü**en
   The verb **apaciguar** follows the same pattern.

4. Verbs ending in **-guir** change **gu** to **g** before **o** and **a** in the first person of the present indicative and in all persons of the present subjunctive.

   conseguir   *to get*
   Pres. Ind.:   consigo, consigues, consigue, etc.
   Pres. Subj.:   consiga, consigas, consiga, consigamos, consigáis, consigan
   Verbs that follow the same pattern: **distinguir, perseguir, proseguir, seguir.**

5. Verbs ending in **-car** change **c** to **qu** before **e** in the first person of the preterit and in all persons of the present subjunctive.

   tocar   *to touch; to play (a musical instrument)*
   Preterit: toqué, tocaste, tocó, etc.
   Pres. Subj.:   toque, toques, toque, toquemos, toquéis, toquen
   Verbs that follow the same pattern: **atacar, buscar, comunicar, explicar, indicar, pescar, sacar.**

6. Verbs ending in **-cer** or **-cir** preceded by a consonant change **c** to **z** before **o** and **a** in the first person of the present indicative and in all persons of the present subjunctive.

   torcer   *to twist*
   Pres. Ind.:   tuerzo, tuerces, tuerce, etc.
   Pres. Subj.:   tuerza, tuerzas, tuerza, torzamos, torzáis, tuerzan
   Verbs that follow the same pattern: **convencer, esparcir, vencer.**

7. Verbs ending in **-cer** or **-cir** preceded by a vowel change **c** to **zc** before **o** and **a** in the first person of the present indicative and in all persons of the present subjunctive.

   conocer   *to know, be acquainted with*
   Pres. Ind.:   conozco, conoces, conoce, etc.
   Pres. Subj.:   conozca, conozcas, conozca, conozcamos, conozcáis, conozcan
   Verbs that follow the same pattern: **agradecer, aparecer, carecer, entristecer** *(to sadden)*, **establecer, lucir, nacer, obedecer, ofrecer, padecer, parecer, pertenecer, reconocer, relucir.**

8. Verbs ending in **-zar** change **z** to **c** before **e** in the first person of the preterit and in all persons of the present subjunctive.

   rezar   *to pray*
   Preterit: recé, rezaste, rezó, etc.
   Pres. Subj.:   rece, reces, rece, recemos, recéis, recen
   Verbs that follow the same pattern: **abrazar, alcanzar, almorzar, comenzar, cruzar, empezar, forzar, gozar.**

9. Verbs ending in **-eer** change the unstressed **i** to **y** between vowels in the third-persons singular and plural of the preterit, in all persons of the imperfect subjunctive, and in the present participle.

   creer   *to believe*
   Pres. Part: creyendo
   Preterit: creí, creíste, creyó, creímos, creísteis, creyeron
   Imp. Subj.:   creyera(-ese), creyeras, creyera, creyéramos, creyerais, creyeran
   Past Part.:   creído
   Verbs that follow the same pattern: **leer, poseer.**

10. Verbs ending in **-uir** change the unstressed **i** to **y** between vowels (except **-quir**, which has the silent **u**) in the following tenses and persons.

    huir   *to escape, flee*
    Pres. Part.:   huyendo
    Pres. Ind.:   huyo, huyes, huye, huimos, huís, huyen
    Preterit: huí, huiste, huyó, huimos, huisteis, huyeron
    Imperative: huye, huya, huyamos, huid, huyan

Pres. Subj.:   huya, huyas, huya, huyamos, huyáis, huyan
Imp. Subj.:   huyera(-ese), huyeras, huyera, huyéramos, huyerais, huyeran
Verbs that follow the same pattern: **atribuir, concluir, constituir, construir, contribuir, destituir, destruir, disminuir, distribuir, excluir, incluir, influir, instruir, restituir, sustituir.**

11. Verbs ending in **-eír** lose the **e** in the third-person singular and plural of the preterit, in all persons of the imperfect subjunctive, and in the present participle.

reír   *to laugh*
Pres Ind.:   río, ríes, ríe, reímos, reís, ríen
Preterit: reí, reíste, rio, reímos, reísteis, rieron
Pres. Subj.:   ría, rías, ría, riamos, riáis, rían
Imp. Subj.:   riera(-ese), rieras, riera, riéramos, rierais, rieran
Pres. Part.:   riendo
Verbs that follow the same pattern: **freír, sonreír.**

12. Verbs ending in **-iar** add a written accent to the **i,** except in the first- and second-persons plural of the present indicative and subjunctive.

fiar(se)   *to trust*
Pres. Ind.:   (me) fío, (te) fías, (se) fía, (nos) fiamos, (os) fiáis, (se) fían
Pres. Subj.:   (me) fíe, (te) fíes, (se) fíe, (nos) fiemos, (os) fiéis, (se) fíen
Verbs that follow the same pattern: **ampliar, criar, desviar, enfriar, enviar, guiar, telegrafiar, vaciar, variar.**

13. Verbs ending in **-uar** (except **-guar**) add a written accent to the **u,** except in the first- and second-persons plural of the present indicative and subjunctive.

actuar   *to act*
Pres. Ind.:   actúo, actúas, actúa, actuamos, actuáis, actúan
Pres. Subj.:   actúe, actúes, actúe, actuemos, actuéis, actúen
Verbs that follow the same pattern: **acentuar, continuar, efectuar, exceptuar, graduar, habituar, insinuar, situar.**

14. Verbs ending in **-ñir** lose the **i** of the diphthongs **ie** and **ió** in the third-person singular and plural of the preterit and all persons of the imperfect subjunctive. They also change the **e** of the stem to **i** in the same persons in the present indicative and present subjunctive.

teñir   *to dye*
Pres. Ind.:   tiño, tiñes, tiñe, teñimos, teñís, tiñen
Preterit: teñí, teñiste, tiñó, teñimos, teñisteis, tiñeron
Pres. Subj.:   tiña, tiñas, tiña, tiñamos, tiñáis, tiñan
Imp. Subj.:   tiñera(-ese), tiñeras, tiñera, tiñéramos, tiñerais, tiñeran
Verbs that follow the same pattern: **ceñir, constreñir, desteñir, estreñir, reñir.**

Some Common Irregular Verbs

Only those tenses with irregular forms are given below.

adquirir   *to acquire*
Pres. Ind.:   adquiero, adquieres, adquiere, adquirimos, adquirís, adquieren
Pres. Subj.:   adquiera, adquieras, adquiera, adquiramos, adquiráis, adquieran
Imperative: adquiere, adquiera, adquiramos, adquirid, adquieran

andar   *to walk*
Preterit: anduve, anduviste, anduvo, anduvimos, anduvisteis, anduvieron
Imp. Subj.:   anduviera (anduviese), anduvieras, anduviera, anduviéramos, anduvierais, anduvieran

avergonzarse   *to be ashamed, to be embarrassed*
Pres. Ind.:   me avergüenzo, te avergüenzas, se avergüenza, nos avergonzamos, os
avergonzáis, se avergüenzan
Pres. Subj: me avergüence, te avergüences, se avergüence, nos avergoncemos, os
avergoncéis, se avergüencen
Imperative: avergüénzate, avergüéncese, avergoncémonos, avergonzaos, avergüénense

caber   *to fit, to have enough room*
Pres. Ind.:   quepo, cabes, cabe cabemos, cabéis, caben
Preterit: cupe, cupiste, cupo, cupimos, cupisteis, cupieron
Future: cabré, cabrás, cabrá, cabremos, cabréis, cabrán
Conditional: cabría, cabrías, cabría, cabríamos, cabríais, cabrían
Imperative: cabe, quepa, quepamos, cabed, quepan
Pres. Subj.:   quepa, quepas, quepa, quepamos, quepáis, quepan
Imp. Subj.:   cupiera (cupiese), cupieras, cupiera, cupiéramos, cupierais, cupieran

caer   *to fall*
Pres. Ind.:   caigo, caes, cae, caemos, caéis, caen
Preterit: caí, caíste, cayó, caímos, caísteis, cayeron
Imperative: cae, caiga, caigamos, caed, caigan
Pres. Subj.:   caiga, caigas, caiga, caigamos, caigáis, caigan
Imp. Subj.:   cayera (cayese), cayeras, cayera, cayéramos, cayerais, cayeran
Past Part.:   caído

conducir   *to guide, to drive*
Pres. Ind.:   conduzco, conduces, conduce, conducimos, conducís, conducen
Preterit: conduje, condujiste, condujo, condujimos, condujisteis, condujeron
Imperative: conduce, conduzca, conduzcamos, conducid, conduzcan
Pres. Subj.:   conduzca, conduzcas, conduzca, conduzcamos, conduzcáis, conduzcan
Imp. Subj.:   condujera (condujese), condujeras, condujera, condujéramos, condu-
jerais, condujeran
(All verbs ending in **-ducir** follow this pattern.)

convenir   *to agree (see* **venir***)*

dar   *to give*
Pres. Ind.:   doy, das, da, damos, dais, dan
Preterit: di, diste, dio, dimos, disteis, dieron
Imperative: da, dé, demos, dad, den
Pres. Subj.:   dé, des, dé, demos, deis, den
Imp. Subj.:   diera (diese), dieras, diera, diéramos, dierais, dieran

decir   *to say, tell*
Pres. Ind.:   digo, dices, dice, decimos, decís, dicen
Preterit: dije, dijiste, dijo, dijimos, dijisteis, dijeron
Future: diré, dirás, dirá, diremos, diréis, dirán
Conditional: diría, dirías, diría, diríamos, diríais, dirían
Imperative: di, diga, digamos, decid, digan
Pres. Subj.:   diga, digas, diga, digamos, digáis, digan
Imp. Subj.:   dijera (dijese), dijeras, dijera, dijéramos, dijerais, dijeran
Pres. Part.:   diciendo
Past Part.:   dicho

detener   *to stop; to hold; to arrest (see* **tener***)*

entretener   *to entertain, amuse (see* **tener***)*

errar *to err; to miss*
Pres. Ind.:   yerro, yerras, yerra, erramos, erráis, yerran
Imperative: yerra, yerre, erremos, errad, yerren
Pres. Subj.:   yerre, yerres, yerre, erremos, erréis, yerren

estar *to be*
Pres. Ind.:   estoy, estás, está, estamos, estáis, están
Preterit: estuve, estuviste, estuvo, estuvimos, estuvisteis, estuvieron
Imperative: está, esté, estemos, estad, estén
Pres. Subj.:   esté, estés, esté, estemos, estéis, estén
Imp. Subj.:   estuviera (estuviese), estuvieras, estuviera, estuviéramos, estuvierais, estuvieran

haber *to have*
Pres. Ind.:   he, has, ha, hemos, habéis, han
Preterit: hube, hubiste, hubo, hubimos, hubisteis, hubieron
Future: habré, habrás, habrá, habremos, habréis, habrán
Conditional: habría, habrías, habría, habríamos, habríais, habrían
Pres. Subj.:   haya, hayas, haya, hayamos, hayáis, hayan
Imp. Subj.:   hubiera (hubiese), hubieras, hubiera, hubiéramos, hubierais, hubieran

hacer *to do, to make*
Pres. Ind.:   hago, haces, hace, hacemos, hacéis, hacen
Preterit: hice, hiciste, hizo, hicimos, hicisteis, hicieron
Future: haré, harás, hará, haremos, haréis, harán
Imperative: haz, haga, hagamos, haced, hagan
Pres. Subj.:   haga, hagas, haga, hagamos, hagáis, hagan
Imp. Subj.:   hiciera (hiciese), hicieras, hiciera, hiciéramos, hicierais, hicieran
Past Part.:   hecho

imponer *to impose; to depose (see* **poner***)*

ir *to go*
Pres. Ind.:   voy, vas, va, vamos, vais, van
Imp. Ind.:   iba, ibas, iba, íbamos, ibais, iban
Preterit: fui, fuiste, fue, fuimos, fuisteis, fueron
Imperative: ve, vaya, vayamos, id, vayan
Pres. Subj.:   vaya, vayas, vaya, vayamos, vayáis, vayan
Imp. Subj.:   fuera (fuese), fueras, fuera, fuéramos, fuerais, fueran

jugar *to play*
Pres. Ind.:   juego, juegas, juega, jugamos, jugáis, juegan
Imperative: juega, juegue, juguemos, jugad, jueguen
Pres. Subj.:   juegue, juegues, juegue, juguemos, juguéis, jueguen

obtener *to obtain (see* **tener***)*

oír *to hear*
Pres. Ind.:   oigo, oyes, oye, oímos, oís, oyen
Preterit: oí, oíste, oyó, oímos, oísteis, oyeron
Imperative: oye, oiga, oigamos, oíd, oigan
Pres. Subj.:   oiga, oigas, oiga, oigamos, oigáis, oigan
Imp. Subj.:   oyera (oyese), oyeras, oyera, oyéramos, oyerais, oyeran
Pres. Part.:   oyendo
Past Part.:   oído

oler *to smell*
Pres. Ind.:   huelo, hueles, huele, olemos, oléis, huelen
Imperative: huele, huela, olamos, oled, huelan
Pres. Subj.:   huela, huelas, huela, olamos, oláis, huelan

poder *to be able to*
Preterit: pude, pudiste, pudo, pudimos, pudisteis, pudieron
Future: podré, podrás, podrá, podremos, podréis, podrán

Conditional: podría, podrías, podría, podríamos, podríais, podrían
Imperative: puede, pueda, podamos, poded, puedan
Pres. Subj.: pueda, puedas, pueda, podamos, podáis, puedan
Imp. Subj.: pudiera (pudiese), pudieras, pudiera, pudiéramos, pudierais, pudieran
Pres. Part.: pudiendo

poner *to place, put*
Pres. Ind.: pongo, pones, pone, ponemos, ponéis, ponen
Preterit: puse, pusiste, puso, pusimos, pusisteis, pusieron
Future: pondré, pondrás, pondrá, pondremos, pondréis, pondrán
Conditional: pondría, pondrías, pondría, pondríamos, pondríais, pondrían
Imperative: pon, ponga, pongamos, poned, pongan
Pres. Subj.: ponga, pongas, ponga, pongamos, pongáis, pongan
Imp. Subj.: pusiera (pusiese), pusieras, pusiera, pusiéramos, pusierais, pusieran
Past Part.: puesto

querer *to want, wish; to like, love*
Preterit: quise, quisiste, quiso, quisimos, quisisteis, quisieron
Future: querré, querrás, querrá, querremos, querréis, querrán
Conditional: querría, querrías, querría, querríamos, querríais, querrían
Imp. Subj.: quisiera (quisiese), quisieras, quisiera, quisiéramos, quisierais, quisieran

resolver *to decide on*
Past Part.: resuelto

saber *to know*
Pres. Ind.: sé, sabes, sabe, sabemos, sabéis, saben
Preterit: supe, supiste, supo, supimos, supisteis, supieron
Future: sabré, sabrás, sabrá, sabremos, sabréis, sabrán
Conditional: sabría, sabrías, sabría, sabríamos, sabríais, sabrían
Imperative: sabe, sepa, sepamos, sabed, sepan
Pres. Subj.: sepa, sepas, sepa, sepamos, sepáis, sepan
Imp. Subj.: supiera (supiese), supieras, supiera, supiéramos, supierais, supieran

salir *to leave; to go out*
Pres. Ind.: salgo, sales, sale, salimos, salís, salen
Future: saldré, saldrás, saldrá, saldremos, saldréis, saldrán
Conditional: saldría, saldrías, saldría, saldríamos, saldríais, saldrían
Imperative: sal, salga, salgamos, salid, salgan
Pres. Subj.: salga, salgas, salga, salgamos, salgáis, salgan

ser *to be*
Pres. Ind.: soy, eres, es, somos, sois, son
Imp. Ind.: era, eras, era, éramos, erais, eran
Preterit: fui, fuiste, fue, fuimos, fuisteis, fueron
Imperative: sé, sea, seamos, sed, sean
Pres. Subj.: sea, seas, sea, seamos, seáis, sean
Imp. Subj.: fuera (fuese), fueras, fuera, fuéramos, fuerais, fueran

suponer *to assume (see* **poner***)*

tener *to have*
Pres. Ind.: tengo, tienes, tiene, tenemos, tenéis, tienen
Preterit: tuve, tuviste, tuvo, tuvimos, tuvisteis, tuvieron
Future: tendré, tendrás, tendrá, tendremos, tendréis, tendrán
Conditional: tendría, tendrías, tendría, tendríamos, tendríais, tendrían
Imperative: ten, tenga, tengamos, tened, tengan
Pres. Subj.: tenga, tengas, tenga, tengamos, tengáis, tengan
Imp. Subj.: tuviera (tuviese), tuvieras, tuviera, tuviéramos, tuvierais, tuvieran

traducir   *to translate (see* **conducir***)*

traer   *to bring*
Pres. Ind.:   traigo, traes, trae, traemos, traéis, traen
Preterit: traje, trajiste, trajo, trajimos, trajisteis, trajeron
Imperative: trae, traiga, traigamos, traed, traigan
Pres. Subj.: traiga, traigas, traiga, traigamos, traigáis, traigan
Imp. Subj.: trajera (trajese), trajeras, trajera, trajéramos, trajerais, trajeran
Pres. Part.: trayendo
Past Part.:   traído

valer   *to be worth*
Pres. Ind.:   valgo, vales, vale, valemos, valéis, valen
Future: valdré, valdrás, valdrá, valdremos, valdréis, valdrán
Conditional: valdría, valdrías, valdría, valdríamos, valdríais, valdrían
Imperative: vale, valga, valgamos, valed, valgan
Pres. Sub.:   valga, valgas, valga, valgamos, valgáis, valgan

venir   *to come*
Pres. Ind.:   vengo, vienes, viene, venimos, venís, vienen
Preterit: vine, viniste, vino, vinimos, vinisteis, vinieron
Future: vendré, vendrás, vendrá, vendremos, vendréis, vendrán
Conditional: vendría, vendrías, vendría, vendríamos, vendríais, vendrían
Imperative: ven, venga, vengamos, venid, vengan
Pres. Subj.: venga, vengas, venga, vengamos, vengáis, vengan
Imp. Subj.: viniera (viniese), vinieras, viniera, viniéramos, vinierais, vinieran
Pres. Part.: viniendo

ver   *to see*
Pres. Ind.:   veo, ves, ve, vemos, veis, ven
Imp. Ind.:   veía, veías, veía, veíamos, veíais, veían
Preterit: vi, viste, vio, vimos, visteis, vieron
Imperative: ve, vea, veamos, ved, vean
Pres. Subj.: vea, veas, vea, veamos, veáis, vean
Imp. Subj.: viera (viese), vieras, viera, viéramos, vierais, vieran
Past Part.:   visto

volver   *to return*
Past Part.:   vuelto

APPENDIX C

GLOSSARY OF GRAMMATICAL TERMS

adjective: A word that is used to describe a noun: *tall* girl, *difficult* lesson.

adverb: A word that modifies a verb, an adjective, or another adverb. It answers the questions "How?" "When?" "Where?": She walked *slowly*. She'll be here *tomorrow*. She is *here*.

agreement: A term applied to changes in form that nouns cause in the words that surround them. In Spanish, verb forms agree with their subjects in person and number (**yo** habl**o**, **él** habl**a**, etc.). Spanish adjectives agree in gender and number with the noun they describe. Thus, a feminine plural noun requires a feminine plural ending in the adjective that describes it (ca**s**as amarilla**s**) and a masculine singular noun requires a masculine singular ending in the adjective (libro negr**o**).

auxiliary verb: A verb that helps in the conjugation of another verb: I *have* finished. He *was* called. She *will* go. He *would* eat.

command form: The form of the verb used to give an order or a direction: *Go! Come* back! *Turn* to the right!

conjugation: The process by which the forms of the verb are presented in their different moods and tenses: I *am*, you *are*, he *is*, she *was*, we *were*, etc.

contraction: The combination of two or more words into one: *isn't, don't, can't*.

definite article: A word used before a noun indicating a definite person or thing: *the* woman, *the* money.

demonstrative: A word that refers to a definite person or object: *this, that, these, those*.

diphthong: A combination of two vowels forming one syllable. In Spanish, a diphthong is composed of one *strong* vowel (**a, e, o**) and one *weak* vowel (**u, i**) or two weak vowels: **ei, ua, ui**.

exclamation: A word used to express emotion: *How* strong! *What* beauty!

gender: A distinction of nouns, pronouns, and adjectives, based on whether they are masculine or feminine.

indefinite article: A word used before a noun that refers to an indefinite person or object: *a* child, *an* apple.

infinitive: The form of the verb generally preceded in English by the word *to* and showing no subject or number: *to do, to bring*.

interrogative: A word used in asking a question: *Who? What? Where?*

main clause: A group of words that includes a subject and a verb and by itself has complete meaning: *They saw me. I go now.*

noun: A word that names a person, place, or thing: *Ann, London, pencil*.

number: Refers to singular and plural: *chair, chairs*.

object: Generally a noun or a pronoun that is the receiver of the verb's action. A direct object answers the question *"What?"* or *"Whom?"*: We know *her*. Take *it*. An indirect object answers the question *"To whom?"* or *"To what?"*: Give *John* the money. Nouns and pronouns can also be objects of prepositions: The letter is *from Rick*. I'm thinking *about you*.

past participle: Past forms of a verb: *gone, worked, written*.

person: The form of the pronoun and of the verb that shows the person referred to: *I* (first-person singular), *you* (second-person singular), *she* (third-person singular), and so on.

possessive: A word that denotes ownership or possession: This is *our* house. The book isn't *mine*.

preposition: A word that introduces a noun or pronoun and indicates its function in the sentence: They were *with* us. She is *from* Nevada.

present participle: A verb form in English that ends in *-ing: eating, sleeping, working*. In Spanish, this form cannot be used as a noun or after a preposition.

pronoun: A word that is used to replace a noun: *she, them, us*, and so on. A **subject pronoun** refers to the person or thing spoken of: *They* work. An **object pro-**

noun receives the action of the verb: They arrested *us* (direct object pronoun). She spoke to *him* (indirect object pronoun). A pronoun can also be the object of a preposition: The children stayed with *us*.

reflexive pronoun: A pronoun that refers back to the subject: *myself, yourself, himself, herself, itself, ourselves,* and so on.

subject: The person, place, or thing spoken of: *Robert* works. *Our car* is new.

subordinate clause: A clause that has no complete meaning by itself but depends on a main clause: They knew *that I was here.*

tense: The group of forms in a verb that show the time in which the action of the verb takes place: *I go* (present indicative), *I'm going* (present progressive), *I went* (past), *I was going* (past progressive), *I will go* (future), *I would go* (conditional), *I have gone* (present perfect), *I had gone* (past perfect), *that I may go* (present subjunctive), and so on.

verb: A word that expresses an action or a state: We *sleep.* The baby *is* sick.

APPENDIX D   ENGLISH TRANSLATIONS OF DIALOGUES

Lección preliminar

GREETINGS AND FAREWELLS

At the university

Good morning, Professor.
Good morning, Miss. What is your name?
My name is María Teresa Rojas.

Good afternoon, Doctor Vegas.
Good afternoon, ma'am. How are you?
Very well, thank you. And you?
Fine, thank you.

Good evening, Mr. Acosta.
Good evening, Ana María. How's it going?
Fine, and you?
Not very well . . .
Gee! I'm sorry.

At the club

Hi, Juan Carlos.
Hello, Silvia. How are you?
Fine, and you?
Fine, thank you.
What's new?
Nothing.
See you later.
Good-bye.

See you tomorrow, Mirta.
See you tomorrow, Daniel. Say hello to
    Roberto.

Bye, Tito.
Bye. See you on Monday.

Lección 1

THE FIRST DAY OF CLASSES

MISS A. *(At the door)* Excuse me. Good
    morning, professor.
PROF. Good morning. Come in and have
    a seat.
MISS A. Thank you very much.
PROF. Miss Alba, (this is) Dr. Díaz.
MISS A. It's a pleasure, Dr. Díaz.

DR. D. The pleasure is mine, Miss Alba.
MISS A. Excuse me, professor, what time is
    it?
PROF. It's two o'clock.
MISS A. At what time is the class today?
PROF. It's at three o'clock.

M. Where are you from?
R. We are from Ecuador. You are from
    Mexico, right?
M. Yes. Listen, how many students are
    there in the class?
R. There are forty students.
L. What's your address, Mario?
M. Ninety-eight Magnolia Street.

S. Professor, how do you say *"de
    nada"* in English?
PROF. You say, "you're welcome."
S. What does "please" mean?
PROF. It means *"por favor."*

L. Hello. My name is Laura Vargas.
    What's your name?
S. My name is Silvia Cruz.
L. Where are you from, Silvia?
S. I'm from Costa Rica, and you?
L. I'm from Chile.
S. Good-bye, Laura.
L. I'll see you later, Silvia.

Lección 2

ON THE PHONE

Raquel wishes to speak with Marta.

M. Yes?
R. Hello. Is Marta there?
M. No, she's not. I'm sorry.
R. What time is she coming back?
M. At nine o'clock at night.
R. Then I'll call later.
M. Very well. Good-bye.

Carmen speaks with her friend María.

M. Hello.
C. Hello. Is María there?
M. Yes, speaking . . . Carmen?
C. Yes. How's it going, María?

M. Very well, thank you. What's new?

C. Nothing. Listen! When are we studying English? Today?

M. Yes, and tomorrow we are studying French.

C. Where? At the university?

M. No, at Amanda's house.

C. Very well. See you later, then.

Pedro wishes to speak with Ana.

R. Hello.

P. Hello. Is Ana there?

R. Yes. Who is speaking?

P. Pedro Morales.

R. One moment, please.

A. *(To Rosa)* Who is it?

R. It's your friend Pedro.

A. Hi, Pedro. How's it going?

P. Fine, and you?

A. So-so.

P. Why? Love problems?

A. No, financial problems. I need money!

P. So do I! Listen, are you working at the hospital tonight?

A. No, I'm not working tonight. (Today, I'm not working at night.) On Mondays my boyfriend and I study at the library.

Lección 3

SUSANA APPLIES FOR A JOB

Susana and her friend Quique are talking in the college cafeteria while they eat ham and cheese sandwiches and drink coffee. The young woman is blonde, pretty, and very intelligent. Quique is tall, dark, handsome, and charming. Susana reads an ad in the paper and decides to apply for the job. Quique thinks that she shouldn't work.

> The IBM Company needs a receptionist. Must speak English and have knowledge of computers. Come or send your application to 342 Simón Bolívar Avenue, Caracas.

Q. Susana, you have four classes! You don't have time to work.

S. All my classes are in the morning. I have the afternoon free.

Q. But you have to study . . .

S. Well, my classes aren't very difficult.

Q. Dr. Peña's class is not easy!

S. It's not difficult. *(She looks at the ad.)* Simón Bolívar Avenue . . . I live near there . . .

Q. Near? You live on Sixth Street.

S. It's not (located) far. Well, I'm leaving.

Q. What time are you coming tomorrow?

S. I'm coming at nine. See you.

Q. We have a French exam and we should study. Why don't you come at eight?

S. No, because at eight I am taking my brother to the gym.

Q. Then, see you tomorrow, and good luck!

(At the IBM Company, Susana fills out the application and later calls Quique on the phone.)

Lección 4

AT A PARTY

Adela, a young Uruguayan woman, gives a New Year's Eve party at her house and invites many of her classmates from the university. At the party, Humberto and Adela talk while they dance.

A. Humberto, where is your cousin?

H. She is coming later. She has to bring my Mom.

A. She is also going to bring some CDs. Listen, where are we going to celebrate the new year?

H. We're going to go to the dance at the Yacht Club.

A. You're right! The party is there. Julio and his girlfriend are going to go, too.

H. Great! They're very nice. Besides, tomorrow is Julio's birthday.

A. Really? How old is Julio?

H. I think he's twenty-two.

A. Listen, are you hungry? Do you want chicken, hors d'oeuvres, salad . . . ? The chicken is delicious.

H. No, thank you. I'm not very hungry, but I'm thirsty.

A. Do you want a cocktail, cider, champagne, beer, sangría . . . ?

H. I prefer a soft drink.

A. What time does the dance at the Club start?

H. At ten-thirty. I'm going to call Julio and Teresa.

A. And Silvia, is she planning to go with us also?

H. No, she is not going because she is sick.

Later, at the Yacht Club, everyone celebrates the New Year.

A. This group is great. Shall we dance, Humberto?

H. Yes.

J. *(To his girlfriend)* Are you tired, Teresa?

T. No, I'm hot. Why don't we all go to the terrace now?

J. Good idea. Shall we take the drinks?

T. Yes, I'm very thirsty.

J. Don't they have grapes? In Spain we always eat twelve grapes at midnight.

M. Here in Montevideo we toast with cider.

A. It's twelve o'clock! Happy New Year!

E. Happy New Year! Happy New Year . . . !

H. And happy birthday, Julio!

Lección 5

PLANS FOR A WEEKEND

Carol, a student from the United States, is in Spain. She attends the University of Salamanca and lives in a boarding house near the Plaza Mayor. She wants to learn to speak Spanish perfectly, and that is why she never misses the opportunity to practice the language. Now she is at a café with two Spanish friends.

L. Listen, Carol, can you go with us to Madrid this weekend?

CL. I don't know . . . I have to write a lot of letters: to my grandmother, to my uncle, to my brother . . .

L. You miss your family very much, don't you?

CL. Yes, . . . especially my older brother.

CN. What is your brother like?

CL. He's blond, slim, and medium height. He is studying medicine.

CN. Very interesting! When is he coming to Spain? In the summer?

CL. No, he's going to travel to Mexico with his wife and two daughters.

CN. Bah! He's married . . . What a pity! Don't you have another brother?

CL. No, I'm sorry. Do you want to see a photograph of my nieces?

CN. Yes. *(She looks at the photo.)* They're very pretty!

CL. They start attending school on September fifteenth.

L. Listen! Why don't you come to Madrid with us? It's more interesting than writing letters . . .

CL. Are you going by car?

L. No, we prefer to go by bus. It's as comfortable as the car, it doesn't cost much, and we don't have to drive.

CL. Good idea! I never drive in Madrid. And where do you plan to go?

CN. To the Prado Museum. They have there some of the most famous paintings in the world.

L. It's very interesting! And Madrid has some very good restaurants! We always have lunch at Casa Botín.

CL. Okay. Let's go to Madrid! . . . If it doesn't rain! Because if it rains, I don't leave the house.

CN. No, dear, it isn't going to rain.

CL. When do we return?

L. Saturday night or Sunday.

Lección 6

A TRIP TO PERU

Teresa, a Mexican teacher, is going to spend her vacation in Peru. She has just arrived in Lima, where she's planning to spend a few days before going to Machu Picchu to visit the famous Incan ruins. She is now at the airport, which is big and very modern. Teresa shows her passport and then goes through customs.

At the customs desk, Teresa is talking with the inspector.

I. You must open your suitcases. Do you have anything to declare?

T. I have a camera and a tape recorder. Nothing else.

I. It's not necessary to declare them. Everything is in order.

T. Is there a tourist office near here?

I. Yes, it's over there, to the left.

At the airport they sell gold and silver objects, and Teresa buys some for her family.

At the tourist office, Teresa asks for information.

T. Good morning, sir. Do you have a list of hotels and boarding houses?

E. Yes, Miss. We also have a list of restaurants and places of interest. Here they are.

T. Thanks. Where can I find a taxi?

E. The second door on the right. There is also a bus that takes you downtown.

Teresa takes the bus and goes to a hotel downtown, where she asks for a room.

T. I need a single room with a private bathroom, please. I don't have a reservation.

E. We have one overlooking the street that costs 208 soles per day. There's also another interior one on the second floor for 130 new soles.

T. They are very expensive for me. Don't you have any cheaper rooms?

E. No, there isn't any. There are few vacant rooms now.

T. I prefer the interior room. Do you accept traveler's checks?

E. Yes, we accept them, and we also accept credit cards.

T. What is the exchange rate?

E. It's at 2.6 soles per dollar.

Teresa signs the register and asks if they have room service.

T. I want to have dinner in my room. Until what time do they serve dinner?

E. They serve it until eleven.

T. Can someone take my suitcases to the room, please?

E. Yes, the bellhop will come to take them right away. Here's the key.

Lección 7

SPEAKING OF VACATIONS

Teresa arrived yesterday from her trip to Peru, and now she is talking on the phone with her friend Silvia. The girls have been talking for a half hour, and Teresa is telling her about her trip.

T. I liked the capital very much, but I liked Machu Picchu better.

S. And you didn't send me a postcard!

T. I bought you two, but I didn't send them. Listen, I have to return (to you) the suitcase and the carry-on bag that you lent me.

S. There is no hurry. Did you take a lot of luggage?

T. Yes, I took three suitcases. I paid excess baggage fees.

S. How much did the plane ticket cost you? Did you travel first class?

T. Are you crazy? I traveled in tourist class. It cost me three thousand five hundred pesos! Round-trip, of course . . .

S. How was the flight?

T. A little long . . . And since the plane left two hours behind schedule, we arrived very late.

S. Did anything interesting happen to you in Lima?

T. Well . . . at the travel agency where I bought the ticket to Machu Picchu, I met a very charming young man.

S. Did he travel with you? You have to tell me everything that happened.

T. Yes, I traveled with him by plane to Cuzco, where we had lunch together. Then we talked during the entire train ride to Machu Picchu.

S. I don't know why your vacations are always great and my vacations are so boring.

T. Next time we have to travel together.

S. Okay, but only if we go by train or by boat. I don't like to travel by plane.

T. Okay, we'll travel by train. Listen, this Saturday, I'm going to the movies with Cecilia. Do you want to go with us?

S. Who is Cecilia?

T. She is the girl that I introduced to you at the library last month.

S. Oh, that one . . . I remember now. Yes, let's go together.

T. Do you want to go have lunch with me now?

S. No, thanks, I already had lunch.

T. Okay, then I'll see you tomorrow.

Lección 8

AT A CUBAN RESTAURANT

Today is December fifteenth. It's Lidia and Jorge Torres's wedding anniversary. They are going to dinner at one of the best restaurants in Miami to celebrate it. They arrive at the El Caribe Restaurant.

L. What a surprise! This is a very elegant restaurant!

J. And the food is excellent.

W. This way, please. Here is the menu.

L. Thanks. *(She reads the menu.)* Steak, roast lamb with mashed potatoes, stuffed turkey, shrimp . . .

J. Why don't you order a tenderloin steak? They prepare some delicious steaks here. Or lobster?

L. No, last night I went to dinner at the Ruiz's, and they served lobster.

W. I recommend to you the specialty of the house: roast pork and rice with black beans. For dessert, ice cream, caramel custard, or ice cream cake.

J. I want roast pork and rice with black beans. And you?

L. I want soup, shrimp, and rice.

W. And to drink?

J. First a vermouth and then a half bottle of red wine.

W. Very well, sir. *(He writes down the order.)*

Before eating dinner, Lidia and Jorge drink vermouth and talk.

L. Did your parents go to the party that Eva gave yesterday?

J. Yes. It was at the Los Violines Club.

L. Did they give her the bracelet (that) they bought for her in Mexico?

J. Yes, they gave it to her. She loved it.

L. Did they show it to you before they gave it to her?

J. Yes, they showed it to me when I went for them the day before yesterday in the afternoon.

L. They got it at a very good price in a very elegant store.

The waiter brings the food. After eating, Lidia and Jorge drink coffee. It's now nine o'clock. Jorge asks for the bill, pays it, leaves the waiter a good tip, and they leave. They have tickets for the theater to see a comedy. Since it is raining cats and dogs, they take a taxi.

J. Happy anniversary, my love. *(He gives her a kiss.)*

L. *(She hugs him.)* Happy anniversary, dear.

Lección 9

A VERY BUSY DAY

Although today is Saturday, Mirta and Isabel got up early to finish cleaning the apartment. Tonight, the two girls are invited to a concert at the House of Paraguayan Culture. Isabel is a little tired because last night she went to bed late.

M. Why did you come (home) so late last night? Where were you?

I. At the store. I had to buy a present for Eva because tomorrow is her birthday. Well, shall we start cleaning?

M. Yes, I'm going to sweep the kitchen and I'm going to vacuum the rug.

I. Then I'm going to clean the bathroom. Later I'm going to cook and iron my red dress. I'm going to wear it tonight.

M. I don't know what to wear.

I. Why don't you wear your blue dress? It's very pretty.

M. No, I tried it on yesterday and it doesn't fit. Oh! Where's the dustpan?

I. On the terrace. Oh! I need to bathe the dog, shower, and get dressed . . . and I have an appointment at the hairdresser's at three!

M. I want to wash my hair and I didn't remember to buy shampoo. May I use yours?

I. Yes, it's in the medicine cabinet.

M. Thanks. I couldn't go to the pharmacy yesterday.

When she arrived at the beauty parlor, Isabel asked the hairdresser for a magazine and sat down to wait for her turn.

I. *(To the hairdresser)* I want a haircut, shampoo, and set.

P. You have very straight hair. Don't you want a perm?

I. No, when I want curls, I use the curling iron. Oh, my hair is very long!

P. Short hair is in style now. *(He cuts her hair and, when he finishes, Isabel looks at herself in the mirror.)*

I. Very good! Now I want to make an appointment for my friend for next week.

P. Wednesday, February first, at nine-thirty? Generally, there are fewer people in the morning.

I. That's fine. My friend's name is Mirta Ortega.

Isabel leaves her purse on the counter. The hairdresser calls her.

P. Miss! Is this purse yours?

I. Yes, it's mine. Thank you.

Lección 10

VACATION PLANS

Marisa and Nora, two Chilean girls who live in Buenos Aires, are sitting at a café on Avenida de Mayo. They are planning their summer vacation, but they can't come to an agreement because Nora likes outdoor activities and Marisa hates them.

M. I brought some tourist brochures about excursions to Punta del Este to show (them to) you.

N. I was there last year. I liked the beach very much, but there were too many people.

M. When I was a little girl, my family and I always used to go on vacation to Montevideo or to Rio de Janeiro.

N. We generally went to the country or to the mountains. We used to camp, ride horses and bikes, fish for trout in a lake . . .

M. How horrible! For me, sleeping in a tent in a sleeping bag is like a punishment.

N. Well, do you know what I did yesterday? I bought a fishing rod to go fishing with you.

M. I have an idea. We can stay at the Hotel del Lago and you can fish while I swim in the pool.

N. Why don't we rent a cabin in the mountains for a few days? You're going to have fun . . .

M. Last year I stayed in a cabin with my family and I was terribly bored. My mother told me that I didn't know how to appreciate nature.

N. *(Kidding)* That happened because I wasn't there to teach you how to fish.

M. Luckily! Listen, seriously, we have to go to the beach because my bathing suit cost me an arm and a leg.

N. I wanted to buy myself one too, but unfortunately I couldn't go to the store.

M. I'll go with you to buy it if we leave for Punta del Este on Saturday.

N. Fine, but in July we're going to Bariloche to ski.

M. I didn't know you liked to ski . . .

N. Yes, I learned to ski last year. I met Gustavo, who was one of the instructors there.

M. No wonder you want to return! Well, let's go to the store and then we'll pack.

The girls went shopping and when they finally arrived home, it was already eight o'clock in the evening.

Lección 11

RUNNING ERRANDS

In a house on Ponce Street in San Juan, Puerto Rico, lives the Vargas family. Sergio is very tired today and wants to sleep late. His mother wants him to run several errands, so the poor boy has to get up as soon as the alarm goes off at seven in the morning.

At nine, he arrives at the dry cleaner's.

S. I'm here to pick up my clothes. Here's the claim check. *(Thinking)* I hope my trousers are ready.

E. *(Reads)* A woman's overcoat and a pair of trousers. *(To Sergio)* One moment, please. *(He comes back a while later.)* The pants are pink, right?

S. They were white when I brought them in . . . !

At ten, Sergio is in the photo section of the La Francia store.

S. I brought in a roll of color film a week ago. I hope it's ready.

E. Let's see . . . Sergio Vargas . . . ? Yes, the pictures came out very well.

S. And how much do you charge to develop a roll of film?

E. Six dollars, sir.

S. Very well. *(He looks at the photographs.)* But who is this lady? These pictures aren't mine!

At eleven, Sergio parks his motorcycle in front of the bank.

S. I want to deposit this check, which is in my mother's name. Is it necessary for her to sign it?

C. If you're going to deposit in her checking account, no.

S. Very well, that's what I want to do. I also want to withdraw two hundred dollars from my savings account.

C. You have to fill out this card.

S. I need you to give me the balance of my savings account.

C. You only have twenty dollars. I'm sorry, Mr. Vargas, but you don't have enough money.

When Sergio leaves the bank, he doesn't find his motorcycle.

S. *(Screaming)* Oh no! Somebody stole my motorcycle!

L. The young man who took (away) your motorcycle said he was your brother . . .

S. I'm an only child!

L. *(Thinking)* They look a lot like each other. I'm surprised they're not brothers.

S. *(As he walks to the police station)* Next Tuesday the thirteenth I'm not leaving the house!

Lección 12

ASKING FOR INFORMATION

Julia, a girl from Honduras, arrived in Madrid a week ago. With her Spanish friends she visited the Parque del Retiro, the Palacio Real, and the old cities of Segovia, Avila, and Toledo. At each place, she bought a pile of postcards to send to her parents and friends. Today she decided to go to the post office to send the postcards and to pick up a package and a money order.

J. *(Thinking)* I doubt that the post office is open at this hour. I think it opens at nine. *(To a gentleman who is standing on the corner)* Tell me, sir, where is the post office located?

MR. G. It's five blocks from here, at the Plaza de La Cibeles.

J. The fact is . . . I'm a foreigner, and I don't know the streets. Can you tell me how to get there?

MR. G. Oh! Continue straight ahead on this street until you get to the Plaza de Colón.

J. How many blocks?

MR. G. Two. Then turn right when you get to the traffic light, on Alcalá Street.

J. Is the post office on that street?

MR. G. Yes, right there. It's an old building, and it's across from the subway station.

At the post office, Julia speaks with the employee who is at the information window.

J. I'm here to pick up a package and a money order. My name is Julia Reyes.

E. Do you have an I.D.?

J. My passport . . . but I left it at the hotel.

E. I don't think they'll give it to you without identification.

J. Fine, I'll come back this afternoon. Where can I buy stamps?

E. Go to window number two, to the left.

At window number two, Julia asks the employee for the stamps she needs.

J. I want to send these postcards by air mail and a registered letter to Honduras.

E. It's one thousand five hundred pesetas, miss.

J. Can you tell me how to get from here to El Corte Inglés?

E. Go out through the main door, cross the Plaza de La Cibeles and walk along the Gran Vía until you get to the Plaza Callao. El Corte Inglés is next to the plaza.

At El Corte Inglés, Julia meets her friend Pilar, with whom she is going to go shopping.

J. I thought you wouldn't be here.

P. Listen, girl, it's not true that Spaniards always arrive late. Sometimes we're punctual.

The girls go up to the third floor, where the ladies' department is.

Lección 13

APARTMENT FOR RENT

Irene and Lucía, two Columbian girls who study at the Universidad Nacional Autónoma in Mexico and live in a boarding house, want to move because they need an apartment which is closer to the university.

L. Irene! In the newspaper they are advertising an apartment that has two bedrooms and is in a good neighborhood.

I. Let's see! Give me the newspaper. *(She reads the ad.)*

Classified Ads

For rent: furnished apartment: two bedrooms, living room, dining room, kitchen, and bathroom. Central heating, air conditioning. Colonia Uno. Phone 481-3520 between 1 and 5 P.M. Rent: $3200.

L. We can call to go see it.

I. I don't know . . . It's very expensive for us, Lucía. Besides, we need an apartment that has a garage . . .

L. Well, call and ask if it has a garage. Let's see . . . what's the phone number?

The following day, as soon as they return from the university, the girls go see the apartment.

L. I love the furniture and the curtains!

I. With the salary we're earning, we're not going to be able to pay the rent.

L. Then, instead of working part-time, we can work full-time.

I. You're crazy! There's nobody who can work full-time and at the same time study at the university.

L. Don't be so pessimistic, Irene!

I. I'm not pessimistic; I'm realistic. Besides, we will need money to buy blankets, sheets, pillowcases, and kitchen utensils.

L. *(She doesn't pay attention to her and goes to the kitchen.)* Irene, come to the kitchen. Look, it has a refrigerator, a microwave, a dishwasher, a new stove . . . and a big sink.

I. We can't make a decision until we see other apartments.

L. But, Irene, we're not going to find any apartment that's as good as this one.

I. Maybe, but we will not be able to pay the rent for this apartment.

L. Listen, and if we win the lottery?

I. Do me a favor, don't talk nonsense. Let's go!

L. *(Angry)* Spoilsport!

Lección 14

PLANNING A DINNER

Oscar and Jorge, two Cuban students who live in Miami, decide to go to the market to do the weekly shopping. This evening they are planning on going out with two girls, Elsa and Adela. They have a date to go to the movies, but first they are going to cook dinner for them at their apartment. The supermarket opens at nine, and the boys are the first to arrive.

O. We need many things: butter, milk, a dozen eggs, bread, sugar . . .

J. Aren't we going to buy meat?

O. Yes, let's buy meat, fish, and chicken. Also oil, two cans of beans and six (cans) of tomato sauce.

J. No man, let's not buy so much tomato sauce, unless you want to eat Italian food for the rest of the month.

O. You're right. Let's see . . . we need apples, grapes, oranges, melon, grapefruit, and pears for the fruit salad . . .

J. Where are the vegetables? We have to buy lettuce, potatoes, carrots, onions, and tomatoes.

O. The tomato is not a vegetable but a fruit. Gee! Now that I think about it, this is going to cost a fortune. We'll have to go on a diet.

J. Good idea. Let's go on a diet, provided that we can eat hot dogs and hamburgers from time to time.

O. Listen, let's hurry up because we have to clean the apartment before the girls arrive.

After dinner, Oscar, Elsa, Jorge, and Adela go to the movies. Now they are standing in line to buy the tickets.

A. This movie won the prize for best film of the year.

E. It's a drama, right? I prefer comedies.

J. Next Saturday, when we go to the movies, we can see a musical.

O. No, let's not go to the movies again. Let's go to a club to dance.

A. I feel like having something to drink. Why don't we go to the Versailles cafeteria when the movie ends? My treat.

J. This is the last show, no? What time does the movie end?

O. About twelve.

As soon as the movie ends, the group goes to the cafeteria to have something to drink and to talk a while.

E. Since tomorrow is a holiday, why don't we go to the beach?

O. Yes, and let's take something to eat.

A. Perfect! As soon as I get up I'm going to prepare a Spanish omelet.

Lección 15

SHOPPING

Anita and her husband Hugo (have) opened the closet and (have) said, almost at the same time, "I have nothing to wear!" They have decided, therefore, to go shopping at El Corte Inglés, a department store which is in the center of Madrid.

When they arrive, the store is not yet open, but there are already many people (there) because there is a big sale today. At nine they enter the store. Anita takes the escalator to the first floor, where the women's department is located. Hugo stays in the men's department, which is on the ground floor.

In the women's department, Anita meets her friend Tere.

A. How's it going? Taking advantage of the sales, right? Tell me, Tere, how much does that silk blouse cost?

T. Twenty-eight hundred pesetas. What size do you wear?

A. I wear size thirty-eight. I'm going to try it on.

T. Wait, don't you like this skirt? It goes very well with the blouse, and it's a medium. Try it on. The fitting room is to the left.

A. *(From the fitting room)* Tere, do me a favor. Bring me a size thirty-six skirt.

T. Wait . . . I'm sorry, there are no smaller sizes. Why don't you try on this sweater?

A. No . . . I don't like it . . .

Anita bought the blouse, but she did not buy the skirt because it was too big on her and it was too expensive. Afterwards, she went to the shoe department because she needed to buy a pair of red shoes to match a red purse Hugo had given her.

A. Do you have any red shoes?

C. I'm sorry, Miss, but in red I only have these sandals.

A. They're pretty. I take size thirty-six. Do you have them in my size? *(To Tere)* They match my purse.

C. Yes, I'll be right back.

The clerk tries the sandals on her.

A. They're tight on me . . . They're a little narrow . . . but I'll take them.

C. Shall I wrap them for you, or do you want to wear them?

A. Wrap them *(up)* for me, please. *(To Tere)* They're a bargain!

In the men's department, Hugo has bought a wool suit, three cotton shirts, two T-shirts, a vest, and a linen jacket. He has also exchanged a pair of boots that he had bought, because they were very wide. Hugo, Anita, and Tere meet at the exit.

A. Hugo, take us to have something to eat. We're starving!

H. Me too! Wait for me here. I'll go get the car.

A. Have you ever been to the Villa Alegre restaurant?

T. Yes, it's very good. Let's go to that one.

Lección 16

CAREERS

Alina and Daniel are two young Latin Americans who are studying at the University of California in Los Angeles. Alina is Cuban and Daniel is Argentinian. They are both taking a class in business administration.

A. I'll have to register for Dr. Saldívar's sociology class. I won't be able to take Professor Wilson's class because at that time I have to take physics.

D. I would take that class with you, but I need to take other subjects. My advisor has suggested (that) I take chemistry, calculus, and geology.

A. Your major is chemistry, right? Have you always liked science?

D. Yes, my father wants me to be a lawyer, like him, but I attended law school in Buenos Aires and I didn't like it.

A. If I had followed my parent's advice, I would have studied engineering or accounting, but I decided to study journalism.

D. And you'll be a great journalist!

A. Thanks. Listen, you will have graduated by next year, right? What will you do then?

D. I want to work in a laboratory, because I like research a lot. And you? What are your plans?

A. Probably I will work for a newspaper . . . I know I'll have to worry about that later, but for the moment my plans are to finish the report I'm preparing for my literature class and to get an "A" on the psychology exam.

D. But, Alina, grades aren't the only important thing! You have to enjoy yourself a little. Would you like to come with me to the stadium tonight? There's a soccer game and our team is playing.

A. I can't. I have a scholarship and I need to maintain a good grade point average. If I get a bad grade, I'll lose the scholarship. Besides, I don't like sports.

D. Speaking of grades . . . now I remember that tomorrow I have a midterm exam in my math class.

A. I suppose you want me to lend you my calculator, as usual.

D. Thanks, buddy. I'm leaving, because David wants me to help him with his biology report, and it's late. Bye!

A. See you tomorrow. Are we having lunch together at noon?

D. Yes, by that time I'll have finished the exam and I will be free.

Lección 17

MEDICAL PROBLEMS

Mirta and her husband are in a restaurant to have lunch. She doesn't feel very well today.

M. I don't know what's wrong. I have a fever and my head hurts a lot. I already took four aspirins.

H. I told you to go to the doctor so he could give you a good check up . . .

M. Teresa suggested that I see Dr. Vargas. I have an appointment for this afternoon.

Later in Dr. Vargas' office.

DR. You have a temperature of 102 degrees. How long have you had those headaches?

M. A week. I have a cough and my throat aches. Do you think I have a cold or the flu?

DR. Yes, you have the flu. I am going to prescribe an antibiotic for you. Are you allergic to any medication?

M. Yes. I am allergic to penicillin.

DR. Are you pregnant?

M. No, doctor.

DR. Take these pills four times a day. Start taking them this very day. Here is the prescription.

In the emergency room of the same hospital. Oscar had an accident and they brought him to the hospital in an ambulance. Now he is talking with the doctor.

M. What happened to you?

O. A car hit me. My leg hurts a lot. I think I broke it.

M. We are going to take some X-rays. I see you also have a wound on your arm. I am going to call the nurse.

With the nurse

N. The doctor told me to disinfect and bandage your wound in order to avoid an infection. When was the last time you had (they gave you) a tetanus shot?

O. Two years ago.

The nurse takes Oscar to the X-ray room.

Lección 18

THIS CAR IS NO GOOD!

Gloria and Julio, a newlywed couple, are on vacation in Costa Rica. Now they're on the highway, on the way to San José.

G. Julio, you're driving very fast! The speed limit is ninety kilometers per hour. If a police officer sees you, he's going to give you a ticket!

J. Don't worry. Where are we? Do you have the map?

G. It's in the glove compartment but, according to that sign, we are forty kilometers from San José.

J. Is there a gas station nearby? The tank is almost empty.

G. It's a pity that you didn't fill the tank before . . .

J. If you had told me (it) before, I would have done it.

G. You talk as if it were my fault!

J. *(Kidding)* And who am I going to blame? Look, there's a service station . . .

Julio stops at the service station to buy gasoline.

J. *(To the attendant)* Fill the tank, please. Also, could you check the oil and the tires?

A. Yes, sir.

J. Yesterday I had a flat, and when I went to the repair shop, the mechanic told me that I needed new tires.

A. Yes, if I were you, I would change them . . . and I would also buy a new battery.

G. Gee! He also told you to fix the brakes and install a new water pump.

J. We'll do all that in San José, if it's necessary.

G. Didn't you also say that you'd change the oil filter and that you'd buy new windshield wipers?

J. If I had known that we were going to have so many problems, I would have bought a new car before leaving on this trip.

G. Yes, because we're going to spend a fortune on repairs.

J. And yesterday, the motor was making a strange noise . . . !

When Julio tries to start (it), the car doesn't work.

J. Oh, no! We'll have to call a tow truck to tow the car to San José.

G. It's not worth it. I would leave it here.

J. I agree with you! If I could, I would buy a new car right now.

APPENDIX E

ANSWER KEY TO THE SELF TESTS

Self Test Lecciones 1–3

Lección 1

A. 1. la / una   2. el / un   3. el / un   4. la / una   5. el / un   6. el / un   7. la / una   8. el / un   9. el / un   10. la / una

B. 1. los señores y las señoritas   2. unos relojes   3. las doctoras y los profesores   4. unos lápices   5. las lecciones   6. unas mujeres   7. las ventanas   8. las plumas y los cuadernos

C. treinta y dos   cincuenta y cinco cuarenta y tres   sesenta y nueve ochenta y seis   noventa y dos   setenta y uno   cien

D. eres / soy / son / Somos / es

E. 1. Es la una y media.   2. Son las tres menos cuarto.   3. Son las cuatro y diez.   4. Son las doce.   5. Son las dos y cuarto.

F. 1. f   2. i   3. g   4. a   5. c   6. e   7. h   8. k   9. m   10. l   11. d   12. j   13. b

G. 1. Inglés.   2. Las ocho.

Lección 2

A. 1. Nosotras hablamos inglés y español.   2. Uds. trabajan en el hospital.   3. Ellas llaman más tarde.   4. Ellos estudian ruso y chino.   5. Nosotros necesitamos dinero.   6. Nosotros deseamos hablar con Eva.

B. 1. la   2. las   3. la   4. los   5. la   6. el   7. la   8. las   9. el   10. el   11. las   12. los

C. 1. —¿Habla Ud. francés, Srta. Peña? —No, (yo) no hablo francés.   2. —¿Él necesita el dinero? —No, (él) no necesita el dinero.   3. —¿Ellos llaman más tarde? —No, (ellos) no llaman más tarde.   4. —¿Trabaja Ud. en la universidad, Srta. Rojas? —No, (yo) no trabajo en la universidad.

D. 1. ¿Cuál es la dirección de Javier?   2. ¿Cuál es el número de teléfono de Rosa?   3. Yo necesito los libros de Teresa.

E. 1. mis / tus   2. nuestra   3. su   4. su   5. nuestras

F. 1. el año mil cuatrocientos noventa y dos   2. el año mil setecientos setenta y seis   3. el año mil ochocientos sesenta y cinco   4. el año mil novecientos noventa y ocho   5. Calle Paz, número dos mil quinientos cincuenta y dos   6. Calle Bolívar, número cinco mil ciento veintitrés

G. 1. i   2. d   3. l   4. a   5. c   6. k   7. b   8. g   9. j   10. f   11. e   12. h

H. 1. Bueno.   2. castellano

Lección 3

A. 1. La chica es alta.   2. La doctora es española.   3. Las señoras son inglesas.   4. La profesora es mexicana.   5. Las hijas de ella no son felices.

B. 1. como   2. vive   3. aprenden   4. Beben   5. crees   6. lee   7. escribimos   8. recibe   9. decido (debo)   10. debe (decide)

C. 1. tienen   2. viene   3. tenemos   4. viene   5. tengo / vienen   6. vengo

D. 1. Yo llevo a mis hermanos a la universidad.   2. Nosotros llevamos

477

los papeles a la clase.   3. Ellos llevan a Julio y a su novia.   4. Nosotros tenemos cuatro hijos.

E. 1. al señor Varela   2. del gimnasio 3. de la biblioteca   4. a las chicas 5. del Sr. Soto

F. 1. conocimiento   2. rubio 3. solicitud   4. difícil   5. café / comen / jamón   6. lee / periódico 7. libre   8. lejos

G. 1. Nombre y apellido   2. Dirección 3. Edad   4. Ciudad (Lugar de nacimiento)   5. Estado civil 6. Profesión (Ocupación)   7. Sexo

H. 1. Marité   2. Luis Miguel Vargas Peña

Self Test Lecciones 4-6

Lección 4

A. 1. Mis compañeros de clase tienen prisa.   2. Yo no tengo hambre, pero tengo mucha sed.   3. ¿Tienes (Tiene Ud.) calor? ¡Yo tengo frío!   4. Mis amigos tienen sueño.   5. (Nosotros) no tenemos miedo.   6. (Ud.) tiene razón, Srta. Peña. Mary tiene treinta años.

B. 1. voy   2. damos   3. está   4. está 5. van   6. dan   7. estoy   8. van 9. estás   10. doy

C. 1. Yo no voy a hablar con mi mamá hoy.   2. Mis hijos van a estudiar en España.   3. Mi amiga va a leer el anuncio.   4. Uds. van a bailar en la fiesta.   5. Tú no vas a vivir cerca de la universidad.   6. Nosotros vamos a brindar con sidra.

D. 1. Ella es la mamá de María.   2. El Club Náutico está en la calle Siete. 3. ¡Hmmm! El pollo está delicioso. 4. Roberto es de España y ahora está en California.   5. La cerveza está fría. 6. El escritorio es de metal.   7. Hoy es martes y mañana es miércoles. 8. Elsa es profesora.   9. La fiesta es

en casa de Lucía.   10. La orquesta es magnífica.   11. Ellos están enfermos. 12. María Laura es uruguaya.

E. 1. quiere (piensa)   2. entendemos (empezamos, comenzamos)   3. pierde 4. Cierras   5. empiezan (comienzan) 6. empezamos (comenzamos) 7. pienso (quiero)   8. preferimos (queremos, pensamos)

F. 1. Invitamos   2. comemos   3. sidra 4. magnífica   5. Nuevo   6. cocteles 7. brindamos   8. discos compactos

G. 1. no existe   2. santo   3. no existe 4. ¡Salud!

Lección 5

A. 1. conduzco   2. sé   3. quepo 4. salgo   5. traduzco   6. veo 7. hago   8. pongo   9. conozco 10. traigo

B. 1. sé   2. conoce / sabe 3. conoce / sabe   4. saben

C. 1. Alfredo es el estudiante más inteligente de la clase.   2. La Lección 2 es menos interesante que la Lección 7.   3. Mi novia es más bonita que tu novia.   4. Roberto es el más guapo de la familia.   5. El profesor tiene menos de veinte estudiantes.   6. Ana es tan alta como Roberto.

D. 1. más grande   2. mejor   3. mejor / peor   4. mayor   5. más pequeño

E. 1. cuesta   2. pueden   3. Recuerda 4. cuento   5. almorzamos 6. vuelves

F. 1. nieto   2. las pinturas   3. cartas 4. almorzar   5. echas de menos 6. ¡Qué lástima!   7. conducen su auto 8. fotos   9. conocen   10. mediana

G. 1. V   2. F   3. F   4. V   5. V

Lección 6

A. 1. En el restaurante México sirven la cena a las nueve.   2. Ella pide una habitación con vista a la calle.

3. (Nosotros) seguimos al botones a la habitación.   4. ¿Consiguen Uds. reservaciones en diciembre?   5. (Yo) digo que él debe firmar el registro ahora.

B. 1. mí   2. ti   3. ellos   4. nosotros   5. conmigo   6. contigo

C. 1. Ellos van a querer algo.   2. Hay alguien en el baño.   3. Tengo algunos objetos de oro y de plata.   4. Ellos siempre pasan por la aduana.   5. Yo también ceno a las nueve.   6. Siempre tiene las listas de los hoteles. 7. Puedes ir o a la derecha o a la izquierda.   8. Ellos siempre quieren algo también.

D. 1. está diciendo   2. estoy hablando 3. estamos leyendo   4. estás comiendo   5. está durmiendo 6. están pidiendo

E. 1. comprarlo   2. te llamo   3. la sirven   4. declararla   5. me lleva 6. las necesito   7. los aceptan 8. llevarlo   9. las tengo 10. llamarla

F. 1. b   2. a.   3. b   4. c   5. b   6. a 7. b   8. a   9. a   10. b   11. c 12. c

G. 1. Perú   2. 25%   3. dólar   4. fácil

Self Test Lecciones 7–9

Lección 7

A. 1. estas tarjetas y aquéllas   2. esa maleta y ésta   3. estas agencias de viajes y aquéllas   4. este avión y aquél 5. este barco y ése   6. estas cartas y ésas

B. 1. Ella les trae la lista.   2. Yo te voy a preparar (voy a prepararte) un sándwich.   3. Él le trae el equipaje. 4. Ana me va a comprar (va a comprarme) las tarjetas.   5. El agente de viajes nos trae los pasajes.   6. Les traen los cheques de viajeros.

C. 1. No me gusta esa agencia de viajes. 2. A él le gusta el asiento de pasillo. 3. ¿Le (Te) gusta este bolso de mano? 4. No nos gusta viajar por avión. 5. ¿Les gusta (a ellos) su hotel?

D. 1. Hace dos días que yo no duermo. 2. Hace un mes que tú no me llamas. 3. Hace media hora que nosotros estamos aquí.   4. Hace un año que ellos viven en España.   5. Hace doce horas que mi hija no come.

E. 1. Ayer Luisa y yo compramos los billetes.   2. La semana pasada yo viajé.   3. Ayer ella me presentó a sus padres.   4. ¿No pagaron Uds. los pasajes ayer?   5. Al mediodía ellos abrieron las ventanas.   6. El lunes nosotros comimos en la cafetería. 7. ¿Empezaste a estudiar esta mañana? 8. Ayer yo le presté las maletas.

F. 1. viajes   2. Buen viaje   3. turista 4. ida   5. retraso   6. devolver 7. próxima   8. salida   9. mano 10. aburridas   11. exceso 12. barco

G. 1. Cuzco está situada a más de diez mil pies de altura.   2. Es la antigua capital del imperio de los incas.   3. Es un gran centro turístico y artístico. 4. Se conoce como "la ciudad perdida de los incas".   5. Se extendió desde el sur de Colombia hasta el norte de Chile y Argentina.

Lección 8

A. 1. Se lo van a mandar (Van a mandárselo) mañana.   2. Elsa me las va a comprar (va a comprármelas). 3. Luis nos las va a traducir (va a traducírnoslas).   4. Se (Te) lo voy a traer (voy a traérselo / traértelo) esta tarde.   5. La profesora me la va a dar (va a dármela).

B. 1. Nosotros fuimos al restaurante y comimos pavo asado.   2. Él no fue mi profesor el año pasado.   3. ¿Tú le diste la botella, querido?   4. ¿Quién pidió el bistec? ¿Fue Ud., señorita? 5. Nosotras no le dimos el flan a Pedro.   6. Yo fui al teatro.   7. Yo no le di la cuenta.   8. ¿Fuiste tú al restaurante anoche?   9. Ellos fueron a la fiesta la semana pasada.   10. ¿Raúl y Eva fueron mis estudiantes el año pasado?   11. Yo te di la propina.   12. Ellos nos dieron una torta helada.

C. 1. ¿Durmieron ellos en el hotel el jueves?   2. Los chicos siguieron a sus padres a la tienda.   3. Nosotros servimos / pedimos sándwiches de jamón y queso.   4. Ella me mintió. No tiene viente años; tiene diez y siete.   5. ¿No consiguió Ud. el dinero para ir de vacaciones?   6. ¿Qué le pidieron los niños a Santa Claus?   7. El hombre murió en un accidente.   8. Ella me repitió la pregunta.

D. 1. Llueve   2. Hace mucho frío   3. calor   4. nieva   5. hace mucho sol   6. lluvia

E. para / para / por / para / por / Por / para / para / por / para / por / por / por / para

F. 1. s   2. i   3. a   4. m   5. q   6. t   7. o   8. d   9. g   10. h   11. c   12. f   13. b   14. r   15. e   16. k   17. n   18. j   19. l   20. p

G. l. latinoamericanos   2. cubanos   3. después   4. sobremesa   5. 10%

Lección 9

A. 1. Tú te vistes muy bien.   2. Ellos se afeitan todos los días.   3. Ellos se acuestan a las once.   4. ¿Ud. no se preocupa por sus hijos?   5. Yo me pongo el vestido.   6. Juan se sienta aquí.   7. Tú te lavas la cabeza todos los días.   8. Yo no me corté el pelo.   9. Yo no me acordé de eso.   10. Uds. se fueron.   11. ¿Cómo te llamas (tú)?   12. Daniel no se despertó hasta las diez.

B. 1. ¿Tú te quitas el suéter?   2. El barbero me corta el pelo.   3. La peluquera me lava la cabeza.   4. Uds. no se lavan las manos.   5. Nosotros preferimos el té.   6. Las madres se preocupan por sus hijos.   7. La comunicación es lo más importante.

C. 1. El mío   2. las suyas   3. las nuestras   4. las tuyas   5. los nuestros   6. El suyo

D. 1. tuvieron   2. estuvieron   3. traduje   4. pude   5. pusiste   6. hubo   7. hizo   8. vino   9. no dijeron   10. trajo

E. 1. tercer   2. quinto   3. cuarto   4. décimo   5. octavo   6. primer

F. 1. escoba   2. lavado / peinado   3. moda   4. aspiradora   5. cocinar   6. champú   7. lacio   8. revista   9. peine   10. máquina (crema) / afeitar 11. regalo

G. 1. F   2. V   3. F   4. F   5. V

Self Test Lecciones 10–12

Lección 10

A. 1. especialmente   2. frecuentemente   3. lenta y claramente   4. recientemente   5. Generalmente   6. Desafortunadamente

B. 1. acampábamos / gustaba   2. montaba / pescaba   3. se divertían   4. veíamos   5. era / iba   6. vivíamos / asistía   7. trabajábamos   8. servías

C. 1. vino / conversamos   2. fueron   3. Eran / llegué   4. dijo / quería   5. era / vivía   6. dijo / estaba   7. hubo   8. estuvimos   9. íbamos / vimos   10. era / empezaron

D. 1. Yo conocí a mi esposo en 1995.   2. Ana no quiso ir a la fiesta anoche; se quedó en casa.   3. Carlos no sabía que ella era casada.

E. 1. l   2. h   3. o   4. a   5. j   6. b   7. d   8. n   9. c   10. m   11. e   12. f   13. i   14. g   15. k   16. p

F. 1. Argentina, Chile y Uruguay   2. Durante los meses de junio, julio y agosto.

Lección 11

A. 1. Hace dos días que ellos depositaron el dinero.   2. Hace tres meses que él reveló esos rollos.   3. Hace una semana que mi perro murió.   4. ¿Cuánto tiempo hace que Ud. vio a su padre?   5. ¿Cuánto tiempo hace que ellos robaron la motocicleta?

B. 1. vayas   2. abrir   3. depositar   4. lo compremos   5. fechen / firmen   6. yo le pague   7. pagarle   8. depositen   9. ahorrar   10. traiga   11. yo lleve   12. estacione (aparque / parquee)   13. cobrarles   14. dejes   15. abrir   16. salga   17. ahorren   18. viva

C. 1. —Espero que Ud. tenga el comprobante, Sr. Vega.   2. —(Yo) siento que ellos no puedan quedarse.   3. —Tememos que Juana no venga.   4. —Me alegro de que tú no tengas que pedir prestado dinero, querido(-a).   5. —Espero que las fotos estén listas.

D. 1. despertador   2. corriente   3. firma   4. diligencias   5. saldo   6. cajero automático   7. revelar   8. plazos   9. frente   10. parezca   11. robaron   12. estacionar (aparcar / parquear)   13. quedarme

E. 1. Borinquen   2. el español y el inglés   3. Están encargados de emitir el dinero y de controlar la actividad de los bancos comerciales.

Lección 12

A. 1. mande   2. Estén   3. Vaya   4. camine / doble   5. sean   6. Caminen   7. Compre   8. Cierren   9. den   10. deje

B. 1. Tráigamelas   2. Désela   3. Escríbanselas   4. Llévesela   5. Dígale   6. Déjelo   7. no se lo diga   8. No me los traiga

C. 1. Ésta es la señorita que le va a dar los pantalones.   2. Éstos son los vestidos que están de moda.   3. Ayer vi a las profesoras de quienes ellos nos hablaron.   4. Ésta es la señora a quien yo le mostré las fotos.   5. Él compró una maleta que es cara.

D. 1. No creo que el correo quede en la esquina.   2. Es verdad que ella está en la oficina de correos.   3. Dudo que tengamos que subir.   4. Niego que él maneje muy bien.   5. No estoy seguro de que Luis sepa dónde está el paquete.   6. No es verdad que necesitemos un documento de identidad.

E. 1. ¿Qué idioma se habla en Chile?   2. ¿A qué hora se cierran los bancos?   3. ¿A qué hora se abre el correo?   4. ¿Dónde se venden sellos?   5. ¿Por dónde se sube al segundo piso?

F. 1. l   2. g   3. o   4. i   5. c   6. a   7. k   8. e   9. b   10. d   11. m   12. h   13. f   14. j   15. n   16. p

G. 1. la fuente de La Cibeles   2. el metro   3. el Palacio Real   4. Segovia

Self Test Lecciones 13–15

Lección 13

A. 1. Dime   2. Haz / limpia   3. Sal   4. Ve / compra   5. Ponlos   6. Ven   7. Sé / tráeme   8. Ten / Espérame   9. No compres   10. No lo sirvas   11. No te vayas   12. Levántate / trabaja

B. 1. ¿Cuál es su (tu) número de teléfono?   2. ¿Cuál es el apellido de su (tu) madre?   3. ¿Qué es un pasaporte?   4. ¿Cuáles son las lecciones que Uds. necesitan?   5. ¿Cuál es su (tu) dirección?   6. ¿Qué es la paella?

C. 1. ¿Hay alguien aquí que sepa hablar español?   2. Tenemos una casa que tiene cinco dormitorios (recámaras).   3. No conozco a nadie que sea de España.   4. ¿Quiere (Quieres) una casa que tenga piscina (alberca)?   5. Necesito un sillón que sea cómodo.   6. Hay una chica que habla francés, pero no hay nadie que hable ruso.

D. 1. m 2. f 3. k 4. o 5. a 6. i
7. c 8. b 9. e 10. n 11. d
12. h 13. g 14. l 15. j 16. p

E. 1. V 2. V 3. F 4. F 5. V

Lección 14

A. 1. llegue 2. vuelvan (regresen)
3. van 4. veas 5. vendan
6. vayas 7. vean 8. necesite
9. des 10. consiga

B. 1. sino 2. pero 3. sino 4. pero
5. sino 6. sino

C. 1. Vamos al supermercado.
2. Vamos a las dos. 3. Compremos
frutas y vegetales. 4. Pidámoselo a
mamá. 5. No, no vayamos al teatro.
Vamos al cine. 6. Volvamos a las
siete. 7. Acostémonos a las once.
8. Levantémonos a las seis.

D. 1. azúcar 2. lata 3. margarina
4. verduras 5. poner 6. cita
7. película 8. feriado 9. docena
10 higiénico 11. diversiones
12. zoológico

E. 1. F 2. V 3. F 4. F 5. V

Lección 15

A. 1. escrito 2. abierto 3. visto
4. hecho 5. roto 6. ido
7. hablado 8. comido 9. bebido
(tomado) 10. recibido

B. 1. rotos 2. abiertas 3. muerto
4. cerrado 5. hechas

C. 1. has usado 2. ha envuelto 3. han
dicho 4. hemos comido 5. me he
quedado 6. han hecho

D. 1. había terminado 2. habían ido
3. había dicho 4. había abierto
5. habíamos comprado 6. habías
preguntado

E. 1. b 2. a 3. a 4. c 5. b 6. c
7. a 8. b

F. 1. al segundo piso 2. utilizar los
servicios de una modista 3. existen
4. a veces

Self Test Lecciones 16–18

Lección 16

A. 1. Le diremos la verdad. 2. ¿Qué
harán Uds.? 3. No querrán ir.
4. Lo sabré mañana. 5. No podrán
venir. 6. ¿Adónde iremos?
7. ¿Dónde lo pondrás? 8. Nosotros
vendremos con él. 9. Tendré que
trabajar. 10. Saldremos mañana.

B. 1. Yo iría a México. 2. Nosotros les
escribiríamos. 3. ¿Tú se lo dirías?
4. Ellos hablarían con Ana. 5. ¿Ud.
lo pondría en el banco? 6. ¿Uds.
vendrían el domingo? 7. Julio
pediría ensalada. 8. Nosotros lo
haríamos hoy. 9. Tú no saldrías con
ella. 10. Ella no caminaría, iría en
coche.

C. 1. habrá dicho 2. habrán vuelto
3. habré terminado 4. habremos
comido 5. habrás escrito

D. 1. Yo habría estudiado y habría
aprobado el examen. 2. Julio me
habría ayudado con el informe.
3. Luis y yo habríamos ido al partido.
4. De haber sabido que yo no tenía el
dinero, mis padres habrían pagado la
matrícula. 5. ¿Qué habrías hecho tú,
Anita?

E. 1. d 2. f 3. h 4. j 5. i 6. k
7. l 8. e 9. g 10. c 11. a
12. b

F. 1. existe 2. especializarse
3. facultades 4. especialización
5. 3 ó 6

Lección 17

A. 1. Mi amiga Marta y yo nos
escribimos frecuentemente y a veces
nos llamamos por teléfono. 2. Olga
y mi hermano se ven los domingos
pero nunca se hablan. 3. ¿Tú y tus
amigos (Ud. y sus amigos) se ayudan
los fines de semana?

B. 1. Quería que fuera con ellos. 2. Les
dije que no se preocuparan. 3. Me

alegré de que el doctor te viera hoy.
4. Temí que me pusiera una inyección.
5. Necesitaba una enfermera que
supiera español. 6. No creí que
tuvieran que desinfectarme la herida.
7. ¿Había alguien que pudiera escribir
una receta para penicilina? 8. Me
alegré de que te sintieras bien. 9. No
era verdad que necesitáramos una
ambulancia. 10. No creí que
estuviera embarazada.

C. 1. me olvido de 2. sueñan con
3. insiste en 4. venimos a 5. se
comprometió con 6. me enamoré de

D. 1. penicilina 2. los dientes 3. la
lengua 4. los ojos 5. los pies
6. la herida 7. rompiste 8. la
pierna 9. el tobillo 10. grados
11. pusieron 12. dolor de cabeza
13. el estómago 14. embarazada
15. gripe

E. 1. El gobierno subvenciona los
hospitales. 2. Van a las clínicas
privadas. 3. En muchos pueblos
remotos, la gente va a un curandero.
4. Las ayuda una partera. 5. Sí, se
pueden comprar medicinas como la
penicilina sin receta médica.

Lección 18

A. 1. Es una lástima que no hayan
encontrado el coche. 2. Me alegro
de que hayas instalado nuevos frenos,
Pedro. 3. ¿Hay alguien que haya
revisado las llantas (los neumáticos,
las gomas)? 4. Él espera que no
hayamos gastado todo el dinero.
5. No creo que hayas arreglado el
motor, Luis.

B. 1. hubiera visto 2. hubieran tenido
3. hubiéramos pagado 4. te hubieras
roto (quebrado) 5. hubiera vuelto

C. 1. tengo 2. pudiéramos
3. hubieran ido 4. quieren
5. hubieras visto 6. fuera

D. 1. Yo quería que ellos instalaran una
batería nueva (un acumulador nuevo).
2. Espero que puedan hablar con el
mecánico. 3. Dile que me llame si
quiere ir, Paquito. 4. No creo que
podamos ir al partido, pero creo que
podemos ir al cine. 5. ¿Hay alguien
que haya tomado administración de
empresas? 6. Yo voy a ayudar a mi
madre (mamá) cuando llegue a casa.
7. Le di dinero para que pudiera pagar
la multa. 8. No es cierto (verdad)
que este coche no sirva.

E. 1. velocidad 2. recién 3. frenos
4. conducir 5. servicio 6. limpiaparabrisas 7. vacío 8. maletero
9. remolcar 10. acumulador
11. guantera 12. culpa 13. vale
14. viaje 15. gasta

F. 1. contaminación 2. malas 3. cara
4. motocicleta 5. 0,6

APPENDIX F PROFESSIONS AND TRADES

accountant **contador(-a)**

actor **actor**

actress **actriz**

administrator **administrador(-a)**

agent **agente**

architect **arquitecto(-a)**

artisan **artesano(-a)**

artist **artista**

baker **panadero(-a)**

bank officer **empleado(-a), bancario(-a)**

bank teller **cajero(-a)**

banker **banquero(-a)**

barber **barbero(-a)**

bartender **barman, cantinero(-a)**

bill collector **cobrador(-a)**

bookkeeper **tenedor(-a) de libros**

brickmason (bricklayer) **albañil**

butcher **carnicero(-a)**

buyer **comprador(-a)**

camera operator **camarógrafo(-a)**

carpenter **carpintero(-a)**

cashier **cajero(-a)**

chiropractor **quiropráctico(-a)**

clerk **dependiente(-a)** *(store)*, **oficinista** *(office)*

computer operator **computista**

construction worker **obrero(-a) de la construcción**

constructor **constructor(-a)**

contractor **contratista**

cook **cocinero(-a)**

copilot **copiloto(-a)**

counselor **consejero(-a)**

dancer **bailarín(-ina)**

decorator **decorador(-a)**

dental hygienist **higienista dental**

dentist **dentista**

designer **diseñador(-a)**

detective **detective**

dietician **especialista en dietética**

diplomat **diplomático(-a)**

director **director(-a)**

dockworker **obrero(-a) portuario(-a)**

doctor **doctor(-a), médico(-a)**

draftsman **dibujante**

dressmaker **modista**

driver **conductor(-a)**

economist **economista**

editor **editor(-a)**

electrician **electricista**

engineer **ingeniero(-a)**

engineering technician **ingeniero(-a) técnico(-a)**

eye doctor **oculista**

farmer **agricultor(-a)**

fashion designer **diseñador(-a) de alta costura**

fire fighter **bombero(-a)**

fisherman **pescador(-a)**

flight attendant **auxiliar de vuelo**

foreman **capataz, encargado(-a)**

funeral director **empresario(-a) de pompas fúnebres**

garbage collector **basurero(-a)**

gardener **jardinero(-a)**

guard **guardia**

guide **guía**

hairdresser **peluquero(-a)**

home economist **economista doméstico(-a)**

housekeeper **mayordomo, ama de llaves**

inspector **inspector(-a)**

instructor **instructor(-a)**

insurance agent **agente de seguros**

interior designer **diseñador(-a) de interiores**

interpreter **intérprete**

investigator **investigador(-a)**

janitor **conserje**

jeweler **joyero(-a)**

journalist **periodista**

judge **juez(-a)**

lawyer **abogado(-a)**

librarian **bibliotecario(-a)**

machinist **maquinista**

maid **criada**

mail carrier **cartero(-a)**

manager **gerente**

mechanic **mecánico(-a)**

midwife **comadrón(-ona), partero(-a)**

miner **minero(-a)**

model **modelo**

musician **músico(-a)**

nurse **enfermero(-a)**

optician **óptico(-a)**

optometrist **optometrista**

painter **pintor(-a)**

paramedic **paramédico(-a)**

pharmacist **farmacéutico(-a)**

photographer **fotógrafo(-a)**

physical therapist **terapista físico(-a)**

physician **médico(-a)**

pilot **piloto** *(masc., fem.)*, **aviador(-a)**

plumber **plomero(-a)**

police officer **policía**

printer **impresor(-a)**

psychologist **psicólogo(-a)**

public relations agent **agente de relaciones públicas**

real estate agent **agente de bienes raíces**

receptionist **recepcionista**

reporter **reportero(-a), periodista**

sailor **marinero(-a)**

sales representative **vendedor(-a)**

scientist **científico(-a)**

secretary **secretario(-a)**

security guard **guardia**

social worker **trabajador(-a) social**

sociologist **sociólogo(-a)**

soldier **soldado, militar**

stenographer **estenógrafo(-a)**

stockbroker **bolsista**

student **estudiante**

supervisor **supervisor(-a)**

surgeon **cirujano(-a)**

systems analyst **analista de sistemas**

tailor **sastre**

taxi driver **chofer de taxi, taxista**

teacher **maestro(-a)** *(elem. school)*, **profesor(-a)** *(high school and college)*

technician **técnico(-a)**

telephone operator **telefonista**

television and radio announcer **locutor(-a)**

television and radio technician **técnico(-a) de radio y televisión**

teller **cajero(-a)**

therapist **terapista**

travel agent **agente de viajes**

truck driver **camionero(-a)**

typist **mecanógrafo(-a), dactilógrafo(-a)**

undertaker   **director(-a) de pompas fúnebres**
veterinarian   **veterinario(-a)**

waiter   **mozo, camarero**
waitress   **camarera**
watchmaker   **relojero(-a)**

worker   **obrero(-a)**
writer   **escritor(-a)**

Vocabulary

The Spanish-English vocabulary contains all active and passive vocabulary that appears in the student text. Active vocabulary includes words and expressions that appear in the vocabulary lists that follow the dialogues and in charts and word lists that are part of the grammar explanations. Passive vocabulary consists of words and expressions that are given an English gloss in photo captions, the **Panorama hispánico** and **¿Lo sabía Ud.?** sections, readings, exercises, activities, and authentic documents.

The English-Spanish Vocabulary contains only those words and expressions that are considered active.

The following abbreviations are used in the vocabularies:

abbr.	abbreviation	*inf.*	informal	*pron.*	pronoun
adj.	adjective	*lang.*	language	*p.p.*	past participle
adv.	adverb	*m.*	masculine noun	*sing.*	singular
aux.	auxiliary	*Mex.*	Mexico	*Sp.*	Spain
f.	feminine noun	*pl.*	plural	*Sp. Am.*	Spanish America
form.	formal	*prep.*	preposition		

Spanish–English

A

a at, to, 2; toward
_____ **cuadros** checked, 15
_____ **eso de** at about, 14
_____ **la española** Spanish style, 8
_____ **la(s)...** at (*hour*), 1
_____ **lunares** dotted, 15
_____ **menos que** unless, 14
_____ **menudo** often
_____ **pesar de** in spite of
_____ **plazos** in installments, 11
_____ **rayas** striped, 15
_____ **todas partes** everywhere
_____ **través de** throughout
_____ **veces** sometimes, 12
_____ **ver** let's see, 11
abajo downstairs, 12
abierto(-a) (*p.p.* of **abrir** *and adj.*) open(ed), 12
abogado(-a) (*m., f.*) lawyer, 16
abrazar to hug, 8
abrigo (*m.*) overcoat, 11
abril April, LP

abrir to open, 3
abuela (*f.*) grandmother, 5
abuelo (*m.*) grandfather, 5
aburrido(-a) boring, 7
aburrirse to be bored, 10
acabado (*m.*) decoration
acabado(-a) finished
acabar to finish
_____ **de** to have just, 6
acampar to camp, 10
accidente (*m.*) accident, 17
aceite (*m.*) oil, 14
aceituna (*f.*) olive
aceptar to accept, 6
acero (*m.*) steel
aclamar to applaud
aclarar to clarify, 4
aconsejar to advise, 11
acordarse (o:ue) (de) to remember, 9
acostar (o:ue) to put to bed, 9
_____**se** to go to bed, 9
actividad (*f.*) activity, 10
actor (*m.*) actor
actriz (*f.*) actress
actuación (*f.*) act
actualmente nowadays
actuar to perform
acumulador (*m.*) battery, 18
adelantado(-a) advanced
además besides, 4

adiós good-bye, LP
administración de empresas (*f.*) business administration, 16
admirar to admire
adolescencia (*f.*) adolescence
adónde where? (*destination*), 4
adoquinado(-a) tiled
adoquinar to tile
aduana (*f.*) customs, 6
aeropuerto (*m.*) airport, 6
afeitar(se) to shave, 9
afueras (*f. pl.*) outskirts
agencia de viajes (*f.*) travel agency, 7
agente (*m., f.*) agent
_____ **de viajes** (*m., f.*) travel agent, 7
agosto August, LP
agregar to add
agrícola (*invariable adj.*) agricultural
agua (*f.*) water
_____ **caliente** (*f.*) hot water
_____ **mineral** (*f.*) mineral water, 8
aguafiestas (*m., f.*) spoilsport, 13
águila (*f.*) eagle
ah oh, 4
ahora now, 4
_____ **mismo** right now, 18
_____ **que lo pienso** now that I think about it, 14

ahorrar to save, 11
ahorros (*m. pl.*) savings, 11
aire acondicionado (*m.*) air conditioning, 13
al (*m. sing.*) (*contraction*) to the, 3
    _____ aire libre outdoors, 10
    _____ contado in cash, 11
    _____ día a day, 17
    _____ día siguiente the following day, 13
    _____ extranjero abroad
    _____ lado de next to, 12
    _____ mismo tiempo at the same time, 13
    _____ rato a while later, 11
    _____ teléfono on the phone
ala (*f.*) wing
alberca (*f.*) (*Mex.*) swimming pool, 10
albóndiga (*f.*) meatball, 8
alcalde (*m.*) mayor
alcaldesa (*f.*) mayor
alcanzar to achieve, to reach
aldea (*f.*) small town
alegrarse (de) to be glad, 11
alegre merry
alemán (*m.*) German (*lang.*), 2
Alemania Germany, 2
alérgico(-a) allergic, 17
alfabetizar to alphabetize
alfabeto (*m.*) alphabet
alfombra (*f.*) carpet, rug, 9
algo something, anything, 6
algodón (*m.*) cotton, 15
alguien someone, somebody, anyone, 6
alguno(-a), algún any, some, 6
    alguna vez ever, 15
algunos(-as) some, 5
allí there, 3
    _____ mismo right there, 12
alma (*f.*) soul
almacén (*m.*) department store
almohada (*f.*) pillow, 13
almorzar (o:ue) to have lunch, 5
almuerzo (*m.*) lunch, 6
alojamiento (*m.*) lodging
alquilar to rent, 10
    se alquila for rent, 13
alquiler (*m.*) rent, 13
alto(-a) tall, 3; ¡Alto! Stop!, 12
altura (*f.*) height
alumno(-a) (*m., f.*) student
amante (*m., f.*) lover
amarillo(-a) yellow, LP
ambiente (*m.*) atmosphere

ambos(-as) both
ambulancia (*f.*) ambulance, 17
amigdalitis (*f.*) tonsilitis
amigo(-a) (*m., f.*) friend, 2
amistad (*f.*) friendship
amor (*m.*) love, 8
    mi _____ darling, 8
amparo (*m.*) shelter
amueblado(-a) furnished, 13
amurallado(-a) walled in
análisis (*m.*) analysis, test
anaranjado(-a) orange, LP
anciana (*f.*) old lady
ancho(-a) wide, 15
anhelar to yearn for
aniversario (*m.*) anniversary, 8
    _____ de bodas wedding anniversary, 8
anoche last night, 8
anotar to write down, 8
ansiosamente anxiously
anteayer the day before yesterday, 8
antes (de) before, 6
    _____ de que before, 14
antibiótico (*m.*) antibiotic, 17
anticipado(-a) advance
antiguo(-a) old, 12
antipático(-a) unpleasant, 3
antiquísimo(-a) ancient, very old
anunciar to announce, to advertise, 13
anuncio (*m.*) ad, 3
añadido(-a) added
año (*m.*) year, LP
    tener... _____s to be . . . years old, 4
apagar to quench
aparato electrodoméstico (*m.*) home appliance, 13
aparcar to park, 11
apartamento (*m.*) apartment, 9
apellido (*m.*) surname, 3
apenas hardly
apendicitis (*f.*) appendicitis
apio (*m.*) celery, 14
apreciar to appreciate, 10
aprender (a) to learn, 3
apretado(-a) cramped
apretar (e:ie) to be tight, 15
    me aprietan they feel tight (on me), 15
aprobar (o:ue) to pass (*an exam or course*), 16
aprovechar to take advantage of, 15
apuesta (*f.*) bet
apurarse to hurry (up), 14

apuro (*m.*): No hay apuro. There's no hurry., 7
aquel(los), aquella(s) (*adj.*) that, those (*distant*), 7
aquél(los), aquélla(s) (*pron.*) that one, those (*distant*), 7
aquello (*neuter pron.*) that, 7
aquí here, 4
    _____ las tiene. Here they are. (Here you have them.), 6
árbol (*m.*): árbol de Navidad Christmas tree, 4
arena (*f.*) sand
argentino(-a) Argentinian, 16
armario (*m.*) closet, wardrobe, 15
arrancar to start (*car*), 18; to tear out
arreglar to fix, to repair, 18
arreglo (*m.*) repair, 18
arriba upstairs, 12
arroyo (*m.*) brook
arroz (*m.*) rice, 8
    _____ con leche (*m.*) rice pudding, 8
    _____ con pollo (*m.*) chicken with rice, 8
arrugado(-a) wrinkled
arruinar to ruin
artesanía (*f.*) handicrafts
artículo (*m.*) article
    _____s deportivos (*m. pl.*) sporting goods
asado(-a) roasted, 8
ascendencia (*f.*) origin
ascensor (*m.*) elevator, 6
asegurarse to make sure
así como as well as
Asia Asia, 2
asiento (*m.*) seat
    _____ de pasillo (*m.*) aisle seat, 7
    _____ de ventanilla (*m.*) window seat, 7
    Tome _____. Have a seat., 1
asignatura (*f.*) subject, 16
asistir (a) to attend, 5
asma (*f.*) asthma
aspiradora (*f.*) vacuum cleaner, 9
aspirina (*f.*) aspirin, 17
asunto (*m.*) matter
aterrizar to land (*plane*)
atraer to attract
atraso (*m.*) delay, 7
    tener... de _____ to be . . . behind schedule, 7

atravesar (e:ie) to go through
atropellar to run over, 17
aumentar to gain
aún still
aunque although, 9
auto (*m.*) car, 5
autobús (*m.*) bus, 5
automóvil (*m.*) car, 5
autopista (*f.*) freeway, highway, 18
auxiliar de vuelo (*m., f.*) flight attendant, 7
avenida (*f.*) avenue, 3
avergonzado(-a) ashamed
avión (*m.*) plane, 7
ayer yesterday, 7
ayuda (*f.*) assistance, help, aid
ayudar (a) to help, to assist, 16
azafata (*f.*) female flight attendant, 7
azúcar (*m.*) sugar, 14
azul blue, LP

B

¡Bah! Bah!, 5
bahía (*f.*) bay
bailar to dance, 4
¿Bailamos? Shall we dance?, 4
baile (*m.*) dance, 4
bajar to descend, to go down, 12
bajo (*prep.*) under
bajo(-a) (*adj.*) short, 3
banano (*m.*) banana tree
banco (*m.*) bank, 11
bañadera (*f.*) bathtub, 6
bañar(se) to bathe, 9
baño (*m.*) bathroom, 6
_____ **María** (*m.*) double boiler
barato(-a) cheap, inexpensive, 6
barbería (*f.*) barber shop, 9
barbero(-a) (*m., f.*) barber, 9
barca de remos (*f.*) rowboat
barco (*m.*) boat, ship, 7
barrer to sweep, 9
barrio (*m.*) neighborhood, 13
barro (*m.*) clay
básquetbol (*m.*) basketball
bastante enough
bastar to be enough, suffice
batallón (*m.*) battalion
batería (*f.*) battery, 18
_____ **de cocina** (*f.*) cookware, 13
beber to drink, 3
bebida (*f.*) drink, beverage, 4
beca (*f.*) scholarship, 16

béisbol (*m.*) baseball
belleza (*f.*) beauty
salón de _____ (*m.*) beauty salon, 9
bello(-a) beautiful
Bellas Artes Fine Arts
beso (*m.*) kiss, 8
biblioteca (*f.*) library, 2
bibliotecario(-a) (*m., f.*) librarian, 16
bicicleta (*f.*) bicycle, 10
montar en _____ to ride a bicycle, 10
bien well, fine, LP; okay, 7
está _____ fine, all right, 10
muy _____ very well, LP
no muy _____ not very well, LP
billete (*m.*) ticket, 7
_____ **de ida** (*m.*) one-way ticket, 7
_____ **de ida y vuelta** (*m.*) round-trip ticket, 7
_____ **de primera clase** (*m.*) first-class ticket, 7
billetera (*f.*) wallet, 15
biología (*f.*) biology, 16
bistec (*m.*) steak, 8
blanco(-a) white, LP
blue jeans (*m. pl.*) jeans
blusa (*f.*) blouse, 15
boca (*f.*) mouth, 17
bocadillo (*m.*) (*Sp.*) sandwich, 3
boda (*f.*) wedding
boleto (*m.*) ticket (*for a show*), 8
bolsa (*f.*) (*Mex.*) purse, handbag, 9
_____ **de dormir** (*f.*) sleeping bag, 10
bolso (*m.*) purse, handbag, 9
_____ **de mano** (*m.*) carry-on bag, 7
bomba de agua (*f.*) water pump, 18
bonito(-a) pretty, 3
borrador (*m.*) eraser, 1
bosque (*m.*) forest
bota (*f.*) boot, 15
bote (*m.*) (*Mex.*) can, 14
botella (*f.*) bottle, 8
botica (*f.*) drugstore
botiquín (*m.*) medicine cabinet, 9
botones (*m.*) bellhop, 6
bóveda (*f.*) dome
brazo (*m.*) arm, 17
breve brief
brindar to toast, 4
brindis (*m.*) toast (*wine*), 4
broma (*f.*) practical joke

bromear to joke, to kid, 10
bronquitis (*f.*) bronchitis
bueno(-a), buen good, 4; hello (*phone*), 2; fine, okay, 7; well, 3
buen provecho enjoy your meal
¡Buen viaje! Have a nice trip!, 7
buena suerte good luck, 3
buenas noches good evening, good night, LP
buenas tardes good afternoon, LP
buenos días good morning, LP
bufanda (*f.*) scarf
burlarse de to make fun of
buscar to look for, to search for, 7
butaca (*f.*) armchair, 13
buzón (*m.*) mailbox, 12

C

caballo (*m.*) horse, 10
montar a _____ to ride a horse, 10
cabaña (*f.*) cabin, 10
cabello (*m.*) hair, 17
caber to fit, 5
cabeza (*f.*) head, 17
dolor de _____ (*m.*) headache, 17
lavarse la _____ to wash (one's) hair, 9
cacerola (*f.*) saucepan, 13
cada (*invariable adj.*) each, 12
_____ **año** each year
caer(se) to fall
café (*m.*) coffee, 3; cafe, 5; brown, LP
_____ **al aire libre** (*m.*) sidewalk cafe
cafetera (*f.*) coffeepot, 13
cafetería (*f.*) cafeteria, 3
cajero automático (*m.*) automatic teller, 11
cajuela (*f.*) (*Mex.*) trunk (*car*), 18
calcetín (*m.*) sock, 15
calculadora (*f.*) calculator, 16
cálculo (*m.*) calculus, 16
calefacción (*f.*) heater
_____ **central** (*f.*) central heating, 13
calentar (e:ie) to heat up, to warm up
calidad (*f.*) quality

cálido(-a) hot, warm
caliente hot, 7
calle (*f.*) street, 1
_____ de dos vías (de doble vía) (*f.*) two-way street
calor (*m.*) heat, 4
hacer _____ to be hot (*weather*), 8
tener _____ to be hot, 4
caluroso(-a) warm, hot
calzar to take (*a certain size in shoes*), 15
cama (*f.*) bed, 11
cámara (fotográfica) (*f.*) camera, 6
_____ de video (*f.*) video camera, 6
camarada (*m., f.*) comrade
camarero(-a) (*m., f.*) waiter, waitress, 8
camarones (*m. pl.*) shrimp, 8
cambiar to change, to exchange, 15
cambio (*m.*) exchange
¿A cómo está el _____ de moneda? What is the exchange rate?, 6
camello (*m.*) camel
caminar to walk, 11
camino (*m.*) road, 18
_____ a on the way to, 18
camión (de pasajeros) (*m.*) (*Mex.*) bus, 5
camisa (*f.*) shirt, 15
camiseta (*f.*) T-shirt, 15
camisón (*m.*) nightgown, 15
campestre rustic
campo (*m.*) country, 10
_____ de batalla (*m.*) battlefield
canasto (*m.*) basket
cancelar to cancel
canción (*f.*) song
cansado(-a) tired, 4
cantante (*m., f.*) singer
cantar to sing, 4
cántaro (*m.*) jug
llover a _____s to rain cats and dogs, 8
caña de pescar (*f.*) fishing rod, 10
capa (*f.*) layer
capaz capable
capital (*f.*) capital (city), 7
capó (*m.*) hood, 18
cara (*f.*) face, 17
¡caramba! gee!, LP
carburador (*m.*) carburetor, 18
cárcel (*f.*) jail

cardo (*m.*) thistle
Caribe (*m.*) Caribbean
carmín encendido bright red
carne (*f.*) meat, 8
carnet de conducir (*m.*) driver's license
carnicería (*f.*) meat market
caro(-a) expensive, 6
carpintero(-a) (*m., f.*) carpenter, 16
carrera (*f.*) university studies, career, 16; race
carretera (*f.*) highway, 18
carro (*m.*) car, 5
carroza (*f.*) float
carta (*f.*) letter, 5; menu, 8
cartera (*f.*) handbag, 9; wallet, 15
cartero (*m.*) mailman, 12
casa (*f.*) house, home, 2
casado(-a) married, 3
casarse (con) to get married (to), 17
casete (*m.*) cassette, tape, 4
casi almost, 15
casillero (*m.*) mailbox, 12
caso (*m.*) case, 14
en _____ de que in case, 14
hacer _____ to pay attention, 13
castaño brown (*hair, eyes*), 3
castellano (*m.*) Spanish (*lang.*)
castigo (*m.*) punishment, 10
castillo (*m.*) castle
catarata (*f.*) waterfall
catarro (*m.*) cold, 17
catorce fourteen, LP
caudaloso(-a) abundant
causa (*f.*) cause
causar to cause
cazar to hunt, 10
cebolla (*f.*) onion, 14
celebrar to celebrate, 4
cementerio (*m.*) cemetery
cena (*f.*) dinner, supper, 6
cenar to have dinner, 6
centro (*m.*) downtown (*area*), 6; center, 15
cepillo (*m.*) brush, 9
cerca (*adv.*) near, 3
_____ de (*prep.*) close to, near, 3
cereal (*m.*) cereal
cero zero, LP
cerrar (e:ie) to close, 4
certidumbre (*f.*) certainty, 2
certificado(-a) certified, registered 12
cerveza (*f.*) beer, 4
cesta (*f.*) basket

chaleco (*m.*) vest, 15
champán (*m.*) champagne, 4
champú (*m.*) shampoo, 9
chapa (*f.*) license plate, 18
chaqueta (*f.*) jacket, 15
charlar to talk, chat, 3
chau bye, LP
cheque (*m.*) check, 11
_____ de viajero (*m.*) traveler's check, 6
chequear to check, 18
chequeo (*m.*) checkup, examination, 17
chequera (*f.*) checkbook, 11
chica (*f.*) girl, young woman, 3
chico (*m.*) boy, young man, 3
chileno(-a) Chilean, 10
chimenea (*f.*) fireplace
chino (*m.*) Chinese (*lang.*), 2
chocolate (*m.*) chocolate, 8
_____ caliente (*m.*) hot chocolate, 8
chorizo (*m.*) sausage
cibernética (*f.*) computer science
cielo (*m.*) sky, heaven
cien, ciento one hundred, 1
ciencia (*f.*) science, 16
cierto true
No es _____. It's not true., 12
ciervo (*m.*) deer
cinco five, LP
cincuenta fifty, 1
cine (*m.*) movie theater, movies, 7
cinta (*f.*) cassette, tape, 4
circo (*m.*) circus, 14
cita (*f.*) appointment, 9; date, 14
ciudad (*f.*) city, 3
clarificar to clarify
claro(-a) light; clear
claro of course, 7
clase (*f.*) class, 1
_____ electiva (*f.*) elective
_____ optativa (*f.*) elective
_____ turista (*f.*) tourist class, 7
primera _____ first class, 7
primer día (*m.*) de clases, first day of classes, 1
clasificado(-a) classified, 13
clasificarse to qualify
clavar la pupila to stare
clima (*m.*) climate, 2
club (*m.*) club, LP
cobija (*f.*) blanket, 13
cobrar to charge, 11
cochino (*m.*) pig

cocina (*f.*) kitchen, 9; stove, 13; cuisine
cocinar to cook, 9
cocinero(-a) (*m., f.*) cook, chef, 16
coctel (*m.*) cocktail, 4
coche (*m.*) (*Sp.*) car, 5
cojera (*f.*) limp
cola (*f.*) line
    hacer _____ to stand in line, 14
colchón (*m.*) mattress, 13
colgado(-a) hung
colombiano(-a) Colombian, 13
Colón: Cristóbal Colón Christopher Columbus
color (*m.*) color, LP
colorado(-a) red
combinar to match, to go together, 15
comedia (*f.*) comedy, 8
comedor (*m.*) dining room, 13
comenzar (e:ie) (a) to begin, 4
comer to eat, 3
    _____ algo to have something to eat, 14
cómico(-a) funny
comida (*f.*) meal, food, 8
    cuarto y _____ room and board
como since, 7; like, as, 10
    _____ si as if, 18
    _____ siempre as usual, 16
cómo how?, 1; what?
    ¿A _____ está el cambio de moneda? What is the exchange rate?, 6
    ¿_____ es...? What is ... like?
    ¿_____ está usted? How are you? (*form.*), LP ¿_____ estás? How are you? (*inf.*), LP
    ¿_____ se dice...? How do you say ... ?, 1
    ¿_____ se escribe? How do you spell it?
    ¿_____ se llama usted? What's your name? (*form.*), LP
    ¿_____ te llamas? What's your name? (*inf.*), 1
    ¿_____ te va? How is it going (for you) (*inf.*)?
cómoda (*f.*) bureau, chest of drawers, 13

comodidad (*f.*) comfort
cómodo(-a) comfortable, 5
compañero(-a) de clase (*m., f.*) classmate, 4
compañía (*f.*) company, 3
complacer to please
componer to fix (*car*)
comprar to buy, 6
compras: de _____ shopping, 15
    hacer (las) _____ to shop, to do the shopping, 14
comprobante (*m.*) claim check, 11
comprobar (o:ue) to check
comprometerse con to get engaged to, 17
computador(-a) (*m., f.*) computer, 3
con with, 2
    _____ ella habla this is she (*speaking*), 2
    _____ razón no wonder, 10
    _____ tal (de) que provided that, 14
    _____ vista a overlooking, 6
concierto (*m.*) concert, 9
conducir to conduct; to drive (*Sp.*), 5
conferencia (*f.*) lecture
confirmar to confirm, 6
conjunto (*m.*) development (*housing*)
conmigo with me, 6
conocer to know, to be acquainted with, 5; to meet, 7
conocido(-a) known
    muy _____ well-known
conocimiento (*m.*) knowledge, 3
conseguir (e:i) to get, to obtain, 6
consejero(-a) (*m., f.*) advisor, 16
consejo (*m.*) advice, 16
construir to build, to construct
consultorio (*m.*) doctor's office, 17
contabilidad (*f.*) accounting, 16
contador(-a) (*m., f.*) accountant, 16
contaminación del aire (*f.*) smog
contar (o:ue) to tell, 5; to count, 5
contento(-a) happy, 4
contestar to answer
contigo (*inf. sing.*) with you, 6
contra against
conversación (*f.*) conversation
conversar to talk, to chat, 3
convertirse (e:ie) **en** to turn into
copa (*f.*) goblet, 8; glass of wine
corazón (*m.*) heart
corbata (*f.*) tie, 15
cordero (*m.*) lamb, 8

cordillera (*f.*) mountain range
coro (*m.*) choir
correo (*m.*) mail, 12; post office, 12
    _____ electrónico (*m.*) E-mail, 12
correr to run
correspondencia (*f.*): tener _____ to correspond
corrida de toros (*f.*) bullfight
cortar to cut, 9
cortar(se) to cut (oneself), 9
    cortarse el pelo to get a haircut, 9
corte (*m.*) haircut, cut, 9
cortesía (*f.*) politeness
cortina (*f.*) curtain, 13
corto(-a) short, 9
cosa (*f.*) thing, 14
costa (*f.*) coast
costar (o:ue) to cost, 5
    _____ un ojo de la cara to cost an arm and a leg, 10
costillas (*f. pl.*) ribs
costumbre (*f.*) custom, habit
creado(-a) created
crecer to grow
crecimiento (*m.*) growth
creer to believe, think, 3
crema (*f.*) cream, 8
    _____ de afeitar (*f.*) shaving cream, 9
criada (*f.*) maid
cruz (*f.*) cross
cruzar to cross, 12
cuaderno (*m.*) notebook, 1
cuadra (*f.*) (*Sp. Am.*) city block, 12
cuadro (*m.*) picture, painting, 5
cuál what?, which?, 1
    ¿_____ es tu (su) dirección? What's your address?, 1
    ¿_____ es tu (su) número de teléfono? What is your telephone number?, LP
cualquier(a) any, anybody
cualquier cosa anything
cuando when, 8
    de vez en _____ from time to time
cuándo when?, 2
cuánto(-a) how much?, 4
    ¿_____ tiempo...? How long ...?, 7
cuántos(-as) how many?, 1
cuarenta forty, 1
cuartel general (*m.*) headquarters

cuarto (*m.*)   room, 6
_____ de baño (*m.*)
   bathroom, 6
_____ y comida   room and
   board
menos _____   quarter of/to
   (*time*), 1
y _____   quarter after/past
   (*time*), 1
cuarto(-a)   fourth, 9
cuatro   four, LP
cuatrocientos   four hundred, 2
cubano(-a)   Cuban, 8
cubierto(-a) (*p.p.* of cubrir *and adj.*)
   covered, 15; cloudy, overcast
cubiertos (*m. pl.*)   place settings, 8
cubrir   to cover
cucaracha (*f.*)   cockroach
cuchara (*f.*)   spoon, 8
cucharita (*f.*)   teaspoon, 8
cuchillo (*m.*)   knife, 8
cuello (*m.*)   neck, 17
cuenca (*f.*)   (river) basin
cuenta (*f.*)   account, 11; bill, 8
_____ corriente (*f.*)   checking
   account, 11
_____ de ahorros (*f.*)   savings
   account, 11
culpa (*f.*)   blame, fault, 18
tener la _____   to be one's fault,
   18
culpable   guilty
culpar   to blame, 18
cultura (*f.*)   culture, 9
cumpleaños (*m.*)   birthday, 4
cumplir... años   to turn _____ (*age*)
cuñada (*f.*)   sister-in-law, 5
cuñado (*m.*)   brother-in-law, 5
curandero (*m.*)   healer
curso (*m.*)   course

D

dar   to give, 4
_____ una multa   to give a
   ticket (fine), 18
darse: darse por vencido(-a)   to give
   up
darse prisa   to hurry (up), 14
datos (*m. pl.*)   data, 3
de   about, 7; from, 1; of, 2
_____ compras   shopping, 15
¿_____ dónde?   from where?,
   1

¿_____ dónde eres?   Where
   are you from?, 1
_____ estatura mediana   of
   medium height, 5
_____ haber sabido   had I
   known, 17
_____ haber seguido   had I
   followed, 16
_____ la mañana (noche,
   tarde)   in the morning
   (evening, afternoon), 2
_____ lana   made of wool
_____ manera que   so, 11
_____ moda   in style, 9
_____ modo que   so, 11
_____ nada   you're welcome,
   1
_____ nuevo   again
¿_____ parte de quién?   Who
   is speaking?, 2
_____ postre   for dessert, 8
_____ pronto   suddenly
_____ quién(es)   whose?, 4
Soy _____...   I'm from . . . , 1
_____ vacaciones   on
   vacation, 10
_____ vez en cuando   from
   time to time, 14
deber (+ *infinitive*)   must, to have to,
   should, 3
_____se a   to be due to
debilidad (*f.*)   weakness
decidir   to decide, 3
décimo(-a)   tenth, 9
decir (e:i)   to say, to tell, 6
¿Cómo se dice...?   How do
   you say . . . ?, 1
_____ tonterías   to talk
   nonsense, 13
¿Qué quiere _____...?   What
   does . . . mean?, 1
Quiere _____...   It means
   . . . , 1
Se dice...   You say . . . , One
   says . . . , 1
decisión (*f.*)   decision, 13
declarar   to declare, 6
dedo (*m.*)   finger, 17
_____ del pie (*m.*)   toe, 17
dejar   to leave (*behind*), 8
del (*m. sing.*) (*contraction*)   of the,
   from the, 3
delante de   in front of
deleitarse (en)   to delight (in)
deletrear   to spell

delgado(-a)   thin, slender, 3
delicioso (-a)   delicious, 4
demasiado(-a)(s)   too much, too
   many
demasiada gente   too many
   people, 10
departamento (*m.*)   department,
   section, 11; apartment
_____ de (ropa para)
   caballeros (*m.*)   men's
   department, 15
_____ de (ropa para) señoras
   (damas) (*m.*)   women's
   department, 12
dependiente(-a) (*m., f.*)   store clerk,
   15
deporte (*m.*)   sport, 16
deportivo(-a)   sports-related
artículos _____s (*m. pl.*)
   sporting goods
depositar   to deposit, 11
derecho (*m.*)   law, 16; (*adv.*) straight
   ahead, 12
derecho(-a) (*adj.*)   right
a la derecha   to (on, at) the
   right, 6
derramar   to spill
derretir (e:i)   to melt
desafiar   to challenge
desafortunadamente   unfortunately,
   10
desarrollarse   to develop
desayuno (*m.*)   breakfast, 6
descomponerse   to break down
descompuesto(-a) (*p.p.* of
   descomponer *and adj.*)   out of
   order, not working, 18
describir   to describe, 4
descubrir   to discover
desde   from, 12
desdeñar   to disdain
desear   to want, to wish, 2
desgraciado(-a)   unfortunate
desierto (*m.*)   desert, 10
desilusión (*f.*)   disappointment
desinfectar   to disinfect, 17
despedida (*f.*)   farewell
despertador (*m.*)   alarm clock, 11
despertarse (e:ie)   to wake up, 9
después   then, 7
_____ de   after, 8
destacar   to stand out
desvestirse (e:i)   to get undressed, 9
detallado(-a)   detailed
detenerse   to stop

devolver (o:ue) to return (*something*), 7

devuelto(-a) (*p.p. of* **devolver** *and adj.*) returned, 15

día (*m.*) day, 1

al _____ siguiente the next day, 13

_____ de fiesta (*m.*) holiday, 14

primer _____ de clases first day of classes, 1

¿Qué _____ es hoy? What day is today?, LP

diario (*m.*) newspaper, 3

dibujo (*m.*) design

diccionario (*m.*) dictionary, LP

diciembre December, LP

dictado (*m.*) dictation, LP

dictadura (*f.*) dictatorship

dicho(-a) (*p.p. of* **decir** *and adj.*) said, told, 15

diecinueve nineteen, LP

dieciocho eighteen, LP

dieciséis sixteen, LP

diecisiete seventeen, LP

diente (*m.*) tooth, 17

dieta (*f.*) diet, 14

diez ten, LP

difícil difficult, 3

¡dígame! hello! (*phone*), 2

diligencia (*f.*) errand, 11

hacer _____s to run errands, 11

dinero (*m.*) money, 2

Dios (*m.*) God

dirección (*f.*) address, 1

¿Cuál es tu (su) _____? What's your address?, 1

Mi _____ es... My address is . . . , 1

dirigir to direct, conduct

_____se a to head for

disco (*m.*) record

_____ compacto (*m.*) compact disc (CD), 4

discoteca (*f.*) discothèque

discusión (*f.*) discussion

diseñar to design

diseño (*m.*) design, 15

disfrutar to enjoy

diversión (*f.*) diversion, amusement

divertido(-a) entertaining

divertirse (e:ie) to have a good time, to enjoy oneself, 10

divorciado(-a) divorced, 3

divorciarse to get divorced

doblar to turn, to bend, 12; to dub

doble double, 6

_____ vía two-way

doce twelve, LP

docena (*f.*) dozen, 14

doctor(-a) (*m., f.*) doctor, LP

documento (*m.*) document, 12

_____ de identidad (identificación) (*m.*) I.D., 12

dólar (*m.*) dollar, 6

doler (o:ue) to ache, to hurt, 17

dolor (*m.*) pain, 17

_____ de cabeza (*m.*) headache, 17

domicilio (*m.*) address, 1

domingo (*m.*) Sunday, LP

dónde where?, 2

¿de _____? from where?, 1

¿De _____ eres? Where are you from?, 1

dormir (o:ue) to sleep, 5

_____se to fall asleep, 9

dormitorio (*m.*) bedroom, 13

dos two, LP

doscientos two hundred, 2

drama (*m.*) drama, play, 14

dramático(-a) dramatic

ducha (*f.*) shower, 6

ducharse to take a shower, 9

dudar to doubt, 12

dulces (*m. pl.*) sweets

durante during, 7

durar to last

durazno (*m.*) peach, 14

E

e and

económico(-a) financial, economic, 2

echar to pour out

_____ de menos to miss, 5

_____ su suerte to share one's destiny

_____ una carta al correo to mail a letter, 12

edad (*f.*) age, 3

Edad Media Middle Ages

edificio (*m.*) building, 12

educación (*f.*) education, 3

efectivo (*m.*) cash, 11

en _____ in cash, 11

ejemplo (*m.*) example

por _____ for example

ejercicio (*m.*) exercise, LP

ejército (*m.*) army

el the (*m. sing.*), 1

él he, 1; him, 6

electricista (*m., f.*) electrician, 16

elegante elegant, 8

elegido(-a) chosen

elevador (*m.*) elevator, 6

ella she, 1; her, 6

ellas (*f. pl.*) they, 1; them, 6

ellos (*m. pl.*) they, 1; them, 6

embajada (*f.*) embassy, 6

embarazada pregnant, 17

emergencia (*f.*) emergency, 17

emparedado (*m.*) (*Sp.*) sandwich, 3

emperador (*m.*) emperor

empezar (e:ie) (a) to begin, to start, 4

empleado(-a) (*m., f.*) clerk, 6; employee

empleo (*m.*) job, 3

en in, at, 1; on, 2

_____ caso de que in case, 14

_____ cuanto as soon as, 11

_____ efectivo in cash, 11

_____ el club at the club, LP

_____ inglés in English

_____ la universidad at the university, LP

_____ regla in order

_____ seguida right away, 6

_____ seguida vuelvo I'll be right back, 15

_____ serio seriously, 10

_____ vez de instead of, 13

enamorado(-a) in love

enamorarse de to fall in love with, 17

encaje (*m.*) lace

encantado(-a) charmed, it's a pleasure

encantador(-a) charming

encantar to love, to like very much, 8

me encanta... I love . . .

encargado(-a) de in charge of

encima de above, on top of

encontrar (o:ue) to find, 5

_____se (con) to meet, 12

encuentro (*m.*) encounter

enemigo (*m.*) enemy

enero January, LP

enfadado(-a) angry, 4

enfermedad (*f.*) disease, sickness

_____es de la niñez childhood diseases

enfermero(-a) (*m., f.*) nurse, 17

enfermo(-a) sick, 4
enfriar to cool down
engañar to deceive
enojado(-a) angry, 4
enrollado(-a) wrapped around
ensalada (*f.*) salad, 4
enseñanza (*f.*) teaching
enseñar (a) to teach, 10; to show, 6
ensuciar(se) to get (oneself) dirty, 9
entender (e:ie) to understand, 4
enterrado(-a) buried
entonces then, in that case, 2
entrada (*f.*) entrance, 7; ticket (*for a show*), 8
entrar (en) to go in, to enter, 15
entre between, among
    _____ **la espada y la pared**
    between a rock and a hard
    place
entregar to deliver, to turn in, 16
entremeses (*m. pl.*) hors d'oeuvres, 4
entretener(se) (*like tener*) to
    entertain (oneself)
entrevista (*f.*) interview, LP
entrevistar to interview
enviar to send, 3
envolver (o:ue) to wrap, 15
envuelto(-a) (*p.p. of* **envolver** *and adj.*)
    wrapped, 15
equilibrado(-a) balanced
equipaje (*m.*) luggage, 7
equipo (*m.*) team, 16
    _____ **estereofónico** (*m.*)
    stereo system, 4
equivocado(-a) wrong
    estar _____ to be wrong, 4
equivocarse to be wrong
es que... the fact is . . . , 12
es (una) lástima it's a pity, 10
escalar to climb, 10
escalera (*f.*) stairs, 6
    _____ **mecánica** (*f.*) escalator,
    15
escenario (*m.*) setting, stage
esclusa (*f.*) lock (*canal*)
escoba (*f.*) broom, 9
escribir to write, 3
escrito(-a) (*p.p. of* **escribir** *and adj.*)
    written, 15
escritor(-a) (*m., f.*) writer
escritorio (*m.*) desk, 1
escuchar to listen to
escuela (*f.*) school, 5
    _____ **secundaria** (*f.*) high
    school
escultura (*f.*) sculpture

ese(-os), esa(s) (*adj.*) that, those,
    (*nearby*), 7
ése(-os), ésa(s) (*pron.*) that one,
    those (*nearby*), 7
esfuerzo (*m.*) effort
eso (*neuter pron.*) that, 7
    a _____ **de** at about, 14
Esopo Aesop
espalda (*f.*) back, 17
España Spain, 2
español (*m.*) Spanish (*lang.*), 2
español(-a) (*m., f.*) Spaniard, 12
especial special
especialidad (*f.*) specialty, 8
especialización (*f.*) major (*field of study*), 16
especialmente especially, 5
especie (*f.*) sort
espectáculo (*m.*) show, spectacle
espejo (*m.*) mirror, 9
esperar to wait (for), 9; to hope, 11
espinaca (*f.*) spinach
esposa (*f.*) wife, 3
esposo (*m.*) husband, 3
esquí (*m.*) ski
esquiar to ski, 10
esquina (*f.*) corner, 12
estación (*f.*) season, LP; station, 12
    _____ **de policía** (*f.*) police
    station, 11
    _____ **de servicio** (*f.*) gas
    (service) station, 18
estacionar to park, 11
estadio (*m.*) stadium, 16
estado (*m.*) state
    _____ **civil** (*m.*) marital
    status, 3
Estados Unidos (*m. pl.*) United
    States, 5
estampado(-a) printed, 15
estampilla (*f.*) stamp, 12
estanque (*m.*) pond
estar to be, 4
    _____ **a... de aquí** to be . . .
    from here, 12
    _____ **de acuerdo** to agree,
    18
    _____ **de moda** to be in style,
    9
    _____ **de vuelta** to be back
    _____ **enamorado(-a) de** to
    be in love with
    _____ **equivocado(-a)** to be
    wrong, 4
    _____ **invitado(-a)** to be
    invited, 9

    _____ **muerto(-a) de hambre**
    to be starving, 15
    _____ **seguro(-a)** to be sure,
    12
¿Cómo está usted? How are
    you? (*form.*), LP
¿Cómo estás? How are you?
    (*inf.*), LP
está bien fine, all right, 10
no está he (she) is not here, 2
estatua (*f.*) statue
estatura (*f.*) height, 5
este east, 10
este(-os), esta(s) (*adj.*) this, 5; these,
    7
éste(-os) ésta(s) (*pron.*) this one;
    these, 7
estilo (*m.*) style
esto (*neuter pron.*) this, 7
estómago (*m.*) stomach, 17
estrecho(-a) narrow, 15
estrella (*f.*) star
estudiante (*m., f.*) student, 1
estudiar to study, 2
Europa Europe, 2
evitar to avoid, 17
examen (*m.*) exam, 3; checkup, 17
    _____ **de mitad de curso** (*m.*)
    midterm exam, 16
    _____ **parcial** (*m.*) midterm
    exam, 16
excelente excellent, 8
exceso (*m.*) excess, 7
    _____ **de equipaje** (*m.*) excess
    baggage, 7
excursión (*f.*) excursion, 10
exigente demanding
éxito (*m.*) success, hit
experiencia (*f.*) experience, 3
expresión (*f.*) expression, LP
extranjero(-a) foreigner, 12
    al extranjero abroad
extrañar to miss, 5
extraño(-a) strange, 18

F

fácil easy, 3
fácilmente easily, 10
facsímil (*m.*) fax (*letter*), 12
facultad (*f.*) college, 16
    _____ **de derecho** (*f.*) law
    school, 16
falda (*f.*) skirt, 15
faltar to be missing
fama (*f.*) fame, reputation

familia (*f.*)   family, 5
famoso(-a)   famous, 5
farmacia (*f.*)   pharmacy, drugstore, 9
favor (*m.*)   favor, 13
fax (*m.*)   fax (*letter*), 12
favorito(-a)   favorite
febrero   February, LP
fecha (*f.*)   date, LP
    ¿Qué _____ es hoy?   What's
    the date today?, LP
fechar   to date (*check or letter*), 11
feliz   happy, 4
femenino(-a)   feminine, 3
feo(-a)   ugly, 3
feria (*f.*)   fair
feriado (*m.*)   holiday, 14
festivo (*m.*)   holiday
fiebre (*f.*)   fever, 17
fiesta (*f.*)   party, 4
    día de _____ (*m.*)   holiday, 14
fijarse en   to notice, 17
filete (*m.*)   tenderloin steak, 8
filtro (*m.*)   filter, 18
fin (*m.*)   end
    _____ de año (*m.*)   New
    Year's Eve, 4
    _____ de semana (*m.*)
    weekend, 5
firma (*f.*)   signature, 11
firmar   to sign, 6
física (*f.*)   physics, 16
flan (*m.*)   caramel custard, 8
flor (*f.*)   flower
floreciente   flourishing
florería (*f.*)   flower shop
flota (*f.*)   fleet
folleto (*m.*)   brochure
    _____ turístico (*m.*)   tourist
    brochure, 10
fondo (*m.*)   background; depth
fortaleza (*f.*)   fortress
fortuna (*f.*)   fortune, 14
foto (*f.*)   photograph, 5
fotografía (*f.*)   photograph, 5
francés (*m.*)   French (*lang.*), 2
Francia   France, 2
franco(-a)   open
frazada (*f.*)   blanket, 13
frecuente   frequent
frecuentemente   frequently
fregadero (*m.*)   kitchen sink, 13
freír (e:i)   to fry
freno (*m.*)   brake, 18
frente a   in front of, 11; across from,
    12
fresa (*f.*)   strawberry, 14

frijoles (*m. pl.*)   beans, 8
frío (*m.*)   cold
    hacer _____   to be cold
    (*weather*), 8
    tener _____   to be cold, 4
frito(-a)   fried, 8
fruncir el ceño   to frown
fruta (*f.*)   fruit, 8
frutería (*f.*)   fruit store
fuente (*f.*)   fountain; source
    _____ de ingresos (*f.*)   source
    of income
fuera (de)   outside
fuerte   strong
fuerza (*f.*)   strength, force
fumar   to smoke
función (*f.*)   show, 14
funcionar   to work, to function, 18
funda (*f.*)   pillowcase, 13
fundar   to found
fútbol (*m.*)   soccer, 16
    _____ americano (*m.*)
    football

G

gamba (*f.*)   shrimp (*Sp.*), 8
ganadería (*f.*)   cattle raising; livestock
ganar   to earn, 13; to win, 13
ganas: tener _____ de   to feel like, 14
ganga (*f.*)   bargain, 15
garaje (*m.*)   garage, 13
garganta (*f.*)   throat, 17
gasolina (*f.*)   gasoline, 18
gasolinera (*f.*)   gas (service) station,
    18
gastar   to spend (*money*), 18
gato (*m.*)   car jack, 18
general   general
generalmente   generally, 9
gente (*f.*)   people, 9
geología (*f.*)   geology, 16
gimnasio (*m.*)   gym, 3
gira (*f.*)   tour
giro postal (*m.*)   money order, 12
gobierno (*m.*)   government
goma (*f.*)   tire, 18
gordo(-a)   fat
gozar (de)   to enjoy
grabadora (*f.*)   tape recorder, 6
gracias   thank you, thanks, LP
    Muchas _____. Thank you
    very much., 1
grado (*m.*)   degree, 17
graduarse   to graduate, 16
gran, grande   big, large, 5

grasa (*f.*)   grease
gratis   free (*of charge*), 11
gripe (*f.*)   flu, 17
gris   gray, LP
gritar   to scream, 11
grúa (*f.*)   tow truck, 18
guante (*m.*)   glove, 15
guantera (*f.*)   glove compartment, 18
guapo(-a)   handsome, 3
guardar   to keep
güero(-a) (*Mex.*)   blond, 3
guerra (*f.*)   war
guía telefónica (*f.*)   telephone book
gustar   to like, to be pleasing to, 7
    me gusta(n)…   I like …
gusto (*m.*)   pleasure, 1
    El _____ es mío.   The pleasure
    is mine., 1
    Mucho _____.   Pleased to
    meet you., 1

H

haber (*aux.*)   to have, 15
habitación (*f.*)   room, 6
    _____ doble (*f.*)   double
    room, 6
habitante (*m., f.*)   inhabitant
habla (*f.*)   speech
    de _____ hispana   Spanish-
    speaking
hablado(-a)   spoken
hablar   to speak, to talk, 2
hacer   to do, to make, 5
    _____ buen tiempo   to be
    good weather, 8
    _____ calor   to be hot, 8
    _____ caso   to pay attention,
    13
    _____ cola   to stand in line,
    14
    _____ diligencias   to run
    errands, 11
    _____ frío   to be cold, 8
    _____ juego   to match, to go
    together, 15
    _____ (las) compras   to do the
    shopping, to shop, 14
    _____ las maletas   to pack, 10
    _____ mal tiempo   to be bad
    weather, 8
    _____ sol   to be sunny, 8
    _____ una radiografía   to take
    an x-ray, 17
    _____ viento   to be windy, 8
hace + *time*   ago, 11

hace + *time* + que + *verb* (*present*) to have been doing something for a length of time, 7

hace + *time* + que + *verb* (*preterit/imperfect*) to have done something in the past (ago), 11

hacerse   to become

hacia   toward, 11

hacienda (*f.*)   farm

hambre (*f.*)   hunger, 4

   tener _____   to be hungry, 4

haragán(-ana)   lazy

harto(-a) de   fed up

hamburguesa (*f.*)   hamburger, 8

hasta   until, 6; up to

   _____ la vista   until I see you again, I'll see you later, 1

   _____ llegar   until you get, 12

   _____ luego   see you later, LP

   _____ mañana   see you tomorrow, LP

   _____ que   until, 14

hay   there is, there are, 1

   _____ niebla   it's foggy, 8

hecho(-a) (*p.p. of* hacer *and adj.*)   done, made, 15

   ropa hecha (*f.*)   ready-to-wear clothing

helado (*m.*)   ice cream, 8

helado(-a)   iced, ice cold, 8

   torta helada (*f.*)   ice cream cake, 8

herencia (*f.*)   inheritance

herida (*f.*)   wound, 17

hermana (*f.*)   sister, 3

hermano (*m.*)   brother, 3

hermoso(-a)   beautiful

hierba (*f.*)   herb; grass

hija (*f.*)   daughter, 5

hijastra (*f.*)   stepdaughter, 5

hijastro (*m.*)   stepson, 5

hijo (*m.*)   son, 5

hijo(-a) único(-a) (*m., f.*)   only child, 11

hijos (*m. pl.*)   children, 3

hilo (*m.*)   linen, 15

hipoteca (*f.*)   mortgage

hola   hello, hi, LP

hombre (*m.*)   man, 1

   _____ de negocios (*m.*)   businessman, 16

hora (*f.*)   time, 1; hour, 7

   ¿A qué _____...?   (At) what time . . . ?, 1

¿Qué _____ es?   What time is it?, 1

horario (*m.*)   schedule, 16

   _____ de clases (*m.*)   class schedule, LP

horno de microondas (*m.*)   microwave oven, 13

horrible: ¡Qué _____!   How horrible!, 10

horriblemente   horribly, 10

hospedarse en   to stay (*at a hotel*), 10

hospital (*m.*)   hospital, 2

hotel (*m.*)   hotel, 6

hoy   today, 1

   _____ en día   today, nowadays

   _____ es...   today is . . . , LP

   _____ mismo   this very day, 17

   ¿Qué día es _____?   What day is today?, LP

   ¿Qué fecha es _____?   What's the date (today)?, LP

huerto (*m.*)   orchard

huevo (*m.*)   egg, 8

I

ida (*f.*): de _____   one-way (*ticket*), 7

   de _____ y vuelta   round-trip, 7

ido (*p.p. of* ir)   gone, 15

idea (*f.*)   idea, 4

identidad (*f.*)   identity

   documento de _____ (*m.*)   I.D., 12

   número de _____ (*m.*)   identification number, 3

identificación (*f.*)   identification, 12

idioma (*m.*)   language, 2

idiota (*m., f.*)   idiot

iglesia (*f.*)   church

imperio (*m.*)   empire

impermeable (*m.*)   raincoat

importante   important, 16

incómodo(-a)   uncomfortable

indígena (*invariable adj.*)   native

infección (*f.*)   infection, 17

información (*f.*)   information, 6

informe (*m.*)   report, paper, 16

ingeniería (*f.*)   engineering, 16

ingeniero(-a) (*m., f.*)   engineer, 16

Inglaterra   England

inglés (*m.*)   English (*lang.*), 1

   en _____   in English, 1

inglés(-esa)   English (*nationality*), 3

ingreso (*m.*)   income

inigualable   unequalled

inodoro (*m.*)   toilet, 6

insistir en   to insist on, 17

inspector(-a) (*m., f.*)   inspector, 6

instalar   to install, 18

institución (*f.*)   institution, 3

instituto (*m.*)   high school

instructor(-a) (*m., f.*)   instructor, 10

inteligente   intelligent, 3

interés (*m.*)   interest, 6

interesante   interesting, 5

interior   interior, 6

invertir (e:ie)   to invest

investigación (*f.*)   research, 16

invierno (*m.*)   winter, LP

invitar (a)   to invite, 4; ¡Yo invito! My treat!, 14

inyección (*f.*)   injection, shot, 17

   _____ antitetánica (*f.*)   tetanus shot, 17

   poner una _____   to give a shot, an injection, 17

ir (a)   to go, 4

   ir a + *infinitive*   to be going (to) + *infinitive*, 4

   _____ de compras   to go shopping, 10

   _____ de pesca   to go fishing, 10

   _____ de vacaciones   to go on vacation, 10

irresponsable   irresponsible

irse   to go away, to leave, 9

   me voy   I'm leaving, 3

Italia   Italy, 2

italiano (*m.*)   Italian (*lang.*), 2

izquierdo(-a)   left, 6

   a la izquierda   to (on, at) the left, 6

J

jabón (*m.*)   soap, 6

jamás   never, 6

jamón (*m.*)   ham, 3

japonés (*m.*)   Japanese (*lang.*), 2

jardín (*m.*)   garden, 13

jefe(-a) (*m., f.*)   chief, head

joven (*m., f.*)   young person, 16

joyas (*f. pl.*)   jewels, jewelry

joyería (*f.*)   jewelry store

juego (*m.*): hacer _____   to match, to go together, 15

jueves (*m.*)   Thursday, LP
juez (*m.*)   judge
jugador(-a) (*m., f.*)   player
jugar (**u:ue**)   to play (*game, sport*)
  _____ **al golf**   to play golf, 10
  _____ **al tenis**   to play tennis, 10
jugo (*m.*)   juice, 8
julio   July, LP
junio   June, LP
junto a   next to
juntos(-as)   together, 7

K

kilómetro (*m.*)   kilometer, 18

L

la (*f. sing.*)   the, 1; (*pron.*) her, it, you (*form.*), 6
laborales (*m. pl.*)   workdays
laboratorio (*m.*)   laboratory, 16
  _____ **de lenguas** (*m.*)   language lab
labrador(-a) (*m., f.*)   farmer
lacio(-a)   straight (*hair*), 9
ladrón (*m.*)   robber
lago (*m.*)   lake, 10
lágrima (*f.*)   tear
lámpara (*f.*)   lamp, 13
lápiz (*m.*)   pencil, 1
largo(-a)   long, 7
  a lo largo   along the length of
las (*f. pl.*)   the, 1; (*pron.*) them, 6
lástima (*f.*)   pity, shame
  es una _____   it's a pity, 11
  ¡Qué _____**!**   What a pity!, 5
lata (*f.*)   can, 14
latinoamericano(-a)   Latin American, 16
laureles (*m. pl.*)   laurels
lavabo (*m.*)   sink, 6
lavado (*m.*)   shampoo, wash, 9
lavadora (*f.*)   washing machine, 13
lavaplatos (*m.*)   dishwasher, 13
lavar(se)   to wash (oneself), 9
  _____ **la cabeza**   to wash one's hair, 9
le   (to, for) her, (to, for) him, (to, for) you (*form.*), 7
lección (*f.*)   lesson, LP
leche (*f.*)   milk, 8

lechera (*f.*)   milkmaid
lechón (*m.*)   suckling pig (pork), 8
lechuga (*f.*)   lettuce, 14
lector(-a) (*m., f.*)   reader
leer   to read, 3
lejos (*adv.*)   far, 3
  _____ **de** (*prep.*)   far from, 3
lengua (*f.*)   tongue, 17
lentamente   slowly, 10
lento(-a)   slow, 10
león (*m.*)   lion
les   (to, for) them, (to, for) you, (*form. pl.*), 7
letra (*f.*)   handwriting
letrero (*m.*)   sign, 18
levantar   to lift, to raise, 9
levantarse   to get up, 9
leyenda (*f.*)   legend
libertad (*f.*)   liberty, 2
libra (*f.*)   pound
libre   free, 3; vacant, 6
libreta de ahorros (*f.*)   savings passbook, 11
libro (*m.*)   book, 1
licencia de conducir (*f.*)   driver's license, 3
licuadora (*f.*)   blender, 13
liebre (*f.*)   hare
liga (*f.*)   league
  grandes _____**s** (*f. pl.*)   major leagues
ligeramente   slightly
limitar con   to border
limpiaparabrisas (*m.*)   windshield wiper, 18
limpiar(se)   to clean (oneself), 9
limpio(-a)   clean
lindo(-a)   pretty, 3
lino (*m.*)   linen, 15
liquidación (*f.*)   sale, 15
liso(-a)   solid-color, plain
lista (*f.*)   list, 6; menu, 8
  _____ **de espera** (*f.*)   waiting list, 6
listo(-a)   ready, 11
literatura (*f.*)   literature, 16
llamar   to call, 2
llamarse   to be called, 9
  ¿Cómo se llama usted?   What is your name? (*form.*), LP
  ¿Cómo te llamas?   What's your name? (*inf.*), 1
  Me llamo...   My name is . . . , LP
llanero (*m.*)   plainsman
llano (*m.*)   plain

llanta (*f.*)   tire, 18
llanura (*f.*)   plain
llave (*f.*)   key, 6
llegada (*f.*)   arrival
llegar   to arrive, 6
  _____ **tarde**   to be late, 7
  _____ **temprano**   to be early, 7
llenar   to fill, to fill out, 3
lleno(-a)   full, 18
llevar   to take (*someone or something someplace*), 3; to wear, to use, 15
  _____ **a cabo**   to carry out
  _____ **puesto(-a)**   to wear, to have on, 15
llevarse   to take away, 11; to buy, to take, 15
llover (**o:ue**)   to rain, 5
  _____ **a cántaros**   to rain cats and dogs, to pour down raining, 8
lloviznar   to drizzle, 8
lluvia (*f.*)   rain, 8
lo   him, it, you (*form.*), 6
  _____ + *adjective*   the + *adjective* thing
  _____ **cual**   which
  _____ **que**   what, 10
  _____ **siento**   I'm sorry, LP
  _____ **único**   the only thing, 16
localidad (*f.*)   location, seat
localizado(-a)   located
loco(-a)   crazy, 7
locutor(-a)   (*m., f.*)   announcer
Londres   London
los (*m. pl.*)   the, 1; (*pron.*) them, you, 6
lotería (*f.*)   lottery, 13
luchar   to fight
luego   afterwards, then, 6
  hasta _____   see you later, LP
lugar (*m.*)   place, 3
  _____ **donde trabaja** (*m.*)   place of employment, 3
  _____**es de interés** (*m. pl.*)   places of interest, 6
  tener _____   to take place
lujo (*m.*)   luxury
  de _____   deluxe
lujoso(-a)   luxurious
lumbre (*f.*)   fire
lunar (*m.*)   mole
lunes (*m.*)   Monday, LP
luz (*f.*)   light, 1; headlight, 18

M

madera (*f.*) wood
madrastra (*f.*) stepmother, 5
madre (*f.*) mother, 4
maduro(-a) ripe
maestro(-a) (*m., f.*) teacher
magia (*f.*) magic
magnífico(-a) magnificent, great, 4
mago(-a) (*m., f.*) magician, wizard
maíz (*m.*) corn
mal bad, badly, 5
malabarismo (*m.*) juggling
maleta (*f.*) suitcase, 6
    hacer las _____s to pack, 10
maletero (*m.*) (*car*) trunk, 18
malo(-a) bad, 4
mamá mom, 4
manada (*f.*) herd
mandar to send, 3; to order, 11
manejar to drive, 5
manera (*f.*) way
    de _____ que so, 11
mano (*f.*) hand, LP
manta (*f.*) blanket, 13
mantecado (*m.*) ice cream (*Mex.,
    Puerto Rico*), 8
mantel (*m.*) tablecloth, 8
mantelería (*f.*) table linens
mantener (*conj. like* **tener**) to
    maintain, 16
mantequilla (*f.*) butter, 14
manzana (*f.*) apple, 14; (*Sp.*) city
    block, 12; block (*of buildings*), (*Sp.
    Am.*), 12
mañana (*f.*) morning, 2; (*adv.*)
    tomorrow, 2
    de la _____ in the morning, 2
    hasta _____ see you
        tomorrow, LP
    por la _____ in the morning, 2
mapa (*m.*) map, 1
maquillarse to apply makeup
máquina de afeitar (*f.*) razor, 9
mar (*m.*) sea, 10
    _____ Mediterráneo
        Mediterranean Sea, 10
maravilla (*f.*) marvel
marca (*f.*) brand
marchito(-a) faded, withered
marea (*f.*) tide
mareo (*m.*) dizziness, dizzy spell
margarina (*f.*) margarine, 14
margarita (*f.*) daisy
mariscos (*m. pl.*) seafood, shellfish,
    8

marrón brown, LP
Marte (*m.*) Mars
martes (*m.*) Tuesday, LP
marzo March, LP
más more, 5
    el (la) _____... de the most
        ... in, 5
    _____ de more than, 5
    _____ o menos so-so, more
        or less, 2
    _____... que more ... than, 5
    _____ tarde later, 2
máscara (*f.*) mask
masculino male, 3
matar to kill
matemáticas (*f. pl.*) mathematics, 16
materia (*f.*) subject matter, 16
materno(-a) maternal
matrícula (*f.*) registration, tuition,
    16
matricularse to register, 16
mayo May, LP
mayor older, 5
    el (la) _____ the oldest, 5
mayoría (*f.*) majority
me me, 6; (to, for) me, 7; (to)
    myself, 9
mecánico (*m.*) mechanic, 18
mediano(-a) medium, 15
medianoche (*f.*) midnight, 4
    a la _____ at midnight, 4
medicina (*f.*) medicine, 5
médico(-a) (*m., f.*) doctor, 17
médico(-a) medical, 17
medida (*f.*) size, 15
medio(-a) half, 8
    media hermana (*f.*) half
        sister, 5
    media hora half an hour, 7
    medio ambiente (*m.*)
        environment
    medio día half a day; part-
        time, 13
    medio hermano (*m.*) half
        brother, 5
    y media half-past (*telling
        time*), 1
mediodía (*m.*) noon, 4
    al _____ at noon, 4
medios (*m. pl.*) means
medir (e:i) to measure
mejor best; better, 5
    el (la) _____ the best, 5
mejorar to improve
melocotón (*m.*) peach, 14
melodía (*f.*) melody

melón (*m.*) melon, 14
menaje (*m.*) household
menor younger, 5
    el (la) _____ youngest, 5
menos till, to (*telling time*), 1; less, 5
    a _____ que unless, 14
    el (la) _____... de the least
        ... in, 5
    más o _____ so-so, more or
        less, 2
    _____ de + *number* less than
        + *number*, 5
    _____... que less ... than, 5
mentir (e:ie) to lie, 8
menú (*m.*) menu, 8
mermelada (*f.*) jam
mercado (*m.*) market, 14
mes (*m.*) month, LP
    el _____ pasado last month,
        7
mesa (*f.*) table, 4
mesero(-a) (*Mex.*) waiter, waitress, 8
mesita de noche (*f.*) nightstand, 13
metro (*m.*) subway, 12
mexicano(-a) Mexican, 6
mezcla (*f.*) mix, mixture
mezclar to mix, to blend
mezquita (*f.*) mosque
mi (*adj.*) my, 2
mí (*pron.*) me, 6
microondas microwave, 13
    horno de _____ (*m.*)
        microwave oven, 13
miedo (*m.*) fear, 4
    tener _____ to be afraid, 4
miembro (*m.*) member
mientras while, 3
    _____ tanto meanwhile
miércoles (*m.*) Wednesday, LP
mil one thousand, 2
milla (*f.*) mile, 18
minoritario(-a) (*adj.*) minority
mío(s), mía(s) (*pron.*) mine, 9
mirada (*f.*) glance
mirar to look at, to watch (T.V.), 3
    _____ vidrieras to window
        shop, 15
mismo(-a) same, 13
    al mismo tiempo at the same
        time, 13
    lo mismo the same thing
mochila (*f.*) backpack, 10
moda (*f.*) fashion
    estar de _____ to be in style,
        9
moderno(-a) modern, 6

módico(-a)   modest
modista (*f.*)   dressmaker
modo (*m.*)   way
    de _____ **que**   so, 11
mojar   to dip
molino de viento (*m.*)   windmill
momento (*m.*)   moment, 2
    un _____   one moment, 2
moneda (*f.*)   currency
montaña (*f.*)   mountain, 10
    _____ **rusa** (*f.*)   roller coaster, 14
montar   to mount, to ride, 10
    _____ **a caballo**   to ride a horse, 10
    _____ **en bicicleta**   to ride a bicycle, 10
montón (*m.*): **un montón de**   a pile of, 12
morado(-a)   purple, LP
moraleja (*f.*)   moral
moreno(-a)   dark, brunette, 3
morir (o:ue)   to die, 5
moro(-a)   Moorish, Moor
mortal   fatal
mostrador (*m.*)   counter, 9
mostrar (o:ue)   to show, 6
moto (*f.*)   motorcycle, 11
motocicleta (*f.*)   motorcycle, 11
motor (*m.*)   motor, 18
mozo (*m.*)   waiter, 8
muchacha (*f.*)   girl, young woman, 3
muchacho (*m.*)   boy, young man, 3
muchedumbre (*f.*)   crowd
mucho(-a)   much, a lot (of), 4
    Muchas gracias.   Thank you very much., 1
    Mucho gusto.   Pleased to meet you., 1
    no mucho   not much, LP
muchos(-as)   many, 4
mudarse   to move (*from one house to another*), 13
muebles (*m. pl.*)   furniture, 13
muerto(-a) (*p.p. of* **morir** *and adj.*)   dead, 15
    _____ **de hambre**   starving, 15
muestra (*f.*)   sample
mujer (*f.*)   woman, 1
    _____ **de negocios** (*f.*)   businesswoman, 16
multa (*f.*)   fine, 18
    poner una _____   to give a ticket (*fine*), 18
mundo (*m.*)   world, 5
muralla (*f.*)   wall

museo (*m.*)   museum, 5
musical   musical, 14
muy   very, LP
    _____ **bien**   very well, LP

N

nacer   to be born
nacimiento (*m.*)   birth, 3
nacionalidad (*f.*)   nationality, 3
nada   nothing, LP; not anything, 6
    de _____   you're welcome, 1
    _____ **más**   nothing else, 6
nadar   to swim, 10
nadie   nobody, no one, not anyone, 6
naranja (*f.*)   orange, 14
nariz (*f.*)   nose, 17
naturaleza (*f.*)   nature, 10
Navidad (*f.*)   Christmas, 4
necesario(-a)   necessary, 6
necesitar   to need, 2
negar (e:ie)   to deny, 12
negro(-a)   black, LP
neumático (*m.*)   tire, 18
nevado(-a)   snow-covered
nevar (e:ie)   to snow, 8
ni   nor, 6
    _____ **... ni...**   neither . . . nor . . . , 6
niebla (*f.*)   fog, 8
    hay _____   it's foggy, 8
nieta (*f.*)   granddaughter, 5
nieto (*m.*)   grandson, 5
nieve (*f.*)   snow, 10
ninguno(-a), ningún   no, none, not any, 6
niñez (*f.*)   childhood
niño(-a) (*m., f.*)   child, 10
nivel (*m.*)   level
no   no, not, LP
    no muy bien   not very well, LP
noche (*f.*)   evening, night, 2
    de la _____   in the evening, 2
    esta _____   tonight, 2
    por la _____   in the evening, 2
nombre (*m.*)   noun, 1; name, 3
    segundo _____   middle name
noroeste   northwest
norte   north, 10
norteamericano(-a)   North American, 3
nos   us, 6; (to, for) us, 7; (to, for) ourselves, 9
    _____ **vemos.**   See you., LP
nosotros(-as)   we, 1; us, 6

nota (*f.*)   grade, 16
noticias (*f. pl.*)   news
novecientos   nine hundred, 2
novedades (*f. pl.*)   novelties
noveno(-a)   ninth, 9
noventa   ninety, 1
novia (*f.*)   girlfriend, fiancée, bride, 2
noviembre   November, LP
novio (*m.*)   boyfriend, fiancé, groom, 2
nublado(-a)   cloudy
nudos (*m. pl.*)   knots
nuera (*f.*)   daughter-in-law, 5
nuestro(-a)   our, 2; (*pron.*) ours, 9
nueve   nine, LP
nuevo(-a)   new, 4
número (*m.*)   number, 1; size (*of shoes*), 15
    _____ **de identidad** (*m.*)   identification number, 3
    _____ **de la licencia de conducir** (*m.*)   driver's license number, 3
    _____ **de seguro social** (*m.*)   social security number, 3
nunca   never, 5

O

o   or, 2
    _____ **... o...**   either . . . or . . . , 6
objeto (*m.*)   object, 6
obra (*f.*)   work
    _____ **de teatro** (*f.*)   play
    _____ **maestra** (*f.*)   masterpiece
océano (*m.*)   ocean, 10
    _____ **Atlántico**   Atlantic Ocean, 10
octavo(-a)   eighth, 9
octubre   October, LP
ocupación (*f.*)   occupation, 3
ocupado(-a)   busy, occupied, 4
ochenta   eighty, 1
ocho   eight, LP
ochocientos   eight hundred, 2
odiar   to hate, 10
odio (*m.*)   hatred
oeste   west, 10
oferta (*f.*)   special offer
oficina (*f.*)   office, 6
    _____ **de correos** (*f.*)   post office, 12
    _____ **de turismo** (*f.*)   tourist office, 6

oficio (*m.*) trade, 16

ofrecer to offer

oído (*m.*) ear (*inner*), 17; (*p.p. of* oír) heard, 15

oír to hear, 15

ojalá God grant, I hope, 11

ojo (*m.*) eye, 17

un _____ de la cara an arm and a leg, 10

ola (*f.*) wave

olor (*m.*) smell, fragrance

olvidar(se) (de) to forget, 9

ómnibus (*m.*) bus, 5

once eleven, LP

onza (*f.*) gold coin

operación (*f.*) surgery

operar to operate

oportunidad (*f.*) opportunity, 5

oprimido(-a) oppressed

optativo(-a) elective

optimista (*invariable adj.*) optimistic

ordenador (*m.*) computer (*Sp.*), 3

oreja (*f.*) ear, 17

orgullo (*m.*) pride

orgulloso(-a) proud

oriental eastern

orilla (*f.*) bank (*river*); shore

oro (*m.*) gold, 6

orquesta (*f.*) orchestra, 4

ortiga (*f.*) nettle

os you (*inf. pl.*), 6; (to, for) you, 7; (to) yourselves, 9

oscuro(-a) dark

otoño (*m.*) autumn, fall, LP

otro(-a) another, other, 5

otra vez again, 14

oveja (*f.*) sheep

oye listen, 1

P

pacer to graze

padrastro (*m.*) stepfather, 5

padre (*m.*) father, 5

padres (*m., pl.*) parents, 5

paella (*f.*) (*Sp.*) chicken and seafood with rice

pagar to pay, 7

página (*f.*) page, LP

país (*m.*) country, 10

País Vasco (*m.*) Basque Country

pájaro (*m.*) bird

palabra (*f.*) word, LP

palacio (*m.*) palace, 12

palita (*f.*) dustpan, 9

pan (*m.*) bread, 14

panqueque (*m.*) pancake

pantalón (*m.*) pants, trousers, 11

pantalones (*m. pl.*) pants, trousers, 11

pantalones cortos shorts

pantimedias (*f. pl.*) pantyhose, 15

pantorrilla (*f.*) calf (*of leg*)

pañuelo (*m.*) handkerchief, 15

papa (*f.*) potato, 8

_____s fritas (*f. pl.*) French fries, 8

papá dad, 5

papel (*m.*) paper, 1

_____ higiénico (*m.*) toilet tissue, 14

paperas (*f. pl.*) mumps

paquete (*m.*) package, 12

par (*m.*) pair, 15

para to, in order to, 3; for, 6; by, 8

_____ que in order that, 14

parabrisas (*m.*) windshield, 18

parado(-a) standing, 12

paraguas (*m.*) umbrella

paraguayo(-a) Paraguayan, 9

parar to stop, 18

parecer to seem

parecerse (a) to look like, 11

pared (*f.*) wall, 1

pareja (*f.*) couple, 18

pareo (*m.*) two-piece outfit

parque (*m.*) park, 12

_____ de diversiones (*m.*) amusement park, 14

parquear to park, 11

parte (*f.*): a alguna _____ somewhere

a todas _____s everywhere

partera (*f.*) midwife

partido (*m.*) game, 16

pasado(-a) last, 7

pasaje (*m.*) ticket, 7

_____ de ida (*m.*) one-way ticket, 7

_____ de ida y vuelta (*m.*) round-trip ticket, 7

_____ de primera clase (*m.*) first-class ticket, 7

pasaporte (*m.*) passport, 6

pasar to pass; to spend (*time*), 6; to happen, 7

_____ la aspiradora to vacuum, 9

_____ por to go by, through, 6

pasatiempo (*m.*) pastime, 10

Pase. Come in., 1

pasear to take a stroll or walk

paseo (*m.*) median, walkway

pasillo (*m.*) aisle, 7

paso (*m.*) step

pastilla (*f.*) pill, 17

patata (*f.*) potato, 8

paterno(-a) paternal

patinaje (*m.*) skating

patria (*f.*) country

pavo (*m.*) turkey, 8

paz (*f.*) peace

pecho (*m.*) chest, 17

pedido (*m.*) order, 8

pedir (e:i) to ask for, to request, 6; to order, 8

_____ prestado to borrow, 11

_____ turno (cita) to make an appointment, 9

_____ un préstamo to apply for a loan, 11

peinado (*m.*) hairstyle, hairdo, 9

peinarse to comb or style one's hair, 9

peine (*m.*) comb, 9

película (*f.*) film (*for camera*), 11; movie, 14

_____ de acción (*f.*) action, adventure movie

_____ de ciencia-ficción (*f.*) science fiction movie

_____ de guerra (*f.*) war movie

_____ de horror (*f.*) horror movie

_____ de misterio (*f.*) mystery movie

pelirrojo(-a) red-headed, 3

pelo (*m.*) hair, 9

peluquería (*f.*) beauty parlor, 9

peluquero(-a) hairdresser, 9

pena: (no) vale la _____ it's (not) worth the trouble, 18

penicilina (*f.*) penicillin, 17

pensamiento (*m.*) thought

pensar (e:ie) to think, 4; to plan, 4

_____ en to think about, 17

pensión (*f.*) boarding house, 5

peor worse, 5

el (la) _____ the worst, 5

pequeño(-a) small, little, 5

pera (*f.*) pear, 14

perder (e:ie) to lose, 4

Perdón. (*m.*) Pardon me., 1

perdonar to forgive

perezoso(-a)   lazy
perfectamente   perfectly, 5
perfecto(-a)   perfect, 14
perfume (*m.*)   perfume
perfumería (*f.*)   perfume shop
periódico (*m.*)   newspaper, 3
periodismo (*m.*)   journalism, 16
periodista (*m., f.*)   journalist, 16
permanente (*m., f.*)   permanent
   (wave), 9
permiso (*m.*)   permission
         Con _____.   Excuse me., 1
pero   but, 3
perro(-a) (*m., f.*)   dog, 9
         _____ caliente (*m.*)   hot dog,
         14
perseverar   to persevere
personaje (*m.*)   character
personal   personal, 3
pesar   to weigh
pesca (*f.*)   fishing, 10
         ir de _____   to go fishing, 10
pescado (*m.*)   fish, 8
pescar   to fish, to catch (a fish), 10
         caña de _____ (*f.*)   fishing
         rod, 10
peseta   monetary unit (*Sp.*)
pesimista (*invariable adj.*)
   pessimistic, 13
peso (*m.*)   weight, monetary unit
   (*Mex.*)
pesquero(-a)   fishing
picado(-a)   choppy
picnic (*m.*)   picnic
pico (*m.*)   bill (*bird*)
pie (*m.*)   foot, 17
piedra (*f.*)   stone
piel (*f.*)   leather
pierna (*f.*)   leg, 17
pieza de repuesto (*f.*)   spare part, 18
pimienta (*f.*)   pepper, 8
pinchazo (*m.*): tener un _____   to
   have a flat tire, 18
pintor (*m.*)   painter
pintura (*f.*)   painting, 5
piña (*f.*)   pineapple, 14
piscina (*f.*)   swimming pool, 10
piso (*m.*)   floor, 6; (*Sp.*) apartment
pizarra (*f.*)   chalkboard, 1
placa (*f.*)   license plate (*Mex.*), 18
plan (*m.*)   plan, 5
plancha (*f.*)   iron, 13
planchar   to iron, 9
planear   to plan, 10
planta baja (*f.*)   ground floor, 15
plata (*f.*)   silver, 6

platicar (*Mex.*)   to talk, to chat, 3
platillo (*m.*)   saucer, 8
plato (*m.*)   dish, plate, 8
playa (*f.*)   beach, 10
playero (*m.*)   beach coverup or shirt
plaza (*f.*)   town square, 5
         Plaza Mayor   main square
plazo: a _____s   in installments, 11
plomero(-a) (*m., f.*)   plumber, 16
pluma (*f.*)   pen, 1
población (*f.*)   population
pobre   poor, 11
poco(-a)   little (*quantity*), 5
         un poco + *adjective*   a little +
         adjective, 7
pocos(-as)   few, 6
poder (o:ue)   to be able to, can, 5;
   (*m.*) power
poema (*m.*)   poem, 2
policía (*m.*)   police officer, 18; (*f.*)
   police, 11
policíaco(-a) (*adj.*)   detective
políticos (*m. pl.*)   politicians
pollo (*m.*)   chicken, 4
         _____ frito (*m.*)   fried chicken
pomelo (*m.*)   grapefruit, 14
ponche (*m.*)   punch, 4
poner   to put, to place, 5
         _____ el aire acondicionado
         to turn on the air
         conditioning, 13
         _____ la calefacción   to turn
         on the heat, 13
         _____ la mesa   to set the
         table, 8
         _____ una inyección   to give
         an injection, shot, 17
         _____ un multa   to give a
         ticket (*fine*), 18
         _____ una obra de teatro   to
         put on a play
ponerse   to put on, 9
         _____ a dieta   to go on a diet,
         14
         _____ de acuerdo   to agree, 10
no tener nada que _____   not
   to have anything to put on,
   15
por   along, 8; around, 8; because of,
   8; by, 8; during, 8; for, 6; in, 8; in
   exchange for, 8; in search of, 8; on
   account of, 8; on behalf of, 8; per,
   6; through, 8
         _____ aquí   around here, 6;
         this way, 8
         _____ encima   above

         _____ eso   that is why, 5
         _____ favor   please, 1
         _____ fin   finally, 10
         _____ la mañana (noche,
         tarde)   in the morning
         (evening, afternoon), 2
¿_____ qué?   why?, 2
         _____ suerte   luckily, 10
         _____ supuesto   of course, 7
         _____ teléfono   by phone; on
         the phone, 2
         _____ vía aérea   by airmail,
         12
porque   because, 3
portaguantes (*m. sing.*)   glove
   compartment, 18
Portugal   Portugal, 2
portugués (*m.*)   Portuguese (*lang.*), 2
poseer   to have, to own, to possess
posibilidad (*f.*)   possibility
postre (*m.*)   dessert, 8
         de _____   for dessert, 8
practicar   to practice, 5
precio (*m.*)   price, 8
preferir (e:ie)   to prefer, 4
pregunta (*f.*)   question, LP
preguntar   to ask (a question), 6
premio (*m.*)   prize, 14
prender   to pin
prensa (*f.*)   press
preocuparse (por)   to worry (about),
   9
preparar   to prepare, 8
presentación (*f.*)   introduction
presentar   to introduce, 7
presente   present, here, LP
presión (*f.*): _____ arterial   blood
   pressure
préstamo (*m.*)   loan
         pedir un _____   to apply for a
         loan, 11
prestar   to lend, 7
primavera (*f.*)   spring, LP
primero(-a), primer   first, 9
         primer día de clases   first day
         of classes, 1
         primera clase   first class, 7
primo(-a) (*m., f.*)   cousin, 4
prisa (*f.*)   haste, hurry
         darse _____   to hurry (up), 14
         No hay _____.   There's no
         hurry., 7
         tener _____   to be in a hurry,
         4
privado(-a)   private, 6
probablemente,   probably, 16

probador (*m.*) fitting room, 15
probar (o:ue) to try, 9; to taste, 9
probarse (o:ue) to try on, 9
problema (*m.*) problem, 2
procedente de coming from
profesión (*f.*) profession, 3
profesor(-a) (*m., f.*) professor, teacher, instructor, LP
programa (*m.*) program, 2
programador(-a) (*m., f.*) programmer, 16
prohibido(-a) prohibited
promedio (*m.*) grade point average, 16
pronóstico del tiempo (*m.*) weather forecast
pronto soon
propietario(-a) (*m., f.*) owner
propina (*f.*) tip, 8
propio(-a)(s) own
  propia página (*f.*) home page
proseguir (e:i) to continue
próximo(-a) next, 7
  próxima vez next time, 7
prueba (*f.*) quiz, LP
psicología (*f.*) psychology, 16
psicólogo(-a) (*m., f.*) psychologist, 16
pueblo (*m.*) town
puente (*m.*) bridge
puerta (*f.*) door, 1; gate, 7
  _____ de salida (*f.*) airline departure gate, 7
  _____ principal (*f.*) main exit (door), 12
puerto marítimo (*m.*) seaport
pues then, 7; therefore, 15; well, 10
puesto (*m.*) stand
puesto(-a) (*p.p. of* **poner** *and adj.*) set, placed, put, 15
  llevar _____ to wear, to have on, 15
pulmonía (*f.*) pneumonia
pulsera (*f.*) bracelet, 8
puntual punctual, 12
pupitre (*m.*) desk, 1
puré de papas (*m.*) mashed potatoes, 8

Q

que (*rel. pron.*) that, 3; who, 12; which, 6; (*conj.*) than, 5
qué what?, LP; **¡qué...!** how . . . !
  ¿A _____ hora? (At) what time?, 1
  ¿_____ día es hoy? What day is today?, LP
  ¿_____ hay de nuevo? What's new?, LP
  ¿_____ hora es? What time is it?, 1
  ¡_____ horrible! How horrible!, 10
  ¡_____ lástima! What a pity!, 5
  ¿_____ quiere decir... ? What does . . . mean?, 1
  ¡_____ sorpresa! What a surprise!, 8
  ¿_____ tal... ? How's it going? (*inf.*), LP; How was (is) . . . ?, 7
  ¿_____ tiempo hace? What's the weather like?, 8
quebrar(se) (e:ie) to break, 17
quedar to be located, 3; to fit, 9
  _____le grande (chico) a uno to be too big (small) on someone, 15
  _____ suspendido(-a) to fail (*exam or course*), 16
quedarse to remain, to stay, 10
  _____ en la cama hasta tarde to sleep late, 11
  _____ sentado to remain seated
queja (*f.*) complaint
querer (e:ie) to want, to wish, to love, 4
  no quise I refused, 11
  ¿Qué quiere decir? What does . . . mean?, 1
  Quiere decir... It means . . . , 1
querido(-a) dear, darling, 8
queso (*m.*) cheese, 3
quien(es) whom, that, 12
quién who?, 2
  ¿de _____? whose?, 4
  ¿_____ es? Who is it?, 2
  ¿_____ habla? Who is speaking?, 2
  ¿De parte de _____? Who is speaking?, 2
química (*f.*) chemistry, 16
quince fifteen, LP
quinientos five hundred, 2
quinto(-a) fifth, 9
quitar to take away, 9
quitarse to take off, 9

R

racimo (*m.*) bunch (*i.e. of grapes*)
radiador (*m.*) radiator
radicarse to gather
radiografía (*f.*) X-ray, 17
rallado(-a) grated
rama (*f.*) branch
rápidamente rapidly, 10
rápido (*adv.*) fast, rapidly, 18
raro(-a) rare
  ¡Qué raro! How odd!
rascacielos (*m. sing.*) skyscraper
rato (*m.*) while, short time
  al _____ a while later, 11
  un _____ a while, 14
rayón (*m.*) rayon
razón (*f.*): **tener _____** to be right, 4
real royal, 12
realista (*invariable adj.*) realistic, 13
rebaja (*f.*) sale, 15
recámara (*f.*) (*Mex.*) bedroom, 13
recepción (*f.*) registration, 6
recepcionista (*m., f.*) receptionist, 3
receta (*f.*) prescription, 17; recipe
recetar to prescribe, 17
recibir to receive, 3
recién casados (*m. pl.*) newlyweds, 18
reciente recent, 10
recientemente recently, 10
recogedor (*m.*) dustpan, 9
recoger to pick up, 11
recomendar (e:ie) to recommend, 8
recordar (o:ue) to remember, 5
recorrer to travel all over (*a place*)
recurrir to turn to
red (*f.*) net
refresco (*m.*) soft drink, soda pop, 4
refrigerador (*m.*) refrigerator, 13
regalar to give (*as a gift*), 9
regalo (*m.*) gift, 9
regazo (*m.*) lap
registro (*m.*) register, 6
regla: en _____ in order
regresar to return, 2
reírse (e:i) to laugh
relajarse to relax
reloj (*m.*) clock, 1
relojería (*f.*) watch store
relleno(-a) stuffed, 8
remar to row
remolcador (*m.*) tow truck, 18
remolcar to tow, 18
renacentista (*invariable adj.*) Renaissance

repasar   to review
repetir (e:i)   to repeat, 8
repollo (*m.*)   cabbage, 14
represa (*f.*)   dam
representación (*f.*)   show
requisito (*m.*)   requirement, 16
reserva (*f.*)   reservation, 16
reservación (*f.*)   reservation, 6
resfriado (*m.*)   cold, 17
resfrío (*m.*)   cold, 17
residencia universitaria (*f.*)   dorm
respaldo (*m.*)   back (*chair*)
responsable   responsible
respuesta (*f.*)   answer, LP
resta (*f.*)   subtraction
restaurante (*m.*)   restaurant, 5
resto (*m.*)   rest, 14
retraso (*m.*)   delay, 7
    tener... de _____   to be . . .
      behind schedule, 7
retrato (*m.*)   portrait
retroceder   to go back
reunión (*f.*)   meeting
revelar   to develop (*film*), 11
reventa (*f.*)   resale
revisar   to check, 18
revista (*f.*)   magazine, 9
revolver (o:ue)   to mix
rey (*m.*)   king
rezar   to pray
rico(-a)   tasty, delicious, 8; rich
río (*m.*)   river, 10
riqueza (*f.*)   riches, wealth
ritmo (*m.*)   rhythm
rizador (*m.*)   curling iron, 9
rizo (*m.*)   curl, 9
robar   to steal, 11
rodeado(-a) (de)   surrounded (by)
rodear   to surround
rodilla (*f.*)   knee, 17
rogar (o:ue)   to beg, to plead, 11
rojo(-a)   red, LP
rollo de película (*m.*)   roll of film, 11
románico(-a)   Romanesque
romper(se)   to break, 17
ropa (*f.*)   clothes, clothing, 11
    _____ hecha (*f.*)   ready-to-
      wear clothes
    _____ interior (*f.*)   underwear,
      15
ropero (*m.*)   closet, wardrobe, 15
rosado(-a)   pink, LP
roto(-a)   (*p.p. of* romper *and adj.*)
    broken, 15
rubio(-a)   blond, 3

ruido (*m.*)   noise, 18
ruinas (*f. pl.*)   ruins, 6
Rusia   Russia, 2
ruso (*m.*)   Russian (*lang.*),   2

S

sábado (*m.*)   Saturday, LP
sábana (*f.*)   sheet, 13
saber   to know, 5; to find out, 10
saborear   to taste
sabroso(-a)   tasty, delicious, 8
sacar   to take out, to withdraw, 11;
    to get, to receive (*a grade*), 16
saco de dormir (*m.*)   sleeping bag, 10
Sagrada Familia (*f.*)   Holy Family
sal (*f.*)   salt, 8
sala (*f.*)   living room, 13
    _____ de emergencia (*f.*)
      emergency room, 17
    _____ de rayos X (equis) (*f.*)
      X-ray room, 17
salario (*m.*)   salary, 13
saldo (*m.*)   balance, 11
salida (*f.*)   exit, 7; departure, 7
salir   to leave, to go out, 5
    _____ de viaje   to leave on a
      trip, 18
salmón (*m.*)   salmon, 8
salón (*m.*)   room
    _____ de belleza (*m.*)   beauty
      parlor, 9
    _____ de estar (*m.*)   family
      room, 13
salsa (*f.*)   sauce, 14
saltar   to leap
Salto Ángel   Angel Falls
salud (*f.*)   health
    ¡Salud!   cheers!
    ¡Salud, amor y pesetas!
      Health, love, and pesetas!
saludo (*m.*)   greeting
    _____s a...   Say hello to . . . ,
      LP
salvavidas (*m., f.*)   lifeguard, 10
sandalia (*f.*)   sandal, 15
sandía (*f.*)   watermelon, 14
sándwich (*m.*)   sandwich, 3
sangrar   to bleed
sangría (*f.*)   sangría, 4
santo (*m.*)   saint
sarampión (*m.*)   measles
sarape (*m.*)   poncho
sartén (*f.*)   skillet, 13
sastre (*m.*)   tailor

se   (to) himself, (to) herself, (to)
    yourself (*form.*), (to) yourselves,
    (to) themselves, 9
    _____ dice...   You say . . . ,
      One says . . . , 1
    _____ prohíbe fumar.   No
      smoking.
    _____ sale por la derecha   exit
      to the right
    _____ usa   it is used
    _____ vende   for sale
secadero (*m.*)   dryer (*coffee*)
secador (*m.*)   blow dryer, 9
secadora (*f.*)   dryer, 13
sección (*f.*)   section, 11
    _____ de (no) fumar (*f.*)   (no)
      smoking section, 7
secretario(-a) (*m., f.*)   secretary, 1
sed (*f.*)   thirst, 4
    tener _____   to be thirsty, 4
seda (*f.*)   silk, 15
sede (*f.*)   headquarters; campus
seguir (e:i)   to follow, to continue, 6
    de haber seguido   had I
      followed, 16
según   according to, 18
segundo(-a)   second, 6
    segundo nombre (*m.*)   middle
      name
seguro(-a)   sure, 12
    estar _____   be sure, 12
seguro (*m.*)   insurance, security
    _____ de automóvil (*m.*)   auto
      insurance
    _____ social (*m.*)   social
      security, 3
seis   six, LP
seiscientos   six hundred, 2
sello (*m.*)   stamp, 12
semáforo (*m.*)   traffic light, 12
semana (*f.*)   week, 9
    Semana Santa   Holy Week
semanal   weekly
semestre (*m.*)   semester, 16
sencillo(-a)   single, 6; simple, 6
sentado(-a)   seated, sitting, 10
sentarse (e:ie)   to sit (down), 9
sentimental   love (*adj.*), 2
sentir(se) (e:ie)   to feel, 9; to be sorry,
    to regret, 11
    lo siento   I'm sorry, LP
señal (*f.*)   sign
señalar   to point
señor (*abbr.* Sr.)   Mr., sir, gentleman,
    LP

señora (*abbr.* **Sra.**)   Mrs. madam, lady, LP

señorita (*abbr.* **Srta.**)   Miss, young lady, LP

septiembre   September, LP

séptimo(-a)   seventh, 9

ser   to be, 1
    Es la…, Son las…   It's … (*referring to time*), 1
    Soy de…   I'm from … , 1

servicio de habitación (cuarto) (*m.*)   room service, 6

servilleta (*f.*)   napkin, 8

servir (e:i)   to serve, 6
    no sirve   it's no good, 18

sesenta   sixty, 1

setecientos   seven hundred, 2

setenta   seventy, 1

sexo (*m.*)   sex, 3

sexto(-a)   sixth, 9

si   if, 5

sí   yes, 1

sidra (*f.*)   cider, 4

siempre   always, 4

siesta (*f.*)   nap

siete   seven, LP

siglo (*m.*)   century

signo (*m.*)   sign (*zodiac*)

siguiente   following, 3; next

silla (*f.*)   chair, 1

sillón (*m.*)   armchair, 13

simpático(-a)   nice, charming, 3

sin   without, 12
    _____ **embargo**   however
    _____ **que**   without, 14

sino   but, 14
    _____ **que**   but rather

sistema (*m.*)   system, 2
    _____ **de calificaciones** (*m.*)   grading system

sitio (*m.*)   place

situación (*f.*)   situation

sobre   about, 10; over

sobrecama (*f.*)   bedspread, 13

sobremesa (*f.*)   after-dinner conversation

sobrenombre (*m.*)   nickname

sobresalir   to be outstanding

sobrina (*f.*)   niece, 5

sobrino (*m.*)   nephew, 5

sobrio(-a)   somber

Sociedad Anónima (*f.*)   Incorporated

sociología (*f.*)   sociology, 16

sofá (*m.*)   couch, sofa, 13

sol (*m.*)   sun, 8

hacer _____   to be sunny, 8

tomar el _____   to sunbathe, 10

solamente   only, 15

soleado(-a)   sunny

solicitar   to apply for, 3

solicitud (*f.*)   application, 3
    _____ **de trabajo** (*f.*)   job application

solo(-a)   alone

sólo   only, 7

soltar (o:ue)   to turn loose

soltero(-a)   single, 3

sollozar   to weep

sombrero (*m.*)   hat

sonar (o:ue)   to ring, 11

sonreír (e:i)   to smile

sonrisa (*f.*)   smile

soñar (o:ue) **con**   to dream about (of), 17

sopa (*f.*)   soup, 8

sorprender   to surprise, 11

sorpresa (*f.*)   surprise, 8

sorteo (*m.*)   drawing (*lottery*)

su   his, her, its, your (*form.*), their, 2

subir   to climb, to go up, 12

subterráneo (*m.*)   subway, 12

subvencionado(-a)   subsidized

sucio(-a)   dirty

sucursal (*f.*)   branch (*office*)

suegra (*f.*)   mother-in-law, 5

suegro (*m.*)   father-in-law, 5

sueldo (*m.*)   salary, 13

suelto(-a)   loose

sueño (*m.*)   dream
    tener _____   to be sleepy, 4

suerte (*f.*)   luck, 3
    buena _____   good luck, 3
    mala _____   bad luck
    por _____   luckily

suéter (*m.*)   sweater, 15

suficiente   enough, sufficient, 11

sufrir   to suffer

sugerir (e:ie)   to suggest, 11

Suiza   Switzerland

suma (*f.*)   addition

supermercado (*m.*)   supermarket, 14

suponer (*conj. like* **poner**)   to suppose, 16

sur   south, 10

suspendido(-a): quedar _____   to fail (*exam or course*), 16

suspiro (*m.*)   sigh

suyo(s), suya(s) (*pron.*)   his, hers, theirs, yours, 9

T

tal vez   maybe, perhaps, 13

talla (*f.*)   size, 15

tallado(-a)   carved

taller (de mecánica) (*m.*)   repair shop, 18

talonario de cheques (*m.*)   checkbook, 11

tamaño (*m.*)   size

también   also, too, 2

tampoco   neither, not either, 6

tan   as, so, 5
    _____ **… como…**   as … as … , 5
    _____ **pronto como**   as soon as, 11

tanque (*m.*)   tank, 18

tanto(-a)   as much, 5; so much, 14
    _____ **como**   as much as, 5

tantos(-as)   as many, 5
    _____ **como**   as many as, 5

tapa (*f.*) (*Sp.*)   hors d'oeuvre

tapete (*m.*)   small rug

tarde (*f.*)   afternoon, 2; (*adv.*) late, 7
    de la _____   in the afternoon, 2
    llegar _____   to be late, 7
    más _____   later, 2
    por la _____   in the afternoon, 2

tarea (*f.*)   homework, LP

tarjeta (*f.*)   card, 7
    _____ **de crédito** (*f.*)   credit card, 6
    _____ **de embarque** (*f.*)   boarding pass, 7
    _____ **de turista** (*f.*)   tourist card, 6
    _____ **postal** (*f.*)   postcard, 7

taxi (*m.*)   taxi, 6

taza (*f.*)   cup, 8

te (*pron.*)   you (*inf.*), 6; (to, for) you, 7; (to) yourself, 9

té (*m.*)   tea, 8

teatro (*m.*)   theater, 8

tejer   to weave

tejido (*m.*)   weaving

teléfono (*m.*)   telephone, 3
    al _____   on the phone, 2
    por _____   by phone, on the phone, 2

televisión (*f.*)   television, 2

televisor (*m.*)   television (set), 13

tema (*m.*)   subject, theme, topic, 2

temer to fear, to be afraid, 11
temperatura (*f.*) temperature, 17
temporada (*f.*) season
temprano early, 9
    llegar ——— to be early, 7
tenedor (*m.*) fork, 8
tener to have, 3
    no ——— **nada que ponerse** not to have anything to put on, 15
    no ——— **razón** to be wrong, 4
    ——— **algo que declarar** to have something to declare, 6
    ——— **... años (de edad)** to be ... years old, 4
    ——— **calor** to be hot, 4
    ——— **correspondencia** to correspond
    ——— **cuidado** to be careful, 4
    ——— **frío** to be cold, 4
    ——— **ganas (de)** to feel like (*doing something*), 14
    ——— **hambre** to be hungry, 4
    ——— **la culpa** to be one's fault, 18
    ——— **lugar** to take place
    ——— **miedo** to be afraid, 4
    ——— **prisa** to be in a hurry, 4
    ——— **que** to have to, 3
    ——— **razón** to be right, 4
    ——— **sed** to be thirsty, 4
    ——— **sueño** to be sleepy, 4
    ——— **... de retraso (atraso)** to be ... behind schedule, 7
    ——— **un pinchazo** to have a flat tire, 18
tenista (*m., f.*) tennis player
tensión (*f.*) stress
tercamente stubbornly
tercero(-a), tercer third, 9
terminar to finish, 9
ternero (*m.*) calf
terraza (*f.*) terrace, 4
terremoto (*m.*) earthquake
tétano (*m.*) tetanus
ti you (*inf. sing.*), 6
tía (*f.*) aunt, 5
tiempo (*m.*) time, 3; weather, 8
    ——— **completo** full-time, 13
tienda (*f.*) store, 8
    ——— **de campaña** (*f.*) tent, 10

——— **por departamentos** (*f.*) department store, 15
tierra (*f.*) earth, land
timbre (*m.*) (*Mex.*) stamp, 12
tímido(-a) timid
tinto red (*wine*), 8
tintorería (*f.*) dry cleaner's, 11
tío (*m.*) uncle, 5
tirar basura to litter
título (*m.*) title
tiza (*f.*) chalk, 1
toalla (*f.*) towel, 6
tobillo (*m.*) ankle, 17
tocadiscos compacto (*m.*) CD player, 4
tocar to play (*music, an instrument*)
tocino (*m.*) bacon
todavía yet, still, 15
todo(-a) all, whole, 7
    todo el día all day long
    todo el viaje the whole trip, 7
todo all, everything (*pron.*), 7
    ——— **está en regla.** Everything is in order., 6
    ——— **lo que pasó** everything that happened, 7
    ——— **me fue mal.** Everything went wrong for me.
tomar to take, 6; to drink, 3
    ——— **algo** to have something to drink, 14
    ——— **el sol** to sunbathe, 10
    ——— **una decisión** to make a decision, 13
    Tome asiento. Have a seat., 1
tomate (*m.*) tomato, 14
tonterías (*f.*): **decir** ——— to talk nonsense, 12
tormenta (*f.*) storm
toronja (*f.*) grapefruit, 14
torre (*f.*) tower
torta (*f.*) cake, 8
    ——— **helada** (*f.*) ice cream cake, 8
tortilla a la española (*f.*) omelette, 8
tortilla mexicana (*f.*) Mexican corn tortilla, 8
tortuga (*f.*) tortoise
tos (*f.*) cough, 17
tostadora (*f.*) toaster, 13
trabajador(-a) hard-working
trabajar to work, 2
trabajo (*m.*) job, 3
traducir to translate, 5
traer to bring, 4
tráfico (*m.*) traffic

trágico(-a) tragic
traje (*m.*) suit, 15
    ——— **de baño** (*m.*) bathing suit, 10
tramo (*m.*) set
traslado (*m.*) transportation
tratar to treat
    ——— **(de)** to try (to), 18
trato (*m.*) deal
travesía (*f.*) voyage
trece thirteen, LP
treinta thirty, LP
tren (*m.*) train, 7
tres three, LP
trescientos three hundred, 2
trimestre (*m.*) quarter, 16
triste sad, 4
tropezar (e:ie) to trip
trozo (*m.*) piece
trucha (*f.*) trout, 8
tu your (*inf. sing.*), 2
tú you (*inf. sing.*), LP
turbonadas (*f. pl.*) gusts
turismo (*m.*) tourism, 6
turista (*m., f.*) tourist, 7
    clase ——— (*f.*) tourist class, 7
turístico(-a) tourist (*adj.*), 10
turno (*m.*) turn, appointment, 9
    pedir ——— to make an appointment, 9
tutear to use the **tú** form
tuyo(s), tuya(s) (*pron.*) yours (*inf. sing.*), 9

U

últimamente lately
último(-a) last, 14
    última vez the last time, 17
un(a) a, an, one, 1
único(-a) only, 11
    hijo(-a) único(-a) (*m., f.*) only child, 11
    lo único the only thing, 16
unido(-a) united
uniforme (*m.*) uniform
unir to unite
universidad (*f.*) university, LP
uno (*m.*) one, LP
unos(-as) a few, some, 1
uruguayo(-a) Uruguayan, 4
usar to wear, to use, 9
    se usa it is used
usted (Ud.) you (*form., sing.*), LP
ustedes (Uds.) you (*form. pl.*), 1

utensilio (*m.*) utensil, 13
útil useful
uva (*f.*) grape, 4

V

vaca (*f.*) cow
vacaciones (*f. pl.*) vacation, 6
　　ir de _____ to go on vacation, 10
vacío(-a) empty, 18
vale okay (*Sp.*), 5
valer to be worth
　　(no) vale la pena it's (not) worth the trouble, 18
valija (*f.*) suitcase, 6
valor (*m.*) value
vámonos let's go, 13
¡vamos! let's go!, 5
vaquero (*m.*) cowboy
　　_____s (*m. pl.*) bluejeans
varicela (*f.*) chickenpox
varios(-as) several, 11
vasija (*f.*) pot
vaso (*m.*) glass, 8
veces: a _____ at times, sometimes, 12
vecino(-a) (*m., f.*) neighbor
vegetal (*m.*) vegetable, 14
veinte twenty, LP
veintidós twenty-two, LP
veintiséis twenty-six, LP
veintitrés twenty-three, LP
veintiuno twenty-one, LP
vela (*f.*) candle
velocidad (*f.*) speed, 18
　　_____ máxima (*f.*) speed limit, 18
vencer to beat, defeat
vendar to bandage, 17
vendedor(-a) (*m., f.*) salesperson, 16
vender to sell, 3
venezolano(-a) Venezuelan, 3
venir (a) to come, 3
venta (*f.*) sale
ventaja (*f.*) advantage
ventana (*f.*) window, 1
ventanilla (*f.*) window (*of a vehicle or booth*), 12
　　asiento de _____ (*m.*) window seat, 7
ver to see, 5
　　a _____ let's see, 11
veranear to spend the summer
verano (*m.*) summer, LP

¿verdad? true?, 1; right?
　　No es _____. It's not true., 12
verde green, LP
verdulería (*f.*) greengrocer's
verdura (*f.*) vegetable, 14
vermut (*m.*) vermouth, 8
vestido (*m.*) dress, 9
　　_____ de noche (*m.*) evening gown, 15
vestirse (e:i) to get dressed, 9
vez (*f.*) time (occasion), 7
　　a veces at times, 12
　　alguna _____ ever, 15
　　de _____ en cuando from time to time
　　en _____ de instead of, 13
　　otra _____ again, 14
　　próxima _____ next time, 7
　　tal _____ maybe, 13
　　última _____ last time, 17
vía (*f.*) street, way
　　por _____ aérea air mail, 12
　　la Gran Vía Main Street
viajar to travel, 5
viaje (*m.*) trip, 6
　　de _____ traveling, 7
　　salir de _____ to leave on a trip, 18
　　todo el _____ the whole trip, 7
viajero(-a) (*m., f.*) traveler, 7
vid (*f.*) vine
vida (*f.*) life
viejo(-a) old, 12
viento (*m.*) wind, 8
　　hacer _____ to be windy, 8
viernes (*m.*) Friday, LP
vinagre (*m.*) vinegar, 14
vino (*m.*) wine, 4
　　_____ blanco (*m.*) white wine, 8
　　_____ tinto (*m.*) red wine, 8
virrey (*m.*) viceroy
visitar to visit, 6
vista (*f.*) view
　　con _____ a overlooking, 6
　　hasta la _____ until I see you again, I'll see you later, 1
visto(-a) (*p.p. of ver and adj.*) seen, 15
viudo(-a) widowed, 3
vivir to live, 3
vocabulario (*m.*) vocabulary, LP
volante (*m.*) steering wheel, 18
volar (o:ue) to fly, 5
volver (o:ue) to return, 5

en seguida vuelvo I'll be right back, 15
vosotros(-as) (*subject pron.*) you (*inf. pl.*), 1; (*object of preposition*), you (*inf. pl.*), 6
vuelo (*m.*) flight, 7
vuelta (*f.*) tour
　　de ida y _____ round-trip, 7
vuelto(-a) (*p.p. of volver and adj.*) returned, 15
vuestro(-a) your (*inf. pl.*), 2; (*pron.*) yours (*inf. pl.*), 9

Y

y and, LP
ya now, already, 7
　　_____ no no longer
yerno (*m.*) son-in-law, 5
yo I, 1
　　¡_____ invito! My treat!, 14
yogur (*m.*) yogurt

Z

zanahoria (*f.*) carrot, 14
zapatería (*f.*) shoe department, shoe store, 15
zapato (*m.*) shoe, 15
zona postal (*f.*) zip code, 3
zoológico (*m.*) zoo, 14
zorro(-a) (*m., f.*) fox

English–Spanish

A

a, an un(a), 1
about de, 7; sobre, 10
accept aceptar, 6
accident accidente (*m.*), 17
according to según, 18
account cuenta (*f.*), 11
　　checking _____ cuenta corriente (*f.*), 11
　　on _____ of por, 8
　　savings _____ cuenta de ahorros (*f.*), 11
accountant contador(-a) (*m., f.*), 16
accounting contabilidad (*f.*), 16
ache doler (o:ue), 17
across from frente a, 12
activity actividad (*f.*), 10
ad anuncio (*m.*), 3

address dirección (*f.*), 1; domicilio (*m.*), 1

    My _____ **is . . .** Mi dirección es..., 1

    What's your _____? ¿Cuál es tu dirección?, 1

advantage: to take _____ **of** aprovechar, 15

advertise anunciar, 13

advice consejo (*m.*), 16

advise aconsejar, 11

advisor consejero(-a) (*m., f.*), 16

afraid: to be _____ tener miedo, 4

after después (de), 8

afternoon tarde (*f.*), 2

    good _____ buenas tardes, LP

    in the _____ de (por) la tarde, 2

afterwards luego, 6

again otra vez, 14

age edad (*f.*), 3

ago: . . . ago hace + *time*, 11

agree ponerse de acuerdo, 10; estar de acuerdo, 18

air: _____ **conditioning** aire acondicionado (*m.*), 13

airmail por vía aérea, 12

airport aeropuerto (*m.*), 6

aisle: _____ **seat** asiento de pasillo (*m.*), 7

alarm clock despertador (*m.*), 11

    the alarm goes off suena el despertador, 10

all todo(-a), 7; (*pron.*) todo, 7

    _____ **right** está bien, 10

allergic alérgico(-a), 17

almost casi, 15

along por, 8

alphabet alfabeto (*m.*), LP

already ya, 7

also también, 2

although aunque, 9

always siempre, 4

ambulance ambulancia (*f.*), 17

amusement park parque de diversiones (*m.*), 14

and y, LP

angry enfadado(-a), enojado(-a), 4

ankle tobillo (*m.*), 17

anniversary aniversario (*m.*), 8

    wedding _____ aniversario de bodas (*m.*), 8

another otro(-a), 5

answer respuesta (*f.*), LP

antibiotic antibiótico (*m.*), 17

any alguno(-a), algún, 6

    not _____ ninguno(-a), ningún, 6

anyone alguien, 6

anything algo, 6

    not _____ nada, 6

apartment apartamento (*m.*), 9; departamento (*m.*)

apple manzana (*f.*), 14

application solicitud (*f.*), 3

    job _____ solicitud de trabajo (*f.*), 3

apply (for) solicitar, 3

    _____ **for a loan** pedir (e:i) un préstamo, 11

appointment cita (*f.*); turno (*m.*), 9

    to make an _____ pedir (e:i) turno, cita, 9

appreciate apreciar, 10

April abril, LP

Argentinian argentino(-a), 16

arm brazo (*m.*), 17

armchair butaca (*f.*); sillón (*m.*), 13

around por, 8

    _____ **here** por aquí, 6

arrive llegar, 6

as como, 10

    _____ **. . .** _____ tan... como, 5

    _____ **if** como si, 18

    _____ **many** tantos(-as), 5

    _____ **many . . .** _____ tantos(-as)... como, 5

    _____ **much** tanto, 5

    _____ **much** _____ tanto como, 5

    _____ **soon** _____ en cuanto, 11; tan pronto como, 11

    _____ **usual** como siempre, 16

Asia Asia, 2

ask preguntar, 6

    _____ **(for)** pedir (e:i), 6

asleep: to fall _____ dormirse (o:ue), 9

aspirin aspirina (*f.*), 17

assist ayudar (a), 16

at a, 2; en, 1

    _____ **about** a eso de, 14

    _____ **the club** en el club (*m.*), LP

    _____ **the university** en la universidad (*f.*), LP

    _____ **what time . . . ?** ¿a qué hora... ?, 1

    at + *time* a la (las) + *time*, 1

Atlantic Ocean océano Atlántico, 10

attend asistir (a), 5

attention: to pay _____ hacer caso, 13

August agosto, LP

aunt tía (*f.*), 5

automatic teller cajero automático (*m.*), 11

automobile automóvil (*m.*), auto (*m.*), carro (*m.*); coche (*m.*), 5

autumn otoño (*m.*), LP

avenue avenida (*f.*), 3

average promedio (*m.*), 16

avoid evitar, 17

B

back espalda (*f.*), 17

backpack mochila (*f.*), 10

bad malo(-a), 4

badly mal, 5

baggage equipaje (*m.*), 7

Bah! ¡Bah!, 5

balance (*bank*) saldo (*m.*), 11

bandage vendar, 17

bank banco (*m.*), 11

barber barbero(-a), (*m., f.*), 9

    _____ **shop** barbería (*f.*), 9

bargain ganga (*f.*), 15

bathe bañar(se), 9

bathing suit traje de baño (*m.*), 10

bathroom baño (*m.*), 6; cuarto de baño (*m.*), 6

bathtub bañadera (*f.*), 6

battery acumulador (*m.*), batería (*f.*), 18

be estar, 4; ser, 1

    _____ **able to** poder (o:ue), 5

    _____ **acquainted with** conocer, 5

    _____ **afraid** temer, 11; tener miedo (de), 4

    _____ **bad weather** hacer mal tiempo, 8

    _____ **. . . behind schedule** tener... de atraso (retraso), 7

    _____ **bored** aburrirse, 10

    _____ **careful** tener cuidado, 4

    _____ **cold** (*weather*) hacer frío, 8; tener frío, 4

    _____ **. . . from here** estar a... de aquí, 12

    _____ **glad** alegrarse (de), 11

    _____ **good weather** hacer buen tiempo, 8

_____ **hot** (_weather_) hacer calor, 8; tener calor, 4

_____ **hungry** tener hambre, 4

_____ **in a hurry** tener prisa, 4

_____ **invited** estar invitado(-a), 9

_____ **located** quedar, 3

_____ **named** llamarse, 9

_____ **pleasing to** gustar, 7

_____ **right** tener razón, 4

_____ **scared** tener miedo, 4

_____ **sleepy** tener sueño, 4

_____ **sorry** sentir (e:ie), 11

_____ **starving** estar muerto(-a) de hambre, 15

_____ **sunny** hacer sol, 8

_____ **sure** estar seguro(-a), 12

_____ **thirsty** tener sed, 4

_____ **tight** apretar (e:ie), 15

_____ **too big (small) on someone** quedarle grande (chico) a uno, 15

_____ **windy** hacer viento, 8

_____ **worth** valer, 16

_____ **wrong** estar equivocado(-a), no tener razón, 4

_____ **. . . years old** tener... años, 4

beach playa (_f._), 10

beans frijoles (_m. pl._), 8

beautician peluquero(-a) (_m., f._), 9

beauty parlor peluquería (_f._), 9; salón de belleza (_m._), 9

because porque, 3

_____ **of** por, 8

bed cama (_f._), 11

to go to _____ acostarse (o:ue), 9

to put to _____ acostar (o:ue), 9

bedroom dormitorio (_m._); recámara (_f._) (_Mex._), 13

bedspread sobrecama (_f._), 13

beer cerveza (_f._), 4

before antes (de), 6; antes de que, 14

beg rogar (o:ue), 11

begin comenzar (e:ie) (a); 4; empezar (e:ie) (a), 4

behalf: on _____ **of** por, 8

believe creer, 3

bellhop botones (_m._), 6

bend doblar, 12

besides además, 4

best el (la) mejor, 5

better mejor, 5

beverage bebida (_f._), 4

bicycle bicicleta (_f._), 10

big grande, 5

to be too _____ quedar grande, 15

bill cuenta (_f._), 8

biology biología (_f._), 16

birth nacimiento (_m._), 3

birthday cumpleaños (_m._), 4

black negro(-a), LP

blame culpa (_f._), 18; culpar, 18

blanket cobija (_f._), frazada (_f._), manta (_f._), 13

blender licuadora (_f._), 13

block (_city_) cuadra (_f._) (_Sp. Am._), manzana (_f._) (_Sp._), 12

_____ (_of buildings_) manzana (_f._) (_Sp. Am._), 12

blond rubio(-a), güero(-a) (_Mex._), 3

blouse blusa (_f._), 15

blow dryer secador (_m._), 9

blue azul, LP

boarding house pensión (_f._), 5

boarding pass tarjeta de embarque (_f._), 7

boat barco (_m._), 7

book libro (_m._), 1

boot bota (_f._), 15

bored: to be _____ aburrirse, 10

boring aburrido(-a), 7

borrow pedir (e:i) prestado, 11

bottle botella (_f._), 8

boy chico (_m._), muchacho (_m._), 3

boyfriend novio (_m._), 2

bracelet pulsera (_f._), 8

brake freno (_m._), 18

bread pan (_m._), 14

break romper(se), quebrar(se) (e:ie), 17

breakfast desayuno (_m._), 6

bride novia (_f._), 2

bring traer, 4

brochure: tourist _____ folleto turístico (_m._), 10

broken roto(-a), 15

broom escoba (_f._), 9

brother hermano (_m._), 3

brother-in-law cuñado (_m._), 5

brown (_hair, eyes_) castaño, 3; marrón, café, LP

brunette moreno(-a), 3

brush cepillo (_m._), 9

building edificio (_m._), 12

bureau cómoda (_f._), 13

bus autobús (_m._), camión de pasajeros (_m._) (_Mex._), ómnibus (_m._), 5

business administration administración de empresas (_f._), 16

businessman (woman) hombre (mujer) de negocios (_m., f._), 16

busy ocupado(-a), 4

but pero, 3; sino, 14

butter mantequilla (_f._), 14

buy comprar, 6; llevarse, 15

by para, 8; por, 8

_____ **airmail** por vía aérea, 12

to go _____ pasar (por), 6

bye chau, LP

C

cabbage repollo (_m._), 14

cabin cabaña (_f._), 10

cafe café (_m._), 5

cafeteria cafetería (_f._), 3

cake torta (_f._), 8

ice cream _____ torta helada (_f._), 8

calculator calculadora (_f._), 16

calculus cálculo (_m._), 16

call llamar, 2

called: to be _____ llamarse, 9

camera cámara fotográfica (_f._), 6

video _____ cámara de video (_f._), 6

camp acampar, 10

can poder (o:ue), 5

can bote (_m._) (_Mex._), lata (_f._), 14

cancel cancelar, 6

capital capital (_city_) (_f._), 7

car auto (_m._), automóvil (_m._), carro (_m._), coche (_m._), 5

caramel custard flan (_m._), 8

carburetor carburador (_m._), 18

card tarjeta (_f._), 7

credit _____ tarjeta de crédito (_f._), 6

tourist _____ tarjeta de turista (_f._), 6

career carrera (_f._), 16

carpet alfombra (_f._), 9

carpenter carpintero(-a), (_m., f._), 16

carrot zanahoria (_f._), 14

carry-on bag bolso de mano (_m._), 7

case caso (_m._), 14

in _____ en caso de que, 14

cash efectivo (*m.*), 11
 in _____ al contado, en efectivo, 11
cassette casete (*m.*), cinta (*f.*), 4
catch (*a fish*) pescar, 10
celebrate celebrar, 4
celery apio (*m.*), 14
center centro (*m.*), 15
central heating calefacción central (*f.*), 13
certainty certidumbre (*f.*), 2
certified certificado(-a), 12
chair silla (*f.*), 1
chalk tiza (*f.*), 1
chalkboard pizarra (*f.*), 1
champagne champán (*m.*), 4
change cambiar, 15
charge cobrar, 11
charming simpático(-a), 3
chat conversar, charlar, platicar, 3
cheap barato(-a), 6
check cheque (*m.*), 11; chequear, revisar, 18
 claim _____ comprobante (*m.*), 11
 traveler's _____ cheque de viajero (*m.*), 6
checkbook talonario de cheques (*m.*), chequera (*f.*), 11
checked a cuadros, 15
checking account cuenta corriente (*f.*), 11
checkup examen (*m.*), chequeo (*m.*), 17
cheese queso (*m.*), 3
chef cocinero(-a), (*m., f.*), 16
chemistry química (*f.*), 16
chest pecho (*m.*), 17
 _____ of drawers cómoda (*f.*), 13
chicken pollo (*m.*), 4
 _____ with rice arroz con pollo (*m.*), 8
child niño(-a), 10
 only _____ hijo(-a) único(-a), 11
children hijos (*m. pl.*), 3
Chilean chileno(-a), 10
Chinese (*lang.*) chino (*m.*), 2
chocolate chocolate (*m.*), 8
 hot _____ chocolate caliente (*m.*), 8
Christmas Navidad (*f.*), 4
 _____ tree árbol de Navidad (*m.*), 4

cider sidra (*f.*), 4
circus circo (*m.*), 14
city ciudad (*f.*), 3
claim check comprobante (*m.*), 11
clarify aclarar, 4
class clase (*f.*), 1
 first-_____ (de) primera clase, 7
 _____ schedule horario de clases (*m.*), LP
 tourist-_____ clase turista (*f.*), 7
classified clasificado(-a), 13
classmate compañero(-a) de clase (*m., f.*), 4
clean (oneself) limpiar(se), 9
clerk empleado(-a) (*m., f.*), 6
climate clima (*m.*), 2
climb escalar, 10, subir, 12
clock reloj (*m.*), 1
 alarm _____ despertador (*m.*), 11
close cerrar (e:ie), 4
 _____ to (*prep.*) cerca de, 3
closet amario (*m.*), ropero (*m.*), 15
clothes ropa (*f.*), 11
clothing ropa (*f.*), 11
club: at the _____ en el club (*m.*), LP
cocktail coctel (*m.*), 4
coffee café (*m.*), 3
coffeepot cafetera (*f.*), 13
cold catarro (*m.*), resfriado (*m.*), resfrío (*m.*), 17
 to be _____ (*weather*) hacer frío, 8; tener frío, 4
color color (*m.*), LP
Colombian colombiano(-a), 13
comb peine (*m.*), 9
 _____ (one's hair) peinar(se), 9
come venir (a), 3
 _____ in! ¡pase!, 1
comedy comedia (*f.*), 8
comfortable cómodo(-a), 5
compact disc disco compacto (*m.*), 4
 _____ player tocadiscos compacto (*m.*), 4
company compañía (*f.*), 3
computer computador(-a), (*m., f.*), ordenador (*m.*) (*Sp.*), 3
concert concierto (*m.*), 9
conduct conducir, 5
confirm confirmar, 6
continue seguir (e:i), 6

conversation conversación (*f.*), 2
cook cocinero(-a) (*m., f.*), 16; cocinar, 9
cookware batería de cocina (*f.*), 13
corner (*street*) esquina (*f.*), 12
cost costar (o:ue), 5
 _____ an arm and a leg costar un ojo de la cara, 10
cotton algodón (*m.*), 15
couch sofá (*m.*), 13
cough tos (*f.*), 17
count contar (o:ue), 5
counter mostrador (*m.*), 9
country campo (*m.*), 10; país (*m.*), 10
couple pareja (*f.*), 18
course: of _____! ¡claro!, por supuesto, 7
cousin primo(-a) (*m., f.*), 4
covered cubierto(-a), 15
covers (*place settings*) cubiertos (*m.*), 8
crazy loco(-a), 7
cream crema (*f.*), 8
cross cruzar, 12
Cuban cubano(-a), 8
culture cultura (*f.*), 9
cup taza (*f.*), 8
curl rizo (*m.*), 9
curling iron rizador (*m.*), 9
curtain cortina (*f.*), 13
customs aduana (*f.*), 6
cut corte (*m.*), 9
 _____ (oneself) cortar(se) (9)

D

dad papá (*m.*), 5
dance baile (*m.*), 4; bailar, 4
dark moreno(-a), 3
darling (mi) amor (*m.*), 8; (*adj.*) querido(-a), 8
data datos (*m.*), 3
date cita (*f.*), 14; fecha (*f.*), LP; (*check or letter*) fechar, 11
 What's the _____ today? ¿Qué fecha es hoy?, LP
daughter hija (*f.*), 5
 _____-in-law nuera (*f.*), 5
day día (*m.*), 1
 a _____ al día, 17
 _____ before yesterday anteayer, 8
 the following _____ al día siguiente, 13

What _____ is today? ¿Qué día es hoy?, LP

dear querido(-a), 18

December diciembre, LP

decide decidir, 3

decision decisión (*f.*), 13

to make a _____ tomar una decisión, 13

declare declarar, 6

degree grado (*m.*), 17

delay atraso (*m.*), retraso (*m.*), 7

delicious delicioso(-a), 4; rico(-a), sabroso(-a), 8

deliver entregar, 16

deny negar (e:ie), 12

department departamento (*m.*), 11

men's _____ departamento (de ropa) para caballeros (*m.*), 15

women's _____ departamento (de ropa) para señoras (damas) (*m.*), 12

department store almacén (*m.*), tienda por departamentos (*f.*), 15

departure: _____ **gate** puerta de salida (*f.*), 7

deposit depositar, 11

descend bajar, 12

describe describir, 4

desert desierto (*m.*), 10

design diseño (*m.*), 15

desk escritorio (*m.*), 1; pupitre (*m.*), 1

dessert postre (*m.*), 8

for _____ de postre, 8

develop (*film*) revelar, 11

dictation dictado (*m.*), LP

dictionary diccionario (*m.*), LP

die morir (o:ue), 5

died muerto(-a), 15

diet dieta (*f.*), 14

to go on a _____ ponerse a dieta, 14

difficult difícil, 3

dining room comedor (*m.*), 13

dinner cena (*f.*), 6

to have _____ cenar, 6

dirty: to get (oneself) _____ ensuciar(se), 9

dish plato (*m.*), 8

dishwasher lavaplatos (*m.*), 13

disinfect desinfectar, 17

divorced divorciado(-a), 3

do hacer, 5

_____ **the shopping** hacer las compras, 14

doctor doctor(-a) (*m., f.*), LP; médico(-a), (*m., f.*), 17

_____'**s office** consultorio (*m.*), 17

document documento (*m.*), 12

dog perro(-a), 9

dollar dólar (*m.*), 6

done hecho(-a), 15

door puerta (*f.*), 1

dotted a lunares, 15

double: _____ **room** habitación doble (*f.*), 6

doubt dudar, 12

downstairs abajo, 12

downtown (*area*) centro (*m.*), 6

dozen docena (*f.*), 14

drama drama (*m.*), 14

dream about (of) soñar (o:ue) con, 17

dress vestido (*m.*), 9

dressed: to get _____ vestirse (e:i), 9

drink bebida (*f.*), 4; beber, tomar, 3

drive conducir, manejar, 5

driver's license licencia de conducir (*f.*), 3

drizzle lloviznar, 8

dry cleaner's tintorería (*f.*), 11

dryer secadora (*f.*), 13

drugstore farmacia (*f.*), 9

during durante, 7; por, 8

dustpan palita (*f.*), recogedor (*m.*), 9

E

each cada, 12

ear (*inner*), oído (*m.*), 17; (*external*) oreja (*f.*), 17

early temprano, 9

to be _____ llegar temprano, 7

earn ganar, 13

easily fácilmente, 10

east este, 10

easy fácil, 3

eat comer, 3

to have something to _____ comer algo, 14

economic económico(-a), 2

education educación (*f.*), 3

egg huevo (*m.*), 8

eight ocho, LP

_____ **hundred** ochocientos, 2

eighteen dieciocho, LP

eighth octavo(-a), 9

eighty ochenta, 1

either . . . or o… o, 6

not _____ tampoco, 6

electrician electricista (*m., f.*), 16

elegant elegante, 8

elevator ascensor (*m.*), elevador (*m.*), 6

eleven once, LP

E-mail correo electrónico (*m.*), 12

embassy embajada (*f.*), 6

emergency emergencia (*f.*), 17

_____ **room** sala de emergencia (*f.*), 17

empty vacío(-a), 18

engaged: to get _____ **to** comprometerse con, 17

engine motor (*m.*), 18

engineer ingeniero(-a) (*m., f.*), 16

engineering ingeniería (*f.*), 16

English (*lang.*) inglés (*m.*), 1; (*nationality*) inglés(-a), 3

enjoy oneself divertirse (e:ie), 10

enough suficiente, 11

enter entrar (en), 15

entrance entrada (*f.*), 7

eraser borrador (*m.*), 1

errand diligencia (*f.*), 11

to run _____s hacer diligencias, 11

escalator escalera mecánica (*f.*), 15

especially especialmente, 5

Europe Europa, 2

evening noche (*f.*), 2

_____ **gown** vestido de noche (*m.*), 15

in the _____ de la noche, 2; por la noche, 2

ever alguna vez, 15

everybody todos(-as), 4

everything todo, 7

_____ **is in order.** Todo está en regla., 6

_____ **that happened** todo lo que pasó, 7

exam examen (*m.*), 3; (*checkup*) examen (*m.*), 17

midterm _____ examen parcial (*m.*), examen de mitad de curso (*m.*), 16

excellent excelente, 8

excess exceso (*m.*), 7

_____ **baggage** exceso de equipaje (*m.*), 7

exchange   cambiar, 15
   in _____ for   por, 8
exchange rate: What is the _____?
   ¿A cómo está el cambio de
   moneda?, 6
excursion   excursión (*f.*), 10
excuse me   perdón, con permiso, 1
exercise   ejercicio (*m.*), LP
exit   salida (*f.*), 7
   main _____   puerta principal
   (*f.*), 2
expensive   caro(-a), 6
experience   experiencia (*f.*), 3
eye   ojo (*m.*), 17

F

face   cara (*f.*), 17
fact: the _____ is . . .   es que... , 12
fail   (*course or exam*) quedar
   suspendido(-a), 16
fall   otoño (*m.*), LP
fall asleep   dormirse (o:ue), 9
fall in love with   enamorarse de, 17
family   familia (*f.*), 5
family room   salón de estar (*m.*), 13
famous   famoso(-a), 5
far (from)   lejos (de), 3
farewell   despedida (*f.*), LP
fast   rápido(-a), 10; (*adv.*)
   rápidamente, 10; (*adv.*) rápido, 18
fat   gordo(-a), 3
father   padre (*m.*), 5
father-in-law   suegro (*m.*), 5
fault   culpa (*f.*), 18
   to be one's _____   tener la
   culpa, 18
favor   favor (*m.*), 13
fax   facsímil (*m.*), fax (*m.*), 12
fear   miedo (*m.*), 4; temer, 11
February   febrero, LP
feel   sentir(se) (e:ie), 9
   _____ like (*doing something*)
   tener ganas de, 14
feminine   femenino(-a), 3
fever   fiebre (*f.*), 17
few   pocos(-as), 6; unos(-as), 1
fiancé   novio (*m.*), 2
fiancée   novia (*f.*), 2
fifteen   quince, LP
fifth   quinto(-a), 9
fifty   cincuenta, 1
fill   llenar, 3
   _____ out   llenar, 3

film   (*for camera*) película (*f.*), 11
filter   filtro (*m.*), 18
finally   por fin, 10
find   encontrar (o:ue), 5
   _____ out   saber, 10
fine   (*adv.*), bien, LP; bueno, 7; está
   bien, 10; multa (*f.*), 16
   give a _____   poner (dar) una
   multa, 18
finger   dedo (*m.*), 17
finish   terminar, 9
first   primero(-a), primer, 9
   _____ class   primera clase, 7
   _____ day of classes   primer
   día de clases, 1
fish   pescado (*m.*), 8; pescar, 10
fishing   pesca (*f.*), 10
   to go _____   ir de pesca, 10
fishing rod   caña de pescar (*f.*), 10
fit   caber, 15; quedar, 9
fitting room   probador (*m.*), 15
five   cinco, LP
   _____ hundred   quinientos, 2
fix   arreglar, 18
flat tire: have a _____   tener un
   pinchazo (*m.*), 18
flight   vuelo (*m.*), 7
   _____ attendant   auxiliar de
   vuelo (*m.*), 7; azafata (*f.*), 7
floor   piso (*m.*), 6
flu   gripe (*f.*), 17
fly   volar (o:ue), 5
fog   niebla (*f.*), 8
foggy: it's _____   hay niebla, 8
follow   seguir (e:i), 6
following   siguiente, 13
food   comida (*f.*), 8
foot   pie (*m.*), 17
for   para, 6; por, 6
   _____ rent   se alquila, 13
foreigner   extranjero(-a), 12
forget   olvidar(se) (de), 9
fork   tenedor (*m.*), 8
fortune   fortuna (*f.*), 14
forty   cuarenta, 1
four   cuatro, LP
   _____ hundred   cuatrocientos,
   2
fourteen   catorce, LP
fourth   cuarto(-a), 9
France   Francia, 2
free   (*of charge*) gratis; libre, 3
freedom   libertad (*f.*), 2
freeway   autopista (*f.*), 18
French   (*lang.*) francés (*m.*), 2

   _____ fries   papas fritas (*f.
   pl.*), 8
Friday   viernes (*m.*), LP
fried   frito(-a), 8
friend   amigo(-a), (*m., f.*), 2
from   de, 1
   _____ the   (*contraction*) del, 3
   ¿_____ where?   ¿de dónde?, 1
   I'm _____ . . .   Soy de..., 1
   to be . . . _____ here   estar a...
   de aquí, 12
   Where are you _____?   ¿De
   dónde eres?, 1
front: in _____ of   frente a, 11
fruit   fruta (*f.*), 8
full   lleno(-a), 18
   _____-time   tiempo completo,
   13
function   funcionar, 18
furnished   amueblado(-a), 13
furniture   muebles (*m. pl.*), 13

G

game   partido (*m.*), 16
garage   garaje (*m.*), 13
garden   jardín (*m.*), 13
gas station   gasolinera (*f.*), estación
   de servicio (*f.*), 18
gasoline   gasolina (*f.*), 18
gate   puerta (*f.*), 7
   departure _____   puerta de
   salida (*f.*), 7
gee!   ¡caramba!, LP
generally   generalmente, 9
gentleman   señor (*m.*), LP
geology   geología (*f.*), 16
German   (*lang.*) alemán (*m.*), 2
Germany   Alemania, 2
get   conseguir (e:i), 6; (*grade*) sacar,
   16
   _____ a haircut   cortarse el
   pelo, 9
   _____ dirty   ensuciar(se), 9
   _____ dressed   vestirse (e:i), 9
   _____ married   casarse con,
   17
   _____ out   salir, 5
   _____ undressed   desvestirse
   (e:i), 9
   _____ up   levantarse, 9
gift   regalo (*m.*), 9
girl   chica (*f.*), muchacha (*f.*), 3
girlfriend   novia (*f.*), 2

give   dar, 4; (*as a gift*) regalar, 9
_____ **a ticket** (*fine*)   poner (dar) una multa, 18
_____ **an injection**   poner una inyección, 17
glad: to be _____   alegrarse de, 11
glass   vaso (*m.*), 8
glove   guante (*m.*), 15
_____ **compartment**   guantera (*f.*), portaguantes (*m.*), 18
go   ir (a), 4
_____ **away**   irse, 9
_____ **by**   pasar por, 6
_____ **camping**   acampar, 10
_____ **down**   bajar, 12
_____ **fishing**   ir de pesca, 10
_____ **on a diet**   ponerse a dieta, 14
_____ **on vacation**   ir de vacaciones, 10
_____ **out**   salir, 5
_____ **shopping**   ir de compras, 10
_____ **through**   pasar por, 6
_____ **to bed**   acostarse (o:ue), 9
_____ **together**   hacer juego, combinar, 15
_____ **up**   subir, 12
I'm leaving   me voy, 3
Let's go!   ¡Vámonos!, 13; ¡Vamos!, 5
to be going (to) + *infinitive*   ir a + *infinitive*, 4
goblet   copa (*f.*), 8
gold   oro (*m.*), 6
gone   ido, 15
good   bueno(-a), buen, 4
_____ **afternoon**   buenas tardes, LP
_____ **evening**   buenas noches, LP
_____ **luck!**   ¡buena suerte!, 3
_____ **morning**   buenos días, LP
_____ **night**   buenas noches, LP
it's no _____   no sirve, 18
good-bye   adiós, LP
grade   nota (*f.*), 16
_____ **point average**   promedio (*m.*), 16
graduate   graduar(se), 16
granddaughter   nieta (*f.*), 5
grandfather   abuelo (*m.*), 5

grandmother   abuela (*f.*), 5
grandson   nieto (*m.*), 5
grape   uva (*f.*), 4
grapefruit   toronja (*f.*), pomelo (*m.*), 14
gray   gris, LP
great   magnífico(-a), 4
green   verde, LP
greeting   saludo (*m.*), LP
groom   novio (*m.*), 2
ground floor   planta baja (*f.*), 15
group (*music*)   orquesta (*f.*), 4
gym   gimnasio (*m.*), 3

H

hair   cabello (*m.*), 7; pelo (*m.*), 9
to comb one's _____   peinarse, 9
to wash one's _____   lavarse la cabeza, 9
haircut   corte (*m.*), 9
to get a _____   cortarse el pelo, 9
hairdo   peinado (*m.*), 9
hairdresser   peluquero(-a) (*m.*, *f.*), 9
hairstyle   peinado (*m.*), 9
half   medio(-a), 8
_____ **an hour**   media hora, 7
_____ **brother**   medio hermano, 5
_____ **past**   y media (*time*), 1
_____ **sister**   media hermana, 5
ham   jamón (*m.*), 3
hamburger   hamburguesa (*f.*), 8
hand   mano (*f.*), LP
handbag   bolsa (*f.*), bolso (*m.*), cartera (*f.*), 9
handkerchief   pañuelo (*m.*), 15
handsome   guapo(-a), 3
happen   pasar, 7
happy   contento(-a), 4; feliz, 4
hate   odiar, 10
have   haber (*aux.*), 15; tener, 3
_____ **a good time**   divertirse (e:ie), 10
_____ **a nice trip**   buen viaje, 7
_____ **a seat.**   Tome asiento., 1
to _____ **been doing something for a length of time**   hace + *time* + que + *verb* (*present*), 7

_____ **dinner**   cenar, 6
to _____ **done something in the past**   hace + *time* + que + *verb* (*preterit/imperfect*), 11
_____ **just ...**   acabar de..., 6
_____ **lunch**   almorzar (o:ue), 5
_____ **on**   llevar puesto(-a), 15
_____ **something to declare**   tener algo que declarar, 6
_____ **something to eat**   comer algo, 14
_____ **something to drink**   tomar algo, 14
_____ **to**   deber, 3; tener que, 3
he   él, 1
head   cabeza (*f.*), 17
headache   dolor de cabeza (*m.*), 17
headlight   luz (*f.*), 18
hear   oír, 15
heat   calor (*m.*), 4
central _____   calefacción central (*f.*), 13
height   estatura (*f.*), 5
hello   hola, LP; (*on the phone*) bueno, 2; (*on the phone*) dígame, 2
say _____ **to ...**   saludos a..., 1
help   ayudar (a), 16
her   ella, 6; la, 6; le, 7; su, 2
here   aquí, 4; presente, LP
_____ **they are.**   Aquí las (los) tiene., 6
hers   suyo(-a)(s), 9
herself   se, 9
hi   hola, LP
highway   autopista (*f.*), carretera (*f.*), 18
him   él, 6; le, 7; lo, 6
himself   se, 9
his   su, 2; suyo(-a)(s), 9
holiday   feriado (*m.*), día de fiesta (*m.*), 14
home   casa (*f.*), 2
_____ **appliance**   aparato electrodoméstico (*m.*), 13
homework   tarea (*f.*), LP
hood   capó (*m.*), 18
hope   esperar, 11
I _____ **...**   ojalá..., 11
horrible: How _____**!**   ¡Qué horrible!, 10
horribly   horriblemente, 10

hors d'oeuvres   entremeses (*m. pl.*), 4
horse   caballo (*m.*), 10
hospital   hospital (*m.*), 2
hot   caliente, 7
    to be _____ (*weather*) hacer calor, 8; tener calor, 4
    _____ **chocolate**   chocolate caliente (*m.*), 8
    _____ **dog**   perro caliente (*m.*), 14
hotel   hotel (*m.*), 6
hour   hora (*f.*), 7
house   casa (*f.*), 2
how   cómo, 1
    _____ **are you?**   ¿Cómo está Ud.? (*form.*), ¿Cómo estás? (*inf.*), LP
    _____ **do you say . . . ?**   ¿Cómo se dice...?, 1
    _____ **long . . . ?**   ¿cuánto tiempo...?
    _____ **many**   cuántos(-as), 1
    _____ **much**   cuánto(-a), 4
    _____**'s it going?**   ¿Qué tal?, LP
    _____ **was (is) . . . ?**   ¿Qué tal...?, 7
hug   abrazar, 8
hundred   cien, ciento, 1
hungry: to be _____   tener hambre, 4
hunt   cazar, 10
hurry (up)   apurarse, darse prisa, 14
    to be in a _____   tener prisa, 4
    There's no _____.   No hay apuro (prisa)., 7
hurt   doler (o:ue), 17
husband   esposo (*m.*), 3

I

I   yo, 1
ice cream   helado (*m.*), mantecado (*m.*) (*Mex.*, *Puerto Rico*), 8
    _____ **cake**   torta helada (*f.*), 8
iced   helado(-a), 8
idea   idea (*f.*), 4
identification (card)   documento de identidad (de identificación) (*m.*), 12
if   si, 5
important   importante, 16
in   en, 1
    _____ **case**   en caso de que, 14
    _____ **cash**   al contado, 12; en efectivo, 12

    _____ **English**   en inglés, 1
    _____ **exchange for**   por, 8
    _____ **front of**   frente a, 12
    _____ **order that**   para que, 14
    _____ **order to**   para, 3
    _____ **search of**   en busca de, 8
    _____ **that case**   entonces, 2
    _____ **the afternoon**   de la tarde, 2; por la tarde, 2
    _____ **the evening**   de la noche, 2; por la noche, 2
    _____ **the morning**   de la mañana, 2; por la mañana, 2
inexpensive   barato(-a), 6
infection   infección (*f.*), 17
information   información (*f.*), 6
injection   inyección (*f.*), 17
    to give an _____   poner una inyección, 17
insist on   insistir en, 17
inspector   inspector(-a) (*m., f.*), 6
install   instalar, 18
installments   plazos (*m. pl.*), 11
    in _____   a plazos, 11
instead of   en vez de, 13
institution   institución (*f.*), 3
instructor   instructor(-a) (*m., f.*), 10; profesor(-a) (*m., f.*), LP
intelligent   inteligente, 3
interest   interés (*m.*), 6
interesting   interesante, 5
interior   interior, 6
interview   entrevista (*f.*), LP
introduce   presentar, 7
invite   invitar (a), 4
    invited: to be _____   estar invitado(-a), 9
iron   planchar, 9; plancha (*f.*), 13
it   la, 6; lo, 6
Italian   (*lang.*) italiano (*m.*), 2
Italy   Italia, 2
its   su, 2

J

jack   gato (*m.*), 18
jacket   chaqueta (*f.*), 15
January   enero, LP
Japanese   (*lang.*) japonés (*m.*), 2
job   empleo (*m.*), trabajo (*m.*), 3
    _____ **application**   solicitud de trabajo (*f.*), 3
joke   bromear, 10

journalism   periodismo (*m.*), 16
journalist   periodista (*m., f.*), 16
juice   jugo (*m.*), 8
July   julio, LP
June   junio, LP

K

key   llave (*f.*), 6
kid: to _____ (*joke*)   bromear, 10
kilometer   kilómetro (*m.*), 18
kiss   beso (*m.*), 8
kitchen   cocina (*f.*), 9
    _____ **sink**   fregadero (*m.*), 13
knee   rodilla (*f.*), 17
knife   cuchillo (*m.*), 8
know   conocer, 5; saber, 5
knowledge   conocimiento (*m.*), 3

L

laboratory   laboratorio (*m.*), 16
lady   señora (*f.*), LP
    young _____   señorita (*f.*), LP
lake   lago (*m.*), 10
lamb   cordero (*m.*), 8
lamp   lámpara (*f.*), 13
language   idioma (*m.*), 2
large   grande, 5
last   pasado(-a), 7; último(-a), 14
    _____ **month**   mes pasado (*m.*), 7
    _____ **night**   anoche, 8
    _____ **time**   última vez (*f.*), 17
late   tarde, 7
    to be _____   llegar tarde, 7
later   más tarde, 2
    a while _____   al rato, 11
    (I'll) see you _____   hasta luego, LP; hasta la vista, 1
Latin American   latinoamericano(-a), 16
law school   facultad de derecho (*f.*), 16
lawyer   abogado(-a) (*m., f.*), 16
learn   aprender (a), 3
least   el (la) menos, 5
leave   dejar, 8; irse, 9; salir, 5
    I'm leaving   me voy, 3
    _____ **on a trip**   salir de viaje, 18
left   izquierdo(-a), 6
    on the _____   a la izquierda, 6
leg   pierna (*f.*), 17
lend   prestar, 7
less   menos, 5

_____ . . . **than** menos... que, 5

_____ **than** + *number* menos de + *number*, 5

more or _____ más o menos, 2

lesson lección (*f.*), LP
letter carta (*f.*), 5
lettuce lechuga (*f.*), 14
liberty libertad (*f.*), 2
librarian bibliotecario(-a) (*m., f.*), 16
library biblioteca (*f.*), 2
license licencia de conducir (*f.*), 3
_____ **plate** chapa (*f.*), placa (*f.*) (*Mex.*), 18
lie mentir (e:ie), 8
lifeguard salvavidas (*m., f.*), 10
lift levantar, 9
light luz (*f.*), 1
traffic _____ semáforo (*m.*), 12
like como, 10
to feel _____ tener ganas de, 14
to _____ gustar, 7
to _____ **very much** encantar, 8
line: to stand in _____ hacer cola, 14
linen hilo (*m.*), lino (*m.*), 15
list lista (*f.*), 6
waiting _____ lista de espera (*f.*), 6
listen! ¡oye!, 1
literature literatura (*f.*), 16
little pequeño(-a), 5
a _____ + *adjective* un poco + *adjective*, 7
live vivir, 3
living room sala (*f.*), 13
loan préstamo (*m.*), 11
to apply for a _____ pedir (e:i) un préstamo, 11
lobster langosta (*f.*), 8
located: to be _____ quedar, 3
long largo(-a), 7
look (at) mirar, 3
_____ **for** buscar, 7
_____ **like** parecerse (a), 11
lose perder (e:ie), 4
lot (of) mucho(-a), 4
lottery lotería (*f.*), 13
love amor (*m.*), 8; encantar, 8; querer (e:ie), 4; sentimental (*adj.*), 2
luck suerte (*f.*), 3
good _____ buena suerte, 3

luckily por suerte, 10
luggage equipaje (*m.*), 7
lunch almuerzo (*m.*), 6
to have _____ almorzar (o:ue), 5

M

madam señora (*f.*), LP
made hecho(-a), 15
magazine revista (*f.*), 9
magnificent magnífico(-a), 4
mail correo (*m.*), 12
E-_____ correo electrónico (*m.*), 12
_____ **a letter** echar una carta al correo, 12
mailbox buzón (*m.*), 13; casillero (*m.*), 12
mailman cartero (*m.*), 12
maintain mantener, 16
major especialización (*f.*), 16
make hacer, 5
_____ **a decision** tomar una decisión, 13
_____ **an appointment** pedir (e:i) turno, cita, 9
man hombre (*m.*), 1
young _____ chico (*m.*), muchacho (*m.*), 3
many muchos(-as), 4
as _____ tantos(-as), 5
how _____ cuántos(-as), 1
map mapa (*m.*), 1
March marzo, LP
margarine margarina (*f.*), 14
marital status estado civil (*m.*), 3
market mercado (*m.*), 14
married casado(-a), 3
marry casarse (con), 17
mashed potatoes puré de papas (*m.*), 8
match combinar, hacer juego, 15
mathematics matemáticas (*f. pl.*), 16
mattress colchón (*m.*), 13
May mayo, LP
maybe tal vez, 13
me me, 6, 7; mí, 6
meal comida (*f.*), 8
mean: What does . . . _____**?** ¿Qué quiere decir...?, 1
It _____**s . . .** Quiere decir..., 1
meat carne (*f.*), 8
meatball albóndiga (*f.*), 8
mechanic mecánico (*m.*), 18

medical médico(-a), 17
medicine medicina (*f.*), 5
_____ **cabinet** botiquín (*m.*), 9
Mediterranean Sea mar Mediterráneo, 10
medium mediano(-a), 15
meet conocer, 7; encontrarse (o:ue) (con), 12
Pleased to _____ **you.** Mucho gusto., 1
meeting reunión (*f.*), 12
melon melón (*m.*), 14
men's department departamento de (ropa para) caballeros (*m.*), 15
menu menú (*m.*), lista (*f.*), carta (*f.*), 8
Mexican mexicano(-a), 6
microwave (oven) (horno de) microondas (*m.*), 13
midnight medianoche (*f.*), 4
at _____ a la medianoche, 4
midterm exam examen de mitad de curso (*m.*), examen parcial (*m.*), 16
mile milla (*f.*), 18
milk leche (*f.*), 8
mine mío(-a), míos(-as), 9
mineral water agua mineral (*f.*), 8
mirror espejo (*m.*), 9
miss echar de menos, 5; extrañar, 5
Miss señorita, Srta. (*f.*), LP
modern moderno(-a), 6
mom mamá (*f.*), 4
moment momento (*m.*), 2
one _____ un momento, 2
Monday lunes (*m.*), LP
money dinero (*m.*), 2
_____ **order** giro postal (*m.*), 12
month mes (*m.*), LP
last _____ mes pasado, 7
more más, 5
_____ **or less** más o menos, 2
_____ **. . . than** más... que, 5
_____ **than** + *number* más de + *number*, 5
morning mañana (*f.*), 2
good _____ buenos días, LP
in the _____ de la mañana, 2; por la mañana, 2
most el (la) más, 5
mother madre (*f.*), 4
mother-in-law suegra (*f.*), 5
motor motor (*m.*), 18
motorcycle motocicleta (*f.*), moto (*f.*), 11

mountain   montaña (*f.*), 10
mouth   boca (*f.*), 17
move   mudarse, 13
movie   película (*f.*), 14
movie theater   cine (*m.*), 7
movies   cine (*m.*), 7
Mr.   señor (*m.*), Sr., LP
Mrs.   señora (*f.*), Sra., LP
much   mucho(-a), 4
    as _____ as   tanto(-a), 5
    how _____   cuánto(-a), 4
museum   museo (*m.*), 5
musical   musical, 14
must   deber, 3
my   mi(s), 2
myself   me, 9

N

name   nombre (*m.*), 3
    husband's (wife's) name
       nombre del esposo (de la
       esposa) (*m.*), 3
    My _____ is . . .   Me llamo...,
       LP
    What's your _____?   ¿Cómo
       se llama Ud.? (*form.*), LP;
       ¿Cómo te llamas? (*inf.*), 1
napkin   servilleta (*f.*), 8
narrow   estrecho(-a), 15
nationality   nacionalidad (*f.*), 3
nature   naturaleza (*f.*), 10
near   (*adv.*), cerca, 3; (*prep.*), cerca
    de, 3
necessary   necesario(-a), 6
neck   cuello (*m.*), 7
need   necesitar, 2
neighborhood   barrio (*m.*), 13
neither   tampoco, 6
    _____ . . . nor   ni... ni, 6
nephew   sobrino (*m.*), 5
never   nunca, 5; jamás, 6
new   nuevo(-a), 4
New Year's Eve   fin de año (*m.*), 4
newlyweds   recién casados (*m. pl.*),
    18
newspaper   diario (*m.*), periódico
    (*m.*), 3
next   próximo(-a), 7
    _____ time   la próxima vez, 7
    _____ to   al lado de, 12
nice   simpático(-a), 3
niece   sobrina (*f.*), 5
night   noche (*f.*), 2
    at _____   por la noche, 2

good _____   buenas noches,
    LP
last _____   anoche, 8
nightgown   camisón (*m.*), 15
nightstand   mesita de noche (*f.*), 13
nine   nueve, LP
    _____ hundred   novecientos,
       2
nineteen   diecinueve, LP
ninety   noventa, 1
ninth   noveno(-a), 9
no   no, LP; ningún, ninguna, 6
    _____ one   nadie, 6
    _____ wonder   con razón, 10
nobody   nadie, 6
noise   ruido (*m.*), 18
none   ninguno(-a), ningún, 6
nonsense: to talk _____   decir
    tonterías, 12
noon   mediodía (*m.*), 4
    at _____   al mediodía, 4
nor   ni, 6
    neither . . . _____ . . .   ni...
       ni..., 6
north   norte (*m.*), 10
North American   norteamericano(-a),
    3
nose   nariz (*f.*), 17
not   no, LP
notebook   cuaderno (*m.*), 1
nothing   nada, LP
    _____ else   nada más, 6
notice   fijarse en, 17
November   noviembre, LP
now   ahora, 4; ya, 7
    _____ that I think about it
       ahora que lo pienso, 14
    right _____   ahora mismo, 18
number   número (*m.*), 1
    driver's license _____   número
       de la licencia de conducir
       (*m.*), 3
    social security _____   número
       de seguro social (*m.*), 3
nurse   enfermero(-a) (*m., f.*), 17

O

object   objeto (*m.*), 6
obtain   conseguir (e:i), 6
occupation   ocupación (*f.*), 3
occupied   ocupado(-a), 4
ocean   océano (*m.*), 10
October   octubre, LP

of   de, 2;
    _____ course!   ¡claro!, ¡por
       supuesto!, 7
    _____ the   del (*contraction*),
       3
office   oficina (*f.*), 6
    doctor's _____   consultorio
       (*m.*), 17
    post _____   oficina de correos
       (*f.*), correo (*m.*), 12
    tourist _____   oficina de
       turismo (*f.*), 6
oh   ah, 4
oil   aceite (*m.*), 14
okay   bien, 7; bueno, 7; vale, 5
old   antiguo(-a), 12; viejo(-a), 12
    to be . . . years _____   tener...
       años, 4
older   mayor, 5
oldest   el (la) mayor, 5
omelette   tortilla (*f.*), 8
on   en, 2
    _____ account of   por, 8
    _____ behalf of   por, 8
    _____ the phone   por
       teléfono, 2
    _____ the way to   camino a,
       18
    _____ vacation   de
       vacaciones, 10
one   uno, LP
    _____ hundred   cien, 1;
       ciento, 1
    _____-way (ticket)   de ida, 7
onion   cebolla (*f.*), 14
only   solamente; sólo, 7; único(-a),
    11
    _____ child   hijo(-a) único(-a),
       11
    _____ thing   lo único, 16
open   abrir, 3
open(ed)   abierto(-a), 12
opportunity   oportunidad (*f.*), 5
or   o, 2
orange   naranja (*f.*), 14;
    anaranjado(-a), LP
orchestra   orquesta (*f.*), 4
order   pedir (e:i), 8; mandar, 11;
    pedido (*m.*), 8
    in _____ that   para que, 14
    in _____ to   para, 3
    out of _____
       descompuesto(-a), 18
other   otro(-a), 5
our   nuestro(-a)(s), 2
ours   nuestro(-a)(s), 9

out of order   descompuesto(-a), 18
outdoors   al aire libre, 10
overcoat   abrigo (*m.*), 11
overlooking   con vista a, 6

P

pack   hacer las maletas, 10
package   paquete (*m.*), 12
page   página (*f.*), LP
pain   dolor (*m.*), 17
painting   cuadro (*m.*), 5; pintura (*f.*), 5
pair   par (*m.*), 15
palace   palacio (*m.*), 12
pants   pantalón (*m.*), pantalones (*m. pl.*), 11
pantyhose   pantimedias (*f. pl.*), 15
paper   papel (*m.*), 1; (*report*) informe (*m.*), 16
Paraguayan   paraguayo(-a), 9
parcel   paquete (*m.*), 12
Pardon me.   Perdón (*m.*), 1
parents   padres (*m. pl.*), 5
park   parque (*m.*), 12; aparcar, estacionar, parquear, 11
   amusement ____   parque de diversiones (*m.*), 14
part-time   medio día, 13
party   fiesta (*f.*), 4
   New Year's Eve ____   fiesta de fin de año (*f.*), 4
pass (*an exam or course*)   aprobar (o:ue), 16
   ____ through   pasar por, 6
passbook   libreta de ahorros (*f.*), 11
passport   pasaporte (*m.*), 6
pastime   pasatiempo (*m.*), 10
pay   pagar, 7
   ____ attention   hacer caso, 13
peach   durazno (*m.*), melocotón (*m.*), 14
pear   pera (*f.*), 14
pen   pluma (*f.*), 1
pencil   lápiz (*m.*), 1
penicillin   penicilina (*f.*), 17
people   gente (*f.*), 9
pepper   pimienta (*f.*), 8
per   por, 6
perfect   perfecto(-a), 14
perfectly   perfectamente, 5
perhaps   tal vez, 13
permanent wave   permanente (*m., f.*), 9

personal   personal, 3
pessimistic   pesimista (*m., f.*), 13
pharmacy   farmacia (*f.*), 9
phone   teléfono (*m.*), 3
   on the ____   por teléfono, 2
photograph   fotografía (*f.*), 5; foto (*f.*), 5
physics   física (*f.*), 16
pick up   recoger, 11
picture   cuadro (*m.*), 5; pintura (*f.*), 5
pile: a ____ of   un montón de (*m.*), 12
pill   pastilla (*f.*), 17
pillow   almohada (*f.*), 13
pillowcase   funda (*f.*), 13
pineapple   piña (*f.*), 14
pink   rosado(-a), LP
pity: it's a ____   es una lástima, 11
   What a ____!   ¡Qué lástima!, 5
place   lugar (*m.*), 3; poner, 5
   ____ of employment   lugar donde trabaja (*m.*), 3
   ____s of interest   lugares de interés (*m. pl.*), 6
placed   puesto(-a), 15
plan   plan (*m.*), 5; pensar (e:ie), 4; planear, 10
plane   avión (*m.*), 7
plate   plato (*m.*), 8
play: ____ golf   jugar (u:ue) al golf (*m.*), 10;
   ____ tennis   jugar (u:ue) al tenis (*m.*), 10
plead   rogar (o:ue), 11
please   por favor, 1
pleased: ____ to meet you.   Mucho gusto., 1
pleasing: to be ____ to   gustar, 7
pleasure   gusto (*m.*), 1
   The ____ is mine.   El gusto es mío., 1
plumber   plomero(-a) (*m., f.*), 16
poem   poema (*m.*), 2
police   policía (*f.*), 11
police officer   policía (*m.*), 18
police station   estación de policía (*f.*), 11
pool   piscina (*f.*), alberca (*f.*) (*Mex.*), 10
poor   pobre, 11
Portugal   Portugal, 2
Portuguese   (*lang.*) portugués (*m.*), 2
post office   correo (*m.*), oficina de correos (*f.*), 12
postcard   tarjeta postal (*f.*), 7

potato   papa (*f.*), 8; patata (*f.*) (*Sp.*), 8
   mashed ____es   puré de papas (*f.*), 8
pour down raining   llover (o:ue) a cántaros, 8
practice   practicar, 5
prefer   preferir (e:ie), 4
pregnant   embarazada, 17
prepare   preparar, 8
prescribe   recetar, 17
prescription   receta (*f.*), 17
present   presente, LP; regalo (*m.*), 9
pretty   bonito(-a), lindo(-a), 3
price   precio (*m.*), 8
printed   estampado(-a), 15
private   privado(-a), 6
prize   premio (*m.*), 14
probably   probablemente, 16
problem   problema (*m.*), 2
   financial ____s   problemas económicos (*m.*), 2
   love ____s   problemas sentimentales (*m.*), 2
profession   profesión (*f.*), 3
professor   profesor(-a) (*m., f.*), LP
program   programa (*m.*), 2
programmer   programador(-a), (*m., f.*), 16
provided that   con tal (de) que, 14
psychologist   psicólogo(-a) (*m., f.*), 16
psychology   psicología (*f.*), 16
punch   ponche (*m.*), 4
punctual   puntual, 12
punishment   castigo (*m.*), 10
purse   bolsa (*f.*) (*Mex.*), bolso (*m.*), cartera (*f.*), 9
put   poner, 5; puesto(-a), 15
   not to have anything to ____ on   no tener nada que ponerse, 15
   ____ on   ponerse, 9
   ____ to bed   acostar (o:ue), 9

Q

quarter   trimestre (*m.*), 16
   ____ after/past   ...y cuarto (*time*), 1
   ____ of/to   ... menos cuarto (*time*), 1
question   pregunta (*f.*), LP
quiz   prueba (*f.*), LP

R

rain lluvia (*f.*), 8; llover (o:ue), 5

    _____ cats and dogs llover a cántaros, 8

raise levantar, 9

rapid rápido(-a), 10

rapidly rápidamente, 10; rápido, 18

rayon rayón (*m.*)

razor máquina de afeitar (*f.*), 9

read leer, 3

ready listo(-a), 11

realistic realista (*m., f.*), 13

receive recibir, 3; (*grade*) sacar, 16

recent reciente, 10

recently recientemente, 10

receptionist recepcionista (*m., f.*), 3

recommend recomendar (e:ie), 8

red rojo(-a), LP; (*wine*) tinto, 8

red-headed pelirrojo(-a), 3

refrigerator refrigerador (*m.*), 13

refuse no querer (e:ie) (*preterit*), 11

register registro (*m.*), 6; matricularse, 16

registered certificado(-a), 12

registration matrícula (*f.*), 16; recepción (*f.*), 6

regret sentir (e:ie), 11

remain quedarse, 10

remember recordar (o:ue), 5; acordarse (o:ue) (de), 9

rent alquiler (*m.*), 13; alquilar, 10

    for _____ se alquila, 13

repair arreglo (*m.*), 18; arreglar, 18

    _____ shop taller (de mecánica) (*m.*), 18

repeat repetir (e:i), 8

report informe (*m.*), 16

request pedir (e:i), 6

requirement requisito (*m.*), 16

research investigación (*f.*), 16

reservation reserva (*f.*), reservación (*f.*), 6

rest resto (*m.*), 14

restaurant restaurante (*m.*), 5

return devolver (o:ue), 7; regresar, 2; volver (o:ue), 5

returned devuelto(-a), 15; vuelto(-a), 15

rice arroz (*m.*), 8

    _____ pudding arroz con leche (*m.*), 8

ride (*a bicycle*) montar en bicicleta, 10; (*a horse*) montar a caballo, 10

right: to (on, at) the _____ a la derecha, 6

I'll be _____ back en seguida vuelvo, 15

_____? ¿verdad?

_____ away en seguida, 6

_____ now ahora mismo, 18

_____ there allí mismo, 12

to be _____ tener razón, 4

ring (*phone*) sonar (o:ue), 11

river río (*m.*), 10

road camino (*m.*), 18

roasted asado(-a), 8

roll of film rollo de película (*m.*), 11

roller coaster montaña rusa (*f.*), 14

room cuarto (*m.*), 6; habitación (*f.*), 6

    _____ service servicio de habitación (cuarto) (*m.*), 6

round-trip de ida y vuelta, 7

royal real, 12

rug alfombra (*f.*), 9

ruins ruinas (*f. pl.*), 6

run errands hacer diligencias, 11

run over atropellar, 17

Russia Rusia, 2

Russian (*lang.*) ruso (*m.*), 2

S

sad triste, 4

said dicho(-a), 15

salad ensalada (*f.*), 4

salary salario (*m.*), sueldo (*m.*), 13

sale liquidación (*f.*), rebaja (*f.*), 15

salesperson vendedor(-a) (*m., f.*), 16

salmon salmón (*m.*), 8

salon salón (*m.*), 9

salt sal (*f.*), 8

same mismo(-a), 13

sandal sandalia (*f.*), 15

sandwich bocadillo (*m.*) (*Sp.*), 3; emparedado (*m.*) (*Sp.*), 3; sándwich (*m.*), 3

Saturday sábado (*m.*), LP

sauce salsa (*f.*), 14

saucepan cacerola (*f.*), 13

saucer platillo (*m.*), 8

save ahorrar, 11

savings ahorros (*m. pl.*), 11

    _____ account cuenta de ahorros (*f.*), 11

    _____ passbook libreta de ahorros (*f.*), 11

say decir (e:i), 6

_____ hello to . . . Saludos a..., LP

How do you _____ . . . ? ¿Cómo se dice...?, 1

You _____ . . . , One says . . . Se dice..., 1

scared: to be _____ tener miedo, 4

schedule horario (*m.*), 16

    class _____ horario de clases (*m.*), LP

    to be . . . behind _____ tener... de retraso (atraso), 7

scholarship beca (*f.*), 16

school escuela (*f.*), 5

science ciencia (*f.*), 16

scream gritar, 11

sea mar (*m.*), 10

seafood mariscos (*m. pl.*), 8

search for buscar, 7

season estación (*f.*), LP

seat: aisle _____ asiento de pasillo (*m.*), 7

    Have a _____. Tome asiento., 1

    window _____ asiento de ventanilla (*m.*), 7

seated sentado(-a), 10

second segundo(-a), 6

secretary secretario(-a) (*m., f.*), 1

section: (no) smoking _____ sección de (no) fumar (*f.*), 7

see ver, 5

    let's _____ . . . a ver..., 11

    (I'll) _____ you later hasta luego, LP; hasta la vista, 1

    _____ you tomorrow hasta mañana, LP

    _____ you. Nos vemos., LP

    until I _____ you again hasta la vista, 1

seen visto(-a), 15

sell vender, 3

semester semestre (*m.*), 16

send enviar, mandar, 3

September septiembre, LP

seriously en serio, 10

serve servir (e:i), 6

service station gasolinera (*f.*), estación de servicio (*f.*), 18

set the table poner la mesa, 8

seven siete, LP

    _____ hundred setecientos, 2

seventeen diecisiete, LP

seventh séptimo(-a), 9

seventy setenta, 1

several varios(-as), 11

sex sexo (*m.*), 3

shame: it's a _____ es una lástima, 11

What a _____! ¡Qué lástima!, 5

shampoo champú (*m.*), 9; lavado (*m.*), 9

shave afeitar(se), 9

shaving cream crema de afeitar (*f.*), 9

she ella, 1

sheet sábana (*f.*), 13

shellfish mariscos (*m. pl.*), 8

ship barco (*m.*), 7

shirt camisa (*f.*), 15

shoe zapato (*m.*), 15

_____ department zapatería (*f.*), 15

_____ store zapatería (*f.*), 15

shopping: to do the _____ hacer (las) compras, 14

to go _____ ir de compras, 10

shopping de compras, 15

to window shop mirar vidrieras, 15

short bajo(-a), 3; corto(-a), 9

shot inyección (*f.*), 17

tetanus _____ inyección antitetánica (*f.*), 17

to give a _____ poner una inyección, 17

should deber, 3

show enseñar (a), 6; mostrar (o:ue), 6

show función (*f.*), 14

shower ducha (*f.*), 6

to take a _____ ducharse, 9

shrimp camarones (*m. pl.*), gambas (*f. pl.*) (*Sp.*), 8

sick enfermo(-a), 4

sign letrero (*m.*), 18; firmar, 6

signature firma (*f.*), 11

silk seda (*f.*), 15

silver plata (*f.*), 6

simple sencillo(-a), 6

since como, 10

sing cantar, 4

single sencillo(-a), 6; soltero(-a), 3

sink (*kitchen*) fregadero (*m.*), 13; lavabo (*m.*), 6

sir señor, LP

sister hermana (*f.*), 3

sister-in-law cuñada (*f.*), 5

sit down sentarse (e:ie), 9

sitting sentado(-a), 10

six seis, LP

_____ hundred seiscientos, 2

sixteen dieciséis, LP

sixth sexto(-a), 9

size medida (*f.*), talla (*f.*), 15; (*of shoes*) número (*m.*), 15

to take _____ ... (*in shoes*) calzar..., 15

ski esquiar, 10

skillet sartén (*f.*), 13

skirt falda (*f.*), 15

sleep dormir (o:ue), 5

_____ late quedarse en la cama hasta tarde, 11

sleeping bag saco de dormir (*m.*), bolsa de dormir (*f.*), 10

sleepy: to be _____ tener sueño, 4

slender delgado(-a), 3

slow lento(-a), 10

slowly lentamente, 10

small pequeño(-a), 5

to be too _____ (on someone) quedar(le) chico(-a) (a uno), 15

smoking: (no) smoking section sección de (no) fumar (*f.*), 7

no _____ se prohíbe fumar, 12

snow nieve (*f.*), 10; nevar (e:ie), 8

so tan, 5; de manera que, 11; de modo que, 11

_____ much tanto, 14

so-so más o menos, 2

soap jabón (*m.*), 6

soccer fútbol (*m.*), 16

social security seguro social (*m.*), 3

sociology sociología (*f.*), 16

sock calcetín (*m.*), 15

soda pop refresco (*m.*), 4

sofa sofá (*m.*), 13

soft drink refresco (*m.*), 4

some alguno(-a), algún, 6; algunos(-as), 5; unos(-as), 1

somebody alguien, 6

someone alguien, 6

something algo, 6

sometimes a veces, 12

son hijo (*m.*), 5

son-in-law yerno (*m.*), 5

soon: as _____ as en cuanto, 11; tan pronto como, 11

sorry: to be _____ sentir (e:ie), 11

I'm _____ lo siento, LP

soup sopa (*f.*), 8

_____ of the day sopa del día (*f.*), 8

south sur (*m.*), 10

Spaniard español(-a) (*m., f.*), 12

Spanish (*lang.*) español (*m.*), 2

_____ style a la española, 8

spare part pieza de repuesto (*f.*), 18

speak hablar, 2

specialty especialidad (*f.*), 8

speed velocidad (*f.*), 18

_____ limit velocidad máxima (*f.*), 18

spend (*money*) gastar, 18; (*time*) pasar, 6

spoilsport aguafiestas (*m., f.*), 13

spoon cuchara (*f.*), 8

sport deporte (*m.*), 16

spring primavera (*f.*), LP

stadium estadio (*m.*), 16

stairs escalera (*f.*), 6

stamp estampilla (*f.*), sello (*m.*), timbre (*m.*) (*Mex.*), 12

stand in line hacer cola, 14

standing parado(-a), 12

start arrancar (*car*), 18; comenzar a (e:ie), empezar a (e:ie), 4

starving: to be _____ estar muerto(-a) de hambre, 15

station estación (*f.*), 12

police _____ estación de policía (*f.*), 11

service _____ estación de servicio (*f.*), gasolinera (*f.*), 18

stay quedarse, hospedarse (en) (*at a hotel*), 10

steak bistec (*m.*), 8

steal robar, 11

steering wheel volante (*m.*), 18

stepdaughter hijastra (*f.*), 5

stepfather padrastro (*m.*), 5

stepmother madrastra (*f.*), 5

stepson hijastro (*m.*), 5

stereo system equipo estereofónico (*m.*), 4

still todavía, 15

stomach estómago (*m.*), 17

stop parar, 18

store tienda (*f.*), 8

store clerk dependiente(-a) (*m., f.*), 15

stove cocina (*f.*), 13

straight (*hair*) lacio(-a), 9

_____ (ahead) derecho, 12

strange extraño(-a), 18

strawberry fresa (*f.*), 14

street calle (*f.*), 1

_____ corner esquina (*f.*), 12

striped   a rayas, 15
student   estudiante (*m., f.*), 1
study   estudiar, 2
stuffed   relleno(-a), 8
style: to be in _____   estar de moda, 9
_____ one's hair   peinarse, 9
subject   asignatura (*f.*), materia (*f.*), 16; tema (*m.*), 2
subway   metro (*m.*), subterráneo (*m.*), 12
suckling pig (pork)   lechón (*m.*), 8
sufficient   suficiente, 11
sugar   azúcar (*m.*), 14
suggest   sugerir (e:ie), 11
suit   traje (*m.*), 15
suitcase   maleta (*f.*), 6; valija (*f.*), 6
summer   verano (*m.*), LP
sun   sol (*m.*), 8
sunbathe   tomar el sol, 10
Sunday   domingo (*m.*), LP
sunny: to be _____   hacer sol, 8
supermarket   supermercado (*m.*), 14
supper   cena (*f.*), 6
to have _____   cenar, 6
suppose   suponer, 16
sure   seguro(-a), 12
to be _____   estar seguro(-a), 12
surname   apellido (*m.*), 3
surprise   sorpresa (*f.*), 8; sorprender, 11
What a _____!   ¡Qué sorpresa!, 8
sweater   suéter (*m.*), 15
sweep   barrer, 9
swim   nadar, 10
swimming pool   piscina (*f.*), alberca (*f.*) (*Mex.*), 10
system   sistema (*m.*), 2

T

T-shirt   camiseta (*f.*), 15
table   mesa (*f.*), 4
set the _____   poner la mesa, 8
tablecloth   mantel (*m.*), 8
take   llevar, 3; llevarse, 11; tomar, 6
_____ a shower   ducharse, 9
_____ advantage of   aprovechar, 15
_____ an X-ray   hacer una radiografía, 17
_____ away   quitar, 9
_____ off   quitarse, 9

_____ out   sacar, 12
_____ size . . .   (*in shoes*) calzar..., 15
talk   hablar, conversar, charlar, 2; platicar, 3
_____ nonsense   decir tonterías, 13
tall   alto(-a), 3
tank   tanque (*m.*), 18
tape   casete (*m.*), cinta (*f.*), 4
tape recorder   grabadora (*f.*), 6
taste   probar (o:ue), 9
tasty   delicioso(-a), 4; sabroso(-a), rico(-a), 8
taxi   taxi (*m.*), 6
tea   té (*m.*), 8
teach   enseñar (a), 10
teacher   profesor(a) (*m., f.*), LP
team   equipo (*m.*), 16
teaspoon   cucharita (*f.*), 8
teeth   dientes (*m. pl.*), 17
telegram   telegrama (*m.*), 2
telephone   teléfono (*m.*), 3
on the _____   por teléfono, 2
television   televisión (*f.*), 2; (*set*) televisor (*m.*), 13
tell   contar (o:ue), 5; decir (e:i), 6
teller: automatic _____   cajero automático (*m.*), 11
temperature   temperatura (*f.*), 17
ten   diez, LP
tenderloin steak   filete (*m.*), 8
tent   tienda de campaña (*f.*), 10
tenth   décimo(-a), 9
terrace   terraza (*f.*), 4
tetanus shot   inyección antitetánica (*f.*), 17
than   que, 5
thank you   gracias, LP
_____ very much   muchas gracias, 1
thanks   gracias, LP
that (*adj.*) aquel(la), 7; (*adj.*) ese, 7; (*adj.*) esa, 7; (*neuter pron.*) aquello, 7; (*neuter pron.*) eso, 7; (*rel. pron.*) que, 3
_____ one   aquél(la),7; ése, 7; ésa, 7
the   el, 1; la, 1; las, 1; los, 1
theater   teatro (*m.*), 8
their   su(s), 2
theirs   suyo(-a)(s), 9
them   ellas, 6; ellos, 6; las, 6; les, 7; los, 6
theme   tema (*m.*), 2
themselves   se, 9

then   después, 7; entonces, 2; luego, 6; pues, 7
there   allí, 3
Is . . . _____?   ¿Está... ?, 2
right _____   allí mismo, 12
_____ is (are)   hay, 1
There's no hurry.   No hay apuro (prisa)., 7
therefore   pues, 15
these (*adj.*) estos(-as), 7; (*pron.*) éstos(-as), 7
they   ellos 1; ellas, 1
thin   delgado(-a), 3
thing   cosa (*f.*), 14
think   creer, 3; pensar (e:ie), 4
_____ about   pensar en, 17
third   tercero(-a), tercer, 9
thirsty: to be _____   tener sed, 4
thirteen   trece, LP
thirty   treinta, LP
this (*adj.*) este, 5; (*adj.*) esta, 7; (*neuter pron.*), esto, 7
_____ is she (speaking)   con ella habla, 2
_____ one (*pron.*)   éste(-a), 7
_____ very day   hoy mismo, 17
_____ way   por aquí, 8
those (*adj.*) aquellos(-as), 7; (*pron.*) aquéllos(-as), 7; (*adj.*) esos(-as), 7; (*pron.*) ésos(-as), 7
thousand   mil, 2
three   tres, LP
_____ hundred   trescientos, 2
throat   garganta (*f.*), 17
through   por, 8
Thursday   jueves (*m.*), LP
ticket   (*fine*) multa (*f.*), 16; (*for plane, train, bus*) billete (*m.*) (*Sp.*), pasaje (*m.*), 7; (*for a show*) boleto (*m.*), entrada (*f.*), 8
first-class _____   billete (pasaje) de primera clase (*m.*), 7
to give a _____   poner (dar) una multa, 18
one-way _____   billete (pasaje) de ida (*m.*), 7
round-trip _____   billete (pasaje) de ida y vuelta (*m.*), 7
tie   corbata (*f.*), 15
tight: to be _____   apretar (e:ie), 15
they feel _____ (on me)   me aprietan, 15
till   menos (*telling time*), 1

time hora (*f.*), 1; tiempo (*m.*), 3; vez (*occasion*) (*f.*), 7

    at the same _____ al mismo tiempo, 13

    At what _____ ...? ¿A qué hora...?, 1

    have a good _____ divertirse, (e:ie), 10

    last _____ la última vez, 17

    What _____ **is it?** ¿Qué hora es?, 1

tip propina (*f.*), 8

tire goma (*f.*), llanta (*f.*), neumático (*m.*), 18

    have a flat _____ tener un pinchazo (*m.*), 18

tired cansado(-a), 4

to a, 2; para, 3

    _____ **the** al (*m. sing.*) (*contraction*), 3

toast (*wine*) brindar, 3; brindis (*m.*), 4

toaster tostadora (*f.*), 13

today hoy, 1

    What day is _____? ¿Qué día es hoy?, LP

    _____ **is ...** hoy es..., LP

toe dedo del pie (*m.*), 17

together juntos(-as), 11

toilet inodoro (*m.*), 6

toilet tissue papel higiénico (*m.*), 14

told dicho(-a), 15

tomato tomate (*m.*), 14

tomorrow mañana, 2

    see you _____ hasta mañana, LP

tongue lengua (*f.*), 17

tonight esta noche, 2

too también, 2

    _____ **many people** demasiada gente, 10

tooth diente (*m.*), 17

tourism turismo (*m.*), 6

tourist turista (*m., f.*), 7; (*adj.*) turístico(-a), 10

    _____ **brochure** folleto turístico (*m.*), 10

    _____ **card** tarjeta de turista (*f.*), 6

    _____ **class** clase turista (*f.*), 7

    _____ **office** oficina de turismo (*f.*), 6

tow remolcar, 18

    _____ **truck** grúa (*f.*), remolcador (*m.*), 18

toward hacia, 11

towel toalla (*f.*), 6

town square plaza (*f.*), 5

trade oficio (*m.*), 16

traffic light semáforo (*m.*), 12

tragic trágico(-a), 11

train tren (*m.*), 7

translate traducir, 5

travel viajar, 5

    _____ **agency** agencia de viajes (*f.*), 7

    _____ **agent** agente de viajes (*m., f.*), 7

traveler viajero(-a) (*m., f.*), 7

traveler's check cheque de viajeros (*m.*), 6

traveling de viaje, 7

treat: My _____! ¡Yo invito!, 14

trip viaje (*m.*), 6

    Have a nice _____! ¡Buen viaje!, 7

    leave on a _____ salir de viaje, 18

    whole _____ todo el viaje, 7

trousers pantalón (*m.*), pantalones, (*m. pl.*), 11

trout trucha (*f.*), 8

true cierto, verdad, 12

    It's not _____. No es cierto (verdad)., 12

    true? ¿verdad?, 1

trunk (*car*) cajuela (*f.*) (*Mex.*), maletero (*m.*), 18

try probar (o:ue), 9; tratar (de), 18

    _____ **on** probarse (o:ue), 9

Tuesday martes (*m.*), LP

tuition matrícula (*f.*), 16

turkey pavo (*m.*), 8

turn turno (*m.*), 9; doblar, 12

    _____ **in** entregar, 16

    _____ **on the air conditioning** (**heat**) poner el aire acondicionado (la calefacción), 13

twelve doce, LP

twenty veinte, LP

    _____-**one** ventiuno, LP

    _____-**two** ventidós, LP

    _____-**three** veintitrés, LP

    _____-**four** veinticuatro, LP

    _____-**five** veinticinco, LP

    _____-**six** veintiséis, LP

    _____-**seven** veintisiete, LP

    _____-**eight** veintiocho, LP

    _____-**nine** veintinueve, LP

two dos, LP

    _____ **hundred** doscientos, 2

U

ugly feo(-a), 3

uncle tío (*m.*), 5

understand entender (e:ie), 4

underwear ropa interior (*f.*), 15

undress, get undressed desvestir(se) (e:i), 9

unfortunately desafortunadamente, 10

United States Estados Unidos (*m. pl.*), 5

university universidad (*f.*), LP

    _____ **studies** carrera (*f.*), 16

unless a menos que, 14

unpleasant antipático(-a), 3

until hasta, 6; hasta que, 14

    _____ **I see you again** hasta la vista, 1

    _____ **you get** hasta llegar, 12

up: to get _____ levantarse, 9

upstairs arriba, 12

Uruguayan uruguayo(-a), 4

us nosotros(-as), 6; nos, 6, 7

use usar, 9; llevar, 15

usual: as _____ como siempre, 16

utensil utensilio (*m.*), 13

V

vacant libre, 6

vacation vacaciones (*f. pl.*), 6

    to go on _____ ir de vacaciones, 10

vacuum pasar la aspiradora, 9

    _____ **cleaner** aspiradora (*f.*), 9

vegetable verdura (*f.*), vegetal (*m.*), 14

Venezuelan venezolano(-a), 3

vermouth vermut (*m.*), 8

very muy, LP

    (**not**) _____ **well** (no) muy bien, LP

vest chaleco (*m.*), 15

video camera cámara de video (*f.*), 6

vinegar vinagre (*m.*), 14

visit visitar, 6

vocabulary vocabulario (*m.*), LP

W

wait (for) esperar, 9

waiter camarero (*m.*), mesero (*m.*) (*Mex.*), mozo (*m.*), 8

waiting list lista de espera (*f.*), 6

waitress camarera (*f.*), mesera (*f.*) (*Mex.*), 8

wake up despertarse (e:ie), 9

walk caminar, 11

wall pared (*f.*), 1

wallet billetera (*f.*), cartera (*f.*), 15

want desear, 2; querer (e:ie), 4

wardrobe armario (*m.*), ropero (*m.*), 15

wash lavar(se), 9

_____ **one's hair** lavarse la cabeza, 9

washing machine lavadora (*f.*), 13

watch mirar, 3

water agua (*f.*)

_____ **pump** bomba de agua (*f.*), 18

mineral _____ agua mineral (*f.*), 7

watermelon sandía (*f.*), 14

way: on the _____ **to** camino a, 18

we nosotros(-as), 1

wear llevar puesto(-a), usar, 9; llevar, 15

not to have anything to _____ no tener nada que ponerse, 15

weather tiempo (*m.*), 8

to be good (bad) _____ hacer buen (mal) tiempo, 8

wedding anniversary aniversario de bodas (*m.*), 8

Wednesday miércoles (*m.*), LP

week semana (*f.*), 9

weekend fin de semana (*m.*), 5

welcome: you're _____ de nada, 1

well bien, LP; bueno, 3; pues, 10

not very _____ no muy bien, LP

very _____ muy bien, LP

west oeste (*m.*), 10

what cuál, 1; qué, LP, lo que, 10

_____ **day is today?** ¿Qué día es hoy?, LP

_____ **does . . . mean?** ¿Qué quiere decir...?, 1

_____ **is your address?** ¿Cuál es tu dirección?, 1

_____ **is your name?** ¿Cómo se llama Ud.? (*form.*), LP; ¿Cómo te llamas? (*inf.*), 1

_____ **time is it?** ¿Qué hora es?, 1

_____ **'s new?** ¿Qué hay de nuevo?, LP

when cuándo, 2

where adónde, 4; dónde, 2

_____ **are you from?** ¿De dónde eres?, 1

which cuál, 1; (*rel. pron.*) que, 6

while rato (*m.*), 14; (*conj.*) mientras, 3

a _____ un rato, 14

a _____ **later** al rato, 11

white blanco(-a), LP

who (*rel. pron.*) que, 12; quién, 2

_____ **is it?** ¿Quién es?, 2

_____ **is speaking?** ¿De parte de quién?, ¿Quién habla?, 2

whole todo(-a), 7

whom quien, quienes, 12

whose de quién, 4

why por qué, 2

that is _____ por eso, 5

wide ancho(-a), 15

widowed viudo(-a), 3

wife esposa (*f.*), 3

win ganar, 13

window ventana (*f.*), 1; (*of a vehicle or booth*) ventanilla (*f.*), 12

_____ **seat** asiento de ventanilla (*m.*), 7

to _____ **shop** mirar vidrieras, 15

windshield parabrisas (*m.*), 18

windshield wiper limpiaparabrisas (*m.*), 18

windy: to be _____ hacer viento, 8

wine vino (*m.*), 4

red _____ vino tinto (*m.*), 8

white _____ vino blanco (*m.*), 8

winter invierno (*m.*), LP

wish desear, 2; querer (e:ie), 4

with con, 2

_____ **me** conmigo, 6

_____ **you** (*inf. sing.*) contigo, 6

withdraw sacar, 11

without sin, 12; sin que, 14

woman mujer (*f.*), 1

young _____ chica (*f.*), muchacha (*f.*), 3

word palabra (*f.*), LP

work trabajo (*m.*), 3; funcionar, 18; trabajar, 2

world mundo (*m.*), 5

worry (about) preocuparse (por), 9

worse peor, 5

worst el (la) peor, 5

worth: to be _____ valer

it's (not) _____ **the trouble** (no) vale la pena, 18

wound herida (*f.*), 17

wrap envolver (o:ue), 15

wrapped envuelto(-a), 15

write escribir, 3

_____ **down** anotar, 8

written escrito(-a), 15

wrong: to be _____ estar equivocado(-a), no tener razón, 4

X

X-ray radiografía (*f.*), 17

_____ **room** sala de rayos X (*f.*), 17

to take an _____ hacer una radiografía, 17

Y

year año (*m.*), 3

to be . . . _____ **s old** tener... años, 4

New Year's Eve fin de año (*m.*), 4

yellow amarillo(-a), LP

yes sí, 1

yesterday ayer, 7

yet todavía, 15

you (*subj.*) tú (*inf.*), usted (*form.*), LP; ustedes, vosotros(-as), 1; (*d.o. pron.*) la(s), lo(s), os, te, 6; (*i.o. pron.*) le(s), os, te, 7; (*obj. of prep.*) ti, usted(es), vosotros(-as), 6

_____ **'re welcome** de nada, 1

with _____ contigo (*inf.*) con usted, 6

young person joven (*m., f.*), 16

younger menor, 5

youngest el (la) menor, 5

your su, tu, vuestro(-a), 2

yours suyo(-a)(s), tuyo(-a)(s), vuestro(-a)(s), 9

yourself se, te, 9

yourselves os, se, 9

Z

zero cero, LP

zip code zona postal (*f.*), 3

zoo zoológico (*m.*), 14

PHOTOGRAPH CREDITS